Financial Innovation and Technology

Series Editor

Thomas Puschmann, Swiss FinTech Innovation Lab, University of Zurich, Zurich, Switzerland

The book series 'Financial Innovation and Technology' features scholarly research on the latest developments in the world of finance such as AI, FinTech startups, Big Data, Cryptocurrencies, Robo-Advisors, Machine Learning, and Blockchain applications among others. The book series explores the main trends and technologies that will transform the finance industry in the years to come. The series presents essential insights into the financial technology revolution, and the disruption, innovation, and opportunity it entails. The books in this series will be of value to both academics and those working in the finance industry.

Alex Zarifis • Xusen Cheng
Editors

Fintech and the Emerging Ecosystems

Exploring Centralised and Decentralised Financial Technologies

Springer

Editors
Alex Zarifis
University of Southampton
Southampton, UK

Cambridge Centre for Alternative Finance
Cambridge, UK

Xusen Cheng
Renmin University of China
Beijing, China

ISSN 2730-9681 ISSN 2730-969X (electronic)
Financial Innovation and Technology
ISBN 978-3-031-83401-1 ISBN 978-3-031-83402-8 (eBook)
https://doi.org/10.1007/978-3-031-83402-8

This Springer imprint is published by the registered company Springer Nature Switzerland AG
The registered company address is: Gewerbestrasse 11, 6330 Cham, Switzerland

Contents

The New Centralised and Decentralised Fintech Technologies, and Business Models, Transforming Finance

Alex Zarifis and Xusen Cheng

1 Introduction

Financial technologies, Fintech, are revolutionising and reorganising the whole financial sector including insurance (Cosma & Rimo, 2024). This digital transformation affects society and our everyday life in many ways, as financial services cut across many other services we use. Many relationships, such as that between a customer and a retailer, are changing and whole business models are being re-drawn. Fintech not only offers new financial services, but reduces barriers to entry, allowing for innovation in business models. The far-reaching role of Fintech and the degree of disruption from this digital transformation means everything has been 'thrown up in the air' and nobody knows exactly where everything will fall. Because of this, it is necessary to understand the various forms of Fintech, what their role is now and their potential role in the future.

There are some proven Fintech technologies, services and business models but there is still a lot of uncertainty. There are alternative visions of finance's future which compete but also learn from each other. The research presented here extends an existing model and finds six Fintech business models that are optimised for AI and blockchain. The main technologies driving Fintech are AI and blockchain. Blockchain is now widely used in cryptocurrencies such as Bitcoin, decentralised finance, stablecoins and non-fungible tokens (NFTs). Blockchain-based finance is now widely accepted by traditional finance and regulators (Proskalovich et al.,

A. Zarifis (✉)
University of Southampton, Southampton, UK

Cambridge Centre for Alternative Finance, Cambridge, UK
e-mail: a.zarifis@soton.ac.uk

X. Cheng
Renmin University of China, Beijing, China

A. Zarifis, X. Cheng (eds.), *Fintech and the Emerging Ecosystems*, Financial Innovation and Technology, https://doi.org/10.1007/978-3-031-83402-8_1

2023). Some changes driven by Fintech can be achieved purely by competition but wider change needs collaboration. Trust remains a challenge for Fintech, particularly when generative AI is used. Trust must be built by leaders even if this means sacrificing some of generative AI's capabilities.

The context of each country influences how much the pull for Fintech is from the people and how it is regulated. Even after the transitional period of disruption, it is unlikely that we will be left with a 'one size fits all' approach by all countries. This research identifies three themes in Fintech: (a) Fintech utilising blockchain, decentralised finance, cryptocurrencies and NFTs, (b) Fintech utilising AI and the metaverse, and (c) Fintech management, consumer behaviour, regulation and cybersecurity.

The digital transformation with Fintech is not driven just by tech-savvy startups, with business models created to utilise new technological capabilities, such as the latest versions of generative AI. The transformation is driven by many different organisations including incumbents, often referred to as traditional finance, regulators, national governments and supranational organisations such as the European Union. These different organisations have different motivations and different visions for the future that they want to encourage.

In addition to the typical considerations of balancing the risk and reward of new Fintech solutions, one of the undercurrents in Fintech is that of a longing for financial independence. This applies to individuals as many would expect, but this also applies to countries and supranational organisations such as the EU. An example is the new initiative WERO, which should give the EU its own transaction alternative to VISA and Mastercard (Teng, 2024). This balance between smooth collaboration and financial independence comes at a time when extreme globalisation is no longer seen as the panacea. An extreme version of globalisation is not seen by most as the best solution for either finance or technology. This can be seen in the efforts for smoother financial transactions between BRICS countries, without the stronger financial integration that a de jure shared currency such as the euro, or a de facto shared currency, would bring.

2 Six Fintech Business Models That Are Optimised for AI and Blockchain

In a similar way to the broad strategic issues around what vision countries have for Fintech to shape the relationships between them, different organisations see this period of transition and adjustment as either an opportunity or a threat. Some from outside the financial sector such as bigtech see it as an opportunity to take market share. Others that have managed to limit competition and have regulatory 'moats' around the financial services they provide would prefer to maintain them. Whether an existing financial organisation decides to keep its existing model, disrupt themselves in a drastic way, or evolve gradually into a new business model, it is important that they understand this multifaceted transformation. While startups are like agile speedboats that can change direction easily, large financial organisations more closely resemble large cruise ships that need to know where they will be in five or ten years time, and set a course to get there. It is necessary to understand how new technologies such as the latest versions of generative AI, blockchain, virtual worlds, the internet of things (IoT) and 5G are triggering this disruption, but they are not the only issues driving it.

If Fintech is not simply driven by the financial sector and new technology then who is it driven by? There are some obvious players driving Fintech innovation who are, to some degree, predictable, such as bigtech, technology providers offering new solutions for part of the value chain and startups offering services directly to customers or collaborating with incumbents. There are also some less obvious, and less predictable, players such organisations involved in decentralised finance, and entrepreneurs such as Elon Musk and Donald Trump. Whether Elon Musk's app X becomes the 'everything app', or Donald Trump and his sons can 'make finance great again' (Katanich, 2024), these initiatives at least show the potential, and appetite, for innovation and disruption. This potential for disruption is not only because of more capable technology that can offer better services to customers becoming available, but also because the barriers to entry to offering financial services are reduced. Fintech reduces barriers to entry so others can offer financial services. If an organisation is strong in one part of the financial value chain illustrated in Fig. 1, it can add the other parts of the value chain more easily.

Figure 1 illustrates an extended model with six Fintech business models that are optimised for AI and blockchain. Previous research identified five optimised business models (Zarifis & Cheng, 2024), but endeavours such as Donald Trump's World Liberty Financial cryptocurrency platform illustrate a distinct sixth model, that also signifies a different stage in the diffusion of Fintech innovations. While the sixth model has similarities to the fourth and fifth, as it is an organisation from outside the financial sector encroaching on it, it also has some distinct features. The key characteristics are that it has an existing user base, or fan base, with which trust has already been built, and unlike the fifth model, it uses advanced but commoditised financial technology. Therefore, unlike the fourth and fifth models, the key advantage does not come from the Fintech technology, but from the existing fanbase with trust already 'baked in'. Despite the ongoing innovation, some Fintech transitioning into a commoditised service that is easily deployed can be seen as a sign of a maturing sector expanding in adoption.

It is important to appreciate that existing trust with customers or fans, or the ability to build trust, are important parts of the value chain. Having the capability to build trust can be the starting point, with financial services added to it. Is the technology still the most critical factor in a Fintech at this stage, or the ability to build trust in it? Words such as modularity and ecosystem are often used, but it is important to understand how a new Fintech can be created, its journey and how it can build momentum and carve out a niche with technology and trust.

It remains to be seen whether this period of many different players getting involved in Fintech will continue or there will be some winners, some losers,

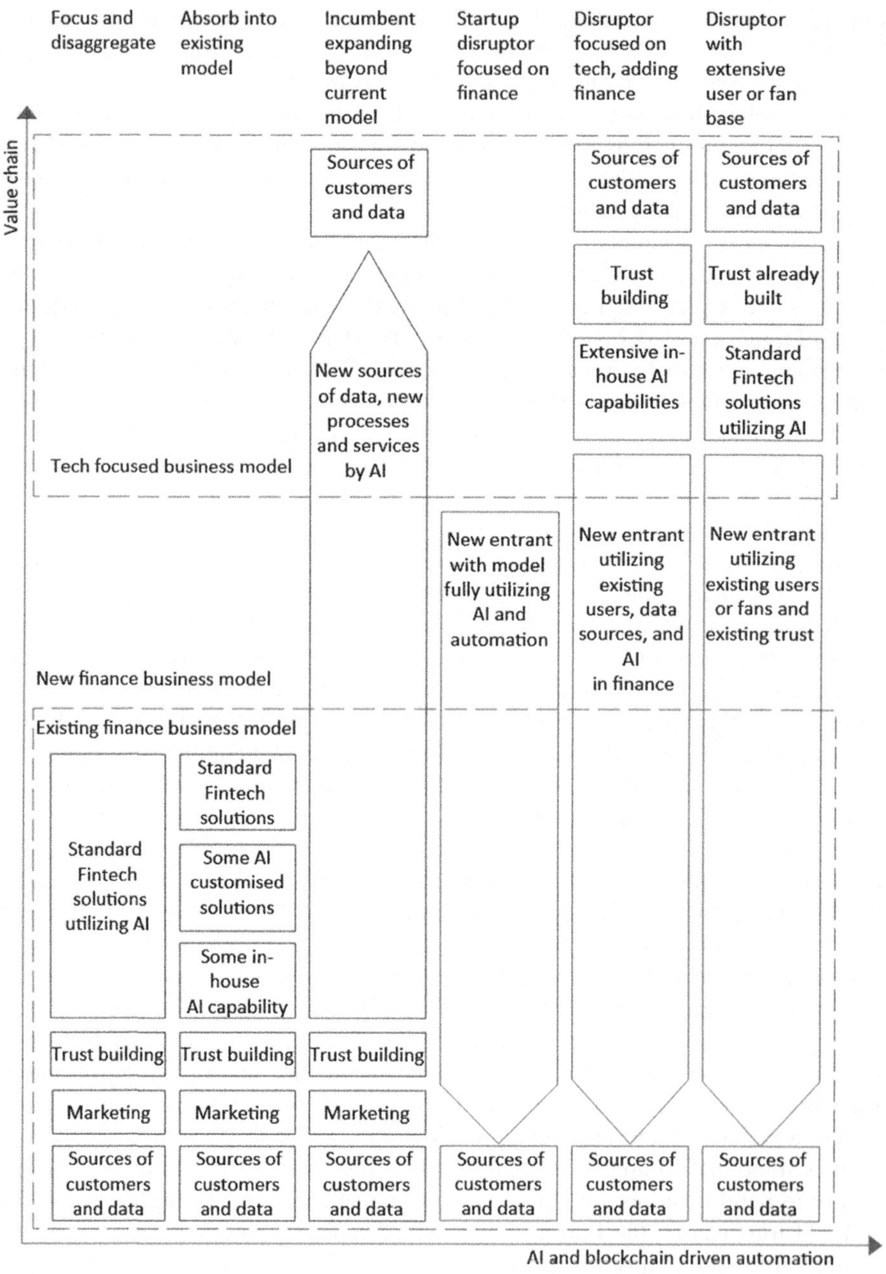

Fig. 1 Six Fintech business models that are optimised for AI and blockchain

and a period of consolidation will follow. Regardless of which players in Fintech will prevail the influence of Fintech cannot just be measured by the success of its proponents, but also the change in the sector they encourage. For example, Revolut and Robinhood have encouraged traditional finance to add similar services to what they offered. Robinhood encouraged traditional banks to not charge fees for investments, and Revolut encouraged some banks to offer spending abroad without fees and disposable digital bankcards for online purchases.

3 Common Themes in Fintech

The chapters here from leading researchers in this area give a more complete understanding of this multifaceted transformation. A meta-analysis of the 19 research projects in Fintech is implemented here across three themes. The research illustrates the breadth of topics in Fintech but at the same time there are some common themes that emerge. Three areas of Fintech are covered: (a) Fintech based on blockchain and solutions that utilise it, such as decentralised finance, cryptocurrencies, central bank digital currencies (CBDC) and NFTs, (b) Fintech utilising AI and the metaverse, and (c) the various issues related to Fintech management such as consumer behaviour, regulation and cybersecurity. The research in these chapters covers new financial technologies such as cryptoassets and the increasing role of generative AI. The change brought about by these technologies is coming together with other drivers of change in finance. The chapters do not only focus on the technology of Fintech but also other aspects of finance driving transformation alongside Fintech. This research does not only benefit researchers and academics. There are many practical lessons for professionals in finance, regulators and others affected by Fintech such as retail. The technology of Fintech and the management of Fintech can be seen as the two pillars of its success as illustrated in Fig. 2.

Significant opportunities are created by Fintech. The speed of technological innovation is increasing with the ability of generative AI expanding regularly. The appetite for Fintech that utilises new technology to offer better solutions seems to be universal. However, the context of each country, and the stakeholders there, shape the local implementations of Fintech. While blockchain is more predictable as a technology, generative AI brings many challenges (Sampat et al., 2023). As the reliance on technology increases, so do the cybersecurity risks. As a larger volume of sensitive data is often collected by Fintech, the potential damage from a breach may be more severe. For many central issues in Fintech, whether they are an opportunity, or a threat, depends on each person's perspective and can change week by week. For example, whether the emerging regulation is seen as an opportunity or as a threat are two sides of the same coin.

One common theme that comes out strongly is that collaboration is needed for large change. While a startup, designed from the start with a business model to fully utilise the latest forms of AI and blockchain, may be able to offer better and cheaper services and gain market share, larger, more fundamental changes need

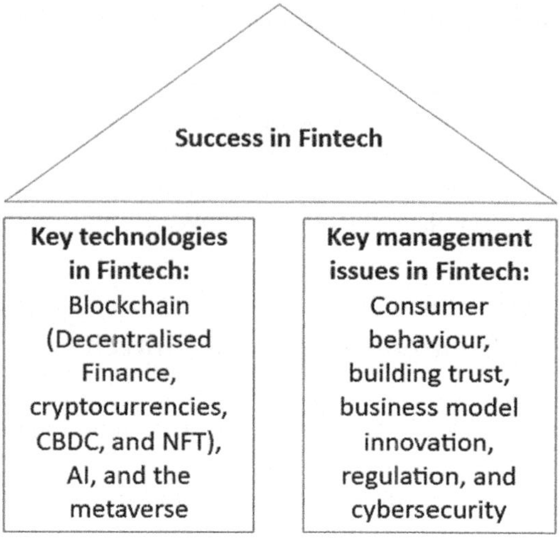

Fig. 2 The three main technologies, and the main management issues, that are the pillars for success in Fintech

collaboration. This collaboration across traditional incumbents, disruptors and those that regulate them is the best way forward. If the incumbents and regulators try to lock out the disruptors, the economy will lose the growth they would bring, and there will be a parallel system the authorities have limited influence over (Auer, 2019). If the disruptors do not collaborate, they will not have the benefits of becoming an incumbent and having influence over future regulation. The many discussions around CBDCs and the Brazilian implementation are examples of the benefits of moving forward and bringing all the stakeholders with you as far as possible.

3.1 Fintech Utilising Blockchain, Decentralised Finance, Cryptocurrencies and NFTs

Blockchain based finance such as Bitcoin seem to regularly be at an important turning point where they can gain, or lose, credibility and wider appeal. Nevertheless, after many years of popularity, especially with younger people, they are now more mature and have wider popularity across traditional finance and regulators. For example, a recent study found that over 80% of regulators in Latin America see blockchain based finance favourably (Proskalovich et al., 2023). Furthermore, the journey until now and the research in this area mean utilising blockchain-based Fintech is no longer a step into the dark reserved for the bravest souls.

Blockchain technology was initially used as a way to offer decentralised financial services. While this is still its primary application, it is also being used to offer centralised solutions such as central bank digital currencies. CBDCs are in some ways more centralised than the current form of money, as more information can be collected on those that use them. Stablecoins have elements of a decentralised

Table 1 Themes in Fintech related to blockchain, DeFi, cryptocurrencies and NFTs

Fintech using blockchain	Major themes
Blockchain technology and cryptocurrencies	-Decentralised, borderless and permissionless. -Secure, incorruptible, immutable and trustless to some degree. -Eliminates the need for intermediaries, and resistant to censorship. -Interoperability between blockchains should go further.
Bitcoin	-Bitcoin price changes are mostly driven by the self-reinforcing effect of market sentiment.
Stablecoins	-Offer the stability of fiat currencies while retaining the benefits of cryptocurrencies.
Central bank digital currency (CBDC)	-Trust in a two-tier CBDC is formed by (a) Trust in government and central bank offering it, (b) expressed guarantees, (c) reputation of other CBDCs, (d) the technology, (e) the trust building features of the retail bank's CBDC wallet app, and (f) the privacy features of the retail bank's CBDC wallet app. -Large informal economies will probably resist a central bank digital currency more.
Decentralised finance (DeFi)	-Five main layers: (1) consensus or settlement, (2) smart contract, (3) business model or service, (4) performance or optimisation, (5) and governance. -Decentralised exchanges (DEX) are a type of DeFi that allows users to trade anonymously on a blockchain. Their popularity is influenced by the expansion of the DeFi industry, community support and trust.
Non-fungible tokens (NFT)	-NFTs in the sports card collectibles market offer many new opportunities such as fractional ownership. -NFTs can create new opportunities in virtual worlds and the metaverse.
Regulation	-Regulation of Fintech using blockchain plays an important role, but organisations offering cryptoassets and DeFi can choose regions with more favourable regulation. -Different implementations of blockchain-based tokens are regulated very differently. -Most stakeholders in DeFi do not want hard or soft regulation, they want good regulation.

currency and a centralised one. As their price is intended to be tied to a regular currency such as the Euro, they are intended to have a more stable value, but if the popularity of the stablecoin suddenly drops it may be hard to keep the pegging, as the Terra collapse in 2022 showed (Briola et al., 2023). Table 1 summarises the main emerging themes related to blockchain-based Fintech.

3.2 *Fintech Utilising AI and the Metaverse*

Generative AI gives you many things but in most implementations, it does not give you a certainty, a confidence in the information given and the process it took. There is usually limited transparency. This is not a criticism, but it is important to appreciate the strengths and weaknesses of each technology, so organisations can get the best out of them by combining them together. Generative AI does not typically encourage trust, but blockchain does. AI needs blockchain and new business models. Many people say blockchain is a trustless technology. This is not the whole story, but it is true that when blockchain is used in a solution less trust is needed. If the blockchain is implemented well less people need to be trusted in terms of the process itself.

If someone is naive and bases their views on what is talked about most, then they may think that the hype around AI is to the detriment of blockchain, but AI with blockchain together can deliver the most effective Fintech solutions for all kinds of organisations such as art galleries, manufacturing, banks and Forex. Organisations such as the Bank of International Settlements (BIS) are encouraging the use of blockchain for central banks (Auer et al., 2023). They are very much the establishment, traditional finance, they are not startups or decentralised finance so it is clear that both incumbents and disruptors see the value of blockchain in an AI-centric world. In a similar way, virtual worlds and the metaverse offer new opportunities, but they also benefit from the certainty blockchain-based technologies such as NFTs can provide (Banaeian Far et al., 2023). Table 2 summarises the main emerging themes related to how AI and the metaverse support Fintech.

Table 2 Themes in Fintech related to utilising AI and the metaverse

Fintech using AI and the metaverse	Major themes
AI	-Robo-advisors offer low-cost, efficient investment advice and portfolio management -Robo-advisors offer sophisticated customised and actionable financial advice -Generative AI implementation in finance raises serious ethical challenges -AI use in finance requires robust regulation
Metaverse	-Create value by improving and extending the customer experience, and improving and extending the business operations -Opportunity for banks to differentiate themselves

3.3 Fintech Management, Consumer Behaviour, Regulation and Cybersecurity

There is a-lot more to Fintech than new technologies. Fintech is not mainly about new technologies but about the new processes, services and business models the technologies enable. A good example of this are NFTs. With NFTs, similarly to other technologies, the most important question is whether the technology solves a problem. If it solves a problem, then it has a very good chance of being widely adopted regardless of whether this adoption is immediate, gradual, or as is often the case you go through some hype first, people are often drawn in from the hype and then realise it is not for them, but after the hype the adoption picks up gradually (Zarifis & Cheng, 2022). NFTs solve the problem of ownership of digital content, so they have a future. The creator of art utilising the NFT, and the platform selling them, are two valid business models. The creator can be paid for selling their art or receive royalties on an ongoing basis. The technology enables a more effective and secure solution for the financial aspect of an artist's work.

This is a very positive thing for art because once someone can earn a living, more art will be created. It fits in the zeitgeist of our time in many ways, e.g. many people have to move regularly for work, change town or country, so they have to have a limited number of personal possessions, and they prefer to have things they can move easily. This kind of person may not want to own a large painting because they know they will have to move house in a few months, but they love art and they want to own something.

The example of NFTs in the art market illustrates how many management issues emerge, how an understanding of consumer behaviour is necessary, and the important role of cybersecurity and regulation in protecting those involved. Table 3 summarises the main emerging themes related to the various issues of Fintech management.

4 Overview of the Chapters

The following 19 chapters cover three areas. There are nine chapters on blockchain technologies, three on AI and the metaverse and seven on the management issues in Fintech.

A. Fintech Utilising Blockchain, Decentralised Finance, Cryptocurrencies and NFTs

Chapter 2. The following chapter 'Digital alchemy: The allure of blockchain technology and cryptocurrency in a modern economy' by Annette Hofmann and Chad Dulle, offers a fascinating discussion on how cryptocurrencies, such as Bitcoin, are far more than just a new form of money. They are a revolution in the financial system, with their ability to offer decentralised, secure and bor-

Table 3 Themes related to Fintech management, consumer behaviour, regulation and cybersecurity

Fintech management	Major themes
Consumer behaviour with Fintech	-The responses to Fintech by different kinds of consumers, in different contexts, shape the specific implementation that affects them -Fintech is appealing across the globe, but the implementations are very different. For example, advanced financial centres have different priorities to developing economies -The pull of undeserved consumers is being met in many developing countries by mobile operators, offering Fintech services
Building trust in Fintech using AI	-Leadership from the board level, should build trust in AI with all the stakeholders. This needs a trustworthy implementation of AI, and building trust by communicating how AI is used in a way that addresses the stakeholders' concerns
Fintech strategies and business models	-Traditional finance such as incumbent banks must choose whether to compete or collaborate with Fintech organisations. If they don't have sufficient knowledge of new technologies to compete, they should collaborate
Regulation and Regtech	-The increasing use of technology in finance is also increasing regulation -Seven critical drivers of Regtech adoption are: compliance automation, risk management, data management and analytics, regulatory technology platforms, ESG compliance, regulatory reporting and compliance monitoring
Cybersecurity risks	-As the reliance on technology increases, so do the cybersecurity risks -As a larger volume of sensitive data is often collected by Fintech, the potential damage from a breach will be more severe -Effective risk management and understanding the potential cost of breaches is necessary

derless alternatives to traditional currencies. By utilising blockchain technology, they provide a transparent and tamper-proof transaction ledger, avoiding the need for intermediaries and allowing for trustless international transactions that are immutable and have some resistance to censorship. Stablecoins have also emerged, attempting to offer the stability of fiat currencies while retaining the benefits of cryptocurrencies. It is becoming important to have interoperability between blockchains so that assets and data can move seamlessly across. Despite the benefits, there are concerns about the environmental impact of energy-intensive proof-of-work consensus mechanisms used by some cryptocurrencies. More sustainable alternatives such as proof-of-stake are being implemented. Decentralised finance is another emerging trend, leveraging blockchain to provide financial services without intermediaries, but it faces challenges particularly regulatory uncertainty and smart contract vulnerabilities. The attraction of cryptocurrencies is that they have the potential to reshape the financial system, encouraging a shift towards a more digital, decentralised and efficient economy.

Chapter 3. The study on the 'Informal economy and central bank digital currency' by Eun Young Oh and Shuonan Zhang explores the relationship between the informal economy and the adoption of central bank digital currency (CBDC) by households and businesses. The findings suggest that a CBDC may have difficulty being widely accepted by end users when there is a large informal economy primarily using cash. Once a CBDC is adopted it can reduce the informal economy, but this effect is lower in countries with large informal economies. CBDC adoption can be promoted by tax reduction when they are used and CBDC interest rates, so that there is a move from the informal sector to the formal sector.

Chapter 4. The research 'A model of trust in central bank digital currency (CBDC) in Brazil: How trust in a two-tier CBDC with both the central and retail banks involved changes consumer trust' by Alex Zarifis and Xusen Cheng finds six ways to build trust in a CBDC in this context. The consumer has an increasing range of financial services to choose from, including decentralised blockchain based cryptocurrencies. A CBDC may use blockchain technology, but it is centralised, so the institutions that support it play an important role. Despite the centralised top-down nature of this financial technology, it still needs to be adopted so the consumer's perspective, particularly their trust in it, is very important. Each CBDC implementation can be different, and each country's context can be different, therefore it is important to understand each case separately. This research models the Brazilian consumer's trust in their two-tier CBDC, where the central bank and the retail banks retain their current role. The six ways to build trust in a CBDC, identified by previous research in a different region, are supported for this case also. These are: (a) trust in government and central bank offering the CBDC, (b) expressed guarantees for those using it, (c) the favourable reputation of other active CBDCs, (d) the CBDC technology, the automation and limited human involvement necessary, (e) the trust building features of the retail bank's CBDC wallet app, and (f) the privacy features of the retail bank's CBDC wallet app, and back-end processes.

Chapter 5. The research 'Modularising decentralised finance: The DeFi layered stack revisited' by Enrico Rossi gives a thorough analysis of DeFi. DeFi can be seen as several logical layers, where each layer performs a different role and a different function. Unlike most discussions of the DeFi stack that usually include heterogeneous elements, such as protocols, assets or services, this work discusses the DeFi stack from a modular point of view. This work decomposes the DeFi stack into functionally independent modules, each representing a set of functionally independent protocols. Five main layers of the DeFi stack are identified: (1) consensus or settlement, (2) smart contract, (3) business model or service, (4) performance or optimisation, and (5) and the governance layer. Each layer has a set of functionally homogeneous and independent protocols. There is a decentralisation-efficiency trade-off for each of these layers. The role played by cryptoassets (tokens) at the various layers is explored. A distinction is made between instrumental tokens (necessary means to an end that are valuable in that they support the operation of decentralised protocols) and tokens-as-instruments (ends in themselves that can retain value and utility independently from the operations of a decentralised protocol at any layer of the stack). This layered understanding of value in DeFi ecosystems, is defined as 'the DeFi pyramid of value'.

Chapter 6. The research 'Modelling persistence in cross-market Bitcoin prices with a break and a memory' by Ahmad Maaitah and Tapas Mishra looks at how Bitcoin investors are driven. Both endogenous and exogenous switching are unavoidable recurring features of financial time series, especially Bitcoin prices. Bitcoin prices are driven by frequent changes in investors' sentiment as there is no fundamental value in crypto assets. Frequent switching in Bitcoin prices is nevertheless primordially endogenous in nature. Therefore, endogenous switches of such a nature may not be at odds with empirical studies which find that long-memory persistence in financial time series may be spuriously dominated by break points in the data. The theoretical lengths of the switches (i.e. the expected convergence behaviour of shocks to the zero mean) often encounter the intervention of another break point (of an unclaimed length) masking the inherent pattern of the series as being perennially persistent. In the empirical finance literature, both memory (persistence feature) and breaks (types of switching) have implications for the efficiency of the market. This chapter presents a theory-driven empirical apparatus to demonstrate that Bitcoin investors are driven, although not beaten by 'memory' as well as a number of endogenous switches in the price level. Both memory and endogenous switches are compatible with what we call an endogenous growth mechanism in the Bitcoin market. The finding of persistence has also relevance to the theory of learning: an agent that learns synchronously is an agent that will depict fewer persistence behaviours. Bitcoin markets depict true long memory and price dynamics is mostly driven by endogenous feedback mechanisms or market reflexivity.

Chapter 7. The research 'External factors that affect the adoption of decentralised exchanges (DEX) for cryptocurrencies: The case of CURVE DEX' by Yuan Yao and Alex Zarifis sheds light on this increasingly popular form of exchange. Decentralised exchanges (DEX) are a type of DeFi that allow users to trade freely and anonymously on a blockchain. This study focuses on how external factors affect the adoption of DEXs and provides suggestions for the development of the entire DEX industry. The study finds that the development of the DeFi industry has a significant impact on the adoption of DEXs, so DEXs should cooperate to develop the industry instead of focusing on competing for a larger share of the existing market. Some other external factors also have an impact, such as technological innovation, partner integration and community support. As DeFi is closely related to the adoption of DEX, the study also discusses the external factors that may affect the adoption of DeFi, namely trust, infrastructure and regulation.

Chapter 8. The work on 'Arena club: A case study in Web3 and Fintech innovation in the collectibles market' by David Krause examines Arena Club's innovative application of Web3 technologies within the sports card market. This is a key segment of the broader collectibles and alternative investment landscape. Fintech is evolving and blockchain and non-fungible tokens (NFTs) are being further integrated into traditional markets offering new solutions to challenges such as authenticity verification, secure ownership transfer and efficient secondary market transactions. Arena Club addresses these issues by utilising blockchain to enhance security and transparency, while NFTs enable new investment opportunities such as fractional ownership. This case study explores Arena Club's impact on the sports card collectibles market, analysing its competitive positioning, technology infrastructure and the broader implications for the Fintech industry. The chapter concludes with insights into the future of Web3 applications in collectibles and suggests directions for further research into the convergence of Fintech and digital assets.

Chapter 9. The second chapter by David Krause is on 'The rise of Web3: Opportunities and challenges'. This research explores Web3, the next phase of Internet evolution characterised by decentralisation and blockchain technology. Web3 is contrasted with its predecessors, Web1 and Web2, highlighting its transformative potential across industries such as finance, art, gaming and governance. Key applications such as decentralised finance (DeFi), non-fungible tokens (NFTs), metaverses and decentralised autonomous organisations (DAOs) are examined to illustrate Web3's models and implications. Web3 also faces some challenges however such as scalability, security, regulatory ambiguity and user experience concerns. This research concludes by discussing the future trajectory of Web3 and suggests areas for future research.

Chapter 10. The study 'From the exclusion of the concept of blockchain to the delimitation of the concept of distributed ledger technology under MiCAR' by Diogo Pereira Coelho sheds light on the important legal and regulatory frameworks for blockchain based Fintech. The entry into force of Markets in Crypto-Assets Regulation (MiCA or MiCAR), raises many questions regarding the case-by-case analysis of the legal framework of crypto-assets that are in its scope. This research contributes to the understanding of the legal definition of distributed ledger technology (DLT). The first part of this research explores the concept of blockchain, namely the phenomenon of decentralisation, blockchain technology and cryptocurrencies, its disruptive potential, functions and main characteristics. This contributes to the understanding of the issues raised in the second and last part of this chapter, which focuses on the exclusion of the concept of blockchain from the legal definition of DLT under MiCAR. In addition to the analysis of the legal definition of DLT, there is a critical analysis of the distinction between blockchain technology and distributed ledger technology.

B. Fintech Utilising AI and the Metaverse

Chapter 11. The first chapter of the second section is 'An introduction to robo-advisors, notable Fintech implementations and underlying theory' by Fabio Dias. This research on robo-advisors offers an overview of the landscape of automated financial advisory services. First it explains how robo-advisors rely on advanced algorithms and artificial intelligence to deliver low-cost, efficient investment advice and portfolio management. There is extensive growth in the use of robo-advisors. Some interesting Fintech implementations, such as Betterment and Wealthfront, are examined for their innovative approaches and market impact. There are several advantages of robo-advisors, including cost efficiency, 24/7 availability and personalised recommendations. The chapter also explores the quantitative techniques employed by robo-advisors, such as mean-variance optimisation, the Black–Litterman model and Monte Carlo simulations, along with the use of advanced machine learning methods for portfolio management.

Furthermore, the chapter discusses the promise and the pitfalls of robo-advisors, their potential for enhancing diversification and reducing behavioural biases, and their appeal to more active and wealthy investors. The customisation of investment portfolios through client questionnaires and algorithmic optimisation is also discussed, showcasing how robo-advisors tailor strategies to individual financial goals and tolerances to risk.

Chapter 12. The work on 'Artificial intelligence in financial technology: Challenges, opportunities, and global trends' by Sonam Rani, Gaurav Gupta, Sailaja Bohara and Amitabh Bhargava explores the transformative role of AI in Fintech. AI is reshaping traditional financial services by enhancing operational efficiency, reducing costs and improving customer experiences. The study categorises the key theories and trends in AI-driven Fintech solutions. AI's integration within Fintech not only drives innovation but also brings new challenges, particularly ethical considerations and the need for robust regulatory frameworks. This research provides valuable insights into the rapidly evolving role of Fintech for academics, industry professionals and policymakers.

Chapter 13. The third important technology in Fintech is virtual worlds so the research on 'Metaverse: Where is it going to add value for the financial services industry and banks' by Anna Omarini and Gulnaz Rakhmatullina is very useful. Fintech is changing the way the finance industry is developing, producing and distributing services. The metaverse is being explored and utilised extensively. This chapter explains how value in the metaverse can be created for financial services. It is proposed that value in the metaverse is co-created through active participation, interaction, collaboration and resource integration among different stakeholders. A 2×2 framework is created that categorises metaverse opportunities into physical vs. virtual world support and customer vs. company orientation, demonstrating the value creation opportunities in a comprehensive manner. Financial institutions can benefit from value creation within each quadrant of the proposed framework. This chapter contributes to academic literature by offering a clear explanation of value creation in the metaverse, and provides industry participants with a framework to integrate into their metaverse strategies. By understanding how value is created, and how stakeholders can benefit, the metaverse can be adopted further in finance and new business ecosystems can be developed.

C. Fintech Management, Consumer Behaviour, Regulation and Cybersecurity

Chapter 14. The first chapter of the third section is on 'The digital evolution of Italian financial services client behaviour and market shifts' by Laura Grassi, Filippo Renga, Alessandro Faes and Claudio Garitta. Digital transformation is reshaping industries across the globe, and the financial sector is certainly no exception. Moving from traditional to digital and hybrid models is a fundamental evolution driven by consumer demand, and innovative new technologies. This chapter delves into how various types of clients, from individual retail consumers to small and medium-sized enterprises (SMEs), are adapting and driving this digitalisation. In finance, it is crucial to understand these dynamics so that new strategies achieve the best balance between digital and physical channels while considering the complexities of the services offered. These dynamics are explored by looking at the specific case of Italy.

Chapter 15. The research on 'Building trust in AI: Leadership insights from Malaysian Fintech boards' by Alex Zarifis and Larisa Yarovaya explores the role of trust in this context. Fintech companies face the challenge of trying to lead in AI adoption while avoiding the many potential pitfalls. The board of directors must show leadership and build trust in their implementation of AI with the main stakeholders.

This research interviewed Malaysian Fintech board members to identify the most effective ways for a board to build trust for shareholders, staff and customers. This research finds that the most effective ways to build trust for these three stakeholders are different. Leaders should build trust for these three stakeholders in two ways: First, by building trust with an effective and trustworthy implementation of AI, and second building trust by communicating how AI is used in a way that addresses the stakeholders concerns.

The findings show that some ways of applying generative AI make it easier to build trust in AI, even if they are a more limited application, and some performance is sacrificed. There are trade-offs between unleashing generative AI in an unrestricted way and a more constrained, transparent and predictable application that builds trust in shareholders, staff and customers. This balancing act, between a fast adoption of generative AI and a more cautious adoption of a more controlled AI is at the heart of the challenge the board faces.

Chapter 16. The study on 'Opportunities and challenges of Fintech in Southeast Asia' by Jianzheng Shi and Yue Wang highlights how the adoption of Fintech is shaped by each country's context. This research examines the current state, trends and influencing factors of the financial technology (Fintech) industry in Southeast Asia. The region's rapid economic growth and thriving e-commerce sector have provided fertile ground for Fintech innovation. Despite significant differences in population, economy and culture among Southeast Asian countries, there is a universal need for more effective financial services. The improvement of Internet infrastructure and the rise of new economic sectors have created favourable conditions for the development of Fintech services such as mobile payments and online lending. There are differences in Fintech development between traditional economic centres such as Singapore, and emerging markets such as Indonesia and the Philippines. Fintech companies expanding into Southeast Asian markets need to take the time to fully understand the local policy environments, establish localised partnerships and effectively integrate into local cultures.

Chapter 17. The analysis of 'New cooperation models between banks and Fintech: A path toward digital transformation in the emerging financial ecosystem' by Agata Wolska, covers the impact of digitalisation on financial services resulting from the constantly changing environment, driven by the emergence of the Internet, mobile phones and new regulations. The digitalisation of banking has led to the rise of new players, Fintechs, forcing traditional banks to choose between cooperation and competition. Many banks prefer to cooperate with Fintechs to remain competitive. The first reason is their limited knowledge of the new technology. The second reason is to avoid the risks that would come from the long-term investments in new technologies they would have to make, to go it alone. New cooperation models have emerged, such as partnerships with Fintech, which have improved financial products and led to the emergence of new business models such as the sharing economy, embedded finance or the implementation of blockchain technology. This highlights the significant impact of Fintech companies on the digital transformation in the emerging financial ecosystem.

Chapter 18. The research on 'Fintech, banks and mobile operators: Interplays for increasing financial inclusion' by Charles Bélanger, Arvind Ashta and Geri Mason, explores the influence of these three players. They enhance financial inclusion through network effects and technological innovations. Mobile operators leverage Fintech solutions, such as mobile payments and value-added services, to reduce customer churn and enhance loyalty. Mobile payments are increasingly reaching the financially excluded, especially in rural areas. Disruptive innovations of Fintechs such as Alipay, JD Finance and Revolut, are rapidly growing in influence, but their role in developing countries is under-researched. By investigating the competitive dynamics among Fintechs, telecoms and traditional financial institutions, key factors are identified that are driving the evolution of financial services and their potential impact on underserved populations. Interviews in Africa and the Middle East uncover both opportunities and challenges for future development. The findings reveal the importance of innovation, strategic collaboration and market orientation among the top managers of institutions in this space.

Chapter 19. The research on 'Understanding the RegTech drivers in the financial ecosystem' by Ivan Sosa Gomez and Sergio Sosa Gomez looks at the technology that can support regulation in finance. There is an increasing focus on the need to understand the drivers of regulatory technology (RegTech) adoption, and its impact on regulatory compliance processes, across the financial ecosystem. This research analyses global RegTech firms, developing a theoretical framework that explains the dynamics driving RegTech adoption. There are seven critical drivers of RegTech adoption: (1) Compliance automation, (2) risk management, (3) data management and analytics, (4) regulatory technology platforms, (5) ESG compliance, (6) regulatory reporting, and (7) compliance monitoring. These drivers improve the efficiency, accuracy and effectiveness of compliance management. The adoption of RegTech is not just a response to increasing regulatory demands in the financial industry but represents a strategic shift driven by technological innovation. These drivers are interconnected, each contributing to a more robust and efficient compliance framework that enables financial organisations to navigate the complexities of the regulatory landscape. This research provides a comprehensive understanding of the drivers of RegTech adoption across the multiple phases of compliance processes: regulation, monitoring, reporting and supervision. Consequently, as regulatory requirements evolve, this chapter offers valuable insights for academics and practitioners as RegTech firms will perform an essential role in the financial ecosystem.

Chapter 20. The last research here, by Narmin Nahidi is on 'Cybersecurity in Fintech from a corporate finance perspective'. Cybersecurity breaches can have a particularly serious financial cost for Fintechs. Fintech firms are especially vulnerable to cyber threats due to their reliance on digital technologies and the sensitive data they handle. In the Fintech sector, the potential costs of cyber breaches can encompass both direct and indirect financial impacts. These costs are not only immediate but can also have long-term repercussions on a firm's financial health and market position. Therefore, understanding and mitigating these risks is essential for the sustainability and growth of Fintechs. This research explores the various financial implications of cybersecurity risks, including the direct costs of breaches, the importance of effective risk management, the role of regulatory compliance and the need for continuous investment in cybersecurity technologies.

References

Auer, R. (2019). Embedded supervision: How to build regulation into blockchain finance. *Bank for International Settlements, 371*, 31. https://doi.org/10.24149/gwp371

Auer, R., Cornelli, G., & Frost, J. (2023). Rise of the Central Bank Digital currencies. *International Journal of Central Banking, 19*(4), 185–214.

Banaeian Far, S., Imani Rad, A., & Rajabzadeh Asaar, M. (2023). Blockchain and its derived technologies shape the future generation of digital businesses: A focus on decentralized finance and the Metaverse. *Data Science and Management, 6*(3), 183–197. https://doi.org/10.1016/j.dsm.2023.06.002

Briola, A., Vidal-Tomás, D., Wang, Y., & Aste, T. (2023). Anatomy of a Stablecoin's failure: The Terra-Luna case. *Finance Research Letters*, Elsevier Inc., *51* No. August 2022, p. 103358, https://doi.org/10.1016/j.frl.2022.103358.

Cosma, S., & Rimo, G. (2024). Redefining insurance through technology: Achievements and perspectives in Insurtech. *Research in International Business and Finance*, Elsevier B.V. *70* No. PA, p. 102301. https://doi.org/10.1016/j.ribaf.2024.102301

Katanich, D. (2024). How to 'make finance great again': Trump's new cryptocurrency debuts.... *Euronews*.

Proskalovich, R., Jack, C., Zarifis, A., Serralde, D. M., Vershinina, P., Naidoo, S., Njoki, D., et al. (2023). *Cryptoasset ecosystem in Latin America and the Caribbean*. Cambridge Centre for Alternative Finance.

Sampat, B., Mogaji, E., & Nguyen, N. P. (2023). The dark side of FinTech in financial services: a qualitative enquiry into FinTech developers' perspective. *International Journal of Bank Marketing*. https://doi.org/10.1108/IJBM-07-2022-0328

Teng, T. (2024). Wero set to become Europe's first unified payment solution | Euronews. *Euronews*.

Zarifis, A., & Cheng, X. (2022). The business models of NFTs and fan tokens and how they build trust. *Journal of Electronic Business & Digital Economics*. https://doi.org/10.1108/JEBDE-07-2022-0021

Zarifis, A., & Cheng, X. (2024). The five emerging business models of Fintech for AI adoption, growth and building trust. In A. Zarifis, D. Ktoridou, L. Efthymiou, & X. Cheng (Eds.), *Business digital transformation* (pp. 73–97). Palgrave Macmillan. https://doi.org/10.1007/978-3-031-33665-2_4

Alex Zarifis research and teaching are on the practical applications of technology in business. Before the University of Southampton, he worked at several academic institutions including the University of Cambridge, University of Manchester and the University of Mannheim. He is currently a research affiliate of the Cambridge Center for Alternative Finance (CCAF).

He has explored cryptoassets such as cryptocurrencies since 2012. As part of this research, he published the first peer-reviewed research on trust in digital currencies in the world in 2014. He also participated in creating the first government recognised, university degree in blockchain technologies in the world.

Dr Alex has published extensively on trust in different technologies and business models. His research has explored the role of trust in AI, blockchain, financial technology—Fintech and insurance technology—Insurtech.

Xusen Cheng is a Full Professor of Information Systems in the School of Information at Renmin University of China. He is also a research fellow in the Metaverse Research Center and School of Interdisplinary Studies at Renmin University of China. He obtained his PhD degree from the University of Manchester, UK. His research interests include trust and information systems, design and behaviour issues of digital business, digital economy and Metaverse. His research has been published in leading journals such as MIS Quarterly and Journal of Management Information Systems.

Part I
Fintech Utilising Blockchain, Decentralised Finance, Cryptocurrencies and NFTs

Digital Alchemy: The Allure of Blockchain Technology and Cryptocurrency in a Modern Economy

Annette Hofmann and Chad Dulle

1 Introduction

At its core, money embodies value—a powerful, intangible force that drives our world. It's the universal language of exchange, effortlessly facilitating the flow of goods and services. Imagine a world without money, where every transaction hinges on the cumbersome barter system, trading items directly in a tangled web of inefficiency. Money's elegance lies in its simplicity, a sleek, indispensable tool that fuels the pulse of any thriving economy. It's not just essential; it's the lifeblood of our interconnected financial reality. For money to be truly effective and universally embraced, it must possess a few crucial qualities that make it irresistible: First, it needs the flexibility to break down into small units, allowing for transactions of all sizes. In ancient times, this meant slicing up gold or silver into precise portions. Today, divisibility is even more crucial, enabling digital transactions to be as accurate as a fraction of a cent. Second, portability is essential. In other words, the ease of carrying and transferring money is a game-changer. Early civilizations dealt with cumbersome items like cattle, grain, or bulky metals as currency. But now, money travels light—zipping across the globe in seconds with the tap of a button, redefining what it means to be portable. Third, money must withstand time, maintaining its form and value. Whether it's a sturdy coin or a crisp bill, physical money needs to endure. But as we edge closer to a digital world, durability also means safeguarding electronic funds from the perils of hacking and data

A. Hofmann (✉)
Lindner Center for Insurance and Risk Management, University of Cincinnati, Cincinnati, OH, USA
e-mail: Annette.Hofmann@uc.edu

C. Dulle
University of Cincinnati, Cincinnati, OH, USA
e-mail: dullecd@ucmail.uc.edu

A. Zarifis, X. Cheng (eds.), *Fintech and the Emerging Ecosystems*, Financial Innovation and Technology, https://doi.org/10.1007/978-3-031-83402-8_2

loss, ensuring that digital money remains untouchable. Fourth, money must be unmistakable, and counterfeiting should be nearly impossible. In the past, coins were stamped with intricate designs to prevent fraud. Today, advanced encryption and digital signatures do the trick, ensuring electronic money is secure and easily identifiable. Finally, to hold its allure, money must be scarce. If there's too much of it, inflation kicks in, and the value plummets. With its rarity and the effort required to extract it, gold was once the epitome of valuable currency. Central banks control the money supply to preserve this scarcity, though managing fiat currencies—those not tied to physical assets—comes with its own set of seductive challenges. Each of these qualities enhances money's power, making it more than just a medium of exchange but a dynamic force that shapes economies and influences the rhythm of our daily lives.

These properties enable money to fulfill its three main social functions: a unit of account, a medium of exchange, and a store of value. Money provides a standard measure of the value of goods and services, a function that allows for consistent pricing across different markets, making trade more efficient (Ostroy & Starr, 1990). Money is also a symbol with functions assigned by consent or legitimate authority (Davis, 2020). As such, it facilitates transactions by eliminating the need for a double coincidence of wants, which is required in a barter system. This means that individuals can trade their goods or services for money, which can then be used to purchase other goods or services. Finally, money preserves value over time, allowing individuals to save and plan for the future. This function is critical for economic stability, enabling long-term investment and consumption.

1.1 The Emergence of Money

The history of money is a tale of human innovation driven by the need for more efficient ways to trade and store value. In the earliest days of human civilization, barter was the primary method of exchange. People traded goods and services directly, but this system had significant limitations, particularly the need for a double coincidence of wants. For example, if a farmer who grew wheat wanted to trade with a shoemaker, the shoemaker had to want wheat while the farmer wanted shoes. This inefficiency led to the development of commodity money. These early forms of money were commodities with intrinsic value, such as cattle, grain, or precious metals. These commodities were valuable because they could be used directly or exchanged for other goods. However, the practicality of carrying large amounts of grain or cattle made trade cumbersome. This led to adopting more portable commodities, such as gold and silver, which were universally recognized and valued.

As economies grew more complex, carrying large quantities of gold or silver became impractical. To solve this problem, representative money was introduced. This form of money was backed by a physical commodity stored in a secure location, such as a bank. Paper notes were issued to claim the gold or silver held in reserve, making transactions more accessible and safer. This system worked well for centuries and laid the foundation for modern banking.[1]

The move from representative money to fiat money was a significant shift in the history of money. Fiat money has no intrinsic value and is not backed by a physical commodity. Instead, its value comes from government decree and the public's trust in that government. The most common example of fiat money today is paper currency. The US dollar, the Euro, and other national currencies are all forms of fiat money. The transition to fiat money allowed governments more control over their economies, particularly in managing inflation and responding to financial crises. However, it also introduced the risk of hyperinflation if too much money is printed without corresponding economic growth.

In the late twentieth and early twenty-first centuries, the rise of the internet and digital technology gave birth to new forms of money. Digital money includes any money that exists electronically, whether fiat currency held in bank accounts or new forms like cryptocurrencies. Cryptocurrencies, such as Bitcoin, represent the latest evolution in the history of money. Unlike traditional forms of money, cryptocurrencies are decentralized and operate on a blockchain. This technology allows for peer-to-peer transactions without the need for intermediaries like banks. Cryptocurrencies challenge conventional notions of money and can potentially disrupt the global financial system.

1.2 The Emergence of Cryptocurrencies

In recent years, cryptocurrencies have emerged as a revolutionary innovation in the world of finance. They are digital or virtual currencies that use cryptographic techniques to secure transactions and control the creation of new units. Unlike traditional currencies, which are issued and regulated by governments, cryptocurrencies operate on decentralized networks based on blockchain technology. With El Salvador boldly adopting Bitcoin as an official currency, others celebrate cryptocurrencies as high-reward investment assets, offering a tantalizing hedge against inflation. While debates rage over whether Bitcoin is truly a currency or just an asset, the true added value of this revolutionary technology continues to spark curiosity and skepticism among researchers (Huynh et al., 2022).

Cryptocurrencies embody an idealized form of money that offers several key advantages over traditional financial systems:

1. *Trustless*: Traditional financial systems rely on trust in intermediaries such as banks, payment processors, and governments. Cryptocurrencies eliminate the need for trust by using cryptographic algorithms and decentralized networks to

[1] See Hart and Ortiz (2014), p. 3f.

validate transactions. This means that participants do not need to know or trust each other to transact securely.

2. *Borderless*: Cryptocurrencies are not bound by national borders. They can be transferred globally with minimal friction, making them a truly global currency. This borderless nature has significant implications for international trade, remittances, and financial inclusion, particularly in regions with limited access to traditional banking services.
3. *Permissionless*: In traditional financial systems, access to banking services and payment networks is often restricted by regulations, fees, and geographical limitations. Cryptocurrencies are open to anyone with an internet connection, allowing users to participate in the financial system without needing permission from any central authority.
4. *Immutable*: Once a transaction is recorded on a blockchain, it cannot be altered or deleted. This immutability ensures the integrity of the transaction history and protects against fraud. In traditional financial systems, transactions can be reversed or altered, leading to potential disputes and uncertainties.
5. *Incorruptible*: Cryptocurrencies' decentralized nature makes them resistant to censorship, manipulation, and interference by governments or other centralized entities. This incorruptibility is particularly important in regions with unstable political systems or high levels of corruption, where traditional financial systems may be vulnerable to abuse.

These attributes make cryptocurrencies an attractive alternative to traditional forms of money, particularly in an increasingly digital and globalized world.

1.3 Blockchain Technology

Blockchain technology is the foundation of most cryptocurrencies and is considered one of the most significant technological innovations of the twenty-first century. A blockchain is a distributed ledger that records transactions across multiple computers in a network. This decentralized approach ensures that the data is secure, transparent, and resistant to tampering. A blockchain consists of a series of "blocks," each containing a list of transactions. These blocks are linked together in a chronological sequence, forming a "chain." The name "blockchain" comes from this structure, where each block is securely connected to the one before.

To understand how blockchains work, consider the Glassbox Analogy. Imagine a glass box where anyone can deposit a piece of information. Everyone can see the information inside the box, but only the person with the correct key can access or remove it. This analogy illustrates the transparency and security features of blockchain technology. In a blockchain, *every transaction is visible to all participants in the network*. However, the data is protected by cryptographic algorithms, ensuring that only authorized parties can modify it. This transparency and security are what make blockchain ideal for recording and verifying transactions in a trustless environment. The combination of a tamper-proof ledger and digital signatures is what makes blockchain technology so revolutionary. The ledger is tamper-proof because each block in the chain is cryptographically linked to the previous one. If someone tries to alter a block, they must change all subsequent blocks, which is practically impossible without controlling most of the network's computing power.[2]

Digital signatures play a crucial role in ensuring the authenticity and integrity of transactions. When a transaction is made, it is signed with a private key unique to the user. Anyone can verify this signature with the corresponding public key, ensuring that the rightful owner authorized the transaction. Using digital signatures ensures that the data recorded on the blockchain is secure and verifiable, making it difficult for malicious actors to alter or forge transactions.

Blockchain databases have several essential qualities that distinguish them from traditional databases:

1. *Immutability*: Once recorded on a blockchain, data cannot be changed or deleted. This immutability is critical for ensuring the integrity of the transaction history and protecting against fraud and tampering. In contrast, administrators can modify traditional databases, making them more vulnerable to unauthorized changes.
2. *Security*: Blockchain uses advanced cryptographic techniques to secure data. These include hashing algorithms, digital signatures, and encryption to protect the data from unauthorized access. The decentralized nature of blockchain also enhances security, as there is no single point of failure that attackers can exploit.
3. *Transparency*: All transactions on a blockchain are visible to all network participants. This transparency helps build trust among users and reduces the risk of fraud. In traditional financial systems, transactions are often opaque, with only authorized parties having access to the details. Blockchain's transparency ensures that all participants have a clear view of the transaction history.
4. *Decentralization*: Unlike traditional databases, which are usually controlled by a single entity, blockchain is decentralized. This means no single party controls the entire network, reducing the risk of manipulation or censorship. Decentralization also makes the network more resilient, as it is not dependent on a central server or authority.

[2] Cryptography is the science of secure communication. It involves techniques for encoding and decoding information to prevent unauthorized access. In the context of blockchain, cryptography is used to secure transactions and ensure the integrity of the data. In symmetric encryption, the same key is used for encryption and decryption. This method is fast and efficient but has a significant drawback: anyone can decrypt the data if the key is compromised. Symmetric encryption is often used to encrypt large amounts of data quickly. On the other hand, asymmetric encryption uses two keys: a public key and a private key. The public key is used to encrypt data, while the private key is used to decrypt it. This method is more secure because even if the public key is known, decrypting the data without the private key is impossible. Asymmetric encryption is used in blockchains to secure transactions and ensure that only the intended recipient can access the data.

These features collectively make blockchain technology a robust and trustworthy foundation for modern digital transactions, offering unparalleled security, transparency, and resilience compared to traditional systems.

In a blockchain network, each user has a pair of keys: a private key and a public key. The private key is known only to the user and is used to sign transactions, while the public key is shared with others and is used to verify the authenticity of the signed transactions. This system ensures that transactions are secure and verifiable and that only the rightful owner can authorize a transaction. In this framework, a hashing function is a mathematical algorithm that takes an input (or "message") and returns a fixed-size string of characters, typically a hexadecimal number. In blockchain, hashing creates a *unique identifier* for each block. This identifier, or hash, is based on the block's contents and the previous block's hash, ensuring that the blocks are securely linked together. The hashing function is crucial for the security and integrity of the blockchain. It ensures that even a tiny change in the input data will produce a completely different hash, making it easy to detect tampering. Hashing also plays a vital role in the proof-of-work consensus mechanism, where miners compete to find a hash that meets specific criteria.

Remember that decentralization is one of the most important features of blockchain technology. In a decentralized network, control is distributed across multiple nodes rather than concentrated in a single entity. This reduces the risk of censorship, manipulation, and single points of failure. Every participant (or node) has a copy of the entire blockchain in a blockchain network. This ensures that the network remains operational even if some nodes fail or are compromised. Decentralization also makes it difficult for any single party to alter the data on the blockchain, as they would need to control most of the network's computing power. This makes blockchain networks more secure and resilient than traditional centralized systems.

Mining is the process by which new Bitcoins are created and transactions are added to the blockchain. Bitcoin uses a proof-of-work (PoW) consensus mechanism, which requires miners to solve complex mathematical puzzles in order to validate transactions and add them to the blockchain. This process is resource-intensive, requiring significant computational power, but it also ensures the security and integrity of the Bitcoin network.

2 Bitcoin and Ethereum

Cryptocurrencies are digital or virtual currencies that use cryptography for security. They operate on decentralized networks based on blockchain technology. The most well-known cryptocurrency is Bitcoin, but there are many others, including Ethereum, which have their own unique features and use cases. The number of actively traded cryptocurrencies has been increasing ever since their creation (see Fig. 1).

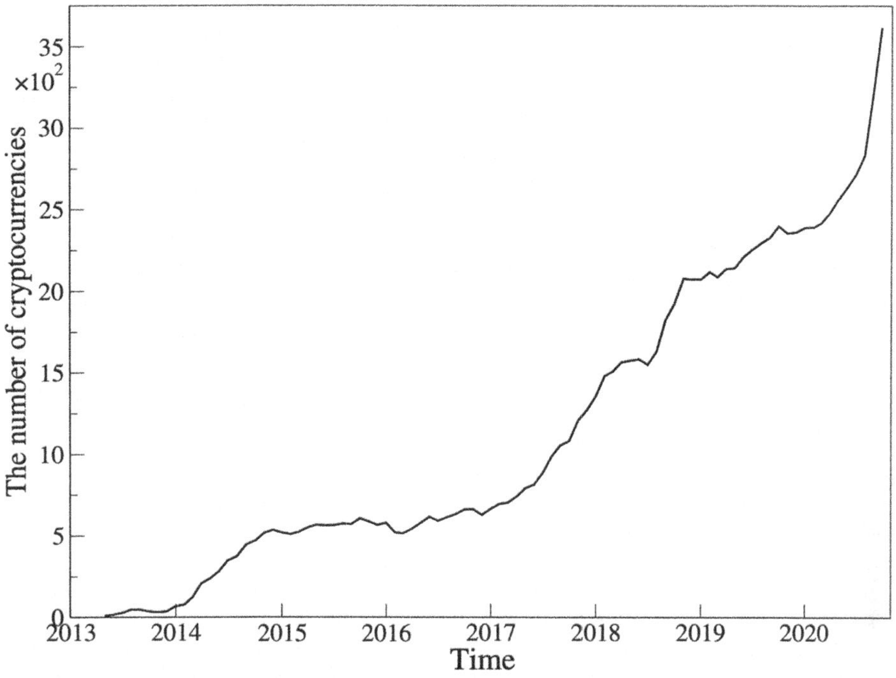

Fig. 1 Number of actively traded cryptocurrencies

2.1 *Bitcoin*

The first and most widely recognized cryptocurrency, Bitcoin (BTC), was introduced in 2008 by an entity under the nickname *Satoshi Nakamoto* during the global financial crisis of 2008 to 2010. Bitcoin was designed as a peer-to-peer digital currency that could operate without a central authority like a bank or government. Central banks began to significantly increase the monetary base ("printing money") to mitigate the crisis. This led to weakened trust in the traditional currencies. Bitcoin is often called "digital gold" because, like gold, it is scarce and requires effort (in the form of computational work) to obtain. However, Bitcoin also has the added benefits of being easily transferable and divisible, making it a more practical medium of exchange in the digital age. Bitcoin is sometimes called "the internet of money" because it enables the transfer of value over the internet without intermediaries. Just as the internet revolutionized communication by allowing information to be exchanged freely and globally, Bitcoin aims to revolutionize finance by enabling the free and global exchange of value.

The comparison to gold is apt because Bitcoin shares several characteristics with precious metals: it is scarce, durable, and difficult to counterfeit. However, Bitcoin can be sent worldwide in minutes, unlike gold, which makes it a more versatile asset. The Bitcoin whitepaper, published by Satoshi Nakamoto in 2008, outlines the

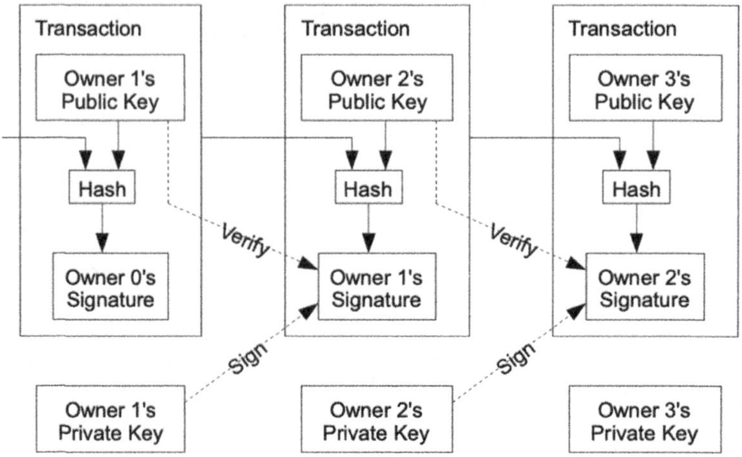

Fig. 2 Electronic coins as chains of digital signatures. *Source*: Nakamoto (2008)

principles behind Bitcoin, describing it as a "peer-to-peer electronic cash system" that allows online payments to be sent directly from one party to another without going through a financial institution. The whitepaper is considered a foundational document in cryptocurrency and has inspired the creation of many other digital currencies (see Nakamoto, 2008). The Bitcoin protocol revolutionized finance by combining a peer-to-peer network with cutting-edge cryptographic techniques—public and private keys—and introducing a groundbreaking consensus mechanism known as *Proof of Work* (PoW). PoW is essential for securing the blockchain and ensuring that all transactions are legitimate. It requires significant computational power, making it expensive and difficult to attack the network. However, the high energy consumption associated with PoW has led to the development of alternative consensus mechanisms, such as *Proof of Stake* (PoS). For the first time in history, Bitcoin offered a way for people across the globe to trust each other and conduct transactions over the internet without the need for a central authority. It shifted the foundation of trust from traditional institutions like states and central banks to the power of technology itself, redefining how we perceive and manage value in the digital age.

Figure 2 illustrates how the network "timestamps transactions by hashing them into an ongoing chain of hash-based proof-of-work, forming a record that cannot be changed without redoing the proof-of-work. (. . .) Electronic coins are defined as chains of digital signatures. Each owner transfers the coin to the next by digitally signing a hash of the previous transaction and the public key of the next owner and adding these to the end of the coin. A payee can verify the signatures to verify the chain of ownership".[3]

[3] Nakamoto (2008), pp. 3 and 6.

Fig. 3 Bitcoin price in US Dollars

Bitcoin's uniqueness lies in its combination of decentralization, security, and scarcity. Unlike traditional currencies, which governments can print at will, Bitcoin has a fixed supply. This hard cap ensures that Bitcoin is deflationary by nature, meaning its value will likely increase over time as demand grows. The identity of Bitcoin's creator, Satoshi Nakamoto, remains a mystery. Nakamoto's decision to remain anonymous has added to Bitcoin's intrigue and mythology. What is known is that Nakamoto was deeply influenced by the 2008 financial crisis and was motivated by a desire to create an economic system that governments or central banks could not manipulate. The price of Bitcoin has increased dramatically since then (see Fig. 3).

Mining is the process by which new Bitcoins are created, and transactions are added to the blockchain. Bitcoin uses a proof-of-work (PoW) consensus mechanism, which requires miners to solve complex mathematical puzzles to validate transactions and add them to the blockchain. This process is resource-intensive, requiring significant computational power, but it also ensures the security and integrity of the Bitcoin network.

One of the most important features of Bitcoin is its *fixed supply* of 21 million coins. This limit was hard-coded into the Bitcoin protocol by Satoshi Nakamoto to prevent inflation. As more people adopt Bitcoin and its supply remains fixed, the value of each Bitcoin is expected to increase, making it a valuable store of wealth.

The halving algorithm is another unique aspect of Bitcoin. Approximately every four years, miners' reward for validating transactions is cut in half. This process, known as "halving," reduces the rate at which new Bitcoins are created and ensures that the total supply of Bitcoin does not exceed 21 million. Halving events are highly anticipated in the Bitcoin community because they often lead to increased scarcity and, consequently, higher prices.

Bitcoin can be traded on cryptocurrency exchanges, where users can buy and sell Bitcoin for other cryptocurrencies or fiat currencies. It can also be used for peer-to-peer transactions, where individuals transfer Bitcoin directly to each other's wallets without needing an exchange. The Bitcoin Lightning Network is a second-layer solution designed to improve Bitcoin's scalability by enabling faster and cheaper transactions. The Lightning Network allows users to open payment channels between each other, through which multiple transactions can be conducted off-chain. These transactions are then settled on the Bitcoin blockchain, reducing the load on the network and making it more efficient. The value of Bitcoin is a subject of much debate. Some view it as a speculative asset, while others consider it a revolutionary form of money. Unlike traditional investments like stocks or bonds, Bitcoin does not generate cash flows or dividends, making it difficult to value using conventional financial metrics. Bitcoin's value proposition lies in its ability to serve as a decentralized store of value, a medium of exchange, and a unit of account. Its fixed supply, security, and global accessibility make it an attractive alternative to traditional currencies and assets. For many, Bitcoin represents a hedge against inflation and a way to preserve wealth in an increasingly uncertain global economy.

Bitcoin, despite its rising popularity, faces criticism in several key areas. Its extreme price volatility makes it an unreliable store of value, with frequent fluctuations deterring long-term investment. The environmental impact of Bitcoin mining, which consumes vast amounts of energy, raises concerns about its sustainability, especially as global efforts focus on reducing carbon emissions. Additionally, Bitcoin's pseudonymous nature makes it difficult to trace transactions, leading to its association with illegal activities like money laundering and tax evasion. These challenges present hurdles to Bitcoin's broader acceptance and long-term viability. Table 1 in the Appendix provides a balanced view of cryptocurrencies' advantages and disadvantages, highlighting both their potential benefits and inherent risks.

2.2 Ethereum

Ethereum is another primary cryptocurrency that has gained significant attention since its creation.[4] Unlike Bitcoin, which was designed primarily as a digital cur-

[4] Technically speaking, "Ethereum" is referring to the blockchain network. It is a major blockchain-based platform for smart contracts but has been often referred to as the cryptocurrency itself. The native coin (the Ethereum blockchain records transactions for many cryptocurrencies which is

rency, Ethereum was created as a platform for decentralized applications (DApps) and smart contracts. It is a decentralized, open-source blockchain that allows developers to build and deploy smart contracts and decentralized applications. It was created in 2013 by Vitalik Buterin, a Canadian computer programmer who saw the potential for blockchain technology to be used for more than just digital currency.[5]

While Bitcoin is often compared to digital gold, Ethereum is more like a decentralized supercomputer. The critical difference between the two lies in their use cases: Bitcoin is primarily a store of value and a medium of exchange. Ethereum serves as a platform for decentralized applications and smart contracts. Additionally, Ethereum uses a different consensus mechanism, known as proof of stake, which is less energy-intensive than Bitcoin's proof of work. Ethereum has several essential qualities that make it unique:

1. *Smart contracts*: These are self-executing contracts with the terms of the agreement directly written into code. Smart contracts automatically enforce and execute agreements when predefined conditions are met, eliminating the need for intermediaries.
2. *Decentralized applications (DApps):* Ethereum allows developers to build decentralized applications that run on the blockchain. These applications are open-source, censorship-resistant, and can operate without downtime.
3. *Proof of Stake (PoS) consensus mechanism*: Unlike Bitcoin's PoW, Ethereum uses PoS, where validators are chosen to add new blocks based on the amount of cryptocurrency they hold and are willing to "stake" as collateral. This method is more energy-efficient and promotes greater decentralization.[6]

Smart contracts are one of Ethereum's most significant innovations. These contracts are written in code and automatically execute when certain conditions are met. For example, a smart contract could be used to automatically transfer ownership of a digital asset once payment is received. Using smart contracts eliminates the need for intermediaries, reduces the risk of fraud, and increases the efficiency of transactions.

The value of Ethereum, like Bitcoin, is influenced by various factors, including its adoption, utility, and overall market sentiment towards cryptocurrencies.

---

unlike Bitcoin) is called "Ether". However, today no one really refers to it as "Ether", especially in the finance world. For example, if we asked the average person about Ethereum they would assume we were referring to the cryptocurrency (although it's technically called Ether) and not the blockchain network. This is not confused with Bitcoin because the cryptocurrency and the blockchain are both called Bitcoin.

[5] Buterin has published a few articles on blockchains and cryptocurrencies on his website, see https://vitalik.eth.limo.

[6] Note that proof of stake and proof of work are two different methods for achieving consensus in a blockchain network. In proof of work, miners compete to solve complex puzzles to validate transactions, which requires a significant amount of computational power. In proof of stake, validators are chosen based on the amount of cryptocurrency they hold and are willing to stake as collateral. PoS is generally considered more energy-efficient and scalable than PoW.

Ethereum's value proposition lies in its ability to serve as a platform for decentralized applications and smart contracts. Unlike Bitcoin, which is primarily a store of value, Ethereum is a programmable blockchain that can create a wide range of applications. This flexibility and utility give Ethereum a unique value proposition, enabling innovation in decentralized finance (DeFi), supply chain management, and digital identity (Tikhomirov, 2018).

3 Key Concepts in Cryptocurrency and Blockchain

3.1 Stablecoins

Stablecoins are a class of cryptocurrencies that aim to provide price stability by being pegged to a reserve asset, such as a fiat currency (e.g., USD) or a commodity (e.g., gold). Unlike traditional cryptocurrencies like Bitcoin and Ethereum, which can experience significant volatility, stablecoins are designed to maintain a stable value. This stability is achieved through various mechanisms, including:

1. *Fiat-collateralized stablecoins*: These are backed by fiat currencies held in reserve by a central issuer. An equivalent amount of fiat currency is kept in reserve for every stablecoin issued. Examples include Tether (USDT) and USD Coin (USDC).
2. *Crypto-collateralized stablecoins*: These are backed by other cryptocurrencies, often over-collateralized to account for the volatility of the backing assets. An example is DAI, which brings Ethereum and other cryptocurrencies back.
3. *Algorithmic stablecoins*: These use algorithms and smart contracts to manage the stablecoin supply, maintaining its peg without direct collateral. An example is TerraUSD (UST), which uses an algorithm to adjust its supply based on demand.

Stablecoins play a crucial role in the cryptocurrency ecosystem by providing a stable medium of exchange and store of value. They are widely used in trading, allowing traders to move in and out of volatile assets without converting to fiat currency. Moreover, stablecoins facilitate cross-border payments and remittances, offering a faster and cheaper alternative to traditional financial systems.

In decentralized finance (DeFi), stablecoins are often used as collateral for loans, liquidity in decentralized exchanges (DEXs), and as a base currency for trading pairs. Their stability and versatility make them essential to the growing DeFi ecosystem.[7]

[7] DEXs are an important application of Ethereum. DEXs are peer-to-peer marketplaces where cryptocurrency traders can conduct transactions directly without the need for an intermediary. Compared to centralized exchanges, DEXs offer benefits such as increased privacy, lower fees, and reduced risk of hacking.

3.2 *The Role of Regulation*

As cryptocurrencies have grown in popularity, they have attracted the attention of regulators worldwide. The regulatory landscape for cryptocurrencies is complex and varies significantly from one jurisdiction to another. Some countries have embraced cryptocurrencies, enacting laws to regulate their use and encourage innovation. Others have taken a more cautious approach, imposing strict regulations or outright bans.

For example, in the United States, the Securities and Exchange Commission (SEC) has been actively involved in regulating cryptocurrencies, particularly with regard to Initial Coin Offerings (ICOs) and whether certain cryptocurrencies qualify as securities. The regulation of cryptocurrencies and blockchain technologies in the United States is inconsistent, with individual states adopting varied approaches. New York, for example, has strict regulations with its BitLicense, while Wyoming has created a crypto-friendly environment. Other states take moderate or cautious stances.[8] Efforts to create a uniform regulatory framework, such as the Uniform Regulation of Virtual Currency Businesses Act by the Uniform Law Commission, aim to standardize laws across states. At the federal level, agencies like the SEC, CFTC, and FinCEN regulate cryptocurrencies from different perspectives, complicating the regulatory landscape. While initiatives like the Token Taxonomy Act seek to harmonize rules, achieving nationwide consistency remains challenging due to differing state and federal views. In contrast, countries like China have taken a more restrictive stance, banning cryptocurrency exchanges and mining operations while simultaneously exploring the development of their own central bank digital currency (CBDC).

Regulation has a profound impact on the cryptocurrency market. On one hand, transparent and fair rules can provide legitimacy to the market, protect consumers, and encourage institutional adoption. On the other hand, overly stringent regulations can stifle innovation and drive cryptocurrency activities underground. The evolving regulatory environment also influences investor sentiment and market dynamics. Announcements of regulatory actions, such as crackdowns on exchanges or changes in tax policy, often lead to significant price movements in the cryptocurrency market. As the industry matures, regulation will be crucial in determining the future trajectory of cryptocurrencies and blockchain technology.

3.3 *Interoperability and Cross-Chain Technology*

Interoperability refers to the ability of different blockchain networks to communicate and work together. The number of independent blockchains has grown as

[8] For more information, see Girasa (2018).

the cryptocurrency ecosystem expands, each with its rules, consensus mechanisms, and native tokens. However, the lack of interoperability between these blockchains creates silos, limiting the potential of decentralized applications (DApps) and restricting the flow of assets and information across networks.

Cross-chain technology aims to solve this problem by enabling different blockchains to interact with each other (Han et al., 2023). Projects like Polkadot, Cosmos, and Chainlink are leading the way in creating protocols and platforms that facilitate cross-chain communication and asset transfers.

- *Polkadot*: Polkadot is a multi-chain platform that allows different blockchains to connect and share information through its relay chain. It supports "parachains," custom blockchains that can interact with each other within the Polkadot network.
- *Cosmos*: Cosmos is another project focused on interoperability. It uses the Inter-Blockchain Communication (IBC) protocol to enable blockchains to securely transfer tokens and data between each other.
- *Chainlink*: Chainlink is a decentralized oracle network that connects intelligent contracts with external data sources. It plays a crucial role in interoperability by allowing smart contracts on different blockchains to access off-chain data, such as price feeds and weather data.

Interoperability is crucial for the future of blockchain technology and the broader cryptocurrency ecosystem. It allows for greater collaboration and innovation, enabling developers to build more complex and robust applications that can leverage the strengths of multiple blockchains. For example, a DeFi application could use the security of Bitcoin, the innovative contract capabilities of Ethereum, and the scalability of a third blockchain, all in one seamless experience.

Moreover, interoperability can create a more inclusive and connected blockchain ecosystem, where users are not locked into a single platform but can freely move their assets and data across different networks. This interconnectedness will likely drive further adoption and integration of blockchain technology into mainstream applications.

3.4 The Environmental Impact of Cryptocurrencies

One of the most significant criticisms of cryptocurrencies, particularly Bitcoin, is their environmental impact. Bitcoin's proof-of-work (PoW) consensus mechanism, which requires miners to solve complex mathematical puzzles to validate transactions and secure the network, is highly energy-intensive. The Bitcoin network's energy consumption has been compared to that of entire countries, leading to concerns about its sustainability. The high energy usage is primarily due to the competitive nature of PoW, where miners use increasingly powerful hardware to gain an advantage in solving puzzles. This has led to the proliferation of large-scale mining operations, often located in regions with cheap electricity, such as China, Russia, and Iceland.

Several alternative consensus mechanisms have been developed in response to the environmental concerns associated with PoW. One of the most prominent is proof of stake (PoS), which Ethereum and other cryptocurrencies use. In a PoS system, validators are chosen to create new blocks and validate transactions based on the amount of cryptocurrency they hold and are willing to "stake" as collateral. This method is significantly more *energy-efficient* than PoW, as it does not require the same level of computational power. It is also a more transparent solution (Sedlmeir et al., 2020). As a result, PoS has been promoted as a more sustainable alternative to PoW. Additionally, other consensus mechanisms, such as delegated proof of stake (DPoS), proof of authority (PoA), and proof of space (PoSpace), are being explored for their potential to reduce the environmental footprint of blockchain networks. A systematic review of the environmental impact of cryptocurrencies using proof of work and proof of stake consensus algorithms is offered by Wendl et al. (2023).

Some projects are specifically focused on reducing the environmental impact of blockchain technology. For example, the *Chia Network*: Chia uses a consensus mechanism called proof of space and time, which relies on unused hard drive space rather than energy-intensive computations. This approach aims to create a more sustainable blockchain network. Another example is *Algorand*, a blockchain that uses a pure proof-of-stake (PPoS) consensus mechanism designed to be energy-efficient. The Algorand Foundation has committed to becoming a carbon-negative blockchain by purchasing carbon offsets.

The environmental impact of cryptocurrencies remains a topic of intense debate. While alternative consensus mechanisms offer potential solutions, the scale and complexity of the transition from PoW to PoS or other methods pose significant challenges. Furthermore, the broader implications of blockchain technology on energy consumption, resource allocation, and environmental sustainability will continue to be critical considerations as the industry evolves (Goodkind et al., 2020).

3.5 The Complexity of Markets for Cryptocurrencies

Once an independent entity with little to no correlation to traditional financial markets, the cryptocurrency market has undergone a dramatic shift. Previously, prices of major cryptocurrencies moved independently of fiat currencies, stock indices, and commodities. However, this changed abruptly during the market upheaval caused by the COVID-19 pandemic. Suddenly, cryptocurrencies began to show cross-correlations, initially with safer assets like the Japanese yen and later with riskier ones like the S&P 500, other currencies, and commodities.[9] This trend emerged during the initial panic of the pandemic's first wave in early Spring 2020

[9] See Wątorek et al. (2021), p. 101.

and persisted through the recovery phase and the subsequent slowdown in Summer 2020. Investors no longer view the cryptocurrency market as a “haven” but as an integrated global financial network component.

Modern financial markets are complex systems characterized by rapid information flow, diverse participant behavior, and various feedback mechanisms, leading to phenomena like speculative bubbles and crashes. These markets display common complexity characteristics, such as “fat tails” in return distributions, volatility clustering, extended memory, non-linear correlations, persistence, and fractality. As noted by Wątorek et al. (2021):

> The striking development of the cryptocurrency market over the last few years– from being entirely peripheral to capitalizing at the level of an intermediate-size stock exchange – provides a unique opportunity to observe its evolution in a short period.

A crucial distinction sets the cryptocurrency market apart from traditional markets: the opportunity to observe its evolution from the beginning. Traditional markets have long histories, so their structural development can only be studied retrospectively. In contrast, the cryptocurrency market, established just over a decade ago, offers a rare glimpse into the process of structural self-organization from its inception to a relatively mature form in a remarkably short time. The critical question now is to what extent, after such rapid development, the complex characteristics of the cryptocurrency market mirror those of more established markets. This raises an intriguing question: is this newfound coupling a temporary reaction to unprecedented circumstances, or does it signal a more profound, ongoing maturation of the cryptocurrency market that will continue?

4 A Look Into the Future

The future of blockchain and cryptocurrency is poised to be transformative, with significant implications across various sectors. In this section, we will discuss some key trends and potential developments.

As *blockchain technology* matures, we can expect broader adoption across industries beyond finance, including supply chain management, healthcare, real estate, and more. Cryptocurrencies may become more integrated into daily transactions, with consumers and businesses increasingly accepting them as payment methods. The technology underlying blockchain is expected to continue advancing, with improvements in scalability, speed, and energy efficiency. Innovations such as sharding, proof-of-stake, and other consensus mechanisms could make blockchain networks more efficient and environmentally sustainable.

Decentralized finance will grow significantly, offering alternatives to traditional financial services such as lending, borrowing, and trading without intermediaries. This could democratize access to financial services, particularly in regions underserved by conventional banks. It already represents one of the most exciting developments in the cryptocurrency space. DeFi refers to financial services built on blockchain technology that operates without intermediaries like banks or brokerages. These services include lending, borrowing, trading, and yield farming. The DeFi ecosystem has proliferated, with the total value locked in DeFi protocols reaching tens of billions of dollars in just a few years. This growth is driven by the promise of greater financial inclusion, lower costs, and increased transparency compared to traditional financial systems. DeFi applications are typically built on Ethereum, which provides the infrastructure for smart contracts and decentralized applications. However, other blockchains, such as Binance Smart Chain, Solana, and Avalanche, are also emerging as important players in the DeFi space. While the potential of DeFi is immense, it also comes with significant risks. For instance, smart contracts are self-executing and cannot be altered once deployed. If a smart contract contains a bug or vulnerability, it can be exploited by malicious actors, leading to the loss of funds. Several high-profile DeFi hacks have occurred due to smart contract vulnerabilities. Also, DeFi operates in a legal gray area, with many services not subject to the same regulations as traditional financial institutions. This lack of regulation can lead to user risks, including the potential for fraud and the absence of consumer protections. Finally, DeFi protocols often rely on liquidity provided by users, who are incentivized with rewards. However, sudden changes in market conditions can lead to liquidity crises, where users cannot withdraw their funds.

As the *regulatory environment* evolves, DeFi is likely to gain more mainstream acceptance, attracting institutional investors and more extensive user bases. Integrating DeFi with traditional finance through mechanisms like tokenized assets and regulated DeFi platforms could also bridge the gap between these two worlds. The regulatory landscape for cryptocurrencies and blockchain will likely evolve, with governments and international bodies working to establish more explicit frameworks. This could help legitimize cryptocurrencies, encouraging institutional investment and broader public acceptance while addressing security, fraud, and environmental impact concerns.[10] The regulatory landscape for cryptocurrencies and blockchain is likely to evolve, particularly with governments and international bodies working to establish more explicit frameworks. This could help legitimize cryptocurrencies, encouraging institutional investment and broader public acceptance while addressing security, fraud, and environmental impact concerns. The future of blockchain and cryptocurrency holds immense potential for reshaping how we conduct transactions, store value, and interact with digital systems. However, this future will also depend on how challenges such as regulation, security, and scalability are addressed.

[10] The future will likely see increased focus on interoperability, allowing different blockchain networks to communicate and share data seamlessly. This will enable a more interconnected blockchain ecosystem, enhancing the utility of blockchain applications and cryptocurrencies. Many governments are exploring the creation of *Central Bank Digital Currencies* or CBDCs, which are digital versions of their national currencies. These could coexist with cryptocurrencies, potentially leading to new forms of competition and collaboration between centralized and decentralized digital currencies.

Appendix

Table 1 Overview of advantages and disadvantages of cryptocurrencies

Pros	Cons
Decentralization—Cryptocurrencies operate on decentralized networks, reducing reliance on central authorities like banks or governments.	**Volatility**—Cryptocurrency prices are highly volatile, leading to significant fluctuations in value.
Security—Advanced cryptography and blockchain offer security against fraud and hacking.	**Regulatory Uncertainty**—The regulatory environment is still developing, creating uncertainty for investors and users.
Transparency—Blockchain transparency allows anyone to verify transactions, fostering trust.	**Scalability Issues**—Bitcoin faces challenges in scaling to handle high transaction volumes.
Low Transaction Costs—Transactions, especially across borders, are cheaper than traditional methods.	**Environmental Impact**—The energy-intensive "Proof of Work" consensus mechanism contributes to a significant environmental footprint.
Financial Inclusion—Cryptocurrencies provide access to financial services for people in regions with limited banking infrastructure.	**Potential for Illegal Activity**—The pseudonymous nature of cryptocurrencies can facilitate illegal activities, money laundering, and tax evasion.
Global Accessibility—Cryptocurrencies can be accessed and used anywhere with an internet connection, breaking down geographical barriers.	**Irreversibility of Transactions**—Transactions on the blockchain are irreversible, which can be a drawback in cases of fraud or error.
Innovation and Flexibility—The technology allows for innovative financial products like smart contracts and DeFi platforms.	**Complexity and User Knowledge**—The technical nature of cryptocurrencies can be difficult for the average user to understand and navigate.
Ownership and Control—Users have full control over their assets without the need for intermediaries.	**Adoption and Acceptance**—While growing, the acceptance of cryptocurrencies for everyday transactions is still limited.
Potential for High Returns—Cryptocurrencies have the potential for significant investment returns due to their rapid growth and market expansion.	**Security Risks**—Despite strong security measures, exchanges, and wallets can still be vulnerable to hacking and theft.
Resistance to Censorship—Decentralized networks are less susceptible to censorship and government control.	**Lack of Consumer Protections**—Cryptocurrencies often lack the consumer protections found in traditional financial systems, such as insurance contracts.

References

Davis, A. E. (2020). Money as a social institution: Its historical emergence and political implications. *How Social Forces Impact the Economy*, 81–96.

Girasa, R. (2018). *Regulation of cryptocurrencies and blockchain technologies. National and International Perspectives*. Palgrave Macmillan.

Goodkind, A. L., Jones, B. A., & Berrens, R. P. (2020). Cryptodamages: Monetary value estimates of the air pollution and human health impacts of cryptocurrency mining. *Energy Research & Social Science, 59*, 101281.

Han, P., Yan, Z., Ding, W., Fei, S., & Wan, Z. (2023). A survey on cross-chain technologies. *Distributed Ledger Technologies: Research and Practice, 2*(2), 1–30.

Hart, K., & Ortiz, H. (2014). The anthropology of money and finance: Between ethnography and world history. *Annual Review of Anthropology, 43*(1), 465–482.

Huynh, A. N. Q., Duong, D., Burggraf, T., Luong, H. T. T., & Bui, N. H. (2022). Energy consumption and Bitcoin market. *Asia-Pacific Financial Markets, 29*(1), 79–93.

Nakamoto, S. (2008). Bitcoin: A peer-to-peer electronic cash system. *Satoshi Nakamoto*. Available online: https://static.upbitcare.com/931b8bfc-f0e0-4588-be6e-b98a27991df1.pdf

Ostroy, J. M., & Starr, R. M. (1990). The transactions role of money. *Handbook of Monetary Economics, 1*, 3–62.

Sedlmeir, J., Buhl, H. U., Fridgen, G., & Keller, R. (2020). Ein Blick auf aktuelle Entwicklungen bei Blockchains und deren Auswirkungen auf den Energieverbrauch. *Informatik Spektrum, 43*(6), 391–404.

Tikhomirov, S. (2018). Ethereum: state of knowledge and research perspectives. In *Foundations and practice of security: 10th International Symposium, FPS 2017, Nancy, France, October 23–25, 2017, Revised Selected Papers 10* (pp. 206–221). Springer International Publishing.

Wątorek, M., Drożdż, S., Kwapień, J., Minati, L., Oświęcimka, P., & Stanuszek, M. (2021). Multiscale characteristics of the emerging global cryptocurrency market. *Physics Reports, 901*, 1–82.

Wendl, M., Doan, M. H., & Sassen, R. (2023). The environmental impact of cryptocurrencies using proof of work and proof of stake consensus algorithms: A systematic review. *Journal of Environmental Management, 326*, 116530.

Annette Hofmann is the Great American Insurance Group Endowed Professor and Director of the Lindner Center for Insurance and Risk Management with the University of Cincinnati's Lindner College of Business. She previously served as the Robert F. Corroon Chair in Risk Economics at the Maurice R. Greenberg School of Risk Management, Insurance, and Actuarial Science at St. John's University in New York. She also held risk management and insurance faculty appointments with other business schools in Germany before she came to the United States.

Chad Dulle is a PhD candidate in finance at the University of Cincinnati's Lindner College of Business, specializing in corporate governance, behavioral finance, and executive characteristics. His research focuses on how traits such as overconfidence and gender influence firm outcomes, with particular emphasis on mergers and acquisitions (M&A), innovation, and social media behavior. Chad is on track to complete his PhD by May 2025, with a dissertation titled "Executive Traits and Firm Outcomes: How Overconfidence and Gender Impact M&As, Innovation, and Social Media Behavior."

Informal Economy and Central Bank Digital Currency

Eun Young Oh and Shuonan Zhang

JEL Classification: E26, E40, E42, E58

1 Introduction

Technological advances in the digital economy have opened the possibility for central banks to issue digital fiat currency—*Central Bank Digital Currency* (CBDC).[1] Ongoing research has spurred a broad discussion about whether central banks should issue CBDC. Proponents argue that CBDC has lower transaction costs than cash (Griffoli et al., 2018), could avoid potential instability caused by private money creation (Brunnermeier & Niepelt, 2019), and improves macroeconomic management as well as the control of money[2] (Bindseil, 2020). The main moti-

This research did not receive any specific grant from funding agencies in the public, commercial, or not-for-profit sectors.

[1] By definition, CBDC is "an electronic form of central bank money that could be used by households and businesses to make payments and store value." (Bank of England)

[2] Bindseil (2020) suggests that CBDC could be helpful to overcome illicit payments and strengthen monetary policies.

E. Y. Oh
Kookmin University, Seoul, Republic of Korea
e-mail: ey.oh@kookmin.ac.kr

S. Zhang (✉)
University of Southampton, Southampton, UK
e-mail: huonan.zhang@soton.ac.uk

A. Zarifis, X. Cheng (eds.), *Fintech and the Emerging Ecosystems*, Financial Innovation and Technology, https://doi.org/10.1007/978-3-031-83402-8_3

vations for emerging economies are a broader tax base from limiting tax evasion and other illicit activities, as well as improved financial inclusion by allowing the unbanked to have access to electronic payment systems (Boar & Wehrli, 2021). Prior research has commonly focused on issuer-related perspectives of CBDC; however, little information is available on the preferences and motivations of consumers and businesses related to the adoption of CBDC. The goal of our paper is to assess the extent to which CBDC can be accepted by end users and circulated in the economy when end user's tax avoidance activities are taken into account, and how the use of CBDC impacts the informal economy.

We build a two-sector dynamic stochastic general equilibrium (DSGE) model with formal and informal productions to understand the relationship between CBDC and the informal economy based on Fernández and Meza (2015) and Orsi et al. (2014). The end users value anonymity in transactions offered by cash payments, especially in countries where significant informal incomes discourage people from using digital payments for tax evasion.[3] Following Agur et al. (2022), the CBDC in our model is designed to blend the characteristics of cash (i.e., peer-to-peer transactions) and the digital nature of deposits (i.e., interest rates). Compared with cash, CBDC is a more efficient means of payment because of lower transaction costs (Hasan et al., 2013; Kosse et al., 2017; Griffoli et al., 2018)[4] but is subject to central bank monitoring and spillover effects on the enforcement of tax payments. Consequently, CBDC leads to a trade-off between cost efficiency and anonymity for households who determine the optimal allocation between cash and CBDC. This decision, in turn, affects labor allocation through the income gap between formal and informal sectors.

To quantitatively evaluate the implications of our model, we calibrate parameters for multiple cases, which allow us to conduct cross-country comparisons. Our results suggest an L-shaped relationship between the informal economy and CBDC, thereby implying that countries with large informal economies—typically developing countries—might be less likely to adopt and widely use CBDC. Moreover, we show a formalization effect on the informal sector due to the spillover effect of CBDC in detecting informal incomes. However, the magnitude of the formalization effect diminishes with the scale of the informal economy.

In order to simultaneously promote the adoption of CBDC and the formalization effect, we consider two policy tools—tax reduction and CBDC interest rates. A tax reduction weakens household incentives to evade taxes, leading to lower opportunity costs of detection when using CBDC. A positive CBDC interest rate directly

[3] There are many reasons why people value anonymity, which is unnecessary to be monetary reasons, such as a desire for privacy (Low et al., 1994), or their own beliefs and morality (Goldberg & Lewis, 2000). In our framework, the preference for anonymity stems from informal incomes. We choose such a monetary reason due to modeling simplicity. Cash allows people to preserve their privacy. One may consider other forms of anonymity which could strengthen our argument.

[4] Existing literature mainly focuses on transaction costs in cash management. In addition, the low transaction costs could be achieved by promoting financial inclusion since CBDC provides a gateway to access formal financial services (Griffoli et al., 2018).

increases incentives for households to hold CBDC. Both policies can encourage the adoption of CBDC. The increased CBDC share in money, in turn, leads to improved monitoring of informal earnings and thus strengthens formalization effects.

In light of model mechanisms, we apply the CBDC informal economy relationship in a business cycle framework to study the implications of adjusting the CBDC interest rate for macroeconomic fluctuations. Following the impulse response analysis, we find that adjusting the CBDC interest rate triggers a reallocation effect between formal and informal sectors, which in turn leads to a more pronounced impulse response of formal output to policy shocks. Given counter-cyclical implementation of government policies, the CBDC rate adjustment could contribute to stabilization of measured business cycles. Such a finding, when combined with the effects of tax rate adjustment, suggests the importance of coordination between fiscal authorities and central banks in macroeconomic management. Moreover, we also show an efficiency gain from CBDC. When more CBDC is used in transactions, the aggregate transaction costs would be lower, which, in turn, stimulates consumption.

Following the quantitative analysis, we further examine the welfare implications of CBDC based on different scenarios. Overall, the presence of CBDC leads to welfare gains by reducing transaction costs to stimulate consumption and by formalizing the economy so that labor forces can enjoy better social protection. The welfare-enhancing effects could become larger if (i) we further account for the interactions between CBDC and stochastic disturbances, (ii) the share of the informal economy becomes small, and (iii) productivity gaps between formal and informal sectors become large. However, if users strongly prefer payment anonymity, the welfare gains could be significantly dampened.

This chapter relates to the growing area of CBDC (e.g., Brunnermeier & Niepelt, 2019; Fernández-Villaverde et al., 2020). Focusing on the design of CBDC, Andolfatto (2021) and Agur et al. (2022) analyze factors that determine the demand for CBDC among different types of money. Based on DSGE models, a strand of literature analyzes implications of CBDC (Barrdear & Kumhof, 2016; Mehl et al., 2020; Uhlig & Xie, 2021) for monetary policies and open economy issues. By extending DSGE modeling of CBDC, our contribution is to highlight the demand for CBDC from the end-user perspective, with a greater focus on the trade-off between cost efficiency and anonymity in payments. Our study proposes the informal economy as another important determinator which affects CBDC through the anonymity feature. Although CBDC can reduce transaction costs by promoting financial inclusion, which is particularly important for developing countries, this benefit could be outweighed by households being in favor of informal incomes. As a result, it could be more difficult for developing countries than for developed countries to adopt CBDC, since informality is more pronounced in the former.

This study is also related to the literature on the informal economy. Existing literature suggests that the informal economy acts as an alternative source of growth and as a cushion in business cycles (Loayza & Rigolini, 2011; Fernández & Meza, 2015). However, the coexistence of formal and informal economies is only a second-best situation. Low productivity (Prado, 2011), lack of social protection (Orsi et al., 2014), and financial exclusion (Capasso & Jappelli, 2013) render informality an undesirable component of an economy. Moreover, the presence of informality causes measurement errors (Gomis-Porqueras et al., 2014; Restrepo-Echavarria, 2014) and weakens the propagation of government policies (Alberola & Urrutia, 2020). This chapter contributes to the literature by highlighting how the introduction of CBDC is conducive to the formalization process not only in the long run but also in a short-run business cycle framework, albeit the benefits are asymmetric across countries. Our findings also connect to interactions between the informal economy and fiscal or monetary policies. Building on Orsi et al. (2014) who find that a high tax rate stimulates the informal economy and Alberola and Urrutia (2020) who show that informality dampens the transmission of monetary policies, we show how adjusting the CBDC interest rate triggers a reallocation between formal and informal labor. We therefore complement the literature on how to improve the formalization effect of fiscal policies and bridge the gap regarding implications of monetary policies for the informal economy.

The rest of this chapter is organized as follows. Section 2 reviews some facts and motivational evidence followed by Sect. 3 that presents the model with CBDC and the informal economy. Section 4 presents our parameter calibrations, and Sect. 5 uses the calibrated model parameters for steady-state analyses. In Sect. 6, the implications of the relationship between the informal economy and CBDC for business cycles is examined followed by Sect. 7 that examines the welfare implications of CBDC. Section 8 concludes with comments.

2 The Informal Economy and Payments

Cash is the crucial medium for undeclared monetized exchanges, as it is not traceable by public authorities in an informal economy. In this way, businesses can evade tax and social security contributions, and employees can avoid paying income taxes. However, cash payments aggravate the tax enforcement problem (Gordon & Li, 2009), which is one of the key aspects of the informal economy. The size of informal activities is larger in developing economies than in developed economies (Capasso & Jappelli, 2013), which is linked to cash being dominant in developing economies. This is despite the rapid development of financial innovation in developing countries (Bech et al., 2018) because cash provides anonymity for users which allows them to hide their transaction histories. For numerous reasons, such as tackling tax evasion and increasing financial inclusion, policymakers encourage the use of digital payments and have tried to change the payment behavior of individuals.[5] Most forms of electronic money or digital payments can be easily traced by public authorities. For instance, bank account records and the use of credit

[5] Numerous countries have applied tax incentives to encourage the use of electronic payments (Sung et al., 2017). For instance, Japan introduced the consumption tax reward point program

Table 1 Informal economies and digital payments

Variables	(1) 2013		(2) 2016	
Informal economy	**−2.128*****	**−0.513***	**−1.779*****	−0.219
	(−8.32)	(−1.69)	(−9.21)	(−0.93)
Control variables				
Financial depth		**31.614*****		**19.811****
		(3.95)		(2.43)
Financial access		6.734		12.614
		(0.72)		(1.21)
Log of GDP per capita		**11.879*****		**13.468*****
		(3.13)		(3.72)
Trade openness		−0.005		−0.006
		(−0.29)		(−0.24)
Inflation		0.026		−0.382
		(0.08)		(−1.47)
R^2	0.525	0.805	0.494	0.775
Observations	60	58	60	57

Note: This table reports cross-section estimation results for the years 2013 and 2016. The dependent variable is digital payments. Numbers in parenthesis are ordinary least squares standard errors. ***, **, and * represent 1%, 5%, and 10% significance.

or debit cards have a high probability of detection as they can be cross-checked via third-party reporting. VAT invoice data and third-party reporting data enable tax authorities to identify and cluster taxpayers, which enhances tax evasion detection.

Among the inhibitors of the adoption of digital payments, the size of the informal economy plays a major role. To better understand the effect of the informal economy on digital payments, and the implications of the effect for the adoption of CBDC, we undertake a preliminary analysis and estimated a multivariate cross-country regression analysis for a sample of 60 economies for the years 2013 and 2016 (the results are shown in Table 1). The negative relationship between the informal economy and digital payments indicates that countries with large informal sectors tend to have a small number of digital payment transactions. In order to fight tax evasion, promote business transparency, and formalize the economy, several countries[6] have employed specific tax measures to promote cashless transactions and banking channels (Awasthi & Engelschalk, 2018). Despite these efforts, digital payment adoption in developing economies is relatively low among businesses and

for electronic payments in October 2019. In this system, cashless payment will receive certain percentage points (2% or 5%) or cash back.

[6] For example, a 2% VAT refund is applied to any purchases made by credit card in Colombia, and some European countries, such as Greece, Hungary, and Italy, have introduced cash payment limits since 2012.

households. Ligon et al. (2019) confirm that concerns about increased tax liabilities will hinder the adoption of digital payments by businesses and consumers.

In accordance with this trend, there has been growing discussion among policymakers about the new payment technology—CBDC. Auer et al. (2020) analyze the economic and institutional drivers for CBDC issuance from the issuer's perspective (i.e., central banks).[7] They find that an economy's digitization, innovation, informal economy, and financial development are positively related to a CBDC index that captures willingness to issue CBDC. Given the positive relationship between the informal economy and the CBDC index, it is likely that the authorities in a large informal economy will have greater interest in a trail of transaction data, as well as a desire to reduce the use of cash. However, even if there were a fully functioning CBDC in operation, a monetary authority would prevent the government from completely phasing out cash as not everyone is willing or able to make digital payments. Vulnerable populations in many countries still live in digital poverty, and populations are aging. Millions of people in developing countries live in areas without broadband infrastructure and lack relevant digital skills. Vulnerable groups, which include retirees, people on low incomes, and those with certain health conditions, find it much easier to pay in cash than to use electronic payments, meaning access to cash is vital for these groups (Evans, 2020).

Authorities often fail to include end-user preferences, that is, the demand side of CBDC, in decision-making processes.[8] It is still unclear whether end users would prefer CBDC over other forms of payment, such as cash in an informal economy. CBDC is a new form of money that can be distinguished from cash and electronic money issued by commercial banks (Carstens, 2018; Berentsen & Schar, 2018). Physical cash is accessible to everyone on a peer-to-peer basis, offers full anonymity, and has no associated counterparty or cyber risk. However, it also has high transaction costs, does not offer interest, and has a fixed nominal value. The time costs of cash transactions include shoe leather costs—the distance between a customer and an ATM or bank branch—and cash withdrawal fees (Attanasio et al., 2002). Transaction costs also increase in places where individuals have limited access to formal financial services. CBDC could serve as a digital substitute for cash. It can have blend feature of cash and deposits (Agur et al., 2022). CBDC could be designed with no service or intermediary fees at the point of transaction and offer relatively cheap payment services. It can also provide high-speed electronic transaction services, since the payments are settled immediately at the point of transaction without going through the clearing process. An interest-bearing feature also offers a store of value as CBDC serves as a risk-free asset. Although an interest-bearing CBDC could lead to a risk of disintermediation as the users can switch their

[7] They develop a global CBDC project index capturing the central bank's progress toward CBDC. 0 indicates no announced project, 1 is in the case of public research studies, and 2 is an active or completed pilot.

[8] Acknowledging the preferences of the end users is the key element for the high adoption rates of e-government services (Pleger et al., 2020).

money (e.g., cash and deposits) into CBDC rapidly, such risk could be mitigated by complementary arrangements. For example, central banks can temporarily set a ceiling on the holdings of CBDC (Bindseil, 2020).

Taken together, the empirical findings and characteristics of CBDC imply that both the adoption and the effect of CBDC on the economy may differ depending on the size of the informal economy. The traceability of CBDC can benefit the government, which can efficiently trace tax evasion and other illegal activities and can help increase financial inclusion and the fluidity of the overall economy. However, consumers and businesses are unlikely to adopt a CBDC if it is less beneficial compared with cash payments. This argument provides motivation and guidance for our theoretical exploration.

3 The Model

We extend some DSGE-based informal economy models such as Fernández and Meza (2015) and Orsi et al. (2014), to quantitatively study the relationship between CBDC and the informal economy. First, a money-in-utility (MIU) setup is used to capture liquidity services provided by multiple types of money (Uhlig & Xie, 2021). The MIU setup is also helpful in capturing several types of monetary friction, such as a "shopping time" friction in which real balances help to economize time spent on the purchase of consumption goods (Mehl et al., 2020; Niepelt, 2020). Moreover, we distinguish two types of money, namely cash and CBDC. Compared with cash, CBDC has negligible transaction costs but incurs government monitoring on household informal income. Hence, the use of CBDC creates a trade-off between cost efficiency and anonymity for households. Furthermore, we also consider the interest-bearing feature of CBDC, which could be remunerated similarly to bank deposits.

In theory, there are two possible designs for CBDC, including a cash-like and a deposit-like form. A purely cash-like CBDC could allow anonymous payments. However, many central banks are considering limiting the anonymity of CBDC since a fully anonymous CBDC design could allow for tax evasion, money laundering, illicit transactions, and financing terrorism (e.g., Bahamas Sand Dollar). Riksbank (2017) suggests that the Swedish CBDC, e-krona, will require registration and hence be traceable. ECB (2019) considers anonymity in small payment amounts only. Following the cases of traceable CBDC and the theoretical framework of Agur et al. (2022), CBDC in our framework has the mixed features of deposits and cash, along with a monitoring feature. Such a framework allows us to study the implications of the CBDC interest rate for the propagation of a set of conventional shocks, as well as a CBDC policy shock. We also consider the hybrid payment anonymity of CBDC in Sect. 3.1.2 as an extended analysis and robustness check.

3.1 Households

The representative household derives utility from consumption, money holding, and leisure. Households supply formal (H_t^f) and informal labor (H_t^I) measured in hours, which is used for the production of formal and informal goods. Following Orsi et al. (2014), there is an informal labor-specific disutility which captures the lack of social protection in the informal sectors.

The household maximizes lifetime expected utility function:

$$E_t \sum_{l=0}^{\infty} \beta^l [log(C_{t+l}) + \xi log(\frac{M_{t+l}}{P_{t+l}}) - \frac{\psi_1 (H_{t+l}^f + H_{t+l}^i)^{1+\eta} + \psi_2 (H_{t+l}^i)^{1+\eta}}{1+\eta}] \tag{1}$$

subject to the budget constraint

$$\begin{aligned} C_t(1+\phi\frac{M_t^c}{M_t}) + I_t + \frac{B_t}{P_t} + \frac{M_t}{P_t} =& R_{t-1}\frac{B_{t-1}}{P_t} + \frac{M_{t-1}^c + R_{t-1}^m M_{t-1}^{cbdc}}{P_t} \\ &+(1-\tau)(w_t^f H_t^f + r_t^{kf} K_t^f) \\ &+(1-\tau pr_t)(w_t^i H_t^i + r_t^{ki} K_t^i) \end{aligned} \tag{2}$$

where C_t denotes consumption, I_t investment, B_t holding of bonds, M_t aggregate money, M_t^{cbdc} CBDC money, M_t^c cash, R_t interest rate, R_t^m CBDC interest rate, P_t price, w_t^f formal wage, H_t^f formal labor, w_t^i informal wage, H_t^i informal labor, r_t^{kf} formal capital rent, K_t^f formal capital, r_t^{ki} informal capital rent, and K_t^i informal capital. ϕ measures the transaction cost, η measures the elasticity of labor supply with respect to wage, τ is the tax rate, and Pr_t is the detection rate of informal income. Broadly, ϕ captures costs due to the relative inefficiency of cash payments compared with CBDC.[9] Our framework assumes that households only pay taxes on formal and detected informal incomes.

The inclusion of CBDC could make the monitoring of informal incomes more efficient. This is because a central bank can trace patterns of CBDC-based transactions and money flows. pr_t is modeled as the sum of a basic detection rate Pr and an enhancing component due to the use of CBDC, as follows:

$$pr_t = Pr + \frac{(M_t^{cbdc}/M_t)^{1+\theta}}{1+\theta}, \quad \theta > 0 \tag{3}$$

[9] CBDC could potentially promote financial access by providing an infrastructure on which financial services could be constructed.

where θ is the elasticity of detection probability with respect to the CBDC share in money. Equation (3) implies that the more CBDC used by households, the more likely their informal income will be detected.

The total capital stock K_t is held by households and evolves according to the following law of motion:

$$K_{t+1} = (1-\delta)K_t + [1 - \frac{\Omega_k}{2}(\frac{I_t}{(1+g^y)I_{t-1}} - 1)^2]I_t \tag{4}$$

where δ is the capital depreciation rate. We assume that changes in investment are subject to a quadratic adjustment cost and its magnitude is measured by Ω_k.

The household maximizes lifetime utility subject to (2)–(4). Essentially, the first-order conditions for CBDC and cash are:

$$\frac{\xi}{M_t/P_t} = \lambda_t[(1 - C_t\phi\frac{M_t^c}{M_t^2}) + (\frac{M_t^{cbdc}}{M_t})^\theta \frac{M_t^c}{M_t^2}\tau(w_t^i H_t^i + r_t^{ki}K_t^i) - \frac{R_t^m}{R_t}] \tag{5}$$

$$\frac{\xi}{M_t/P_t} = \lambda_t[(1 + C_t\phi\frac{M_t^{cbdc}}{M_t^2}) - (\frac{M_t^{cbdc}}{M_t})^\theta \frac{M_t^{cbdc}}{M_t^2}\tau(w_t^i H_t^i + r_t^{ki}K_t^i) - \frac{1}{R_t}] \tag{6}$$

Combining (5) and (6) and rearranging, we obtain

$$\underbrace{(\frac{M_t^{cbdc}}{M_t})^\theta \tau(w_t^i H_t^i + r_t^{ki}K_t^i)}_{\text{cost due to the detection}} = \underbrace{\frac{R_t^m - 1}{R_t}M_t}_{\text{benefit due to interest payment}} + \underbrace{C_t\phi}_{\text{benefit due to transaction cost deduction}} \tag{7}$$

Equation (7) suggests that in equilibrium, the marginal cost of CBDC, namely the detection cost, should be equal to the marginal benefits from interest payments and the transaction costs deduction. By defining the CBDC share in money as $s_t^{cbdc} = M_t^{cbdc}/M_t$, we can solve Eq. (7) to obtain

$$s_t^{cbdc} = [\frac{\frac{R_t^m - 1}{R_t}M_t + C_t\phi}{\tau(w_t^i H_t^i + r_t^{ki}K_t^i)}]^{\frac{1}{\theta}} \tag{8}$$

Equation (8) implies a negative relationship between CBDC money shares and the size of the informal economy given others remain constant. A sizeable informal economy could prevent people from using CBDC as the detection cost is large.

3.1.1 With Another Digital Payment

In Sect. 1, we do not distinguish cash and CBDC from other digital payment or E-money. In this section, we further include a form of digital money D_t. Following Niepelt (2020), we assume that real digital money D_t/P_t is a component of real balance which yields utility. The household problem becomes

$$\max E_t \sum_{l=0}^{\infty} \beta^l [log(C_{t+l}) + \xi log(\frac{M_{t+l} + D_{t+l}}{P_{t+l}}) - \frac{\psi_1(H^f_{t+l} + H^i_{t+l})^{1+\eta} + \psi_2(H^i_{t+l})^{1+\eta}}{1+\eta}] \tag{9}$$

subject to the budget constraint with CBDC

$$\begin{aligned} C_t(1+\phi\frac{M^c_t}{M_t + D_t}) + I_t + \frac{B_t}{P_t} + \frac{D_t}{P_t} + \frac{M_t}{P_t} =& R_{t-1}\frac{B_{t-1}}{P_t} + \frac{M^c_{t-1} + R^m_{t-1}M^{cbdc}_{t-1}}{P_t} \\ &+ \frac{D_{t-1}}{P_t} + (1-\tau)(w^f_t H^f_t + r^{kf}_t K^f_t) \\ &+ (1-\tau pr_t)(w^i_t H^i_t + r^{ki}_t K^i_t) \end{aligned} \tag{10}$$

Compared with cash and CBDC, the digital payment is as convenient as CBDC, noninterest bearing, and moderately traceable. The presence of D_t changes the equilibrium for CBDC as follows:

$$s^{cbdc}_t = [\frac{\frac{R^m_t - 1}{R_t}M_t + C_t\phi\frac{M_t}{M_t + D_t}}{\tau(w^i_t H^i_t + r^{ki}_t K^i_t)}]^{\frac{1}{\theta}} \tag{11}$$

Given others remain constant, Eq. (11) implies that the CBDC share would be smaller where a higher amount of digital payment is already in use in the economy. The presence of digital payment D_t reduces the convenience benefits of CBDC and dampens household's willingness to further replace cash with another form of digital payment (CBDC).

3.1.2 With Tiering Payment Anonymity

In this subsection, we consider a scenario in which payment anonymity based on the CBDC has a hybrid structure, such as in the ECB (2019). An anonymous payment option is partially available (i.e., for small amounts), while identification is required for other payments (i.e., large or frequent payments).

To incorporate such a scheme, we assume that a proportion of CBDC payment is traceable, while the other proportion is anonymous. The detection probability function (3) can be rewritten as follows:

$$pr_t = \begin{cases} Pr + \dfrac{(M_t^{cbdc}/M_t)^{1+\theta}}{1+\theta} & \nu \text{ proportion of payment} \\ Pr & 1-\nu \text{ proportion of payment} \end{cases} \tag{12}$$

where ν is the proportion of payment traceable by CBDC. The expected detection probability is

$$E(pr_t) = Pr + \nu \frac{(M_t^{cbdc}/M_t)^{1+\theta}}{1+\theta} \tag{13}$$

With the expected detection, the budget constraint becomes

$$\begin{aligned} C_t(1+\phi\frac{M_t^c}{M_t}) + I_t + \frac{B_t}{P_t} + \frac{M_t}{P_t} =& R_{t-1}\frac{B_{t-1}}{P_t} + \frac{M_{t-1}^c + R_{t-1}^m M_{t-1}^{cbdc}}{P_t} \\ &+ (1-\tau)(w_t^f H_t^f + r_t^{kf} K_t^f) \\ &+ [1-\tau E(pr_t)](w_t^i H_t^i + r_t^{ki} K_t^i) \end{aligned} \tag{14}$$

The equilibrium share of CBDC becomes

$$s_t^{cbdc} = [\frac{\frac{R_t^m - 1}{R_t} M_t + C_t\phi}{\nu\tau(w_t^i H_t^i + r_t^{ki} K_t^i)}]^{\frac{1}{\theta}} \tag{15}$$

3.2 *Intermediate Goods Producers*

The intermediate goods sector consists of two subsectors, namely formal and informal firms. In each subsector, the representative firm j uses labor and capital to produce output based on the following Cobb-Douglas production function:

$$Y_{jt}^o = A_t^o (K_{jt}^o)^\alpha (H_{jt}^o)^{1-\alpha}, \quad o = f, i \tag{16}$$

where indices f and i denote formal and informal variables, respectively. Productivity A_t^o has two components common to both types of firms, including a deterministic trend $(1+g^y)^t$ and a common productivity shock ε_t^a following an AR(1) process. For formal firms, there is a formal-specific productivity shock ε_t^f following an AR(1) process:

$$A_t^f = (1 + g^y)^t \varepsilon_t^a \varepsilon_t^f \tag{17}$$

$$A_t^i = (1 + g^y)^t \varepsilon_t^a \tag{18}$$

Profit maximization for each type of firm yields the following first-order conditions:

$$w_t^o = (1 - \alpha) p_{jt}^{m,o} \frac{Y_{jt}^o}{H_{jt}^o}, \quad o = f, i \tag{19}$$

$$r_t^{ko} = \alpha p_{jt}^{m,o} \frac{Y_{jt}^o}{K_{jt}^o}, \quad o = f, i \tag{20}$$

where $p_{jt}^{m,o}$ are the price of intermediate goods.

3.3 Final Goods Producers

There is a continuum of monopolistic competitive final goods producers z, each of which is like a retailer, that buys intermediate goods and transfers them into differentiated final goods Y_t^z (Chang et al., 2019). The firms face nominal price adjustment costs following Rotemberg's approach $0.5\Omega_p(P_t^z/\pi P_{t-1}^z - 1)^2 Y_t$, where Ω_p measures the size of the adjustment cost, π is the steady-state inflation, and Y_t is the aggregate output.

The final goods producer chooses P_t^z to maximize expected profit from which we obtain the optimal price:

$$\max E_t \sum_{l=0}^{\infty} \Lambda_{t+l}[(\frac{P_{t+l}^z}{P_{t+l}} - p_{t+l}^m) Y_{t+l}^z - \frac{\Omega_p}{2}(\frac{P_{t+l}^z}{\pi P_{t+l-1}^z} - 1)^2 Y_{t+l}] \tag{21}$$

where Λ_{t+l} is the stochastic discount factor decided by the household.

3.4 Equilibrium

With symmetric equilibrium, we obtain the aggregate output, formal output, and informal output as follows:

$$Y_t = Y_t^f + Y_t^i \tag{22}$$

$$Y_t^o = A_t^o (K_t^o)^\alpha (H_t^o)^{1-\alpha}, \quad o = f, i \tag{23}$$

From the first-order conditions of households, we obtain the informal labor function as follows:

$$H_t^i = \begin{cases} \lambda_t[(1-\tau pr_t)w_t^i - (1-\tau)w_t^f]/\psi_2 & \text{if } (1-\tau pr_t)w_t^i > (1-\tau)w_t^f \\ 0 & \text{otherwise} \end{cases} \tag{24}$$

which suggests a negative relationship between the detection rate and the incentive to engage in informal work.

We obtain the relationship between r_t^{kf} and r_t^{ki} as follows:

$$(1-\tau pr_t)r_t^{ki} = (1-\tau)r_t^{kf} \tag{25}$$

The optimal price-setting decision implies the Phillips curve relation:

$$p_t^m = \frac{1}{\mu} + \frac{\mu-1}{\mu}\frac{\Omega_p}{Y_t}[(\frac{\pi_t}{\pi}-1)\frac{\pi_t}{\pi}Y_t - E_t\Lambda_t(\frac{\pi_{t+1}}{\pi}-1)\frac{\pi_{t+1}}{\pi}Y_{t+1}] \tag{26}$$

The labor and capital markets must be clear $H_t = H_t^f + H_t^i$, $K_t = K_t^f + K_t^i$. The resource constraint is

$$Y_t = C_t + I_t + G_t + \frac{\Omega_p}{2}(\frac{\pi_t}{\pi}-1)^2 Y_t \tag{27}$$

G_t is an exogenous spending shock following an AR(1) process. The interest rate is given by a Taylor rule as follows:

$$R_t = (R_{t-1})^{\psi_r}[R^m(\frac{\pi_t}{\overline{\pi}})^{\psi_\pi}(\frac{Y_t^f}{(1+g^y)Y_{t-1}^f})^{\psi_y}]^{1-\psi_r}\varepsilon_t^m \tag{28}$$

where ε_t^m is a conventional monetary policy shock. In order to close the model, we need to specify a CBDC interest rate rule. We assume a Taylor rule for R_t^m which is likely to be used (Barrdear & Kumhof, 2016; Mehl et al., 2020) after CBDC is issued.

$$R_t^m = (R_{t-1}^m)^{\rho_r}[R^m(\frac{\pi_t}{\overline{\pi}})^{\rho_\pi}(\frac{Y_t^f}{(1+g^y)Y_{t-1}^f})^{\rho_y}]^{1-\rho_r}\varepsilon_t^r \tag{29}$$

where ε_t^r is a CBDC monetary policy shock.

4 Calibration

Our calibration strategy is similar to that of Restrepo-Echavarria (2014). For parameters that are well identified in the literature and typically less variant across countries, we give them fixed values. For other parameters which show significant cross-country differences or affect the CBDC informal economy relationship, we consider a benchmark and some alternative values. In terms of the benchmark values, we mainly focus on Mexico, as it is considered as a representative emerging economy and has been extensively studied (see Aguiar and Gopinath (2007) among others).

Table 2 shows calibrated parameters. We set capital share α and capital depreciation rate δ as 0.35 and 0.05, respectively, in line with Fernández and Meza (2015). The discount factor β is calibrated as 0.99 to match the interest rate of 1.0145. The inverse labor elasticity is calibrated as 2, which is a standard value used in the literature. The money preference parameter ξ is calibrated as 0.02 based on money to output ratio (105%) for low- and middle-income countries. The ϕ is calibrated as 0.01, which implies that transaction costs account for 0.6% of output. This level is found in some Latin American countries such as Uruguay (Griffoli et al., 2018), European countries (Hasan et al., 2013), and Canada (Kosse et al., 2017). Following Restrepo-Echavarria (2014), we set the benchmark tax rate τ as 0.22. Given that the CBDC has not been issued, there is no target available to calibrate θ. We use a quadratic function to model the detection cost for households. A quadratic form is often used to model a cost function. This implies the elasticity of detection with respect to the CBDC share as unity. Our findings do not fundamentally change for

Table 2 Calibrated parameters

Parameters	Description	Value
α	Capital share	0.35
β	Discount factor	0.992
δ	Capital depreciation	0.05
η	Labor elasticity	2
ξ	Money preference	0.02
μ	Final goods markup	1.1
Ω_p	Price adj. cost parameter	22
Ω_k	Capital adj. cost parameter	4
ϕ	Transaction cost	0.01
τ	Tax rate	0.22
θ	Elasticity of detection rate	1
Steady state (ss)		
$1+g^y$	ss per capita GDP growth	1.006
G/Y	ss exogenous demand share	0.15
H	ss labor hour	0.33
H^I/H	ss informal labor share	0.32
Pr	No CBDC detection rate	0.02

alternative values of θ.[10] Following Comin et al. (2014), the final goods markup parameter μ is calibrated as 1.1. The two adjustment cost parameters Ω_p and Ω_k are set to 22 and 4, respectively, which lie in the ranges considered in the literature (Christiano et al., 2005; Smets & Wouters, 2007; Chang et al., 2019).

The lower part of Table 2 shows the calibrated values of the steady-state parameters. We set the quarterly output growth rate as 1.006, consistent with Fernández and Meza (2015). The exogenous demand share is calibrated as 0.15 to be consistent with data. We set ψ_1 and ψ_2 to match steady-state labor hour and informal labor share, respectively. The steady-state labor hour is calibrated as 0.33 as commonly used in the literature. In terms of informal labor share, we use 0.32 as in Fernández and Meza (2015) as the benchmark. This is a moderate level among others. For the detection rate Pr without CBDC, we choose 0.02 as the value based on Italy (Orsi et al., 2014) in the absence of other references. Finally, we defer the calibration of monetary policy parameters and shock processes to Sect. 6 as they do not affect the steady state.

5 Steady-State Analysis

As detailed in this section, we initially undertake a steady-state analysis by simulating the model to analyze the relationship between the informal economy and CBDC. Then in the following section, we further the analysis by considering the relationship within a business cycle framework using impulse response functions.

5.1 The Effects of the Informal Economy on CBDC

Table 3 shows the model-predicted CBDC share based on the benchmark calibration and alternative informal economy shares as well. The experiment is done by changing the parameter ψ_2, while the other parts of the model kept intact in order to capture the effect of the informal economy holding everything else constant. We do not claim that ψ_2 is the only factor driving the informal economy. There are other factors that also affect informality, such as the tax rate and intensity of monitoring. What matters for this experiment is not the reason for determining informality, but only that it is determined. We begin our analysis with a noninterest-bearing CBDC for ease of comparison. Starting with a moderate informal economy share, such as the benchmark case (0.32), the CBDC share in money would be around 9%. This share indicates the economy has a low capacity to accommodate CBDC, and the likelihood of replacing a large amount of cash by CBDC would be low. As

[10] For the reason of brevity, we do not include results based on alternative values of θ. They are available upon request.

Table 3 Comparisons of steady-state CBDC shares

Informal share	USA (0.1)	Spain (0.22)	Benchmark (Mexico, 0.32)	Brazil (0.43)	Thailand (0.55)
CBDC share	0.291	0.130	0.089	0.067	0.052

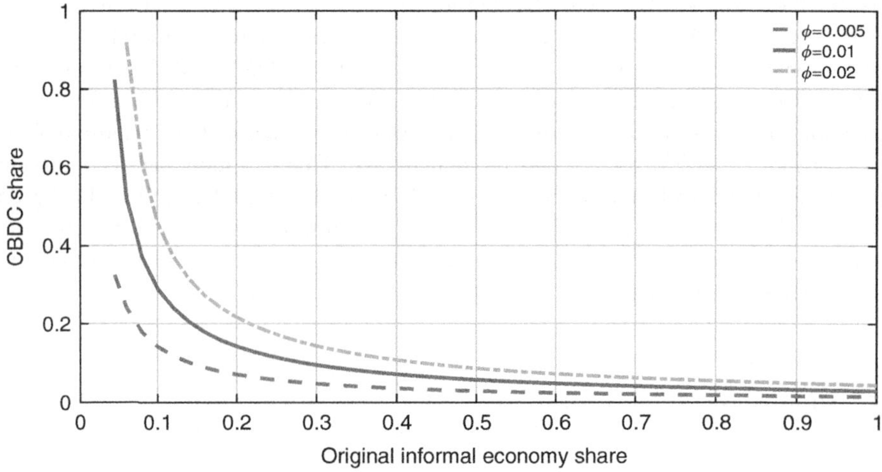

Fig. 1 The relationship between the CBDC share and the original informal economy share

the informal economy share increases, such as the values for Brazil (0.43) and Thailand (0.55), the cost of holding CBDC (i.e., detection costs) would become higher relative to the benefits (i.e., efficiency and convenience gains) and hence would lead to even lower CBDC shares. On the contrary, with smaller informal economy shares, such as values for the USA (0.1) and Spain (0.22), the detection costs relative to the benefits would be lower, and hence CBDC could be more acceptable in the economy. To summarize, Table 3 shows a negative relationship between the informal economy and the CBDC share, consistent with the theory proposed in Sect. 3.

While Table 3 displays some specific cases, Fig. 1 plots the relationship between the informal economy and the CBDC share in a more general way. In addition to the negative relationship as shown in Table 3, Fig. 1 shows an L-shaped relationship. The main mechanism driving the L-shaped pattern relies on disproportional effects of the detection costs and the benefits with regard to convenience. In order to understand the mechanism, we rewrite Eq. (8) in steady state and set R^m as unity to satisfy a noninterest-bearing CBDC condition as follows:

$$(s^{cbdc})^{\theta} = \frac{C\phi}{\tau(w^i H^i + r^{ki} K^i)} = \frac{C\phi}{\tau\mu Y^i} = \frac{\phi}{\tau\mu} y^i \tag{30}$$

$$\frac{\partial s^{cbdc}}{\partial y^i} = -\frac{1}{\theta}\left(\frac{\phi}{\tau\mu}\right)^{\frac{1}{\theta}}\left(\frac{1}{y^i}\right)^{\frac{1}{\theta}+1} < 0$$

$$\frac{\partial \text{detection cost effect}}{\partial y^i} = \left|\frac{\partial s^{cbdc}}{\partial y^i}\right| / \partial y^i = -\frac{1}{\theta}\left(\frac{\phi}{\tau\mu}\right)^{\frac{1}{\theta}}\left(\frac{1}{\theta}+1\right)\left(\frac{1}{y^i}\right)^{\frac{1}{\theta}+2} < 0$$

where $y^i = Y^i/C$ is a measure of the informal economy share. The convenience benefit which appears as nominator in Eq. (30) has a fixed marginal impact on the CBDC share, while the detection cost, which appears as the denominator, has negative and diminished marginal effects on the CBDC share. Such an L-shaped pattern is robust to different levels of transaction cost ϕ. Furthermore, Fig. 1 suggests that the curves become flat when the informal economy share becomes higher than approximately 30%. Considering that informal economy shares in developed countries tend to be below 30%, while in many developing countries they are greater than 30%,[11] Fig. 1 delivers two important insights. Shrinking the informal economy would be useful in promoting the acceptance of CBDC in developed countries. However, implementing the same policy might not be effective for developing countries since the presence of a sizeable informal economy would lead to the marginal effect of detection costs being insensitive to changes in the informal economy share.

Figure 2 compares the benchmark CBDC informal economy relationship with two alternative cases, including a case with another digital payment and the other one with a partial detection feature of CBDC. Not surprisingly, the presence of another form of digital money shifts the relationship downward. In the other case with a partial detection feature of CBDC, the relationship shifts upward, indicating that CBDC is more likely to be accepted given others remain constant. However, the negative and nonlinear relationship remains robust, especially when the original informal economy share becomes high.

5.2 The Implications of CBDC

Table 4 shows the impacts of CBDC on the economy. We focus on three key variables, namely detection probability, formal output share, and formalized output share. The formalized output is defined as the sum of formal output and detected informal output $y_t^f + pr_t y_t^i$.

Similar to what is shown in Table 3, we consider five original informal economy shares. Table 4 shows negative relationships between original informal economy

[11] In 2016, the USA, Japan, and the United Kingdom show low levels of informal economic activities at 8%, 8.1%, and 9.5%, respectively. In contrast, Nigeria, Ukraine, and Sri Lanka show high level of informal economies at 53.4%, 43.9%, and 36.4%, respectively.

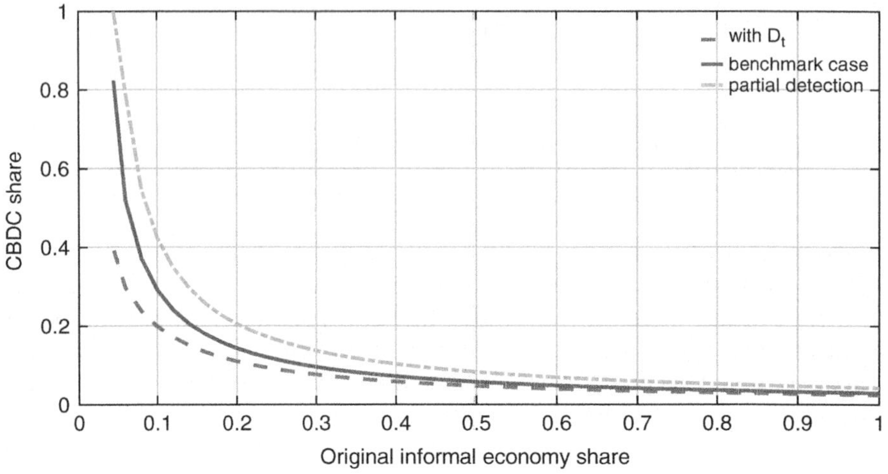

Fig. 2 Alternative CBDC-informality relationships

Table 4 Impacts of CBDC

Original informal share	0.1	0.22	0.32	0.43	0.55
Increase in detection prob (pr_t)	4.250%	0.840%	0.400%	0.220%	0.140%
Increase in formal output share (y_t^f)	0.310%	0.130%	0.083%	0.061%	0.045%
Increase in formalized output share $(y_t^f + pr_t y_t^i)$	0.690%	0.300%	0.200%	0.155%	0.124%

shares and their impacts on the three variables. With the original informal economy share increases, the increase in detection probability becomes smaller, thereby leading to less of an increase in formal and formalized outputs. As suggested by our previous analysis in Sect. 5.1, high original informal economy shares decrease household acceptance of CBDC, and through the spillover of CBDC on detection, the increases in formal and formalized outputs become smaller.

Among the five cases considered in Table 4, the most significant impacts from CBDC occur when the original informal economy share is 10%. In this case, the issuance of CBDC stimulates the detection rate from 2% to 6% and increases formal and formalized output shares by 0.3% and 0.7%, respectively. The increase in formalized output is larger than that of formal output because not only do some informal employees shift to formal production (increasing y_t^f), but also the detection of informal output becomes more effective (increasing $pr_t y_t^i$).

5.3 Roles of Tax Rates and CBDC Interest Rates

In this section, we consider alternative values of the tax rate τ and the CBDC interest rate R^m to study their implications and further understand the relationship between

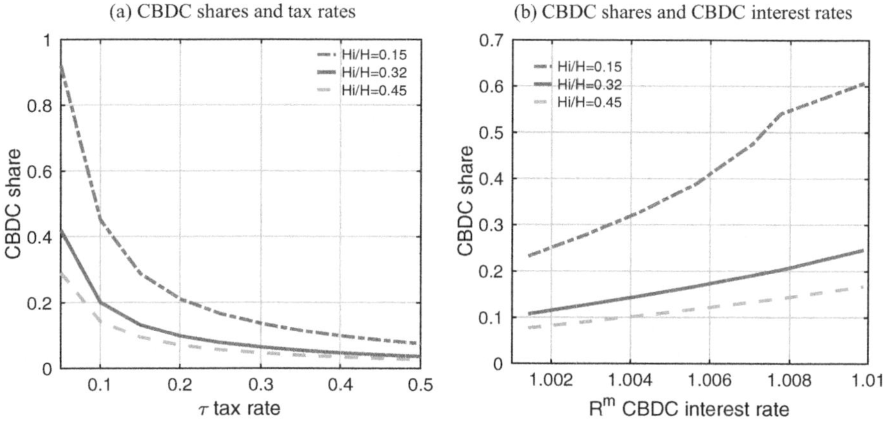

Fig. 3 The relationship between the CBDC share and the tax rate or the CBDC interest rate

the informal economy and CBDC. As suggested by Eq. (8), the tax rate and the CBDC interest rate are important determiners of the CBDC share.

Figure 3a suggests a negative relationship between the tax rate and the CBDC share. As the tax rate increases, incentives to engage in informal activities would be larger and the potential detection loss could be more significant. With such concerns, households would avoid detection due to the use of CBDC, which results in a lower CBDC share. This mechanism has important implications for the issuance of CBDC because a tax cut has the potential to encourage people to use CBDC. Compared to the benchmark result in Table 3 (8.9% of CBDC share), cutting the tax rate from 22% to 10% alongside CBDC issuance leads to a much larger CBDC share (20%). However, it should be noted that, on average, the tax rates in developing countries tend to be relatively low. Moreover, public debts in developing countries tend to be relatively high, and tax is a key component of fiscal revenue. These facts imply limited policy space for tax reductions to promote the acceptance of CBDC. Given the aforementioned concerns, developing countries may consider limited usage of tax reductions when issuing CBDC.

Shifting our attention to the CBDC interest rate as an alternative policy tool, Fig. 3b suggests a positive relationship between the CBDC interest rate and the CBDC share. A higher CBDC interest rate therefore adds one more benefit to hold CBDC in addition to the convenience gain, making CBDC more attractive to households. This mechanism implies that a positive CBDC interest rate enhances the acceptance of CBDC, which complements the effect of tax reduction. For instance, setting the CBDC interest rate as 70% of the deposit rate could double the CBDC share compared to the benchmark result.

Next, we investigate how the tax reduction and positive CBDC interest rate affect the role of CBDC in formalizing output. We consider three alternative tax rates in Table 5a, all of which are lower than the benchmark value (0.22). Unlike in Table 4 in which issuance of the CBDC only has minor impacts on formalized output share,

Table 5 Impacts of CBDC on formalized output shares

(a) with lower tax rates				(b) with CBDC interest rates			
Original informal share	0.15	0.32	0.45	Original informal share	0.15	0.32	0.45
τ=0.05	8.45%	4.19%	2.85%	r^m=0.3r	1.29%	0.55%	0.38%
τ=0.10	2.30%	0.99%	0.70%	r^m=0.5r	2.65%	0.92%	0.62%
τ=0.15	0.97%	0.44%	0.31%	r^m=0.7r	4.19%	1.53%	0.98%

Note: τ is the tax rate. r^m is the CBDC interest rate, shown as percentage of the conventional interest rate

Table 5a suggests more significant effects when the tax rate is lower. For example, when the tax rate is 10% and the original informal economy share is 32%, the issuance of CBDC could stimulate about 1% of formalized output share rather than 0.2% as in Table 4 (see the last entry in the fourth column of Table 4). If we further cut the tax rate to 5%, this effect can rise to 4.2%. A more formalized economy also provides a larger tax base, which partially offsets the fiscal burden which results from the tax reduction.

Turning to the CBDC interest rate, Table 5b suggests that a positive CBDC interest rate can also boost formalized output share. For instance, when the CBDC interest rate reaches 70% of the deposit rate and the original informal economy share is 32%, the issuance of CBDC could stimulate about 1.5% of formalized output share. This effect is much larger than the case of a zero CBDC rate (0.2%). The presence of a positive CBDC interest rate increases the CBDC share and strengthens its spillover effect on detection, which promotes both formal output and detected informal output.

6 Impulse Response Analysis

In this section, we exploit the negative relationship between the informal economy and the CBDC share as established in Sect. 5 to investigate the implications of the relationship for business cycles.

We calibrate the Taylor parameters of conventional money policy ψ_r, ψ_y and ψ_π as 0.8, 1.5, and 0.1, respectively, which are commonly used in the literature (e.g., Galí, 2015). These values are also used for counterpart parameters in the CBDC rate policy ρ_r, ρ_y and ρ_π. In terms of shock processes, we estimate the persistence and volatility of TFP and government spending shocks using OLS based on the Mexican TFP and government spending data during the period 1990Q1–2018Q4. The estimated AR(1) parameters of the TFP shock (ρ_a) and that of the government spending shock (ρ_g) are 0.95 and 0.89, respectively. The shock volatility σ_a and σ_g are estimated as 0.91 and 1.02. The two monetary policy shock persistence parameters are set as 0.4 which is in line with the existing literature (e.g., Galí, 2015).

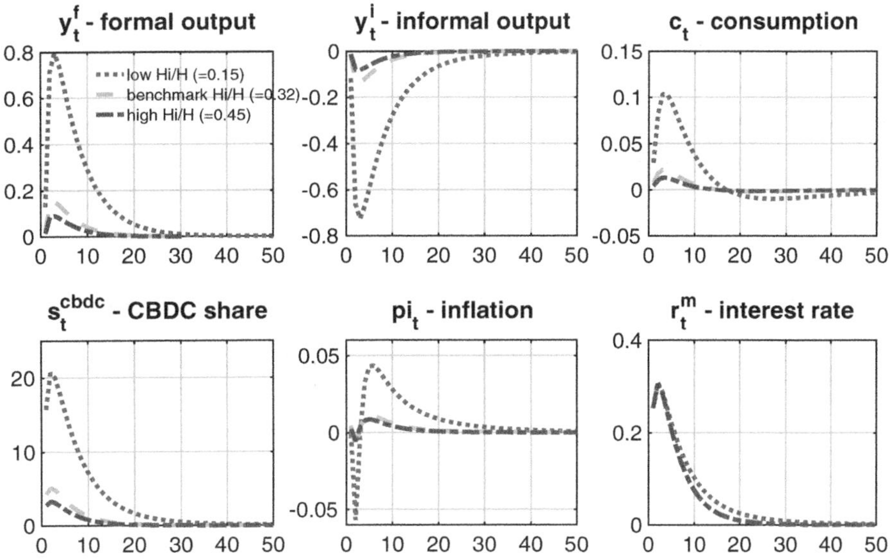

Fig. 4 IRFs to the CBDC shock. *Note*: We compare the cases with low (red lines), benchmark (green lines), and high (blue lines) informal economy shares

Figure 4 plots impulse responses of some key variables given a rise of 25 basis points of CBDC interest rate. An increase in the CBDC interest rate makes CBDC more attractive than cash, resulting in a higher CBDC share in the economy. Through the spillover effect on detection, the higher CBDC rate discourages tax evasion and triggers labor reallocation from the informal to the formal sector, thereby leading to an increase in formal output and a decrease in informal output. In addition to this reallocation effect, a higher CBDC share reduces the transaction cost and hence stimulates consumption. Owing to both the reallocation and the cost-reduction effects, an increase in CBDC rate has an expansionary effect on the measured economy and is helpful to formalize the economy. Furthermore, we find that the effect of a CBDC policy shock can be stronger when the original informal economy share becomes smaller. In line with the steady-state analysis in Sect. 5, a small share of the informal economy results in more CBDC circulated in the economy, which makes the CBDC policy more powerful.

Figure 5 plots impulse responses to a tightened conventional monetary policy shock with an interest rate risen by 25 basis points. Consistent with findings in the literature, an increase in the conventional policy rate reduces output and curbs inflation. Responding to this, the central bank reduces the CBDC interest rate, leading to a decrease in CBDC share. Due to the spillover effect on detection, there would be a reallocation effect from formal to informal production. We can interpret the differences between the black line and the other lines in Fig. 5 as additional effects of the monetary policy due to the CBDC rate adjustment. In this sense, the presence of CBDC can strengthen the effects of the conventional monetary

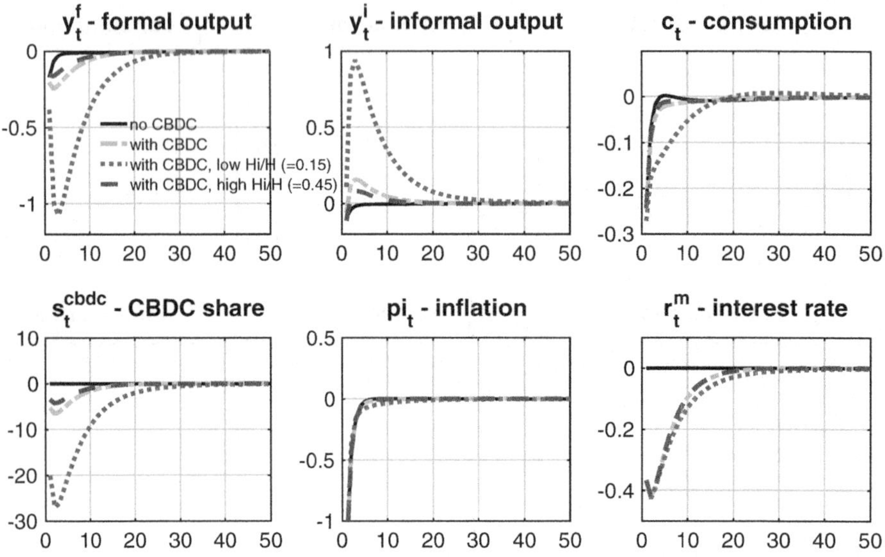

Fig. 5 IRFs to the interest rate shock. *Note*: We conduct two comparisons. The first one is comparing the cases with (green lines) and without CBDC (black lines); the second one is comparing the cases with low (red lines) and high (blue lines) informal economy shares

policy on the formal output but dampen or even reverse the movement of informal output. Moreover, our results provide another angle (i.e., the informal economy) to address the coordination between CBDC and the conventional monetary policy (see Barrdear & Kumhof, 2016, Brunnermeier & Niepelt, 2019 among others). Furthermore, Fig. 5 suggests that the additional effects provided by adjusting CBDC rates diminish with the original informal economy share.

In terms of the government spending shock, Fig. 6 shows that the presence of CBDC amplifies the response of formal output. Expansionary government spending heats the economy and results in increased CBDC interest rates. Consequently, there is an increase in CBDC shares which triggers a reallocation effect on labor toward the formal sector, and thereby increase in formal output would be amplified. Comparing the difference between blue and red lines and that between green and black lines, we find that the amplification effect provided by adjusting CBDC rates diminishes with original informal economy shares. Such a finding is similar to that of conventional monetary policy shock. Furthermore, our results suggest that government spending is helpful to formalize an economy, which is consistent with existing literature (Mauricio, 2011; Restrepo-Echavarria, 2014).[12] Unlike the literature in which government spending is linked to detection, we model a spillover

[12] In the literature, government spending could be in the form of purchasing formal goods and enhanced monitoring. They either provide direct support to the formal sector or discourage informal production, both of which contribute to a formalized economy.

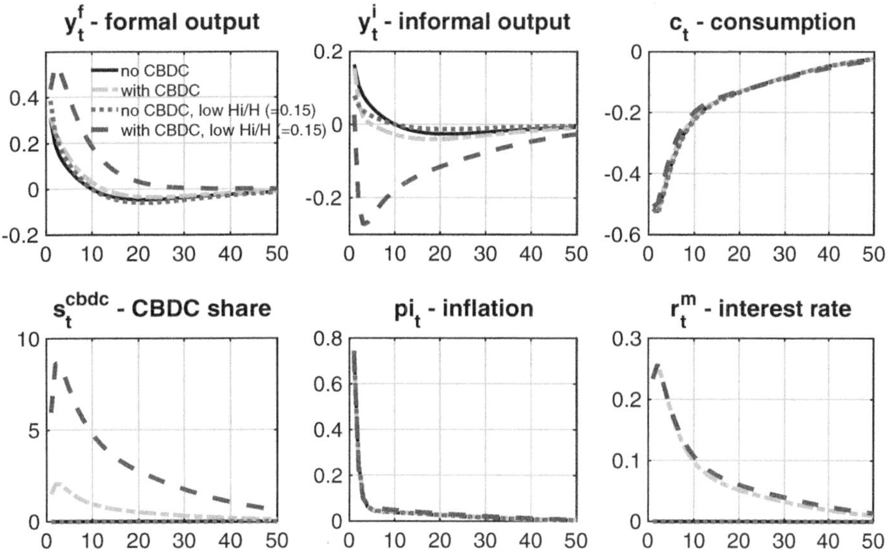

Fig. 6 IRFs to the government spending shock. *Note*: We conduct two comparisons. The first one compares the cases with CBDC (green lines) and without CBDC (black lines); we also make a similar comparison (red lines vs. blue lines) when the informal economy share is low

effect of CBDC on detection and suggest coordination between monetary and fiscal policy in promoting formality.

Contrary to the amplification effects from policy shocks, Fig. 7 shows that the presence of CBDC dampens the response of formal output to a positive TFP shock. The positive TFP shock pushes down the price level, lowering inflation. The monetary authority decreases the CBDC policy rate, which leads to a decline in the CBDC share. This triggers a reallocation effect on labor toward the informal sector, which in turn leads to a decline in formal output.

7 Welfare Analysis

This section examines the welfare implications of CBDC. We start by discussing alternative measures of welfare gains, followed by presentations and discussions of the results.

Welfare is measured as the lifetime expected utility of households, defined in Eq. (1). To compute welfare, the set of equilibrium conditions, including the welfare measure, are solved using a second-order approximation, as in Schmitt-Grohé and Uribe (2004). Following Ascari et al. (2018), welfare gains in the case with CBDC relative to the no-CBDC regime are computed as consumption-equivalent differences based on non-stochastic steady-state and stochastic means.

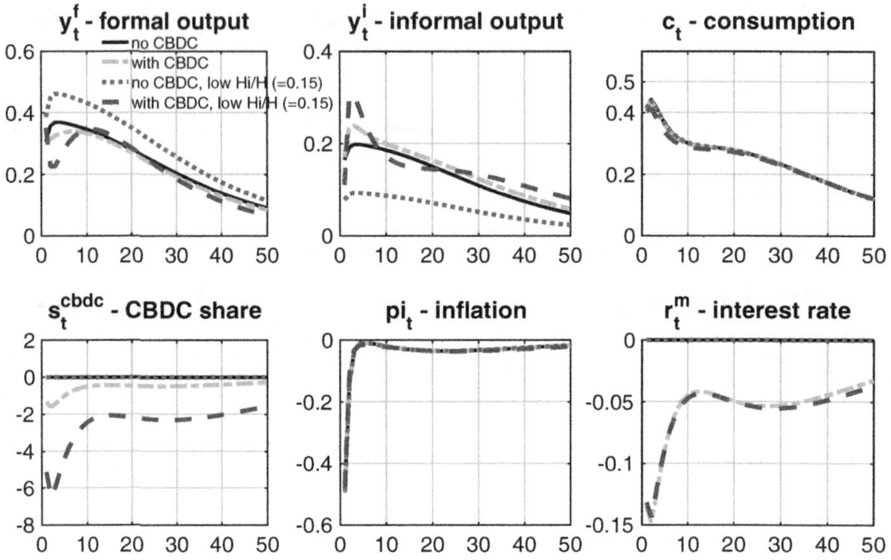

Fig. 7 IRFs to the TFP shock. *Note*: the same as above

For the second measure, we incorporate information on how the presence of CBDC interacts with stochastic disturbances. More specifically, we start by computing the welfare under the benchmark economy (i.e., no-CBDC regime) V^b and under the alternative economy (i.e., CBDC regime) V^a. A welfare gain Δ is then computed as the percentage change in consumption that would leave households indifferent between living under the CBDC regime and under the no-CBDC regime, such that

$$E_t \sum_{l=0}^{\infty} \beta^l [log(C_{t+l}^b (1+\Delta)) + \xi log(m_{t+l}^b) - \frac{\psi_1 (H_{t+l}^{f,b} + H_{t+l}^{i,b})^{1+\eta} + \psi_2 (H_{t+l}^{i,b})^{1+\eta}}{1+\eta}] = V^a \tag{31}$$

where C_t^b, m_t^b, $H_t^{f,b}$ and $H_t^{i,b}$ are consumption, real money holding, and formal and informal labor hours in the no-CBDC regime. Based on non-stochastic steady states, a welfare gain (Δ_{ss}) is given by

$$\Delta_{ss} = exp[(1-\beta)(V_{ss}^a - V_{ss}^b)] - 1 \tag{32}$$

Based on stochastic means, a welfare gain (Δ_m) is given by

$$\Delta_m = exp\{(1-\beta)[E(V_m^a) - E(V_m^b)]\} - 1 \tag{33}$$

Table 6 Welfare gains of CBDC

	Steady state	Stochastic mean	
		TFP shock only	All shocks
$Hi/H = 0.15$	1.3069%	1.5527%	2.5903%
$Hi/H = 0.32$	0.4908%	0.5275%	0.6782%
$Hi/H = 0.45$	0.3390%	0.3610%	0.4500%

Note: This table shows consumption-equivalent welfare gains of CBDC at different levels of informal economy shares

Table 7 Welfare gains of CBDC: with productivity gap and alternative welfare measure

Relative productivity	Benchmark welfare measure	Preference on anonymous payment
$A^f/A^i = 1$	0.6782%	0.1414%
$A^f/A^i = 1.1$	0.8049%	0.1899%
$A^f/A^i = 1.2$	1.2430%	0.4699%

Note: This table shows consumption-equivalent welfare gains of CBDC conditional on stochastic means at different levels of productivity gaps. The informal economy share is fixed at the benchmark case (0.32)

where subscript ss denotes non-stochastic steady states and subscript m denotes stochastic means.

Table 6 reports the welfare gains of CBDC at different levels of informal economy shares. Overall, this table shows a positive welfare implication of CBDC conditional on both steady states and stochastic means. Focusing on the benchmark informal economy share (0.32), the issuance of CBDC would generate a consumption-equivalent welfare gain of 0.49% conditional on steady states and 0.53% conditional on stochastic means with TFP shock only. If we further account for interactions between CBDC and other shocks, the consumption-equivalent welfare gain would increase to 0.68%, indicating a larger welfare benefit from CBDC. Moreover, the welfare gain would decrease if the original informal economy share becomes high.

Next, we investigate how welfare gains interact with the relative productivity of the formal to the informal economy. By focusing on the stochastic means and the benchmark informal economy share, we compute welfare gains for different relative productivity (A^f/A^i) which are summarized in Table 7.[13] It shows that welfare gains from CBDC increase with higher levels of relative productivity. The increase in the productivity gap could raise the income gap between formal and informal sectors, leading to larger beneficial effects from formality on consumption and hence larger welfare-enhancing effects from CBDC.

We further consider an extended case in which households may have stronger preferences related to payment anonymity than in the benchmark welfare measure. For instance, households might derive utility from a proportion of money holding which can fully ensure payment anonymity, namely cash. With this consideration,

[13] Results based on non-stochastic steady states and stochastic means are qualitatively similar.

we use an alternative measure of welfare and compute welfare gains as in Eqs. (32) and (33). The alternative welfare is given by

$$E_t \sum_{l=0}^{\infty} \beta^l [log(C_{t+l}) + \xi log(m^c_{t+l}) - \frac{\psi_1(H^f_{t+l} + H^i_{t+l})^{1+\eta} + \psi_2(H^i_{t+l})^{1+\eta}}{1+\eta}] \tag{34}$$

Welfare gains based on the alternative measure are reported in the last column of Table 7. There is an apparent decrease in the welfare gains compared to the benchmark analysis at each level of relative productivity. Taking 10% of the productivity gap as an example, the consumption-equivalent welfare gain of CBDC would be 0.19%, nearly a quarter of the benchmark result (0.8%). However, the relative rank of the welfare gain remains the same.

8 Conclusion

The ongoing development of CBDC spurs extensive discussions regarding the consequences of CBDC issuance. However, it remains questionable if CBDC would be accepted by end users. In this chapter, we fill this gap by examining the relationship between the adoption of CBDC by end users and the informal economy, and further investigating the benefits of CBDC by exploiting cross-country differences in the informal economy. To this end, we develop a two-sector monetary model featuring three important elements of CBDC: cash-like convenience of use, deposit-like money, and a spillover effect on detection of the informal economy. These three factors formulate a trade-off between cost efficiency and anonymity for end users, and thus an endogenous relationship between CBDC and informal economic activities.

The theoretical result shows an L-shaped relationship between CBDC and the informal economy, suggesting that a sizeable informal economy would decrease the adoption and usage of CBDC by end users. On the other hand, it confirms that the presence of CBDC is conducive to formalizing an economy by improving detection rates when households use CBDC services. Based on these relationships, we further investigate important economic implications of CBDC for business cycle stabilization. By adjusting the CBDC interest rate, the presence of CBDC can trigger a reallocation effect between the formal and informal sectors. Such an adjustment is helpful to stabilize measured output variation and enhance welfare. However, the welfare-enhancing effects become small if users strongly prefer payment anonymity.

Our results deliver a number of important policy implications. The presence of CBDC is helpful to formalize an economy. However, such benefits are not symmetric across countries. Developed countries with a lower share of the informal economy would find it easier to adopt CBDC; hence policymakers in such countries have greater flexibility to advance monetary and fiscal policies. On the contrary, developing countries which have high shares of the informal economy would find it harder to circulate CBDC and thus would only enjoy limited benefits. Our study also implies that tax reduction and a positive CBDC interest rate are useful tools to enhance the successful adoption of CBDC.

References

Aguiar, M., & Gopinath, G. (2007). Emerging market business cycles: The cycle is the trend. *Journal of Political Economy, 115*(1), 69–102.

Agur, I., Ari, A., & Dell'Ariccia, G. (2022). Designing central bank digital currencies. *Journal of Monetary Economics, 125*, 62–79.

Alberola, E., & Urrutia, C. (2020). Does informality facilitate inflation stability? *Journal of Development Economics*, 102505.

Andolfatto, D. (2021). Assessing the impact of central bank digital currency on private banks. *The Economic Journal, 131*(634), 525–540.

Ascari, G., Phaneuf, L., & Sims, E. R. (2018). On the welfare and cyclical implications of moderate trend inflation. *Journal of Monetary Economics, 99*, 56–71.

Attanasio, O. P., Guiso, L., & Jappelli, T. (2002). The demand for money, financial innovation, and the welfare cost of inflation: An analysis with household data. *Journal of Political Economy, 110*(2), 317–351.

Auer, R., Cornelli, G., Frost, J. et al. (2020). *Rise of the central bank digital currencies: drivers, approaches and technologies*. Centre for Economic Policy Research.

Awasthi, R., & Engelschalk, M. (2018). *Taxation and the shadow economy: how the tax system can stimulate and enforce the formalization of business activities*. The World Bank.

Barrdear, J., Kumhof, M. (2016). The macroeconomics of central bank issued digital currencies, Technical report, Bank of England working paper.

Bech, M. L., Faruqui, U., Ougaard, F., & Picillo, C. (2018). Payments are a-changin'but cash still rules. *BIS Quarterly Review*.

Berentsen, A., & Schar, F. (2018). *The case for central bank electronic money and the non-case for central bank cryptocurrencies*. Federal Reserve Bank of St. Louis.

Bindseil, U. (2020). Tiered CBDC and the financial system. *ECB Working Paper*, No. 2351

Boar, C., & Wehrli, A. (2021). Ready, steady, go?-results of the third BIS survey on central bank digital currency. *BIS Papers*, No. 114

Brunnermeier, M. K., & Niepelt, D. (2019). On the equivalence of private and public money. *Journal of Monetary Economics, 106*, 27–41.

Capasso, S., & Jappelli, T. (2013). Financial development and the underground economy. *Journal of Development Economics, 101*, 167–178.

Carstens, A. (2018). Money in the digital age: what role for central banks? *Lecture at the House of Finance, Goethe University, Frankfurt, 6*.

Chang, C., Liu, Z., Spiegel, M. M., & Zhang, J. (2019). Reserve requirements and optimal Chinese stabilization policy. *Journal of Monetary Economics, 103*, 33–51.

Christiano, L. J., Eichenbaum, M., & Evans, C. L. (2005). Nominal rigidities and the dynamic effects of a shock to monetary policy. *Journal of Political Economy, 113*(1), 1–45.

Comin, D., Loayza, N., Pasha, F., & Serven, L. (2014). Medium term business cycles in developing countries. *American Economic Journal: Macroeconomics, 6*(4), 209–45.

ECB. (2019). Exploring anonymity in central bank digital currencies. *ECB in Focus* (4).

Evans, J. (2020). *Protecting access to cash*. University of Bristol.

Fernández, A., & Meza, F. (2015). Informal employment and business cycles in emerging economies: The case of Mexico. *Review of Economic Dynamics, 18*(2), 381–405.

Fernández-Villaverde, J., Sanches, D., Schilling, L., & Uhlig, H. (2020). Central bank digital currency: Central banking for all? *Review of Economic Dynamics, 41*, 225–242.

Galí, J. (2015). *Monetary policy, inflation, and the business cycle: an introduction to the new Keynesian framework and its applications*. Princeton University Press.

Goldberg, H., & Lewis, R. T. (2000). *Money madness: The psychology of saving, spending, loving, and hating money*. Wellness Institute, Inc.

Gomis-Porqueras, P., Peralta-Alva, A., & Waller, C. (2014). The shadow economy as an equilibrium outcome. *Journal of Economic Dynamics and Control, 41*, 1–19.

Gordon, R., & Li, W. (2009). Tax structures in developing countries: Many puzzles and a possible explanation. *Journal of Public Economics, 93*(7–8), 855–866.

Griffoli, M. T. M., Peria, M. M. S. M., Agur, M. I., Ari, M. A., Kiff, M. J., Popescu, M. A., & Rochon, M. C. (2018). *Casting light on central bank digital currencies*. International Monetary Fund.

Hasan, I., De Renzis, T., & Schmiedel, H. (2013). Retail payments and the real economy, Technical report, ECB Working Paper.

Kosse, A., Chen, H., Felt, M.-H., Jiongo, V. D., Nield, K., & Welte, A. (2017). The costs of point-of-sale payments in Canada, Technical report, Bank of Canada Staff Discussion Paper.

Ligon, E., Malick, B., Sheth, K., & Trachtman, C. (2019). What explains low adoption of digital payment technologies? evidence from small-scale merchants in Jaipur, India. *PloS One, 14*(7), e0219450.

Loayza, N. V., & Rigolini, J. (2011). Informal employment: safety net or growth engine? *World Development, 39*(9), 1503–1515.

Low, S. H., Paul, S., & Maxemchuk, N. F. (1994). Anonymous credit cards. In *Proceedings of the 2nd ACM Conference on Computer and Communications Security* (pp. 108–117).

Mauricio, P. (2011). Government policy in the formal and informal sectors. *European Economic Review, 55*, 1120–1136.

Mehl, A., Stracca, L., & Ferrari, M. (2020). Central bank digital currency in an open economy. *Journal of Monetary Economics, 127*, 54–68.

Niepelt, D. (2020). Monetary policy with reserves and CBDC: Optimality, equivalence, and politics. CESifo Working Paper No. 8712.

Orsi, R., Raggi, D., & Turino, F. (2014). Size, trend, and policy implications of the underground economy. *Review of Economic Dynamics, 17*(3), 417–436.

Pleger, L. E., Mertes, A., Rey, A., & Brüesch, C. (2020). Allowing users to pick and choose: A conjoint analysis of end-user preferences of public e-services. *Government Information Quarterly, 37*(4), 101473.

Prado, M. (2011). Government policy in the formal and informal sectors. *European Economic Review, 55*(8), 1120–1136.

Restrepo-Echavarria, P. (2014). Macroeconomic volatility: The role of the informal economy. *European Economic Review, 70*, 454–469.

Riksbank, S. (2017). The Riksbank's e-krona project–Report 1. E-krona reports.

Schmitt-Grohé, S., & Uribe, M. (2004). Solving dynamic general equilibrium models using a second-order approximation to the policy function. *Journal of Economic Dynamics and Control, 28*(4), 755–775.

Smets, F., & Wouters, R. (2007). Shocks and frictions in us business cycles: A Bayesian DSGE approach. *American Economic Review, 97*(3), 586–606.

Sung, M. J., Awasthi, R., & Lee, H. C. (2017). Can tax incentives for electronic payments reduce the shadow economy. *Korea's attempt to reduce underreporting in retail businesses. World Bank policy research working paper*, No. 7936.

Uhlig, H., & Xie, T. (2021). Parallel digital currencies and sticky prices, Technical report, National Bureau of Economic Research.

Dr Eun Young (EY) Oh has a PhD in Economics from Durham University and a MLitt in Finance from the University of St Andrews. During her PhD, she investigated the role of money in monetary policy and how money supply and seigniorage impact on output growth using a DSGE model and Hansen's panel threshold (Non-linear) methodology. Her research interests include monetary policy, Fintech including P2P lending and crowdfunding, digital currency and Central Bank Digital Currency, and the digital economy.

Dr Shuonan Zhang is a lecturer at the University of Southampton. Before taking his current position, he was a research fellow in Macroeconomics at the University of Portsmouth. He obtained a Ph.D in Economics from the University of Manchester.

Dr Zhang's current research focuses on macroeconomic implications of financial development (e.g., traditional finance and shadow banking) and technology innovation (or broadly intangibles). He is particularly interested in the interactions between business cycles and long-run growth or development issues through various channels.

A Model of Trust in Central Bank Digital Currency (CBDC) in Brazil: How Trust in a Two-Tier CBDC with Both the Central and Retail Banks Involved Changes Consumer Trust

Alex Zarifis and Xusen Cheng

1 Introduction

This research puts forward a model of consumer's trust in central bank digital currencies (CBDC) in Brazil. Three institutional, and three technological factors, are found to play a role. It is important to develop user-centred services in Brazil so that trust is built in the services themselves, and the government institutions that deliver them, sufficiently for broad adoption (OECD, 2023). Brazil, as one of the largest economies in Latin America has been seen as a leader in financial technology for some time in that part of the world, but more recently, as a member of BRICS it is starting to have an influential role globally. Brazil has taken initiatives to update its own internal central bank services, but has also been involved in several initiatives as part of BRICS. As part of this, Brazil is also leading in the implementation of CBDCs. This top-down innovation in financial technologies at national and international levels must also be supported by a bottom-up adoption by citizens. The citizen now has a variety of options for their financial services. Not all of the options that are popular and easily available to citizens are fully regulated or secure. Some of the easily available options such as meme coins can be quite risky (Huber & Sornette, 2022). Brazilian citizens can support, or push back, on a CBDC for a variety of reasons that are not necessarily easy to predict. A CBDC is a complex innovation, and it is not straightforward to predict which characteristic of the solution, or the general context, will have the most decisive influence. It

A. Zarifis (✉)
University of Southampton, Southampton, UK

Cambridge Centre for Alternative Finance, Cambridge, UK
e-mail: a.zarifis@soton.ac.uk

X. Cheng
Renmin University of China, Beijing, China

A. Zarifis, X. Cheng (eds.), *Fintech and the Emerging Ecosystems*, Financial Innovation and Technology, https://doi.org/10.1007/978-3-031-83402-8_4

is therefore important to understand the citizens perspective in the adoption of the Brazilian CBDC. Consumer trust in their CBDC can make the adoption more effective and reduce the risk of a partial or complete failure.

1.1 Central Bank Digital Currencies (CBDC)

With various versions of CBDCs being implemented or explored, a general definition cannot go beyond its fundamental characteristics of being money that is digital, without a physical note or coin, and issued by a central bank. Unlike most cryptocurrencies that are decentralized, a CBDC is typically centralized. While being centralized may reduce some risks, it may inadvertently increase others. Furthermore, unlike most cryptocurrencies, blockchain is not necessarily always utilized in a CBDC.

There are wholesale and retail CBDCs (Auer et al., 2023; Auer & Böhme, 2020). The Brazilian consumer can use the retail version for their daily payments. A wholesale version can be used to move large amounts of money between banks efficiently. While most Latin American central banks are focusing mainly on the retail version (Proskalovich et al., 2023), Brazil, through its involvement in BRICS, is also moving forward with a wholesale version.

A retail CBDC can either be issued directly to individuals, or to commercial banks that then offer them to individual consumers. A CBDC using the two-tier system is closer to existing solutions while a one-tier solution is potentially more disruptive. Many countries exploring CBDCs are considering a hybrid implementation, with both one-tier and two-tiers offered. While this is a more complicated solution, offering some flexibility to consumers may be beneficial and reduce push-back.

Despite the first initiative to explore CBDCs in Latin America being in 2014 by Ecuador, most Latin American countries seem to be moving forward cautiously. However, more recently, Brazil along with Mexico seems to be moving forward more enthusiastically with CBDCs having pilots and putting some of the necessary regulations in place. At the same time, Latin America is also home to El Salvador which took a different approach to innovation in financial technology by adopting Bitcoin as a legal tender and supporting Bitcoin adoption enthusiastically (Alvarez et al., 2023).

The motivation to implement a CBDC can include wanting to increase efficiency, offer new services and encourage innovation, reduce tax evasion, reduce money laundering, de-dollarisation and fight off competition from new financial alternatives such as Bitcoin (Chen et al., 2022; Morales-Resendiz et al., 2021).

An innovation on this scale, and with something so sensitive, is not without challenges. Some of these challenges are typical for all CBDC implementations while others are specific to the region or the specific country. There is limited financial and digital knowledge and a lack of identity documents among some people. Cash is still popular and there is a large informal economy. The occasional challenges in the economy such as inflation also cause people to move their wealth abroad (Proskalovich et al., 2023).

The large project of implementing a CBDC will not only affect the finances of the country but also many aspects of the citizens personal and professional lives. This change will influence the relationship between the government, the regulators, the central bank, retail banks and other financial institutions offering services to individuals and merchants. It also affects countries and people outside Brazil. Firstly, it is happening with some co-ordination with other countries that are members of BRICS building on previous efforts to link CBDCs of several countries (BIS Innovation Hub, 2023). Secondly, many Latin American countries are waiting for the regional leaders to move forward with CBDCs so they follow. It will be easier for other Latin American countries once there is a strong regional example of a CBDC so there is a model of the technology and the process to implement it (Proskalovich et al., 2023).

1.2 Consumer Trust in a CBDC

While there is a breadth of stakeholders that need to support this innovation, it is critical that consumers adopt it. In the current environment the consumer has many options, some that are fully regulated and supported by the government, others that are partially regulated, and others that are illegal but are still available and hard to shut down. In addition to the financial dimension of a currency such as it holds its value, being widely accepted and so on, it needs to be trusted to be used. Traditionally, the government institutions involved in delivering the currency build trust sufficiently, but government institutions are not trusted as much as they were in the past with around seven in ten Brazilians not trusting them (OECD, 2023). While it is likely that a citizen will use their country's currency, it is not inevitable that they will use their country's currency for all their needs. The consumer's trust is challenged by the risks that a new digital currency brings so it is important to build trust to mitigate this. Therefore, the research question is:

How can consumer trust be built in the Brazilian Central Bank Digital Currency (CBDC)?

Existing research that identified six ways to build trust in a different CBDC (Zarifis & Cheng, 2024a) was used as a basis. This research tested a model with seven ways to build trust in the Brazilian CBDC. The seventh hypothesized way to build trust that was added to the model is not supported by the analysis. It was hypothesized that the implementation process, including pilot implementations, was a seventh way to build trust, but that is not supported by the data. The data supported six out of the seven ways to build trust that came from the original model. Therefore, despite the differences in the Brazilian CBDC, the original model applies there also which suggests the model applies to both two-tier solutions, and mixed one and two-tier solutions. The six ways to build trust that are supported are: (a) trust in government and central bank offering the CBDC, (b) expressed guarantees for those using it, (c) the favourable reputation of other active CBDCs, (d) the CBDC technology, the automation and limited human involvement necessary, (e) the trust building features of the CBDC wallet app, and (f) the privacy features of the CBDC wallet app and back-end processes.

The theoretical foundation that follows concludes with the initial research model. The methodology section explains the quantitative approach used to explore this model. The analysis section presents the many statistical tests that are implemented. Finally, the theoretical and practical implications of the findings are discussed.

2 Theoretical Foundation

The implementation of this new currency and the technology that supports it in Brazil is a very large project with far-reaching implications, for the various stakeholders, and the consumers using it in particular. This interdisciplinary topic is discussed extensively in the literature on Fintech but it is also covered by the broader literature on finance and information systems. The literature review here first covers the main forms of CBDCs, then it looks at the Brazilian implementation so far, and finally, the role trust has in similar contexts. These three sections of the literature, provide the foundation for the research model that will be tested.

2.1 The Different Forms of Central Bank Digital Currencies (CBDC)

A variety of reasons, including the reduced popularity of cash, and the increasing popularity of cryptocurrencies, have made CBDCs more appealing to governments and central banks (Auer et al., 2023). There are some existing implementations of CBDCs and there are many more planned. However, there isn't one solution in terms of the digital currency, or the technology that supports it. Beyond the fundamental principle that it is a currency issued by a central bank, and for which the central bank is liable, there are many differences. Firstly, there can be a CBDC that is only used between banks to transfer large amounts of money efficiently, which is sometimes referred to as a wholesale CBDC (BIS Innovation Hub, 2023). Then there is a retail CBDC that is used by regular citizens for all their purchases from a retailer, and to send money to each other, peer-to-peer (Auer & Böhme, 2020; León et al., 2024). Retail CBDCs can have two tiers like the current system with the central bank, retail banks and the consumers, or one tier, where the central bank interacts directly with the consumer. In a one-tier system, the central bank will typically have to offer consumers a digital wallet to use their CBDCs, so they do not need an account with a retail bank for this process.

In terms of technology, while CBDCs are seen as a government version of cryptocurrencies, the use of blockchain is not entirely necessary, as this is a centralised currency, and not decentralised. Nevertheless, some digital currencies use blockchain as it can, in some cases, support faster and more secure transactions.

The current implementations of CBDCs include China's digital Renminbi RMB, India's Digital Rupee, Russia's Digital Ruble, Bahamas Sand Dollar, the Eastern Caribbean Central Bank Dcash, the Nigerian e-Naira and the Jamaican JamDex (Flores Gálvez & Mata Hernández, 2023; Xu, 2022). These cases are sufficiently used to be considered a real live implementation, and not just a trial. At the same time, they have not reached the level of adoption to fully replace the traditional currency. In Latin America, the other large country to be moving forward is Mexico, but progress is not as fast as Brazil (Flores Gálvez & Mata Hernández, 2023; Zarifis & Cheng, 2024b).

2.2 The Brazilian Central Bank Digital Currency (CBDC) Drex

2.2.1 The Implementation Process and Pilots

Brazil is the largest, most populous country in Latin America, and it also has the largest economy. It is therefore no surprise that it is also expected to be one of the leaders in financial innovation, and CBDCs in particular (Proskalovich et al., 2023; Tombini, 2023). Leading in this complex financial innovation requires a long commitment to develop technologies, processes and people's skills. While it is unrealistic to expect such a large project to be completed without any setbacks, limiting the problems, and keeping the disruption as low as possible, reduces the financial cost to all the stakeholders.

Brazil started this process by successfully implementing a project for an instant payment system called PIX. This system uses a unique key to complete a transaction from one account to another instantly (Rodrigues et al., 2022). The adoption was helped by people's habit of using their phones, the perceived value, and the expected performance of this solution (Amboage et al., 2024). The successful implementation of the PIX project was an interim step that moved the technology and the people towards a CBDC.

Through a series of working groups and consultations, some priorities were identified for the CBDC in Brazil. These include (a) the need for better cross-border interoperability than current solutions, (b) encouraging financial innovation by supporting technologies such as smart contracts, and (c) encouraging financial innovation by supporting other organisations that want to provide integrated financial services (Brazilian Central Bank, 2024).

It is easy to see how the Brazilian CBDC fits into its national strategy, but also that of BRICS, which it is a member of. The scale of the project, and the high level of interconnectedness in finance, mean that even large countries like Brazil benefit from international collaboration. Limiting currency substitution, typically with the dollar is another area where international collaboration with BRICS is beneficial.

2.2.2 The Specific Challenges Brazil Faces for Its CBDC

Brazilian citizens want user-centred designs, appreciate being involved in the creation of new services that affect them, and do not want to simply receive services planned by others passively (OECD, 2023). These beliefs are similar around the world, but it cannot be assumed that what works in one place, works in another, so it is important to evaluate new solutions in different contexts.

The large informal economy in Brazil is around 40% (Statista Research Department, 2023) and cash is still popular. On the one hand, those using cash may be more resistant to a CBDC, but on the other hand, if the CBDC is a superior payment system it might entice them more than previous options.

Millions of Brazilians do not have identity documents (Agencia Brazil, 2024). As with other challenges to a Brazilian CBDC identified here, this can be seen as an opportunity to make progress on several fronts. It is also important for the solution to show resilience to Internet and power losses. An offline capability through a wallet app would be helpful. If consumers do not know if they will have reliable access to the CBDC they will probably continue to use cash instead.

2.2.3 The Architecture of the Brazilian CBDC Drex

Drex has wholesale functionality that enables banks to move money between themselves efficiently, and retail functionality for individuals to use. The retail functionality is not provided directly by the central bank, but through retail banks, mirroring the current system (Brazilian Central Bank, 2024). This is an example of the importance that has been put on moving forward with all the stakeholders, and not causing unnecessary disruption to the financial ecosystem. Drex has been designed from the start to work with blockchain-based smart contracts. This means many automated financial services that execute contracts, based on some predefined criteria, can be provided. Smart contracts are particularly useful in enabling financial services from different organisations to be combined. Therefore, while Drex, like all CBDCs is centralised, it supports some decentralised financial services. Drex utilises a 'permissioned' Ethereum Hyperledger Besu (Brazilian Central Bank, 2024).

2.3 *Trust in Cryptocurrencies and CBDCs*

2.3.1 Trust in Technology

When using technology to make a payment there are several risks that challenge the consumer's trust in the process. There is the risk of losing the money being spent, the account details, or other personal information. Typically, if the consumer's trust is not enough they will not use the technology (McKnight et al., 2011). There may be some exceptions such as a scenario where the consumer has no choice but to use something they do not trust. However, typically there are alternatives, and the use of a specific financial technology is not compulsory. In most parts of the world, including Latin America, the alternative financial services available are increasing. One example of the increase in choice is the bank licence awarded to the purely online bank Revolut in Mexico. A second example of the increase in choice is the many leaders that state that they are positive towards cryptocurrencies.

2.3.2 Trust in Financial Services and Currencies

Trust in many government institutions around the world is considered to be lower than usual for a variety of reasons and this is also the case in Brazil, where seven out of ten do not trust their government institutions (OECD, 2023). A CBDC, particularly in the way Drex is being implemented, with a whole ecosystem of services being built around it, offers many new services that bring with them new risks. Therefore, the role of trust, may be even more critical for a wide-ranging CBDC ecosystem than a simpler financial innovation like an Internet-only bank.

2.4 *Research Model*

This research attempts to identify the factors that build trust in CBDCs in Brazil. An existing model with three variables covering trust in institutions, and three variables covering trust in technology, is used as a basis (Zarifis & Cheng, 2024a). A seventh variable covering trust in the implementation process is added to the existing model to capture the specific context of the Brazilian implementation of CBDCs more comprehensively. Two more changes are made to the original model so that it captures the Brazilian two-tier CBDC model better. Two variables from the existing model related to the wallet app that enables the use of the CBDC are adjusted to reflect that this functionality is provided by a retail bank in a two-tier system. The functionality to use the CBDC is provided by a central bank directly in a one-tier system, unlike the typical situation we have now where a retail bank provides it. Figure 1 illustrates the initial research model of how consumer trust is built in the Brazilian CBDC with seven methods.

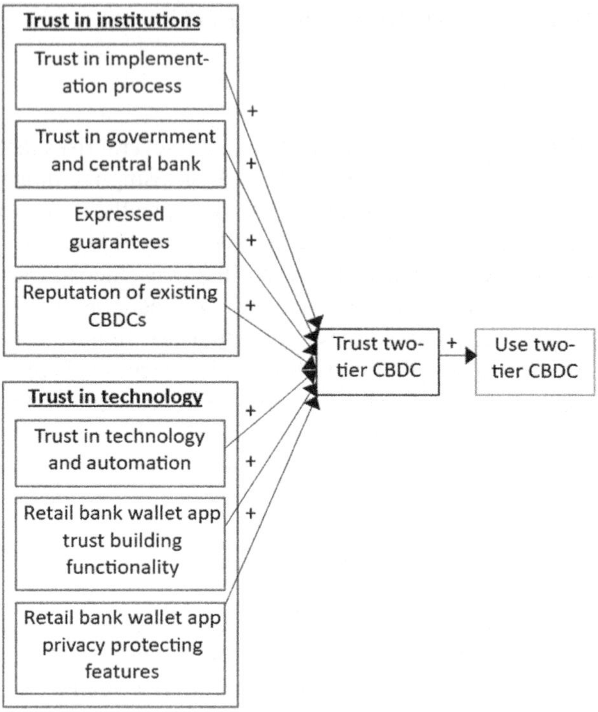

Fig. 1 Initial research model of trust in a two-tier CBDC in Brazil, adapted from (Zarifis & Cheng, 2024a)

2.4.1 Trust in Implementation Process

Citizens' trust in Brazil's government and the services it offers is believed to benefit from having a transparent, clear process, being involved extensively, and having the opportunity to give feedback (OECD, 2023). While a CBDC may be seen as a type of currency with standard characteristics this is not the case as the literature review shows. There is both a range of characteristics and a range of different implementation processes. The implementation process has been proven to influence the rate of adoption of a CBDC significantly (León et al., 2024). The Brazilian implementation process has been very gradual and built on previous successes. This gradual, confident and transparent implementation process was designed to make all the stakeholders comfortable moving forward and is expected to build trust. Therefore the first hypothesis is:

H1 Trust in CBDC implementation process will build a user's trust in the CBDC.

2.4.2 Trust in the Institutions Supporting the CBDC

Trust in many government institutions around the world is lower than usual for a variety of reasons and this is also the case in Brazil (OECD, 2023). Trust in the related institution usually play a role in the adoption of a technology (Pavlou & Gefen, 2004). While it is clear that the institutions supporting the CBDC will influence trust in it, it is not so easy to identify in what way this will happen. Not everything a government or central bank will do will have an influence. Even actions that may seem influential may not play a decisive role in the end. Based on the literature, in addition, to trust in the government and central bank issuing the CBDC, trust will be built by expressed guarantees (Martínez-López et al., 2020), and the positive reputation of CBDCs already operating elsewhere (Dupont & Karpoff, 2020; Einwiller, 2003). These three dimensions of institutional trust are expected to play a significant role. Therefore the second, third and fourth hypotheses are:

H2 Trust in the Brazilian government and central bank issuing the CBDC will build a user's trust in their CBDC.

H3 Expressed guarantees for the user of a Brazilian CBDC will increase trust in that CBDC.

H4 A positive reputation of CBDCs already implemented in other countries increases a consumer's trust in the Brazilian CBDC.

2.4.3 Trust in Technology Used by the Central Bank and the Retail Banks to Operate a CBDC

As the name of a CBDC suggests, technology plays a central role in this digital currency. Many technologies spread across several organisations come together to support the CBDC, and ecosystem of financial services it provides. The consumer may be more comfortable with technologies and solutions they are familiar with, and find it challenging to trust something new like a CBDC that uses blockchain (Brazilian Central Bank, 2024). The Brazilian CBDC is a two-tier system with the central bank and retail banks playing their traditional roles. Therefore, the technology of both the central bank and retail banks plays a role. Based on the literature trust can be built by, (a) the automation and reduced human involvement achieved by a CBDC technology (Ahn & Chen, 2022), (b) the retail bank's wallet app trust-building functionality (Chang et al., 2013), and (c) the retail bank's wallet app privacy protecting features such as not sharing personal information with other organisations (Dinev et al., 2013; Pocher & Veneris, 2022). Therefore, the fifth, sixth and seventh hypotheses are:

H5 The automation and reduced human involvement achieved by a CBDC technology increases trust.

H6 The trust-building functionality of the retail bank's wallet app will increase trust in the CBDC.

H7 The retail bank's wallet app privacy-protecting features, and back-end processes such as anonymity, will increase trust in the CBDC.

2.4.4 Trust Increases Willingness to Use a CBDC

In addition to identifying the factors that build trust in the Brazilian context, it is important to confirm that trust does indeed influence the adoption of this technology in this context, as it does in similar contexts (Lankton et al., 2015; McKnight & Chervany, 2002). The seven factors listed above are expected to build trust in the Brazilian CBDC. The consumer's trust is expected to increase the use of the CBDC as there is extensive literature supporting the positive relationship between trust and the adoption of a technology. This positive relationship however needs to be tested and verified in this context. Furthermore, validating this relationship will complete a model from the ways to build trust in a CBDC, to using the CBDC. This is a sufficiently comprehensive way to frame these issues. Therefore, the eighth hypothesis is:

H8 Consumer trust in the Brazilian CBDC will increase their willingness to use it.

3 Methodology

3.1 Data Analysis

As this research attempts to explore and validate a model a quantitative method is chosen. In order to test the nine hypotheses and the whole model they create, Partial Least Squares-Structural Equation Modelling (PLS-SEM) is applied with the SmartPLS 4.1 software. PLS-SEM is considered to be more geared toward exploring a model than Covariance Based Structural Equation Modelling which is more focused on validating a model (Hair et al., 2021).

3.2 Data Collection

This study adapts an established model of trust in CBDCs to the particular context of Brazil which has some distinct characteristics (Zarifis & Cheng, 2024a). There are two main distinct characteristics this CBDC has. The first is the gradual and successful build-up to its implementation, and the second is the architecture with two tiers, where consumers still interact with retail banks and not directly with the central bank.

Consequently, the research instrument must reflect four factors that build trust in a CBDC that remain the same as the established model (Zarifis & Cheng, 2024a), two factors that are adapted to reflect the two-tier model, and one new factor to reflect the significance of the journey to implementation. The seven variables that build trust, along with the variable of trust in a CBDC, and a variable of using a CBDC, are illustrated in Table 1. These nine variables are latent variables, as each of them is measured by three measured variables. This is done because beliefs such as trust and privacy often have several dimensions to them and are hard to measure directly. Using several measured variables ensures the latent variables are captured more accurately. The ninth variable willingness to use a CBDC is arguably a simpler concept and may have been captured sufficiently with two latent variables, as some other research does, but three were used for this also to ensure its accuracy.

For data collection, a self-administered questionnaire was made available via the SoSci Survey cloud service (www.soscisurvey.de) that meets privacy requirements such as GDPR. The study was promoted on social media in Brazil and participants could use a URL link directing them to where they could complete the questionnaire.

Participants could use a seven-step bipolar scale from one, representing strongly disagree, to seven, representing strongly agree. No incentive was given, firstly because it was not considered necessary to give extra motivation on this new and important issue, secondly to avoid biasing in some way, and thirdly to avoid collecting personal information. Established scales were used as the basis for the questions of this study as illustrated in Table 1.

Table 1 Latent variables and their measures

Latent variables	Measures	Source of construct measures adapted
Trust in CBDC implementation process	TP1, TP2, TP3	Lankton et al. (2015), McKnight and Chervany (2002)
Trust in government and central bank (TG)	TG1, TG2, TG3	Grimmelikhuijsen and Knies (2017)
Expressed guarantees (EG)	EG1, EG2, EG3	Dinev et al. (2013), Martínez-López et al. (2020), Yun et al. (2019)
Reputation of existing CBDCs (R)	R1, R2, R3	Einwiller (2003)
Trust in technology and automation (TA)	TA1, TA2, TA3	Lankton et al. (2015), McKnight and Chervany (2002)
Retail bank's wallet app trust building functionality (AF)	AF1, AF2, AF3	Pavlou (2002)
Retail bank's wallet app privacy protecting features (PF)	PF1, PF2, PF3	Dinev et al. (2013)
Trust in CBDC (TC)	TC1, TC2, TC3	Lankton et al. (2015), McKnight and Chervany (2002)
Intention to use CBDC (UC)	UC1, UC2, UC3	Venkatesh et al. (2003)

The minimum sample size necessary was estimated in three ways. Firstly, the G*Power software 3.1.9.7 estimated a minimum sample size of 263 for a predictive power of 95% Based on the maximum number of arrows being seven, for a significance level of 1% and a minimum R2 of 0.10, the minimum number required is 228 (Hair et al., 2021). Lastly, a rule of thumb that is popular is to ensure there are ten participants per measured variable, which suggests a minimum sample of 270.

Some quality checks were made on the 512 submissions and the final number of valid completed surveys is 453. The quality checks ruled out unreasonably fast submissions, submissions that chose the same number throughout, and incomplete submissions. The survey did not have any questions that could not be answered by someone that lived in Brazil (Table 2).

4 Analysis and Results

The analysis starts by evaluating the measurement model, which covers the relationship between each latent variable and its measured variables. This is followed by the analysis of the structural model, the relationship between the latent variables that form the model.

4.1 Measurement Model

The measurement model is evaluated in several ways to check if the measured variables are indeed strongly associated with their latent variable and not another latent variable. The results are presented in Tables 3 and 4. The convergent validity of the variables is evaluated with two methods. The lowest factor loading is 0.862 for PF3, above the minimum acceptable value of 0.7. For the Average Variance Extracted (AVE) the lowest value is 0.798 for R, above the minimum acceptable value of 0.5. Composite Reliability (CR) is used to test the reliability of the latent variables. The lowest value for CR is 0.868 for TC, above the recommended threshold of 0.7. The Fornell–Larcker criterion evaluated the discriminant validity as illustrated in Table 4. As the results in Table 4 show the latent variables are sufficiently distinct statistically. Overall, the tests carried out at this stage support the measurement model.

4.2 Structural Model

Several criteria must be met to support the structural model. In the initial model, TP had a weak negative effect on trust of 0.33 and was therefore removed from the model. The hypothesis related to TP, trust in the process is not supported. The model

Table 2 Participants demographic information

Measure	Variable	Participants	Percentage
Gender	Female	196	43%
	Male	257	57%
Age	18–24	182	40%
	25–39	147	33%
	40–59	84	19%
	60 or older	40	9%
Educational level (highest qualification)	No high school education	46	1%
	High school graduate	254	56%
	University bachelor's degree	135	30%
	University postgraduate degree	18	4%
Income (Brazilian Real per month)	No income	74	16%
	Up to 6000	62	14%
	6001–9000	143	32%
	9001–12,000	151	33%
	Over 12,001	23	5%
Brazilian nationality and Brazilian resident		404	89%
Without Brazilian nationality but a Brazilian resident		49	11%

Table 3 Measurement model results for convergent validity, consistency and reliability

Variables		Loadings	CR	AVE
TP	TP1	0.943	0.916	0.853
	TP2	0.918		
	TP3	0.910		
TG	TG1	0.943	0.947	0.904
	TG2	0.958		
	TG3	0.951		
EG	EG1	0.886	0.909	0.843
	EG2	0.960		
	EG3	0.907		
R	R1	0.934	0.878	0.798
	R2	0.897		
	R3	0.846		
TA	TA1	0.934	0.917	0.855
	TA2	0.911		
	TA3	0.929		
AF	AF1	0.906	0.900	0.832
	AF2	0.898		
	AF3	0.932		
PF	PF1	0.928	0.892	0.818
	PF2	0.922		
	PF3	0.862		
TC	TC1	0.916	0.868	0.789
	TC2	0.856		
	TC3	0.892		
UC	UC1	0.913	0.914	0.853
	UC2	0.938		
	UC3	0.938		

Table 4 Measurement model results for discriminant validity (Fornell–Larcker criterion)

	TP	TG	EG	R	TA	AF	PF	TC	UC
TP	0.924								
TG	0.813	0.951							
EG	0.745	0.900	0.918						
R	0.687	0.815	0.866	0.893					
TA	0.771	0.884	0.851	0.816	0.925				
AF	0.912	0.720	0.766	0.754	0.683	0.912			
PF	0.550	0.648	0.710	0.740	0.635	0.897	0.904		
TC	0.714	0.862	0.884	0.861	0.888	0.852	0.825	0.888	
UC	0.669	0.777	0.806	0.794	0.767	0.755	0.747	0.885	0.924

Table 5 Results of the final structural model

Path	Sample Mean	Standard Deviation	T Statistics
TG-TC	1.658	89.737	0.008**
EG-TC	2.001	118.657	0.007**
R-TC	0.860	67.784	0.004**
TA-TC	1.106	34.822	0.020**
AF-TC	0.437	31.447	0.027**
PF-TC	0.059	33.493	0.010**
TC-UC	0.994	0.014	70.972**

Note: *$p < 0.10$; **$p < 0.05$; ***$p < 0.01$

was therefore retested without TP. PLS-SEM and SmartPLS are designed to support exploring a model and generating a revised, stronger model (Hair et al., 2021).

The results of the evaluation of the structural model are presented in Table 5 which shows the path coefficients and the coefficient of determination R-square values. For the endogenous variable, 'trust CBDC', the coefficient of determination R-square is 0.905, and for the second endogenous variable 'use CBDC' it is 0.783 so they are both substantial as they are above 0.67 (Chin, 1998).

The effect size (f2) for the paths TG-TC (0.022), EG-TC (0.035), R-TC (0.021), TA-TC (0.143), AF-TC (0.052), PF-TC (0.100) are weak but significant. TC-UC (3.604) is strong as it is above 0.35 (Chin, 1998).

Bootstrapping with 5500 resamples was utilised to evaluate the path significance levels. The results of the bootstrapping statistics are presented in Table 5. The bootstrapping results give further support to the relationship between TG, EG, R, TA, AF, PF and TC.

The priority of the PLS-SEM is not to evaluate model fit (Hair et al., 2021) but nevertheless, the Standardized Root-Mean Residual (SRMR) for the estimated model is 0.063 suggesting a good model fit as it is below 0.08 (Hu & Bentler, 1999).

5 Discussion

Trust is necessary for a CBDC to be widely adopted and used enthusiastically across all economic activity. As trust in the government institutions including those in Brazil, seem to be lower than usual it is important to identify and utilize all the ways that trust can be built (OECD, 2023).

5.1 Implications for Theory

This research extends an existing model of consumer trust in a CBDC (Zarifis & Cheng, 2024a) to cover the Brazilian CBDC and other two-tier CBDC implementations. In two-tier CBDC implementations the central bank and commercial banks

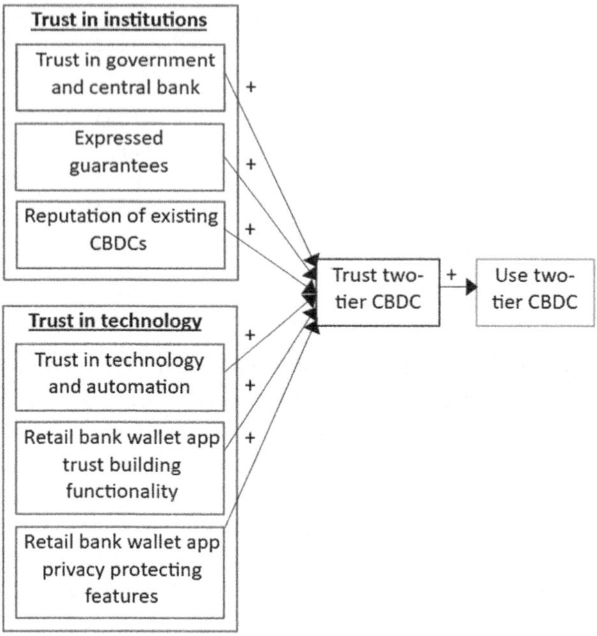

Fig. 2 Model of consumer trust in Brazil's two-tier CBDC, adapted from (Zarifis & Cheng, 2024a)

retain similar roles to the ones they have today, unlike a one-tier system where the central bank interacts directly with the user. The supported model of trust in Brazil's two-tier CBDC is illustrated in Fig. 2.

While it is obvious that a different country, in this case Brazil, may have some idiosyncrasies in how users perceive CBDCs, what might be less obvious is that the Brazilian CBDC is a different solution with a different implementation process. The implementation is a clear two-tier solution meaning that the current two-tier system with the central bank and the commercial banks is mirrored. The implementation process in Brazil is also distinctive due to its gradual, and successful, implementation that built on previous successes like the PIX instant payment platform.

This research first clarified what the key characteristics of the Brazilian CBDC are. It then proposed a model of consumer trust in a CBDC based on an existing model (Zarifis & Cheng, 2024a) with one addition. The addition made was that the implementation process in Brazil, because of its cautious, gradual and successful nature would build trust. The analysis supports the original model but does not support the addition made. One possible explanation is that the successful implementation process avoided problems that would reduce trust but did not necessarily build trust. A second possible explanation is that many people were not aware, or did not think about the implementation process.

An additional adjustment to the model used as a starting point is that the wording of the two variables related to the wallet app is changed to reflect that in a two-tier CBDC the wallet app used, will be that of the retail bank.

As the implementation process does not have a significant influence, it is three institutional factors and three features of the technology that influence trust. Therefore this model finds that trust in the Brazilian CBDC is built in the following ways: (a) trust in government and central bank offering the CBDC, (b) expressed guarantees for those using it, (c) the favourable reputation of other active CBDCs, (d) the CBDC technology, the automation and limited human involvement necessary, (e) the trust building features of the retail bank's CBDC wallet app, and (f) the privacy features of the retail bank's CBDC wallet app and back-end processes.

It is an important theoretical contribution to show that the model of consumer trust in a CBDC is valid in at least two countries and that it is valid for both a mixed implementation, and a clear two-tier implementation. The two countries where this model has now been tested have distinct cultures, and the two solutions and implementation processes are also quite different, so it is useful to show that the same model is useful in these two cases. This is a strong indication that the model will be valid in many countries, although it cannot be assumed it would be valid for a strict one-tier implementation.

Lastly, this research informs the broader literature on trust illustrating the influence on consumer trust by the institutions involved in the service, and the technology characteristics (Ratnasingham et al., 2005; Stouthuysen et al., 2018). While the institutions and the technology characteristics often influence trust, this is not always the case, and there is therefore an ongoing debate on the relationship between institutions and trust.

5.2 *Implications for Practice*

This research has practical implications for several stakeholders in a CBDC and can inform action to build consumer trust. It is widely believed that on the topic of CBDCs, as with other financial innovations Brazil is a regional leader with some countries in Latin America waiting to see what CBDC will be offered, how it will be implemented, and received by the public, before moving forward (Proskalovich et al., 2023). Therefore, clearly framing the Brazilian CBDC model makes it easier for the countries in Latin America primarily, but also elsewhere, to learn lessons. The first two important implications for practise from the Brazilian model are the choice of a two-tier CBDC which is close to the existing system people are familiar with, and the gradual implementation that is transparent to the public without surprises, and also enables expertise to be built up. While these do not build trust directly they may stop trust being reduced.

The final implication for practice is the model of how to build trust in a CBDC that shows what to focus on. While one person or a focus group could come up with a long list of possible issues affecting trust, this model identifies the six issues that do indeed influence trust. This is a manageable number for stakeholders such as the government, regulators, commercial banks or other financial institutions. A stakeholder that is affected by CBDCs may try to influence as many of the six factors shaping trust as possible, or they may focus on some of the six.

A government may be able to influence five of the six either directly or indirectly. It is unlikely that a government can influence (c) the reputation of existing CBDCs. A government can probably influence (a) trust in the government and central bank, and (b) expressed guarantees directly. A government should also be able to have some indirect influence over (d) trust in the technology and automation, (e) retail bank wallet app trust-building functionality and (f) retail bank wallet app privacy features.

Other stakeholders such as retail banks, depending on their role will probably have to focus on the last three trust-building methods. As the two-tier system is close to the current system, the role of banks and other financial institutions offering services to private individuals, in building trust is also similar. Nevertheless, given that in a typical banking app, a customer has several currencies to choose from, the retail banks will have to think about how trust in the CBDC can be built sufficiently so that it is preferred to the alternatives that have been available for longer and are more familiar.

5.3 Limitations and Future Research

This research hypothesised that the gradual and successful implementation of the Brazilian CBDC positively influenced consumer trust in it. Despite this being a logical hypothesis, supported by some literature, this was not supported by the data. This does not mean this gradual cautious implementation was not beneficial. It may have avoided failures that would have damaged trust and it may have built trust in other stakeholders, other than the consumers.

If the implementation was not so cautious with several pilots, there may have been problems that weakened trust. Future research can explore this further, although it is not easy to measure the potential effect of an event that did not happen. An experiment may be suitable.

Future research can also explore whether the gradual implementation built trust in the other stakeholders such as regulators, retail banks, other financial institutions and technology providers. These stakeholders may have followed the developments more closely and may have been more positively influenced by the gradual implementation process.

While the model is supported in two countries and two different implementations of CBDCs, it would be useful to validate it in additional countries especially if they have very different implementations such as a strict one-tier implementation.

6 Conclusion

This research extends an existing model of consumer trust in a CBDC (Zarifis & Cheng, 2024a) to cover the Brazilian CBDC, and other two-tier CBDC implementations where the central bank and commercial banks retain similar roles to the ones they have today. The model was explored with survey data.

The implementation process does not have a significant influence on trust, so it is three institutional factors, and three features of the technology that influence trust. Therefore trust in the Brazilian CBDC is built in the following ways: (a) Trust in government and central bank offering the CBDC, (b) expressed guarantees for those using it, (c) the favourable reputation of other active CBDCs, (d) the CBDC technology, the automation and limited human involvement necessary, (e) the trust building features of the CBDC wallet app, and (f) the privacy features of the CBDC wallet app and back-end processes.

References

Agencia Brazil. (2024) *CNJ Counts 100,000 Attendances in the Civil Registration Week.*

Ahn, M. J., & Chen, Y. C. (2022). Digital transformation toward AI-augmented public administration: The perception of government employees and the willingness to use AI in government. *Government Information Quarterly*, Elsevier Inc., *39*(2), 101664. https://doi.org/10.1016/j.giq.2021.101664.

Alvarez, F., Argente, D., & Van Patten, D. (2023). Are cryptocurrencies currencies? Bitcoin as legal tender in El Salvador. *Science, 382*(6677). https://doi.org/10.1126/science.add2844

Amboage, G. B., Monteiro, G. F. d. A., & Bortoluzzo, A. B. (2024). Technological adoption: the case of PIX in Brazil. *Innovation and Management Review*. https://doi.org/10.1108/INMR-10-2022-0133

Auer, R., & Böhme, R. (2020). The technology of Retail Central Bank Digital Currency. *BIS Quarterly Review*.

Auer, R., Cornelli, G., & Frost, J. (2023). Rise of the Central Bank Digital Currencies. *International Journal of Central Banking, 19*(4), 185–214.

BIS Innovation Hub. (2023). *Project MBridge Update: Experimenting with a Multi-CBDC Platform for Cross-Border Payments*.

Brazilian Central Bank. (2024). *Drex – Digital Brazilian Real.*

Chang, M. K., Cheung, W., & Tang, M. (2013). Building trust online: Interactions among trust building mechanisms. *Information and Management, Elsevier B.V., 50*(7), 439–445. https://doi.org/10.1016/j.im.2013.06.003

Chen, S., Goel, T., Qiu, H., & Shim, I. (2022). CBDCs in emerging market economies. *BIS Papers*, https://doi.org/10.2139/ssrn.4085690.

Chin, W. W. (1998). The partial least squares approach to structural equation modelling. In G. A. Marcoulides (Ed.), *Modern methods for business research* (pp. 295–336). Lawrence Erlbaum Associates.

Dinev, T., Xu, H., Smith, J. H., & Hart, P. (2013). Information privacy and correlates: An empirical attempt to bridge and distinguish privacy-related concepts. *European Journal of Information Systems, Nature Publishing Group, 22*(3), 295–316. https://doi.org/10.1057/ejis.2012.23

Dupont, Q., & Karpoff, J. M. (2020). The trust triangle: Laws, reputation, and culture in empirical finance research. *Journal of Business Ethics, Springer, 163*(2), 217–238. https://doi.org/10.1007/s10551-019-04229-1

Einwiller, S. (2003). When reputation engenders trust: An empirical investigation in business-to-consumer electronic commerce. *Electronic Markets, 13*(3), 196–209. https://doi.org/10.1080/1019678032000092246

Flores Gálvez, J. N., & Mata Hernández, J. M. (2023). CBDC-MXN: Challenges and perspectives in the implementation as a Mexican digital currency. *Mercados y Negocios, 2023*(49), 3–20. https://doi.org/10.32870/myn.vi49.7689

Grimmelikhuijsen, S., & Knies, E. (2017). Validating a scale for citizen trust in government organizations. *International Review of Administrative Sciences, 83*(3), 583–601. https://doi.org/10.1177/0020852315585950

Hair, J., Hult, T., Ringle, C., & Sarstedt, M. (2021). *A primer on partial least squares structural equation modeling (PLS-SEM)* (3rd ed.). Sage Publishing.

Hu, L. T., & Bentler, P. M. (1999). Cutoff criteria for fit indexes in covariance structure analysis: Conventional criteria versus new alternatives. *Structural Equation Modeling, 6*(1), 1–55. https://doi.org/10.1080/10705519909540118

Huber, T. A., & Sornette, D. (2022). Boom, bust, and Bitcoin: Bitcoin-bubbles as innovation accelerators. *Journal of Economic Issues, Informa UK Limited, 56*(1), 113–136. https://doi.org/10.1080/00213624.2022.2020023

Lankton, N., McKnight, H., & Tripp, J. (2015). Technology, humanness, and trust: Rethinking trust in technology. *Journal of the Association for Information Technology, 16*(10), 880–918.

León, C., Moreno, J. F., & Soramäki, K. (2024). Simulating the adoption of a retail CBDC. *Journal of Economics and Statistics*, 1–33. https://doi.org/10.1515/jbnst-2024-0002

Martínez-López, F. J., Li, Y., Feng, C., & Esteban-Millat, I. (2020). Purchasing through social platforms with buy buttons: A basic hierarchical sequence. *Journal of Organizational Computing and Electronic Commerce, Taylor & Francis, 30*(1), 67–87. https://doi.org/10.1080/10919392.2020.1713698

McKnight, H., Carter, M., Thatcher, J. B., & Clay, P. (2011). Trust in a specific technology: An investigation of its components and measures. *ACM Transactions on Management Information Systems, 2*(2). https://doi.org/10.1145/1985347.1985353

McKnight, H., & Chervany, N. L. (2002). What trust means in E-commerce customer relationships: An interdisciplinary conceptual typology. *International Journal of Electronic Commerce, 6*(2), 35–59.

Morales-Resendiz, R., Ponce, J., Picardo, P., Velasco, A., Chen, B., Sanz, L., Guiborg, G., et al. (2021). Implementing a retail CBDC: Lessons learned and key insights. *Latin American Journal of Central Banking, 2*(1), 1–10. https://doi.org/10.1016/j.latcb.2021.100022

OECD. (2023). Drivers of trust in public institutions in Brazil. *OECD Publishing*. https://doi.org/10.1787/fb0e1896-en

Pavlou, P. A. (2002). Institution-based trust in interorganizational exchange relationships: The role of online B2B marketplaces on trust formation. *The Journal of Strategic Information Systems, 11*(3–4), 215–243. https://doi.org/10.1016/S0963-8687(02)00017-3

Pavlou, P., & Gefen, D. (2004). Building effective online marketplaces with institution-based trust. *Information Systems Research, 15*(1), 667–675. https://doi.org/10.1287/isre.1040.0015

Pocher, N., & Veneris, A. (2022). Privacy and transparency in CBDCs: A regulation-by-design AML/CFT scheme. *IEEE Transactions on Network and Service Management, IEEE, 19*(2), 1776–1788. https://doi.org/10.1109/TNSM.2021.3136984

Proskalovich, R., Jack, C., Zarifis, A., Serralde, D. M., Vershinina, P., Naidoo, S., Njoki, D., et al. (2023). *Cryptoasset ecosystem in Latin America and the Caribbean*. Cambridge Centre for Alternative Finance.

Ratnasingham, P., Gefen, D., & Pavlou, P. A. (2005). The role of facilitating conditions and institutional trust in electronic markets. *Journal of Electronic Commerce in Organizations, 14*(5), 69–82.

Rodrigues, V. F., Policarpo, L. M., da Silveira, D. E., da Rosa Righi, R., da Costa, C. A., Barbosa, J. L. V., Antunes, R. S., et al. (2022). Fraud detection and prevention in e-commerce: A systematic literature review. *Electronic Commerce Research and Applications, Elsevier B.V, 56*. August 2021. https://doi.org/10.1016/j.elerap.2022.101207

Statista Research Department. (2023). *Informal Employment as Percentage of Total Employment in Brazil from 2011 to 2022.*

Stouthuysen, K., Teunis, I., Reusen, E., & Slabbinck, H. (2018). Initial trust and intentions to buy: The effect of vendor-specific guarantees, customer reviews and the role of online shopping experience☆. *Electronic Commerce Research and Applications, Elsevier B.V., 27*, 23–38. https://doi.org/10.1016/j.elerap.2017.11.002

Tombini, A. (2023). The future of money: A possible role for central bank digital currencies and their implications digitalisation and benefits for society. *BIS Speeches*, 1–14.

Venkatesh, V., Morris, M. G., Davis, G. B., & Davis, F. D. (2003). User acceptance of information technology: *Toward a unified view. MIS Quarterly, 27*(3), 425–478

Xu, J. (2022). Developments and implications of Central Bank Digital Currency: The case of China e-CNY. *Asian Economic Policy Review*, John Wiley and Sons Inc, 1 July, https://doi.org/10.1111/aepr.12396.

Yun, H., Lee, G., & Kim, D. J. (2019). A chronological review of empirical research on personal information privacy concerns: An analysis of contexts and research constructs. *Information and Management, Elsevier B.V., 56*(4), 570–601. https://doi.org/10.1016/j.im.2018.10.001

Zarifis, A., & Cheng, X. (2024a). *The six ways to build trust and reduce privacy concern in a Central Bank Digital Currency (CBDC)* (pp. 115–138). Business Digital Transformation, Springer International Publishing. https://doi.org/10.1007/978-3-031-33665-2_6

Zarifis, A., & Cheng, X. (2024b). *Trust in Central Bank Digital Currency (CBDC) in Mexico* (pp. 1–3). European Conference on Infomation Systems (ECIS).

Alex Zarifis's research and teaching are on the practical applications of technology in business. Before the University of Southampton, he worked at several academic institutions including the University of Cambridge, the University of Manchester and the University of Mannheim. He is currently a research affiliate of the Cambridge Center for Alternative Finance (CCAF).

He has explored cryptoassets such as cryptocurrencies since 2012. As part of this research, he published the first peer-reviewed research on trust in digital currencies in the world in 2014. He also participated in creating the first government recognised, university degree on blockchain technologies in the world.

Dr Alex has published extensively on trust in different technologies and business models. His research has explored the role of trust in AI, blockchain, financial technology (Fintech) and insurance technology (Insurtech).

Xusen Cheng is a Full Professor of Information Systems in the School of Information at Renmin University of China. He is also a research fellow in the Metaverse Research Center and School of Interdisplinary Studies at the Renmin University of China. He obtained his PhD degree from the University of Manchester, UK. His research interests include trust and information systems, design and behaviour issues of digital business, digital economy and Metaverse. His research has been published in leading journals such as MIS Quarterly and Journal of Management Information Systems.

Modularizing Decentralised Finance: The DeFi Layered Stack Revisited

Enrico Rossi

1 Introduction: Overview of the Work

Decentralised finance (DeFi) has gained significant attention since early 2020 due to the "DeFi boom" starting during the "DeFi summer" of 2020. This has spurred a substantial amount of literature on DeFi (Amler et al., 2021; Bartoletti et al., 2021b; IOSCO, 2022; Makarov & Schoar, 2022; Meyer et al., 2021; Qin et al., 2021a; Rossi, 2022a; Schär, 2021; Werner et al., 2021; Zetzsche et al., 2020). Many of these works provide exhaustive definitions of DeFi, highlight the main business models and discuss critical aspects that should be considered from economic, legal, and policy-making points of view.

Many of these works on DeFi point out the layered nature of DeFi (Makarov & Schoar, 2022; Schär, 2021; Werner et al., 2021; Wieandt & Heppding, 2022). As discussed by a variety of authors, DeFi can be understood as a stack of logical layers, where each layer represents a separate element or component of DeFi performing a different role within the stack. The relevance of the stack derives from the fact that layers can be treated as independent analytical elements, so that different DeFi services and business models, competitive dynamics, and risks can be assessed by comparing the different natures and characteristics of the various layers across the various solutions. Based on this approach, layers become the fundamental building blocks of DeFi. This layered understanding of DeFi is also consistent with the main characterizations of blockchain architectural and logical solutions, which often distinguish between layer 1 and layer 2 solutions (Gangwal et al., 2022; Gudgeon et al., 2020a; Jourenko et al., 2019).

E. Rossi (✉)
Cambridge Centre for Alternative Finance, Cambridge, UK

UCL Centre for Blockchain Technologies, London, UK
e-mail: enrico.rossi@ucl.ac.uk

A. Zarifis, X. Cheng (eds.), *Fintech and the Emerging Ecosystems*, Financial Innovation and Technology, https://doi.org/10.1007/978-3-031-83402-8_5

The main limitation of standard discussions of the DeFi stack mainly derives from the fact that the logic and approach followed to discern and identify the various modules is not explicitly stated; the main outcome is that the various elements of the stack do not always emerge from coherent and consistent top-down modularization approaches of DeFi systems (Simon, 1962). This often leads to a multiplicity of seemingly arbitrary definitions and characterizations of the stack that are not only inconsistent with each other but are also often composed of (ontologically and logically) heterogeneous elements. It therefore becomes hard to understand the overarching and common logic that is used to construct the stack so as to clearly (if not univocally) derive its various elements. As a result, the question that mainly motivates and drives this paper is: how can we make sense of the DeFi layered stack?

This work provides an alternative systematic assessment of, and perspective on, the DeFi stack. In contrast to the standard discussion of the DeFi stack that usually includes heterogeneous elements, such as protocols, assets, or services, this work reinterprets and reconstructs the DeFi stack from a modular point of view, in a way that is more consistent with the standard definition of layered modularity provided by the literature (Baldwin & Woodard, 2009; Hylving & Schultze, 2020; Van Schewick, 2012; Yoo, 2013; Yoo et al., 2010) and system modularization (Baldwin, 2008; Baldwin & Clark, 2000; Garud et al., 2009; Langlois, 2002; Langlois & Robertson, 1992; Schilling, 2000; Simon, 1962).

Consistent with the literature on layered modular architectures, this work decomposes the DeFi stack into functionally independent modules (Baldwin & Clark, 2000; Ulrich, 1995), each representing a set of functionally-independent (and functionally-specific) protocols. The proposed stack then is made up of layers of functionally-independent logical modules, each composed of sets of protocols that retain functional homogeneity internally (within each module) and are characterised by functional heterogeneity externally (with respect to the clusters of protocols belonging to different logical modules). This is consistent with the principles of modular systems that prescribe modules to be functionally interdependent internally and operating according to their idiosyncratic rules, but functionally independent externally (independence from other modules) (Baldwin, 2008; Baldwin & Clark, 2000; Cabigiosu & Camuffo, 2016; Schilling, 2000; Simon, 1962; Ulrich, 1995).

The proposed DeFi stack is therefore only composed of one single homogeneous building block (element)—the protocol—rather than a variety of possibly heterogenous elements (spanning from assets to services). At the same time, the present work only considers one single feature to modularize DeFi eco-systems into modules: protocols' main functions. As a result, protocols developed in order to perform a certain function and fulfil a certain role are all clustered together into the same module, while protocols performing different functions are allocated to separate (functionally-independent) modular layers. This novel interpretation of the stack based on functional homogeneity and independence (rather than the ontology of elements) is discussed in Sect. 3 of the paper.

Based on that, the paper identifies five main layers (DeFi logical modules) clustered into two main macro-layers (discussed in Sect. 4). First (Sect. 4.1), the paper identifies an infrastructural macro-layer composed of two well-known layers: the consensus layer and the smart contract layer. The former mainly fulfils "writing functions" (it includes protocols enforcing the right consensus in order to validate changes in states and status updates over the blockchain), while the latter mainly includes protocols dedicated to the autonomous initiation, automatic enforcement, and automatic executions of changes in states (i.e. transactions) and/or contractual clauses.

Second (Sect. 4.2), the paper identifies three separate layers belonging to the application macro-layer: a business model or service layer, a performance optimization layer, and a governance layer. The first includes all protocols dedicated to the operation of a DeFi system, the correct provision of its services, and the issuance of its claim-tokens (Sect. 4.2.1). This layer includes all those protocols whose ultimate goal is to operate a system and provide a certain outcome or service; different business models and DeFi applications can be distinguished at this layer as they provide different types of services to their users.

The second layer includes all those protocols developed in order to ensure that services are provided in an efficient manner and the application is operated according to some optimization mechanisms (Sect. 4.2.2). This layer includes protocols that optimize the DeFi business models, incentivize actors' participation and adoption, ensure short-term stability, liquidity, and the long-term solvency of applications. Being able to provide a service and operate a decentralised business is different, and independent from, operating it efficiently, profitably, and in a sustainable and viable manner.

Finally, Sect. 4.2.3 discusses the last layer, called the governance layer. This third layer includes all (smart contract) protocols that operate and enforce on-chain governance mechanisms and align incentives. This third layer clusters all those protocols that use smart contract functionalities to bridge the on-chain vs. off-chain rift and address the problem of implementing governance and decision-making practices on-chain.

The paper therefore breaks down the DeFi stack into five core layers, each characterised by a specific set of protocols sharing a core functionality. Each layer is also analysed in function of the specific nature and meaning of the decentralization-efficiency trade-off. For each of these layers, the work discusses how the specific meanings of core concepts, such as those of decentralization and efficiency, change in light of the specific layer they refer to. For instance, while decentralization in the smart contract layer (layer 2) mainly refers to the concept of autonomy (vs. discretion), decentralization in the governance layer may assume a variety of meanings all somewhat linked to the problem of procedural decision-making power (and so on). The same applies to efficiency which can be understood either in operational terms, in economic terms, in production terms, and so forth. Given the multifaceted meanings of decentralization, the work also discusses the various types of risks involved in any of the five layers.

Lastly, the paper provides two further contributions.

First, in Sect. 4.3 the paper shows that cryptoassets (tokens) can operate at any of these five layers. On the one hand, every layer of the stack is supported by a token in the performance of its functions and defines the right incentives to operate in a decentralised manner; on the other hand, tokens are functionally amorphous and agnostic and can therefore fulfil various functions and operate at multiple layers based on the specific way in which they are employed and the specific functionality provided. For instance, so-called governance tokens can be used for governance purposes to support protocols at layer 5, they can be used for stability, solvency, or liquidity purposes to support incentive mechanisms at layer 4, and also for operational purposes at layer 3. For this reason, the paper suggests avoiding the concept of a governance token and substituting it with the broader concept of "application-native tokens" (ANTs). The same is valid for a variety of other tokens performing different functions at different layers.

As a result, the work argues that it may be more convenient to avoid the explicit identification of a specific asset layer: not only because it would be inconsistent with the modularization adopted here (based on functional protocols rather than data objects), but also because it would create logical overlaps across layers and would violate the necessary independence requirement to separate one modular layer from another.

Given that any layer can have one (or multiple) tokens linked to it, the work proposes a novel classification of tokens that identifies two types of tokens: instrumental tokens and tokens-as-instruments. While the first type groups all those tokens that play a key role in supporting the functionalities of the various protocols of the stack (and therefore derive their usefulness and value from the operation of the various protocols at any layer), the second type includes all those tokens that can be useful and valuable independently from the operation of a protocol of the DeFi stack. The first type of tokens are necessary to support the operation of decentralised protocols; for this reason, they are a "means to an end" and cannot be clearly decoupled from the functionalities performed by some protocols of the stack. The second set of tokens (such as fiat-backed stablecoins) are ends in themselves and can be severed from the operation of all protocols; these are tokens that do not need to support decentralised protocols and, for this reason, they can retain value and utility even in a centralised context, independently from the operation of decentralised protocols.

Second, the final section of the work proposes a novel way to understand value along the DeFi stack. Section 5 develops a novel "pyramid of value" that breaks down the value of a DeFi application into fundamental layers of value, each characterised by the value of a specific token and the incentive mechanism supported and enabled by it. As discussed in the final section of the work, the tokens composing the five layers of value are: the claim-token issued by the application (which can be a stablecoin or wrapped token or something akin to these), the token the claim-token is pegged to, the token used as collateral or backing of the issued claim-token, the governance token (or, more appropriately, the ANT) and, finally, the layer-1 native token. Each of these five layers relies on, and is supported by, the underlying one through specific value-stability (or value-support) mechanisms. As a result, each interaction between any two adjacent layers of value is characterised by the operation of a specific stability mechanism.

In conclusion, it is important to highlight that this paper can be interpreted as the second part of a previously written piece (Rossi, 2022a) on the meaning of DeFi. While the latter provides a univocal definition and characterization of DeFi (it tries to answer the question of what DeFi is), this work breaks down (modularizes) DeFi into its main logical elements (the five-layered set of protocols) and discusses the issue of how DeFi operates and what constitutes a DeFi eco-system. For this reason, the discussion and framework provided in Sect. 2 derives from Rossi (2022a).

2 Some Necessary Terminological Clarifications

DeFi is a complex and multidimensional concept formed by a multiplicity of heterogeneous elements. These various elements are not equivalent: some elements are more general and high-level than others and are defined at different levels of aggregation. For the sake of precision and clarity, in what follows, we will employ the following terminology.

First, the concept of (DeFi) application refers to the abstract overall set of elements, logics, protocols, procedures, data, operations, relationships, activities, and performances that are usually identified by a specific name (i.e. MakerDAO, or Aave). A DeFi application is usually created and managed by a set of individuals and its goal is to provide certain DeFi services to their users. In traditional (centralized) environments, the "application" refers to the legal business entity or the company.

The DeFi service is the outcome provided by the specific application. A DeFi service provides some added value to the users benefitting from it and it refers to what an application ultimately does.

For DeFi protocols we mean the set of actions and functionalities logically embedded into code. Protocols are the lines of codes instructing applications on what has to be done in each circumstance or for each command or request. Protocols enable the provision of services.

A DeFi architecture refers to the specific way in which the various physical and logical elements of a DeFi application are connected, linked, and composed, including the broader rules defining the ways in which these are supposed to interact and interoperate. While protocols represent specific logical building blocks (lines of code and logic fulfilling specific roles and providing specific functionalities), a DeFi system architecture captures the way in which the various protocols interact and are interlinked.

For DeFi systems we refer to the overall set of logical and physical elements, architectures, and rules that are linked and interoperate in order to provide a specific service so to achieve a specific goal. A system therefore includes protocols and architectures. This is consistent with the standard characterization of systems provided by the literature (Grewatsch et al., 2021; Lee, 2010; Parnas, 1972; Simon, 1962), which highlights a few core characteristics of systems, namely the fact that they are constituted of sub-elements or subsystems (in this case the protocols) that perform specific functions with their own process dynamics (Schad & Bansal,

2018), and are combined and interlinked in complex ways (in this case, according to architectural or design rules), thus generating both combinatorial and dynamic complexity (Sterman, 2002). Although systems can be characterized by a variety of different ontologies, and be decomposed into a variety of different ontological sub-systems (i.e. social and organizational, technological or physical, and data or informational—see Lee et al. (2015) and Simon (1962)—, with the term "system" in this case we only refer to the technological (physical or logical) aspect of DeFi systems, including protocol logics (as building blocks, or a system's elements) and their organizing architecture (as their design rules). For this reason, it is possible to use the expressions 'system protocols' and a 'system architecture' instead of referring to DeFi protocols and DeFi architectures. On the other hand, a DeFi application can therefore be understood as a specific DeFi system operating in a certain way for the provision of a specific service (application = system + service).

Finally, a DeFi ecosystem enlarges the focus beyond the single application in order to capture the set of contextual social, human, organizational, symbolic, semantic, technological, legal, and economic aspects and factors that interact with the application and somehow constrain and shape its operations and affect its outcomes.

In this classification, protocols become logical elements fulfilling the role of the fundamental unit of analysis (input side) of DeFi, while the service becomes DeFi's fundamental output; the set of DeFi's protocols are linked and organized according to specific architectures and the system's rules in order to provide a specific (set of) services (Fig. 1).

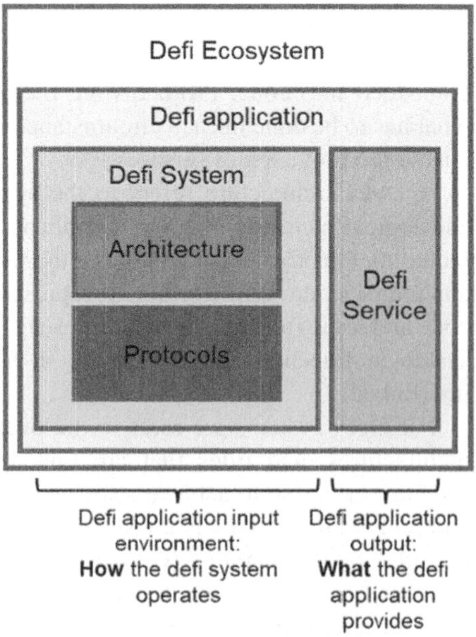

Fig. 1 A terminological taxonomy of DeFi and its constitutive concepts—from Rossi (2022a)

3 Typical Characterization of DeFi: Main Elements and Properties

Typical introductions to DeFi tend to define and characterize it according to two different perspectives: the set of elements composing its layered stack, and the set of idiosyncratic properties and novel characteristics of DeFi's services that distinguish them from the provision of financial services in the traditional financial sector. Discussions of the various DeFi services, or protocols, are usually added to these. Neither represents a proper definition of DeFi, but they both highlight interesting aspects to better capture and understand DeFi's nature. The former is typically used to identify the set of elements and conditions usually shared by all DeFi applications and playing a (direct or indirect) role in the provision of DeFi services. The latter is typically used to distinguish DeFi from traditional financial services in light of idiosyncratic advantages and possible limitations.

As a result, while the DeFi stack can be used to provide a comprehensive and complete overview of all elements characterizing a DeFi ecosystem that play a role in the provision of DeFi services, the discussion of DeFi's idiosyncratic properties of DeFi is usually used to univocally distinguish DeFi services from traditional financial services.

3.1 The Traditional Overview of DeFi's Idiosyncratic Properties: Limitations

The literature usually provides a detailed discussion of DeFi idiosyncratic properties, such as composability, flexibility, decentralization, accessibility, innovativeness, interoperability, borderlessness, transparency, automation of business processes, and finality, amongst others (Meegan & Koens, 2021; Werner et al., 2021). The typical list of properties provides an in-depth overview of the various characteristics of DeFi that distinguish it from traditional financial services. An exhaustive list of properties provides a comprehensive overview of the univocal characteristics of DeFi, but it also reveals certain shortcomings and limitations, consistent with the discussion developed in Sect. 2 above.

First, it often highlights properties of the blockchain itself (such as transparency or borderlessness) that are not specific to DeFi but rather characterize any service operated over a blockchain. As a result, it is important to distinguish those DeFi properties that characterise the underlying blockchain infrastructure from idiosyncratic DeFi properties that specifically distinguish DeFi from any other possible service operated over the blockchain.

Second, the typical list often conflates "primary" necessary properties of DeFi and "derived" or secondary properties of DeFi, understood as those non-necessary properties that only emerge as implications, or secondary outcomes, of other more foundational DeFi characteristics. For instance, composability mainly derives from the atomic property of DeFi's smart contracts (Qin et al., 2021a) coupled with standardization, while characteristics such as "finality" derive from the specific design and architectural solutions adopted by the smart contact and settlement layers considered. In other words, it is important to distinguish core, primary, or necessary characteristics of DeFi, from secondary characteristics that are mainly implications, or outcomes, of the former.

Third, some properties suffer from circular reasoning, such as DeFi's decentralised nature, as discussed above. Although many properties of DeFi represent ideal conditions that could be theoretically attainable or conditions that any DeFi application should strive for, this does not mean that they are necessarily attained. Consistent with the previous discussion, it is important to distinguish between ideal or possible properties from actual properties and to characterise DeFi in the function of the latter, not in the function of the former.

In sum, rather than stating a full list of DeFi ideal properties ex-ante that also risks capturing a variety of non-essential and non-unique characteristics of DeFi, it is better to derive DeFi's idiosyncratic properties from a minimal, yet complete, set of its key characteristics.

3.2 The Traditional DeFi Stack: DeFi's Comprehensive Set of Elements

Current treatments of DeFi often characterize DeFi systems according to their logical layered stack, usually called the DeFi stack (Deshmukh et al., 2021; Makarov & Schoar, 2022; Schär, 2021; Werner et al., 2021).

Layered representations of DeFi do not provide proper definitions of DeFi strictly speaking, but they rather provide (more or less exhaustive or schematic) overviews of the main (types of) elements involved in the provision of DeFi services, by mapping these elements into the different logical layers of the stack they belong to. Usually, these representations of the DeFi stack include a variety of heterogenous and diverse elements organized along a variety of heterogenous layers, such as: logical protocols such as smart contracts, application elements such as web pages or application interfaces, infrastructural elements such as network gateways, data objects such as tokens, and various others. This makes usual representations of the stack internally heterogenous, as different layers can refer to different types of elements.

As a result, there is no univocal conceptualization of the DeFi stack in the literature, as different authors interpret the different layers in different ways, depending on the specific set of elements that they decide to include. Typical representations of the DeFi stack include (a varying selection of) the following layers:

- Layers identifying proper logical elements or programs (such as smart contracts); Layers identifying symbolic (legal or economic) elements or data objects (such as tokens or units of value).
- Layers identifying organizational elements (such as specific companies, applications or communities).
- Layers identifying specific services or protocols (such as lending rather than trading, or aggregating).
- Layers identifying physical (hardware) elements (physical infrastructure).
- Layers identifying other miscellaneous elements, such as aggregators, gateways, or interfaces ensuring usability and access to applications, or composability and interoperations among them (such as wallets, oracles and web applications).

Taken together, these layers are not homogenous nor coherent. Nevertheless, the DeFi stack remains a useful tool as it provides a good foundational overview of the elements and concepts playing a role in DeFi applications. This can provide clarity on the complete set of features, properties and characteristics shared by all elements participating in the DeFi ecosystem.

The remainder of the section will therefore provide an overview of the classical representations of DeFi stack, and develop a new one that can be subsequently used for further analysis of DeFi's distinguishing features.

3.3 Reinterpreting the DeFi Stack: Modularization of a DeFi System

Typical representations of the DeFi stack do not adopt a univocal and common rationale to identify the various layers and, for this reason, different interpretations of the DeFi stack identify a variety of different heterogenous elements.

Here we provide a specific reinterpretation of the DeFi stack that takes the protocol as the unit of analysis and distinguishes different layers based on the different functional roles of their respective protocols. On the one hand, this ensures homogeneity across the various layers, as they are all identified by specific protocols performing specific functions. On the other hand, this also ensures a univocal and consistent modularization logic as all modules are identified by grouping protocols performing the same self-contained function within a DeFi system. In this way, each (logical) layer represents a functionally-independent module univocally characterised by the specific (logical) functionality of its protocol. Different protocol-modules can then be linked and recombined according to the specific architectural rules in order to provide a common output (DeFi application's service).

This approach is consistent with the standard definition of modularity and system modularization understood as the decomposition of systems into functionally independent modules (Baldwin & Clark, 2000; Simon, 1962) that can be seamlessly recombined according to modular or architectural logic (Henderson & Clark, 1990). The advantage of this decomposition is that all layers are identified according to their common unit of analysis (the protocol performing a certain function in the provision of a DeFi service), and the rationale of the decomposition is univocal and homogeneous across all layers (functional homogeneity of the protocols for each layer). Logical functions can then be grouped into independent modules that can be separated (decomposed) due to their functional specificity, yet seamlessly recombined thanks to standard interfaces and according to application-specific design rules (Baldwin & Clark, 2000; Cabigiosu & Camuffo, 2016; Schilling, 2000).

Based on that, we employ a two-staged process to construct the DeFi stack. First, we decompose the system into two macro-layers as we distinguish between protocols that perform functions of the underlying common infrastructural macro-layer that are common to all DeFi applications, and protocols that perform functions for the single DeFi application operating over the infrastructural layer. Second, we further decompose the macro-layers themselves into more fundamental layers corresponding to functionally-specific protocols: each module represents a logical layer, and each layer represents a specific function. This second decomposition more closely reflects the usual representation of the DeFi stack given by the literature.

3.3.1 Decomposing the Infrastructural Macro-Layer

The first infrastructural layer can be broken down into two fundamental layers. The first (layer 1) corresponds to those protocols enforcing overall system integrity and eventual consistency through the attainment and verification of consensus among all nodes (native consensus protocols) (Bano et al., 2019), while layer 2 corresponds to those protocols mainly initiating and executing smart contracts functionalities over (or beside) native consensus protocols.

Layer 1: Settlement and Consensus Layer The first set of protocols (layer 1) belongs to a settlement layer module and its main goal is to settle transactions, ensure the attainment of decentralised consensus, and update new agreed states. In other words, the function of the protocol at this layer is to maintain the system's overall consistency and integrity whenever states are changed and need to be updated in a (more or less) decentralised manner. These can be characterised as consensus protocols. States' updates can occur for various reasons: either for the occurrence of predefined contextual events occurring off-chain (monitored and imported on-chain by means of oracles: see layer 3 below), for the verification of certain predefined conditions enforced by smart contracts on-chain (see layer 2 below), or for the deliberate initiation of transactions by the part of users (typically operating in the application macro-layer) or autonomous programs, or "bots" (smart contracts in layer 2 below).

This layer is therefore devoted to the: (i) attainment of consensus (ii) over the new updated state/s of the system (iii) in order to obtain overall consistency and integrity of the system, (iv) by settling transactions, (v) and writing the new updated states into the common ledger (containing and representing the new agreed consensus over the new states of the system). In sum, this layer includes all protocols that ultimately confirm transactions (states' updates) by *writing* them into the common ledger (blockchain).

Layer 2: Smart Contract Layer The second layer is a smart contract layer characterised by smart contract protocols. Modules belonging to this second layer are characterised by protocols whose primary common function is to automatically execute transactions (or any request of states' updates), but that can potentially also autonomously initiate transactions and/or automatically enforce predefined conditions as specified by their 'code'.

While the function of the protocols operating in the previous layer was to achieve (decentralised) consensus and maintain overall consistency od states in the *writing* of transactions, the function of the protocols operating at this layer is to achieve: (i) autonomous initiation of transactions (state-changing activities) and/or (ii) automatic enforcement of conditions and execution of programs, while ensuring the automatic *execution* (processing) of transactions. Automation means that the execution of certain actions does not depend on the discretion and initiative of independent counterparties, but only on the pre-programmed commands of the smart contract protocols. As discussed below, while not all smart contract protocols need to autonomously initiate a transaction, all smart contract protocols are employed to automate the execution of a transaction.

As a result, while layer 1 includes all those protocols that write states' updates into the chain—by ensuring the (decentralised) validation and confirmation of these states' updates—layer 2 includes all those smart contract protocols dealing with the autonomous initiation and/or automatic execution of states' updates. For this reason, the former can be defined as a settlement, or consensus, layer, while the latter is defined as a smart contract, or execution, layer.

Not all blockchain infrastructures complement the consensus layer with a smart contract layer, but all DeFi applications rely on and are deployed over, a smart contract layer: DeFi protocols operate through smart contract functionalities. As a result, layer 2 remains necessary to operate and support the application layers. Moreover, it is important to highlight that this distinction between a layer 1 module and a layer 2 module should not be confused with the common distinction between layer 1 and layer 2 solutions for blockchain scalability (Gudgeon et al., 2020a; Jourenko et al., 2019): as discussed below, the two are closely related but not identical as they capture different aspects of infrastructural layers.

3.3.2 Decomposing the Application Macro-Layer

The DeFi application macro-layer can also be broken down into a variety of functionally independent modules. The way in which this can be done is less clear-cut and is open to a variety of approaches and interpretations.

Here we identify three main layers that correspond to the typical three main types of functionally-independent modules composing a DeFi application: a layer characterised by the application's business model protocols defining the basic functioning and operations of the DeFi system for the provision of a given service; a layer including the protocols defining incentive mechanisms and dealing with the overall economic performance of the system and the achievement of application-specific economic conditions; and a final layer characterised by the set of protocols taking care of an application governance mechanisms, such as decision-making and procedural aspects.

Layer 3: Service or Business Model Layer The first application-specific layered module (layer 3) includes protocols for the operation of the system and the performance and provision of a service's basic functionalities. The protocols are devoted to the deterministic (and possible automatic) execution of all required functionalities and operations for the correct provision of services in the manner expected by stakeholders and users. We call these the operational, or application service, protocols; these are the protocols that are necessary to operate a certain business model and, by so doing, provide a specific service. For this reason, layer 3 can be interpreted as a service, or business model, layer. This layer is similar to infrastructural layer 2 in that they both include smart contract protocols and they both include protocols for the initiation, operation and execution of states' updates. But while layer 3 is characterised by application-specific smart contract protocols, layer 2 includes general-purpose smart contracts operated at the infrastructural level. For this reason, layer 3 protocols could also be defined and understood as application-specific smart contract protocols.

Layer 4: Performance or Optimization Layer The second application-specific layered module (layer 4) includes protocols for the performance of an application's economic mechanisms; its main characteristic is the definition of optimal incentive mechanisms for the optimal provision of the service, consistent with the maximization of the application's economic performances. As a result, these are application-incentive protocols. This layer is similar to layer 1 in that they both deal with economic mechanisms for the alignment of incentives; but while layer 4 includes protocols defining application-specific incentives mechanisms, layer 1 includes protocols for the alignment of incentives among actors participating in the consensus mechanism of the wider blockchain infrastructure.

Layer 5: Governance Layer The third layered module (layer 5) includes protocols for the performance of on-chain governance functionalities; its main characteristic is the definition of mechanisms for the open and democratic participation of all stakeholders in the decision-making processes. These are on-chain governance protocols. The on-chain governance module does not have an obvious equivalent at the infrastructural level.

There may be other types of protocols performing other types of functionalities, but these are probably the most fundamental and most common across a wide spectrum of DeFi applications.

3.3.3 The Modularization of Protocols Is a Modularization of Risks

DeFi can therefore be broken down into homogeneous and functionally-independent protocol layers performing functions shared by a variety of applications (including, but not limited to, DeFi applications) and protocol layers performing functions that are specific and idiosyncratic to a single DeFi application. This modular decomposition into functionally-independent layers (or modules) can also be used to distinguish between different sources of risks, where each risk appertains to, and emerges from, a module's specific functionality (Fig. 2).

First, the consensus layer is mainly characterised by security risks in the form of attacks on the integrity and consistency of the system through the manipulation and gaming of the blockchain's consensus protocol (Azouvi & Hicks, 2021; Bano et al., 2019), such as selfish-mining attacks, Sybil attacks, majority attacks, denial of service attacks, block withholding attacks and so forth (Eyal & Sirer, 2018; Liu et al., 2019; Wang et al., 2019b). In other words, any risk deriving from actions that can undermine the addition (writing) of consistent states' updates to the blockchain ledger belongs to this layer.

Second, the smart contract layer is characterised by all those risks emerging from the inefficiencies, vulnerabilities and limitations of smart contracts. These can be technological such as unbounded computation, authentication issues and contract-

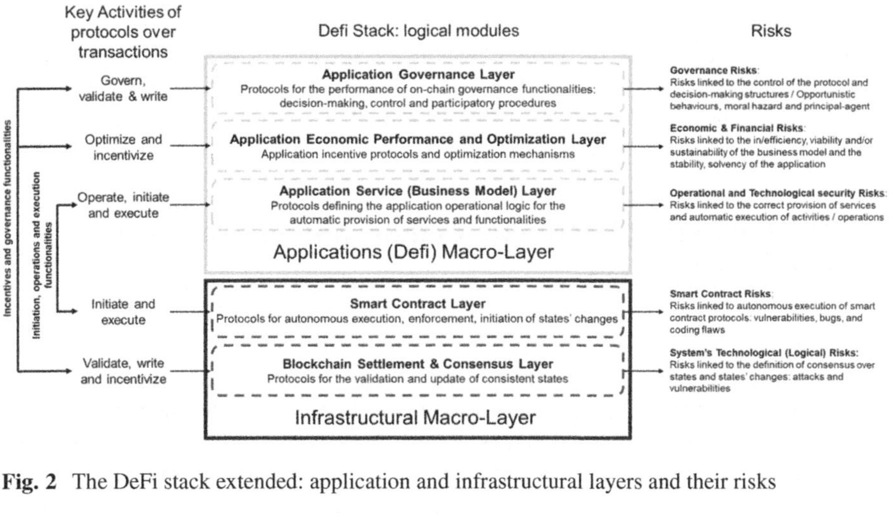

Fig. 2 The DeFi stack extended: application and infrastructural layers and their risks

in-the-middle attacks, unpredictable execution, and so forth (Atzei et al., 2017) or more legal/economic, such as contract incompleteness, ambiguities, undefined liabilities, and so forth (Østbye, 2019; Pasquale, 2019; Sklaroff, 2017; Werbach & Cornell, 2017). In sum, all circumstances that can undermine the automatic execution and autonomous initiation of states' updates belong to this layer.

Third, the service protocol layer is characterised by all those risks undermining the correct functioning of application-specific automated smart contracts and exploiting possible vulnerabilities or DeFi's technological security risks, such as frontrunning risk, single transaction attacks, slippage, divergence losses, failures in the compossibility of DeFi protocols or logical bugs in general (Daian et al., 2019; Eskandari et al., 2020; Li et al., 2022; Qin et al., 2021b; Werner et al., 2021; Xu et al., 2021). These are similar to the smart contracts attacks discussed in the previous points (they are both risks linked to the execution of actions in the operation of smart contracts), but they specifically refer to the functioning of the DeFi protocol in the performance of the specific DeFi services rather than the execution of smart contracts which refer to the functioning of the overall underlying platform. These can be referred to as DeFi operational or technological, risks.

Fourth, the incentive mechanism layer is characterised by all those peculiar economic and financial risks emerging from instabilities or economic vulnerabilities of the protocols and deriving from economic uncertainty, actor opportunism, and misalignments of incentives such as moral hazard (Carter & Jeng, 2021; Darlin et al., 2022; Gudgeon et al., 2020b; Kao et al., 2020; Kozhan & Viswanath-Natraj, 2021; OECD, 2022; Qin et al., 2021c; Wang et al., 2022; Werner et al., 2021; Zetzsche et al., 2020). These are mainly interdependence, market, credit and liquidity risks emerging from the operation of DeFi's incentive mechanisms in the provision of DeFi services.

Finally, the governance layer mainly includes those risks linked to the peculiar way in which a protocol is managed and governed, and therefore those risks emerging from the behaviours of those controlling the protocol and having decision-making authority over it, such as hacks, collusive behaviours, conflicts of interests, opportunistic exploitation of voting power and voting rights and so forth (Aramonte et al., 2021; Barbereau et al., 2022b; Carter & Jeng, 2021; Sun et al., 2022; Zetzsche et al., 2020). These can simply be generally called governance risks (Fig. 2).

4 The DeFi Stack Revisited: Modularization of DeFi into Functional Layers

Each layer is characterised by key aspects and dimensions that distinguish one specific implementation and solution from another. Different DeFi applications and solutions can therefore be understood, compared and contrasted according to the different distinguishing characteristics of each layer composing the DeFi stack. For this reason, it is important to identify the key aspects characterizing each layer in order to distinguish, compare and contrast the different (often competing) solutions adopted by the various DeFi applications.

4.1 The Infrastructural Macro-Layer

The infrastructural macro-layer corresponds to the foundational set of layers supporting the provision of all DeFi applications operating over it. This macro-layer can be broken down into two main functional layers. The first corresponds to the blockchain consensus and settlement functionalities, while the second characterizes the smart contract functionalities. In this case, all DeFi applications sharing the same first two layers will share the same properties and characteristics, while DeFi applications operating over different layers will manifest different properties deriving from the different characteristics of these layers.

4.1.1 The Consensus Layer (Layer 1): Decentralized Validation and Settlement

The blockchain (DLT) consensus or settlement layer represents the first layer in almost all representations and characterizations of the DeFi stack. This layer includes all those protocols devoted to obtaining consensus over a settled status (Bamakan et al., 2020; Xiao et al., 2020). Different solutions to the layer 1 module are mainly to be distinguished and evaluated according to the specific way in which they achieve consensus efficiency while ensuring some degree of decentralization in doing so, as well as the extent of interoperability with other blockchains (mainly in terms of bridges—see Hardjono (2021) and McCorry et al. (2021)). Both efficiency and decentralization in consensus can be understood in different ways and can be implemented differently. As a result, four main aspects should be considered when distinguishing solutions for this first layer, as outlined below.

Consensus Protocols: Decentralization vs. Efficiency First, different blockchain settlement layers adopt different consensus algorithms, such as proof-of-work (PoW) or a proof-of-stake (PoS) consensus mechanisms (Saleh, 2021), or other alternative consensus protocols such as Delegated-proof-of-Stake (DPoS) as in the case of Tron; proof-of-authority (PoA); a combination of the two such as Binance Smart Chain's (BSC) proof-of-staked-authority (PoSA); proof of history (PoH) in case of Solana, amongst others (Bamakan et al., 2020). The key event in this respect was the transition of Ethereum Mainnet from PoW to PoS last September (Buterin & Griffith, 2019).

This aspect is relevant for three main reasons (covering both decentralization and efficiency).

One, different consensus protocols are relevant to understand the decentralised nature of blockchain consensus—as some consensus protocols (such as PoA) are inherently more centralised than others (such as PoS) (Gencer et al., 2018). In this case, decentralization refers to the equal ability of all nodes participating in the network to freely validate and "write" transactions into the chain, and therefore confirm changes in states (permissionless nature). Decentralized layer 1 modules are characterized by consensus protocols conferring equal capabilities to all nodes in the validation and confirmation of states' changes. Different permissionless protocols manifest different aspects of decentralization, so it is not easy to compare and contrast different degrees of decentralization for permissionless protocols such as, for instance, PoW and PoS (Gencer et al., 2018; Kwon et al., 2019; Mueller-Bloch et al., 2022). In general, a variety of metrics should be used (Campajola et al., 2022; Karakostas et al., 2022; Rossi & Sørensen, 2019; Zhang et al., 2022). At the other extreme, there are outright permissioned consensus protocols where only a fixed and predefined set of nodes have the ability (power or rights) to participate in the consensus mechanism. These represent centralised designs of layer 1 and are probably more appropriate for institutional DeFi rather than DeFi proper, which so far has only been developed over permissionless protocols (discussed in Sect. 4.2).

Two, different consensus protocols may be more or less energy efficient: it is well known that the environmental impact of more decentralised protocols such as PoW is much more problematic than the one of other consensus protocols such as PoS (Sedlmeir et al., 2020).

Three, different consensus protocols are also more or less costly to operate as they also require different levels of fees to be paid to miners to add transactions to blocks; similarly to the previous points, protocols where consensus power is more centralised can be implemented much more cheaply. The last two points are two different forms of efficiency, which we call production efficiency (energy consumption) and economic efficiency (fees to be paid to reward miners). These aspects of layer 1 efficiency are usually addressed through a plethora of solutions that are convenient to treat as separate relevant points of a layer 1 module, as discussed in points two-to-four below.

Consensus and Finality Rules Second, different layer 1 consensus protocols adopt different finality rules. Some consensus protocols, such as Bitcoin's PoW, adopt probabilistic finality mechanisms, meaning that there is no certainty about the required time to finalize a transaction (Nabilou, 2022). Although probabilistic finality is a necessary prerequisite of decentralised (permissionless) consensus protocols, they also add an extra dimension of uncertainty and, as a result, inefficiency to the layer. Other consensus protocols adopt different (and more efficient) finality mechanisms, such as absolute finality, ensuring that transactions are considered definitive as soon as the block is added to the chain (Zhang & Lee, 2020). Typically the former ensures a higher degree of decentralisation in consensus than the latter, even though it still does not address the uncertainty deriving from the fact that the probability that a transaction will be processed and added to the main chain remains dependent on the level of fees paid to the miners.

As a result, while the type of consensus protocol adopted mainly captures the extent of decentralization of the layer 1 module, the type of finality mechanism mainly captures the extent of scalability of the layer 1 module. This is yet a different aspect of layer 1's efficiency, which can be characterised as "operational" efficiency (finality is very much a legal as well as a technological concept). Beside finality, there are two important characteristics of layer 1 protocols that have to be considered with respect to scalability.

On-Chain Scalability: Parallelization of Layer 1 Third, it is important to understand whether the blockchain consensus layer implements some parallelization logic by partitioning the blockchain's layer 1 into multiple layer 1 chains, each independently operating its own consensus protocols. This is typically defined as on-chain scaling. Through layer 1 side-chains, novel blockchain designs circumvent the inefficiencies deriving from the serialization of the consensus over a single blockchain that acts as a single bottleneck for the validation and verification of all transactions (states' changes). This serialization results in extremely inefficient solutions that do not scale easily (Croman et al., 2016; Xu et al., 2017) and force the blockchain to process and validate a handful of transactions per second.

Layer 1 parallelization designs vary, but they mainly involve the decomposition and replication of the consensus protocols across a variety of chains that can independently process and validate transactions in parallel. The question is therefore whether the consensus protocol is executed over one single chain (serialization), or it is duplicated and simultaneously executed over a multiplicity of chains operating in parallel. Examples of layer 1 partitioning operating a parallelization of consensus protocols are Polkatod's para-chains, or sharding solutions (Kokoris-Kogias et al., 2018), such as Ethereum's shards (Wang et al., 2019a).

Side-Chains and Off-Chain Consensus Fourth, it is important to understand whether the blockchain separates settlement activities from computation activities by supporting and operating layer 2 solutions that execute transactions off-chain and reduce the computation and validation burdens of the underlying common consensus protocol.

These are usually called off-chain scaling solutions, to be distinguished from on-chain scaling solutions that directly involve the consensus protocols themselves. The goal is to execute as many transactions as possible off-chain without any need to validate, settle and write them on-chain, and to use the blockchain as a common settlement layer that is updated only with a final resulting state that bundles and contains the result of all transactions executed off-chain. In this way, the consensus and settlement layer does not have to constantly operate every single transaction and state's update on-chain whenever an update is required. By so doing, layer 2 solutions improve scalability as the blockchain is no longer used to process every transaction but as a coordinating and reconciling entity. In contrast to the multi-chain solutions, they do not require an ex-ante partitioning of the consensus protocol into multiple independent settlement chains but remain flexible enough to allow for the ex-post addition of a variety of solutions that can independently execute transactions off-chain and subsequently settle and reconcile them over the main chain, thus offloading much of the computational burden from the main chain itself (Gudgeon et al., 2020a; Hafid et al., 2020; Jourenko et al., 2019).

Many types of off-chain scaling solutions exist. Only a specific subset of off-chain scaling solutions can be appropriately treated as a property of the consensus layer, while other off-chain scaling solutions should be included in the discussion of the smart contract layer. Their inclusion into layer 1 scalability solutions depends on whether layer 2 scaling solutions also perform their own validation and settlement (such as sidechains, plasma chains or commit chains), or whether they can simply be treated as smart contract protocols executing transactions off-chain, yet still relying on an underlying settlement layer to ultimately reconcile, confirm, validate, and append states' changes (such as in the case of rollups or channels). The former includes protocols whose primary functionalities are mainly consistent with the consensus and settlement module (layer 1), while the latter includes protocols whose primary functionalities are mainly consistent with the smart contract module (layer 2). A commit chain such as Polygon is an example of a widely adopted off-chain scaling solution that, however, also performs its own settlement and validation and, for this reason, belongs more to the consensus and settlement layer (differently form rollup solutions, that should belong to the smart contract layer instead—see layer 2 below).

As a result, side-chains are not "pure" layer 1 on-chain scaling solutions (such as sharding solutions), yet they are not pure layer 2 of-chain smart contract scaling solutions (such as rollups); in fact, layer 2 scaling solutions such as rollups can be implemented and operated over side-chains such as in the case of Polygon's rollups solutions. For this reason, these off-chain solutions could be defined as layer 1.5, even though it is much more convenient to treat them simply as a further distinguishing property of the layer 1 consensus and settlement module (as many online DeFi data platforms do).

Consensus & Settlement Layer: Layer 1 Wrap Up The four features of the first layered module (consensus and settlement layer) mainly capture the trade-off between layer 1 protocol decentralization and layer 1 protocol efficiency, where decentralization is mainly defined in function of the permissionless nature of the consensus protocol (as discussed above), while efficiency has three different natures: production efficiency (in the form of energy consumption), economic efficiency (the degree of fees to be paid to miners, stakers, or transaction validators in general), and operational efficiency (in the form of scalability and transaction finality). This shows that the usual dichotomy between scalability and decentralization captured in the famous "scalability trilemma" is a specific case (or a subset) of a broader trade-off between consensus efficiency and consensus decentralization, where scalability is one specific aspect, or dimension, of efficiency among others.

It should be noted that solutions that increase economic efficiency (such as optimistic roll-ups) may increase finality time and therefore worsen other aspects of efficiency, such as operational efficiency. As a result, solutions adopted to address one specific type of inefficiency may negatively affect others. These are non-commensurable efficiency trade-offs that have to be taken into account when assessing other solutions.

In conclusion, while point one captures both the extent of a protocol's decentralised nature and its production and economic efficiency, points two-to-four mainly capture different aspects of, or solutions to, layer 1 (in)-efficiency. Both efficiency and decentralization are extremely relevant for the operation of DeFi applications as the performativity of DeFi financial services ("fi"), and their degree of decentralization ("de") both reflect, and depend on, them. As a result, different types of layers 1 (different layer 1 solutions) have to be assessed and compared mainly in function of their performance with respect to: consensus decentralization and consensus efficiency (to be understood mainly, but not only, in terms of transaction finality).

Clearly, these aspects are strictly linked and interwoven. Certain consensus protocols sacrifice decentralisation or are devised in order to be extremely efficient from the outset and do not need any additional or complementary scalability solutions (such as Solana, until very recently), while others operate layer 1 sidechains and do not need (or do not operate yet) layer-2 solutions (such as Polkadot). Some only operate layer 2 solutions but do not operate layer-1 sidechains (such as Bitcoin), while others do both (such as Ethereum).

4.1.2 The Smart Contract Layer (Layer 2): Autonomous Initiation and Execution

The smart contract layer is logically different from the underlying consensus layer as it includes the set of protocols whose function is to autonomously initiate transactions and/or automatically execute and enforce predefined conditions. Although smart contract functionalities and consensus protocols are usually tightly linked, it is important to distinguish between initiating or executing transactions and states' updates (layer 2), and validating, confirming and appending these transactions and states' updates (layer 1). The function of the protocols in layer 1 is mainly centred around the conditions of confirming states' changes and writing them into the common database, the functions of the protocols in layer 2 are mainly concerned with initiating and/or executing states' changes. Their features, characteristics, and main aspects differ as well.

The key characteristic of all protocols operating in layer 2 is their programmability and atomicity (programmable atomicity—see Qin et al. (2021a)), while the two most important aspects characterizing layer 2 protocols in order to assess and compare alternative layer 2 solutions are: the extent in which they can autonomously initiate, enforce and execute states' changes, and the extent in which these can be done efficiently and cheaply. The former provides an overview of the set of operational activities falling within the scope of smart contracts, the latter provides a measure of their economic efficiency. This highlights a trade-off between autonomy (automation) and efficiency. An assessment and comparison of alternative layer 2 solutions will have to focus on these two aspects.

Degrees of Autonomy: From Autonomous Initiation to Automatic Execution The first captures the scope of activities where smart contracts can be used to automate the initiation and/or execution of transactions and effectively and securely enforce legal conditions embedded into code (Østbye, 2019; Sklaroff, 2017; Werbach, 2018; Werbach & Cornell, 2017). In other words, this first aspect captures the scope of autonomy and automation of layer 2. Here we distinguish between three different ways in which smart contracts can play a role in this respect (in decreasing levels of autonomy): autonomous initiation, automatic enforcement, and automatic executions.

One, some transactions can be autonomously initiated by the smart contract protocols; in this case, smart contracts act as fully-flagged autonomous participants to the DeFi ecosystem, and therefore as proper (autonomous) counterparties of bilateral transactions. For this reason, smart contracts can be identified by their own public address, they are typically endowed with their own wallet (treasury, vault, or pool) containing tokens, and they provide their own inputs to the system. In other words, the smart contract in this case autonomously initiates transactions and/or submits states' changes to the underlying consensus protocol. The autonomous initiation of transactions in this case is usually triggered by the verification of some on-chain or off-chain condition or event, often relying on oracles bringing off-chain data on-chain (Liu et al., 2021; Pasdar et al., 2021). Examples are the autonomous issuance or sale of a token held by the smart contract whenever the balance of a smart contract's wallet or vault exceeds a certain threshold (such as in the case of MakerDAO's surplus auctions (Kirillov & Chung, 2022)).

Two, smart contracts can automatically enforce contractual clauses between them and the users, or among the users, such as the automatic update of payable fees for certain activities or transactions for given circumstances, consistent with predefined rules and conditions programmed into code. In contrast to the previous case, the smart contract, in this case, does not operate as an active (and autonomous) counterparty of the transaction (it does not autonomously and unilaterally initiate states' changes), but it simply enforces general (contractual) conditions valid for all counterparties operating over the network and bound by these conditions. While we refer to the previous case as an autonomous initiation of transactions (or states' updates), we call this an automatic enforcement of conditions (supporting or leading to, states' updates). This corresponds to the original main feature of smart contracts that in this case operate as automatic on-chain legal enforcers: the so-called "code is law" (De Filippi & Hassan, 2018; Werbach & Cornell, 2017; Yeung, 2019). This is the case with a large number of applications such as the automatic enforcement of a refund or compensation clause between two counterparties in case certain specific contractual conditions are (not) met and/or verified. The role of legal automation is, of course, opening up opportunities (Holden & Malani, 2019; Meier & Sannajust, 2021) but also raising various concerns of inefficient or ineffective legislation, mainly deriving from the inherent inflexibility and incompleteness of smart contracts (Gans, 2019; Pasquale, 2019; Werbach, 2018).

Three, smart contracts automatically execute states' updates. This final functionality represents the actual automatic execution of transactions or states' updates following the specific commands initiated by the actors or conditions verified by the smart contracts, such as in the case of the execution of transactions by the part of rollups smart contract functionalities. The outcome of these executions will then have to be confirmed and appended to the common database as states' updates by the validators operating at layer 1. This is, in a sense, a base (or necessary) functionality of smart contract: not all smart contracts unilaterally initiate states' updates or enforce contractual conditions, but all smart contracts automatically execute certain actions.

Layer 2 Efficiency: Smart Contract Fees The second main characteristic of smart contracts concerns the level of fees and frictions (transaction costs in general) affecting the execution of transactions (i.e. states' updates). The majority of layer 1 blockchains require fees to be paid to validators in order to align incentives as rewards for their participation in the consensus. These types of fees are mainly linked to a layer-1 blockchain and can be used to align incentives in order to ensure a system's overall consistency and address consensus-linked attacks such as majority attacks. The operation of layer 2 protocol functionalities also requires fees, but these are also paid to prevent technological security risks, attacks—such as denial of service (DDoS) attacks—and vulnerabilities in the execution of smart contract protocols (such as unbounded executions or infinite loops).

The extent of transaction fees can vary for three reasons (in logical descending order). First, different platforms require different levels of fees, and this is often linked to the nature of the underlying consensus layer: in general, more centralised consensus protocols can afford lower fees. Second, the execution of different types of transactions for any given platform typically requires different levels of fees: complex transactions and operations requiring more computation capacity are more costly to operate and, for this reason, require more fees. Third, any given transaction executed on any given platform requires higher fees whenever the network is more congested: transaction initiators will have to dynamically adjust their paid fees to convince validators to process their transaction rather than alternative ones.

General Purpose Smart Contracts vs. Layer 2 Off-Chain Solutions The third main characteristic of the smart contract layer derives from the previous discussion of scalability solutions and concerns the distinction between general-purpose smart contract functionalities that operate independently from (and over-the-top of) the consensus layer, and smart contract functionalities that operate as extensions of the consensus layer in order to address specific purposes and provide specific functionalities, such as in the case of off-chain (layer 2) scalability solutions.

There are many types of layer 2 smart contract-functionalities, but the main ones are: channels such as the Bitcoin Lightning Network (Poon & Dryja, 2016), or rollups such as Ethereum's Optimism or Arbitrum (Gangwal et al., 2022). The key feature of these off-chain solutions is to decouple the execution of smart contracts functionalities (at layer 2) from their settlement and validation (at layer 1). These smart contract scalability solutions can be employed to reduce smart contract fees (increasing layer 2 economic efficiency), often at the expense of layer 1 operational efficiency; this is mainly the case of rollups in the case of the Ethereum platforms. Other times they are mainly developed to increase operational efficiency and transaction outputs; this is mainly the case with the Bitcoin lighting network.

Layer 2 Wrap-Up: Autonomy vs. Efficiency In sum, different smart contract platforms are characterised by different degrees of autonomy, as well as by different degrees of efficiency as they charge different fees for different transactions. Both have important implications for the provision of DeFi services operated on competing smart contract layers (layer 2). High fees may make a smart contract platform extremely inefficient and lead to market manipulations (for instance due to increasing miner extractable value—see below), and this is especially true for complex transactions, such as the ones generated by DeFi applications, which require a higher amount of fees compared to simple payment transactions. Different DeFi applications provide different types of services and, for this reason, they will use a different amount of fees. But in general, the less scalable and more congested a platform, the higher the smart contract fees that the layer 2 smart contract platform requires on average from the various applications operating over it, everything else equal.

4.1.3 The Infrastructural Macro-Layer: Wrap Up

Layer 1 and layer 2 correspond to functionally independent modules in the sense that they perform separate and self-contained functions: while layer 1 includes the protocols that ensure that the system reaches consensus over the way the states have to be updated (validation and writing functions), layer 2 includes the protocols that ensure that the system states' updates can be autonomously initiated and/or automatically enforced and/or executed (initiation and execution functions). Protocols performing the first function are assessed and characterised according to the various ways they address the trade-off between centralization and efficiency, while protocols performing the second function are assessed and characterised according to the various ways in which they address the trade-off between autonomy/automation and efficiency.

It is interesting to note that the two trade-offs mirror one another as both autonomy and decentralised consensus can be treated as two specific instances (or aspects) of decentralization.

On the one hand, both layer 1 and layer 2 protocols can be assessed according to different dimensions of decentralization (Rossi & Sørensen, 2022). In one case (consensus protocols layer) decentralization is intended as an equal and symmetrical endowment of validation (writing) capabilities to all participating nodes—thus, the absence of validation or writing power concentrated in (or delegated to) few nodes. In the other case (smart contract layer) decentralization is mainly intended as the party's ability to enforce and execute states' updates independently from the authorization and discretion of specialised third parties endowed with special powers or capabilities to refute, reject, censor, authorize, discriminate licit activities. In the first case, different types of consensus protocols correspond to different degrees of decentralization of layer 1, in the second case we distinguished between different degrees of autonomy/automation of layer 2 (the autonomous initiation of transactions, the automatic enforcement of conditions, and the basic automatic execution of operations).

On the other hand, both layers compare these degrees of decentralization to a measure of efficiency. In one case (consensus layer) efficiency mainly refers to the cost and rapidity of operating protocols that validate, settle, and therefore confirm and write states' updates. In the other case (smart contract layer) efficiency mainly refers to the cost and rapidity of automatically enforcing conditions and executing states' changes. While efficiency in the first case is equally intended both in value and quantity terms, it is mainly to be intended in value terms in the second case. Moreover, while fees in the first case (layer 1) are always used as a reward (incentive) mechanism, and therefore they are always paid to a counterparty, fees in the second case are not necessarily used as a reward mechanism, but they are necessarily always used as artificially-imposed transaction costs on the initiators of transactions to avoid smart contract inefficiencies, attacks (such as DDoS attacks) and vulnerabilities; for this reason, they can be simply burned by the system, not necessarily "paid" to some address. We define the former as "mining fees" (validation fees), and the latter as "smart contract fees" (execution fees). These twofold trade-offs between some form of decentralisation and some form of efficiency reflect two manifestations of the "scalability trilemma" across both layers of the infrastructural macro-layer.

These two trade-offs not only mirror each other, but they are also linked. For instance, different platforms that require a different time to validate and finalize transactions also require different levels of smart contract fees to operate any type of financial transaction. High fees can incentivize block miners to participate in the consensus protocol but it can also undermine the adoption of DeFi services on those same platforms. Both are key aspects affecting the provision and execution of DeFi services. The former is mainly linked to the characteristics and performances of the underlying (permissionless) blockchain consensus protocol and determines the ability of a specific blockchain to avoid congestion and ensure rapid transaction finality while maintaining decentralized consensus. The latter is an inherent feature of any smart contract platform, and it defines the set of incentives used by the protocol in order to ensure consistency and atomicity in the automatic execution and enforcement of transactions while protecting itself against attacks (such as DDoS attacks). The combination of consensus layer operational efficiency and smart contract operational efficiency can ensure the convergence (and possible conflation) of reconciliation (smart contract layer) and settlement activities (Lima & Rossi, 2022), thus opening up possibilities to move from T3 settlement to T2, T1 and even T0 settlement periods (Feenan et al., 2021).

The interaction and interoperation of layers 1 and 2 not only combine to produce efficiency, but they can also generate dependencies, and even tensions or trade-offs. For instance, the efficiency of layer 2 (the level of the fees charged by smart contract protocols) is not independent of the nature of the properties and characteristics of the underlying layer 1 (the nature of the consensus protocol). For example, blocks in the

Ethereum blockchain are created as a function of the fees paid by the transactions contained (each block has a target size of 15 million gas and a maximum capacity of 30 million gas), and these fees are dynamically adjusted based on the previous block sizes. Table 1 summarizes the main dimensions (or characteristics) of layer 1 and 2 protocols which should be taken into account in order to compare, contrast, and distinguish alternative implementations and solutions.

It is important to stress that the proposed distinction between layers 1 and 2 is not identical to the standard distinction between layers 1 and 2 solutions mainly (but not only) used in the literature on blockchain scalability (Gangwal et al., 2022; Gudgeon et al., 2020a; Jourenko et al., 2019). The latter distinguishes layer 1 and layer 2 based on whether the execution and operation of transactions occur off-chain (layer 2), and therefore separately and independently from their settlement over the underlying consensus chain (layer 1). Here we distinguish layers 1 and 2 consistent with the principles of modularity theory and therefore based on the protocols' idiosyncratic functionalities vis-à-vis the others: all protocols whose function is to settle (confirm and write) states' updates belong to the first layer (regardless of whether they are actually performed separately from an underlying "parent," or "master" chain), while all protocols whose primary function is to automatically initiate or execute states' changes belong to layer 2. Protocols in layer 2 do not, or cannot, deal with settlement. For this reason, while all layer 1 (on-chain) scalability solutions include protocols consistent with our layer 1, and all protocols here grouped under layer 1 can be consistent with standard layer 1 on-chain scalability solutions, not all layer 2 (off-chain) scalability solutions include protocols belonging to our layer 2.

In conclusion, layer 1 and layer 2 share two main characteristics. One, they both include protocols that are common to all applications operating over these layers or, in other words, they operate protocols that are not application-specific. For this reason, they can be grouped within a broader and overarching macro-layer. Two, they can both be assessed, analysed and characterised according to the decentralization-efficiency trade-off, where both decentralization and efficiency acquire different meanings within and across the two layers.

4.2 The DeFi Application Macro-Layer

The various application-specific protocols that perform different roles for the single DeFi applications are located above the infrastructural layer. Similar to the discussion developed for the infrastructural macro-layer, the application macro-layer can also be decomposed into three modular layers according to the specific functionality performed. These three functionally-defined layers can then be linked and combined according to the application-specific architectural rules, in the same way in which layer 1 and layer 2 interact and are combined according to infrastructure design and architectural rules.

Table 1 Layer 1 and layer 2: key relevant aspects to assess and compare DeFi solutions

Infrastructural macro-layer: two-layered modularization of protocols			
Layer 1 module: Consensus protocols	Write and confirm states' changes	Dimensions of decentralization	Different consensus protocols: Distribution of validation capabilities to different nodes
		Dimensions of efficiency	Energy consumption (production efficiency)
			Mining fees (economic efficiency)
			Finality rules (operational efficiency)
			Layer 1 (on-chain) scalability solutions: Parallelization and multi-chains design (operational & economic efficiency)
			Layer 2 (off-chain) settlement solutions: Side-chains operating their settlement chain (operational & economic efficiency)
Layer 2 module: Smart contract protocols	Initiate and execute states' changes	Dimensions of decentralization	Autonomous initiation of transactions
			Automatic enforcement of conditions
			Automatic execution of transactions/conditions
		Dimensions of efficiency	Smart contract fees (economic efficiency & security)
			Layer 2 (off-chain) smart contract solutions: Rollups or channels decoupling smart contract executions from consensus (economic efficiency & security)

4.2.1 The Business Model, or Service, Layer (Layer 3): Ensuring a DeFi System's Operation

The first layer of the DeFi stack represents the set of application-specific protocols that perform all the necessary functions to ensure the provision of the specific DeFi service. This layer captures the set of protocols that contribute to the operational logic of the DeFi application and, by doing so, ensure that the system performs certain functionalities as required by the specific service they are designed to provide: different layer 3 protocols are designed to perform different functionalities and provide different DeFi services. For this reason, when the focus is on layer 3, DeFi applications can be compared and contrasted based on the different services provided and functionalities they perform. Drawing on the standard treatment provided by the literature (Xu & Xu, 2022), five different sets of layer 3 protocols can be distinguished (Amler et al., 2021; Gogel, 2021; Werner et al., 2021), as discussed below.

Collateralised Debt Positions First, protocols enable simple collateralized debt positions (CDPs) and provide the necessary foundational building block for the creation of (decentralized) crypto-backed stablecoins. The single most relevant example belonging to this class is the MakerDAO protocol (operating over the Ethereum platform) supporting the creation of Dai, the first on-chain crypto-backed stablecoin (Brennecke et al., 2022; Maker Team, 2020). In this case, protocols enable users to deposit their (unused) funds in a vault in return for a token retaining stable market value and granting them the right to withdraw the same amount of funds at a later date from the protocol's vault. The service is costly (it charges interests or fees over the borrowed token) and often requires overcollateralization (meaning that issuance and redemption do not usually occur at 1:1, with the exception of some "risk-free" collateral), but it also allows users to possibly earn passive interests on their deposit.

In the literature, this type of protocol is sometimes simply defined as "stablecoins" that, however, characterises a type (or class) of tokens rather than the set of a system's protocols for the provision of a service. Here we characterize the service provided by CDPs as "decentralized savings", or "decentralized deposits", consistent with the ultimate nature of the service, but also consistent with the classification provided by some major DeFi data providers.

In sum, layer 3 protocols for CDPs mainly focus on the set of activities dealing with: the locking of tokenised funds in vaults; the issuance of tokenised claims over the capital; the management of the costs (fees) and earnings over the two; the correct return of the capital and redemption, and destruction of the tokenised claims; as well as the issuance, management, and trading of governance tokens whenever these are used as utility tokens for the correct operations of the system (such as paying fees for the collection of the capital). The architecture of the application system takes care of the overall interactions and linkages between these various protocols.

Protocols for Loanable Funds Second, there are protocols for loanable funds, also called lending and borrowing protocols (Aramonte et al., 2022; Bartoletti et al.,

2021a; Gudgeon et al., 2020c; Saengchote et al., 2022). While CDPs are one-sided services, layer 3 protocols in this case implement two-sided business models and allow two different types of users to interact. On the one hand, they allow investors to deposit funds in a lending pool or vault and obtain a tokenised claim in return that also grants interests over their locked deposit, similar to what CDP protocols do (but following different logics and architectures). On the other hand, they allow users to borrow the available capital from the pools subject to the deposit of collateral and upon payment of a fee. Similarly to CDPs, borrowers' positions are also typically overcollateralized.

Two major applications dominate this category, Aave and Compound (both originally launched over Ethereum), followed by others also operating over other smart contract platforms, such as Venus (BNB Chain), or Euler (still over Ethereum). These protocols also issue their own peculiar type of crypto-backed stablecoin (called cTokens and aTokens in the case of Compound and Aave respectively) that represent a tokenised claim over the deposited funds (backed by, and pegged to, the deposited funds) and therefore are quite different from Maker's Dai as they are much more similar to on-chain tokenized securities.

As a result, layer 3 protocols in the case of lending services perform a variety of basic activities and functions such as acceptance of the deposit of funds, issuance of tokenised claims in return against the funds, managing the accrual of interest, allowing the deposit of collateral, lending funds against collateralised positions, allowing redemption of tokenised claims by the part of the lender, allowing the return of the borrowed capital and withdrawal of the collateral by the part of the borrower, taking care of the payment and transfer of fees to various counterparties, as well as the management of governance tokens whenever these are used to ensure the correct operation of the system.

Decentralised Exchanges Third, there are decentralized exchange (DEX) applications operating automatic market maker (AMM) protocols (Lo & Medda, 2020; Mohan, 2022; Xu et al., 2021). This is currently the biggest type of protocol in terms of TVL, and includes a variety of important protocols across a range of platforms, such as Curve, Uniswap, Balancer, PancakeSwap, and others.

On the one hand, they allow users to deposit a pair of assets in the protocols' pools while issuing liquidity pool tokens (LPTokens) in return: these LP tokens can be understood as a form of tokenized securities that can be redeemed against the deposits, similar to those issued by protocols for loanable funds. Each liquidity pool contains a pair of assets and is characterised by a unique exchange rate between the two. On the other hand, layer 3 protocols make assets deposited in the various liquidity pools available to whoever wants to swap pairs of tokens. Protocols adjust exchange rates accordingly. As a result, layer 3 protocols in this case perform a variety of activities, such as the management of the pools; the issuance of redemption tokens (LPTokens); the swap of pairs of tokens; the charging of fees and interest; and the transfer (pay back) of fees to liquidity providers.

Decentralised Derivatives Fourth, there are derivative protocols, such as Synthetix, or even dYdX (which is also a DEX). These protocols allow users to deposit collateral in the protocol's debt pool and mint a certain amount of tokens (for instance sTokens in the case of Synthetix) that represent synthetic assets or, in other words, derivatives over underlying deposited assets. These tokens can be used for trading purposes on the platforms (derivative protocols in a sense also act as DEXes), but they also act in the same way as cTokens or LPTokens in the sense that they represent claims against the underlying asset and offer the right to be redeemed against the latter. However, these derivative tokens are technically much more similar to crypto-collateralized stablecoins such as Dai in the sense that their price is pegged to a third asset while being backed by collateral locked in the protocol debt pool. In fact, the issuance of sUSD against ETH in Synthetix is conceptually identical to the issuance of Dai against ETH on Maker. As in the other protocols introduced above, debt pools are also overcollateralized. As a result, derivative protocols blend features and aspects of CDPs protocols, loan protocols, and DEXes. The nature and potential uses of sTokens reflect this.

Decentralised Aggregators and Yield Management Protocols Fifth, there are protocol aggregators and decentralized portfolio management services (Cousaert et al., 2022), such as Yearn Finance or Convex Finance. These are often also protocols considered at higher layers of the stack, as they enable users to trade and arbitrage across other DeFi pools moving their funds from one to the other in order to maximize the overall returns of their cryptoasset portfolio. For instance, users can do arbitrage among lending protocols, deposit their funds, and get claim-tokens in return, this time usually called "wrapped tokens" (such as yTokens for Yearn Finance, or cvxCRV for Convex Finance). These wrapped tokens represent claims (shares) against the funds deposited in the protocol's pool. Other functions perform similar portfolio optimization functions for other types of protocols.

The Two Key Common Aspects of Layer 3 Modules All these five service protocols share the same basic logic and architecture that, in its most basic and fundamental form, is composed of a couple of two symmetric atomic transactions, leading to four different overall stages (Xu & Xu, 2022). First, all protocols operate similarly as they: (i) issue claim-tokens, (ii) follow the deposit of some tokenised capital into an application-specific smart contract address (that always represents the backing of the issued token and is often, but not always, also used as a collateral). Second, all protocols: (iii) allow for the repossession of the immobilised capital, (iv) following the redemption of the claim-tokens (Fig. 3). As the transactions are always between a user and a smart contract account, the deposit, locking and repossession of the tokenised funds, as well as the issuances, redemption, and destruction of the claim-tokens are all automatically executed by the smart contract of the specific application. If the issuance of the claim-token and the unlocking and return of the deposited token are automatically triggered and performed independently from an explicit request or command by the part of the user, then these transactions are performed following an automatic enforcement of contractual conditions (and not merely automatically executed).

The operation of DeFi applications is therefore centred around the issuance-redemption of a pair of tokens: the tokens representing deposited funds, and

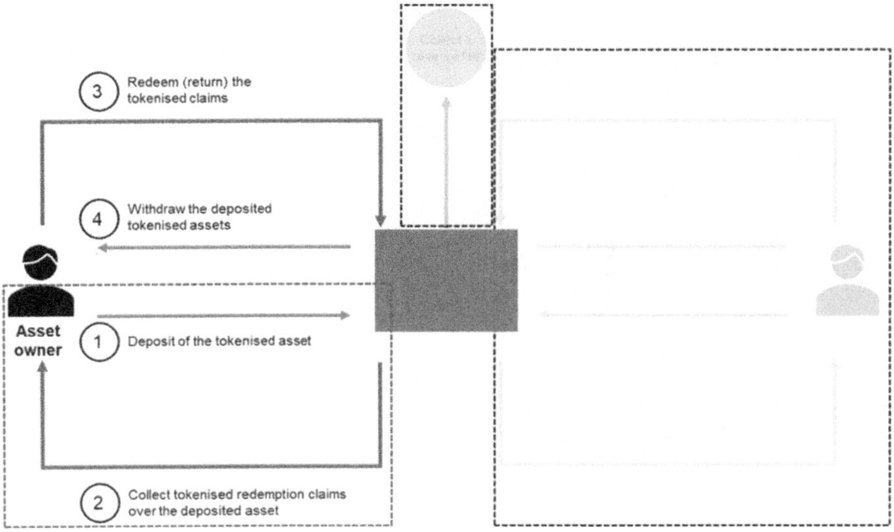

Fig. 3 Foundational and minimal steps of layer 3 protocols (business modules)

the tokens representing redemption claims over these. Different service protocols and business models can interpret these stages differently and can add further stages (such as the payment of fees, the activities of a counterparty, the further accumulation of tokens—yield farming—or rewards, and so on), but they all start the service with the issuance of a claim-token following the deposit of some tokenised capital into a smart contract address (typically known as a vault or pool), and they all close it as these claim-tokens are redeemed in order to recollect the deposited tokens. If the position does not have a mandatory maximum time limit for the position to be closed and the claim redeemed, the minimum amount of stages can be reduced to two only (deposit of tokenised capital and issuance of claim-token). Although both deposited tokens and issued claim-tokens play a role in this layer, it is much more appropriate to include the issuance and management of claim-tokens in layer 3 and to include the management of deposited tokens in layer 4; while the former is integral part of the service provided by the DeFi application, the latter play a key role in the optimization of the operations of the application.

As a result, all layer 3 protocols share two main architectural and logical characteristics shaping the way the application operates and the service it provides. One concerns the issuance of the claim-token, the other the storage and management of the deposited tokens.

First, they all issue claim-tokens in response to the deposit of tokenised capital in a smart contract address, as discussed in Table 2 (Rossi, 2022a). At times these claim-tokens issued by the protocols are also called “wrapped tokens” (Xu & Xu, 2022), but here we define them as “claim-tokens” as these tokens always necessarily represent tokenised claims over the deposited tokenised funds. The common role of these tokens is to allow the token holder to exercise a redemption claim over

Table 2 Different types of services to assess and compare different DeFi layer 3 protocols

Layer 3 protocols		Main examples	Claim-token issued (examples)	Suggested legal classification of claim-tokens
Primary protocols	CDPs	MakerDAO, liquidity	Dai	Derivative
	Protocols for loanable funds	Aave, compound, Venus	aToekn, cToken	Equity
	DEXes	Curve, Uniswap, balancer, PancakeSwap	LPTokens	Equity
	Derivatives	Synthetix, dYdX	sToken	Derivative
	Portfolio management and yield aggregators	Yearn finance, convex finance	yToken	Equity
Additional (auxiliary or complementary) DeFi protocols	Liquid staking	Lido	stETH	Fixed-income security
	Bridges	Synapse, Ren, portal-wormhole	WBTC	Tokenized cryptoasset
	Prediction markets and decentralized oracles	Augur	Long/short tokens	Equity

its deposited tokenised funds for their repossession, even though the services and business models of different applications characterise the specific claims and the associated redemption mechanisms differently. For this reason, although the presence of an application-specific token granting redemption rights over deposited funds is the common characteristic of all DeFi business model protocols at layer 3, different DeFi applications interpret the functionalities of this module differently as they differ in their way of defining issuance, claim, and redemption mechanisms. At a general level, the key aspects of DeFi's claim-tokens that distinguish the service and operations of one business model from the others are:

- Whether the issued token confers claims simply over one's own deposited tokens (proprietary vaults), over a share of the entire pool of tokens in the smart contract's wallets (typically called "pools", or "liquidity pools"), or over a share of the overall protocol operations (staking rewards).
- Whether the issued token confers claims over some additional returns, rewards, or interests over the underlying capital or merely over the deposited tokens (passive income).
- Whether the issued token confers claims over the issuance of additional tokens, such as dual governance tokens (in yield farming, or surplus auctions).
- Whether the token confers redemption claims specifically over the tokens deposited (non-fungibility) or over some alternative tokens (fungibility): these alternative tokens can be equivalent in value, but not necessarily in type (different liquidity, validity, acceptance, etc.).
- Whether the obtainment of the issued token is costly and requires the payment of some variable interest rate or fixed fee.
- Whether redemption can occur at any time "at will", or whether funds are locked for a minimum amount of time: this reveals whether deposited tokens and claim-tokens have the same liquidity, and it affects the risks sustained by the token holder.
- Whether there are some redemption penalties to be paid (either by default or in case redemption claims are exercised against the system's standard smart contract rules).
- Whether the redemption claim can also be automatically enforced by an application's smart contract on behalf of the token holder or not: usually all DeFi applications automatically seize the collateral and liquidate it if the claim-token appreciates too much with respect to the deposited tokens and/or the value of the deposited tokens break a minimum collateralization ratio.
- Whether the token holder has claims specifically against the deposited tokens, or more generally against applications' smart contract protocols. One of the main factors distinguishing between the two in this case is whether claim-tokens behave as stablecoins (or tokenised assets) or not. In the first case, it is reasonable to assume that token holders expect to recoup a certain amount of value when redeeming their claim-tokens, to the value of their tokenised funds originally deposited (discounted of over- or under-collateralization and fees if any); in the second case, it may be that redemption claims cannot be certain and guarantee

but rather uncertain as they may include unexpected extra-returns or losses. In the first case, DeFi applications would behave consistent with banking institutions, in the second with investment funds or similar institutions.

These nine aspects can vary for three different reasons (relevant at three different levels). One, differences may emerge across different users for any given DeFi application; for instance, a two-sided business model such as protocols for loanable funds, charging negative interest rates to borrowers, and accrue positive interest rates to liquidity providers (among other asymmetric policies). Two, differences may emerge across different applications for any given business model: for instance, while Compound v3 uses private vaults and only allows claimants to withdraw their own funds, other protocols for loanable funds (and Compound v2) confer claims over a share of the common liquidity pool. Three, differences emerge across business models altogether; for instance, the MakerDAO protocol does not automatically pay interest rates, while protocols for loanable funds typically do.

Second, all layer 3s are characterised by a non-custodial logic, meaning that all DeFi's applications do not acquire control over the tokenised funds deposited in their addresses, but they leave control over the funds to their owners (Qin et al., 2021a; Werner et al., 2021). For this reason, the deposit of the funds does not entail a transaction of ownership rights (and associated control rights) over the tokenised funds, but rather an endowment of temporary use rights over the deposited tokens. As a result, the tokens issued by DeFi represent "proofs-of-ownership", or ownership claims over the funds exercisable by the owner in order to withdraw and repose the funds. In other words, claim-tokens are either (tokenised) securities or derivates, depending on the specific nature of, and relationship with, the underlying deposited token. Here we only highlight the non-custodial nature of the protocols' architecture and do not discuss the detailed functions and properties of the locked tokens as these will be part of the subsequent layer.

From Primary to Auxiliary Service Protocols Besides these five main protocols, layer 3 includes other auxiliary and complementary sets of protocols that adopt almost identical architecture and logic of DeFi protocols (4 basic atomic transactions) and share the same core features and characteristics of all other DeFi layer 3s: they also issue tokens representing some form of ownership claims over an underlying fund of tokens that has been deposited in non-custodial addresses belonging to an application's smart contract. For this reason, they can be considered fully-fledged DeFi services (business models), even though they are to be used in combination with the five main DeFi protocols, rather than as stand-alone services.

The main three auxiliary business models are: liquid staking protocols (Lido), bridges (Portal-Wormhole), Prediction Markets and decentralised oracles (Augur). The first receives tokens and issues a "staking-claim" (stETH) that confers a claim to obtain a constant return and to redeem the locked tokens. Bridges receive a certain type of tokens and issues a "synthetic version" of that token, called a "wrapped token" that can also be reconverted into the originally locked tokens when "redeemed". Finally, prediction markets allow users to lock a certain quantity of tokens and to purchase tokens representing their betting position on a certain event.

These tokens can always be redeemed for a certain share of the locked tokens as long as the bet is correct (tokens do not confer any claim and become worthless in case of wrong bets). As they all issue claim-tokens in return for the deposit of tokens into a non-custodial smart contract address, they can all be treated as alternative DeFi business models for the provision of specific DeFi services.

Oracles and bridges deserve a separate mention. Oracles are necessary to import information on-chain and enable automatic execution and enforcement of smart contract conditions (Liu et al., 2021). Without oracles, a lot of the decentralized functionalities of DeFi protocols cannot be implemented (this is relevant for both infrastructure and application layers). Decentralized bridges can also be treated as layer 3 protocol types as they enable interoperability between different blockchain settlement layers (wrapped asset bridges) or a blockchain and its layer 2 sidechains for any given settlement layer (sidechain bridges) (Hardjono, 2021). These DeFi services are complementary in the sense that they can be used in combination with other protocols, but they typically either connect different layers of the stack, or they provide the necessary interfaces between the external ecosystem (both traditional centralized and the other DeFi services within the broader DeFi ecosystem) and the various layers themselves.

In sum, all these protocols represent the set of different application-specific smart contracts that ensure the operation and execution of application-specific services and functionalities (i.e. its overall business model). Different protocols can therefore be grouped according to the specific type of service and functionality.

Key Considerations Linking Claim-Tokens and Locked Tokens In conclusion, it is important to highlight an important aspect characterizing the relationship between the two core aspects of DeFi applications. On the one hand, all DeFi claim-tokens are issued following the deposit (and locking) of some tokenised funds; for this reason, their redemption is always against an underlying capital. Claim-tokens issued by a DeFi application are therefore always "backed by" the value of some underlying tokens; this is the value of redemption claims. On the other hand, different claim-tokens can be characterised by different "pegging strategies": some claim-tokens are also pegged to the value of the backing (deposited) tokens (such as in the case of Synthetix sTokens, or wrapped coins), but others are not. As a result, when it comes to the reference value of claim-tokens (the value their redemption claim refers to), three main cases can be identified (Rossi, 2022b):

- Claim-tokens backed and pegged to the value of the tokens deposited and locked into the application's smart contract wallet (vault or pool). This is the case with DeFi applications issuing claim-tokens that behave as cryptoasset-referenced tokens, or tokenised cryptocurrencies. Examples are sTokens and WBTC.
- Claim-tokens that are backed by the value of the underlying locked tokens and pegged to a different entity. This is the case with standard crypto-backed stablecoins (also called decentralised stablecoins) such as Dai. These are usually called decentralised stablecoins as they are pegged to an off-chain stable source of value, such as fiat currencies, but backed on-chain, by a variety of tokens.

- Claim-tokens that are backed by the value of the underlying locked tokens and are not pegged to the value of any particular entity. This can be the case for two main reasons: firstly, claim-tokens are actually pegged to the value of the underlying locked tokens but they also confer extra interests or rewards (such as in the case of aTokens or stETH); secondly, because claim-tokens can acquire a variety of values that are uncertain and completely impossible to account for ex-ante (such as yTokens or Long/Short-Tokens). This is also the case with "unpegged stablecoins", such as Olympus OHM.

The specific legal nature of the various claim-tokens issued by the different DeFi applications therefore depends on their peculiar relationship with the underlying tokens backing them. In general, the relationship between these two components can be complex, leading to a multiplicity of possible typologies and classifications (Rossi, 2022b). In practice, all claim-tokens confer some form of ownership rights over the underlying locked tokens and, for this reason, they can be treated as securities (security-tokens or tokenised securities).

As a result, different application services can be grouped in macro-classes based on the specific type of security that these claim-tokens represent. First, some claim-tokens are very similar to fixed-income securities, and the most glaring case in this sense are staking claims (such as stETH) that confer a predictable and stable flows of income based on the amount of tokens made available by the staker. Second, some claim-tokens are like equities, as they couple ownership rights over the underlying capital with some variable income. This variable income can either derive from the dynamic change and adjustment of contextual conditions (mainly in the case of lending pool tokens), or from the fact that claim-tokens represent shares over the returns generated by common pools (such as in the case of LPTokens, yield aggregators claim-tokens, or prediction market tokens). Finally, claim-tokens can represent pure tokenised assets (as in the case of wrapped tokens) or more generally crypto-derivatives (as in the case of crypto-backed stablecoin Dai or sTokens). This last category includes all synthetic tokens that emerge from complex relationships between the claim-token's pegged value and the underlying tokenised assets they are backed by Rossi (2022b).

Characterizing Layer 3 Protocols: Decentralization vs. Efficiency Trade-Off The business model layer reveals yet another aspect of the trade-off between decentralization and efficiency. Both concepts can be understood in two different ways given the two main architectural and logical characteristics characterizing all DeFi layer 3 protocols, namely: (i) the issuance of claim-tokens by the part of a smart contract following a deposit of tokenised funds, and (ii) the storage and management of the deposited tokens (Table 3).

On the one hand, "decentralization" in the case of layer 3 means two things, depending on whether it applies to claim-tokens or locked tokens. First, in the case of issued tokens, decentralization is to be understood as automation in execution or enforcement of transactions, implying predictability and independence from the discretion of an authorizing third party. This is a characteristic of decentralization shared with layer 2 as both layers operate smart contracts, and therefore both layers

Table 3 Evaluation and comparison between the common characteristics of different layer 3s

Dimensions to contrast and compare different layer 3s	Two main aspects characterizing layer 3		
Two-dimensional trade-off	**Issuance of claim-tokens:** Certifying ownership of, and redemption rights over, locked tokenized funds		**Non-custodial logic** for: Deposit, management, redemption and repossession of tokenized funds
Decentralization	**Automation/autonomy** (no discretion of, and authorization from, a third party)		**Disintermediation** (no delegation of control over tokenized funds to a third party)
Efficiency	**(Non-atomic) economic efficiency**:		**(Atomic) operational efficiency**
	Gas fees application fees interest charged swap fees penalties	Liquidity rewards staking rewards token rewards security rewards	Minimum locking time; illiquidity slippage; Divergence losses; Frontrunning attacks vulnerabilities; Bugs; various attacks; smart contract inefficiencies
Risks (inefficiencies)	Specific operational and technological risks of applications		

are characterised by some degree of automation. Second, in the case of the deposited tokens, decentralization acquires a different meaning, namely disintermediation, to be understood as a lack of delegation and the resulting relationship of dependence: due to the non-custodial nature of the architecture, deposited tokenised funds are not endowed to an intermediary that does not acquire control, nor ownership, over them. Conversely, the depositor retains ownership and control over them. For this reason, there is no delegation or disintermediation. It should be noted that these two meanings of decentralization are independent from one another as automation could be implemented with custodial (intermediated) architectures, while intermediation of course does not entail automation. On the other hand, efficiency can also acquire two different meanings.

First, protocols in layer 3 are characterised by different degrees of economic efficiency, deriving from the trade-off between transaction costs affecting the execution and operations of the various activities involved in the user-smart contract relationship, and the returns or rewards emerging from those. These various transaction costs are composed of smart contract (gas) fees, single application fees (such as stability fees), negative interest charges, swap fees, and withdrawal penalties (Xu et al., 2021). Fundamental smart contract fees will typically affect all parties if they depend on the characteristics of layer 2, while application-specific fees interests, and penalties affect asymmetrically liquidity providers (who enjoy positive returns form their participation in the application) and those borrowing tokens (who usually face some costs). Positive returns countering these costs usually derive from the positive rewards or interest rates accruing to the claim-token holders and/or the capital provider, depending on the specific solutions (as discussed above), such as liquidity rewards, staking rewards, tokenised rewards (rewards in the form of governance tokens as in the case of yield farming), and security rewards (Xu et al., 2021).

These dimensions of efficiency emerge from the inter-temporal exercise of a claim, in the sense that there is a temporal lag between the time period when the token is issued and the time period when the claim comes into force and/or is exercised. However, the incentives and optimization mechanisms operating at this layer are silent with respect to the solvency, stability and viability of the application: in order to assess this, different considerations will have to be developed and different protocols will have to be devised and implemented (layer 4). As a result, the implementation of economic incentives at this layer is still characterised by operational risks, rather than economic risks, which will be addressed by the subsequent layer's protocol.

Second, operational efficiency mainly derives from the ability to operate all transactions instantly and at will, with minimal operational frictions or uncertainties. Characteristics of the system's logic that undermine the smooth and efficient operation of the deposit-issuance-redemption-withdrawal chain of activities are: minimum locking time for tokenised funds, illiquidity (preventing a seamless withdrawal at will), slippage, divergence losses, frontrunning attacks, vulnerabilities of the protocols (such as reetrancy or integer manipulation), bugs, attacks or inefficient smart contract operations in general (such as single transaction sandwich attacks creating price imbalances) (Bichuch & Feinstein, 2022; Cousaert et al., 2022; Daian et al., 2019; Kao et al., 2020; Qin et al., 2022; Werner et al., 2021; Xu et al., 2021; Zhou et al., 2021). These various aspects are also linked to the operational risks and technological security risks (Werner et al., 2021) characterizing the operations of the single application; greater inefficiencies can be both the precondition for, and the outcome of, operational risks and technological security risks. These other dimensions of efficiency are mainly atomic in the sense that they involve the instantaneous operation and execution of smart contracts.

Layer 3 Wrap-Up This layer includes all those protocols and smart contract modules that ensure the correct operation of the system, enact the business model, and execute all the necessary operations to provide the desired service and functionalities. It includes protocols that execute all atomic transactions that also ensure seamless composability of different DeFi services across different applications (Qin et al., 2021a). In this respect, layer 3 of different applications can be compared and contrasted along two main lines.

First, it is possible to focus on the differences and distinguish between different business models and service architectures, as different DeFi applications provide different services and perform different operations. This is the standard method adopted by the literature to distinguish between different types of DeFi applications. However, this only provides a high-level distinction between heterogenous business models; it does not allow a comparison between them.

A second way to distinguish between different layer 3s, is to focus on the two main common characteristics linking the layer 3s of all applications: the automatic issuance of claim-tokens following the deposited tokenised funds, and the non-custodial logic for the management of the locked tokenised funds. Each common aspect can then be assessed according to the decentralization-efficiency trade-off, (while both entail security aspects): while decentralization can either be understood in terms of automation/autonomy (mainly for issued tokens) or in terms of disintermediation (mainly for locked tokens), efficiency can be broken down either into economic efficiency (mainly linked to the possession of claim-tokens) or operational efficiency (mainly linked to the creation, management, and redemption of the deposited tokens). It should be noted that in this case both dimensions of efficiency mainly entail and involve operational risks. The optimal and efficient implementation of incentive mechanisms is independent of the various dimensions of solvency, profitability, and stability that are mainly captured by proper economic risks (such as market and credit risks). These will be discussed in layer 4.

4.2.2 The Performance and Optimization Layer (Layer 4): Defining System Incentives

The protocol sublayer mainly focuses on the nature of the business model and the ways certain services and functionalities can be provided. However, a DeFi protocol can be architecturally and logically sound to provide the desired service as expected, and yet be unviable, unsustainable, or completely unstable from an economic point of view. Logical and operational performativity does not imply economic and financial performativity, in the same way in which operational and technological risks are distinct from the various types of market, financial, and credit risks. For this reason, here we decouple the service protocol layer of the DeFi stack—which distinguishes different applications based on the way they operate and the service they ultimately provide—, from an economic performance and optimization layer that includes the set of protocols that incentivizes the actors in order to ensure stability, efficient operations, and the optimal provision of the service. In other words, this logical module deals with all the incentives and optimization aspects of the system, not with its operational aspects.

This layer typically includes four main aspects linked to the protocol's incentive, performance, and optimization mechanisms. Here, we identify six main functions fulfilled by layer 4.

First, the protocols operating at this layer are typically characterised by a set of predefined parameters that are usually defined ex-ante and represent the high-level outcomes of the community governance and protocol developers' decision-making processes. These parameters can usually be changed by the community through protocols operating at layer 5 (Sect. 4.2.3).

Second, this layer includes protocols dedicated to the optimization of the business model and service provision: different DeFi business models are characterised by different goals and should be evaluated according to different performances.

Third, this layer includes all protocols incentivizing actors to participate, use the application, and deposit tokens. In other words, this layer defines the incentive mechanisms that ensure that the DeFi application is attractive, useful and convenient to those willing to use it and benefit from its services.

Fourth, the layer includes all protocols executing smart contracts ensuring the short-term stability of claim-token values. Fifth, the layer includes smart contract protocols ensuring short-term liquidity and constant solvency of the debt positions. Points four and five also include incentive mechanisms, but the goal of the incentive mechanisms in this case is not to attract users and investors, but rather to shape their behaviour in order to achieve the objective of stability and liquidity. Sixth, there are protocols whose function is to ensure long-term application solvency in case all other incentive mechanisms put in place fail to deliver the desired outcome.

Finally, protocols dealing with stability and solvency across layers should also be included.

The importance of this layer derives from the fact that each DeFi protocol has to optimize its behaviour in function of a variety of contingent parameters, contextual data, usage patterns, and motivations. For this reason, while the operation of the service layer can be defined ex-ante, the system should be able to implement mechanisms that allow it to adjust ex-post to changed conditions and appropriately incentivize the decisions and behaviours of its users. This becomes necessary for the DeFi application to be profitable, efficient, viable, and widely adopted. The market forces requiring constant responses and adaptation can either come from the DeFi ecosystem (a token can increase its value due to its employment in, and demand

Table 4 Typical parameters defining overall tokenomics of DeFi applications

Tokenomics parameters	
Claim-tokens	Locked tokens
Number and types of claim-tokens issued	Set of allowed tokens accepted as deposited funds
Types of claims conferred by the tokens (uses),	Set of tokens accepted as collateral (if different)
Conditions and mechanisms for creation (minting and/or issuance)	Collateral composition & diversification
Conditions and mechanisms for destruction (burning)	Overcollateralization ratio
Presence of a peg	Interests charged over the collateral
Mechanisms ensuring the peg	Rewards accruing to liquidity providers
Positive and negative interest rates generated	Temporal limits (min or max) for locking funds
Participation rewards	Liquidity parameters
Fees and penalties to exercise the claims	Returns and costs generated by the deposited tokens
Minimum yield guaranteed (for liquidity mining or liquid staking)	Fees and penalties for locking tokens
	Utilization and supply rates (for loans)
	Available set of token pairs (for DEXes)

from, other protocols due to the high interconnection between protocols) or from the external economy. For instance, many tokens used in DeFi protocols are pegged to fiat currencies (e.g. Dai), meaning that the mechanisms of the protocol cannot operate in isolation from the external economic context.

Tokenomics: Defining Rules and Parameters Each DeFi protocol relies on the custody and issuance of specific tokens to make sure that users can operate financial transactions and undertake financial activities. The way in which the legal claims and economic value of the various issued tokens are determined depends on specific decisions made by the developers. More generally, a variety of parameters and mechanisms can be included here, organized according to whether they mainly characterize the applications' claim-tokens or their locked tokens (Table 4).

With respect to the former, key parameters include (among others): number and types of claim-tokens issued; types of claims conferred by the tokens (their possible usage); mechanisms that trigger their creation (minting and issuance) and destruction (burning); whether they are pegged to some source of value or not; mechanisms ensuring the peg; returns and costs (interest rates) associated to the tokens; participation rewards; fees and penalties associated with the exercise of the claims; and so forth.

When it comes to the locked tokens, key parameters usually defined by DeFi applications are: the set of allowed tokens accepted as deposited funds; the set of tokens accepted as collateral (if different); allowed collateral composition;

overcollateralization ratio; interests charged over the collateral; rewards accruing to liquidity providers; temporal limits (minimum or maximum) for locking tokens; liquidity parameters; returns and costs generated by the deposited tokens; fees and penalties (for mismanagement of the deposited or collateralization rules); utilization and supply rates (for loans); and the available set of token pairs (for DEXes).

These parameters can be both static (such as how many tokens can remain in a vault or the total amount of tokens that can be issued) and dynamic (such as the level of return rates or fees accrued by the token holders). Moreover, the same type of decisions and parameters may apply to yet other types of tokens, such as governance tokens (discussed in Sect. 4.2.3 below).

The Goals and Optimization Mechanisms of DeFi Applications: Evaluation of Layer 4 Performance Each DeFi application has a different goal and, for this reason, a different optimization mechanism. These optimization mechanisms can also be used to compare the effectiveness and optimality of different DeFi applications providing the same service. As a result, it is important to highlight that different DeFi business models are implemented in order to achieve different results (Table 5).

First, the goal of CDPs is to devise the most efficient collateralization mechanism in order to ensure the constant value of the claim-token issued: absolute constancy of value of the claim-token, in this case, is the primary goal of the application (Bullmann et al., 2019; Catalini et al., 2021; Catalini & Massari, 2021; Klages-Mundt & Minca, 2020, 2021; Li & Mayer, 2021; Saengchote, 2021). The greater the stability and reliability of claim-tokens issued by CDP systems, the more likely it will be for a specific application to gain trust and be adopted. Moreover, the higher the fees and negative interest charged by the application, the less widely adopted an application will be.

Second, the ultimate goal of protocols for loanable funds is to determine the optimal couple of interest rates charged and paid to the users operating on two sides: interest rates charged to token borrowers and interest paid to token providers (Bartoletti et al., 2021a; Gudgeon et al., 2020c; Saengchote et al., 2022; Xu & Xu, 2022). In contrast to CDPs, protocols for loanable funds operate non-custodial two-sided businesses. In this case, the interest rates charged to the token borrowers must be high enough to generate sufficient returns to generate a return for capital providers (and accumulate reserves), but low enough to convince borrowers to use the service and leverage two-sided network externalities (Armstrong, 2006; Rochet & Tirole, 2003). Incentives to participate can also be created through the provision of other benefits and the issuance of further tokens, such as governance tokens in the case of yield farming.

Third, the goal of AMMs is to efficiently define the most accurate exchange rate between any pair of tokens and to do so in the most efficient manner. The more numerous the combinations of token pairings, and the greater the liquidity for each of them, the more accurate the pricing of the tokens. As a result, even in this case, the layer is characterised by a trade-off between effectiveness and efficiency—having enough trading pools to directly measure trading rates, while having enough

Table 5 Different optimization goals for different types of business models issuing different types of claim-tokens

Layer 3 protocols		Layer 4 optimization mechanisms: goals	Claim-token issued (examples)	Suggested legal classification of claim-tokens
Primary protocols	CDPs	Optimal mechanisms for value stability	Dai	Derivative
	Protocols for loanable funds	Optimal interest rates charged	aToken	Equity
	DEXes	Optimal pricing & exchange rates	LPTokens	Equity
	Derivatives	Optimal behaviour of synthetic value	sToken	Derivative
	Portfolio management and yield aggregators	Optimal yield	yToken	Equity
Additional (auxiliary or complementary) DeFi protocols	Liquid staking	Optimize the fixed returns accruing to the stakers	stETH	Fixed-income security
	Bridges	Optimal mechanisms for value stability	WBTC	Tokenized cryptoasset
	Prediction markets and decentralized oracles	Optimal betting pricing for the occurrence of uncertain events	Long/short tokens	Equity

liquidity for each trading pool in order to establish correct and precise prices. Illiquid pools are inefficient as they may suffer from slippage and/or divergence losses, as discussed above (Bichuch & Feinstein, 2022; Kao et al., 2020; Xu et al., 2021).

Fourth, protocols for crypto-derivatives aim at creating synthetic assets that retrace the behaviour of the underlying assets. As a result, the goal of these protocols is to create synthetic assets whose value follows as much as possible the one of the underlying assets. This should be achieved as efficiently as possible.

Fifth, yield aggregators, portfolio optimization and liquidity mining protocols share one simple goal: to maximize the returns generated by the pools where the various users have deposited their tokens (Cousaert et al., 2022). In this case, the maximization of the returns mainly depends on two aspects: first, the operation of efficient mechanisms for the optimization of the arbitrage and trading between protocols and, second, the setup of incentive mechanisms to maximize the number of tokens deposited in the pools by the part of investors.

Finally, there are complementary protocols. First, the goal of liquid staking is to maximize the regular returns accruing to token owners (stakers), while minimizing risks; second the goal of bridges is identical to that of CDPs or derivative protocols (they both operate protocols for the tokenization of cryptoassets), namely to optimally reproduce and track the value and behaviour of an underlying asset; lastly, the goal of prediction markets is to optimally derive the likelihood and betting price for the occurrence of an uncertain event.

In conclusion, DeFi business models can be evaluated along three different dimensions. First, a dimension of effectiveness that takes into account the extent to which the result or performance actually delivered and achieved differs from the expected or promised result or performance (e.g. ideal absolute stability vs. actual stability of the value of claim-tokens). Second, a dimension of efficiency, that takes into account the extent to which results can be achieved with minimum costs; costs can be actual fees or rewards paid, operational transaction costs, extra inefficiencies needed to address risks, and various risks to be discounted, as discussed above (e.g. slippage in case of AMM, or overcollateralisation ratios). Third, a dimension of maximization that takes into account the extent to which the application is able to obtain greater results from an absolute point of view and improve on its performances (e.g. increase the yield paid due to an increasing participation to its pools).

It should be noted that some of these optimization mechanisms only derive from an optimization of the protocol and smart contracts' logic, while others derive from the ability to convince users and incentivize their behaviours. In this second case, optimization requires the definition of incentive mechanisms.

Incentive Mechanisms Third, this layer defines the various incentive mechanisms that shape the optimal and desired responses on the part of the users, such as the incentives to participate and use the service, incentives to provide liquidity, incentives to redeem a token and withdraw a deposit, incentives to liquidate a collateralized position, incentives to trade or mint tokens, incentives to participate in auctions, incentives to swap or trade two applications' tokens to maintain overall stability, and so forth. For instance, DEXes' liquidity mining rates represent typical examples of incentive mechanisms trying to maximize participation (and liquidity provision) into a DEX liquidity pool.

Some of these incentives derive form the economic rewards defined in layer 3 (such as the participation incentives linked to the payment of interest to those providing liquidity and possessing a claim-token), while others derive from mechanisms peculiar to layer 4 (such as the incentives to trigger a liquidation auction). These incentives are mainly linked to the mechanisms characterizing the issuance and possession of claim-tokens, rather than the mechanisms dealing with the management of the deposited funds. Even those incentives that are mainly concerned with actions on the deposited tokens (such as incentives to liquidate collateralized positions) are largely linked to the exercise of claims conferred by the claim-tokens (so that participation in liquidations often can only be possible through the holding and staking of claim-tokens).

Stability and Solvency Mechanisms Applications usually have stability and solvency mechanisms. In general, three main stability mechanisms are usually adopted by the various DeFi applications.

One, DeFi applications have to make sure that the value of the claim-tokens issued remains stable and it carefully reflects the value of the tokenised capital initially deposited. For this reason, DeFi protocols adopt standard mechanisms that reduce or expand the supply of their claim-tokens in order to drive market responses and keep their value stable and anchored to a specific peg (which is typically the reference value provided by the underlying locked tokens). This can either be done directly, such as in the case of rebase algorithmic stablecoins (Zhao et al., 2021), or indirectly, by adjusting the positive and negative interest rates paid or charged by the claim-tokens. The goal of these incentive mechanisms is to retain stability by rebalancing the short-term equilibrium between demand and supply of the claim-tokens. This represents a sort of short-term monetary policy of the application that is mainly concerned with the short-term economic stability of the system and sustains the incentives to participate. For instance, Dai is characterised by a negative stability fee and a positive saving rate: changes in both interest rates contribute to the overall stability of Maker's protocol. The object of these first-level stabilization mechanisms is the claim-token.

Two, DeFi applications have to make sure that they are able to fulfil all their redemption claims at any time. In order to do that, they have to make sure that they are liquid and solvent at any time. For this reason, protocols usually define mechanisms that incentivize actors or smart contract protocols to act on the collateralized positions in case the value of the locked tokens cannot ensure the instantaneous redemption of all circulating claims. They can do so by either incentivizing a recapitalization of the locked tokens, or, alternatively, by triggering liquidations of collateralised positions directly. Almost all different types of DeFi protocols discussed above have functions that automatically liquidate collateral held by smart contracts. These liquidations can either be performed by properly incentivised actors and executed by smart contracts, or directly autonomously initiated and executed by the smart contract itself. These represent necessary mechanisms that mainly counter the possible (il)-liquidity problems or insolvency of the DeFi application due to under-collateralised positions, and potentially leading to fire sales or death spirals (BIS & IOSCO, 2021; Catalini & de Gortari, 2021; Catalini et al., 2021). For example, MakerDAO incentivizes auction-keepers to automatically trigger liquidation auctions and close under-collateralised positions that may undermine the application's stability. The object of these second-level stabilization mechanisms are the deposited (locked) tokens.

The parameters driving and determining liquidation auctions depend on specific governance decisions concerning the collateralization of users' positions. The nature and type of locked funds (the nature of the collateralization of users' positions) can change based on their: (i) composition (mono-asset or baskets of assets); (ii) liquidity (more or less locked funds); (iii) stability with respect to a peg (some funds are more volatile than others); (iv) relationship and correlation with the traded native assets (some locked funds are identical to the traded assets, others are different); (v) extra-mechanisms in which they support value (some collateral accrue interest, pay dividends, or generate rewards); (vi) extra factors that should be compensated for in the support of value (fees, negative interest); (vii) extent of collateralization in relation to the native asset; (viii) liquidation level or liquidation ratio at which collateral is deemed to be insufficient to support the value of the native coin.

Three, DeFi applications have to make sure that, even when external actors are non-cooperative, non-responsive, and cannot be incentivised, they can rely on a certain level of reserves or buffers that can be activated in case of either instability, illiquidity, or under-collateralization to keep ensuring short-term stability of the claim-tokens and/or solvency of the overall debt positions. This is usually done by ensuring that the application itself can operate smart contract protocols that can issue other valuable tokens and, by doing so, can either recapitalise the debt positions with additional deposited tokens or redeem the claim-tokens transacted in the market. As a result, applications devise protocols whose role is to trigger auctions to issue or burn these other types of tokens (secondary, or dual tokens) to incentivize the sale or purchase of the claim-tokens, whose value has to be controlled. Obviously, these secondary tokens will have to be endowed with some value for this third set of mechanisms to work. Usually, the role of these dual tokens is fulfilled by the applications' governance tokens and, for this reason, the ultimate source of value incentivizing actors and maintaining stability in this case derives from the possibility to participate in the application's governance process (layer 5 below).

This third set of solutions represents mechanisms of last resort that can be implemented to ensure both stability and solvency, and they are usually activated whenever the previous two fail to deliver the expected outcome. The object of this third type of stabilization mechanism is the claim-token once again, even though such mechanisms involve the (emergency) reserves of an application. This is the case, for example, with Maker's debt auctions, which involve Maker's reserves.

Inter-layer Stability Fourth, DeFi protocols should also be able to respond to disequilibrium and forces coming from the underlying infrastructural layers. For instance, some native tokens used as collateral can suddenly collapse or become extremely illiquid if their blockchain starts to fail. Additionally, DeFi protocols should also consider the level of the fees required to operate smart contracts and potentially adjust accordingly, also across platforms. Moreover, staking, liquidity provision, and yield management should occur across smart contract platforms, meaning that each DeFi layer should incorporate information on other platforms' ecosystems. More generally, DeFi applications can diversify their dependence on any specific infrastructure in two ways. One, they can operate across different smart contract platforms so that the possible collapse of one single layer 1 native token does not necessarily undermine the solvency of the overall application (mainly through bridges). Two, they can devise ways to manage the composition of their deposits and collateral, by both adjusting economic incentives for depositing different layer 1 native tokens and/or preventing the deposit of certain tokens if the vaults or pools are not sufficiently diversified (mainly using wrapped tokens).

Layer 4 Wrap-Up This level includes all those mechanisms that incentivize actors and ensure the stability, viability and sustainability of the DeFi protocol, while trying to maximise its performances, optimize its functioning and operations, and ensure its solvency. These main goals of DeFi's layer 4 can be exercised by implementing mechanisms that focus on both the claim-token and the tokenised locked funds. For this reason, different DeFi applications should mainly be compared and contrasted (and will mainly differ) in these four respects (Table 6).

In contrast to layer 3 (whose focus is mainly on the efficient and decentralised execution and operation of atomic transactions for a given business model logic and architecture), the focus of layer 4's protocols is mainly on the economic performance of inter-temporal transactions. For this reason, this layer deals with non-atomic economic stability and security risks (Werner et al., 2021). These mainly include the set of market, credit, and liquidity risks emerging from the operation of the various DeFi business models and the provision of their different services. Optimal risk management at this layer necessarily depends on the mitigation of operational and technological risks mainly affecting the execution of protocols and functionalities at layer 3.

The meaning of the decentralization-efficiency trade-off for layer 4 then mainly reflects the dichotomy between automation and/or disintermediation and (non-atomic) operational and/or economic efficiencies. Poorly designed incentive and stability mechanisms (relying on both automation and disintermediation) can lead to fundamental economic security risks of the application for three main reasons (in order): (i) they cannot guarantee stability of the value of the claim-tokens; (ii) they are not sufficiently liquid or creditworthy in order to instantaneously satisfy all issued redemption claims due to a crunch or plunge of the value of the locked tokenised funds (under-collateralization and liquidation); (iii) they do not have sufficient reserves to be able to autonomously recapitalise and/or repurchase claim-tokens in the face of a lack of cooperation due to a lack of trust of users and investors in its long-term solvency.

Table 6 The dimensions of decentralization and efficiency mechanisms for layer 4

Dimensions to contrast and compare different layer 4s	Different types of solutions characterizing layer 4	
Decentralization	**Automation/autonomy** (no discretion of, and authorization from, a third party)	**Disintermediation** (no delegation of control over tokenized funds to a third party)
Loci of efficiency and optimization mechanisms	**Incentivize holders of claim-tokens:** Define automatic smart contract mechanisms to enforce and execute incentive mechanisms	**Directly act on the locked tokens**: Application autonomously resolves and extinguishes its illiquid or insolvent positions
Incentive mechanisms (DApp optimization, growth and profitability)	Incentives to use the service incentives to provide liquidity incentives to redeem a claim-token incentives to withdraw a deposit incentives to liquidate a debt position incentives to trade or mint tokens incentives to participate in auctions incentives to swap or trade DApp native tokens	
Short-term stability mechanisms	**Adjust demand and supply** *Direct*: Automatically adjust supply of a claim-token (rebase mechanisms algo stablecoins) *Indirect*: Adjust interest rates paid or charged by the claim-tokens (majority of DeFi applications)	
Short term liquidity/solvency mechanisms	**Resolve under-collateralized positions** Incentivize liquidation or recapitalization of a debt position	**Resolve under-collateralized positions** Autonomous initiate and execute the liquidation of a debt position
Long-term liquidity/solvency mechanisms	**Application uses own funds to address insolvent, undercapitalized positions**	
	Application smart contracts automatically auction tokens to buy-back and burn claim-tokens from the market	Application smart contract autonomously recapitalizes debt positions with own funds
Inter-layer interdependences mechanisms	Mechanisms to operate across infrastructures Mechanisms to manage the composition of the layer 1 tokens used as deposits and collateral	
Risks	Applications' specific (non-atomic) economic risks	

It should be noted that while interoperability and compatibility between different DeFi protocols can be achieved through the definition of (static) APIs, common programming functions or bridges, interoperability and compatibility at this optimization sublayer requires the constant exchange and update of information. Auxiliary DeFi services such as oracles, prediction markets or bridges are key to implement incentive mechanisms and ensure the economic composability and integrity between protocols. This sublayer also interconnects with other elements of the crypto ecosystem, such as wallets, centralized exchanges, and traditional financial institutions. As a result, interoperability should include both centralized and decentralized systems.

4.2.3 The Governance Layer: Performing on-Chain Control and Decision-Making

DeFi applications usually include a third set of protocols (or smart contract modules) that complement the other two and are dedicated to performing the application's governance functionalities. For "governance" here we mean all those rules, procedures, and social and legal structures that support decision making processes and define accountabilities among actors (Beck et al., 2018; Weill & Ross, 2004).

The Complicated Nature (and History) of the DeFi Governance Layer: Overview The governance module of a DeFi application performs very specific and important functionalities and, for this reason, it can be allocated to its own specific layer (layer 5). More generally, protocols in layer 5 perform three different types of functionalities: two serve as support functionalities to the other two layers, while one is specific and peculiar to the specific governance layer. The common element linking all these is the governance token that, together with applications' claim-tokens, represents the second type of token issued by DeFi applications. Above, the governance token was referred to as a "secondary" or "dual" token; these terms derive from the fact that while the term "governance token" explicitly links this token to the governance functionality, it leaves the other two functionalities of this token out, and ignores the broader role played by the token at all layers of the application stack. For this reason, here we define this second token as the "application native token" (ANTs), and keep in mind that ANTs can also perform the role of governance tokens, but they do not exclusively (or necessarily) do that.

Following Maker's first issuance of its own ANT (MKR) as early as April 2016, and the key role that this played on two fronts—the launch of Maker's on-chain governance voting at the end of 2018, and the solvency of the system during Maker's "black Thursday" of March 2020—a variety of other protocols started issuing their own ANTs in order to address two main goals.

First, application developers started to conceive of ANTs as governance tokens that could decentralise the governance of various applications and projects. Starting in 2020, DeFi protocol communities and developers have started to focus on the development of on-chain governance mechanisms in order to achieve on-chain decentralised governance. This was also (but not exclusively) due to the increasing scrutiny of regulatory agencies around the world, following the SEC lawsuits against EtherDelta (an order-book DEX) at the end of 2018, and especially against Ripple Labs in 2020. This was coupled with an increasing tendency to treat any claim-token issued and/or controlled by centralised organizations as securities. The classification of all claim-tokens as securities lead to the natural conclusion that all centralised DeFi organizations that issue tokens and fall within the Howey Test conduct activities of security offerings. This is the case unless their respective organizations are decentralized, such as in the case of DAOs (Henderson & Raskin, 2019). This leads to the two questions: (i) what does decentralization mean in the case of the Howey test and (ii) how should this be achieved? A key role in this quest for decentralized governance is played by DeFi applications' issuance of governance tokens.

Second, DeFi communities simultaneously started to use governance tokens as proper exchange tokens in order to perform key roles in conveying economic incentives to the actors, while ensuring stability and solvency of the protocol. In this case, ANTs can be used as a dual of claim-tokens as they fulfil a key role in the definition of the application's incentives at layer 4. The key event in this sense was Compound's issuance of its ANT COMP in June 2020, to reward liquidity providers and incentivize adoption and usage of the platform. Since then, all other major DeFi applications have started to issue governance tokens and provide "yield farming" services. This officially kicked-off the exponential rise of token prices during the 2020 "DeFi summer".

As a result, the governance layer of DeFi applications includes all those smart contract protocols that initiate, enforce and execute the functionalities of the various ANTs and that ensure that ANTs can perform all their roles within an application's ecosystem. As ANTs can perform three different roles (operational, economic, and governing), the protocols of the governance layer can also perform three main different functionalities: two complementary and supportive of the other two application layers (operational for layer 3 and economic for layer 4), one idiosyncratic (governance).

ANT as a Utility Token: Using the Governance Layer to Support the Application's Business Model First, ANTs can be used as utility tokens to support and facilitate the operations of some systems that are executed by layer 3 protocols. For example, governance tokens can be required to pay fees in order to redeem the claim-tokens and close a collateralised position. This was the original case in the Maker protocol where the MKR token used to be necessary to pay the required quoted stability fee and should have therefore been purchased in advance from the Maker reserve in exchange for Dai. This is an operational employment of the ANT as it affects the way in which collateralised positions can be opened and closed, and the claim-tokens redeemed. Although fees are involved, it still is a layer 3 employment as the ANT it is not used to determine fees, shape incentives, or ensure stability, but only to operate basic functionalities of the protocol. This is similar to the use of Binance ANT (BNB), or even Ripple XRP, which are both native tokens mainly used for operational purposes, even though there are key differences between these native tokens and pure DeFi ANTs.

Another example of ANTs used to support an application's layer 3 is represented by the employment of ANTs as locked funds for the issuance of claim-tokens. Not all applications allow claim-tokens to be backed by their own ANT. For example, MakerDAO does not allow MKR to be among the available collateral for CDPs. On the other hand, various other protocols do and some protocols only accept ANT as possible locked funds. This used to be the case with the original version of the Synthetix protocol where sTokens could only be minted when SNX holders staked their SNX as collateral using the Synthetix Staking application. In this case, the ANT fulfils a necessary role in allowing the opening of collateralised positions and backing the issuance of claim-tokens. For this reason, even in this case, the ANT can be seen as facilitating the operations of layer 3 of a DeFi application.

In sum, whenever the ANT either facilitates the operations of a DeFi business model and/or enables the provision of the DeFi service, it can be treated as a utility token: the ANT becomes necessary to operate the application as well as to access, and benefit from, its services. This is identical to the role performed by a utility token, defined as a "type of crypto-asset which is only intended to provide access to a good or a service supplied by the issuer of that token" (European Commission, 2020: 56).

ANT as an Exchange or Investment Token: Using the Governance Layer to Support the Application's Incentive Mechanisms The second main employment of ANTs is in relation to their employment as incentive tools to drive users' behaviours and ensure profitability, stability, and eventually the application's ultimate solvency. There are various examples of the flexible and multifaceted nature of ANT when used as an incentive token, as outlined below.

First, ANT can be used to expand the user base of a DeFi application and attract customers. The use of ANT in order to gain extra rewards and to further accumulate additional ANTs is the most common example of ANTs being used as tools to sustain growth, market adoption, and to generate profits. This is the common case of yield farming, where the ownership of a platform's ANT confers the right to gain further ANTs as a reward for participation in liquidity provision. These extra-returns can be obtained either directly in virtue of mere ownership (as in the case of COMP tokens), or indirectly following the staking of an ANT in other complementary pools (as in the case of CRV tokens staked in Convex Finance). These solutions have been adopted to make participation in certain platforms more convenient and profitable than participation in other platforms and, for this reason, to gain users, investors, and ultimately customers.

Second, ANT can be used as dual tokens for short-term rebalancing of the supply and demand of a claim-token, or to ensure liquidity and stability of debt positions. These cases emerge whenever it is possible to ensure the arbitrage between the value of the ANT and the value of a claim-token, or whenever an ANT is used as an application's official currency to place bids in liquidation auctions in order to obtain collateral at discounted prices. In both cases, when used as incentives, claim-tokens can be redeemed or exchanged for ANT.

Finally, ANTs can be also used to trigger debt auctions or, more generally, as tools of last resort to ensure the application's overall stability in the face of systemic shocks. This is a typical case employed by many CDP applications or stablecoin issuers more generally: MakerDAO relies on the fire-issuance of MKR tokens to redeem and burn an oversupply of Dai tokens and/or a critical under-collateralization of CDPs whenever liquidation auctions do not work, as shown during "black Thursday" in 2020 (Klages-Mundt & Minca, 2020, 2021; Salehi et al., 2021). In the same vein, the fire-issuance of the LUNA ANT in order to redeem UST was also the mechanism attempted by Terraform Labs to (try to) avoid the unpegging and collapse of UST last May.

The tragic debacle of UST (as well as the collapse of Alameda Research and its sister company, FTX) has shown that whenever ANTs are used as locked collateral to back the issuance of claim-tokens and ensure the operation of the protocols (tokens supporting layer 3), as well as tools of last resort for the solvency of the application (tokens supporting layer 4), the whole system may behave as a Ponzi scheme and can be subject to uncontrollable death spirals (Catalini & de Gortari, 2021; Catalini et al., 2021). This is especially evident for DeFi applications issuing and managing claim-tokens behaving as on-chain backed (or decentralised) stablecoins (which can be crypto-collateralised or algorithmic).

ANT as a Governance Token Proper: The Governance Layer as a Dedicated Layer to Support On-Chain Governance Protocols The third and final employment of ANTs is the most common and obvious, and occurs whenever ANT is used as a governance token in order to participate in on-chain voting procedures and to the overall on-chain governance of the application. This is the main use case of ANT inherited from DAOs, where a set of protocols manage the way governance tokens are issued, burned, staked, and used in the governance and decision-making process. Almost all DeFi ANTs can perform governance functions and be used as forms of collective governance.

In this case, ANTs can be understood as tokenised shares or equities that confer voting or participation rights to those holding them. In order to participate in voting sessions, tokens can be directly staked or deposited and locked on-chains into dedicated portals or smart contract addresses managed by the application's set of dedicated governance protocols. Alternatively, ANT holders can also delegate their tokens to specialised actors or third parties exercising voting on their behalf. The same locked token can be reused in a variety of vote rounds as governance tokens are typically not burned in the voting process but simply returned to their owner once the voting process ends, or they can be alternatively stored in the governance contract for further voting.

Token holders can vote to change and define a variety of key application-specific parameters characterizing an application's functioning. These parameters are typically a variable set of those highlighted in Table 4, and usually concern aspects of the application's tokenomics and operational dimensions, such as fees, returns, collateralization, and so forth. For example, MKR holders can vote on a variety of parameters, such as:

- Adding a new collateral asset type with a unique set of risk parameters
- Changing the risk parameters of one or more existing collateral asset types, and adding new risk parameters to one or more existing collateral asset types
- Modifying the Dai savings rate
- Modifying the Dai stability fee
- Modifying the collateral auction duration
- Determining the surplus and debt thresholds
- Modifying the sensitivity parameter for Oracles' prices acquisition
- Choosing the set of oracle feeds
- Choosing the set of emergency oracles
- Triggering Emergency shutdown
- Other general upgrades to the system (e.g. voting mechanisms)

Overview of the Multidimensional Nature of the Main ANTs: Summing Up One of the main goals of ANTs is to implement on-chain governance practices in order to introduce decentralised governance and overcome the legal, regulatory and business limitations deriving from a centralised governance in the hands of a few predefined application owners. However, governance tokens are very complex entities that, despite their very specific characterization, perform different functions and fulfil different roles in different protocols. Their role as governance tokens *sricto sensu* is only one specific aspect among many others. For this reason, it is much more appropriate to characterise them as application-native tokens, in the same way in which layer-1 incentive tokens are also application-native tokens whose role is to enforce and execute on-chain consensus. Consistent with the tripartite discussion developed above, the main contractual claims that governance tokens confer to their holders are (among others):

- Voting rights
- Residual claims over funds locked into vaults/pools
- Claims over a share of the fees generated by the platform activity
- Rights to obtain further governance tokens as rewards for participation/liquidity provision.
- Claim over active interest rates (fixed income)
- Rights to trade them against specific assets (transaction facilitators).
- Rights to use the token as a further collateral
- Rights to use them to pay fees or to undertake certain platform activity for free or at a discounted price

Table 7 below provides a very schematic and high-level overview of the main properties, characteristics, and roles of DeFi ANTs (typically called "governance tokens") for a selection of the major DeFi applications consistent with the main business models discussed in Sect. 4.2.1.

Table 7 A schematic summary of the various properties and roles of DeFi ANTs

Application-Native Token (ANT)	Protocol type	Properties
MakerDAO MKR	CDP	• Grants voting rights • Used to ensure value stability and solvency in auctions • Used to pay fees • Used as a claim of last resort on liquidated collateral and emergency shut downs
Aave AAVE	Lending	• Confers voting rights • Used for staking for security and insurance of deposits in auctions • Used for staking to claim fees
Compound COMP	Lending	• Confers voting rights • Used to back liquidity/collateralization • Used as a reward/incentive for liquidity provision
Balancer BAL	DEX	• Confers voting rights • Used as a reward for liquidity provision • Used as a reward for using the protocol in trading
Curve CRV	DEX	• Confers voting rights • Used as a reward/incentive • Used for staking and claim trading fees
Convex CVX	Yield aggregator/Yield farming	
Sushiswap SUSHI	DEX	• Confers voting rights • Used for staking and claim interests • Used to claim rewards when staked
Uniswap UNI	DEX	• Confers voting rights • Used as a reward/incentive • Used as incentive mechanism within the ecosystem • Possibly used as utility tokens
dYdX DYDX	DEX and Derivatives	• Confers voting rights • Used as a reward for liquidity provision and trading
Sinthetix SNX	Derivatives	• Confers voting rights • Confers claims over the value of debt pools • Used as collateral • Used to gain fees generated by the platform (staking rewards)
Yearn.finance YFI	Yield aggregator/Yield farming	• Confers voting rights • Used as a reward for liquidity provision

Decentralization vs. Efficiency Trade-Offs: Dimensions of Decentralization in the Governance Layer ANTs have been historically introduced to implement on-chain decentralised governance and overcome the legal, regulatory and business limitations deriving from a centralised control over DeFi protocols and applications. For this reason, since the so-called "2020 DeFi summer", almost all major DeFi applications have launched their own governance token. Although applications' governance tokens can indeed allow for dispersed control and decision-making procedures, this is not always the case. Some authors have highlighted how the concentration in control rights is not necessarily very "decentralised" in DeFi applications (Aramonte et al., 2021; Barbereau et al., 2022a; Fritsch et al., 2022). This is especially true given that the nature of decentralization in the governance layer entails a variety of dimensions and aspects. Here we highlight nine aspects of layer 5 decentralization that have to be considered.

First, different DeFi applications create, issue and distribute governance tokens in different ways; typically, different shares of governance tokens are distributed to different types of stakeholders based on their roles and engagement with the protocol (whether they were previous users of the protocols, investors, current governance token holders, developers, community participants, and so forth). As a result, not all stakeholders may have the same rights or likelihood to receive the same amount of governance tokens. Different DeFi applications may therefore differ in the way they decide to distribute their ANT to the various stakeholders.

Secondly, in contrast to shares, governance tokens are not necessarily distributed following a monetary investment as mere engagement with the application (in a variety of capacities) is often sufficient to acquire a claim over the governance token. This makes ANTs different from standard equities and, in this case, they may not be classified as securities as there is no initial capital investment (regardless of whether this investment is in a common enterprise). However, similar to shares, many governance tokens give rights to some sort of dividends (stable returns) often in the form of additional governance tokens, thus acting as incentive mechanisms as discussed in Sect. 4.2.2 above.

Third, similar to shares but in contrast to normal "political" voting rights, the power of each token holder is weighted according to the amount of governance tokens that they control; this generates an important form of centralization of DeFi protocols as the control over the protocol can lay in the hands of very few actors controlling few concentrated public addresses (Aramonte et al., 2021). The on-chain governance of these protocols is therefore not properly democratic as voters do not have only one vote, consistent with plutocratic systems (Buterin, 2017; Rossi & Sørensen, 2022).

Fourth, the concentration of voting power into a limited number of accounts also highlights a further problem deriving from the pseudonymity of the public addresses: different public accounts may be controlled by the same entity (physical or legal). For this reason, a fairly diluted governance structure may be in fact much concentrated due to the simultaneous control of multiple accounts by part of the same entity. This reveals a secondary manifestation of a double-spending Sybil attack (Zhang & Lee, 2019) applied to the employment of voting rights rather than the transaction of exchange tokens. In this sense, it is impossible to distinguish between the concentration and distribution of voting rights among addresses and the concentration of voting rights among individuals. At the same time, the transparency of any operation executed on-chain makes on-chain voting processes not private but rather trackable and subject to possible surveillance. This also goes against standard democratic voting procedures that assume that voting should be secret and fully anonymous and not transparent and trackable.

Fifth, governance tokens can be delegated and this means that they are not nominal and/or private: votes can be exercised by specialised counterparties on behalf of the original token holders. This is also a problematic aspect of standard democratic voting process: not only will concentration of delegated voting in the hands of a few big intermediaries increase the concentration of power in the hands of these same intermediaries (Nadler & Schär, 2020), but this delegation creates incentive alignment issues as the decisions made by the counterparty should be aligned (and may be in conflict) with the intentions of the delegating entity. Misalignment, moral hazard and principal-agent problems may therefore emerge.

Sixth, governance tokens are not only not nominal, but they are typically completely fungible as they can be exchanged on the secondary market once they have been issued and distributed by the DeFi platform. This monetary and fungible nature makes their classification as utility tokens problematic (and potentially impossible under MiCA) and reveals new possible sources of centralization, mainly deriving from the leverage of market power in order to indirectly accumulate governance tokens and therefore exercise direct control over DeFi platforms. The possibility to "buy and accumulate votes" on secondary markets leads to problems of potential corruption and vote corruption. While the pseudonymity in accounts generate problems similar to the so-called Sybil attacks, the accumulation of governance tokens through purchases in secondary markets generates problems similar to the well-known majority attacks for consensus protocols (Aramonte et al., 2021; Eyal & Sirer, 2018; Gencer et al., 2018; Narayanan et al., 2016).

Seventh, it is important to distinguish between DeFi applications and protocols that make participation mandatory, or at least introduce clauses or incentives to force token holders to participate into voting, and those where participation in on-chain governance practices is purely voluntary. For instance, when it comes to layer 1 on-chain governance such as PoS protocols, the failure to abide by the required terms of engagement generates penalties, slashing, and even the complete loss of funds. These practices are much less common in DeFi applications where on-chain governance is much more on a voluntary basis. This aspect reveals yet another problem with typical DAOs and on-chain governance practices: dilution of ownership and control "on paper" does not mean that governance is diluted in practice, as the "active" token holders that regularly participate and shape the application's decision-making process may just be a fraction of those entitled to do so (Barbereau et al., 2022b). This asymmetry in participation may also derive from the fact that some decisions require specific expertise and therefore only involve a restricted circle of participants. In this case, the governance of a DeFi application becomes de facto and much more centralised in practise than on paper. This problem also emerged in the implementation of EOS' on-chain governance a few years ago.

Eighth, almost all DeFi applications are characterised by a double-tier governance structure: on-chain voting is typically preceded by preliminary stage characterised by an off-chain selection and acceptance of relevant and worthy changes to be subsequently brought on-chain (Zhao et al., 2022). This two-stage process is usually managed by a restricted circle of maintainers, core developers, administrators or moderators who have the ultimate responsibility to manage and govern the application. This core-periphery structure reveals yet another form of hierarchical centralization deriving from the distinction between two different layers of decision-making authority and responsibility (Ao et al., 2022; Safadi et al., 2020): the circle of those deciding which proposed changes shall be selected and can be put to voting (usually the members of a foundation or "lab"), and those having the right to express their voting over the given proposed changes. Some aspects of the application's protocols do not need to be considered or selected in the first place as they cannot be changed by design.

Ninth, different DeFi applications may be characterised by different supply schedules of their governance tokens: some governance tokens may be redeemed and burned by the protocol, and other times they may be constantly issued by the protocol. This affects the circulating supply of the token and therefore the type of incentive structures they generate and the dynamic distribution of control rights. This is common also for layer 1 ANTs: for example, Binance is planning to halve the circulating supply of its ANT (BNB token) by redeeming and burning 100,000,000 BNB tokens out of its originally-issued 200,000,000 tokens.

Decentralization vs. Efficiency Trade-Offs: Dimensions of Efficiency in the Governance Layer The adoption of on-chain governance procedures are characterised by complicated trade-offs between centralization and decentralization. Another important aspect to be considered is whether the adoption of on-chain governance increases or decreases efficiency of the governance process (Sun et al., 2022). A few aspects of efficiency should be considered when it comes to the employment of ANTs as governance tokens.

First, on-chain governance makes any vote a de facto Ethereum transaction: for this reason, each vote becomes a transaction executed by the platform's smart contract that is subject to standard smart contract fees. From this point of view, the whole spectrum of efficiency dimensions already discussed for layer 2 also applies to the employment of ANT as governance tokens. Among them, the main sources of inefficiency are the high fees and the possible delays for the execution of the voting transactions due to congestion of the network.

Secondly, in order to vote, participants should typically lock their ANT into dedicated protocol smart contracts. This means that token holders are subject to possible lock-in effects due to the possible impossibility of retrieving and unlocking their staked tokens. In case governance tokens are also used for other stability and economic purposes by layer 4 protocols, this may create serious risks of illiquidity and instability of the system whenever tokens are simultaneously required for different reasons. This represents another form of application inefficiency.

Third, the sum of the previous two points highlights a further source of on-chain governance inefficiency: the potential lack of effectiveness and promptness in decision making. Fully open and participatory processes are not always the most efficient and convenient ones. This is especially true in case of long waiting times, lock-in effects, and the impossibility of speeding up the process. As highlighted in some of the recent collapses (UST), sometimes promptness and rapidity may be vital in avoiding catastrophic failures (for instance, the ability to decide whether to "manually" sell extra reserves to sustain the peg of a stablecoin).

Fourth, hierarchical decision-making may be more efficient and effective whenever complicated and extremely technical decisions have to be taken. The general public (or average elector) may not necessarily be able to decide swiftly and effectively if the knowledge and competences are asymmetrically distributed among token holders. Lack of expertise and competence among voters may make the process cumbersome, lengthy, and inefficient. In other words, sometimes it is better to delegate to experts.

Finally, various examples have revealed how transparent and public information is sometimes not optimal, especially in case of protocol vulnerabilities or bugs; hard or soft forks and general updates to the protocols may be required to avoid major damage to, or malicious exploitation of, the system's failures or vulnerabilities. However, the implementation of these changes via the usual transparent and participative procedures may not be feasible nor recommended. In these cases, it is almost always better to amend the protocol "silently" and trying to hide the vulnerability to as many people as possible to avoid that some malicious voter may exploit it. The history of Bitcoin and the Ethereum community reveals various episodes where bugs have been fixed in secret without any discussion to avoid possible leaking and exploitation. In this case, on-chain democratic governance procedures may become extremely inefficient and, in fact, detrimental.

The Governance Layer's Decentralization vs. Efficiency Trade-Off: Final Remarks In conclusion, three aspects of the governance layer are worthy of mention.

First, layer 5 includes all those protocols that deal with ANTs in various capacities. Although ANTs are necessary to implement and support DeFi on-chain governance as they are used as governance tokens, not all ANTs are simply and exclusively governance tokens. ANTs can typically perform a variety of different roles within DeFi applications and be used as key instruments by protocols belonging to other layers. As a result, ANTs can support and enforce key incentive mechanisms at layer 4 to ensure the stability of the application's claim-token, as well as the long-term collateralization and solvency of the whole protocol. In this case, they are mainly used as exchange or payment tokens. On the other hand, ANTs can also be used by layer 3 protocols in order to facilitate the execution of certain operations and ensure the provision of certain functionalities. Although this last employment of ANT is probably less common (and probably less necessary), in this case, they are mainly used and regarded as utility or participation tokens as they ensure that token holders are allowed and/or required to perform certain activities, operations and functionalities.

Secondly, although ANTs have been historically introduced in order to "decentralise" governance of DeFi applications and distribute the control and/or ownership structure, a variety of considerations (and recent works) reveal that this conclusion is less clear and more complicated than it may first appear. The decentralization of applications' governance is a complex and multidimensional concept that depends on a variety of aspects and considerations. The mere ex-ante equal distribution of ANTs to a variety of anonymous and dispersed actors addresses some problems generated by centralised governance, but it also creates other new problems, mainly linked to the ex-post marketability of the tokens, their delegation, the lack of participation, and so forth.

Third, the complicated nature of DeFi's decentralised governance is also affected by its ambiguous trade-off with governance efficiency: at times decentralised governance structures are desirable and effective, other times they may generate more complications and become more inefficient. This is especially true in the case of asymmetric capabilities and insider knowledge of voters, the role played by scale economies and delegation, the necessity to intervene in a prompt and direct manner to avoid the exploitation of glaring vulnerabilities, and so forth.

Table 8 summarizes the various dimensions of the decentralization-efficiency trade-off as applied to layer 5 of DeFi applications.

4.3 The Heterogenous "Asset Layer": Acting as a Support Side-Layer to Other Layers

Typical representations of the DeFi stack also include a distinct asset layer beside other logical layers. Here, we prefer to leave a specific asset out of the picture as this would not be consistent with the standard modularization of the DeFi stack that, in this case, is developed according to heterogenous logical protocols and not logical entities such as assets. In truth, each layer previously mentioned can operate, or be associated with, one or multiple assets. Given the widespread adoption of the "asset layer" and the importance assets have within the layered stack, it is worth briefly mentioning and discussing it and subsequently suggesting an alternative classification of assets across the various layers.

4.3.1 Different Tokens Operating in the Different Layers of the DeFi Stack

In standard characterizations of the DeFi stack, the asset layer normally includes all the types of native and issued assets that are used to operate DeFi services.

Table 8 The nature of the decentralization-efficiency trade-off for DeFi layer 5

Decentralization base case: Equal distribution of ANTs to a variety of dispersed token holders where everyone can exercise the same type of voting right on-chain		
Alternative dimensions of decentralization distinguishing different applications' layer 5s	Equal distribution of different ANTs to various dispersed accounts	
	Unequal likelihood to obtain ANTs due to different status or acquired rights	
	Concentrated control of multiple pseudonymous ANT wallets/addresses by the part of single entity	
	Concentration due to delegation of ANTs to specialized third parties	
	Dynamic concentration of ANTs due to acquisition of ANTs in secondary markets	
	Concentrated voting power due to asymmetric participation in voting sessions	
	Centralization due to multiple-tier governance structure distinguishing core administrators from peripheral ANT holders	
	Concentration emerging from asymmetric redemption and burning of ANT by the part of the application protocol.	
Dimensions of efficiency	Economic inefficiency	Gas costs to execute voting on-chain
	Operational inefficiency	Illiquidity and governance tokens' lock-in effects
		Slow and ineffective voting procedures
		Suboptimal decisions due to lack of diffused expertise among token-holders
		Inefficiencies due to revelation of vulnerabilities as public information

Within this layer, the literature usually includes both native assets (layer 1 and 2 in the infrastructural macro-layer) such as ETH, DeFi native stablecoins (claim-tokens) such as Dai, and even application-specific governance tokens, such as MKR, or COMP. These different types of assets: operate in different layers of the DeFi stack, and are mainly employed in different ways and for different purposes in these different layers. In sum, this layer characterizes the asset in function of the claims it confers and represents, its role and employment in a DeFi protocol, and its market value.

As a result, many types of tokens are involved in DeFi protocols. Table 9 summarizes typical assets used in, and by, DeFi protocols. It can be seen that different tokens represent different claims, they can be used in different ways and employed for different purposes, they are issued for different reasons, they originally belong to different layers of the stack, but they can be used in a variety of different layers to fulfil a variety of roles. For example, ETH is a native token issued at layer 1 and is originally used to fulfil its role at layer 1, while Dai is issued in the DeFi application layer to address needs and fulfil functions in the application layer. At the same time, layer 1 native tokens such as ETH can also be used in higher application layers to fulfil application-specific roles (such as acting as collateral), while ANTs can be used for different purposes at different layers of the application macro-layer, as discussed above.

For this reason, although it is important to keep the various tokens separate according to the layer they originally belong to (in order to retain logical consistency across layers consistent with the logic of modularization previous discussed), it is even more important to distinguish them based on the different types of roles or functions fulfilled within the layered stack. It should be noted that all tokens belonging to the application macro-layer can be conceived of as a form of contractual claim held by the user against a protocol smart contract address (pool or vault) and, for this reason, be understood as a form of claim-token. The specific claims conferred by each token vary as each token can be understood as a variable bundle of contractual claims. Many tokens are practically very similar, yet they may vary in some very specific respects according to the different roles fulfilled.

Although many of the tokens listed in Table 9 are usually grouped together and it is often convenient to group them together as discussed above (for instance, sTokens, cTokens, Dai, stTokens, LPTokens are all claim-tokens issued by DeFi applications, while MKR, UNI, SNX are all ANTs created by the various DeFi applications), it is still important to distinguish seemingly identical or homogeneous tokens due to their different roles and functions performed in different DeFi stacks in order to provide different types of services.

Table 9 Different types of tokens used in different DeFi applications and protocols

Type of DeFi token/claims	Typical use/purpose in DeFi protocols & applications	Examples
Native exchange tokens	Used as locked collateral	ETH
Fiat-backed stablecoins	Used as locked collateral or as a means of application-specific payment	USDC
Crypto-backed stablecoins	Issued to redeem locked collateral, also used as locked collateral themselves	Dai
ANTs (governance tokens)	Issued to enable on-chain voting (governance), pay fees, ensure protocol solvency and stability, and used as locked collateral	MKR
Wrapped tokens (on-chain tokenization)	Issued to enable cross-chain interoperable payments and transactions and as locked collateral	WBTC
Liquidity tokens (wrapped tokens)	Issued to enable liquidity providers to redeem their locked funds and to claim rewards	cTokens
Liquidity pools tokens	Issued to enable liquidity providers to redeem their locked funds, as participation shares in the pools, to claim rewards	LPTokens
Liquidity reward tokens	Issued to vote in on-chain governance and as a reward for liquidity provision	UNI
Crypto-derivatives	Issued to redeem locked collateral, as an ETF, a crypto-derivative and also used as locked collateral themselves	sTokens
Staking tokens	Issued to be used as locked collateral, gain returns and interest, and also provide voting (governance) rights	SNX
Staked token	Issued to be used as a claim over funds locked in a staking pool	stETH
Native staking token	Issued to be an ANT (governance token), as well as an incentive mechanism in DeFi-native staking consensus protocols	LUNA

4.3.2 Distinguishing Tokens Based on Their Functional Relationship with the DeFi Stack

As mentioned above, it is difficult to identify a specific asset layer distinct from all other layers. This is the case for multiple reasons.

First, Modular Inconsistency Assets are more appropriately defined as data objects rather than logical protocols: any system that is modularised according to its various functionally-independent protocols (and their architectural rules defining interdependences) cannot present an idiosyncratic and stand-alone asset layer.

Second, Lack of Specificity All layers of the stack issue or operate assets in order to perform layer-specific functions; as a result, it is not possible to single out a specific asset layer and distinguish it from the other layers. Potentially each layer is associated with some asset and requires assets to perform their operations and deliver their functions.

Third, Functional Indeterminacy Even though many assets are issued by specific layers, it is difficult to provide a clear distinction of assets based on the specific layer they belong to and, vice versa, to distinguish the various layers according to the type of asset they operate. In the same way, in which different layers can be treated as different modules due to their functional specificity and functional independence form the other layers, it is better to distinguish different assets based on their different role at different layers and their different functions performed in these different layers.

For all these reasons, here we propose an alternative, and much more general, classification of tokens based on the verification that tokens are data objects (or entities) that are ontologically amorphous and "ambivalent" (Kallinikos et al., 2013). For this reason, they should be distinguished based on the contingent functions performed and specific roles fulfilled in each layer of the DeFi stack rather than according to their heterogenous intrinsic ontologies. As different layers of the stack are distinguished based on their idiosyncratic functional independence, tokens should be linked to the various layers according to their different functional roles performed in each of these layers, rather than according to their ontological affinity or homogeneity with these logical layers.

As a result, it is possible to distinguish tokens in two broad categories according to their relationship with the various logical layers: *instrumental tokens* and *tokens-as-instruments*.

Instrumental Tokens Tokens are instrumental if they are necessary and indispensable to perform, ensure or enforce a certain function in any of the five layers. Instrumental tokens are means to an end supporting the functionalities and performance of specific protocols and, for this reason, their nature and value are intrinsically linked to the protocol they instrumentally perform a function for.

For example, layer 1 native tokens (such as ETH) are necessary (instrumental) to define the incentive structure required to operate a decentralised consensus protocol; this means that without the incentives generated through the issuance and transaction of a valuable token at layer 1 (as a reward for desired behaviour), the "Byzantine generals problem" cannot be resolved (Lamport et al., 1982) and a decentralised consensus cannot be achieved and implemented. Alternatively, ANTs are often necessary (instrumental) to ensure the stability, collateralization and solvency of many DeFi applications, as discussed above (Sect. 4.2.3); this means that without the creation, issuance and distribution of an ANT, the stability, liquidity and solvency of the DeFi application cannot be maintained and guaranteed, as the specific DeFi application would not be able to provide the right incentive mechanisms not only to attract liquidity providers and investors (such as in the case of liquidity mining), but also to incentivise participation in liquidations and conduct auctions in case of under-collateralization and possible insolvency.

The key characteristic of instrumental tokens derives from the fact that they create necessary incentive mechanisms for the implementations and enforcement of decentralised arrangements, while their value derives from the specific (instrumental) functionalities performed to operate and execute these decentralised protocols. Instrumental tokens are purposefully issued to optimally and efficiently operate a decentralised protocol over the DeFi stack and, for this reason, their value and usefulness are tightly linked to (and cannot be severed from) the value of the protocol. Instrumental tokens are therefore key to address the efficiency-decentralization trade-offs discussed above.

Tokens-as-Instruments Tokens-as-instruments may perform a layer-specific function, but they are mainly issued in order to fulfil functions external to, and independent of, the DeFi stack. In other words, their value can be severed from the operation of the underlying protocol or logical layer, and for this reason, they can be valuable and useful independently of the value and usefulness of any DeFi protocol. The value of tokens-as-instruments comes from their functions and utility outside the DeFi protocol stack. This is the case with pure payment tokens—such as fiat-backed (or even algorithmic) stablecoins—that are issued in order to develop digital payment services that can be operated independently from the operational, economic and procedural dynamics of DeFi protocols (Fig. 4). Tokens-as-instruments are not necessary to support specific incentive mechanisms in order to support and operate decentralised protocols. For this reason, they can be potentially operated independently from the logical and architectural solutions devised and may retain their value even if the underlying infrastructure of protocol becomes useless, is abandoned or replaced.

In sum, instrumental tokens are means to an end, where the "end" is the performance of some necessary functionality over the DeFi stack. On the other hand, tokens-as-instruments are ends in themselves, in the sense that the functionality of the underlying infrastructural logic can perform certain functionalities independently from the issuance and properties of the tokens. Typically, the former are necessary to create the right incentives in order to operate and enforce decentralised protocols and, for this reason, their utility and value cannot be severed from the usefulness and value of these decentralised protocols. Given their mutual instrumentality, a biunivocal relationship can be expected between the two: an

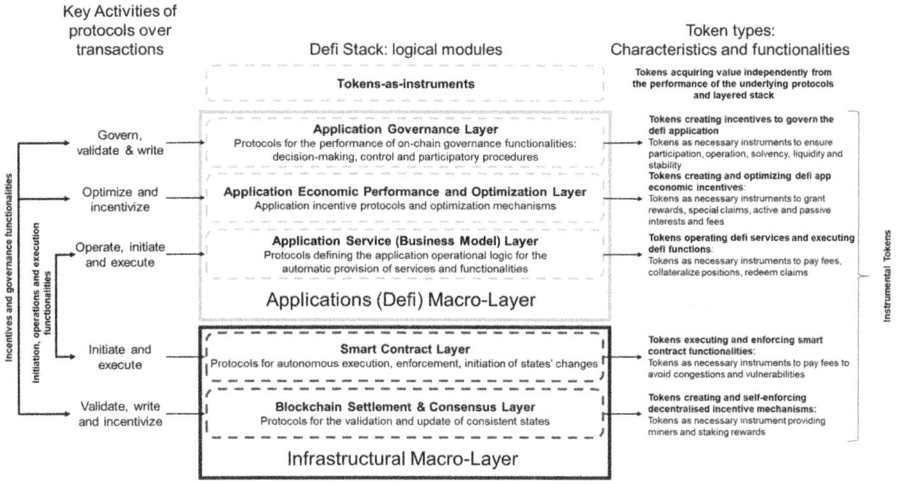

Fig. 4 Tokens-as-instruments (ends) and instrumental tokens (means) and the DeFi stack

increase in usefulness, adoption and value of the underlying protocols associated with the functions of the token automatically increases the utility, adoption and value of the token, and vice versa. On the other hand, the latter become more widespread and common in centralised contexts where the correct operation of a certain protocol, and the trust in its usefulness and value, derive from other types of institutional arrangements and incentive mechanisms.

5 A Final Layered Perspective: The DeFi Pyramid of Value (and Risk)

The previous sections have highlighted two main characteristics of the DeFi stack. First, the DeFi stack can be decomposed into functionally homogeneous protocols, consistent with the standard modularization process discussed by the modularity literature (Baldwin & Clark, 2000). Layers emerge from the modularization of a DeFi application into sets of functionally independent protocols, each operating specific functions for the performance of DeFi services. Second, the previous discussion has also highlighted that these different functions can only be performed with the help of specific instrumental tokens that provide the necessary incentives to correctly (or optimally) operate these protocols and fulfil their functions in a (more or less) decentralised manner. Different tokens operate at different layers for the fulfilment of different functions in the various different layers.

This parallelism between the logical layers of the protocol stack and the incentive mechanisms generated by the various tokens belonging to, or interacting with, the protocols in the various layers can be used to understand the nature and origin of value in DeFi applications. The overall value of a DeFi application or DeFi service is supported by a complex layer of incentive mechanisms operating at different layers of the DeFi stack, and relying on the issuance of different tokens playing different roles in the various functional layers.

As a result, this concluding section proposes a novel layered framework of value that here we rename "*the pyramid of value*" of DeFi applications.

On the one hand, the layers of the pyramid of value correspond to different dimensions of value of the overall DeFi application and, as a result, different types of (valuable) instrumental-tokens. For this reason, each dimension also corresponds to a specific incentive mechanism supported by a specific (layer-specific) token. As a result, in contrast to the standard DeFi stack, where layers correspond to functionally independent protocols, the various layers of the proposed pyramid of value correspond to different tokens playing specific roles in different incentive mechanisms. It is therefore not possible to establish a univocal mapping between the standard layered stack discussed above (which is a proper logical modularization of applications and software into its fundamental functionally-independent protocol modules), and the DeFi pyramid of value. In other words, the two follow two different logics of layered modularization.

On the other hand, the various layers of value are interdependent and logically ordered, so that each incentive mechanism—and dimension of value—relies on, and is supported by, the underlying one: in this way, each layer relies on the incentive structures and the values of tokens at a lower value layer to support its own incentive mechanisms and the value of tokens. Each layer is linked to the underlying one by means of specific stabilization mechanisms that rely on the stability of values of tokens in lower layers to stabilize the value of the token and the risk in the upper layer. In this way, risks at one layer rely on, and are addressed and managed by, mechanisms of the underlying layer, while failures to stabilize and support the value of the DeFi applications at any layer rely on increasingly deep and more fundamentals layers (and therefore more fundamental protocols and tokens) until the most fundamental layer of value is reached.

In sum, the DeFi pyramid of value (and risk) can be understood as a layered stack of instrumental tokens, each supporting a different incentive mechanism, where the value of each token and the incentive mechanisms at each layer are supported by, and rely on, the value of the tokens and the incentive mechanisms of the lower layer. Stabilization mechanisms link each layer to the underlying one and ensure that the loss of value of tokens, or the failure of the protocols and incentive mechanisms at any layer can be supported by, and fall back on, the incentive mechanisms supporting the value of the tokens in the lower layer (Fig. 5). This also means that failures of value of instrumental tokens operating at deeper and foundational layers may undermine the stability and value of the layers above it and therefore, ultimately, of the whole DeFi pyramid of value.

The specific nature of the pyramid of value will depend on the specific architectural solution adopted, as well as on the specific business model operated and service provided. In fact, different DeFi applications may employ different

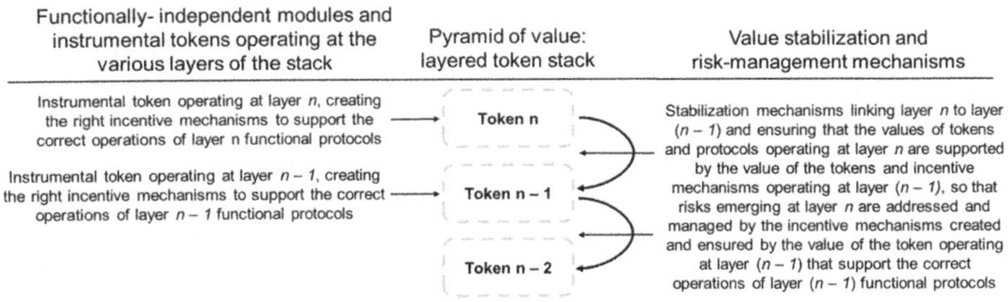

Fig. 5 A schematic representation of the DeFi value stack

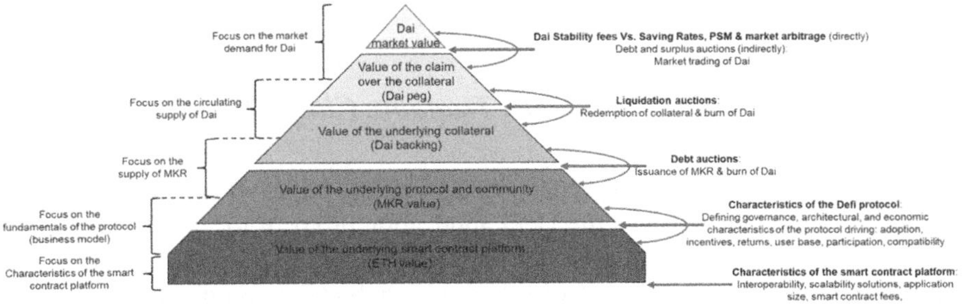

Fig. 6 Characterization of the DeFi pyramid of value as applied to MakerDAO

architecture, logical mechanisms and issue different types of tokens performing different functions and supporting different incentive mechanisms in order to achieve different purposes, as discussed above. This will generate different pyramids of value for different DeFi applications. Here, we try to develop a discussion as general as possible and, for the sake of simplicity, we mainly refer to the pyramid of value characterizing MakerDAO, even though the considerations developed below can be extended to a variety of other DeFi applications. Figure 6 provides a graphical representation of the pyramid of value as applied to MakerDAO. The figure highlights five different layers, each corresponding to the value of five different tokens.

Each layer relies on the one below it through the operation of stabilization mechanisms that use the value of the underlying tokens to support the value of the token operating in the layer above, as discussed above. A short-term stabilization mechanism links the two upper tokens and confers stability to short-term oscillations of value (mainly addressing market and operational risks); a medium-term mechanism ensures stability of value through liquidity and collateralization (mainly addressing counterparty credit and liquidity risk); a more long-term mechanism ensures the DeFi application overall solvency and acceptance (mainly addressing overall business, but also regulatory and application-counterparty risk); finally, a foundational layer, usually including native layer 1 tokens, ensures the viability of the underlying infrastructural macro-layer (mainly addressing foundational technological and cyber risks). Each layer therefore represents a dimension of value, but also a dimension of risk. A failure in any one of the layers relies on the correct support of the underlying layer. As a result, the risk management in one layer depends on the way in which risk is managed in the underlying layer.

It should be noted that, when the pyramid of value is applied to a DeFi service relying on the issuance of a crypto-backed stablecoin (such as Dai), the first three layers (from the top) correspond to the three main dimensions of value of a stablecoin as discussed in Rossi (2022b): the value of the token as means of exchange (top 5th layer), the value of the peg as unit (or reference) of value (4th layer), and the value of the collateral (the actual ultimate support of value of the issued stablecoin—3rd layer).

5.1 First Layer of Value: DeFi Tradable Claim-Tokens

This first, and most superficial, type of tokens are the claim-tokens issued by DeFi applications as claims against the DeFi application protocol for the redemption of the locked capital. These tokens can be freely traded and represent DeFi's first and probably most visible source of value: they embody the economic value of the claim issued by DeFi applications for the redemption of the capital locked into the DeFi's application smart contract wallet (even though in a non-custodial manner). Practically, the market price of these first types of tokens represents the market value of the bundle of contractual claims they grant against the DeFi protocol issuing them. These tokens are usually necessary instruments supporting DeFi services and therefore mainly belong to the business model or service layer of the DeFi stack: their value therefore mainly represents the market value of the DeFi application, which is also the first dimension of the value of a DeFi application.

Regardless of the specific way in which these tokens are defined and intended, their value is typically characterised by two main aspects (see Table 10).

First, they are typically all fungible and tradeable on the market; thus they can all, in principle, appreciate or depreciate based on the interaction between their supply and demand in the market. Given their fungibility, the final user can use these fungible tokens in a variety of ways and for a variety of reasons: (i) to conduct margin trading, (ii) to hedge risks against volatility and/or diversify, (iii) to be exposed to possible investment opportunities that require certain specific tokens (staking, liquidity mining), (iv) to short a token and perform arbitrage, (v) to play the market in general while still being able to retain ownership over its original tokens (that do not have to be traded away).

Second, they are all backed by the funds locked into the protocol's vaults or pools. It is the deposit of the funds to the protocol's address that triggered their minting, creation, and issuance by the protocol in the first place. Some of these tokens are also pegged to their underlying collateral (aTokens), others are pegged to yet a different asset (Dai), and still others are not pegged at all and are free to fluctuate (LP Tokens).

Table 10 DeFi claim-tokens issued in the application layer: dimensions of value

DeFi native claim-tokens: different types	Example	Dimensions of value
Crypto-collateralized stablecoin	Dai, sUSD (only when collateralized by ETH)	• Collateralized by cryptoassets • Pegged to fiat
Wrapped tokens (tokenized shares)	aETH, cDAI	• Collateralized by cryptoassets • Pegged to their collateral
LP tokens	1LP-ETH-USDC (Uniswap LP token)	• Collateralized by a basket (pair) of cryptoassets • Unpegged
Liquidity tokens (shares over funds)	yTokens	• Collateralized by a basket of assets • Unpegged
Synthetic tokens (derivatives)	sETH (when collateralized by SNX)	• Collateralized by a cryptoasset • Pegged to a different cryptoasset

A collapse of the market value of applications' native tokens generates the first degree of value instability of the DeFi value stack, and therefore the first layer of risk for DeFi applications. This is mainly a short-term risk (typically market risk or applications' operational risks). In this case, the second layer of value becomes relevant and plays a role in order to support the value of DeFi's claim-tokens.

5.2 *Second Layer of Value: Claim-Token Reference of Value (Stablecoin Peg)*

The evaluation of any loss of value has to be done against a benchmark, or reference point. The chosen reference of value can be simply based on temporal trends (historical), it can be against other relevant assets or tokens, it can be against a chosen objective or target (for instance a target profit of the application or token's holders), or it can be against a chosen peg if the asset has to track some other asset's underlying value. In other words, value stability and volatility are relative concepts (Rossi, 2022b). The possible unpegging of the claim-token from its reference value is therefore the first source of value instability and risk that a DeFi application can face, as discussed in Sect. 4.2.2. Not all DeFi applications provide services that are based on tokens pegged to other references of value (i.e. stablecoins) (Arner et al., 2020; Bullmann et al., 2019). For this reason, this second layer of value is not shared by all DeFi applications, but only by a specific set of DeFi applications providing services that need, and rely on, the issuance of stablecoins.

As a result, this second layer of the pyramid of value includes those tokens that represent the peg of the claim token operating one layer above them. The value of the peg-token (with respect to the value of the pegged-token) is the second source of value. The value of the peg provides the correct signals shaping and driving the incentive mechanisms operating at this layer.

When considering stablecoins, the de-pegging can emerge for a variety of reasons, such as the loss of value of the token's backing, or simply the short-term market fluctuations characterizing the exchange rate between the peg and the token, as discussed in Sect. 4.2.2. The former represents more fundamental issues addressed by the lower layer, (also defined as demand-side volatility—(Kwon et al., 2021; Lyons & Viswanath-Natraj, 2020)), while the latter includes demand-side mechanisms that rebalance the value of the claim-token through mechanisms acting on the demand and supply of the claim-token. As a result (as already discussed in Sect. 4.2.2 above), the value of the claim-tokens operating in the top layer of the pyramid of value is sustained by short-term (spot-market) stabilization mechanisms that implement specific monetary policy measures, such as the shift in interest rates and passive income granted by the claim-token to its holders, or the costs and fees associated with the holding of the claim-token. Provided that the peg is correctly valued by the market (incentive mechanisms at layer 4), this stabilization mechanism relies on the incentives provided by the market in exchanging the peg for the claim-token (and vice versa).

Failures to sustain the value of the claim-token by means of monetary policy mechanisms force the system to rely on even lower layers, thus introducing supply-side stabilization mechanisms.

5.3 Third Layer of Value: DeFi Collateralised Value Locked (Locked Tokens)

All DeFi applications operate by locking funds into pools or vaults that back, and can be recovered against, DeFi's native tokens. These funds have market value and represent DeFi applications' third layer of value. Even in this case, there is no homogeneity across DeFi applications as different DeFi applications admit different types of funds to be locked in their smart contract addresses, and these can be of different natures: layer-1 native tokens (ETH or BTC), layer-1 wrapped tokens (WBTC), governance tokens (COMP), DeFi native tokens (Dai), (centralized) fiat-backed stablecoins (USDC), or tokenized real assets (Maker's RWAs).

The value of the locked asset represents the backing of the issued claim-tokens and, for this reason, it supports the claim tokens' values, regardless of their short-term fluctuations on the market (also with respect to a possible peg). As discussed in Sect. 4.2.2, this means that the market value of the locked tokens provides the right incentives (at layer 3) to sustain and stabilize the value of the DeFi services and claim-tokens issued.

Table 11 Factors affecting the incentive mechanisms at layer three of the pyramid of value

Relevant dimensions of the collateral acting as the third layer of value
Composition and diversification
Liquidity
Stability with respect to the peg
Relationship with the native token
Additional sources of value
Additional costs generated
Extent of collateralization with respect to the native token
Liquidation ratio

On the one hand, whenever the locked tokens appreciate, the claim-token should appreciate and this should trigger incentives to conduct market arbitrage between locked tokens and claim-tokens. Alternatively, the right incentives can be re-established by the execution of more stringent monetary stabilization mechanisms one layer up (layer 2). On the other hand, whenever the value of the claim-token depreciates due to a fall in the market value of the locked tokens, new (layer 3) stabilization mechanisms are triggered to re-establish the right incentives. Various solutions can be adopted: either some incentive mechanisms are triggered in order to force claim-token holders to deposit more tokens as collateral (this can be done by increasing the fees or interest paid by token holders), or some incentive mechanisms will make it convenient for other actors (i.e. keepers in MakerDAO) to bid for the locked tokens and liquidate positions (Table 11).

This is the third layer of value of DeFi protocols that supports the first one: changes in the value of the collateral should be reflected in a change in value of the traded claims redeemable for this collateral. The collateralized tokens therefore act as the support of value for DeFi's fungible tokens. As discussed above, the incentive mechanisms generated by the collateralised tokens acting as the third layer of value can differ and vary in the various applications across a variety of dimensions (see Sect. 4.2.2). Stability mechanisms at this layer make sure that the collateral's locked value and the claim-token market value retain parity so that the latter can be supported by the former.

However, there are three main reasons why the stability mechanisms operating at this layer of the pyramid of value fail to provide the right incentives to sustain the value of the claim-token. First, the market does not trust the ability of the application to ensure the 1:1 redeemability of the claim-token against the collateral and keep discounting the claim-token price by some (more or less high) risk factor (counterparty risk). Second, the collateral may not be liquid enough to be easily recoverable, thus creating congestion and illiquidity (liquidity and operational risk). Third, there may be a reversed endogeneity between the DeFi native tokens and the locked tokens creating feedback loops of value between the dropping claim-token and the value of the collateral such as in the case of death spirals (Bullmann et al., 2019; Catalini & de Gortari, 2021). In any of these cases, the incentive mechanisms provided by the locked tokens and used by the layer 3 stability mechanisms may not be enough. The pyramid of value then moves one layer down.

5.4 Fourth Layer of Value: Application-Native Tokens (Governance Tokens)

The fourth layer of value of DeFi applications is usually represented by the market value of DeFi's governance tokens. Section 4.2.3 extensively discussed the role that governance tokens play in DeFi applications and the reason why it is better to call these tokens ANTs due to their multiple and variegated roles in DeFi applications. ANTs can be understood as utility, exchange, and governance tokens depending on the role played in DeFi applications. Regardless of its specific employment at various layers of the DeFi stack, ANTs usually provide the necessary incentives for users to participate in the broader ecosystem of the application and become actual shareholders in the DeFi application. In other words, the price of ANTs reveals that the market believes that having the power to shape, and contribute to, the definition of a DeFi application's rules, procedures, and decision making process is itself valuable and useful.

In general, valuable ANTs become necessary to ensure stability whenever the incentives leveraged by layer 3 stabilization mechanisms fail. As a result, layer 4 stabilization mechanisms relying on the value of ANTs become key whenever the value of tokens used as collateral (of backing) cannot provide the right incentives to sustain the value of DeFi applications and claim-tokens. In this case, DeFi applications usually exploit their ANTs to stabilize the value of their claim-tokens and re-establish stability: issuance of ANTs by the part of applications' reserves of governance protocols becomes the new (layer 4) stabilization mechanism. Of course, this novel stabilization mechanism can only fulfil its goal if the market values an application's ANT and, as a result, it values the powers and capabilities that holding ANTs confer on the users.

DeFi applications usually issue two tokens: claim-tokens (operating at layer 1 of the DeFi pyramid—business model or service layer of the DeFi stack), and ANTs (operating at layer 4 of the DeFi pyramid—mainly governance layer of the DeFi stack). For this reason, the latter can be understood as the dual of the former and characterized as the claim-token "dual token". Both are the application's native tokens.

The vital importance of the native ANT acting as the ultimate backer of a decentralized stablecoin can be appreciated by looking at the collapse of Terra UST on the week of 7–15 May 2022. Although there are fundamental differences between Maker and Terra Labs and between Dai and UST, the two share the same "layered backing" logic. As UST first de-pegged on the 7th and the 9th of May due to an oversupply of UST in the ecosystem, the system started to mint LUNA to redeem it for UST and lower its supply in the market. This is the equivalent of a debt auction in MakerDAO. Similar to what happened on "black Thursday", this depressed the market price of LUNA. However, in contrast to "black Thursday", a lack of confidence in the solvency and sustainability of the Terra system pushed redemptions to occur at increasingly lower prices of LUNA. As the capitalization of LUNA in the market fell below the overall value of circulating UST (May 9th), the underlying support of UST collapsed. This fuelled a death spiral where the increasingly low prices of the Terra ecosystem's governance token LUNA brought down the prices of UST and, with it, confidence in the value of the whole project (thus exacerbating the plunge of LUNA further).

The comparison between the MKR-LUNA experience shows that the ability of a dual governance token to maintain value in the face of oversupply represents the key ultimate support of the value of such systems.

5.5 *Fifth Layer of Value: The Layer 1 Consensus Token (Native Token of the Infrastructural Macro-Layer)*

The final layer of the pyramid of value is represented by the only non-application-specific token: the infrastructural layer 1 native token (here we do not distinguish between the two infrastructural layers). Overall, the value of any DeFi application strictly depends on the value of the underlying infrastructure and, for this reason, on the value of the token that provides the right incentive mechanisms to enforce the consensus protocol. For instance, settlement and smart contract layers that are extremely slow, congested, or non-scalable (not very useful or usable), and/or extremely isolated and restricted (not interconnected), and/or extremely vulnerable or unreliable (not secure) are not good solutions to develop DeFi ecosystems. This poor value of the infrastructural layer should be reflected in a low value of their native (layer 1) consensus tokens. In this case, incentives are created in the lowest layer of the stack.

As a result, the last layer of the pyramid of value supporting the value of a DeFi application is represented by the value of the infrastructure native token and the incentive mechanisms that this supports (both from a consensus and settlement point of view and smart contract execution point of view).

There is no doubt that DeFi applications developed over ecosystems relying on unvalued infrastructures will suffer and most likely be valued poorly by the market. As a result, a valuable native token is a necessary condition for sustaining the value of any DeFi application and its claim-tokens. In this case, stability mechanisms sustaining the value of the application can be the likes of: low gas fees, the availability of dedicated bridges to ensure interoperability, the availability of cheap and efficient layer-2 solutions for the application (such as rollups), the possibility to leverage some type of technical or economic support from the community, and so forth.

On the other hand, a high value of the layer-1 native token may not be sufficient to support the value of specific DeFi applications. This will depend on the specific characteristics of the DeFi application and on the peculiar nature of the services provided.

References

Amler, H., Eckey, L., Faust, S., Kaiser, M., Sandner, P., & Schlosser, B. (2021). *Defi-ning defi: Challenges & pathway*. IEEE.

Ao, Z., Horvath, G., & Zhang, L. (2022). *Are decentralized finance really decentralized? A social network analysis of the Aave protocol on the Ethereum blockchain*. arXiv preprint arXiv:2206.08401.

Aramonte, S., Huang, W., & Schrimpf, A. (2021). DeFi risks and the decentralisation illusion. *BIS Quarterly Review*, 21–36.

Aramonte, S., Doerr, S., Huang, W., & Schrimpf, A. (2022). *DeFi lending: Intermediation without information?* Bank for International Settlements.

Armstrong, M. (2006). Competition in two-sided markets. *The RAND Journal of Economics, 37*(3), 668–691.

Arner, D. W., Auer, R., & Frost, J. (2020). *Stablecoins: Risks, potential and regulation*. BIS Working Paper, 905.

Atzei, N., Bartoletti, M., & Cimoli, T. (2017). *A survey of attacks on ethereum smart contracts (SoK)*.

Azouvi, S., & Hicks, A. (2021). *Sok: Tools for game theoretic models of security for cryptocurrencies*.

Baldwin, C. Y. (2008). Where do transactions come from? Modularity, transactions, and the boundaries of firms. *Industrial and Corporate Change, 17*(1), 155–195.

Baldwin, C. Y., & Clark, K. B. (2000). *Design rules: The power of modularity*. MIT Press.

Baldwin, C. Y., & Woodard, C. J. (2009). The architecture of platforms: A unified view. In A. Gawer (Ed.), *Platforms, markets and innovation* (Vol. 32, pp. 19–44). Edward Elgar.

Bamakan, S. M. H., Motavali, A., & Bondarti, A. B. (2020). A survey of blockchain consensus algorithms performance evaluation criteria. *Expert Systems with Applications, 154*, 113385.

Bano, S., Sonnino, A., Al-Bassam, M., Azouvi, S., McCorry, P., Meiklejohn, S., & Danezis, G. (2019). Consensus in the age of blockchains. In *Proceedings of the 1st ACM Conference on Advances in Financial Technologies. Association for Computing Machinery*, pp. 183–198.

Barbereau, T., Smethurst, R., Papageorgiou, O., Rieger, A., & Fridgen, G. (2022a). DeFi, not so decentralized: The measured distribution of voting rights. In *Paper presented at the Proceedings of the 55th Hawaii International Conference on System Sciences*.

Barbereau, T., Smethurst, R., Papageorgiou, O., Sedlmeir, J., & Fridgen, G. (2022b). *Decentralised finance's unregulated governance: Minority rule in the digital wild west*. Available at SSRN.

Bartoletti, M., Chiang, J. H.-Y., & Lafuente, A. L. (2021a). SoK: Lending pools in decentralized finance. In *Paper presented at the Financial Cryptography and Data Security. FC 2021 International Workshops. FC 2021, Berlin, Heidelberg*.

Bartoletti, M., Chiang, J. H.-Y., & Lafuente, A. L. (2021b). *Towards a theory of decentralized finance*.

Beck, R., Müller-Bloch, C., & King, J. L. (2018). Governance in the blockchain economy: A framework and research agenda. *Journal of the Association for Information Systems, 19*(10), 1.

Bichuch, M., & Feinstein, Z. (2022). *Axioms for automated market makers: A mathematical framework in FinTech and decentralized finance*. arXiv preprint arXiv:2210.01227.

BIS, & IOSCO. (2021). *Application of the principles for financial market infrastructures to stablecoin arrangements. BIS Paper(106)*.

Brennecke, M., Guggenberger, T., Schellinger, B., & Urbach, N. (2022). *The De-Central Bank in decentralized finance: A case study of MakerDAO.*

Bullmann, D., Klemm, J., & Pinna, A. (2019). *In search for stability in crypto-assets: Are stablecoins the solution? ECB Occasional Paper(230).*

Buterin, V. (2017). The meaning of decentralization. *Medium.com, 2021.*

Buterin, V., & Griffith, V. (2019). *Casper the friendly finality gadget.* arXiv preprint arXiv:1710.09437.

Cabigiosu, A., & Camuffo, A. (2016). Measuring modularity: Engineering and management effects of different approaches. *IEEE Transactions on Engineering Management, 64*(1), 103–114.

Campajola, C., Cristodaro, R., De Collibus, F. M., Yan, T., Vallarano, N., & Tessone, C. J. (2022). *The evolution of centralisation on cryptocurrency platforms.* arXiv preprint arXiv:2206.05081.

Carter, N., & Jeng, L. (2021). *Defi protocol risks: The paradox of defi. "Regtech, suptech and beyond: Innovation and technology in financial services" RiskBooks–Forthcoming Q*, 3.

Catalini, C., & de Gortari, A. (2021). *On the economic design of stablecoins.* Available at SSRN 3899499.

Catalini, C., & Massari, J. (2021). Stablecoins and the future of money. *Harvard Business Review*, 10.

Catalini, C., de Gortari, A., & Shah, N. (2021). *Some simple economics of stablecoins.*

Cousaert, S., Xu, J., & Matsui, T. (2022). *Sok: Yield aggregators in defi.*

Croman, K., Decker, C., Eyal, I., Gencer, A. E., Juels, A., Kosba, A., Miller, A., Saxena, P., Shi, E., & Gün Sirer, E. (2016). On scaling decentralized blockchains. In *Paper presented at the International conference on financial cryptography and data security, Berlin, Heidelberg.*

Daian, P., Goldfeder, S., Kell, T., Li, Y., Zhao, X., Bentov, I., Breidenbach, L., & Juels, A. (2019). *Flash boys 2.0: Frontrunning, transaction reordering, and consensus instability in decentralized exchanges.* arXiv preprint arXiv:1904.05234.

Darlin, M., Palaiokrassas, G., & Tassiulas, L. (2022). *Debt-financed collateral and stability risks in the DeFi ecosystem.*

De Filippi, P., & Hassan, S. (2018). *Blockchain technology as a regulatory technology: From code is law to law is code.* arXiv preprint arXiv:1801.02507.

Deshmukh, S., Warren, S., & Werbach, K. (2021). *Decentralized Finance: (DeFi) Policy-maker toolkit* (Vol. 8, 6th ed.). WEF.

Eskandari, S., Moosavi, S., & Clark, J. (2020). *Sok: Transparent dishonesty: Front-running attacks on blockchain.*

European Commission. (2020). *Proposal for a regulation of the European Parliament and of the council on markets in crypto-assets, and amending directive. 593 final.*

Eyal, I., & Sirer, E. G. (2018). Majority is not enough: Bitcoin mining is vulnerable. *Communications of the ACM, 61*(7), 95–102.

Feenan, S., Heller, D., Lipton, A., Morini, M., Ram, R., Sams, R., Swanson, T., Yong, S., & Zalles, D. B. (2021). Decentralized financial market infrastructures: Evolution from intermediated structures to decentralized structures for financial agreements. *The Journal of FinTech, 1*(02), 2150002.

Fritsch, R., Müller, M., & Wattenhofer, R. (2022). *Analyzing voting power in decentralized governance: Who controls DAOs?* arXiv preprint arXiv:2204.01176.

Gangwal, A., Gangavalli, H. R., & Thirupathi, A. (2022). A survey of layer-two blockchain protocols. *Journal of Network and Computer Applications, 103539.*

Gans, J. S. (2019). *The fine print in smart contracts.* National Bureau of Economic Research.

Garud, R., Kumaraswamy, A., & Langlois, R. (2009). *Managing in the modular age: Architectures, networks, and organizations.* Wiley.

Gencer, A. E., Basu, S., Eyal, I., Van Renesse, R., & Sirer, E. G. (2018). Decentralization in bitcoin and ethereum networks. In *Paper presented at the Financial Cryptography and Data Security. FC 2018. Lecture Notes in Computer Science*, Vol. 10957.

Gogel, D. (2021). *DeFi beyond the hype: The emerging world of decentralized finance.*

Grewatsch, S., Kennedy, S., & Bansal, P. (2021). Tackling wicked problems in strategic management with systems thinking. *Strategic Organization.* https://doi.org/10.1177/147612702110386

Gudgeon, L., Moreno-Sanchez, P., Roos, S., McCorry, P., & Gervais, A. (2020a). Sok: Layer-two blockchain protocols. In *Paper presented at the Financial Cryptography and Data Security. FC 2020. Lecture Notes in Computer Science*.

Gudgeon, L., Perez, D., Harz, D., Livshits, B., & Gervais, A. (2020b). *The decentralized financial crisis*.

Gudgeon, L., Werner, S., Perez, D., & Knottenbelt, W. J. (2020c). *Defi protocols for loanable funds: Interest rates, liquidity and market efficiency*.

Hafid, A., Hafid, A. S., & Samih, M. (2020). Scaling blockchains: A comprehensive survey. *IEEE Access, 8*, 125244–125262.

Hardjono, T. (2021). *Blockchain gateways, bridges and delegated hash-locks*. arXiv preprint arXiv:2102.03933.

Henderson, R. M., & Clark, K. B. (1990). Architectural innovation: The reconfiguration of existing product technologies and the failure of established firms. *Administrative Science Quarterly, 35*(1), 9–30.

Henderson, M. T., & Raskin, M. (2019). A regulatory classification of digital assets: Toward an operational Howey test for cryptocurrencies, ICOs, and other digital assets. *Columbia Business Law Review, 443*.

Holden, R. T., & Malani, A. (2019). *Can blockchain solve the hold-up problem in contracts?* (Vol. 25833). National Bureau of Economic Research.

Hylving, L., & Schultze, U. (2020). Accomplishing the layered modular architecture in digital innovation: The case of the car's driver information module. *The Journal of Strategic Information Systems, 29*(3), 101621.

IOSCO. (2022). OR01/2022 IOSCO decentralized finance report. *IOSCO Public Reports, 2022*, 1–45.

Jourenko, M., Kurazumi, K., Larangeira, M., & Tanaka, K. (2019). *SoK: A taxonomy for layer-2 scalability related protocols for cryptocurrencies*. Cryptology ePrint Archive.

Kallinikos, J., Aaltonen, A., & Marton, A. (2013). The ambivalent ontology of digital artifacts. *MIS Quarterly*, 357–370.

Kao, H.-T., Chitra, T., Chiang, R., & Morrow, J. (2020). *An analysis of the market risk to participants in the compound protocol*.

Karakostas, D., Kiayias, A., & Ovezik, C. (2022). *SoK: A stratified approach to blockchain decentralization*. arXiv preprint arXiv:2211.01291.

Kirillov, A., & Chung, S. (2022). *StableSims: Optimizing MakerDAO liquidations 2.0 incentives via agent-based modeling*. arXiv preprint arXiv:2201.03519.

Klages-Mundt, A., & Minca, A. (2020). *While stability lasts: A stochastic model of stablecoins*. arXiv preprint arXiv:2004.01304.

Klages-Mundt, A., & Minca, A. (2021). *(In)Stability for the blockchain: Deleveraging spirals and stablecoin attacks*. arXiv preprint arXiv:1906.02152.

Kokoris-Kogias, E., Jovanovic, P., Gasser, L., Gailly, N., Syta, E., & Ford, B. (2018). Omniledger: A secure, scale-out, decentralized ledger via sharding. In *Paper presented at the 2018 IEEE Symposium on Security and Privacy (SP)*.

Kozhan, R., & Viswanath-Natraj, G. (2021). *Decentralized stablecoins and collateral risk. WBS Finance Group Research Paper Forthcoming*.

Kwon, Y., Liu, J., Kim, M., Song, D., & Kim, Y. (2019). Impossibility of full decentralization in permissionless blockchains. In *Paper presented at the Proceedings of the 1st ACM Conference on Advances in Financial Technologies (AFT'19)*. Association for Computing Machinery.

Kwon, Y., Kim, J., Kim, Y., & Song, D. (2021). *The trilemma of stablecoin*. Available at SSRN 3917430.

Lamport, L., Shostak, R., & Pease, M. (1982). The Byzantine generals problem. *ACM Transactions on Programming Languages and Systems, 4*(3), 382–401.

Langlois, R. N. (2002). Modularity in technology and organization. *Journal of Economic Behavior & Organization, 49*(1), 19–37.

Langlois, R. N., & Robertson, P. L. (1992). Networks and innovation in a modular system: Lessons from the microcomputer and stereo component industries. *Research Policy, 21*(4), 297–313.

Lee, A. S. (2010). Retrospect and prospect: Information systems research in the last and next 25 years. *Journal of Information Technology, 25*(4), 336–348.

Lee, A. S., Thomas, M., & Baskerville, R. L. (2015). Going back to basics in design science: From the information technology artifact to the information systems artifact. *Information Systems Journal, 25*(1), 5–21.

Li, Y., & Mayer, S. (2021). *Money creation in decentralized finance: A dynamic model of stablecoin and crypto shadow banking.* CESifo Working Paper, No. 9260, Center for Economic Studies and ifo Institute (CESifo), Munich (2020-03): 030.

Li, W., Bu, J., Li, X., & Chen, X. (2022). *Security analysis of DeFi: Vulnerabilities, attacks and advances.* arXiv preprint arXiv:2205.09524.

Lima, G., & Rossi, E. (2022). Distributed ledger technology and the evolution of post trade. *Journal of Securities Operations & Custody, 14*(3), 248–282.

Liu, Z., Luong, N. C., Wang, W., Niyato, D., Wang, P., Liang, Y.-C., & Kim, D. I. (2019). A survey on blockchain: A game theoretical perspective. *IEEE Access, 7*, 47615–47643.

Liu, B., Szalachowski, P., & Zhou, J. (2021). *A first look into defi oracles.*

Lo, Y., & Medda, F. (2020). *Uniswap and the rise of the decentralized exchange.* Accessed from https://mpra.ub.uni-muenchen.de/103925/

Lyons, R. K., & Viswanath-Natraj, G. (2020). *What keeps stablecoins stable?* National Bureau of Economic Research WP, No. w27136.

Makarov, I., & Schoar, A. (2022). *Cryptocurrencies and Decentralized Finance (DeFi).* National Bureau of Economic Research.

Maker Team. (2020). *The maker protocol: MakerDAO's Mulfi-Collateral Dai (MCD) System.*

McCorry, P., Buckland, C., Yee, B., & Song, D. (2021). *Sok: Validating bridges as a scaling solution for blockchains.* Cryptology ePrint Archive.

Meegan, X., & Koens, T. (2021). *Lessons learned from decentralised finance (DeFi).* ING. Accessed from https://new.ingwb.com/binaries/content/assets/insights/themes/distributed-ledger-technology/defi_white_paper_v2. 0.pdf

Meier, O., & Sannajust, A. (2021). The smart contract revolution: A solution for the holdup problem? *Small Business Economics, 57*(2), 1073–1088.

Meyer, E., Welpe, I. M., & Sandner, P. G. (2021). *Decentralized finance—A systematic literature review and research directions.* Available at SSRN 4016497.

Mohan, V. (2022). Automated market makers and decentralized exchanges: A DeFi primer. *Financial Innovation, 8*(1), 1–48.

Mueller-Bloch, C., Andersen, J. V., Spasovski, J., & Hahn, J. (2022). *Understanding decentralization in proof-of-stake blockchains: An agent-based simulation approach.* Available at SSRN 4149460.

Nabilou, H. (2022). *Probabilistic settlement finality in proof-of-work blockchains: Legal considerations.* Amsterdam Law School Research Paper, 2022-04(2022-04).

Nadler, M., & Schär, F. (2020). *Decentralized finance, centralized ownership? An iterative mapping process to measure protocol token distribution.* arXiv preprint arXiv:2012.09306.

Narayanan, A., Bonneau, J., Felten, E., Miller, A., & Goldfeder, S. (2016). *Bitcoin and cryptocurrency technologies: A comprehensive introduction.* Princeton University Press.

OECD. (2022). *Why Decentralised Finance (DeFi) matters and the policy implications.* OECD.

Østbye, P. (2019). *Who is liable if a cryptocurrency protocol fails?* Available at SSRN 3423681.

Parnas, D. L. (1972). On the criteria to be used in decomposing systems into modules. In *Pioneers and their contributions to software engineering* (pp. 479–498). Springer.

Pasdar, A., Dong, Z., & Lee, Y. C. (2021). *Blockchain oracle design patterns.* arXiv preprint arXiv:2106.09349.

Pasquale, F. (2019). A rule of persons, not machines: The limits of legal automation. *The George Washington Law Review, 87*, 1.

Poon, J., & Dryja, T. (2016). *The bitcoin lightning network: Scalable off-chain instant payments.*

Qin, K., Zhou, L., Afonin, Y., Lazzaretti, L., & Gervais, A. (2021a). *CeFi vs. DeFi–Comparing centralized to decentralized finance.* arXiv preprint arXiv:2106.08157.

Qin, K., Zhou, L., Livshits, B., & Gervais, A. (2021b). *Attacking the defi ecosystem with flash loans for fun and profit*.
Qin, K., Zhou, L., Gamito, P., Jovanovic, P., & Gervais, A. (2021c). *An empirical study of defi liquidations: Incentives, risks, and instabilities*. In Proceedings of the 21st ACM internet measurement conference (pp. 336–350).
Qin, K., Zhou, L., & Gervais, A. (2022). Quantifying blockchain extractable value: How dark is the forest? In *Paper presented at the 2022 IEEE Symposium on Security and Privacy*.
Rochet, J.-C., & Tirole, J. (2003). Platform competition in two-sided markets. *Journal of the European Economic Association, 1*(4), 990–1029.
Rossi, E. (2022a). *Defi Defi-Ned: An analytical framework for the definition and characterization of Defi*. Available at SSRN 4322901.
Rossi, E. (2022b). *Stablecoins in three dimensions: Foundations of value in the crypto-economy*. Available at SSRN 4123691.
Rossi, E., & Sørensen, C. (2019). *Towards a theory of digital network de/centralization: Platform-infrastructure lessons drawn from blockchain*. Available at SSRN 3503609.
Rossi, E., & Sørensen, C. (2022, May 14). *The meaning of de/centralization: A theoretical review, towards a conceptual framing*.
Saengchote, K. (2021, July 26). *Where do DeFi stablecoins go? A closer look at what DeFi composability really means*.
Saengchote, K., Putniņš, T., & Samphantharak, K. (2022). *Does DeFi remove the need for trust? Evidence from a natural experiment in stablecoin lending*. arXiv preprint arXiv:2207.06285.
Safadi, H., Johnson, S. L., & Faraj, S. (2020). Who contributes knowledge? Core-periphery tension in online innovation communities. *Organization Science, 32*(3).
Saleh, F. (2021). Blockchain without waste: Proof-of-stake. *The Review of Financial Studies, 34*(3), 1156–1190.
Salehi, M., Clark, J., & Mannan, M. (2021). *Red-black coins: Dai without liquidations*.
Schad, J., & Bansal, P. (2018). Seeing the forest and the trees: How a systems perspective informs paradox research. *Journal of Management Studies, 55*(8), 1490–1506.
Schär, F. (2021). Decentralized finance: On blockchain-and smart contract-based financial markets. *FRB of St. Louis Review*.
Schilling, M. A. (2000). Toward a general modular systems theory and its application to interfirm product modularity. *Academy of Management Review, 25*(2), 312–334.
Sedlmeir, J., Buhl, H. U., Fridgen, G., & Keller, R. (2020). The energy consumption of blockchain technology: Beyond myth. *Business & Information Systems Engineering, 62*(6), 599–608.
Simon, H. A. (1962). The architecture of complexity. *Proceedings of the American Philosophical Society, 106*(6), 467–482.
Sklaroff, J. M. (2017). Smart contracts and the cost of inflexibility. *University of Pennsylvania Law Review, 166*, 263.
Sterman, J. (2002). *System dynamics: Systems thinking and modeling for a complex world*.
Sun, X., Stasinakis, C., & Sermpinis, G. (2022). *Decentralization illusion in DeFi: Evidence from MakerDAO*. arXiv preprint arXiv:2203.16612.
Ulrich, K. (1995). The role of product architecture in the manufacturing firm. *Research Policy, 24*(3), 419–440.
Van Schewick, B. (2012). *Internet architecture and innovation*. MIT Press.
Wang, G., Shi, Z. J., Nixon, M., & Han, S. (2019a). *Sok: Sharding on blockchain*.
Wang, W., Hoang, D. T., Hu, P., Xiong, Z., Niyato, D., Wang, P., Wen, Y., & Kim, D. I. (2019b). A survey on consensus mechanisms and mining strategy management in blockchain networks. *IEEE Access, 7*, 22328–22370.
Wang, Z., Qin, K., Minh, D. V., & Gervais, A. (2022). Speculative multipliers on defi: Quantifying on-chain leverage risks. In *Financial cryptography and data security*.
Weill, P., & Ross, J. W. (2004). *IT governance: How top performers manage IT decision rights for superior results*. Harvard Business Press.
Werbach, K. (2018). Trust, but verify: Why the blockchain needs the law. *Berkeley Technology Law Journal, 33*, 487.

Werbach, K., & Cornell, N. (2017). Contracts ex machina. *Duke Law Journal, 67*, 313.
Werner, S. M., Perez, D., Gudgeon, L., Klages-Mundt, A., Harz, D., & Knottenbelt, W. J. (2021). *Sok: Decentralized finance (defi)*. arXiv preprint arXiv:2101.08778.
Wieandt, A., & Heppding, L. (2022). *Centralized and decentralized finance: Coexistence or convergence?* Available at SSRN 4046173.
Xiao, Y., Zhang, N., Lou, W., & Hou, Y. T. (2020). A survey of distributed consensus protocols for blockchain networks. *IEEE Communications Surveys & Tutorials, 22*(2), 1432–1465.
Xu, T. A., & Xu, J. (2022). *A short survey on business models of Decentralized Finance (DeFi) protocols*. arXiv preprint arXiv:2202.07742.
Xu, X., Weber, I., Staples, M., Zhu, L., Bosch, J., Bass, L., Pautasso, C., & Rimba, P. (2017). A taxonomy of blockchain-based systems for architecture design. In *Paper presented at the IEEE international conference on software architecture (ICSA)*.
Xu, J., Paruch, K., Cousaert, S., & Feng, Y. (2021). *Sok: Decentralized exchanges (DEX) with automated market maker (AMM) protocols*. arXiv preprint arXiv:2103.12732.
Yeung, K. (2019). Regulation by blockchain: The emerging battle for supremacy between the code of law and code as law. *The Modern Law Review, 82*(2), 207–239.
Yoo, C. S. (2013). Protocol layering and Internet policy. *University of Pennsylvania Law Review*, 1707–1771.
Yoo, Y., Henfridsson, O., & Lyytinen, K. (2010). Research commentary—The new organizing logic of digital innovation: an agenda for information systems research. *Information Systems Research, 21*(4), 724–735.
Zetzsche, D. A., Arner, D. W., & Buckley, R. P. (2020). Decentralized finance. *Journal of Financial Regulation, 6*(2), 172–203.
Zhang, S., & Lee, J.-H. (2019). Double-spending with a Sybil attack in the bitcoin decentralized network. *IEEE Transactions on Industrial Informatics, 15*(10), 5715–5722.
Zhang, S., & Lee, J.-H. (2020). Analysis of the main consensus protocols of blockchain. *ICT Express, 6*(2), 93–97.
Zhang, L., Ma, X., & Liu, Y. (2022). *SoK: Blockchain decentralization*. arXiv preprint arXiv:2205.04256.
Zhao, W., Li, H., & Yuan, Y. (2021). *Understand volatility of algorithmic stablecoin: Modeling, verification and empirical analysis*.
Zhao, X., Ai, P., Lai, F., Luo, X., & Benitez, J. (2022). Task management in decentralized autonomous organization. *Journal of Operations Management*.
Zhou, L., Qin, K., & Gervais, A. (2021). *A2mm: Mitigating frontrunning, transaction reordering and consensus instability in decentralized exchanges*. arXiv preprint arXiv:2106.07371.

Enrico Rossi This paper was developed and written when Enrico was the research lead of the "Distributed Financial Market Infrastructure" group at the Cambridge Center for Alternative Finance (CCAF) at Cambridge University (Judge Business School), and research associate of the UCL Centre for Blockchain Technologies (CBT). Enrico has been named "2020-21 Academic blockchain influencer of the year" by the UK BIG Innovation Centre for his contribution to the UK All-Party Parliamentary Group on Blockchain. Enrico holds a PhD and a Master's degree in management and economics from the London School of Economics (LSE), where he co-created and led LSE's first online course in cryptoassets. Enrico is currently a senior associate at the UK Financial Conduct Authority (FCA) where he develops cryptoasset policy, focussing on wholesale markets and trading policy. All views and positions expressed in this paper have been written while at Cambridge, prior to joining the FCA, and do not represent the FCA's current position.

Modelling Persistence in Cross-Market Bitcoin Prices with a Break and a Memory

Ahmad Maaitah and Tapas Mishra

> No memory is ever alone; it's at the end of a trail of memories, a dozen trails that each have their own associations.—Louis L'Amour (From the book Ride the River, 1983)

1 Introduction

1.1 Background and Context

With a promise to break away from central banks' intervention in the currency-regulation, virtual currencies—particularly Bitcoin, have paved an unshakable pathway of growth—moving from a period of despondency to a sustained period of consolidation and expansion since its inception by Satoshi Nakamoto (2008). Such a growth has yet to be characterized by a financial theoretic foundation and therefore its future movements can be encapsulated partly by a comparison with a theory-backed asset market and partly by modeling the hidden features of the data. It is not always true that a theory drives procedures of empirical testing; a sound empirical analysis of a given data can also sow the seed of designing a theory. It is nowhere so true than in the virtual currency markets because investors have only access to data that may help them identify a realistic pattern by wading through complex waters of methods of heterogeneous efficacy. This chapter focuses on the empirical characterisation of Bitcoin market data and drawing possible parallels to existing economic and financial theories.

A. Maaitah (✉)
Center for Digital Finance, University of Southampton, Southampton, UK
e-mail: Ahmad.Maaitah@soton.ac.uk

T. Mishra
University of Southampton, Southampton, UK

A. Zarifis, X. Cheng (eds.), *Fintech and the Emerging Ecosystems*, Financial Innovation and Technology, https://doi.org/10.1007/978-3-031-83402-8_6

Our primary emphasis is on a 'jointness' exercise, that is, to allow both a memory (or persistence) and a break in the series, where the latter is assumed to be driven by endogenous events. The endogenous fluctuations are largely confounded in the literature as recent work shows that the persistence feature in a time series may be confused with the prevalent effects of a shock (mostly of an exogenous nature). In this chapter, we argue that to model Bitcoin price fluctuations and the hidden memory structure leading to reliable predictive power, one needs to recognise that Bitcoin price changes are largely different from other theory-backed assets in the financial markets. The mediating or moderating effects of theory-driven fundamental values of asset prices with frequently occurring break points (of exogenous nature mostly) work as a 'shock absorber', whereas Bitcoin prices are fundamentally driven by sentiments. Here the theoretical value of sentiment itself is the fundamental value of Bitcoin prices. Psychologically though we know fluctuations of sentiments are not primarily driven by exogeneous shocks. Rather, an innate tendency of sentiment is the endogenous nature of its evolution. Accordingly, in this chapter, we present extensive arguments and empirical evidence that both endogenous switches and persistence (long memory) are compatible with the observed growth pattern of Bitcoin prices across markets.[1] From the tradition of economic growth theory, we know that such 'memory' and 'endogenous switches' are features of an endogenous growth mechanism in the sense that an effective policy intervention can maneuver growth. In the Bitcoin market, such growth dynamics would imply that a policy to impact the 'peer-to-peer impulse response would approximate the hidden growth of this currency to the dynamism in a regular asset market.

An important aspect of our contribution is to uncover the magnitude of memory or the extent of slow convergence of shocks or the extent to which the current value of a system depends on a remote past value. In fact, *emory* is imperishable during the life of a boundedly rational agent. The only characteristic note one can say about the existence of memory is whether it is small or big and the long or short 'trail' of associations it inherently defines over a period of time—just as Louis L'Amour (an American author) has famously quoted. In a recent research, for example, Cheah et al. (2018) employed a fractional cointegrated vector autoregressive approach to understand the nature of memory within the Bitcoin-markets interactive system. Similarly, Caporale et al. (2018) examined long-memory features in cryptocurrency markets.

Our work contributes to the nascent literature on the source and implications of 'memory' in cryptocurrency market, in particular, Bitcoin markets in the following three significant ways. *First*, we propose an identification strategy to demonstrate the source and implications of a long-memory in Bitcoin markets. We discuss them

[1] Chevallier et al. (2019) combine Markov-switching models with Lévy jump-diffusion to capture various sub-period of crises over the business cycle. The authors conclude that cryptocurrencies exhibit high volatility and leverage effects (at least in one regime), whereas two-regime models yield better results in terms of prediction.

with regard to the efficient market hypothesis, one that is commonly discussed in financial economics. We propose a demand-driven long-memory channel for Bitcoin and show that there are waves of Buyer initiated transactions (given a fixed supply for Bitcoin), which follow a Beta distribution with memory, by following a linear algorithm of aggregation and power distribution. *Second*, we model (non-)existence of long-memory to an endogenous/exogenous market system mechanism which might give rise to a persistent shock with or without a mean reversion.[2] We discuss this in light of an endogenous switch in memory and mean of the Bitcoin price process. *Third*, using daily Bitcoin data for five different markets, we study the nature of persistence in Bitcoin returns/volatility while considering an endogenous switch in return/volatility. From this, we shed light on the nature of directional predictability of Bitcoin prices across these markets and quantify to what extent a 'memory' governs the internal dynamics of the system.

The choice of Bitcoin for our empirical examination is led by the fact that it is the biggest and most active cryptocurrency with a market capitalisation of over $150[3] billion. In the absence of strict monetary and financial regulations, cryptocurrency investors seem to be quickly moving from a state of despondency (due to recurrent losses from their investments in regulated financial markets) to one of hope (because Bitcoin prices are fundamentally driven by the 'feeling and the memory' of investors at a point of time. To investigate the nature of such types of investment decisions and help governments design adequate regulations for limiting cross-market movement of shocks, a remarkable growth of research has sprung lately.

1.2 Why Endogenous Switch?

The Efficient Market Hypothesis (EMH) assumes that the market is sufficiently fast and responsive to converge on an equilibrium price that correctly reflects all external, or so-called *exogenous* information. It further assumes that all internal or endogenous processes are already reflected in prices. Hence, following this view, only exogenous inputs (viz., an exchange hack, a central bank announcement, or a geopolitical event) can change investors' anticipations and prices. Consequently, extreme events, such as bubbles or crashes, are shown to result from exogenous

[2] An important endogeneous mechanism, such as halving block rewards in Bitcoin protocol in every four years so that the miners receive when they contribute a so-called 'block' of transactions to the blockchain. Built into the protocol to control Bitcoin's (BTC) inflation, the previous halvings have coincided with massive rallies, for instance, after the first halving, which occurred in November 2012, Bitcoin's price increased from $12 to more than $650. After the second halving in July 2016, the price accelerated to almost $20,000 in late-2017. While it's of course uncertain whether the next halving will accelerate prices, the halvings seemed to have driven Bitcoin's previous hype cycles. Naturally, the next halving has generated an intense debate whether it's already priced in or not.

[3] coinmarketcap.com (June 2019).

news that has not been factored into prices yet. For those who put trust in EMH, for them Bitcoin's supply schedule—which is encoded into the protocol and known since the inception of the network—constitutes *endogenous* information and should, accordingly, already be priced in.

The EMH has poor predictive power as there is a robust evidence that prices move too much compared with what one would expect from the EMH. Research shows that only a small fraction of price movements can be explained by relevant news releases. Such findings suggest that price dynamics are mostly driven by endogenous positive feedback mechanisms between investors' anticipations and prices—a phenomenon popularly known as 'market reflexivity.' Irrespective of whether the stock-to-flow model is valid or not, whether one believes in the EMH what's often under-appreciated in these debates is the fundamentally reflexive nature of financial markets. Markets, and especially bitcoin, are reflexive phenomena. There's a positive feedback mechanism between expectations and prices: expectations affect prices, which, in turn, influence traders' or investors' expectations and behaviour. It's this self-reinforcing positive feedback loop that's also at the core of speculative bubbles and market crashes.

Under this backdrop, we propose the identification of endogenous switches in cross-market Bitcoin prices in a memory-embedded embedded environment. It serves two important purposes: first, endogenous switches imply the effectiveness of policy-controls as these switches are often triggered by policies/manipulation of prices (see Neil Gandal et al., 2018), rather than just any exogenous shocks. Second, such switches also characterise the nature of persistence in the series. In particular, if there is a long-memory (or a slow-convergence of shocks), the price growth system in Bitcoin markets can identify reactions as well as path-dependence of reactions to positive or negative shocks. For our purpose, we employ the rich features of Markov Switching Autoregressive Fractionally Integrated Moving Average (MS-ARFIMA) model.

The findings from this work have two important implications for investors and policy makers. First, the presence of long memory could enable investors to capture speculative profits and this can be achieved through market timing. During a high-volatility regime, investors could buy and then subsequently sell when the market switches to a low-volatility regime in all Bitcoin cross-markets. Investors could also hedge during a high-volatility regime by purchasing Bitcoin futures from the Chicago Board Options Exchange (CBOE). Second, as for policy makers and regulators could introduce circuit breakers to stop trading in Bitcoin cross-markets when the market switches abruptly to a high-volatility regime as the impact of a negative down turn would take a relatively long period of time to dissipate given the nature of persistence in the price behaviour of Bitcoin in the cross-markets.

To investigate further, the rest of the chapter is planned as follows. Section 2 presents a synoptic overview of the literature on long memory in the Bitcoin market. Section 3 discusses empirical methodology. Section 4 presents data and summery statistics and presents preliminary results on stationarity tests. In Sect. 5, we present and discuss the results. Section 6 presents a robustness exercise and finally, Sect. 7 concludes and presents the main implications of our research.

2 Literature Overview

Cryptocurrency market has recently received significant attention due to its important role in global financial markets. Thus, a significant growth of research has sprung recently to help governments and policy makers to design adequate regulations on controlling cross-market movement shocks, also, to discriminate and facilitate the best investment decisions for financial institutions, investors and portfolio managers.

An excellent systematic survey done recently (Corbet et al., 2019) reveals that the literature has focused mainly on three theoretical and empirical research areas; First, regulations and information system research, second financial market and monetary theoretical formulation of cryptocurrency, third, development of econometric and/or statistical mechanism to understand price behaviour under different scenarios. Another systematic review done by Kyriazis (2019) explores the cryptocurrency research under efficient market hypotheses and long-range dependence, which the latter provides us with very crucial inferences in determining the best investment strategies for gaining extraordinary returns. To maintain the flow of our ideas in the chapter and minimise repetition and space of a succinct literature review, interested readers are encouraged to refer to the latter two surveys.

Investigating the regulations and information system of cryptocurrencies allows authorities and legislators to derive suitable laws and regulations with boundaries to increase the efficiency and decrease the frustration and manipulation of the market (Böhme et al., 2015; Dwyer, 2015; Neil Gandal et al., 2018). A growing literature in economics and financial markets simultaneously with the latter phase of research has helped individual investors, investment entities and risk managers to hedge and diversify their investments to maximise the profit with the lowest associated risk (Baur et al., 2018; Gillaizeau et al., 2019; Urquhart & Zhang, 2019). Despite the sparse literature on cryptocurrencies in finance and economics, much excellent research in different areas, such as market efficiency, price and/or bubble dynamics, hedging and diversification strategies and many others, has attempted to examine the cryptocurrency market and Bitcoin in particular.

A plethora of empirical research has systematically presented state-of-the-art estimation techniques to identify, among others, the efficiency of Bitcoin market (Brauneis & Mestel, 2018; Khuntia & Pattanayak, 2018; Wei, 2018) which they adopted different methods to support the efficiency of Bitcoin market and concluded that the level of efficiency is associated with some factors such as liquidity and size. On the contrary, many support the fact that Bitcoin market is in lack of efficiency due to the imbalance between the true value of Bitcoin and its available information in the market (Bouri et al., 2019; Urquhart, 2016; Vidal-Tomás & Ibañez, 2018). Investigating the connectedness/spillovers and market dynamics provides a clear indication of the market inefficiency, also, useful information about the net receiver and net dispenser of Bitcoin volatility (Corbet et al., 2018; Gillaizeau et al., 2019).

A wide range of empirical research focuses also on long-range persistence, cointegration and structural breaks to explain the complex behaviour and non-linear dynamics of Bitcoin prices (Alvarez-Ramirez et al., 2018; Caporale et al., 2018; Cheah et al., 2018). The existence of long-range dependence in return and volatility prices indicate for informational inefficiency in the market, hence, speculation, forecasting and designing profitable investment strategies can be exploited to make abnormal profits, but ignoring the stability of the system during the analysis process could generate misleading information. Many others have analysed the time-varying behaviour of long-range dependence through different tests such as Hurst exponent and detrended fluctuation analysis *DFA* and Exact local whittle estimation with rolling windows (Alvarez-Ramirez et al., 2018; Bariviera, 2017, 2017; Caporale et al., 2018; Cheah et al., 2018). The statistical properties overtime are subjected to change suddenly, especially in Bitcoin market, which may leave some distortion along shocks permanency, hence, structural breaks tests are very crucial to validate the long-range stability process (Al-Yahyaee et al., 2018; Bouri et al., 2019; Charfeddine & Maouchi, 2019; Mensi, 2018; Mensi et al., 2019). A very long debate in the literature discusses that the presence of structural break in a time series could appear as high long-range persistence, thus, level shifts and long memory are easily confused (Diebold & Inoue, 2001).

In contrast, former studies such as Chaim and Laurini (2018), shed light on stochastic volatility models with shifts in mean and variance for a ‘cryptocurrency market’ and ‘other asset markets’ (such as indices and gold), (Cheah et al., 2018) demonstrated the importance of cross-market dynamic interdependence of Bitcoin prices by estimating a system-wide long-memory. The focus on a cross-market rather than a single-market cryptocurrency market in the latter study holds significance in our context: by modelling the theory of endogenous and exogenous growth mechanisms and aligning designed empirical tests to show whether persistence is a product of such a model. Aligning an empirical model to that of a grounded theory is important to generate the best predictions and this is precisely one of the main objectives of this chapter.

We propose a variant of ARFIMA Markov Switching with an endogenous switch governing the internal dynamics of the Bitcoin price or volatility system. This endogenous process is synchronised with growth-theoretic mechanisms and shows the credible role of policy in containing volatility persistence.

3 Methodology

Autoregressive (AR) models are designed to capture the nature of ‘past-dependence’ of a time series. Memory features (viz. short, long or intermediate) are reflections of the nature of past-dependence. In this section, we present and distinguish among three classes of AR models: a Markov Switching AR (MS-AR), a Markov Switching Autoregressive Moving Average (MS-ARMA) and a Markov Switching Autoregressive *fractionally integrated* Moving Average (MS-ARFIMA) models. The MS-ARFIMA is our focal point of application, however, to understand its superiority, it is important to present a brief analytical architecture of both MS-AR and MS-ARMA models.

3.1 Markov Switching Auto-regressive (MS-AR)

Hamilton (1989) introduced a discrete shift in the regime process through an auto-regressive model to trace the dynamic behaviour of a time series. To illustrate that, we should consider that the mean (intercept) of an auto-regressive model is non-constant overtime. Thus, different auto-regressive models should be built after each break point to boost the efficiency of detecting the non-linearity in a time series. Models (1) and (2),[4] below, illustrate how considering two different intercepts could help in solving the turning point problems in time series.

$$x_t = \alpha_1 + \beta x_{t-1} + \epsilon_t, \tag{1}$$

$$x_t = \alpha_2 + \beta x_{t-1} + \epsilon_t, \tag{2}$$

where $\alpha_{1 \wedge 2}$ the constant terms and $\epsilon_t \sim i.\ i.\ dN(0, \sigma^2)$. The concept of the latter models is plausible, but not effective to be processed individually. Econometrically, changing the behaviour of series in the past and in the future (e.g. changing the intercept) should be considered in a unified model to provide a reliable forecasting. In this regard, the above models or more could be compressed in a one framework and then allow the process to switch among intercepts by an unobserved variable S_t, which S_t called regime or state variable (e.g. $S_t = 1, 2, 3, \ldots$).[5] Consequently, Eqs. (1) and (2) can be rewritten as:

$$x_t = \alpha_{S_t} + \beta x_{t-1} + \epsilon_t, \tag{3}$$

where $S_t = 1$ when the process is in state 1 (α_1), in contrast, $S_t = 2$ when the process is in state 2 (α_2). Equation (3) follows a normal distribution with different means and variances. Hamilton (1989) considered latter regimes to be an unobserved random variable or in other words discrete-valued stochastic variable. Mathematically, the Markov chain process is the simplest and proper model to deal with the travelling process among regimes within the system. Before start explaining the Markov chain, let us first set S_t to be an integer number as $(1, 2, 3, \ldots, N)$. Second, Assume that S_t equals a specific amount of j and the probability of obtaining j depends totally on the most recent past value S_{t-1}. Latter specification can be written mathematically as:

$$p = \{S_t = j | S_{t-1} = i, S_{t-2} = m, \ldots\} = p\{S_t = j | S_{t-1} = i\} = p_{ij} \tag{4}$$

[4] Some researchers considering these models as zero mean, see Cochrane (2005), Hamilton (1994).

$$x_t - \alpha_1 = \beta(x_{t-1} - \alpha_1) + \epsilon_t.$$

[5] Notice here, if S_t, $t = 1, 2, \ldots$ is defined as observable variable (known in advance), then the process is simply a dummy variable auto-regressive.

where $p_{ij}, {}_{ij=1,2,3,\ldots N}$ in which p_{ij} is the transition probability, i is the state in time $\{_{t-1}\}$ and j is the state in time $_t\}$. By probability law the sum of all p_{ij} must be equal to 1.

$$p_{i1} + p_{i2} + p_{i3} + \cdots + p = 1, \tag{5}$$

Transition probabilities could be compressed into $(N \times N)$ matrix, called the transition probability matrix or P:

$$P = \begin{pmatrix} p_{11} & p_{21} & \cdots & p_{N1} \\ p_{12} & p_{22} & \cdots & p_{N2} \\ \vdots & \vdots & \cdots & \vdots \\ \vdots & \vdots & \cdots & \vdots \\ p_{1N} & p_{2N} & \cdots & p_{NN} \end{pmatrix} \tag{6}$$

In this transition probabilities matrix, the column indicates to ith and the row indicates the jth of p_{ij} in Eq. (5). For instance, the column 2, row 1 parameter indicates the probability that state 2 will be followed by state 1. In other words, transition probabilities should give some inference for choosing the current state among the states in the system:

$$\begin{aligned} P\{S_t = 2|S_{t-1} = 2\} = p \\ P\{S_t = 1|S_{t-1} = 1\} = q \end{aligned} \tag{7}$$

In case the system has two states (as in our case), four transition probabilities will be generated: staying in the same state (p or q) or switching from state to state $(1 - p)$ or $(1 - q)$. In general, after forecasting the Markov chain the mixture model could be executed by the expectation maximisation (ME) algorithm.[6,7,8]

(a) **Markov Switching Auto-regressive Moving Average (MS-ARMA)**

The latter subsection has introduced a general class of the MS-AR process (Hamilton, 1989). In this subsection, an $MS - ARMA$ model will be introduced to build an initial idea about $MS - ARFIMA$ model. Chen and Tsay (2011) investigated the problem of 'N^t possible routs' when the system contains MA parameters by

[6] Hamilton assumed that the state is just depends on the most recent past value $\{S_{t-1}\}$ and ignore all others $\{S_{t-2}, S_{t-3}, S_{t-4}, \ldots\}$.

[7] For more information about MS-AR see Kim (1994). See also Kim et al. (1999) to explore different calculation methods of Markov switching model.

[8] Markov chain can be represented through vector auto-regression framework to calculate all possible number of ahead forecasts of the process. Notice here, the matrix P must be irreducible $(p_{11} < 1 \wedge p_{22} < 1)$ otherwise the state will be an absorbing state (the process will stay in this process forever), to review the full process see Hamilton (1989, 1994).

building a new algorithm based on Gray's (1996), and Hamilton (1989)'s ideas and calling it the extended Hamilton–Gray (EHG) algorithm. However, the N-state in MS-ARMA (*p*,*q*) model can be written as follows with respect to Eqs. (4)–(7):

$$x_t = \alpha_{st} + \Sigma_{i=1}^{p} \beta \left(x_{t-i} - \alpha_{st-i}\right) + \epsilon_t + \Sigma_{i=1}^{q} \delta_i \epsilon_{t-i}, \epsilon_t \sim i.i.d.N\left(0, \sigma_{st}^2\right) \quad (8)$$

The model above is identical to Eq. (3) plus the MA term $(\delta_i \epsilon_{t-i})$. Some restrictions as invertibility and stationarity on AR MA polynomials among each state should be identified:

$$Y_{s_t}(L) = 1 - \alpha_{1,s_t} L - \cdots - \alpha_{p,s_t} L^p, \; \Xi_{s_t}(L) = 1 + \delta_{1,s_t} L + \cdots + \delta_{q,s_t} L^q. \quad (9)$$

where $Y_{s_t}(L) \wedge \Xi_{s_t}(L)$ are the roots of polynomials and by assumption they should be all outside the unit root circle. Moreover, both polynomials of AR & MA do not share any common roots.[9] However, when $q \neq 0$ EM algorithm cannot be employed, basically, because the possible routs of regimes that run from $t_1 t_i$ is going to expand exponentially '$N^{T'}$'.[10] Consequently, their algorithm is able to trace the past history of x_t up to a particular lag to extract the error terms from x_t instead of tracing the entire past history of x_t. Hence, the approach is recursively analysing the conditional expectation of lagged ϵ_{t-N} the process could be estimated efficiently. For more approaches to resolve the same problem see Billio et al. (1999), Billio and Monfort (1998), Kim (1994).

After calculating the population parameters of the switching-regime model based on EHG algorithm a smooth and efficient process can easily analyse the mixture model in Eq. (8).[11]

(b) **Markov-Switching Auto-regressive Fractional Integral Moving Average (MS-ARFIMA)**

An insightful method has been developed by Tsay and Härdle (2009) will be adopted to investigate the Bitcoin volatility across financial markets. In this subsection ARFIMA process and Markov switching model will be demonstrated in detail.

AR, ARMA or ARIMA are formally a special case of the most generalised model ARFIMA process. The former models functionally capture only the short-range dependence (SRD), per contra the latter process was modified to be able

[9] After forecasting the probabilities, an inference on the regimes can be build through Bayesian theorem, by combining the information of current and past data, transition probabilities and distributions. The latter combination can generate inference for each date t in the sample data, this process called the smoother recursion, see Kim (1994) for more details.

[10] See Chen and Tsay (2011), Assumption 1.

[11] Notice here, this problem arise when the system is going to filter out all the sequence of error terms $(\epsilon_1, \ldots, \epsilon_t)$ to proceed the MLE.

to trace the short-range and long-range (LRD) dependence. However, combining the Markov-switching model with long memory enables us to study the fractional order of integrations with the presence of structural breaks simultaneously and endogenously through a unified framework. This process is known to be more efficient and robust to capture the complex behaviour of exchange rates across financial markets, otherwise, neglecting both latter phenomenon could generate very deceptive inference (Diebold & Inoue, 2001; Haldrup & Nielsen, 2006; Tsay & Härdle, 2009).

Previous subsections explore how auto-regressive and auto-regressive moving-average models with the Markov-switching process can be employed to trace the complex dynamic behaviour of a time series. (Tsay & Härdle, 2009) introduced fractional integration to the above model (MS-ARMA), thus three main parameters are able to switch within MS $-$ ARFIMA(p, d, q) process. A fractional integral process (η), is defined as follows:

$$(1 - L)^d x_t = \epsilon_t \tag{10}$$

where 'L' is the back shift operator, ϵ_t is identically independently distributed and $0 < d < 1$. The long memory process is stationary when $d > 0$ and non-stationary when $d \geq 0.5$. Fractional integration process d features by the slow hyperbolic decaying of the auto-correlation function:

$$\rho\,(\eta) = \frac{\Gamma\,(\eta + d)\,\Gamma\,(1 - d)}{\Gamma\,(\eta - d + 1)\,\Gamma(d)},\ \text{where}\ \rho\,(\eta) \sim \frac{\Gamma\,(1 - d)}{\Gamma(d)}\eta^{2d-1} \tag{11}$$

where $\rho(\eta)$ is the auto-correlation function of x_t at lag η, $\Gamma(\cdot)$ is gamma function, (x_t) in Eq. (10) represents ARFIMA$(0, d, 0)$, η is the lag of x_t.

After introducing MS-AR between Eqs. (3) and (7) the long memory process in the latter equations can be combined with Markov chain to produce MS-ARFIMA(p,d,q) as follows:

$$x_t = \alpha_{st} \cdot I\,(t \geq 1) + (1 - L)^{-d_{st}} \cdot \sigma_{st} \cdot \psi_t \cdot I\,(t \geq 1) = \alpha_{st} I\,(t \geq 1) + y_t \tag{12}$$

where x_t is the observed time series, $I(\cdot)$ is the indicator function, ψ_t is a stationary zero-mean process with spectral density $F_\psi(\lambda) \sim G_0\ as\ \lambda \to 0$ at each state. The ARMA process is stationary and invertiable and y is simple ARFIMA $(0, d, 0)$ process.

The fractional differencing (d_{st}) in the latter process is permitted to be a Markov chain, but considering one condition that s_t is independent of ψ_τ for all t and τ. However, it is well known that Hamilton (1989)'s algorithm cannot be employed to estimate the latter model and the reason is consist with the problem of estimating $MS - ARMA$ in the previous subsection.[12] Thus, the possible routs of regimes that

[12] See Chen and Tsay (2011) for the full process.

running from $t_1 t_i$ are expanding exponentially 'N^T'.[13] Moreover, because of the fractional differencing parameter, $MS - ARFIMA$ process cannot be build in a state-space form. As a consequence, Tsay and Härdle (2009) derived a new algorithm called Durbin–Levinson–Viterbi (*DLV*) to cop with the limitation above. Their new algorithm was built based on a combination of two separate and well-known algorithms in the literature; Durbin–Levinson algorithm and the Viterbi algorithm. Thus, *DLV* algorithm is now solving two major problems: ARFIMA model with a hidden Markov process can be estimated efficiently and the puzzle proposed by Diebold and Inoue (2001) is solved now. *DLV* algorithm now can capture the long memory of a time series with the existence of potential structural breaks in its mean.

To employ Durbin–Levinson (DL) algorithm mathematically let us consider Eq. (12) in its simplest case which the long memory parameters are constant among the states (d_0). ϵ_t is a zero mean and independently and identically distributed. Technically, We can employ (DL) algorithm to execute the latter specification (d_0) and the likelihood function of the process can be written as:

$$L(S_T, X_T; \zeta) = \prod_{(t=1)}^{T} (2\pi)^{(-0.5)} \cdot u_{t-1}^{-0.5} \cdot \exp\left(-\frac{(y_t - \hat{y}_t)^2}{2u_{t-1}}\right) \cdot P(s_t \vee s_{t-1}), \tag{13}$$

where T is the total sample, $X_T = (x_1, \ldots, x_t)^{\perp}$ is the column vector for the whole observation from time 1 to t, $S_t = (s_1, \ldots, s_t)^{\perp}$ is the corresponding regimes and ζ[14] is column vector of both the transition probabilities p_{ij} and the vector parameter ν, which $\nu = (\alpha_1, \ldots, \alpha_N; \sigma_1, \ldots, \sigma_N; Y_{11}, \ldots, Y_{1p}; Y_{21}, \ldots, Y_{Np}; d_1, \ldots, d_N; \Xi_{11}, \ldots, \Xi_{Nq})^{\perp}$. $\hat{y}_t$ is a one-step-ahead predictor of y_t, u_t is the corresponding one-step ahead forecasting variance.

Equation (13) is appropriate to implement the Viterbi algorithm. Therefore, by combining the latter algorithm with Durbin–Levinson algorithm, d_0 can shifts among two states d_{s_t}, which *DLV* now can detect the long memory parameter of a time series with the presence of a Markov-switching in mean.

As we mentioned earlier model (12) is no longer can be written in a state space form because of the long memory parameter and identifying the possible state paths expand exponentially.[15] The path of possible regimes can be rewritten as follows:

$$\begin{aligned}(S_{t-1}(s_t = j), s_t = j) = (&s_1(s_t = j), s_2(s_t = j), \\ &s_3(s_t = j), \ldots, s_{t-1}(s_t = j), s_t = j)\end{aligned} \tag{14}$$

[13] Notice here, if $d_{st} = 0$, then the process is still MS-AR model (Hamilton, 1989).

[14] This problem arise when the process is going to filter out all the sequence of error terms $(\epsilon_1, \cdots, \epsilon_t)$ to proceed the MLE.

[15] Notice here, this parameter is representing the conditional density function (CDF) of X_t.

4 Data and Preliminary Results

4.1 Data

The data collected is daily high and low (H–L) exchange rates of Bitcoin against five major currencies across the world—namely, the U.S. dollar (USD), the Australian dollar (AUD), the Canadian dollar (CAD), the Euro (EUR), the British Pound (GBP). The sample span start from Jan 1st, 2015 to March, 13th, 2019. All the Bitcoin prices were obtained from (Bitcoinity.org),[16] to check the accuracy of prices we compared our sample spans with Quandle and bitcoicharts. As mentioned above, a plethora of literature claimed that the Bitcoin market is isolated from other conventional markets. Consequently, we are interested in investigating the cross-market Bitcoin prices system, as studying the Bitcoin dynamics will provide rich information about the factors that affect price developments and help us in nesting efficient investment strategies.

To choose the ideal Bitcoin prices against each currency, we take into consideration the trading volume across all the platforms of each currency (e.g. USD, CAD, GBP, AUD and EUR) in Bitcoin market. We found that trading volume of USD in Bitfinex platform exceeded 185 Billion over the last five years, which makes the market share of the latter platform is around 40.98% to overtake almost half the market in trading Bitcoin in USD. Kraken platform has executed transactions of BTC/EUR by around 32 Billion over the last five years, and the market share of trading Bitcoin/Eur via this platform is around 34%.[17] GBP, CAD and AUD were traded intensively on Bit-X, Quadrigacx and Btcmarkets platforms respectively. The market share of trading Bitcoin in the latter 3 currencies are 52%, 75% and 85% respectively.

The first difference of natural logarithm was applied to the daily prices to transform them into daily continuously compounded returns, by the following equation:

$$R_t = \ln(P_t) - \ln(P_{t-1}) \tag{15}$$

We compute Parkinson's High-Low historical volatility (HL-HV) model to overcome the weaknesses in the conventional volatility model. Close-to-close volatility model neglects the sensitivity of trading hours, hence, lots of valuable information will be excluded (Bennett & Gil, 2012). Parkinson's model produces more significant signals and improves the efficiency of the volatility estimate (Parkinson, 1980). Bennett and Gil (2012), and Parkinson (1980) claim that Parkinson's volatility measure is more efficient and productive than conventional close-to-close volatility estimates.

---

[16] For the full process of Viterbi algorithm see Tsay and Härdle (2009).

[17] https://data.bitcoinity.org/markets/volume/30d?c=e&t=b

Table 1 Summary statistics, exchange rate volatility

Exchange rate	Mean	S.D	Min	Max	Skewness	Kurtosis
BTC/USD	0.631	0.543	0.051	5.364	2.560	13.79
BTC/EUR	0.609	0.554	0.062	6.975	3.082	21.11
BTC/GBP	0.602	0.556	0.045	7.468	3.507	26.63
BTC/AUD	0.661	0.565	0.050	4.866	2.941	15.47
BTC/CAD	0.617	0.515	0.079	4.838	2.731	14.23
Obs.			1533			

Formally, V for each of our five Bitcoin-to-currency exchange rates is calculated as follows.

$$V = \left(\frac{1}{4\ln(2)} . \ln\left(\frac{h}{l}\right)^2 \right) \tag{16}$$

where h and l are the highest and lowest exchange rates on a given trading day, respectively. The estimator above computes the daily variance, hence, the corresponding estimate of the annualised daily percent standard deviation (volatility) is computed as follows:

$$\text{Vol} = \sqrt{365 * V}.$$

4.2 *Summary Statistics*

Table 1 displays the descriptive statistics of Bitcoin volatility for the 5 major currencies. The number of observations is 1533 across the variables.[18] The average volatility across all variables is fluctuating around 0.6, which is the highest and lowest mean across the sample are AUD (0.661) and GBP (0.602) respectively. Observing the second moment, we can notice that the S.D across the 5 variables is bounded between CAD (0.515) and AUD (0.565).Thus, the average of S.D. is approximately 0.5. The five exchange rates display large positive skewness, suggesting a large concentration of observations to the left of their central tendency, hence, volatility series are asymmetrically distributed. Bitcoin prices are sensitive to major economic and political events, and all extreme shocks can be explained through the four moments. All series show unequivocally leptokurtic behaviours, in which Kurtosis is different across individual series and ranges from around 14 on average (BTC/USD, BTC/CAD and BTC/AUD) to about 25 (BTC/EUR and BTC/GBP).

[18] From Jan 1, 2015 to March 13, 2019.

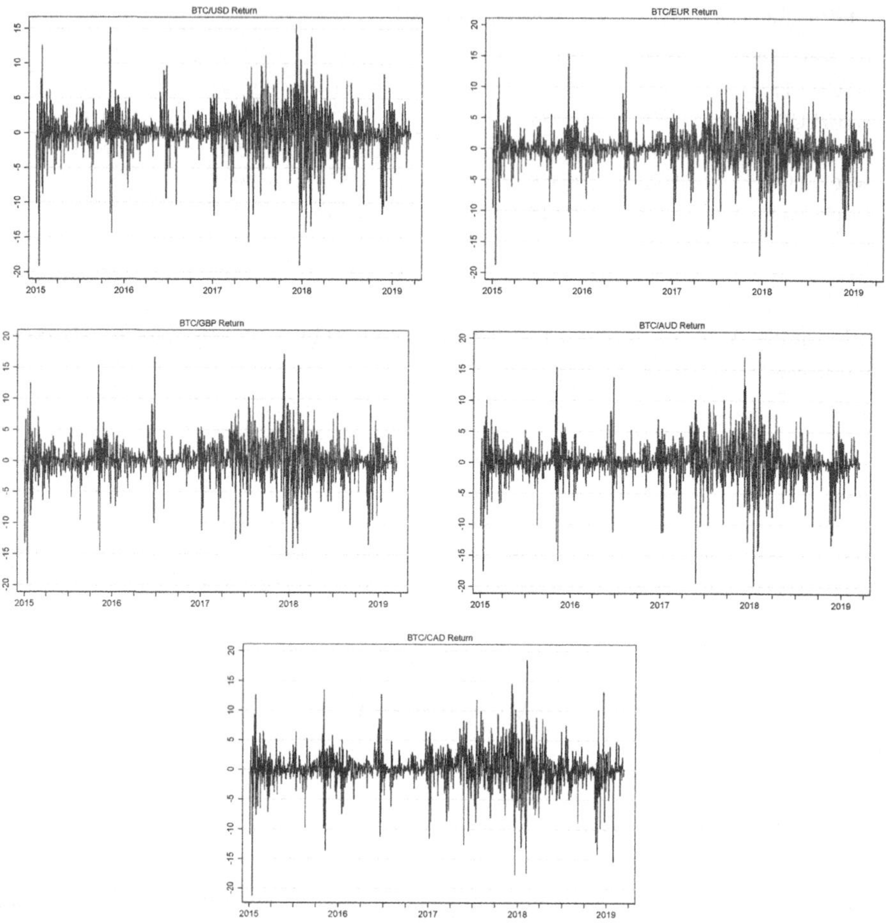

Fig. 1 Bitcoin daily return of five markets. *Note*: top left corner USD, top right EUR, middle left GBP, middle right AUD and bottom CAD. Exchange rate returns, daily. Dates on the *x*-axis indicate the start of the year and ticks are quarterly

Overall, Fig. 1 display the returns series overtime across the five markets. During the first quarter of 2015, an extreme negative shock happened across the five markets. Then, in the end of the same year episodes of high and negative returns were recorded. Tracking the entire return series across the five markets can give us an indication that the most fluctuating period was from the middle of July to the first quarter of 2018. Therefore, Fig. 1 hinting that the instability of return is most notable during three different periods across the five markets (e.g. 2015, 2016 and 2018).

Figure 2 displays the volatility of five Bitcoin markets over the time. BTC/EUR and BTC/GBP show the highest shock across the whole system to record just around 7 in both markets. Visually, we can confirm that BTC/USD and BTC/EUR are the

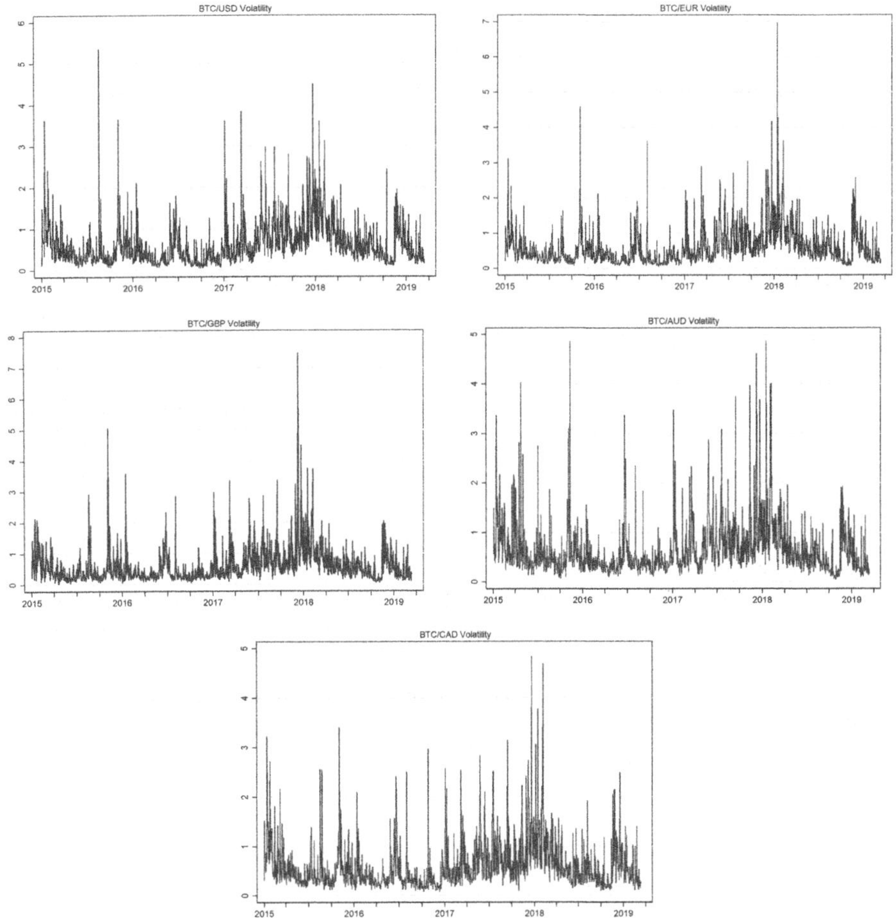

Fig. 2 Bitcoin daily volatility of five markets. *Note*: top left corner USD, top right EUR, middle left GBP, middle right AUD and bottom CAD. Exchange rate volatility, daily. Dates on the x-axis indicate the start of the year and ticks are quarterly

most stable markets which both series most of the time fluctuating below 2 except for the period around 2018. Also, extensive fluctuations across the entire system appear mainly around 2018 and partially between 2015 and 2016 hinting that some events such as Brexit and platform breaches led the Bitcoin prices to be remarkably sensitive.

In the next subsection, the sample properties are diagnosed as stationarity, long memory and structural breaks.

4.3 Stationarity and Long Memory Estimation

Diagnosing the stationarity of exchange rates series through Augmented Dicky Fuller *ADF* and the Kwiatkowski–Phillips–Schmidt–Shin *KPSS* unit root tests is required (Dickey & Fuller, 1979; Kwaitkowski et al., 1992). In order to find an initial evidence of the presence of long memory, the estimated parameters of *ADF* and *KPSS* can give a general indication of the fractional integration. If the conclusions of both tests are different, this means a long memory process may exist in every individual series. Table 2 shows both latter tests, in which *ADF* test rejected the null hypothesis at 1% significant level and *KPSS* has rejected the null hypothesis at 1% significance level except those indicated by a star. On one hand, *ADF* test is admitting the stationarity of the 5 exchange rates series. On the other hand, *KPSS* test fails to reject the alternative hypothesis across the series which indicates that the series are unity. Consequently, the joined rejection of both tests hints that both tests provided insufficient representation of either $I(0)$ or $I(1)$ and a fractional process should be adopted. So, to explore the long memory process, we should employ a long memory time-varying technique to investigate the long-range dependence as 'Local, Exact local, Feasible Exact Local and 2-step Exact local whittle' estimation of fractional integration (more discussion in Sect. 5) (Shimotsu & Phillips, 2005; Shimotsu, 2010). However, before moving directly to the fractional integration we should stop for a while to investigate the potential break points in Bitcoin markets, hence the long memory and turning points phenomena are easily confused[19] (Diebold & Inoue, 2001). In the next section both phenomena will be introduced individually, then combined in a one unified framework.

5 Main Results

We have discussed this far, various methods to analyse fractional integration and switching models. In this section, we discuss results to shed light on the dynamics of the Bitcoin market. The basis for our estimation is the MS-ARFIMA model developed by Tsay and Härdle (2009) in order to analyse the persistency behaviour and dynamics across different Bitcoin markets under scrutiny (BTC/USD, BTC/EUR, BTC/GBP, BTC/AUD and BTC/CAD). The results of the multiple break point test (Bai & Perron, 1998) and fractional integration test (Shimotsu, 2010) are discussed in the beginning to allow us to explain how MS-ARFIMA process aggregates the latter two phenomena and clear the confusion among turning points and long memory in a time series.[20] Indeed, investigating the dynamics of

[19] We find the optimal Bitcoin data can be obtained from bitcoinity.org.

[20] Both phenomena shows slow decaying of the auto-correlation function.

Table 2 ADF and Phillips–Perron unit root tests, exchange rate volatility

Exchange rate	*Test*	Test stat	Critical	Conclusion value 1%	Test stat	Critical	Conclusion value 1%
	Model with constant				**Model without constant**		
BTC/USD	*ADF*	−7.682	−3.43	Rejected	−4.191	−2.58	Rejected
	KPSS	0.952	0.739	Rejected	–	–	–
BTC/EUR	*ADF*	−9.254	−3.43	Rejected	−4.122	−2.58	Rejected
	KPSS	1.044	0.739	Rejected	–	–	–
BTC/GBP	*ADF*	−8.714	−3.43	Rejected	−2.932	−2.58	Rejected
	KPSS	0.991	0.739	Rejected	–	–	–
BTC/AUD	*ADF*	−9.237	−3.43	Rejected	−4.0917	−2.58	Rejected
	KPSS	0.412	0.347**	Rejected	–	–	–
BTC/CAD	*ADF*	−9.291	−3.43	Rejected	−3.680	−2.58	Rejected
	KPSS	0.625	0.463*	Rejected	–	–	–
	Model with trend				**Model with drift**		
BTC/USD	*ADF*	−7.832	−3.96	Rejected	−7.683	−2.328	Rejected
	KPSS	0.402	0.216	Rejected	–	–	–
BTC/EUR	*ADF*	−9.472	−3.96	Rejected	−8.489	−2.328	Rejected
	KPSS	0.368	0.216	Rejected	–	–	–
BTC/GBP	*ADF*	−8.888	−3.96	Rejected	−8.715	−2.328	Rejected
	KPSS	0.405	0.216	Rejected	–	–	–
BTC/AUD	*ADF*	−9.236	−3.96	Rejected	−9.238	−2.328	Rejected
	KPSS	0.385	0.216	Rejected	–	–	–
BTC/CAD	*ADF*	−9.359	−3.96	Rejected	−9.292	−2.328	Rejected
	KPSS	0.354	0.216	Rejected	–	–	–

* At 5% significance level. ** At 10% significance level

Bitcoin markets under MS-ARFIMA will allow us to study simultaneously and endogenously the persistence of fractional integration and the potential break points.

We comment on the results in three distinct sub-sections. The first subsection, the potential break points that have been detected through multiple break point tests will be discussed in scrutiny. In the second subsection Local Whittle, Exact Local Whittle, Feasible Exact Local Whittle and Two-step Exact Local Whittle test will be displayed, compared, rolled into suitable windows, and then discussed in detail. The last subsection will demonstrate the endogenous shifts of long memory, mean and variance parameters to clear the confusion between long memory and break points. Then, a brief illustration of the transition probability among the states for the three parameters will be displayed statically and dynamically and at the end of the section a comparison among the fitted values of ARFIMA and MS-ARFIMA processes.

5.1 Structural Break

Detecting potential breaks in a time series is a crucial matter to validate the performance of an econometric model and control the bias. Bai and Perron (1998, 2003)'s test is applied to detect if there potential turning points over the time. The previous section has confirmed the stationarity across the five exchange rates series. Basically, by holding the stationarity assumption we confirm that the joint statistical probability of our five series does not change overtime (e.g. constant mean, constant variance, and trend less series). The normal stationary tests as ADF and Philips-Perron are not enough powerful to detect the joint statistical distribution among observations and specify the break points. Multiple break points tests were adopted to find if any of the five stationary exchange rate series has any breaks in the joint probability over the time. Figure 3 reveals interesting information that claims on the contrary of stationarity assumption that mean and variance are constant along the sample span.

In Fig. 3 the blue line illustrates the possible turning point in the mean over the sample span across the five exchange rates. We use the global information criterion method to specify the breaks across the five markets. Ten breaks in (BTC/USD, BTC/EUR, BTC/GBP) and eight breaks in (BTC/AUD and BTC/CAD) are selected by Bayesian Information Criteria (BIC). bai2003computation recommended using the highest trimming percentage (15%) if the sample span is small. On the contrary, our sample span is 1533 observations and choosing a lower trimming percentage (5%) to detect the turning points should be acceptable. By allowing for shifts in the constant, we can see clearly from Fig. 3 that the coefficient value during the first break in all series is swinging between 0.7 and 0.94. Upward shifts appear in all series ranging around 1.5 from the second quarter of 2017 to approximately the second quarter of 2018, then start to shift down again to back to the normal shifts. Different upward and downward shifts across the five exchange rates are recorded, but all conclude that the period from 2017 to the middle of 2018 experienced waves of turmoils that distort the distributional propriety in that time.

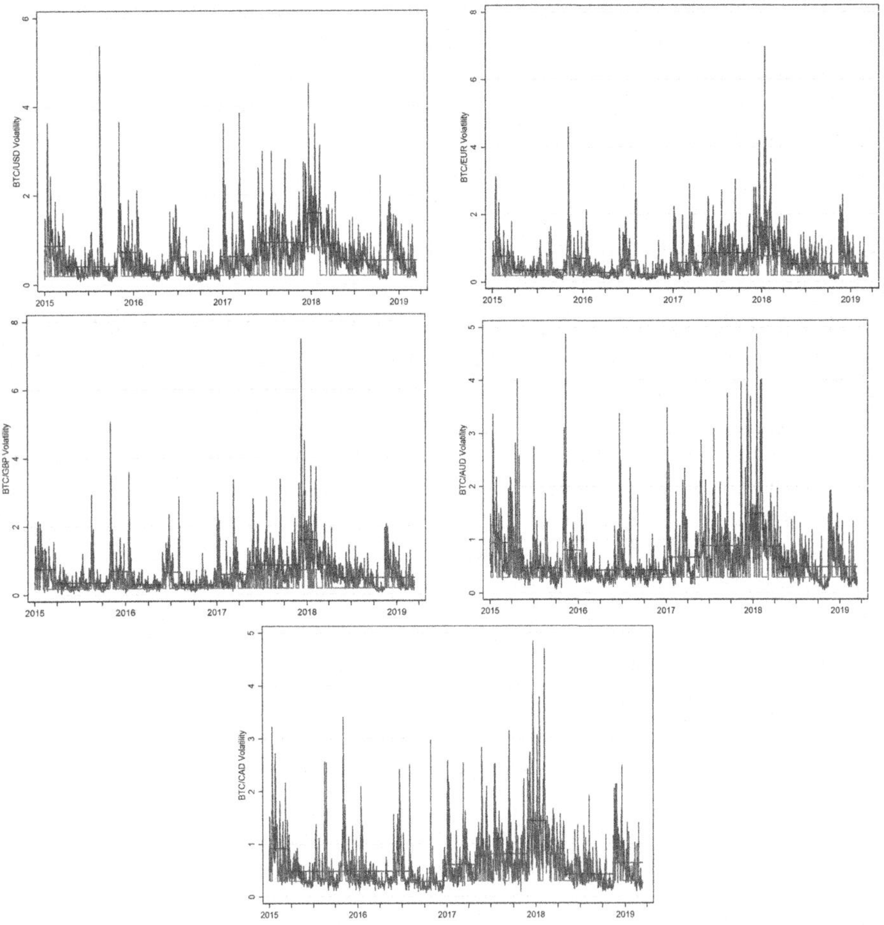

Fig. 3 Estimated breaks in the volatility of Bitcoin exchange markets (Bai and Perron). *Note*: top left corner USD, top right EUR, middle left GBP, middle right AUD and bottom CAD. Blue line represents Bai and Perron multiple structural tests, the red line is the MS-ARFIMA process

As we know some structural break models postulate that the shifting mechanism is deterministic and the switching is determined exogenously. Alternatively, Bai and Perron (2003) developed a model to detect structural breaks endogenously, hence, there is no need to determine the timing of breaks beforehand. However, the trimming percentage and allowing for serial correlation and heterogeneity are restricting the model efficiency. Detecting the structural breaks and identifying the changing points across a series is very helpful especially if the series is displaying a long memory. Why is it important? Because as we mentioned above the slow decaying of the auto-correlation function could be accounted for from both short memory series with potential breakpoints (structural break points phenomenon) or strong dependence among observations within the series (long memory phenomenon). An important question arises here, to clear the confusion among the latter two very similar phenomena 'Should we test both long memory and structural breaks simultaneously in a unified framework?' or 'Should we account for the last two problems separately?'

5.2 *Evidence of Long-Memory Persistence*

To provide evidence on long memory, we have estimated Local Whittle and its extended versions: Exact Local Whittle (ELW), Feasible exact local whittle (FELW) and Two-step exact local whittle (TSELW). The analysis implemented in different bandwidths (e.g. $m = T^{0.5}$, $m = T^{0.6}$, $m = T^{0.7}$, $m = T^{0.8}$) to prove and clarify that the long memory is not sensitive to the choice of a particular bandwidth. Moreover, rolling windows of the estimated d have been applied to diagnose the stability of the estimated parameters d overtime.

Tables 3, 4, 5, and 6 illustrate the degree of fractional integration based on (LW), (ELW), (FELW) and (TSELW) estimations of the volatility under different band

Table 3 Estimates of Local Whittle (LW) for the volatility of the five BTC markets

	$\hat{d}_{LW}$			
	$m = T^{0.5}$	$m = T^{0.6}$	$m = T^{0.7}$	$m = T^{0.8}$
BTC/USD	0.514	0.445	0.410	0.360
BTC/EUR	0.521	0.370	0.389	0.378
BTC/GBP	0.471	0.408	0.340	0.352
BTC/AUD	0.436	0.350	0.362	0.346
BTC/CAD	0.417	0.400	0.334	0.347

Table 4 Estimates of Exact Local Whittle (ELW) for the volatility of the five BTC markets

	$\hat{d}_{ELW}$			
	$m = T^{0.5}$	$m = T^{0.6}$	$m = T^{0.7}$	$m = T^{0.8}$
BTC/USD	0.541	0.463	0.428	0.390
BTC/EUR	0.539	0.368	0.400	0.408
BTC/GBP	0.469	0.410	0.345	0.379
BTC/AUD	0.492	0.376	0.388	0.384
BTC/CAD	0.430	0.423	0.352	0.382

Table 5 Estimates of Feasible Exact Local Whittle (FELW) for the volatility of the five BTC markets

	$\hat{d}_{FELW}$			
	$m = T^{0.5}$	$m = T^{0.6}$	$m = T^{0.7}$	$m = T^{0.8}$
BTC/USD	0.520	0.451	0.417	0.380
BTC/EUR	0.524	0.374	0.396	0.400
BTC/GBP	0.479	0.413	0.346	0.374
BTC/AUD	0.454	0.354	0.368	0.367
BTC/CAD	0.439	0.408	0.341	0.368

Table 6 Estimates of Two-step Exact Local Whittle (TSELW) for the volatility of the five BTC markets)

	$\hat{d}_{\text{TSELW}}$			
	$m = T^{0.5}$	$m = T^{0.6}$	$m = T^{0.7}$	$m = T^{0.8}$
BTC/USD	0.532	0.451	0.417	0.380
BTC/EUR	0.537	0.374	0.396	0.400
BTC/GBP	0.479	0.413	0.346	0.374
BTC/AUD	0.454	0.354	0.368	0.367
BTC/CAD	0.439	0.408	0.341	0.368

width respectively. All tables provide 4 bandwidths (*e. g.* , $m = T^{0.5} | m = T^{0.8}$) to detect the sensitivity of *d*. Results among the latter tables show that each exchange rate series has a significant long memory. All the outcomes display a value higher than zero $d > 0$, which means the series are strong persistent along the sample span. The values of *d* are bounded in the (0.0.5) interval for the five markets across almost all the bandwidths, which indicate that all series are co-variance stationary except $m = T^{0.5}$ across the BTC/USD and BTC/EUR markets. Generally, we can confirm that the major of d values are co-variance stationary and mean-reverting, which implies that the shock effect will die out in the long run. A close look at the series individually, we can see that the value of *d* across different bandwidths for all markets are swinging between ˋ0.35 ∧ 0.54ˊ. All tests provide approximately identical results and hinting for stable estimations, which implies that our series contains long memory and this may have useful implication within our context.

For each *d* value, the asymptotic standard error can be estimated as. The total number of observations in each series is 1533, and the bandwidths range from 0.50.8. For example, in Table 5, $m = T^{0.5}$ the approximate SE is 0.0799. Similarly, the approximate S.E of $m = T^{0.6} m = T^{0.8}$ bandwidths are 0.055, 0.0383, and 0.026 respectively.

We extend our work and take a further step to roll the estimated *d* by setting a suitable window of the (TSELW) estimation in Table 6. A window of 360 days with five days increments after each window is used to detect the sensitivity of *d* within $m = T^{0.6}$ bandwidth across all the markets. Figure 4 displays the stability of long memory parameters across the five markets. We can see that the long memory in BTC/USD market was stable ($d \approx 0.4$) during the first half of 2015 and from the second half of 2016 to the end of the sample span. The period between the middle of 2015 and 2016 shows upward and downward fluctuations hinting that investors might over react to their investment decisions in the BTC/USD market. BTC/GBP market shows stable persistence over the first half of the sample span with stable downwards over the second half of the period before back again to its normal value over the last few days of the rolled *d* parameters. The rest of markets (e.g. BTC/EUR, BTC/AUD and BTC/EUR) display more upward and downward fluctuations over the sample span. All markets show high persistence through the first year, the persistence starts to decline gradually before it increases again.

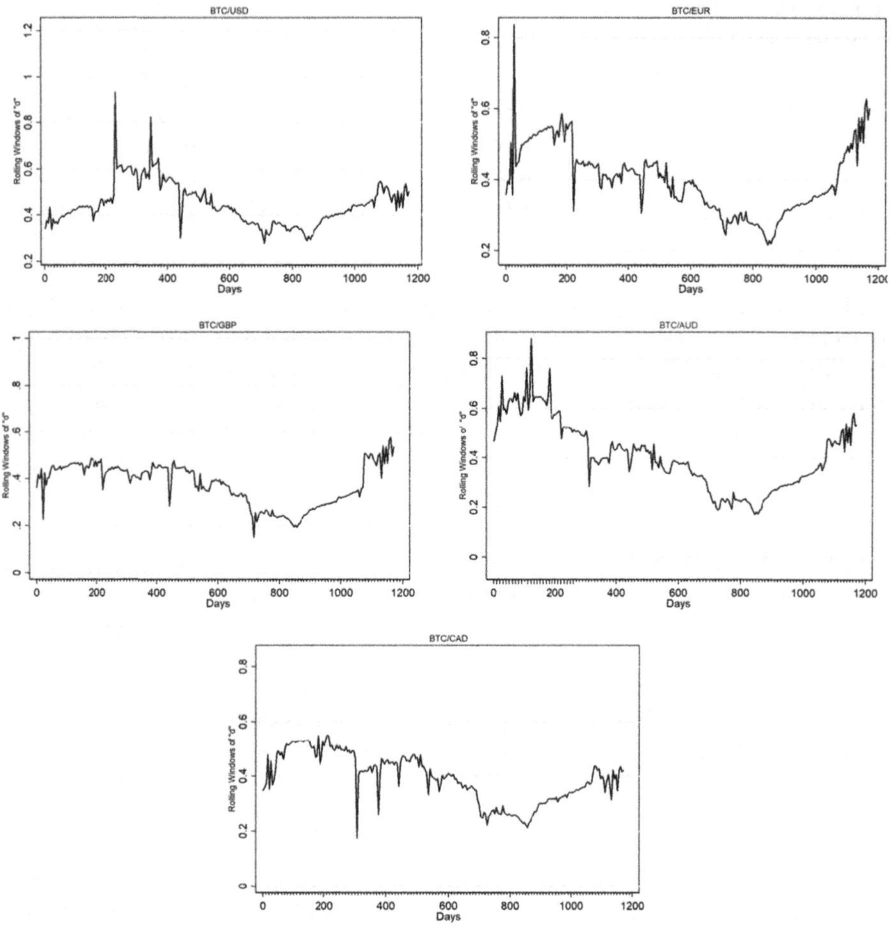

Fig. 4 The rolling windows of estimated '*d*' in Bitcoin markets. *Note*: Top left corner BTC/USD, top right BTC/EUR, middle left BTC/GBP, middle right BTC/AUD and bottom BTC/CAD. Rolling windows, daily. Dates on the *x*-axis indicate the start date by 1 and ticks are 20 days each

Finally, we obtain the time series of the estimated '*d*' in each market, then identify a suitable window for this series and roll it again to find the speed of decaying in the rolling windows of estimated.[21]

[21] see Diebold and Inoue (2001).

5.3 Results from MS-ARFIMA Estimation

Berkes et al. (2006), Diebold and Inoue (2001), Granger and Hyung (2004), Kunsch (1987), and others[22] claimed that long-range dependence and structural breaks are easily confused. In the above sections, long memory tests and multiple structural breaks tests were carried out to prove that each BTC exchange rate series has long-range dependence and turning points over the time. Much research has studied the properties of Bitcoin market by detecting the fractional integration and structural changes by different approaches as we have done in the first two subsections above (Bariviera, 2017, 2017; Bouri et al., 2019; Charfeddine & Maouchi, 2019; Jiang et al., 2018; Mensi, 2018; Mensi et al., 2019).

However, Diebold and Inoue (2001) claimed that a spurious long memory could be generated due to the presence of structural breaks (persistence along the hyperbolic decaying). Indeed, ignoring the structural breaks in a long memory time series could generate instable results, hence, underestimate the long range dependence parameter. To overcome the puzzle proposed by Diebold and Inoue (2001), many authors tried to build a model that aggregates both structural breaks with long memory (Haldrup & Nielsen, 2006; Ray & Tsay, 2002). Many gaps in the latter approaches were cured in MS-ARFIMA (Tsay & Härdle, 2009). The model is computing the degree of fractional integration and structural breaks simultaneously and endogenously by shifting the ARFIMA parameters through the Markov switching process into different states.

Table 7 presents the static results of MS-ARFIMA process. Although the results across different specifications are stable, Table 7 shows the best fit of MS-ARFIMA which each estimation has been selected according to the highest log likelihood for each Bitcoin exchange rate under different MS-ARFIMA orders.[23] The best order of each exchange rate is USD/BTC $\sim$ MS-ARFIMA (1,d,1), EUR/BTC $\sim$ MS-ARFIMA (1,d,0), GBP/BTC $\sim$ MS-ARFIMA (1,d,1), AUD/BTC $\sim$ MS-ARFIMA (1,d,1), CAD/BTC $\sim$ MS-ARFIMA (0,d,1).

Observing Table 7 the first column shows the MS-ARFIMA parameters, from the top left corner (d_1 and d_2) represents the long memory parameters in state 1 and state 2 respectively. The mean and standard deviation of the BTC exchange rate for each market are (μ_1 and μ_2) and (σ_1 and σ_2) parameters respectively. The (p_{11} and p_{22}) are the probability parameters, p_{11} illustrates the probability that the process will stay in state one and $(1 - p_{11})$ is the probability that the process moves from state 1 to state 2. p_{22} inferred about the probability of the process that staying in state 2 and $(1 - p_{22})$ is the probability of moving from state 2 to state 1. ϕ and θ are the auto-regressive and moving average parameters.

Scrutinising Table 7 (USD/BTC), can show us that the estimated standard deviation in regime 1 is higher than the standard deviation in regime 2, ($\sigma_1 = 0.71$)

---

[22] See Appendix 1.

[23] For excellent survey on structural breaks and long memory see Baillie (1996).

Table 7 Estimates of MS-ARFIMA model of volatility across the five Bitcoin markets

	BTC/USD		BTC/EUR		BTC/GBP		BTC/AUD		BTC/CAD	
	MS-ARFIMA		MS-ARFIMA		MS-ARFIMA		MS-ARFIMA		MS-ARFIMA	
	(1, *d*, 1)		(1, *d*, 0)		(1, *d*, 1)		(1, *d*, 1)		(0, *d*, 1)	
	Estimate	S.E.	Estimate	S.E.	Estimate	S.E.	Estimate	S.E	Estimate	S.E.
d_1	0.4224	0.0520	0.3472	0.0314	0.3570	0.0355	0.3427	0.0355	0.2914	0.0445
d_2	0.4249	0.0329	0.3488	0.0199	0.3253	0.0240	0.3100	0.0177	0.2899	0.0221
μ_1	0.8314	0.1095	0.9056	0.0873	0.7206	0.1188	0.9596	0.1249	0.8757	0.0828
μ_2	0.1936	0.0691	0.2350	0.0523	0.1786	0.0541	0.2938	0.0552	0.2997	0.0427
σ_1	0.7098	0.0291	0.7165	0.0296	0.7981	0.0359	0.7956	0.0358	0.6611	0.0249
σ_2	0.1856	0.0038	0.1682	0.0034	0.1762	0.0035	0.1847	0.0037	0.1617	0.0034
p_{11}	0.8339	0.0212	0.7662	0.0244	0.7323	0.0273	0.7303	0.0275	0.8410	0.0191
p_{22}	0.9585	0.0057	0.9433	0.0066	0.9450	0.0064	0.9443	0.0064	0.9496	0.0064
φ	0.3018	0.1022	−0.0328	0.0326	0.4184	0.3289	−0.4565	0.2795	–	–
θ	−0.4734	0.1025	–	–	−0.4446	0.3265	0.4948	0.2696	0.0526	0.0362
L	−358.38933		−310.734501		−333.830679		−392.023359		−292.341567	

Note: d, long memory; μ, mean; σ, standard deviation; P, transition probability; ϕ, Autoregressive parameter; θ, Moving average parameter; L, Log-likelihood of switching model; *S. E*, standard error and ($\sigma_2 = 0.18$), which indicate that state 1 (S_1) is a high-volatility regime and state 2 (S_2) is a low-volatility regime. Relatively, if the variation around the mean shows a particular behaviour, then the associated mean $\mu_1 > \mu_2$ are displaying the same conclusion as the volatility, which $\mu_1 = 0.83$ 'state 1' and $\mu_2 = 0.19$ 'state 2'.

The memory properties explain the persistence in BTC/USD market, if $d > 0$ this means that the past shocks are affecting the BTC price behaviour in the future. We can see that (d_1 and d_2) are greater than zero, which $d_1 = 0.422$ (S_1) and $d_2 = 0.425$ (S_2). The value of fractional integration in both regimes are bounding within $0 < d < 0.5$ interval, which means the process are stationary with strong persistence over the time. Transition probability of S_1 is $p_{11} = 0.83$ and for S_2 is $p_{22} = 0.95$, which implies that the probability to stay in regime 2 is higher than staying in regime 1 by approximately 12%.

Discussing the static data of BTC/USD markets is useful, but visualising the switching parameters is very helpful in exploring the structural breaks in fractional integration and the first two statistical moments ($\mu \wedge \sigma$). Figure 5 illustrates the switching in the mean of all volatile Bitcoin markets. In the left top corner, We can observe that the BTC/USD volatility shifts are clustering during some episodes of high shocks, these episodes can be related to political or economic events that might have happened in Bitcoin market over the time. Switches within the system are treated endogenously which means the model is synchronised with growth-theoretic mechanisms that allowed the process to generate shifts based on the internal dynamics of BTC prices.

Moving to the second column in Table 7 (BTC/EUR market), the analysis displays almost the same behaviour as BTC/USD market. The mean/volatility parameters switch from $\frac{0.9}{0.7}$ in S_1 to $\frac{0.2}{0.16}$ in S_2. Based on the transition probabilities, the probability of staying in S_2 within the system is grater than the probability to stay in S_1 by 18%, which indicates that the process most likely generates its infer when the mean/volatility of data is swinging between $\frac{1.67}{1.44}$ respectively. As previously mentioned, the conduct of statistical properties in S_1 imply that BTC/EUR market has a series of high shocks over the time. Regarding fractional integration, the memory parameters in both regimes indicate that the persistence of auto-correlation is strong over the sample span and the past events will engage in depicting the future price of BTC/EUR. We can see from Table 7 (BTC/EUR) that d parameter is greater than zero and less than 0.5 which indicates that the BTC/EUR series is stationary and mean reverting. In addition, $d_1 \wedge d_2$ almost carry the same persistence value among the regimes, which indicates that the persistence is running continuously throughout the whole period from Jan 2015 to March 2019. Dynamically, the right top corner of Fig. 5 demonstrates the switching mean of BTC/EUR volatility and identifies any intervened point that happened because of abnormal events may have occurred over time. On the contrary of BTC/USD market (left top corner), BTC/EUR market (right top corner) shows significant switches after 2017 over the same period. Consequently, it is likely these fast switches happened due to the high speed of occurring unusual events in cryptocurrency markets.

On the same pattern, in Table 7 the BTC/GBP, BTC/AUD and BTC/CAD markets display interesting parameter behaviours within a two-regime Markov switching

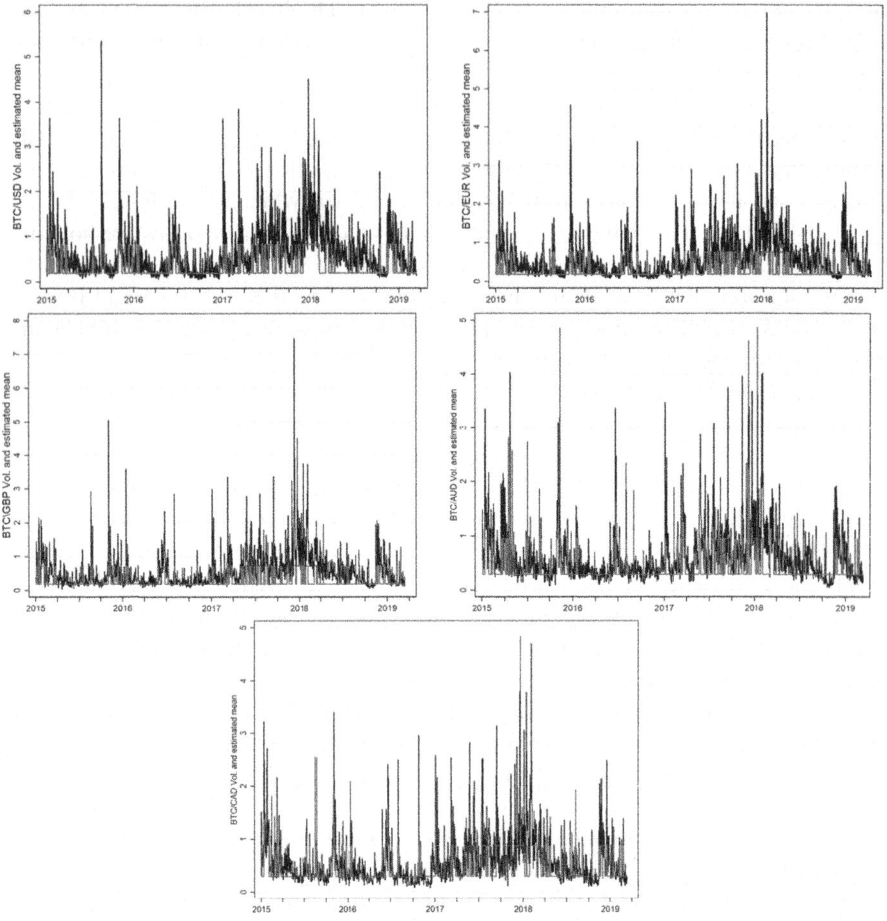

Fig. 5 Bitcoin exchange rates and the path of estimated switching in the mean of volatility. *Note*: Top left corner USD, top right EUR, middle left GBP, middle right AUD and bottom CAD. The red line represents the estimated μ_{st} from MS-ARFIMA model

system. If Bitcoin markets possess episodes of high uncertainty, the markets will react randomly with high volatilities as in S_1 across the latter markets. On the other hand, the low volatility state identified in S_2 within the latter markets. The mean of BTC/GBP, BTC/AUD and BTC/CAD series in S_1 and S_2 are 0.72/0.17, 0.95/0.29 and 0.87/0.29 respectively, Whereas the volatility of the latter series in both regimes are 0.79/0.17, 0.79/0.18 and 0.66/0.16 respectively. The most important parameter across the tables is the fractional integration, BTC/GBP market displays a high persistence stationary behaviour with 0.35 in S_1 and 0.32 in S_1, which refer to stable persistence through the time. In BTC/AUD market the fractional differencing parameter in S_1 shows a persistence by 0.34, while in S_2 reveals 0.31. Long memory parameters $d_1 \wedge d_2$ show almost steady persistence in BTC/CAD markets due to the chosen period. Further, the transition probability parameters for BTC/GBP, BTC/AUD and BTC/CAD p_{22} is greater than p_{11} and the process stay in regime two much longer.

In Fig. 5, the middle row left and right illustrates the BTC/GBP, and BTC/AUD markets respectively and the BTC/CAD market at bottom. Among the five markets, we can observe that BTC/AUD market (middle row right) has the highest transitions number in mean, SD and long memory parameters, albeit, throughout 2016, there were no significant structural breaks, but the rest of anterior and posterior years show remarkable turning points. In all the markets except BTC/AUD, we can aver that the period from 2015 to 2017 has experienced low number of structural breaks than the period from 2017 to 2019. Indeed, after 2017 each market shows different break points over the time depicting almost the same behaviour across the switching parameters.

After all, Fig. 6 shows the BTC volatility for each market with its fitted ARFIMA values. For each market, we can observe how the estimated value of the ARFIMA process (dotted red line) fits the original volatility series (black line) for each market. ARFIMA process performs all the series perfectly in different specifications. It appears that in Fig. 6 the process is detecting the behaviour of each series, but it indicates that most of the values far from the mean are not detected. In contrast, if we examine the fitted MS-ARFIMA plots in Fig. 7, will notice the difference between the estimated values of ARFIMA and the estimated value of MS-ARFIMA. Fitted values (dotted red line) in the latter figures fit the original series exactly and detect the behaviour of markets perfectly and accurately.

6 Robustness

How sensitive are our results to the choice of alternative volatility measure, long memory bandwidth?

We check the robustness of our full sample analysis results based on the volatility measure and the bandwidth of the long memory parameter. Recall that our empirical analysis is based on Parkinson (1980)'s High-Low historical volatility measure. This measure provides more useful information regarding future volatility than a close-to-close estimator, but to follow the literature we can calculate the volatility as the logarithmic difference between high and low Bitcoin prices Return volatility $= \ln P_{\text{high}} - \ln P_{\text{low}}$ (Bariviera, 2017). Hence, as robustness checks, we use the latter estimator to re-estimate the structural breaks, long memory and MS-ARFIMA model to obtain both static and dynamic data. Comparing Parkinson's measure with the Return volatility measure, we find no significant differences among the switches especially during the high fluctuation periods. See Tables (11 to 15) in the appendix. Our conclusion for both measures are same, as all the Bitcoin exchange rate volatility shows high persistence over time (Table 8) with significant structural breaks particularly after 2017. Further, Shimotsu (2010)'s long memory

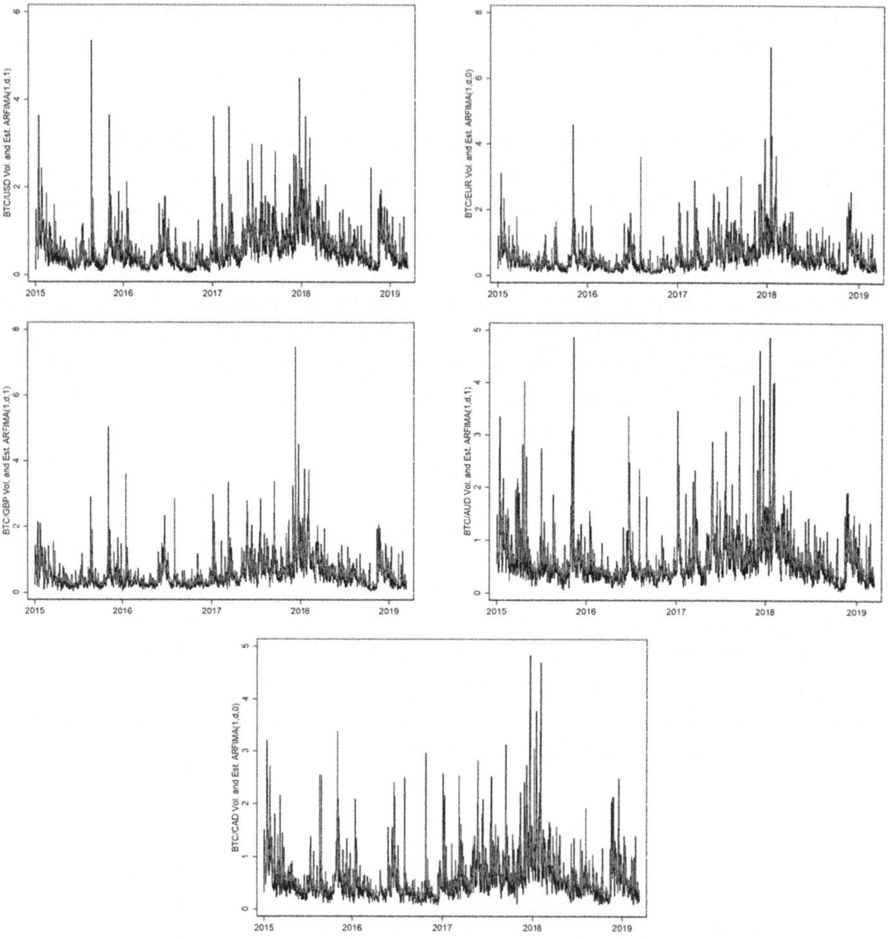

Fig. 6 Bitcoin Exchange rates volatility and the estimated value of the ARFIMA process. *Note*: top left corner USD, top right EUR, middle left GBP, middle right AUD and bottom CAD. The black solid line represents the Bitcoin exchange rate volatility, red dotted line represents the fitted value from the ARFIMA model

measures were applied in different bandwidths to assess the stability of the analysis. Local Whittle, Exact local Whittle, Two-step Exact local Whittle (Table 9), and Feasible Exact Local Whittle (Table 10) with different bandwidths (0.4–0.8) were employed to find the value of *d*. Both, Parkinson's and return volatility measure shows stable and consistent results across the five variables (Figs. 8, 9, and 10).[24]

[24] Different specification have been employed [e.g. (0,d,0), (0,d,1), (1,d,0) and (1,d,1)], the results are available with authors upon requests.

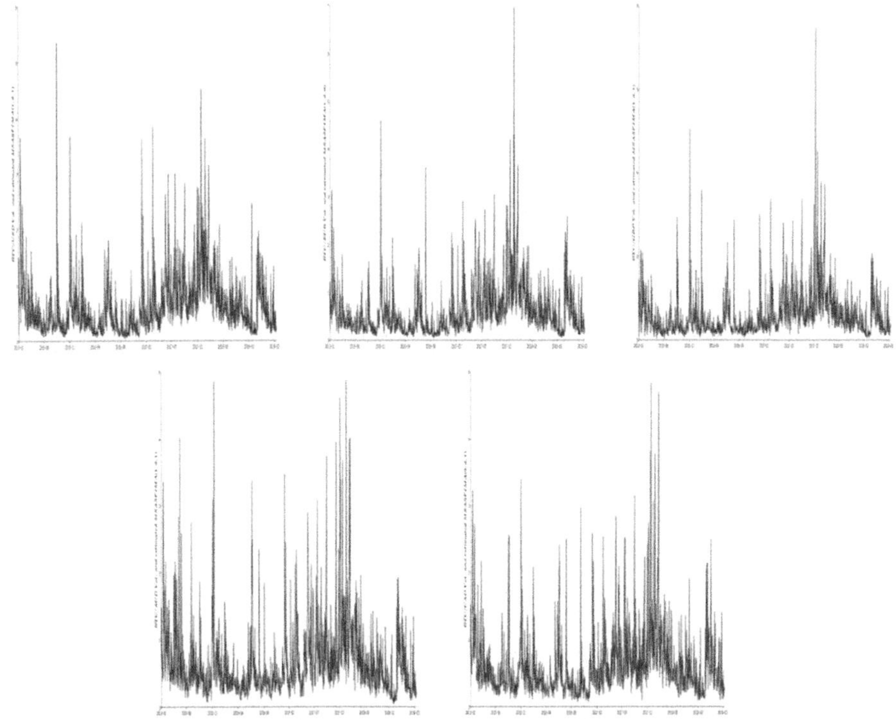

Fig. 7 Bitcoin Exchange rates volatility and the estimated values of the MS-ARFIMA model. *Note*: Top left corner USD, top right EUR, middle left GBP, middle right AUD and bottom CAD. The black solid line represents the Bitcoin exchange rate volatility, red dotted line represents the fitted value from the MS-ARFIMA model

7 Conclusions

The presence of structural breaks may be confused with the presence of a long memory in the volatility of Bitcoin cross-markets. A switching-embedded mechanic can help identify the true nature of memory in the series by mitigating the effects of spurious long-memory. A Markov-switching (MS) ARFIMA model can potentially overcome such a problem. Accordingly, the purpose of this chapter is to exploit the rich features of MS-ARFIMA to model frequent shifts in cross-market Bitcoin prices. Those frequent switches may not always be identified as exogenous. When sentiments drive price changes, switches are invariably endogenous (because one would hardly identify if the regular changes in sentiment are driven primordially by exogenous phenomena). Combining both an endogenous switch and a persistence (memory) in modelling Bitcoin price changes would be a potential optimal strategy.

Table 8 Estimates of MS-ARFIMA model

	BTC/USD		BTC/EUR		BTC/GBP		BTC/AUD		BTC/CAD	
	MS-ARFIMA		MS-ARFIMA		MS-ARFIMA		MS-ARFIMA		MS-ARFIMA	
	(1, *d*, 1)		(0, *d*, 1)		(1, *d*, 0)		(0, *d*, 1)		(1, *d*, 1)	
	Estimate	S.E.	Estimate	S.E.	Estimate	S.E.	Estimate	S.E	Estimate	S.E.
d_1	0.4772	0.0486	0.3563	0.0322	0.3407	0.029	0.3561	0.0316	0.2756	0.0837
d_2	0.4423	0.0336	0.3485	0.0209	0.3117	0.0174	0.2982	0.0194	0.2663	0.0526
μ_1	6.2306	1.3547	7.1305	0.9302	6.4464	1.0258	6.7589	1.1148	6.2231	0.9982
μ_2	1.482	0.767	1.6703	0.5471	1.7022	0.461	2.3365	0.4484	2.1388	0.4621
σ_1	6.1884	0.2546	6.1937	0.2491	6.9928	0.3163	6.4412	0.255	5.4306	0.1790
σ_2	1.6003	0.0324	1.4403	0.0232	1.5378	0.0307	1.4006	0.0289	1.2759	0.0283
p_{11}	0.8224	0.0218	0.7818	0.0232	0.7341	0.0274	0.7406	0.0239	0.8961	0.0138
p_{22}	0.9553	0.0059	0.9425	0.0067	0.9451	0.0064	0.9265	0.0075	0.9516	0.0066
φ	0.2769	0.0896	–	–	−0.0015	0.0194	–	–	−0.0902	0.0919
θ	−0.474	0.0898	−0.0436	0.036	–	–	0.0549	0.0356	0.1382	0.0838
L	−3672.7555		−3628.32752		−3647.5388		−3708.4664		−3612.41	

Note: d, long memory; μ, mean; σ, standard deviation; P, transition probability; ϕ, Auto-regressive parameter; θ, Moving average parameter; L, Log-likelihood of switching model; $S. E$, standard error

Table 9 Estimates of Two-step Exact Local Whittle (TSELW) for the return volatility of the five BTC markets

			$\hat{d}_{TSELW}$		
	$m = T^{0.4}$	$m = T^{0.5}$	$m = T^{0.6}$	$m = T^{0.7}$	$m = T^{0.8}$
BTC/USD	0.558	0.533	0.451	0.418	0.381
BTC/EUR	0.576	0.538	0.375	0.396	0.401
BTC/GBP	0.545	0.479	0.412	0.346	0.374
BTC/AUD	0.487	0.454	0.354	0.368	0.368
BTC/CAD	0.741	0.440	0.407	0.341	0.369

Table 10 Estimates of Feasible Exact Local Whittle (FELW) for the return volatility of the five BTC markets

			$\hat{d}_{FELW}$		
	$m = T^{0.4}$	$m = T^{0.5}$	$m = T^{0.6}$	$m = T^{0.7}$	$m = T^{0.8}$
BTC/USD	0.524	0.516	0.451	0.418	0.381
BTC/EUR	0.542	0.524	0.375	0.396	0.401
BTC/GBP	0.520	0.479	0.412	0.346	0.374
BTC/AUD	0.487	0.454	0.354	0.368	0.368
BTC/CAD	0.587	0.440	0.407	0.341	0.369

To show that MS-ARFIMA is appropriate for our purpose, we tested for structural break and fractional integration separately. Our results provide clear evidence of the presence of multiple breaks in the series: ten breaks in (BTC/USD, BTC/EUR and BTC/GBP) and eight breaks in (BTC/AUD and BTC/CAD), respectively. Furthermore, the results show the presence of long memory across all Bitcoin cross-markets. Therefore, a spurious long memory in volatility could be attributed to the presence of structural breaks if the standard ARFIMA model was applied to each of the Bitcoin cross-markets, respectively. Consequently, we have applied the MS-ARFIMA model instead and find that our Bitcoin price series are fractionally integrated (i.e., long-memory) for all MS-ARFIMA models.

Our findings have important implications for investors and policy makers. First, the presence of long memory could enable investors to capture speculative profits (Cheah et al., 2018). This can be achieved through market timing. During a high-volatility regime, investors could buy and then subsequently sell when the market switches to a low-volatility regime in all Bitcoin cross-markets. Investors could also hedge during a high-volatility regime by purchasing Bitcoin futures from the Chicago Board Option Exchange (CBOE). Second, as for policy makers and regulators could introduce circuit breakers to stop trading in Bitcoin cross-markets when the market switches abruptly to a high-volatility regime as the impact of a negative down turn would take a relatively long period of time to dissipate given the nature of persistence in the price behaviour of Bitcoin in the cross-markets.

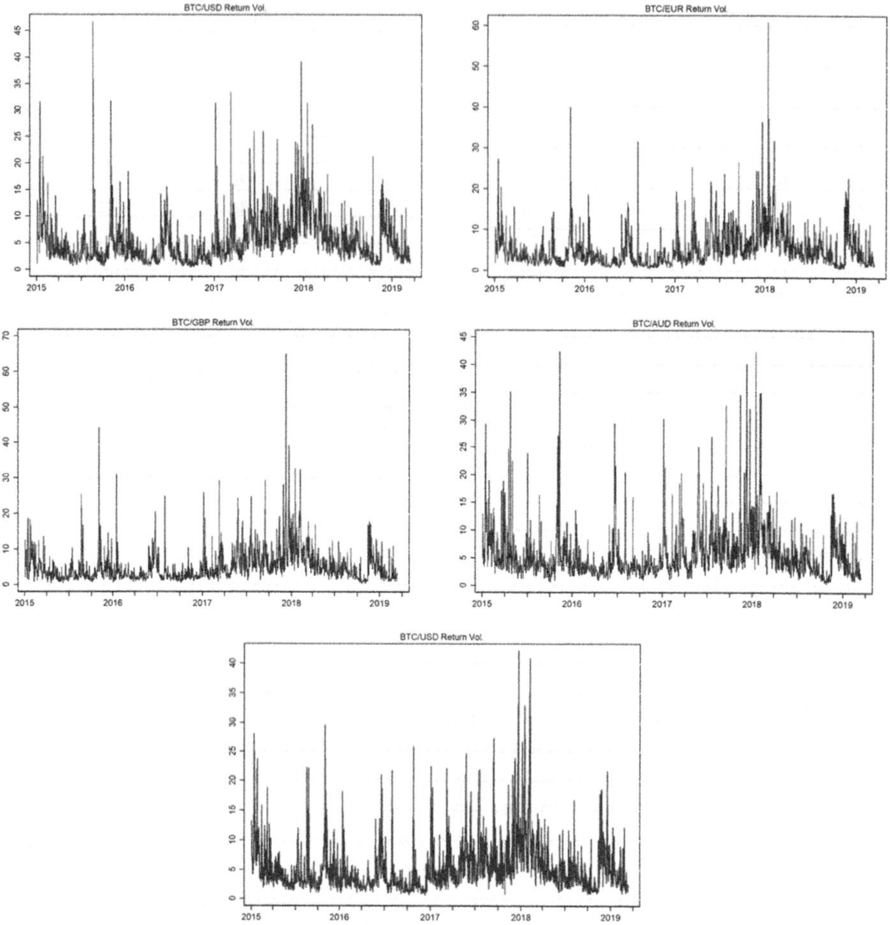

Fig. 8 Exchange rate return volatility. *Note*: (top left corner USD), (top right EUR), (middle left GBP), (middle right AUD) and (bottom CAD)

Apart from purchasing Bitcoin futures from the CBOE, the ability of portfolio investment managers can be further enhanced if speculative and hedging activities between cross-market Bitcoin prices are carried out as well. Indeed, by examining a wide range of financial assets including cryptocurrencies, we will be able to develop a dynamic hedge ratio—one that can help investors formulate appropriate hedging strategies between financial markets and protect their respective portfolios from abrupt structural changes.

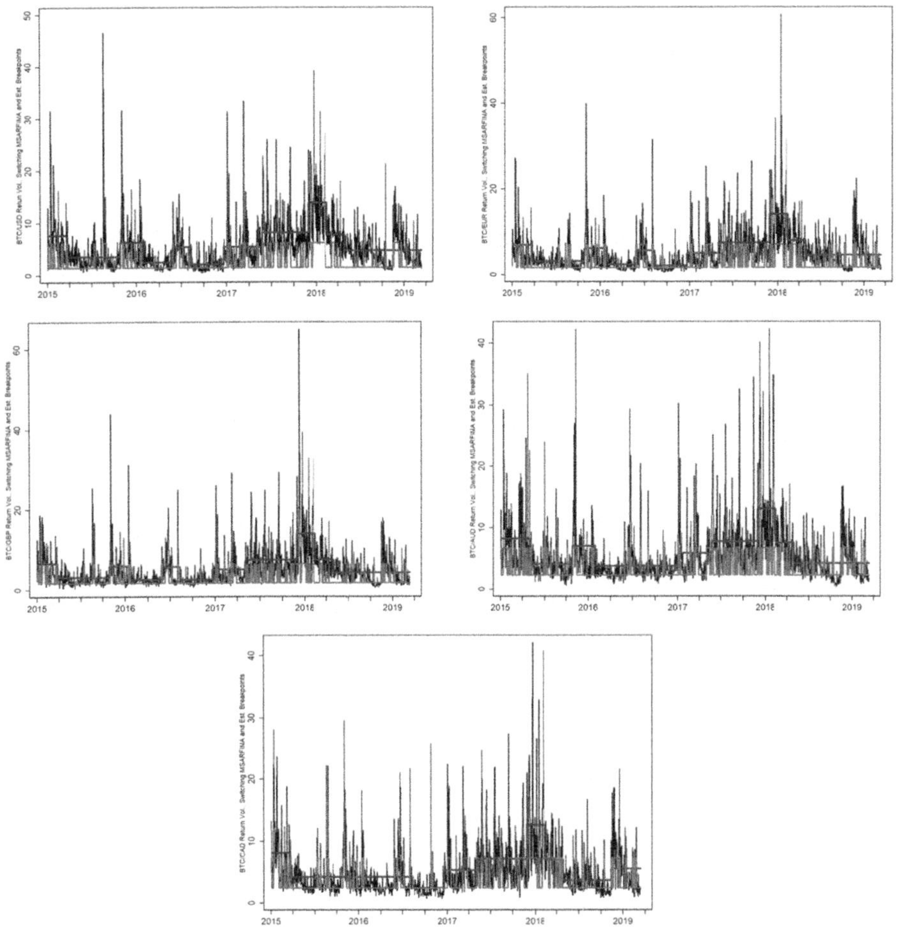

Fig. 9 Estimated breaks in the return volatility of Bitcoin exchange markets (Bai and Perron). *Note*: top left corner USD, top right EUR, middle left GBP, middle right AUD and bottom CAD. Blue line represents Bai and Perron multiple structural test, red line is the MS-ARFIMA process

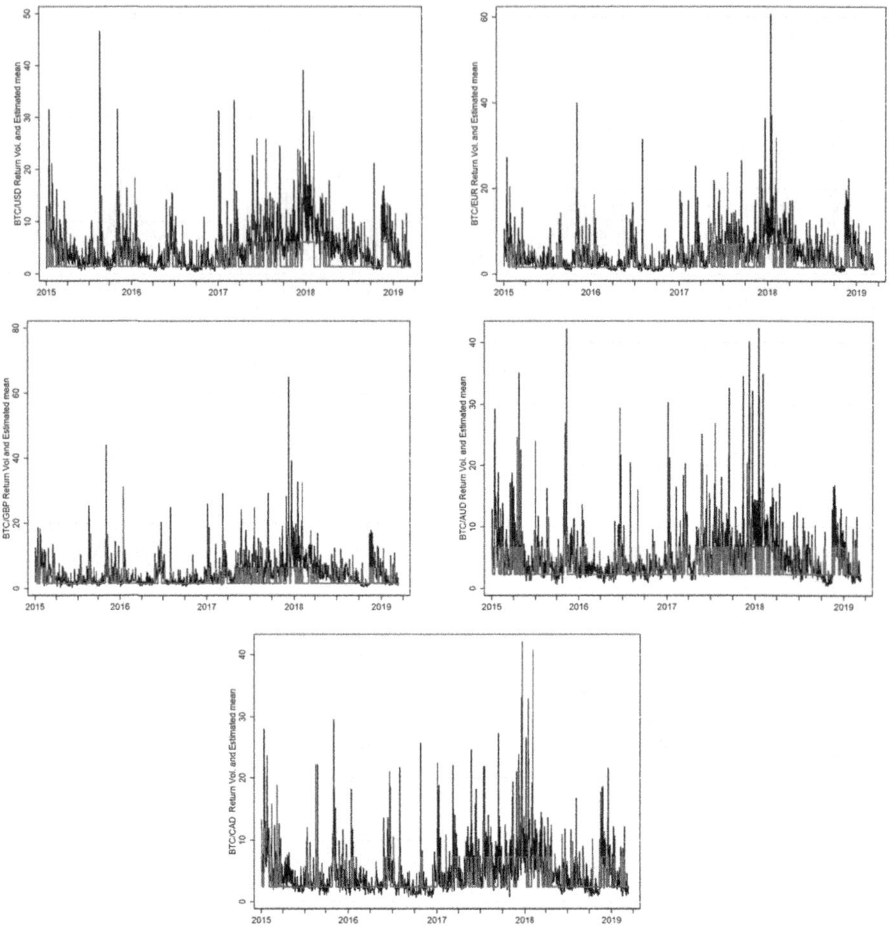

Fig. 10 Bitcoin exchange rates and the path of estimated switching in the mean of return volatility. *Note*: Top left corner USD, top right EUR, middle left GBP, middle right AUD and bottom CAD. Red line represents estimated μ_{st} from MS-ARFIMA model

Appendix

Rolling Windows of the Rolling Windows Series for Each Market

Different Specifications for the Estimated MS-ARFIMA Process

Table 11 Estimates of BTC/USD market volatility under different specifications of MS-ARFIMA process

	MS-ARFIMA (0, *d*, 0)		MS-ARFIMA (0, *d*, 1)		MS-ARFIMA (1, *d*, 0)		MS-ARFIMA (1, *d*, 1)	
	Estimate	S.E.	Estimate	S.E.	Estimate	S.E.	Estimate	S.E
d_1	0.2615	0.0332	0.3838	0.0447	0.3313	0.0391	0.4224	0.0520
d_2	0.3202	0.0156	0.3880	0.0272	0.3630	0.0219	0.4249	0.0329
μ_1	0.9745	0.0697	0.7869	0.1035	0.8872	0.0870	0.8314	0.1095
μ_2	0.2576	0.0490	0.2008	0.0644	0.2184	0.0584	0.1936	0.0691
σ_1	0.7046	0.0296	0.7193	0.0287	0.7148	0.0295	0.7098	0.0291
σ_2	0.1870	0.0038	0.1851	0.0038	0.1857	0.0038	0.1856	0.0038
p_{11}	0.8189	0.0222	0.8544	0.0196	0.8295	0.0215	0.8339	0.0212
p_{22}	0.9564	0.0058	0.9613	0.0055	0.9577	0.0057	0.9585	0.0057
φ	–	–	–	–	−0.0914	0.0331	0.3018	0.1022
θ	–	–	−0.1418	0.0435	–	–	−0.4734	0.1025
L	−365.67568		−363.261213		−362.471718		−358.38933	

Note: *d*, long memory; μ, mean; σ, standard deviation; *P*, transition probability; φ, Autoregressive parameter; θ, Moving average parameter; *L*, Log-likelihood of switching model; *S.E*, standard error

Table 12 Estimates of BTC/EUR market volatility under different specifications of MS-ARFIMA process

	MS-ARFIMA (0, *d*, 0)		MS-ARFIMA (0, *d*, 1)		MS-ARFIMA (1, *d*, 0)		MS-ARFIMA (1, *d*, 1)	
	Estimate	S.E.	Estimate	S.E.	Estimate	S.E.	Estimate	S.E
d_1	0.3306	0.0263	0.3529	0.0321	0.3472	0.0314	0.2874	0.0284
d_2	0.3382	0.0155	0.3474	0.0211	0.3488	0.0199	0.3171	0.0177
μ_1	0.9113	0.0820	0.8362	0.0956	0.9056	0.0873	0.7674	0.0676
μ_2	0.2376	0.0498	0.2004	0.0556	0.2350	0.0523	0.1905	0.0466
σ_1	0.7132	0.0293	0.7090	0.0034	0.7165	0.0296	0.6562	0.0217
σ_2	0.1665	0.0034	0.1653	0.0285	0.1682	0.0034	0.1513	0.0033
p_{11}	0.7627	0.0244	0.7787	0.0233	0.7662	0.0244	0.8919	0.0144
p_{22}	0.9415	0.0067	0.9425	0.0067	0.9433	0.0066	0.9534	0.0064
φ	–	–	–	–	−0.0328	0.0326	−0.5040	0.2178
θ	–	–	−0.0413	0.0376	–	–	0.5469	0.2077
L	−311.252655		−313.96913		−310.734501		−324.6173	

Note: *d*, long memory; μ, mean; σ, standard deviation; *P*, transition probability; φ, Autoregressive parameter; θ, Moving average parameter; *L*, Log-likelihood of switching model; *S.E*, standard error

Table 13 Estimates of BTC/GBP market volatility under different specifications of MS-ARFIMA process

	MS-ARFIMA (0, *d*, 0)		MS-ARFIMA (0, *d*, 1)		MS-ARFIMA (1, *d*, 0)		MS-ARFIMA (1, *d*, 1)	
	Estimate	S.E.	Estimate	S.E.	Estimate	S.E.	Estimate	S.E
d_1	0.3391	0.0272	0.3267	0.0359	0.3250	0.0303	0.3570	0.0355
d_2	0.3121	0.0159	0.3086	0.0213	0.3027	0.0182	0.3253	0.0240
μ_1	0.7375	0.1130	0.7479	0.1107	0.7535	0.1099	0.7206	0.1188
μ_2	0.1885	0.0501	0.1925	0.0510	0.1948	0.0485	0.1786	0.0541
σ_1	0.8013	0.0363	0.7840	0.0339	0.8017	0.0365	0.7981	0.0359
σ_2	0.1765	0.0035	0.1739	0.0035	0.1769	0.0035	0.1762	0.0035
p_{11}	0.7303	0.0275	0.7628	0.0253	0.7293	0.0276	0.7323	0.0273
p_{22}	0.9451	0.0064	0.9465	0.0064	0.9451	0.0064	0.9450	0.0064
φ	–	–	–	–	0.0106	0.0288	0.4184	0.3289
θ	–	–	0.0197	0.0359	–	–	−0.4446	0.3265
L	−333.95178		−336.939603		−334.518996		−333.830679	

Note: d, long memory; μ, mean; σ, standard deviation; P, transition probability; φ, Autoregressive parameter; θ, Moving average parameter; L, Log-likelihood of switching model; *S.E*, standard error

Table 14 Estimates of BTC/AUD market volatility under different specifications of MS-ARFIMA process

	MS-ARFIMA (0, *d*, 0)		MS-ARFIMA (0, *d*, 1)		MS-ARFIMA (1, *d*, 0)		MS-ARFIMA (1, *d*, 1)	
	Estimate	S.E.	Estimate	S.E.	Estimate	S.E.	Estimate	S.E
d_1	0.3670	0.0322	0.2820	0.0316	0.3446	0.0385	0.3427	0.0355
d_2	0.3235	0.0159	0.2627	0.0174	0.3098	0.0200	0.3100	0.0177
μ_1	0.9242	0.1343	0.8686	0.0898	0.9503	0.1290	0.9596	0.1249
μ_2	0.2865	0.0587	0.2841	0.0419	0.2919	0.0561	0.2938	0.0552
σ_1	0.8008	0.0360	0.7210	0.0273	0.7978	0.0360	0.7956	0.0358
σ_2	0.1855	0.0037	0.1631	0.0034	0.1855	0.0037	0.1847	0.0037
p_{11}	0.7331	0.0275	0.8006	0.0208	0.7331	0.0275	0.7303	0.0275
p_{22}	0.9451	0.0064	0.9367	0.0071	0.9451	0.0064	0.9443	0.0064
φ	–	–	–	–	0.0283	0.0336	−0.4565	0.2795
θ	–	–	0.1119	0.0328	–	–	0.4948	0.2696
L	−393.729588		−400.962282		−393.212967		−392.023359	

Note: d, long memory; μ, mean; σ, standard deviation; P, transition probability; φ, Autoregressive parameter; θ, Moving average parameter; L, Log-likelihood of switching model; *S.E*, standard error

Table 15 Estimates of BTC/CAD market volatility under different specifications of MS-ARFIMA process

	MS-ARFIMA (0, *d*, 0)		MS-ARFIMA (1, *d*, 0)		MS-ARFIMA (0, *d*, 1)		MS-ARFIMA (1, *d*, 1)	
	Estimate	S.E.	Estimate	S.E.	Estimate	S.E.	Estimate	S.E
d_1	0.3192	0.0292	0.2757	0.0381	0.2914	0.0445	0.2692	0.0429
d_2	0.2961	0.0001	0.2684	0.0225	0.2899	0.0221	0.2761	0.0234
μ_1	0.6522	0.0848	0.7072	0.0783	0.8757	0.0828	0.8865	0.0765
μ_2	0.2183	0.0416	0.2434	0.0409	0.2997	0.0427	0.3057	0.0394
σ_1	0.6235	0.0201	0.6209	0.0201	0.6611	0.0249	0.6560	0.0244
σ_2	0.1459	0.0032	0.1461	0.1461	0.1617	0.0034	0.1602	0.0034
p_{11}	0.9012	0.0135	0.9024	0.0133	0.8410	0.0191	0.8452	0.0186
p_{22}	0.9522	0.0067	0.9530	0.0066	0.9496	0.0064	0.9492	0.0065
φ	–	–	–	–	0.0526	0.0362	−0.0591	0.2372
θ	–	–	0.0476	0.0355	–	–	0.1216	0.2297
L	−300.4434		−299.755155		−292.341567		−293.877633	

Note: d, long memory, μ, mean, σ, standard deviation, P, transition probability, φ, Autoregressive parameter, θ, Moving average parameter, L, Log-likelihood of switching model, $S.E$, standard error

References

Alvarez-Ramirez, J., Rodriguez, E., & Ibarra-Valdez, C. (2018). Long-range correlations and asymmetry in the Bitcoin market. *Physica A: Statistical Mechanics and its Applications, 492*(C), 948–955.

Al-Yahyaee, K. H., Mensi, W., & Yoon, S.-M. (2018). Efficiency, multifractality, and the long-memory property of the bitcoin market: A comparative analysis with stock, currency, and gold markets. *Finance Research Letters, 27*, 228–234.

Bai, J., & Perron, P. (1998). Estimating and testing linear models with multiple structural changes. *Econometrica, 66*, 47–78.

Bai, J., & Perron, P. (2003). Computation and analysis of multiple structural change models. *Journal of Applied Econometrics, 18*(1), 1–22.

Baillie, R. T. (1996). Long memory processes and fractional integration in econometrics. *Journal of Econometrics, 73*(1), 5–59.

Bariviera, A. F. (2017). The inefficiency of bitcoin revisited: A dynamic approach. *Economics Letters, 161*, 1–4.

Bariviera, A. F., Basgall, M. J., Hasperué, W., & Naiouf, M. (2017). Some stylized facts of the bitcoin market. *Physica A: Statistical Mechanics and its Applications, 484*, 82–90.

Baur, D. G., Hong, K., & Lee, A. D. (2018). Bitcoin: Medium of exchange or speculative assets? *Journal of International Financial Markets, Institutions and Money, 54*, 177–189.

Bennett, C., & Gil, M. A. (2012). *Measuring historical volatility. Technical report, & markets, Santander global banking, equity derivatives division technical note.*

Berkes, I., Horváth, L., Kokoszka, P., Shao, Q.-M., et al. (2006). On discriminating between long-range dependence and changes in mean. *The Annals of Statistics, 34*(3), 1140–1165.

Billio, M., & Monfort, A. (1998). Switching state-space models likelihood function, filtering and smoothing. *Journal of Statistical Planning and Inference, 68*(1), 65–103.

Billio, M., Monfort, A., & Robert, C. P. (1999). Bayesian estimation of switching ARMA models. *Journal of Econometrics, 93*(2), 229–255.

Böhme, R., Christin, N., Edelman, B., & Moore, T. (2015). Bitcoin: Economics, technology, and governance. *Journal of Economic Perspectives, 29*(2), 213–238.

Bouri, E., Gil-Alana, L. A., Gupta, R., & Roubaud, D. (2019). Modelling long memory volatility in the bitcoin market: Evidence of persistence and structural breaks. *International Journal of Finance & Economics, 24*(1), 412–426.

Brauneis, A., & Mestel, R. (2018). Price discovery of cryptocurrencies: Bitcoin and beyond. *Economics Letters, 165*, 58–61.
Caporale, G. M., Gil-Alana, L., & Plastun, A. (2018). Persistence in the cryptocurrency market. *Research in International Business and Finance, 46*, 141–148.
Chaim, P., & Laurini, M. P. (2018). Volatility and return jumps in bitcoin. *Economics Letters, 173*, 158–163.
Charfeddine, L., & Maouchi, Y. (2019). Are shocks on the returns and volatility of cryptocurrencies really persistent? *Finance Research Letters, 28*, 423–430.
Cheah, E.-T., Mishra, T., Parhi, M., & Zhang, Z. (2018). Long memory interdependency and inefficiency in bitcoin markets. *Economics Letters, 167*, 18–25.
Chen, C.-C., & Tsay, W.-J. (2011). A markov regime-switching arma approach for hedging stock indices. *Journal of Futures Markets, 31*(2), 165–191.
Chevallier, J., Goutte, S., Guesmi, K., & Saadi, S. (2019). On the Bitcoin price dynamics: An augmented Markov-Switching model with Lévy jumps.
Cochrane, J. H. (2005). *Time series for macroeconomics and finance*. Manuscript, University of Chicago.
Corbet, S., Meegan, A., Larkin, C., Lucey, B., & Yarovaya, L. (2018). Exploring the dynamic relationships between cryptocurrencies and other financial assets. *Economics Letters, 165*, 28–34.
Corbet, S., Lucey, B., Urquhart, A., & Yarovaya, L. (2019). Cryptocurrencies as a financial asset: A systematic analysis. *International Review of Financial Analysis, 62*, 182–199.
Dickey, D. A., & Fuller, W. A. (1979). Distribution of the estimators for autoregressive time series with a unit root. *Journal of the American Statistical Association, 74*(366), 427–431.
Diebold, F. X., & Inoue, A. (2001). Long memory and regime switching. *Journal of Econometrics, 105*(1), 131–159.
Dwyer, G. P. (2015). The economics of bitcoin and similar private digital currencies. *Journal of Financial Stability, 17*, 81–91.
Gillaizeau, M., Jayasekera, R., Maaitah, A., Mishra, T., Parhi, M., & Volokitina, E. (2019). Giver and the receiver: Understanding spillover effects and predictive power in cross-market bitcoin prices. *International Review of Financial Analysis, 63*, 86–104.
Granger, C. W. J., & Hyung, N. (2004). Occasional structural breaks and long memory with an application to the S&P 500 absolute stock returns. *Journal of Empirical Finance, 11*(3), 399–421.
Gray, S. F. (1996). Modeling the conditional distribution of interest rates as a regime-switching process. *Journal of Financial Economics, 42*(1), 27–62.
Haldrup, N., & Nielsen, M. Ø. (2006). A regime switching long memory model for electricity prices. *Journal of Econometrics, 135*(1–2), 349–376.
Hamilton, J. D. (1989). A new approach to the economic analysis of nonstationary time series and the business cycle. *Econometrica: Journal of the Econometric Society, 57*, 357–384.
Hamilton, J. D. (1994). *Time series analysis* (Vol. 2). Princeton University Press.
Jiang, Y., Nie, H., & Ruan, W. (2018). Time-varying long-term memory in bitcoin market. *Finance Research Letters, 25*, 280–284.
Khuntia, S., & Pattanayak, J. K. (2018). Adaptive market hypothesis and evolving predictability of bitcoin. *Economics Letters, 167*, 26–28.
Kim, C.-J. (1994). Dynamic linear models with markov-switching. *Journal of Econometrics, 60*(1–2), 1–22.
Kim, C.-J., Nelson, C. R., et al. (1999). *State-space models with regime switching: Classical and Gibbs-sampling approaches with applications* (Vol. 1). MIT Press Books.
Kunsch, H. R. (1987). Statistical aspects of self-similar processes. In *Proceedings of the First World Congress of the Bernoulli Society, 1987* (Vol. 1, pp. 67–74). VNU Science Press.
Kwaitkowski, D., Phillips, P. C. B., Schmidt, P., & Shin, Y. (1992). Testing the null hypothesis of stationarity against the alternative of a unit root. *Journal of Econometrics, 54*(1), 159–178.
Kyriazis, N. A. (2019). A survey on efficiency and profitable trading opportunities in cryptocurrency markets. *Journal of Risk and Financial Management, 12*(2), 67.

Mensi, W., Al-Yahyaee, K. H., & Kang, S. H. (2018). Structural breaks and double long memory of cryptocurrency prices: A comparative analysis from bitcoin and ethereum. *Finance Research Letters, 29*, 222–230.
Mensi, W., Lee, Y.-J., Al-Yahyaee, K. H., Sensoy, A., & Yoon, S.-M. (2019). Intraday downward/upward multifractality and long memory in bitcoin and ethereum markets: An asymmetric multifractal detrended fluctuation analysis. *Finance Research Letters, 31*, 19–25.
Nakamoto, S. (2008). Bitcoin whitepaper. https://doi.org/bitcoin. org/bitcoin. pdf-915
Neil Gandal, J. T., Hamrick, T. M., & Oberman, T. (2018). Price manipulation in the Bitcoin ecosystem. *Journal of Monetary Economics, 95*.
Parkinson, M. (1980). The extreme value method for estimating security price volatilities. *Journal of Business, 53*, 61–65.
Ray, B. K., & Tsay, R. S. (2002). Bayesian methods for change-point detection in long-range dependent processes. *Journal of Time Series Analysis, 23*(6), 687–705.
Shimotsu, K. (2010). Exact local whittle estimation of fractional integration with unknown mean and time trend. *Econometric Theory, 26*(2), 501–540.
Shimotsu, K., & Phillips, P. C. B. (2005). Exact local whittle estimation of fractional integration. *The Annals of Statistics, 33*(4), 1890–1933.
Tsay, W.-J., & Härdle, W. K. (2009). A generalized ARFIMA process with Markov-switching fractional differencing parameter. *Journal of Statistical Computation and Simulation, 79*(5), 731–745.
Urquhart, A. (2016). The inefficiency of Bitcoin. *Economics Letters, 148*, 80–82.
Urquhart, A., & Zhang, H. (2019). Is bitcoin a hedge or safe haven for currencies? An intraday analysis. *International Review of Financial Analysis, 63*, 49–57.
Vidal-Tomás, D., & Ibañez, A. (2018). Semi-strong efficiency of bitcoin. *Finance Research Letters, 27*, 259–265.
Wei, W. C. (2018). Liquidity and market efficiency in cryptocurrencies. *Economics Letters, 168*, 21–24.

Dr. Ahmad Maaitah is an Assistant Professor of Finance and FinTech at Southampton Business School, University of Southampton. His research lies at the intersection of traditional finance and digital finance, with particular expertise in volatility modelling, market forecasting, and long-memory dynamics in cryptocurrency and digital asset markets. He has published studies on cross-market Bitcoin price persistence and volatility spillovers, contributing to the evolving landscape of FinTech and digital finance research.

Dr. Maaitah also serves as Programme Director for the BSc Finance and FinTech programme, overseeing curriculum development and mentoring students specializing in FinTech. He leads collaborative research initiatives at the Centre for Digital Finance and fosters industry partnerships focused on digital finance innovation. Earlier in his career, Dr. Maaitah gained extensive experience in the financial industry. He continues to bridge academia and practice by engaging and collaborating with FinTech institutions, banking professionals and regulators internationally.

Tapas Mishra is currently a Professor of Financial Economics and Head of Banking and Finance at the Southampton Business School. He is also the founding director of the Centre for Empirical Research in Finance and Banking—a centre that has got a wide network of leading practitioners and financial sector experts from the IMF, the World Bank, the HSBC Bank and the Nationwide Bank, among others. Tapas is a leading expert in financial economics and advanced econometric modelling, focusing in particular on big data and high-dimensional econometrics, macroprudential policy and stress testing of banks, sustainable finance, corporate finance, and real estate economics. He develops theoretical architecture around these and peripheral themes enabling large-scale empirical testing.

External Factors that Affect the Adoption of Decentralized Exchanges (DEX) for Cryptocurrencies: The Case of Curve DEX

Yuan Yao and Alex Zarifis

1 Introduction

Decentralized finance (DeFi) is increasing in popularity across many parts of the world. Decentralized exchanges (DEX) are a type of DeFi that allows users to trade freely and anonymously on a blockchain. This study focuses on how external factors affect the adoption of DEXs and provides suggestions for the development of the DEX industry. The study finds that the development of the DeFi industry has a significant impact on the adoption of DEXs, so DEXs should cooperate to develop the industry instead of focusing on competing for a larger share of the existing market. Some other external factors also have an impact, such as technological innovation, partner integration and community support. As DeFi is closely related to the adoption of DEX, the study also discusses the external factors that may affect the adoption of DeFi, namely trust, infrastructure and regulation.

Banking services are still the largest providers of payment and money transfer services, but there are still many challenges. First, when clients make overseas transfers, there is a high intermediary fee and it takes several days to complete instead of happening immediately. The second challenge is consumers' trust. Trust is needed to use financial services particularly Fintech (Zarifis & Cheng, 2022). After some banks like Silicon Valley Bank (SVB) collapsed, some people have a distrust of commercial banks (Ali et al., 2024). At the same time, new consumers may be rejected by banks because of their income (Olaleye et al., 2022). Finally,

Y. Yao
University of Southampton, Southampton, UK

A. Zarifis (✉)
University of Southampton, Southampton, UK

Cambridge Centre for Alternative Finance, Cambridge, UK
e-mail: a.zarifis@soton.ac.uk

A. Zarifis, X. Cheng (eds.), *Fintech and the Emerging Ecosystems*, Financial Innovation and Technology, https://doi.org/10.1007/978-3-031-83402-8_7

people are now concerned about privacy. As John McAfee claimed, we are 'slaves' as long as our economic interactions are controlled by other people. Are consumers being controlled? Banks can stop your transaction and ask for asset certifications. Traditional financial activities can easily be affected by powerful entities. Is there a method to lower overseas transfer fees, giving most people the opportunity to participate, and help people regain the autonomy of economic activities?

Blockchain technology is a Distributed Ledger Technology (DLT), which can save time and reduce intermediary costs while making overseas transfers (Banafa, 2020). It is trustless in some ways, due to the technology of blockchain, so it doesn't require a qualification check while consumers use it. It is immutable and anonymous so that no one can change your transaction, and identifying who owns the blockchain address can be difficult. Because of these characteristics blockchain technology can reshape the banking industry in a more disruptive way than ever before (Martino, 2021).

Decentralized Finance (DeFi) is a financial technology that uses blockchain technology as a trust mechanism, so it provides a way to deal with the problems of traditional finance (Ojog, 2021). Today, DeFi is becoming very attractive, and the number of decentralized applications is increasing (Puschmann & Huang-Sui, 2024). DeFi contains a variety of business models, including decentralized exchange (DEX), decentralized lending and collateralized debt position.

There are two platforms for cryptocurrency trading, centralized exchange (CEX) and DEX. Most of the exchange volume is happening at CEX (Aspris et al., 2021) because they are easier to use. However, DEXs volume is catching up. The reasons for the popularity of DEXs are linked to the unique advantages of DeFi. First, CEX is a business that requires Know Your Customer (KYC). It requires customers' identification for registration to comply with anti-money laundering regulations and any other laws from the countries its customers come from. Because of this, users are still concerned about several issues such as privacy and the risk of their wealth being confiscated. It is very difficult to block and confiscate DEX users' wealth because it is anonymous and only an address is needed, unlike KYC. Next, CEXs are always using order books as their business models, which means they have high intermediary fees, and high trading slippage due to generally insufficient liquidity. On the contrary, DEXs are using automatic market makers (AMM) or centralized liquidity automatic market makers (CLAMM) as their business models, which can be a good solution to the above problems. Finally, CEXs only list cryptocurrencies that meet their requirements, if people want to trade a wider variety of cryptocurrencies they will need DEX. DEX is a perfect place for long-tail assets, anyone can make a liquid pool with any asset without needing permission.

DEX has great significance in digital trading as well as some challenges and limitations, so it is necessary to find out what factors are affecting DEX adoption. Different DEXs have their advantages and disadvantages, previous works are mainly focused on the differences between DEXs, for instance, whether people prefer AMM-based DEX (Xu et al., 2023) and how to design a DEX better than others. However, this research will focus on what and how external factors affect DEX's adoption.

DEX adoption can be quantified by two indicators, DEX Total Value Locked (TVL) and DEX trading volume. This research will use Curve Dao DEX (CURVE) as a case to show the impact of external factors on DEX adoption. External factors like market sentiment and influencers' marketing are not easy to quantify, so this research is trying to use chain TVL as an indicator to represent market changes and on-chain users' numbers, and clarify the relationship between chain TVL and DEX TVL. Another indicator is the transaction fee (GAS) to show how transaction costs impact DEX adoption. This research attempts to answer these three questions:

1. What are the external factors that affect retail DEX adoption?
2. What is the relationship between chain TVL and DEX adoption?
3. What is the trend of trading volume changing while transaction fees change?

Understanding what external factors can affect DEX adoption is necessary. DEX is still an emerging incremental market, acquiring new consumers from traditional financial businesses is much more important, and useful, than focusing on the competition between different DEXs. This research identifies how external factors impact DEX adoption, and what should DEXs do to attract more users. The study finds that the development of the DeFi industry has a significant impact on the adoption of DEXs, so DEXs should cooperate to develop the industry instead of focusing on competing for a larger share of the existing market. Some other external factors also have an impact, such as technological innovation, partner integration and community support.

The second section is the literature review, which integrates current work and illustrates the concepts needed for the research. The third section is the methodology and then the analysis. The findings are in section four and section five is the discussion. The last section is the conclusion and limitations of the research.

2 Literature Review

The literature review clarifies the concepts that are necessary to understand the decentralized exchange (DEX) and its adoption. The first section is about DEX and how it is part of DeFi. The second part illustrates the concepts of the variables. This research aims to find how external factors affect DEX adoption, and there are four variables needed to achieve this aim, they are blockchain total value locked (TVL), blockchain GAS price, Curve DEX TVL and its trading volumes. The last part, is the summary of the literature review.

2.1 Decentralized Exchange (DEX)

2.1.1 Decentralized Finance (DeFi)

Markets are typically centralized in classical economic theory (Malamud & Rostek, 2017). However, the development and advancement of modern Fintech have a huge impact on reshaping the financial industry. Customers now have new demands and expectations, such as anonymity and security, which could not be fulfilled by centralized finance. DeFi disintermediates reducing intermediaries and their costs (Puschmann & Huang-Sui, 2024). There are many decentralized applications (dApps) offering various financial services (Jensen et al., 2021). Some DeFi applications are decentralized lending, derivatives decentralized trading, collateralized debt positions (CDP), decentralized exchanges (DEX) and so on.

2.1.2 Decentralized Exchange (DEX)

When people trade goods, tokens or cryptocurrencies, they need a platform to match these transactions. In the past, there were only centralized platforms, like brokers or auction houses. These kinds of intermediaries are susceptible to losses from a single point of failure. In 2015, NYSE faced an "internal technical issue", and it caused a nearly four-hour outage (CNN, 2015). Even in the blockchain industry, centralized exchanges (CEX) have problems. These centralized platforms claim that they would ensure the safety of traders' money and provide an efficient way to match the buyers and sellers. However, firstly they are not safe, exchanges have had cybersecurity breaches and the misappropriation of user funds occurs from time to time. For instance, the world's largest bitcoin exchange at the time, Mt. Gox was breached and lost 650,000 Bitcoins in 2014; the CEO of the exchange FTX, misappropriated users' money. What's more, they are not efficient. CEXs are using order books as their buyers-to-sellers match method, which means they will not have sufficient liquidity, especially in some small CEXs and unpopular trading pairs. In extreme conditions, traders may suffer huge slippage losses or even not be able to complete a transaction.

But now, thanks to the smart contract, it is possible to have a decentralized intermediary. Developers can use smart contracts to deploy decentralized APPs (dAPP) on the blockchain, these dAPPs can be accessed using non-custodial wallets, so they are anonymous instead of needing a Know-Your-Customer (KYC). In addition, a decentralized blockchain with a lot of validators will not face the problem of downtime. Because all the transactions and movements are executed by a smart contract through blockchain, if the code doesn't have a backdoor and is well-written, the safety issues are limited. Traders will control their assets instead of the platform. The popularity of the phrase "Not Your Key, Not Your Coin" illustrates the importance of this to many people. Anyone using the DEX could get rewards by locking their assets into it to provide liquidity (Gogel et al., 2021). Instead of using

Table 1 SWOT analysis of DEX

Strengths	1. DEXs are safer than CEXs, and users can control their assets. 2. KYC is not needed which can fulfill users' need for anonymity. 3. All transaction records are publicly available on the blockchain, enhancing transparency and trust in transactions.
Weaknesses	1. It is harder to teach users how to use a DEX than a CEX. 2. Transactions are slower than CEX due to the blockchain verification, especially in busy times.
Opportunities	1. People are more and more concerned about privacy and security issues; therefore, the DEX market has tremendous growth potential. 2. Innovative technologies and model designs, like governance tokens and vote-escrowed, make DEXs more attractive.
Threats	1. Because it is hard to regulate, governments generally put more pressure on DEXs. 2. The limitations of blockchain technology, such as scalability and speed issues, may affect the development of DEX.

illiquid order books to match buyers and sellers, decentralized exchanges typically use liquidity pools provided by automated market makers (AMM) (Friesendorf & Blütener, 2023). The illustration of DEX business models is in the next section, before that, it is necessary to have a quick summary of DEX by using the SWOT analysis method (Table 1).

Thus, this research uses two independent variables, the Ethereum blockchain TVL to represent the change in the scale of the industry, and the blockchain GAS price to show the market sentiments.

2.1.3 DEX Business Models

DEXs have several business models because they have customers with different needs, some of them are still using order books like CEX while others are using more effective methods such as automated market maker (AMM). It is true that AMM not only can be used on DEXs but also on some other kinds of DeFi.

AMM-based DEX has liquidity pools for each trading pair, when a transaction happens, DEX will calculate the right output amount according to the input amount and the pool balance by using the constant function. As the most representative forms of constant function market maker (CFMM), constant sum and constant product are widely adopted by AMM-based DEX protocols (Xu et al., 2023).

Despite the special algorithm making it possible to have automated pools for traders to use, there are still some questions. If DEXs want to provide a low slippage, low swap fees and a more sufficient liquidity environment to traders, how should they attract more people to provide liquidity as there are some risks when staking on the platform? Curve DEX innovatively built an ecosystem based on their governance token, Curve token (CRV). To attract users to provide liquidity, Curve provides CRV as the reward as well as the original pools' trading fees to the liquidity providers.

2.2 Concepts of Variables

This research includes four variables, the independent variables are Ethereum blockchain TVL and Ethereum blockchain GAS price and the dependent variables are Curve DEX TVL and its trading volumes. This section discusses these variables.

2.2.1 Total Value Lock (TVL)

Which indicator should be used to represent the industry scale of DeFi? Total Value Lock (TVL) can represent the amount of invested funds by expressing in monetary terms, with accuracy and timeliness (Stepanova & Erins, 2021). TVL represents the amount of money that users already deposited into the platform (Dydx, 2024). As mentioned earlier, this research includes two variables related to TVL.

The first one is an independent variable, blockchain TVL, which will be the Ethereum chain TVL in this case because Curve DEX is mainly built on the Ethereum blockchain. What's more, according to Defillama.com, the TVL indicators across all chains clearly show that Ethereum is the most popular. The second one is a dependent variable, Curve DEX TVL to represent its adoption.

2.2.2 Blockchain GAS Price

Another independent variable that has been chosen in this research is the blockchain GAS price. In this case, the GAS price is the Ethereum GAS price. So, what is blockchain GAS and what is blockchain GAS price? GAS measures the computational effort required to execute specific operations on the blockchain (Ethereum Foundation, 2024). There is a question about GAS fees, why do they exist and why does the blockchain need GAS fees? GAS fees could help prevent network spamming by attaching a cost to each transaction to avoid blockchain overloading with unnecessary transactions, and because the fees will be an incentive for validators, they would have the motivation to contribute their ETH to help secure the network. This process is known as proof of Stake. Then how to calculate the GAS fee? According to Coinbase's tutorial (2024), the calculation of GAS fees involves two key components: The GAS limit and its price, therefore, the transaction cost is the product of the GAS limit and the GAS price. The GAS fee system is running automatically when a transaction is called, it will be paid regardless of whether the transaction succeeds or fails.

The reason to choose the GAS price as an independent variable to represent the market sentiment on-chain is because the cost of GAS fees is influenced by supply and demand dynamics, GAS prices may increase while the network experiences high traffic. By using the GAS price indicator, it will show how the GAS price influences the DEX trading volume during network congestion and even the level of DEX adoption.

2.2.3 DEX Trading Volume

As mentioned before, DEX adoption from the seller side can be represented by Curve DEX TVL, but what about the buyer side? The traders are the buyer side of DEX retail users, because trading is to buy an asset by using another asset, so it makes sense to use trading volume to show the DEX adoption.

2.3 Summary

The current work on DEX is more concentrated on which internal factors could bring advantages to one DEX, to help it increase its market share compared to other DEXs. These works are useful because they can help build a better DEX, but the area that also needs to be researched, but has not caught much attention yet is how the external factors affect DEX adoption, in other words, how to expand the scale of the whole DEX industry. In this research, the effect of two external factors is explored.

Decentralized exchange (DEX) is a platform that allows users to trade crypto assets directly peer-to-peer without relying on a centralized intermediary. Curve is an AMM-based DEX that brings low slippage and low fees for users. The independent variables used are Ethereum TVL and GAS price, as they could represent the industry scales and short-term market sentiment. The dependent variables are Curve DEX TVL and its volumes, which can show the DEX adoption trend.

3 Methodology

3.1 Research Design

3.1.1 Research Approach and Method

This research uses secondary data and then applies quantitative methods to analyse it. There are two independent variables, chain TVL and transaction fees (GAS) and two dependent variables, Curve TVL and its volumes. The blockchain which been selected as the instance is the Ethereum chain because it contains the largest TVL, therefore, the GAS price chosen is also from Ethereum. According to this, although Curve is a multiple-chain DEX, its TVL and volumes will be selected only for the Ethereum chain. Considering the feasibility, the two dependent variables should be modelled separately to eliminate their interactions. Therefore, there are expected to be two formulas, all independent variables to Curve TVL, and them to Curve volumes. Then according to the formulas, it should be easy to find the relationships between them. The research is trying to identify the formula of all independent variables and each dependent variable, to show the trends. The data this research needs are four variables, and they are collected from defillama.com and blockchair.com. These formulas are expected to show how external factors influence DEX adoption:

$$\text{Curve DEX TVL} = A^{*}\ \text{chain TVL} + B^{*}\ \text{GAS price}$$

$$\text{Curve volume} = C^{*}\ \text{chain TVL} + D^{*}\ \text{GAS price}$$

3.2 *Data Analysis Processes*

Data analysis typically starts with several steps such as data collection, data cleaning, data integration and structuring (Cai et al., 2023). This section focuses on three stages: data collection, processing and analysis. The first stage is data collection, which is identifying the data sources needed to ensure that there is sufficient and relevant data for analysis. The second stage is data cleaning, by cleaning the null, missing and outlier values, the data set will be more exact and accurate for the analytics. Next, the data exploratory analysis is important, trends and preliminary analysis of the data were obtained through data visualization and descriptive statistics. The last stage of data analytics is data modelling and editing, which could help to find the relationship between variables.

3.2.1 Data Collection

Ethereum TVL, Curve DEX TVL and its volumes were collected from defillama.com, and Ethereum GAS price from blockchain.com. To make them correspond to each other, a timestamp is required, which means that each data should involve both the time and the numerical information. To find the relationship between dependent and independent variables, and avoid the impact between dependent variables, two data tables are used (table A and table B) (Tables 2 and 3).

Table 2 Table A

	Ethereum TVL	Ethereum GAS price	Curve DEX TVL
Day1			
Day2			
Day3			
...			

Table 3 Table B

	Ethereum TVL	Ethereum GAS price	Curve DEX volumes
Day1			
Day2			
Day3			
...			

3.2.2 Data Processing

The goal of data preprocessing is to clean and correct input data so that the results may be later applied faster and with greater accuracy. Then data cleaning removed null values and outliers. This research uses Python language to analyse the data, through the website Colab from Google. The cleaned data has 1589 records.

3.2.3 Data Analysis

Because in this research every variable is numerical instead of content, and the dependent variables do not follow the Bivariate Distribution, a Linear Regression Model should be applied. First, the data is put into train and test datasets to effectively avoid over-fitting or under-fitting problems, which can help to improve the performance of models in practical applications. Then the code used is: $model = LinearRegression\ ()$ to employ the model, after that, predict on the test dataset to evaluate the model. The Ordinary Least Squares (OLS) method is used in analytics, which is a widely used linear regression method to estimate the values of unknown parameters in a regression model. In table A, after the linear regression model has been employed the value of R-squared is 0.746. Typically, data analysis theory suggests that when R-squared is between 0.6 and 0.8, the model has a good ability to explain the data. The last step is to draw a figure to show the relationship between the real value and the predicted value, which will be shown in the result, and calculate the correlation coefficient.

4 Results

As there are two formulas, one uses Curve DEX TVL as the dependent variable, while another uses Curve DEX volume, and there are results for both of them separately. Sections 4.1 and 4.2 are the results for each table, while Sect. 4.3 will introduce the limitations of this research's data analytics, including the small amount of data and the inaccuracy caused by the interaction between variables.

```
corr_matrix:
                      ETH TVL ($)  ETH GAS PRICE (GWei)  Curve DEX TVL ($)
ETH TVL ($)              1.000000              0.245767           0.859413
ETH GAS PRICE (GWei)     0.245767              1.000000           0.275964
Curve DEX TVL ($)        0.859413              0.275964           1.000000
                            OLS Regression Results
==============================================================================
Dep. Variable:      Curve DEX TVL ($)   R-squared:                       0.747
Model:                            OLS   Adj. R-squared:                  0.747
Method:                 Least Squares   F-statistic:                     2342.
Date:                Tue, 16 Jul 2024   Prob (F-statistic):               0.00
Time:                        16:34:05   Log-Likelihood:                -36825.
No. Observations:                1589   AIC:                         7.366e+04
Df Residuals:                    1586   BIC:                         7.367e+04
Df Model:                           2
Covariance Type:            nonrobust
```

Fig. 1 Table A OLS regression results

Table 4 Table A results

	Coef	Std err	t	$P >$ $\|t\|$	[0.025	0.975]
Const	−1.772e+09	1.33e+08	−13.368	0.000	−2.03e+09	−1.51e+09
ETH TVL	0.1706	0.003	61.476	0.000	0.165	0.176
ETH GAS PRICE	0.0108	0.002	6.721	0.000	0.008	0.014

4.1 Curve DEX TVL

This section is about the results and explanation of table A, which contains variables: Ethereum TVL, Ethereum GAS price and Curve DEX TVL. The results can be found in Fig. 1 and Table 4 below. According to Fig. 1, the following views can be drawn. First, the dependent variable is Curve DEX TVL and the R-squared of this model equals 0.747. This is a high value for R-squared, which means that this model has a strong explanatory ability. The independent variables jointly have a significant impact on the dependent variable because the F-statistic value is high.

Then the details can be found in Table 4. According to the results shown in the table, the formula for the dependent variable, Curve DEX TVL, can be summarized as

$$\text{CURVE DEX TVL } (\$) = 0.1706^{*}\text{ETH TVL } (\$) + 0.0108^{*}\text{ETH GAS PRICE } (\text{GWei}) - 1.772E + 09.$$

All independent variables have the $P > |t|$: 0.000, which means they are all very statistically significant. Const term has a wider confidence interval, while both of the independent variables have a narrow one. Therefore, the estimated values for independent variables are more accurate than const.

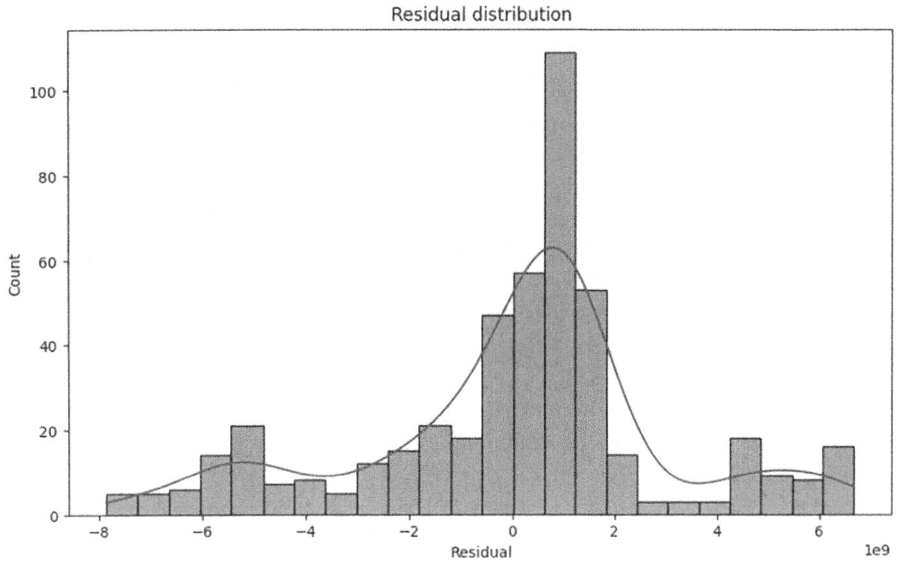

Fig. 2 Table A residual distribution

Table 5 Table A residual analysis

Omnibus: 80.012	Durbin-Watson: 0.011
Prob (Omnibus): 0.000	Jarque-Bera (JB): 100.836
Skew: −0.497	Prob (JB): 1.27e−22
Kurtosis: 3.730	Cond. No. 1.54e+11

Next, use residual analysis to assess the multicollinearity of variables and the autocorrelation. According to Table 4, the results of the autocorrelation can be found. First, the residuals do not follow the normal distribution, according to the indicators Omnibus and Prob (Omnibus). Skew and Kurtosis show residual distribution is skewed (Fig. 2). The Durbin-Watson indicator should be close to 2, while in this case is only 0.011, which means there is severe autocorrelation (Table 5).

In sum, the first model, which uses Curve DEX TVL as the dependent variable, has strong explanatory power because of the high value of R-square. Secondly, all of the independent variables have a significant impact on the dependent variable. However, there are also some problems, multicollinearity of variables and the autocorrelation may affect the accuracy of the model. According to this model, this formula can be used to represent the relationship between variables:

$$\text{CURVE DEX TVL } (\$) = 0.1706^{*}\text{ETH TVL } (\$) + 0.0108^{*}\text{ETH GAS PRICE } (\text{GWei}) - 1.772\text{E} + 09.$$

4.2 Curve DEX Volume

This section is about the results and explanation of Table B, which contains variables: Ethereum TVL, Ethereum GAS price and Curve DEX volume. The results can be found in Fig. 3 and Table 6 below. According to Fig. 3, the following views can be drawn. First, the dependent variable is Curve DEX volume and the R-squared of this model equals 0.328. According to this indicator, this model is not as good as the first one, which means that this model does not have a strong explanatory ability. The adjusted R-squared is 0.324, which shows that the independent variables have some explanatory power, but it is not strong enough. The independent variables jointly can significantly affect the dependent variable because the F-statistic value is high.

Then the details can be found in Table 6. According to the results shown in the table, the formula for the dependent variable, Curve DEX volume, can be summarized as:

$$\text{CURVE DEX volumes (\$)} = 0.0046^{*}\text{ETH TVL (\$)} + 0.0014^{*}\text{ETH GAS PRICE (GWei)} - 1.876\text{e} + 07.$$

All independent variables have the $P > |t|$: 0.000, which means they are all very statistically significant. However, the $P > |t|$ indicator for const is 0.287, higher than

```
corr_matrix:
                    ETH TVL ($)  ETH GAS PRICE ($)  CURVE VOLUMES ($)
ETH TVL ($)            1.000000          -0.136087           0.159918
ETH GAS PRICE ($)     -0.136087           1.000000           0.021638
CURVE VOLUMES ($)      0.159918           0.021638           1.000000
                            OLS Regression Results
==============================================================================
Dep. Variable:      CURVE VOLUMES ($)   R-squared:                       0.328
Model:                            OLS   Adj. R-squared:                  0.324
Method:                 Least Squares   F-statistic:                     88.17
Date:                Wed, 17 Jul 2024   Prob (F-statistic):           6.62e-32
Time:                        13:00:31   Log-Likelihood:                -7220.9
No. Observations:                 364   AIC:                         1.445e+04
Df Residuals:                     361   BIC:                         1.446e+04
Df Model:                           2
Covariance Type:            nonrobust
```

Fig. 3 Table B OLS regression results

Table 6 Table B results

	Coef	Std err	t	$P > \|t\|$	0.025	0.975
Const	−1.876e+07	1.76e+07	−1.067	0.287	−5.33e+07	1.58e+07
ETH TVL	0.0046	0.000	13.045	0.000	0.004	0.005
ETH GAS PRICE	0.0014	0.000	4.211	0.000	0.001	0.002

Table 7 Table B residual analysis

Omnibus: 128.189	Durbin-Watson: 1.332
Prob (Omnibus): 0.000	Jarque-Bera (JB): 412.036
Skew: 1.599	Prob (JB): 3.37e−90
Kurtosis: 7.115	Cond. No. 1.61e+11

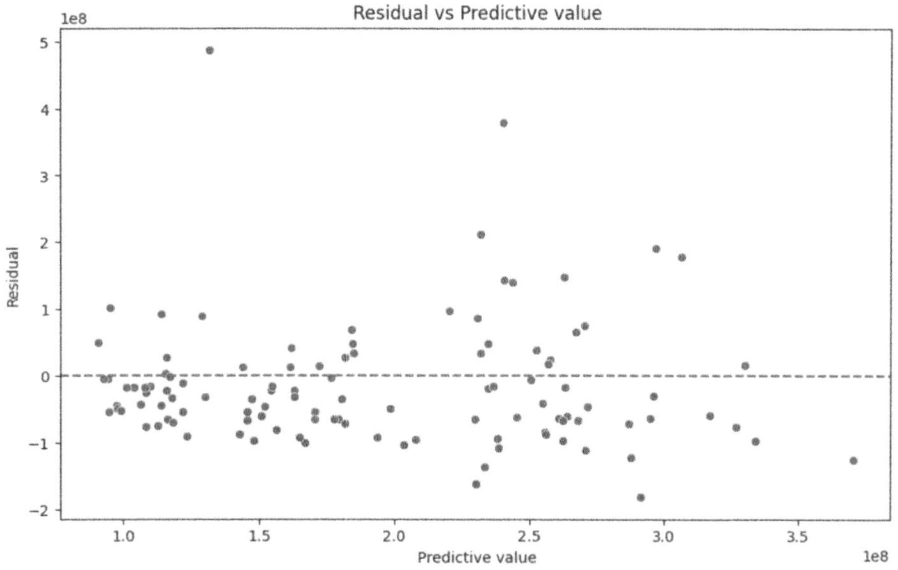

Fig. 4 Table B residual scatter plot

0.05. So, in this model, const is not statistically significant. Like the first model, the const term has a wider confidence interval, while both of the independent variables have a narrow one. Therefore, the estimated values for independent variables are more accurate than const.

Next, residual analysis is used to assess the multicollinearity of variables and the autocorrelation. According to Table 7, the results of the autocorrelation can be found. First, the residuals do not follow the normal distribution, according to the indicators Omnibus and Prob (Omnibus). Skew and Kurtosis show that the residual distribution is right-skewed (Fig. 4). The Durbin-Watson indicator should be close to 2, while in this case is 1.332, better than the first model, but it still has some autocorrelation. Cond.No. is high, and shows severe multicollinearity.

In sum, the second model, which uses Curve DEX volume as the dependent variable, has limited explanatory power because of the low value of R-square. The independent variables explained some of the variation in the Curve DEX volume, but there is still a lot of unexplained variation. Secondly, all of the independent variables have a significant impact on the dependent variable. For the autocorrelation aspect, this model performs better than the first one but has a severe multicollinearity problem which may affect the accuracy of the model. According to this model, this

	ETH TVL ($)	ETH GAS PRICE ($)	CURVE VOLUMES ($)
0	26103330528	26561534518	5.594012e+07
1	26169485872	26283994639	1.405758e+08
2	26252769817	32103618808	1.027090e+08
3	26192577210	38381579868	1.121221e+08
4	27197526760	28760372099	2.228097e+08
..	...	...	...
361	54847100291	12186106860	5.914191e+08
362	52459229878	4122720026	3.164913e+08
363	53841766734	3808631625	1.872676e+08
364	51135824075	6078534017	2.205242e+08
365	53286902418	5644262627	2.206983e+08

[364 rows x 3 columns]

Fig. 5 Table B residual scatter plot

formula cannot be used to represent the relationship between variables:

$$\text{CURVE DEX volumes (\$)} = 0.0046^{*}\text{ETH TVL (\$)} + 0.0014^{*}\text{ETH GAS PRICE (GWei)} - 1.876\text{e} + 07.$$

4.3 Model Limitations

This part is only about the limitations of the model. First, the volume of data affects the accuracy of the model. In model two, there are only 364 records left after the outlier and null values cleaning (Fig. 5). This situation causes the model to not have a strong explanatory ability.

Secondly, autocorrelation affects the model, which means that the Curve DEX TVL and volumes could change over time, even the Ethereum TVL and GAS prices do not change at all. After the check of the independent variables, it shows that they also have autocorrelation (Fig. 6). In model one (Curve DEX TVL), the *R*-square is high at 0.747, thus there may be a small impact from the autocorrelation. On the contrary, model two is suffering from a lot of problems, which means that the model is not reliable.

Therefore, the second model cannot be used until it is improved. The model has problems with non-normality and heteroscedasticity; to solve these problems, it is necessary to use the Weighted Least Squares (WLS) method. The WLS method is a regression analysis technique that is mainly used to deal with data with heteroscedasticity. Heteroscedasticity refers to the fact that the variances of the error terms in the data are not equal at different observation points. In this case, the ordinary least squares (OLS) method may produce biased or inaccurate estimates.

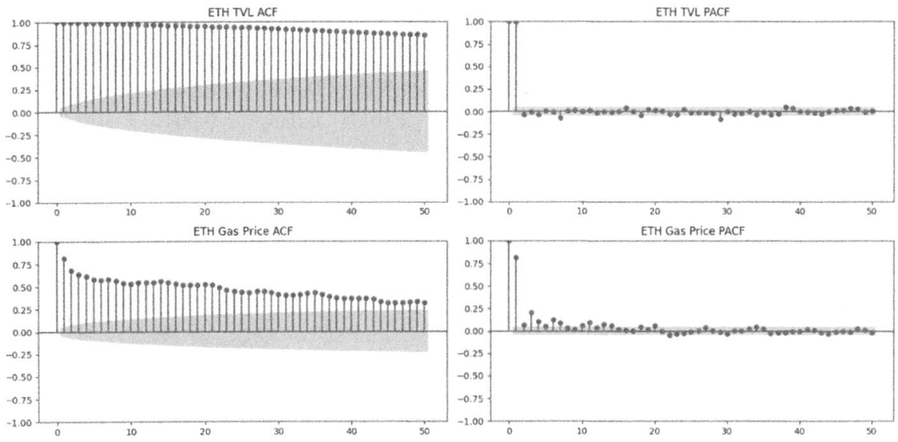

Fig. 6 Independent variables auto-correlation check

OLS Regression Results

Dep. Variable:	CURVE VOLUMES ($)_LOG	R-squared (uncentered):	0.999
Model:	OLS	Adj. R-squared (uncentered):	0.999
Method:	Least Squares	F-statistic:	2.447e+05
Date:	Sun, 21 Jul 2024	Prob (F-statistic):	0.00
Time:	16:03:20	Log-Likelihood:	-273.64
No. Observations:	364	AIC:	551.3
Df Residuals:	362	BIC:	559.1
Df Model:	2		
Covariance Type:	nonrobust		

Fig. 7 Table B OLS weighted least squares (WLS) results

After the logarithmic transformation for the variables and the next analytics, the new results can be summarized. Figure 7 below shows that the adjusted model has a very high *R*-square value, 0.999, thus in this model, the independent variables can strongly explain the dependent variable, the Curve DEX volumes.

Table 8 shows that all of the independent variables have a significant impact on the dependent variable, as all of the $P > |t|$ values are smaller than 0.05. Because we used the uncentered regression, there are no constant values in the new model. The new model can be summarized as the formula:

$$\log\ (\text{CURVE VOLUMES}) = 0.7097 \cdot \log\ (\text{ETH TVL}) + 0.0691 \cdot \log\ (\text{ETH GAS PRICE}),$$

and after the transformation, the formula can be written as:

$$\text{CURVE VOLUMES} = \text{ETH TVL}^{0.7097} \cdot \text{ETH GAS PRICE}^{0.0691}.$$

Table 8 Table B WLS results

	Coef	Std err	t	$P > \|t\|$	[0.025	0.975]
ETH TVL_LOG	0.7097	0.032	21.962	0.000	0.646	0.773
ETH GAS PRICE_LOG	0.0691	0.033	2.101	0.036	0.004	0.134

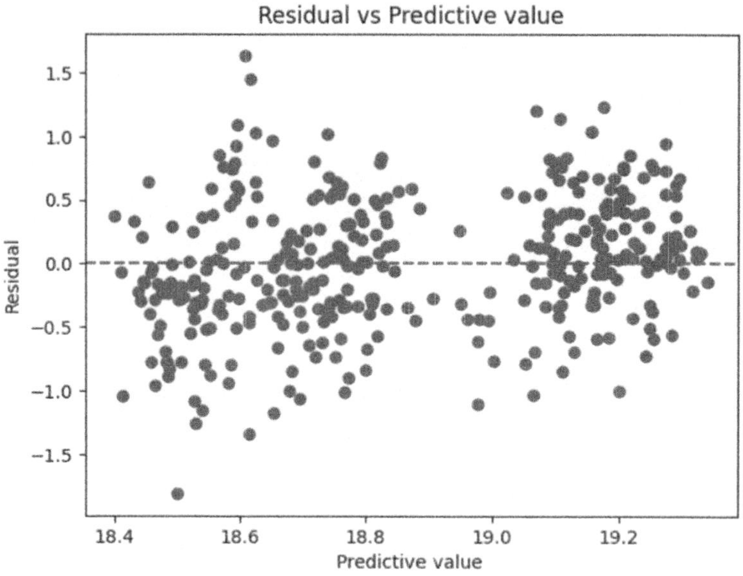

Fig. 8 Table B residual scatter plot

The new model performs better in the residual scatter plot (Fig. 8), and it is more representative.

4.4 Summary

In summary, two formulas that can show the relationships between the variables came out after the data analytics:

$$\text{CURVE DEX TVL } (\$) = 0.1706^{*}\text{ETH TVL } (\$) + 0.0108^{*}\text{ETH GAS PRICE } (\text{GWei}) - 1.772\text{E} + 09.$$

and

$$\text{CURVE VOLUMES} = \text{ETH TVL}^{0.7097} \cdot \text{ETH GAS PRICE}^{0.0691}.$$

The first model is generally good, more than 1.6 thousand records make it reliable, and the *R*-square value shows a strong explanatory ability. In the meanwhile, the limitation of the number of records makes the second model less reliable, increases uncertainty in model parameter estimates and finally leads to poor explanatory ability. Because of this, it is necessary to use the WLS method to improve its reliability, and then the new formula for the new model is above.

5 Discussion

The discussion has two parts. Section 5.1 is the findings of the Curve DEX case. By analysing the models related to the external factors and the DEX adoption indicators, it is expected that the industry scales (Ethereum TVL) and marketing sentiment (Ethereum GAS price) affect the DEX adoption (Curve DEX TVL and its volumes). Some other external factors that can also impact the DEX adoption are discussed in Sect. 5.2.

5.1 *Curve DEX Case*

In the Curve DEX case, two models have been employed, and then according to these models, the relationships between variables can be summarized as two formulas below:

$$\text{CURVE DEX TVL } (\$) = 0.1706^{*}\text{ETH TVL } (\$) + 0.0108^{*}\text{ETH GAS PRICE (GWei)} - 1.772\text{E} + 09.$$

$$\text{CURVE VOLUMES} = \text{ETH TVL}^{0.7097} \cdot \text{ETH GAS PRICE}^{0.0691}.$$

5.1.1 Curve DEX TVL

The formula (CURVE DEX TVL ($) = 0.1706*ETH TVL ($) + 0.0108*ETH GAS PRICE (GWei) − 1.772E+09) shows that both ETH TVL and ETH GAS PRICE have a positive impact on the Curve DEX TVL. ETH TVL indicator in this model is the main affect on Curve DEX TVL, as its coefficient is the largest, 0.1706.

Meanwhile, the ETH GAS price indicator was originally expected to have a huge positive correlation with the DEX adoption, because it shows the market sentiment, a higher GAS price means more transactions are executed on the blockchain at the same time. But in this model, the correlation coefficient is only a little greater than zero, which means ETH GAS price only has a small positive impact on the Curve DEX TVL, and has less impact compared with ETH TVL, as it is only 0.0108.

Why does this happen? First, the GAS prices have their limits. The GAS price distribution has clear upper and lower limits, and the vast majority of gas prices are distributed from zero to 2e+11 Only in extreme situations the gas price is higher than 3e+11. It only floats within a fixed range, so its impact is not large. Furthermore, the GAS price increases due to more transactions, but these transactions not only come from the trading transactions that happen on DEXs but also come from other uses of blockchain and DeFi, so not all of them will be reflected in DEXs. Finally, the dependent variable in this model is Curve DEX TVL has a certain hysteresis. When the market sentiment is high, and more people come to use DEXs, then a high Annual Percentage Yield (APY) for the users' asset that staking in the DEX platform, further attracts more people put their asset into the platform. Therefore, the GAS price indicator cannot reflect the DEX adoption immediately in the Curve DEX TVL aspect.

5.1.2 Curve DEX Volume

The formula ($\text{CURVE VOLUMES} = \text{ETH TVL}^{0.7097} \cdot \text{ETH GAS PRICE}^{0.0691}$) shows that the impact of Ethereum TVL and GAS price on the Curve DEX volumes are the non-linear effects. The exponents of the independent variables show how these factors affect the dependent variable. For the Ethereum TVL indicator, it raised to the power of 0.7097, while another one raised to the power of 0.0691.

According to Table 9, the Ethereum TVL has a huge impact on the Curve DEX volumes. If it increases by 1%, the volume will increase by around 0.7%. However, the exponent is less than one, so the effect is decreasing. The boundary is mainly because the trading need is now limited by the number of users on the blockchain, and the education costs that bring users from traditional finance into the new Fintech are high and take some time. The GAS price also has a positive impact on Curve DEX volumes as expected, but the effect is small. As with the first model, the reason is that its range is very narrow, and not all of the transactions relate to trading on DEXs. Next, the high GAS price will increase the blockchain transaction fee and then cost more when users trade on a DEX. This situation could react to transaction volume, forcing people who are not desperate to trade on-chain immediately to choose the CEXs or trade later.

Table 9 Comprehensive change rate matrix

GAS price ETH TVL	0%	Increase 1%	Increase 2%	Increase 3%
0%	1	1.000686	1.001373	1.002061
Increase 1%	1.007056	1.007742	1.008429	1.009117
Increase 2%	1.014198	1.014898	1.015585	1.016273
Increase 3%	1.021360	1.022063	1.022750	1.023439

In sum, according to the second model, the industry scales have a huge but decreasing positive impact on the Curve DEX volumes, while the market sentiments do not have a significant effect on it.

5.1.3 DEX Adoption

According to the results of the two models of this research, the DEX adoption is closely related to industry scales, but the GAS price has less impact on it. For the DEX volume aspect, the impact from both independent variables is showing a decreasing trend.

Why the increase of the blockchain TVL, which is the expansion of the industry scale, can increase the DEXs TVL and their volumes? In the beginning, when the blockchain TVL increased, more and more assets and money flowed into the blockchain ecosystem, some of them may enter into the DEXs for the real yield because offering the liquidity pools for the DEXs can always get rewards from the trading fees. Passive liquidity pools are token holders who wish to passively invest their assets to accumulate trading fees, thereby the passive liquidity pools directly increase the DEXs TVL.

Then, the increase of the DEX TVL improves the liquidity of the cryptocurrency pairs on the platform, which makes the trading slippages, which means the amount the price moves in a trading pair between when a transaction is submitted and when it is executed, lower to provide a smoother, cheaper and more efficient trading experience to the users. The users trading on the platform increase trading volumes, further which will react to more income for the liquidity providers, improve their annual percentage yield, and then attract more liquidity pools deposit into the DEXs to create a DeFi flywheel loop. Therefore, the blockchain TVL has a huge impact on both the DEX TVL and its volumes. However, because it is hard to teach users how to use blockchain and DeFi, it is not possible to convert a large number of traditional users to on-chain users in a short time. So, after the DEX users and volumes increased reaching a certain level, in this situation, even if the liquidity continues to increase, the speed of trading volumes will slow down. And that is why the impact rate is showing a decreasing trend.

Why the GAS price increase only has a small and positive impact on DEXs TVL and their volumes? The opposite of blockchain TVL is GAS price affects the DEXs TVL partly through impact on its volumes. First of all, the increase in GAS price shows that the transactions on the blockchain are increasing, which means the market sentiment is high at that moment. In this situation, the blockchain ecosystem activity increases and leads to the DEX volumes going up, and then the annual percentage yields (APY) of the liquidity pools increase to be more attractive and push more people to stake assets into the platform. Furthermore, in the high GAS price scenario, some liquidity providers may choose to lock their pools into the DEXs for a longer time to avoid the trading costs from frequent interactions with blockchain. However, when the GAS price is high, the higher costs of executing transactions will be an obstacle to some small transactions, and force the users to use CEX or the DEX on other blockchains. For example, trading on the Ethereum blockchain on June 5th, 2023 with a GAS price of 149.76 GWei, which means a trading call on Uniswap DEX with a 356,190 Gas limit will cost $169.06 for the GAS fee. So, when the blockchain reaches a high level, the marginal growth will be affected by blockchain capabilities (TPS) and its Consensus Algorithm (PoS, PoW or PoH).

Therefore, blockchain TVL has a significant positive impact on DEX adoption. The increase in blockchain TVL has significantly increased the DEX TVL and its volumes. However, the marginal effect is decreased because of the difficulty of converting users on-chain in a short time, so the power of pulling in DEX trading volumes is weakening while the industry scale keeps growing. For the GAS price aspect, although a high GAS price represents a high market sentiment and confidence to attract more funds deposit and trading in the DEX, it also makes the transaction costs higher and suppresses small transactions. So, the short-term market sentiment does not have a significant impact on the DEX adoption.

5.2 *Other External Factors Affect DEX Adoption*

There are three other main factors that affect DEX adoption. The first factor is the technological innovation in the industry, including the blockchain performance, the infrastructure and new entrants on-chain. First, the scalability and performance of the blockchain can directly impact the time it takes for a transaction confirmation, and therefore affect the users' experience of DEX. The majority of users of DEX are people who have cryptocurrency trading needs, so the main competitor of DEX is CEX. Due to the CEX always being built on the internet instead of blockchain technology, they have the characteristics of high transaction speed and low interaction fees, because they don't need to pay the blockchain GAS fees. But for the on-chain products, when the volume of transactions surpasses the network's capacity, it leads to a condition known as blockchain network congestion, provoking processing delays (Algoine, 2023). Therefore, even though DEXs are safer and have anonymity, if the transaction fees are high or the blockchain is congested, more people will go to use CEX instead of DEX. Even though the DEX to CEX spot trade volume is increasing, it still hasn't surpassed 15% yet, and most of the cryptocurrency traders are still using CEX (the block, 2024).

Innovation in the infrastructure and new entrants on-chain could also affect DEX adoption. PUMP.FUN is a new product built on the Solana blockchain, and it is a cryptocurrency token launchpad that simplifies the way that tokens are launched. By using this tool, the only steps that you need to create your token are, to set up a name for your token and add the liquidity pool in DEX. With no coding knowledge required, it makes launching a token easy. Since PUMP.FUN was made available in March 2024, and DEX volume on Solana is increasing, even surpassing Ethereum on some days. Now, more new tokens appear on-chain (almost 20K tokens minted per day), which leads to an increase in trades. Because the trading pairs on CEX need to have permission to start while those on DEX don't, most of the new tokens can only trade on DEX. Therefore, industry innovation could bring advantages to DEX and increase its adoption. Nevertheless, regardless of how simple it is to launch a cryptocurrency or other cryptoasset, it is still necessary to build consumer trust in it (Zarifis & Fu, 2024).

The second factor is partner integration and community support. As mentioned earlier in this research, it is hard to acquire new users for DEX in a short time because the users' education costs are high. Purchasing a cryptoasset can require several steps and the adoption of technologies that are new to the user and they may not trust (Zarifis & Castro, 2022). Using DEX needs more extra steps compared with using CEX, retailers have to learn new things starting from the download of digital wallets, the introduction of public and secret keys, to the use of decentralized applications (DApps) and the permissions of DApps, etc. So, partner integration is necessary to expand the users, especially with partners who can professionally teach users how to use DEX. A lot of CEXs, nowadays, like OKX and COINBASE, started to realize the prospects of DeFi and then developed their WEB3 digital wallets with the integration of many DEXs and published some tutorial videos and articles to educate new users. The OKX WEB3 wallet provides one-stop asset management, secure storage, transfer and other functions so users can access all of the DEXs (OKX, 2023). The integration provides convenience to users and makes it more acceptable for users to use DEX. What's more, community support is also important, a strong and active community can increase projects' visibility and reliability. Community education and promotion activities help more users understand and use DEX.

The last factor is the external environment, including macroeconomics and regulation. Unlike short-term market sentiment, macroeconomics always has long-term cyclical characteristics. Macroeconomics is also reflected in the blockchain industry scales. In the period of macroeconomics going up, market liquidity is sufficient, which makes the investors have more interest in high-tech and risky assets and then push the blockchain industry to grow. However, when the interest rate of traditional currencies increases, the market liquidity shrinks, and this leads to a decline in cryptoasset investment. The regulatory policies of different countries and regions affect the operation and user adoption of DEX, and strict supervision may limit the development of DEX. Even if DEX does not require KYC and is anonymous, some DEXs can block the IP addresses of local users to comply with the laws of different countries and regions.

6 Conclusion

This research uses secondary data from Defillama and blockchair, and quantitative methods to analyse the impact of external factors on DEX adoption. The two formulas tested include Ethereum TVL, GAS price, Curve DEX TVL and its volumes:

$$\text{CURVE DEX TVL }(\$) = 0.1706^{*}\text{ETH TVL }(\$) + 0.0108^{*}\text{ETH GAS PRICE (GWei)} - 1.772\text{E} + 09.$$

$$\text{CURVE VOLUMES} = \text{ETH TVL}^{0.7097} \cdot \text{ETH GAS PRICE}^{0.0691}.$$

Both of the formulas show that ETH TVL has a significant impact on DEX adoption instead of GAS price, this provides important empirical evidence for the liquidity management of DEX.

6.1 Theoretical Contribution

This research is different from most other research in this area as it focuses on external factors instead of internal ones, and has two theoretical contributions:

First, related research is mainly focused on the difference between DEXs, and tries to find how a DEX can gain an advantage over other DEXs, but this research concentrates on the external factors to show how to encourage DEX adoption. While market fluctuations may attract short-term attention and reactions, the long-term development of DEX relies on a stable user base in DeFi and continued expansion of the industry.

Secondly, this research enriches the theoretical framework of DeFi and sheds light on the relationship between DeFi and DEX. A DEX relies on the liquidity of DeFi, with higher liquidity on the blockchain, the DEX liquidity is expected to be higher, leading to slippage (which means the loss that users suffer when trading on DEX) is reduced. This research provides new insights into understanding the liquidity dynamics of Curve DEX, extending existing theory on the interplay between liquidity and transaction costs.

6.2 Practical Contribution

This research offers guidance to the stakeholders of DEX, including the users, blockchain engineers, developers, and regulators. First, it discusses the potential external factors that can affect DEX adoption. In addition to the industry scale, these factors also contain the innovation in the industry, which could improve the user experience, and the support from partners and communities, which could boost the new users of DEX, and the external environment that would affect DEX adoption by affecting the industry scale. The DeFi industry scale, which is the blockchain TVL, has a significant impact on DEX adoption, therefore, it is also important to figure out what could impact the DeFi adoption. According to the discussion, the obstacles to DeFi's increasing adoption are trust, infrastructure and regulation.

Therefore, this research provides some suggestions. From the blockchain layer, the highest priority of blockchain engineers is to build better infrastructures to provide a faster and safer platform for decentralized application developers. From the application layer, developers should find a way to solve the liquidity fragment problem and make it easier to use for users. It will be helpful if users, communities and other partners can introduce and educate new users. Many governments are embracing blockchain technology and new Fintech, reducing counterproductive regulations, and avoiding frequent changes, to help the development of financial technology (Proskalovich et al., 2023). The results of this research emphasize that industry health is much more important than the competition between DEXs. If the large DEX providers such as Uniswap, Curve DEX and Velodrome-swap, work together to expand the industry scale, and attract more users on-chain instead of competing for the market share, the adoption of DEX will be stronger.

6.3 Limitations and Future Research

The first limitation is that the specific case chosen does not represent all DEXs accurately due to there being many different blockchains and DEXs. Other DEXs on other blockchains should be researched to make sure the findings of this research have broad applicability. If future research on other DEXs can also use more data, that represent behaviour over a longer period of time, this will clarify these issues further.

References

Algoine. (2023). *Understanding blockchain network congestion causes, consequences, and mitigation strategies*. Accessed from https://algoine.com/news/Understanding-Blockchain-Network-Congestion-Causes,-Consequences,-and-Mitigation-Strategies/1539?Lang=en

Ali, S., et al. (2024). Reputational contagion from the Silicon Valley Bank debacle. *Research in International Business and Finance, 69*, 102275. https://doi.org/10.1016/j.ribaf.2024.102275

Aspris, A., et al. (2021). Decentralized exchanges: The 'wild west' of cryptocurrency trading. *International Review of Financial Analysis, 77*. https://doi.org/10.1016/j.irfa.2021.101845

Banafa, A. (2020). *Blockchain technology and applications* (River publishers series in security and digital forensics). River. https://doi.org/10.1201/9781003337393

The Block. (2024). Latest crypto news. https://www.theblock.co/

Cai, Q., et al. (2023). A survey on deep reinforcement learning for data processing and analytics. *IEEE Transactions on Knowledge and Data Engineering, 35*(5). https://doi.org/10.1109/TKDE.2022.3155196

CNN. (2015). *Nyse suspends trading*. Accessed from https://money.cnn.com/2015/07/08/investing/nyse-suspends-trading/index.html

Coinbase. (2024). *What are gas fees?* Accessed from https://www.coinbase.com/en-gb/learn/crypto-basics/what-are-gas-fees

Dydx. (2024). *DeFi's pulse: Explaining total value locked in Crypto*. Accessed from https://dydx.exchange/crypto-learning/tvl

Ethereum Foundation. (2024) *Ethereum development documentation*. Accessed from https://ethereum.org/en/developers/docs/gas/

Friesendorf, C., & Blütener, A. (2023). *Decentralized finance (defi): How decentralized applications (dapps) disrupt banking*. Springer. https://doi.org/10.1007/978-3-031-37488-3

Gogel, D., Baker-Taylor, T., Cloots, A. S., Forster, B., Lazaro, J., Schär, F., & Sokolin, L. (2021, May). *Defi beyond the hype*. The Wharton School. Accessed from https://wifpr-wharton-upenn-edu.soton.idm.oclc.org/wp-content/uploads/2021/05/defi-Beyond-the-Hype.pdf

Jensen, J. R., Wachter, V., & Ross, O. (2021). An introduction to decentralized finance (defi). *Complex Systems Informatics and Modeling Quarterly, 0*(26), 46–54. https://doi.org/10.7250/csimq.2021-26.03

Malamud, S., & Rostek, M. (2017). Decentralized exchange. *The American Economic Review, 107*(11), 3320–3362.

Martino, P. (2021). *Blockchain and banking: How technological innovations are shaping the banking industry*. Palgrave Macmillan. https://doi.org/10.1007/978-3-030-70970-9

Ojog, S. (2021). The emerging world of decentralized finance. *Informatică Economică., 25*(4), 43–52. https://doi.org/10.24818/issn14531305/25.4.2021.05

OKX. (2023). *OKX Web3*. Accessed from https://medium.com/@okxweb3/about

Olaleye, S. A., Nuhu, N., & Gallindo, E. (2022). An exploration of card payment services in Mexico: A managerial and customer perspective. *Journal of Technology Management & Innovation, 17*(4). https://doi.org/10.4067/S0718-27242022000400014

Proskalovich, R., Jack, C., Zarifis, A., Serralde, D. M., Vershinina, P., Naidoo, S., Njoki, D., Pernice, I., Herrera, D., & Sarmiento, J. (2023). *Cryptoasset ecosystem in Latin America and the Caribbean*. University of Cambridge - Cambridge Center for Alternative Finance (CCAF). Accessed from https://www.jbs.cam.ac.uk/faculty-research/centres/alternative-finance/publications/crypotasset-ecosystem-in-latin-america-and-the-caribbean/

Puschmann, T., & Huang-Sui, M. (2024). A taxonomy for decentralized finance. *International Review of Financial Analysis, 92*. https://doi.org/10.1016/j.irfa.2024.103083

Stepanova, V., & Erins, I. (2021). Review of decentralized finance applications and their total value locked. *TEM Journal, 10*, 327–333. https://doi.org/10.18421/TEM101-41

Xu, J., Paruch, K., Cousaert, S., & Feng, Y. (2023). SoK: Decentralized exchanges (DEX) with automated market maker (AMM) protocols. *ACM Computing Surveys, 55*(11), 1–50. https://doi.org/10.1145/3570639

Zarifis, A., & Castro, L. A. (2022). The NFT purchasing process and the challenges to trust at each stage. *Sustainability, 14*(24), 16482. https://doi.org/10.3390/su142416482

Zarifis, A., & Cheng, X. (2022). A model of trust in Fintech and trust in Insurtech: How artificial intelligence and the context influence it. *Journal of Behavioral and Experimental Finance, 36*, 1–20. https://doi.org/10.1016/j.jbef.2022.100739

Zarifis, A., & Fu, S. (2024). The second extended model of consumer trust in cryptocurrency payments, CRYPTOTRUST 2. *Frontiers in Blockchain, 7*, 1–11. https://doi.org/10.3389/fbloc.2024.1220031

Yuan Yao graduated from Beijing Forestry University and is currently pursuing a master's degree at the University of Southampton, both degrees majoring in information systems. He became involved with blockchain technology and DeFi in 2021, starting by being attracted by Asymmetric

Cryptography and then finding the charm of Decentralized Finance. As a participant of DeFi, his research interests include Decentralized Exchange, Collateralized Debt Position and platform governance token rewards.

Alex Zarifis research and teaching are on the practical applications of technology in business. Before the University of Southampton, he worked at several academic institutions including the University of Cambridge, University of Manchester and the University of Mannheim. He is currently a research affiliate of the Cambridge Center for Alternative Finance (CCAF). He has explored cryptoassets such as cryptocurrencies since 2012. As part of this research, he published the first peer-reviewed research on trust in digital currencies in the world in 2014. He also participated in creating the first government recognized, university degree on blockchain technologies in the world. Dr Alex has published extensively on trust in different technologies and business models. His research has explored the role of trust in AI, blockchain, financial technology (Fintech) and insurance technology (Insurtech).

Arena Club: A Case Study in Web3 and Fintech Innovation in the Collectibles Market

David Krause

1 Introduction

The intersection of Fintech and Web3 technologies is redefining industries far beyond traditional financial services, including the sports card market—a key segment of the broader collectibles and alternative investment landscape. Originally emerging in the late 19th century, the sports card industry has grown into a multi-billion-dollar enterprise, capturing the interest of collectors and investors alike. However, this market has faced persistent challenges, such as authenticity verification, ownership transfer, and secure secondary market transactions, which have hindered its full potential.

Arena Club, a pioneering entity in this space, is leveraging Web3 technologies—particularly blockchain and non-fungible tokens (NFTs)—to address these challenges and transform the industry.[1] By utilizing these technologies, Arena Club seeks to enhance security, transparency, and efficiency within the market, offering new investment opportunities and redefining the role of digital assets in collectibles. This paper examines Arena Club's innovative approach as a case study, exploring its impact on the sports card market and its implications for the broader Fintech ecosystem. The analysis highlights how the integration of Web3 solutions into the sports card industry exemplifies the evolving role of Fintech in reshaping traditional

[1] Web3 is a decentralized internet ecosystem built on blockchain technology, aiming to return ownership and control of data to users enabling new economic models and digital assets (Krause, 2024a).

D. Krause (✉)
Marquette University, Milwaukee, WI, USA
e-mail: david.krause@marquette.edu

A. Zarifis, X. Cheng (eds.), *Fintech and the Emerging Ecosystems*, Financial Innovation and Technology, https://doi.org/10.1007/978-3-031-83402-8_8

markets, offering insights into future applications of blockchain in the collectibles sector.

2 Sports Cards: An Engaging Alternative Asset

The collectibles market has experienced a surge in popularity as investors seek to diversify their portfolios beyond traditional asset classes (Kleine et al., 2024). Within this realm, sports cards have emerged as a particularly compelling investment opportunity. Offering the potential for substantial returns, sports cards have captivated both seasoned investors and newcomers alike.

Originating as simple inserts in tobacco and gum packages, trading cards initially featured a diverse array of subjects (Bloom, 1997). However, the advent of professional sports leagues in the mid-20th century triggered the growth of sports card collecting. The subsequent expansion of card themes to encompass entertainment, history, and other popular domains—including gaming—have broadened the market's appeal.[2]

Several key factors contribute to the fluctuating value of trading cards, making them a dynamic and intriguing investment. Among the most significant determinants is scarcity (Ghazi & Schneider, 2024). Like fine art and other collectibles, limited production runs, unique variations, and exceptional conditions can exponentially increase a card's desirability and, consequently, its value. Illustrative examples of rare cards include the legendary Honus Wagner T206 card issued in 1909, often likened to the "Mona Lisa" of baseball cards, as well as the record-breaking $12.6 million auction price achieved by a 1952 Mickey Mantle card in 2022 (Hajducky, 2022).

Card condition is another critical factor influencing value (Thompson & Sen, 2024). Professional grading services, such as Professional Sports Authenticator (PSA), meticulously assess a card's authenticity, preservation, and overall quality. A standardized grading scale, ranging from 1 (Poor) to 10 (Gem Mint), provides a transparent framework for evaluating condition. Encapsulation in tamper-evident cases called slabs safeguards cards from damage and enhances their market liquidity.

Beyond their financial potential, trading cards often possess significant historical and cultural value. As tangible artifacts capturing iconic moments and legendary athletes, they resonate deeply with collectors and sports enthusiasts. This intrinsic appeal, coupled with the potential for financial appreciation, creates a compelling investment proposition for those seeking to own a piece of sports and cultural history.

[2] Trading card games (TCG) like Pokémon, Magic: The Gathering, and Yu-Gi-Oh! blend strategy, collection, and competition as players construct decks using unique cards.

3 Arena Club Background

Arena Club is a young company, established in 2021, that has rapidly emerged as a key player in the sports memorabilia industry. Specifically focused on trading cards, the company operates a digital platform that facilitates the buying, selling, and trading of authenticated sports cards. To bolster consumer confidence and provide accurate valuations, Arena Club also offers card grading services. The company's target market primarily consists of sports memorabilia collectors and gaming enthusiasts.

Headquartered in Los Angeles, California, as of July 2024, Arena Club has secured $19 million in funding across a single Series A round led by a consortium of venture investors including M13, BAM Ventures, Defy Partners, Elysian Park Ventures, and Lightspeed Venture Partners. Brian Lee is the founder and Chief Executive Officer, while Jesse Glass is a co-founder who serves as the Chief Financial Officer and Chief Operating Officer. Notably, Hall of Fame baseball player Derek Jeter is also a co-founder, supporter, and investor in the company.

4 Competitive Analysis

In 2024, the eBay Vault partnership with PSA was announced (PR Newswire, 2024). This combined service offers secure storage for valuable trading cards in climate-controlled, high-security facilities. The primary benefit for sports card collectors using PSA, the largest player in the industry, is a seamless integration with eBay, allowing for easy listing and selling of vaulted cards. Ownership of a card transfers instantly upon purchase, eliminating costs and wait times associated with shipping a physical card. Additionally, buyers can leverage PSA's authentication and grading platform.

PSA's acquisition of eBay's vault marks the first step in their movement to online vaulting of sports cards (Rajan, 2024). They indicate that the vaulting option offers comprehensive features such as climate-controlled storage, insurance coverage, and 24-hour security, which is underpinned by expert inspection of all stored items to ensure authenticity and trustworthiness. Integration with eBay streamlines transactions, enabling instant ownership transfer upon purchase which facilitates listing, packaging, and shipping through PSA's dedicated eBay store. This strategic move further solidifies PSA's longstanding expertise in authentication and grading.

Beyond PSA and eBay, other significant players have emerged in the sports card vaulting space. Established marketplaces like PWCC Marketplace, renowned for its auction platform, have expanded to offer secure vaulting services for valuable card collections. Similarly, COMC, originally focused on comic book management, also provides comprehensive storage and management solutions for trading cards. Additionally, Beckett, a respected authority within the collectibles industry, is preparing to enter the vaulting market as it seeks to leverage its brand recognition and extensive expertise. These players bring diverse approaches and strengths to the market, enriching the landscape of options available to collectors and investors alike. While Arena Club offers innovative solutions tailored to tech-savvy collectors, PSA's integration with eBay positions it with broader market reach and enhanced liquidity, underscoring its competitive advantage in the dynamic and evolving sports card ecosystem.

5 Industry Data Analysis

This research leverages data from two key sources: GemRate and Arena Club. GemRate, an independent authority in the trading card industry, tracks and analyzes data from major grading companies (PSA, Beckett, CGC, and SGC) to provide insights for collectors and investors.[3] Their data, based on grading company population reports, reveals the volume and grade distribution of specific cards. Arena Club's published population report offers a similar breakdown for cards they have graded. The analysis considers data from both sources, encompassing the companies' entire history as well as a specific period from January 2022 to July 2024.

Arena Club grades modern, officially licensed sports and gaming cards, potentially including some vintage cards that meet specific criteria. Table 1 reveals that since 2022, Arena Club's graded cards are dominated by major sports categories, with baseball (31.2%) and basketball (27.1%) comprising over 58% of the total. Football cards also hold a significant share (21.0%), while hockey and other sports cards represent a small fraction. Notably, Pokémon cards (9.0%) capture a considerable portion, while "Other" (10.8% estimate) encompasses a diverse range of minor sports, media, and trading game card types.

Exhibit 1, which is a one-week snapshot of reported grading activity by the major players, shows the clear hierarchy within the industry. PSA's weekly grading

Table 1 Arena Club Grading Card Data Inception to July 2024

Card Type	Count	Share
Baseball	57,522	31.2%
Basketball	49,990	27.1%
Football	38, 714	21.0%
Hockey	1715	0.9%
Pokémon	16,695	9.0%
Other (estimate)	20,000	10.8%
Total	184,636	

[3] The four largest sports card grading companies in the industry are: Professional Sports Authenticator (PSA), Beckett Grading Services (BGS), Certified Guaranty Company (CGC), and Sportscard Guarantee Company (SGC).

Fig. 1 One-week snapshot of reported grading activity

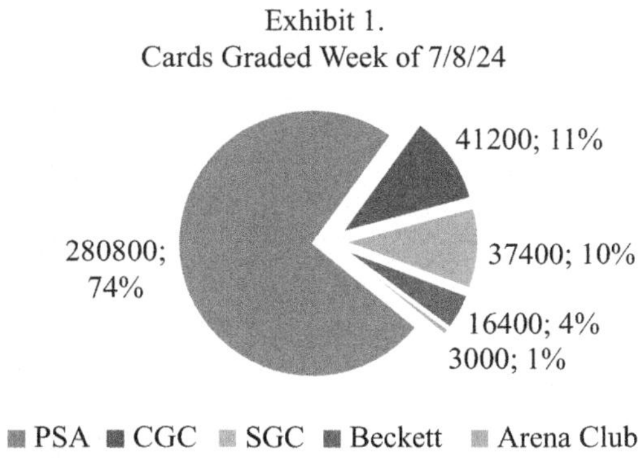

Table 2 Top 10 Sports Cards from PWCC Iconic 100 Tracker

Popularity	Sport	Card
1	Baseball	1952 Topps Mickey Mantle
2	Basketball	1986 Fleer Michael Jordan
3	Baseball	1933 Goudey Babe Ruth
4	Basketball	2003 UD Exquisite Collection LeBron James Patch Autograph
5	Football	2000 Playoff Contenders Tom Brady Autograph
6	Hockey	1979 O-Pee-Chee Wayne Gretzky
7	Basketball	1980 Topps Larry Bird/Julius Erving/Magic Johnson
8	Baseball	1989 Upper Deck Ken Griffey Jr Star Rookie
9	Baseball	1948 Leaf Jackie Robinson
10	Basketball	1961 Fleer Wilt Chamberlain

volume (74% of all cards graded) dwarfs the other established competitors. Arena Club's weekly volume is growing and currently amounts to about 1% of the total grading activity (Fig. 1).

The PWCC Iconic 100 Tracker, compiled by PWCC Marketplace, is a list of the most valuable and classic cards in the sports card hobby. The following table lists the top 10 most coveted sports cards of the past century (Table 2).

Examining a specific card can reveal further insights into the sports card grading industry. The following is a picture of the 1986 Fleer Michael Jordan #57 card (Fig. 2):

Table 3 shows grading data since January 2022 for the 1986 Fleer Jordan card. A gem rating is the top grade assigned by the grading company, signifying a card in mint condition. This highly coveted status significantly increases a card's value compared to ungraded or lower-graded counterparts. Table 3 reveals that PSA and Beckett together graded a combined 88.7% of the Jordan cards suggesting they are the preferred choices for collectors of these valuable cards.[4] Conversely, CGC and Arena Club combined to grade less than 1% of the iconic card during this period.

[4] In March 2023, the 1986 Fleer Jordan card, grade 10, sold for $192,000 in a Goldin Auction.

Fig. 2 1986 Fleer Michael Jordan #57 card (picture of author's card)

Table 3 1986 Fleer Michael Jordan Grading Data January 2022–July 2024

Grading Company	PSA	Beckett	SGC	CGC	Arena Club	Total
Cards Graded	27,099	14,163	3819	102	202	45,385
Gem Rated	1.20%	3.90%	0.80%	1.00%	0.00%	2.00%

Exhibit 2 displays a histogram of the Arena Club grading scores for the 1986 Fleer Michael Jordan card. Of the 202 cards graded, there is a concentration of these towards the higher end of the grading scale, suggesting a sizeable portion of these cards are in very good to mint condition; however, none achieved a 10 gem rating (Fig. 3).

In addition to examining a specific card, it is useful to analyze the grading trend of an entire annual set of cards, in this case, the 1986 Fleer Basketball set. Tables 4 and 5 provide insights into the grading distribution and quality of the 1986 Fleer set, comparing data from the grader's inception date to July 2024 and from January 2022 to July 2024. PSA dominates the market with about 80% of cards graded with a gem rating in the range of 4–5% depending upon the period examined. Beckett is second in grading volume and has a higher gem rate in the range of 7–10% of the cards graded. SGC, CGC, and Arena Club combined to make up about 10% of the graded 1986 Fleer cards since January 2022, with a gem rating of about

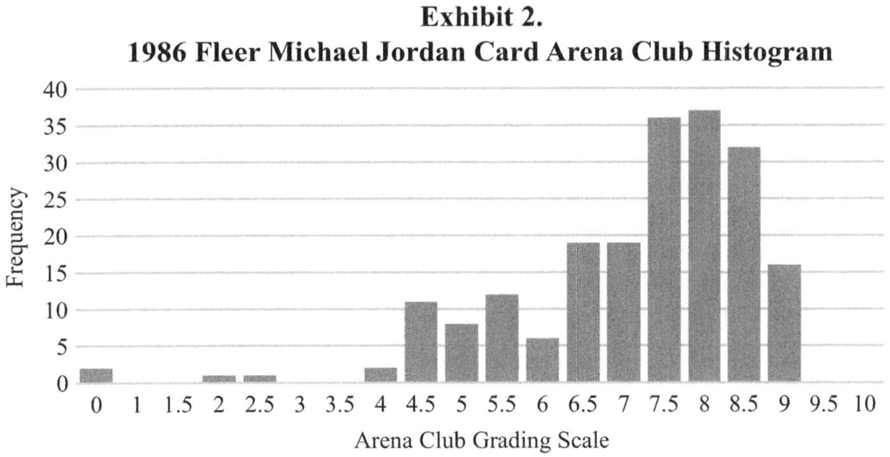

Fig. 3 Histogram of the Arena Club grading scores

Table 4 1986 Fleer Basketball Set Grading Data Inception Date—July 2024

Card Count	PSA	Beckett	SGC	CGC	Arena Club	Total
Cards Graded	506,813	95,708	42,426	7730	202	652,879
Market Share	77.63%	14.66%	6.50%	1.18%	0.03%	
Card Grading	**PSA**	**Beckett**	**SGC**	**CGC**	**Arena Club**	**Total**
Cards Graded Gem	20,610	7234	635	23	0	28,502
Gem Rate	4.10%	7.60%	1.50%	0.30%	0.00%	4.4%

Table 5 1986 Fleer Basketball Set Grading Data January 2022–July 2024

Card Count	PSA	Beckett	SGC	CGC	Arena Club	Total
Cards Graded	132,447	10,636	10,251	6524	202	160,060
Market Share	82.75%	6.65%	6.40%	4.08%	0.13%	
Gem Rate	5.30%	9.80%	2.00%	0.30%	0.00%	5.2%

1%. This analysis confirms PSA's market leadership, although Beckett's higher gem rate suggests it may attract higher-quality submissions.

The research shows that PSA reigns supreme in the grading market, handling a significant portion of total cards graded across all companies and card types. They also hold a dominant share for specific high-value cards like the 1986 Fleer Michael Jordan. However, while trailing PSA in volume, Beckett boasts a higher gem rate for some valuable cards, suggesting they cater to collectors seeking top-quality cards. Additionally, as a growing player, Arena Club focuses on modern cards and has a smaller market share compared to established giants, but their presence indicates potential for future growth.

6 Understanding Arena Club's Web3 Infrastructure

Arena Club is integrating advanced Web3 technologies into the traditional sports card industry. Utilizing artificial intelligence (AI) for image analysis and condition assessment, alongside blockchain for secure and transparent card provenance, Arena Club is transforming the card grading process (Kruszeski, 2024; Krause, 2024b).[5] Additionally, their exploration of NFTs provides collectors with new avenues for digital ownership and trading of physical cards, effectively bridging the gap between analog and digital collectibles. The process of creating and accessing a card's NFT with Arena Club is detailed in Appendix A.

Blockchain as the Foundation Blockchain technology serves as the cornerstone of Arena Club's platform, providing a secure and transparent infrastructure for managing sports card ownership and transactions. By utilizing a blockchain, Arena Club can offer several key advantages:

- **Immutability:** Once recorded on the blockchain, transaction data becomes permanent and cannot be altered, ensuring the integrity of ownership records, and preventing fraudulent modifications.
- **Transparency:** The public nature of the blockchain allows anyone to verify the authenticity of a card and its ownership history, enhancing trust and confidence among market participants.
- **Security:** Blockchain's cryptographic mechanisms protect data from unauthorized access, reducing the risk of hacking and data breaches.

Beyond these core benefits, blockchain's decentralized nature contributes to the platform's robustness. By distributing data across multiple nodes, the risk of data loss or corruption is significantly mitigated. Additionally, the absence of a central authority reduces the potential for censorship or manipulation of transaction records. Furthermore, blockchain's potential for scalability and interoperability can facilitate seamless integration with other digital assets and platforms.

Polygon Offers Efficiency and Scalability While blockchain technology provides a strong foundation, challenges such as scalability and transaction speed can hinder its adoption in certain applications. To address these limitations, Arena Club has leveraged the Polygon network. This is a layer-2 scaling solution built on Ethereum, designed to improve transaction throughput and reduce costs. By utilizing Polygon, they seek to offer faster and more cost-effective transactions while maintaining the

[5] Empirical research found Arena Club's AI grading system to hold promise, offering greater objectivity and faster turnaround times at a lower cost than human-based grading. As more cards are graded, AI models are expected to learn and improve, potentially achieving greater consistency than human graders.

security benefits of the underlying blockchain technology. Polygon's key advantages include:

- **Enhanced scalability:** Polygon's architecture enables significantly higher transaction throughput compared to Ethereum, allowing for smoother operations and faster processing times, even during peak usage periods.
- **Lower transaction costs:** By processing transactions off-chain and bundling them into blocks before submitting them to the Ethereum mainnet, Polygon reduces gas fees and makes transactions more affordable for users.[6]
- **Compatibility with Ethereum:** Polygon is fully compatible with the Ethereum Virtual Machine (EVM), allowing for seamless integration with existing Ethereum-based applications and smart contracts.

Non-Fungible Tokens NFTs are distinctive digital assets that are built on blockchain technology. While cryptocurrencies are fungible and interchangeable, NFTs are non-fungible, which means each item is distinct and irreplaceable. NFTs play a crucial role in digital asset ownership by representing ownership of a specific asset, such as a piece of art, a collectible, or in the case of Arena Club, a digital representation of a physical sports card. By tokenizing these assets, NFTs provide a verifiable and secure method of establishing ownership and facilitating their transfer.

Digital Proof of Claim At the heart of Arena Club's platform is the Digital Proof of Claim (DPOC), a unique digital asset representing ownership of a physical sports card. Each DPOC is minted as an NFT on the Polygon blockchain, providing a verifiable and immutable record of ownership. The following describes the process:

- **Minting:** When a physical card is added to the Arena Club vault, a corresponding DPOC is minted on the Polygon blockchain.[7] This process creates a digital twin of the physical card, linking it to its unique NFT.[8]
- **Ownership Transfer:** When a card is sold or traded on the Arena Club platform, the associated DPOC is transferred from the seller's digital wallet to the buyer's wallet (See Appendix B). This transfer is recorded on the blockchain, establishing a clear and transparent chain of ownership.
- **Burning:** If a user decides to retrieve their physical card from the vault, the corresponding DPOC is "burned," effectively removing it from circulation. This process ensures that only one physical card exists for each DPOC.

---

[6] Ethereum gas fees are the transactional costs paid to miners for processing and validating transactions on the blockchain, with their amount fluctuating based on network congestion.

[7] A trading card platform vault is a secure, climate-controlled storage facility for physical trading cards that integrates with digital platforms for management, valuation, and trading.

[8] A digital twin is a virtual replica of a physical object or system that uses real-time data to simulate and optimize its counterpart.

By utilizing DPOCs, Arena Club offers several advantages to collectors and investors:

- **Enhanced Authenticity:** Each DPOC is uniquely linked to a physical card, providing a verifiable digital certificate of authenticity.
- **Fractional Ownership:** DPOCs can potentially be divided into fractions, allowing multiple investors to own shares of a valuable card.
- **Secondary Market Efficiency:** The blockchain-based trading of DPOCs facilitates faster and more secure transactions compared to traditional methods.
- **Additional Features:** DPOCs can incorporate additional features such as digital signatures from athletes or celebrities, enhancing the collectible value of the card.

Furthermore, DPOCs can serve as a foundation for building a vibrant digital ecosystem around sports cards. For example, they can be integrated with augmented reality experiences, providing interactive elements for collectors. Additionally, DPOCs can be used to create digital collectibles and merchandise, expanding the revenue streams for both Arena Club and card owners.

IPFS and Decentralized Storage An InterPlanetary File System (IPFS) is a decentralized storage and distribution system used to store and access data in a peer-to-peer network. In the context of Arena Club, an IPFS is utilized to store the digital images and metadata associated with sports cards. By leveraging IPFS, Arena Club can reduce reliance on centralized storage providers and improve the security, resilience, and accessibility of card data.

7 Creating New Opportunities in the Sports Card Market

Arena Club's Web3 ecosystem has the potential to revolutionize the sports card industry by facilitating peer-to-peer trading, eliminating intermediaries, and increasing transparency and trust through blockchain technology, while also offering innovative features like digital twin technology and fractional ownership for enhanced accessibility and liquidity.

Fractional Ownership and Tokenization Tokenization presents an unprecedented opportunity to democratize ownership of high-value sports cards. By dividing a card into fractional digital tokens, platforms can enable a broader investor base to participate in the market. This fractional ownership model can dramatically increase liquidity, as tokens can be traded on secondary markets with greater ease compared to physical card ownership. Moreover, tokenization can provide transparency into the card's ownership history, valuation, and any associated benefits, such as a share of potential future profits from the card.

Digital Collectibles NFTs are ideally suited for creating digital collectibles linked to physical sports cards. These digital assets can offer unique ownership verification, enabling collectors to showcase and trade their digital representations. Furthermore,

NFTs can be used to create virtual experiences, such as augmented reality (AR) or virtual reality (VR) showcases, enhancing the overall fan experience. By linking physical cards to digital NFTs, platforms can create a hybrid model that bridges the gap between the physical and digital worlds.

Blockchain and Sports Card Valuation Blockchain technology can revolutionize sports card valuation by providing an immutable record of a card's history, including ownership, grading, and any relevant transactions. This transparency can enhance trust and confidence in the market. Additionally, smart contracts can be utilized to automate valuation processes based on predefined criteria, such as card condition, player performance, and market trends. While challenges remain in accurately capturing physical card condition digitally, advancements in image recognition and AI could potentially address this issue. Blockchain-based valuation systems can contribute to a more efficient, transparent, and reliable sports card market.

8 Potential Legal and Regulatory Challenges

The intersection of blockchain technology and the sports card market introduces a range of legal and regulatory challenges that must be navigated carefully. These challenges span several key areas:

Securities Regulation One critical regulatory issue is the classification of the Digital Proof of Ownership Certificates. Determining whether DPOCs are classified as securities is important. If they are deemed securities, platforms like Arena Club could face stringent regulatory oversight. This would include the necessity for registration and adherence to rigorous investor protection rules, fundamentally altering the operational landscape for these platforms. Such classification could impose extensive compliance requirements, potentially increasing operational costs and impacting the scalability and accessibility of these platforms.

Additionally, the tokenization of high-value sports cards to offer fractional ownership brings another layer of regulatory complexity. Tokenization allows investors to purchase a fraction of a high-value card, democratizing access to rare and expensive items. However, this practice raises regulatory questions about whether these fractional ownership tokens qualify as securities. If deemed securities, these tokens would fall under the purview of the regulation of the Securities and Exchange Commission (SEC), necessitating compliance with laws designed to protect investors. This includes detailed disclosure requirements, registration of the offering, and ongoing reporting obligations. Ensuring compliance with these regulations is essential to protect investors and maintain market integrity, but it also requires platforms to navigate a complex legal framework.

Furthermore, the regulatory classification of DPOCs and tokenized sports cards could influence their market perception and acceptance. Investors may be wary of platforms that fail to clearly address these regulatory issues, potentially limiting the growth and adoption of blockchain-based sports card trading. Therefore, platforms like Arena Club must proactively engage with regulatory authorities, seek clarity on applicable laws, and implement robust compliance measures to foster trust and legitimacy in this emerging market. Addressing these challenges effectively is crucial for the sustainable development of a blockchain-based ecosystem for sports card grading, storing, and trading.

Consumer Protection Protecting customers is a critical consideration in the integration of blockchain technology within the sports card market. While blockchain significantly enhances the verification of authenticity, consumers remain vulnerable to fraud, especially concerning physical card counterfeits. Therefore, ensuring the authenticity of both digital and physical cards is vital in protecting consumers from fraudulent activities. Platforms must implement robust measures to authenticate the cards they manage to maintain consumer trust and market integrity.

Additionally, platforms need to ensure the security of both digital assets and physical cards under their custody. This includes safeguarding against breaches and losses, which could otherwise lead to substantial consumer complaints and potential legal liabilities. Implementing strong security protocols and maintaining comprehensive custody practices are essential to protecting consumer assets and upholding the platform's reputation. Addressing these consumer protection concerns is vital for fostering a safe and trustworthy environment for sports card enthusiasts in the evolving digital marketplace.

Tax Implications Transactions involving Digital Property Ownership Certificates may trigger capital gains tax obligations for collectors. Platforms should provide clear guidance on these tax obligations and potentially integrate with tax reporting systems to streamline compliance. Additionally, the sales tax applicability to digital assets is an evolving area of law. Platforms must stay informed about relevant regulations to avoid legal issues.

Intellectual Property In the realm of sports card grading and trading, safeguarding intellectual property rights is important. Platforms must carefully monitor and prevent trademark and copyright infringement, particularly concerning sports figures, team logos, and card designs. Unauthorized utilization of these protected materials can result in legal conflicts, emphasizing the necessity for strong intellectual property management. Moreover, platforms must adhere to stringent data privacy regulations, such as the General Data Protection Regulation (GDPR) and California Consumer Privacy Act (CCPA), when handling consumer information and transaction histories.[9] Adhering to these regulations helps build user trust while also reducing the legal risks linked to data privacy violations.

Anti-Money Laundering (AML) and Counter-Terrorism Financing (CTF) These are interconnected measures designed to protect the financial system from criminal

[9] These are data privacy laws protecting consumer data rights in their respective jurisdictions.

activities by preventing the movement of illicit funds. In addition, to prevent the misuse of platforms for illicit activities, strong Know Your Customer (KYC) and Customer Due Diligence (CDD) procedures are essential. These measures help identify potential money laundering and terrorist financing risks. Additionally, strict adherence to sanctions regulations is crucial to avoid engaging in transactions with sanctioned individuals or entities.

9 Leveraging Web3 for Customer Loyalty and Community Engagement

Arena Club is poised to harness the transformative potential of its Web3 infrastructure to foster an engaged community. By strategically implementing loyalty programs, cultivating a strong user base, and leveraging data-driven insights, Arena Club can create a thriving ecosystem that drives long-term success.

Gamified Loyalty Programs and Rewards Gamification can be pivotal to incentivizing user engagement. By rewarding activities like buying, selling, and holding sports cards with exclusive digital content, merchandise, and event access, Arena Club can cultivate a loyal customer base. Further enhancing this strategy, utility tokens can provide additional incentives and benefits, deepening user engagement within the platform ecosystem.

Building a Strong User Base It is possible to build a larger community through robust social features, enabling collectors and investors to interact and connect. Strategic partnerships with sports teams, athletes, and brands can enrich the community experience by offering exclusive content and immersive experiences. Moreover, by involving the community in decision-making processes, Arena Club can empower users and foster a sense of ownership.

Data-Driven Insights The use of data analytics will be crucial for understanding user preferences, tailoring marketing efforts, and identifying emerging trends. By leveraging blockchain data, Arena Club can gain valuable insights into user behavior, enabling the platform to provide personalized experiences and make informed decisions about product development and market strategies. Through a combination of these strategies, Arena Club can create a vibrant and loyal community that not only enhances user satisfaction but also drives sustained growth and success in the dynamic realm of sports card trading and grading.

10 Conclusion

Arena Club's integration of Web3 technologies represents a significant advancement in the sports card market, addressing key challenges related to authenticity, ownership transfer, and transaction security. Through the application of blockchain, Arena Club provides enhanced transparency and immutability, fostering greater trust among collectors and investors. The use of NFTs to enable fractional ownership and create new revenue streams further exemplifies the transformative potential of Web3 in this market.

These innovations, while promising, also highlight broader implications for the Fintech industry. Arena Club's model illustrates how Fintech solutions can revolutionize traditional markets by introducing digital assets and decentralized systems, setting a precedent for similar applications in other sectors. However, the success of these technologies depends on navigating complex regulatory landscapes and advancing technological infrastructure to meet the demands of scalability and transaction speed.

Looking forward, continued research into the long-term effects of Web3 adoption in the collectibles market will be crucial. Comparative studies on the performance of different blockchain platforms, along with explorations of AI and machine learning integration, will provide valuable insights into enhancing the security, efficiency, and reliability of digital assets. These developments will guide future innovations in Fintech, solidifying the role of Web3 in transforming industries traditionally outside the realm of financial technology.

Appendix A

Accessing a Card's NFT in Arena Club

The following shows how a user can access a card's asset-backed NFT (which Arena Club refers to as a Digital Proof of Claim or DPOC). Go to the card detail page and click on the "Transactions" button.

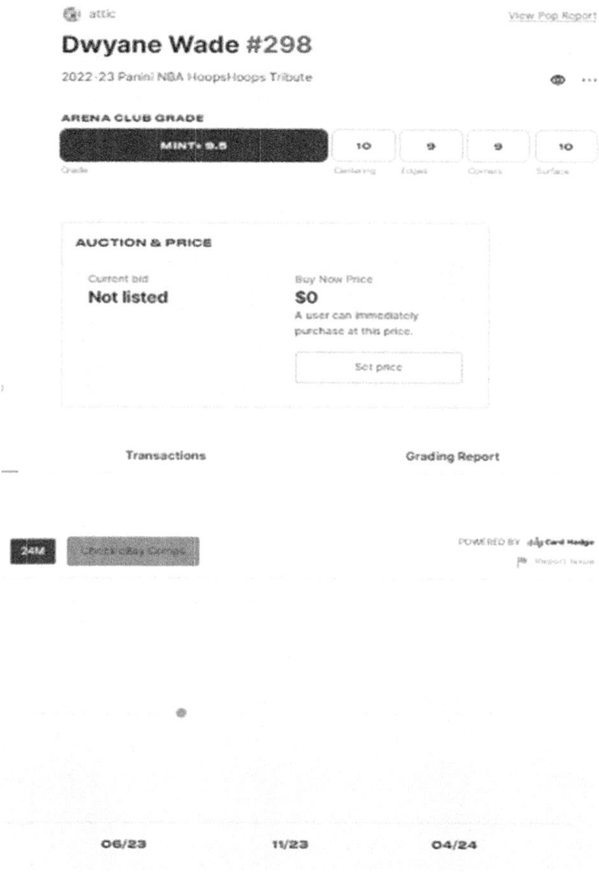

In the Transactions History table, click the "VIEW ON POLYGON" button that will take the user to the PolygonScan.

The PolygonScan view is where the transaction history and the details of the DPOC can be viewed, which mirrors the transaction history of card ownership in the Arean Club vault.

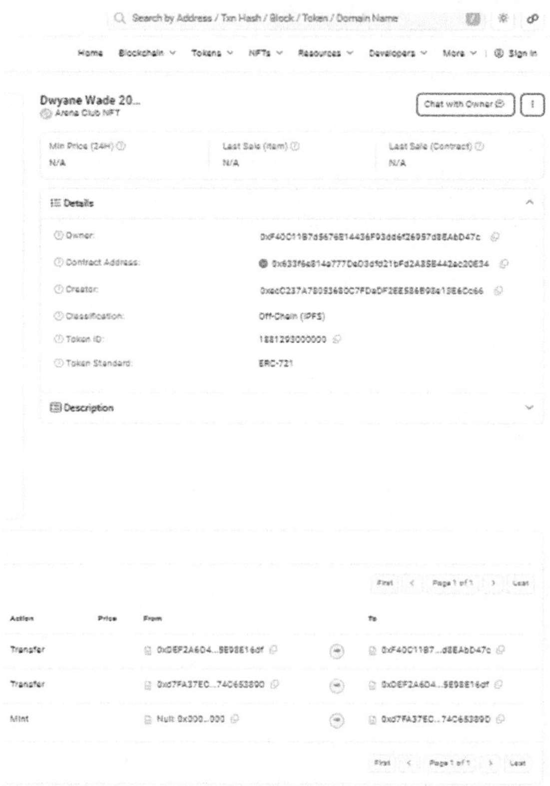

Presently, the DPOC is stored in a Polygon user wallet controlled by Arena Club. They state the reason is to ensure a smooth and secure transaction process—noting they manage the wallet on the user's behalf to ensure security and trust. Shortly after a transaction has occurred, the Polygon button will state "MINTING IN PROGRESS" which means the card is still being recording on the blockchain—a task that can take time due to network factors. Once the process is completed, the button "VIEW ON POLYGON" button will appear.

After a new card is revealed on a user's Arena Club account, it might take up to two weeks for the card image to display on PolygonScan. This is because the image is stored on the InterPlanetary File System (IPFS), which is a secure and decentralized system for storing and accessing files when the card is minted. PolygonScan, which is a separate platform, can take time to retrieve and display the image. They state that this delay is a normal part of blockchain's image processing.

Appendix B

Custodial Wallets and Arena Club's Approach to NFTs

What are Custodial Wallets?
These are a type of digital wallet where a third party, such as a cryptocurrency exchange or service provider (Arena Club), holds and manages the private keys associated with a user's NFTs. This contrasts with non-custodial wallets, where users maintain complete control over their private keys.

Key Features and Benefits:
Convenience: Custodial wallets offer a user-friendly experience. Users do not need to manage private keys themselves, making them ideal for beginners.

Integrated Services: Many providers offer additional features like trading, staking, and sometimes even insurance, creating a comprehensive platform for managing digital assets.

Customer Support: Custodial wallets often come with dedicated customer support, which can be helpful for users unfamiliar with NFTs.

Seamless Integration: Custodial wallets integrate with marketplaces and other platforms, simplifying NFT transactions.

Security Risks and Drawbacks:
Reduced User Ownership: Users rely on the service provider to secure their assets, introducing risks like hacking, fraud, or mismanagement.

Limited Control: Users may have restricted access to their NFTs if the service provider faces technical difficulties or imposes limitations on NFT usage.

Arena Club's Use Case:
Arena Club utilizes custodial wallets on the Polygon blockchain to manage users' NFTs. This approach offers:

Simplified User Experience: New users don't need to learn about private key management.

Centralized Control: Arena Club retains control over minting, pricing, and NFT access, facilitating efficient sales and rentals.

However, there are also drawbacks:

Reduced User Ownership: Users relinquish control over their NFTs to Arena Club.

Security Risks: If Arena Club's systems are compromised, user NFTs could be stolen.

Conclusion:
Custodial wallets offer a user-friendly experience but come with trade-offs in terms of user ownership and security. Arena Club must weigh these factors against their goals and target audience. Opting for a custodial approach might be suitable if user education and initial experience are priorities. However, for long-term security and asset control, exploring non-custodial solutions might be necessary. As the NFT landscape evolves, Arena Club will need a strategic approach that adapts to both current user needs and future market developments.

References

Bloom, J. (1997). *A house of cards: Baseball card collecting and popular culture* (Vol. 12). University of Minnesota Press.

Ghazi, S., & Schneider, M. (2024). Market value of rarity: A theory of fair value and evidence from rare baseball cards. *Journal of Economic Behavior & Organization, 219*, 318–339.

Hajducky, D. (2022, August 28). 1952 Topps Mickey Mantle card sells for $12.6 million, shattering record. ESPN. https://www.espn.com/mlb/story/_/id/34473632/1952-topps-mickey-mantle-card-sells-126-million-shattering-record

Kleine, J., Peschke, T., & Wagner, N. (2024). Beyond financial wealth: The experienced utility of collectibles. *The Quarterly Review of Economics and Finance*, 101865.

Krause, D.. (2024a). *Responsible Development of Internal GenAI Systems*. Available at SSRN: https://ssrn.com/abstract=4834767.

Krause, D. (2024b, July 15). *The Rise of Web3: Opportunities and challenges*. Available at SSRN: https://ssrn.com/abstract=4895353

Kruszeski, M. (2024). *Artificial Intelligence (AI) in grading collectibles: A technological revolution*. Master of Science in Finance Professional Report, College of Business, Marquette University

PR Newswire. (2024, April 10). eBay, Collectors enter into commercial agreement, sign deals for acquisition of eBay vault by PSA. *PR Newswire*. Retrieved from https://www.prnewswire.com/news-releases/ebay-collectors-enter-into-commercial-agreement-sign-deals-for-acquisition-of-goldin-by-ebay-and-acquisition-of-the-ebay-vault-by-psa-302112632.html

Rajan, R. (2024, April 10). eBay acquires Goldin, sells vault to PSA in strategic deals. Investing.com. https://www.investing.com/news/company-news/ebay-acquires-goldin-sells-vault-to-psa-in-strategic-deals-93CH-3372822

Thompson, T. H., & Sen, K. C. (2024). Analytics and baseball card values. *Managerial Finance, 50*(2), 386–395.

David Krause founded the AIM Program in 2004 and was its director until 2022, establishing it as a premier offering for the university. Prior to joining Marquette, Krause was active in several businesses he co-founded that were engaged in manufacturing, health care, medical devices, and financial services. Krause received his BBA, MBA, and Ph.D. degrees in the field of finance. He has concentrated his studies in the areas of investments, economics, and statistics. Over the years he has been published in numerous academic and trade journals. He is currently an Expert level candidate in the Certificate in Investment Performance Measurement (CIPM) program credentialed by the Chartered Financial Analyst (CFA) Institute. He also writes Level II and III investment ethics cases for the CFA Institute. In addition to his academic and business pursuits, David Krause has served on various corporate, charitable, civic boards and foundations.

The Rise of Web3: Opportunities and Challenges

David Krause

1 Introduction

The internet, since its inception, has undergone transformative shifts, fundamentally altering how we interact, communicate, and conduct business.[1] From the static, read-only nature of Web1 to the interactive, user-generated content of Web2, each evolution of the web has introduced new opportunities and challenges. We now stand on the brink of a potential third iteration: Web3.

Web3 represents a revolutionary shift from previous web iterations. Leveraging blockchain technology, it aims to create a decentralized internet where users have greater control over their data, digital assets, and online interactions.[2] This transformation could significantly impact industries, redefine business models, and change the power dynamics between corporations and individuals.

This paper aims to provide a comprehensive overview of Web3, exploring its core principles, underlying technologies, and diverse applications. By examining the key differences between Web3, Web2, and Web1, we will highlight the transformative potential of this emerging landscape. Furthermore, we will explore specific examples of Web3 applications, such as Decentralized Finance (DeFi), Non-Fungible

[1] The internet, established in the late 1960s, is a worldwide network of connected computers facilitating data exchange, while the World Wide Web, introduced in 1989, is a system of interconnected hypertext documents and multimedia accessible through web browsers via the internet.

[2] Blockchain is a technology that creates a secure and transparent digital ledger by recording transactions across a distributed network of computers.

D. Krause (✉)
Marquette University, Milwaukee, WI, USA
e-mail: david.krause@marquette.edu

A. Zarifis, X. Cheng (eds.), *Fintech and the Emerging Ecosystems*, Financial Innovation and Technology, https://doi.org/10.1007/978-3-031-83402-8_9

Tokens (NFTs), Metaverses, and Decentralized Autonomous Organizations (DAOs), to clarify their mechanics and implications.

Achieving a mature and efficient Web3 ecosystem poses several challenges. This paper will examine key hurdles such as scalability, security, regulatory ambiguity, and user experience concerns that may impede widespread adoption.[3] Additionally, we will consider the future trajectory of Web3, assessing its potential influence on the financial sector. The objective is to offer a comprehensive understanding of Web3, encompassing its opportunities and challenges, empowering stakeholders to critically evaluate its potential impact on business, particularly in financial transactions.

2 Understanding Web3

Defining Web3 Web3 signifies a transformative phase in internet evolution aimed at decentralizing control over data, platforms, and services (Wan et al., 2023). Unlike Web2, where centralized tech giants mediate and facilitate user interactions, Web3 promotes an open, transparent, and user-centric digital ecosystem. This change in basic assumptions is underpinned by blockchain technology, facilitating secure and verifiable record-keeping. Key characteristics of Web3 include:

- Decentralization: The distribution of power among network participants reduces dependence on centralized intermediaries (Liu et al., 2023).
- Blockchain: This technology ensures trust, transparency, and immutability, supporting decentralized applications (dApps) and peer-to-peer transactions (Filipčić, 2022).
- Tokenization: Digital assets or tokens often symbolize ownership, governance rights, or utility within Web3 platforms (Lai et al., 2023).[4]
- User Ownership: Individuals attain enhanced control over their data and digital assets, creating a sense of ownership and empowerment (Weyl et al., 2022).

3 Comparison of Web1, Web2, and Web3

To fully appreciate the evolution and potential of Web3, it is essential to contrast it with its predecessors, Web1 and Web2. Each iteration represents a distinct phase in the internet's development, characterized by specific attributes, user experiences, and underlying technologies.

[3] Scalability here refers to the capacity of blockchain networks and decentralized applications to manage increased transaction volumes and user interactions efficiently and economically.

[4] Tokenization is the process of representing real-world assets or rights as digital tokens on a blockchain, enabling fractional ownership, increased liquidity, and efficient trading.

Web1: The Static Web Web1, commonly referred to as the "Read-Only Web," marked the initial phase of the internet, primarily serving as a static platform for information dissemination (Berners-Lee, 2000). During this era, users predominantly acted as passive consumers of content, with limited opportunities for interaction or participation. The architecture of Web1 was defined by HTML pages interconnected through hyperlinks, forming an extensive network of static information.[5] Typical examples of Web1 include early news websites and online encyclopedias, which provided a one-way flow of information from content creators to users without significant user-generated input or dynamic content features.

Web2: The Interactive Web Web2, often referred to as the "Social Web," signified a transformative evolution in the internet landscape, characterized by a shift toward user-generated content and enhanced interactivity (Brynjolfsson & McAfee, 2014). This era ushered in platforms that empowered users to not only consume but also create, share, and engage with content, fostering a more participatory online environment. Centralized platforms emerged as influential intermediaries, playing pivotal roles in facilitating communication and interaction on a global scale. Prominent examples of Web2 platforms include Facebook, YouTube, Twitter, Wikipedia, and TikTok, which have revolutionized the way individuals connect, communicate, and collaborate online.[6]

Web3: The Decentralized Web Web3 represents a change in the internet's architecture, aiming to decentralize control away from centralized intermediaries. By leveraging blockchain technology and smart contracts, Web3 empowers users to own and control their data, digital assets, and online identity (Tapscott, 2023).[7] This decentralized approach fosters a more open, transparent, and censorship-resistant digital ecosystem. Emerging applications such as decentralized finance, non-fungible tokens, and decentralized autonomous organizations exemplify the potential of Web3 to reshape economic and social interactions. Table 1 summarizes the key differences between the three generations of the web.

4 Web3 Applications

The potential applications of Web3 are vast and varied, spanning multiple industries and sectors. While the technology is still in its emerging stages, several promising use cases have emerged. This section will explore some of the most prominent Web3 applications, including DeFi, NFTs, metaverses, and DAOs.

---

[5] HyperText Markup Language is the language used to create and structure web content.

[6] Twitter rebranded itself as X in 2023, offering a wider range of services beyond social media.

[7] Smart contracts are self-executing computer programs that automate the terms of an agreement directly into code, eliminating the need for intermediaries.

Table 1 Differences between the Web generations

Feature	Web1	Web2	Web3
User Role	Consumer	Consumer and Creator	Owner and Creator
Platform	Static	Interactive	Decentralized
Ownership	Platform	Platform	User
Technology	HTML	HTML, JavaScript, databases	Blockchain, smart contracts
Examples	Online news and encyclopedias	Social media, blogs	DeFi, NFTs, DAOs

Decentralized Finance DeFi is a rapidly growing sector within the Web3 ecosystem that aims to disrupt traditional financial systems (Aquilina et al., 2024). By leveraging blockchain technology, DeFi protocols offer a range of financial services, including lending, borrowing, trading, and asset management. Key characteristics of DeFi include:

- **Decentralization:** Financial services are provided through peer-to-peer networks without intermediaries.
- **Transparency:** All transactions are recorded on a public blockchain, enhancing trust and accountability.
- **Accessibility:** DeFi services can be accessed by anyone with an internet connection, regardless of geographic location or financial background.
- **Innovation:** DeFi has fostered the development of novel financial instruments and products, which also has posed a regulatory challenge.[8]

DeFi protocols encompass a wide range of financial applications. Prominent examples include Uniswap, a decentralized exchange facilitating peer-to-peer cryptocurrency trading; Aave, a lending and borrowing platform enabling users to earn interest on deposited assets or borrow funds against collateral; and MakerDAO, which issues the DAI stablecoin through a decentralized system that relies on collateralized debt positions.[9] These protocols illustrate the diverse functionalities offered within the DeFi ecosystem.

Non-Fungible Tokens NFTs are unique digital assets that represent ownership of real-world or virtual items (Mazur and Polyzos, 2024). Built on blockchain

[8] DeFi regulation is complex, with decentralized protocols operating alongside traditional financial entities, creating challenges for US regulators like the Securities and Exchange Commission (SEC) and the Commodity Futures Trading Commission (CFTC).

[9] Stablecoins are cryptocurrencies designed to maintain a stable price by pegging their value to a reference asset like the US dollar.

technology, NFTs provide verifiable proof of ownership and authenticity. Key characteristics of NFTs include:

- **Uniqueness:** Each NFT is distinct and cannot be replicated.
- **Ownership:** NFTs confer ownership rights to the digital asset.
- **Scarcity:** The limited supply of NFTs can contribute to their value.
- **Verifiability:** Blockchain technology ensures the authenticity and provenance of NFTs.[10]

NFT applications encompass a diverse range of uses. In digital art, artists can sell and monetize their creations, gaining direct access to global markets. Collectibles, such as trading cards, sports memorabilia, stamps, and virtual items, can be tokenized, offering unique ownership and trading opportunities.[11] In the gaming industry, NFTs enable the ownership and trading of in-game items and virtual real estate, enhancing the gaming experience and providing new revenue streams for developers and players alike.[12]

Metaverses Metaverses are immersive virtual worlds where users can interact with each other and digital assets. Built on blockchain technology, metaverses offer decentralized ownership, interoperability, and monetization opportunities (Hadi et al., 2024). Key characteristics of metaverses include:

- **Immersive experiences:** Users can interact with a virtual environment through avatars.
- **Digital ownership:** Users can own virtual land, assets, and experiences.
- **Interoperability:** Assets can be transferred between different metaverse platforms.
- **Economic activity:** Users can earn, spend, and invest virtual currencies within the metaverse.

Metaverse platforms offer immersive digital experiences and ownership opportunities. Meta, formerly Facebook, has made a substantial investment in developing the metaverse, a virtual reality universe, reflecting its belief in its potential as the future of social interaction and commerce. Decentraland, based on the Ethereum blockchain, allows users to explore, create, and trade in a virtual world. The Sandbox, another prominent platform, provides a user-generated gaming world where participants can buy, develop, and monetize virtual real estate. These efforts

[10] NFTs can help verify the provenance of rare items like baseball cards, limited edition sneakers, and fine art, ensuring their authenticity and preventing counterfeits.

[11] Arena Club grades sports cards using artificial intelligence, then converts them into NFTs for secure and transparent trading. This platform enhances the buying, selling, and storing of sports cards by merging physical and digital realms.

[12] Axie Infinity allows players to own and trade in-game creatures called Axies as NFTs. This ownership creates a virtual economy where players can earn real-world value through gameplay and trading.

exemplify the potential of the metaverse in combining creativity, ownership, and blockchain technology.

Decentralized Autonomous Organizations DAOs are organizations governed by rules encoded as computer programs known as smart contracts (Riaza & Gnabo, 2023). They operate without central authority, with decision-making power distributed among token holders. Key characteristics of DAOs include:

- **Decentralization:** No central leadership or management structure.
- **Transparency:** All decisions and actions are recorded on the blockchain.
- **Community governance:** Token holders participate in decision-making through voting.
- **Automation:** Smart contracts automate organizational processes.

Examples of DAOs include 'The DAO,' one of the earliest and most notable decentralized autonomous organizations, and MakerDAO, which governs the Maker Protocol and the DAI stablecoin. Both organizations highlight the potential of DAOs to facilitate decentralized governance and decision-making in various blockchain-based projects.

5 Challenges and Criticisms

While promising decentralization and user ownership, challenges such as scalability, user experience, security vulnerabilities, and regulatory uncertainty hinder widespread adoption. Overcoming these obstacles is critical for Web3 to realize its full potential.

Scalability and Performance One of the most significant hurdles facing Web3 is scalability. Many blockchain networks struggle to manage high transaction volumes, resulting in slow transaction speeds and high fees. This limitation could hamper the widespread adoption of Web3 applications, especially those requiring real-time processing or large-scale usage.

Security and Privacy The security of Web3 systems is paramount, as breaches can lead to significant financial losses and reputational damage. Smart contract vulnerabilities, phishing attacks, and private key theft are among the prevalent security threats.[13] Additionally, the public nature of blockchains raises concerns about user privacy, as transaction data can be publicly accessible.[14]

[13] Auditing can help prevent smart contract vulnerabilities by identifying and addressing potential security flaws before deployment.

[14] Blockchain technology offers pseudoanonymity, where users are identified by public addresses but their real-world identities remain hidden, raising privacy concerns due to the transparent nature of transaction records.

Regulatory Uncertainty The rapidly evolving nature of Web3 has created a regulatory vacuum in many jurisdictions. Lack of clear guidelines and regulations can hinder innovation, investor confidence, and the overall development of the Web3 ecosystem (Georgiades, 2023). Regulatory ambiguity also poses challenges for businesses seeking to operate in compliance with legal frameworks.

User Experience Web3 applications often present a steep learning curve for users unfamiliar with blockchain technology and cryptocurrency. Complex interfaces, technical jargon, and the need for digital wallets can create barriers to entry and hinder mass adoption. Improving the user experience is essential for mainstream acceptance of Web3.

Environmental Impact The energy consumption associated with some blockchain networks, particularly those based on proof-of-work consensus mechanisms, has raised concerns about the environmental impact of Web3 (Asif and Hassan, 2023).[15] The need for sustainable and energy-efficient blockchain solutions is becoming increasingly important. One answer could be the proof of stake consensus mechanism that selects validators to process transactions and create new blocks based on the amount of cryptocurrency they hold, incentivizing truthful behavior and reducing energy consumption compared to the proof of work mechanism (Krause, 2024a).

Centralization Risks Despite the decentralization philosophy of Web3, there is a risk of centralization creeping in through various means. For example, reliance on centralized infrastructure, the concentration of mining power, and the dominance of a few key players can undermine the decentralization goals of Web3.

6 The Future of Web3

Web3 has the potential to revolutionize the behavior of individuals, businesses, and society. By decentralizing control and ownership, the technology could foster new economic models, enhance privacy, and create more transparent systems. While still in an early phase of development, Web3's potential to transform sectors like finance, supply chain management, and governance is immense.

Potential Impact on Businesses Web3 offers numerous opportunities for businesses to innovate and create new value propositions. Some potential applications include:

- **Tokenization of assets:** Businesses can tokenize physical and digital assets to facilitate fractional ownership and trading.

[15] Proof of work is a consensus mechanism that secures a blockchain by requiring miners to expend computational effort to solve complex puzzles to validate transactions and create new blocks.

- **Governance model:** DAOs can enable a decentralized corporate governance structure where decisions are made collectively by token holders through voting on proposals.
- **Supply chain transparency:** Blockchain can enhance supply chain visibility, traceability, and efficiency.
- **Customer loyalty programs:** Token-based loyalty programs can foster deeper customer engagement and retention.
- **Decentralized marketplaces:** Businesses can create peer-to-peer marketplaces without intermediaries.

Web3 and Society Beyond the business realm, Web3 has the potential to reshape society in several ways:

- **Enhanced data privacy:** Decentralized systems can empower individuals to control their data.
- **Financial inclusion:** DeFi can provide access to financial services for underserved populations.
- **Democratic governance:** DAOs can foster new forms of democratic participation and decision-making.
- **Creative economy:** NFTs and metaverses can support creators and artists.

Emerging Trends and Developments Several emerging trends are shaping the future of Web3:

- **Interoperability:** Efforts to create bridges between different blockchain networks will enhance the overall Web3 ecosystem.
- **Scalability solutions:** The development of layer-2 solutions and new consensus mechanisms will address scalability challenges.[16]
- **Web3 gaming:** The convergence of gaming and blockchain is creating new opportunities for players and developers.
- **Regulatory frameworks:** The establishment of clear and supportive regulatory environments will foster Web3 innovation.

7 Regulatory Decision Regarding Web3 Needed

Over the past several years, the financial system in the United States has witnessed several noteworthy events related to the cryptocurrency ecosystem. There were the collapses of Silvergate, Silicon Valley Bank, and Signature Bank, all financial institutions with deep connections to cryptocurrency customers (Hamurcu, 2023). The fallout from the FTX cryptocurrency exchange debacle further exacerbated concerns, leading to a loss of confidence and subsequent withdrawals by Web3

[16] Layer-2 solutions are additional protocols built on top of a blockchain to increase transaction speed and efficiency without compromising the security of the underlying blockchain.

institutions banking with these entities, culminating in a scenario reminiscent of bank runs and institutional failures.[17] These events underscore the critical role of regulation - or the lack of it - in ensuring the stability of financial institutions engaged in digital asset transactions.

The US government's response, including the decision to insure all of Silicon Valley Bank assets beyond the standard $250,000 limit, temporarily stabilized confidence in the banking system.[18] However, such measures were seen as a short-term solution, failing to address the underlying systemic issues. To foster a harmonious coexistence between DeFi and traditional finance, robust regulatory frameworks are needed to mitigate potential crises, especially amid increasing cryptocurrency adoption. For instance, a Pew Research Center survey conducted in March 2023 found that 17% of US adults have invested in or used cryptocurrencies (Faverio & Sidoti, 2023). Institutional involvement is also increasing, exemplified by Wisconsin's public pension fund, which allocated $160 million to Bitcoin ETFs in 2024, establishing itself as a significant early institutional investor in digital assets (Krause, 2024b).

Despite prioritizing the regulation of emerging technologies, the Securities and Exchange Commission has yet to establish any clear regulatory frameworks for Web3 technologies. The SEC's strategy to date has primarily involved reactive measures, including enforcement actions against major players such as Kraken, Coinbase, and Ripple, rather than proactive rulemaking (Stanley, 2024).

This uncertainty in US regulation poses a significant risk of pushing the cryptocurrency industry to relocate offshore. Thus far the European Union and Japan, have embraced clearer regulatory guidelines for digital assets. Singapore and the United Arab Emirates (UAE) have also established favorable regulatory environments, positioning themselves as hubs for digital asset innovation.

The European Union has taken significant steps towards establishing clear regulatory guidelines for digital assets through the Markets in Crypto Assets (MiCA) regulation (Schickler, 2023). MiCA, set to become the world's first major comprehensive crypto law, will provide legal certainty for the sector across all 27 E.U. member states, covering a wide range of crypto-assets and related services, including issuance, trading, custody, and portfolio management. The regulation introduces a single authorization system for crypto-asset service providers, aims to protect investors by imposing stricter requirements, and includes specific provisions for stablecoins, with most provisions set to apply from December 30, 2024.

Japan also has been proactive in regulating digital assets, being one of the first countries to recognize cryptocurrencies as legal property under the Payment Services Act in 2017. The country has implemented a licensing system for cryptocurrency exchanges and allowed the industry to engage in self-regulation

[17] The FTX implosion was a massive cryptocurrency exchange fraud that led to billions of dollars in investor losses and criminal charges against its founder, Sam Bankman-Fried.

[18] The Federal Deposit Insurance Corporation (FDIC) insures deposits in banks up to a limit of $250,000 per depositor, per insured bank, for each account ownership category.

through recognized bodies like the Japan Virtual Currency Exchange Association (JVCEA).

Critics of more stringent regulation argue it stifles innovation and imposes cumbersome compliance processes. Others claim that a lack of clear regulatory guidelines not only hampers innovation but also risks the United States losing its competitive edge in the global digital economy. The challenge lies in reconciling the divergent views of regulatory bodies like the SEC, CFTC, and Financial Crimes Enforcement Network (FinCEN), which struggle to classify cryptocurrencies consistently as commodities or securities. Unlike Japan's streamlined approach under the Financial Services Agency (FSA), the US regulatory landscape remains fragmented, hindering clarity and posing challenges for market participants.

Looking forward, the United States must prioritize the establishment of comprehensive regulatory frameworks that provide clarity while fostering innovation within the Web3 ecosystem. This entails overcoming regulatory fragmentation, enhancing coordination among agencies, and adopting a forward-looking approach to anticipate technological advancements. By doing so, the United States can create a conducive environment where digital asset projects feel secure in remaining domestic, thereby promoting innovation, safeguarding investors, and maintaining its leadership in the global digital economy.

The regulation of Web3 technologies presents a complex challenge requiring balanced approaches that protect market integrity while supporting technological advancement. As global jurisdictions forge ahead with regulatory clarity, the United States must expedite its efforts to establish coherent frameworks that ensure stability, encourage innovation, and sustain its competitive edge in the evolving landscape of digital finance.

8 Conclusion

Web3 heralds a transformative shift toward a decentralized internet, offering users unprecedented control over their data and assets. This paradigm promises substantial benefits, including industry disruption, heightened transparency, and enhanced innovation. However, critical challenges such as blockchain scalability, security vulnerabilities, and regulatory uncertainties loom large, hindering its widespread adoption. To fully harness Web3's potential, future research should prioritize improving blockchain scalability, enhancing user interfaces for broader accessibility, establishing clear global regulatory frameworks, and exploring the socio-economic implications of Web3 technologies. Collaborative efforts among stakeholders will be essential in unlocking Web3's full potential and ensuring its positive impact on business, society, and governance.

Web3's evolution presents a fertile ground for future research across various fronts. First, exploring sustainable blockchain solutions to mitigate environmental concerns linked with energy-intensive proof-of-work mechanisms is crucial. Second, investigating governance models within decentralized autonomous organizations to enhance their efficiency and resilience in diverse operational contexts merits attention. Third, examining the integration of Web3 technologies with emerging fields like artificial intelligence and the Internet of Things could unlock new synergies and applications. Finally, longitudinal studies on user adoption patterns and behavioral shifts in Web3 ecosystems will provide valuable insights into its evolving societal impacts. Addressing these research areas will not only advance our understanding but also foster the responsible development of Web3 technologies in the digital age.

References

Aquilina, M., Frost, J., & Schrimpf, A. (2024). Decentralized finance (DeFi): a functional approach. *Journal of Financial Regulation, 10*(1), 1–27.

Asif, R., & Hassan, S. R. (2023). Shaping the future of Ethereum: Exploring energy consumption in Proof-of-Work and Proof-of-Stake consensus. *Frontiers in Blockchain, 6*, 1151724.

Berners-Lee, T. (2000). *Weaving the Web: The original design and ultimate destiny of the World Wide Web*. Harper Business.

Brynjolfsson, E., & McAfee, A. (2014). *The second machine age: Work, progress, and prosperity in a time of brilliant technologies*. W.W. Norton & Company.

Faverio, M., & Sidoti, O. (2023, April 10). *Majority of Americans aren't confident in the safety and reliability of cryptocurrency*. Pew Research Center. https://www.pewresearch.org/short-reads/2023/04/10/majority-of-americans-arent-confident-in-the-safety-and-reliability-of-cryptocurrency/

Filipčić, S. (2022, May). Web3 & DAOs: An overview of the development and possibilities for the implementation in research and education. In *2022 45th Jubilee International Convention on Information, Communication and Electronic Technology (MIPRO)* (pp. 1278–1283). IEEE.

Georgiades, A. (2023, June 26). Web3 is becoming more popular: Where's the regulation? *Forbes*. https://www.forbes.com/sites/forbesfinancecouncil/2023/06/26/web3-is-becoming-more-popular-wheres-the-regulation/

Hadi, R., Melumad, S., & Park, E. S. (2024). The Metaverse: A new digital frontier for consumer behavior. *Journal of Consumer Psychology, 34*(1), 142–166.

Hamurcu, Ç. (2023). Bank failure risk: A study on Silicon Valley Bank, Signature Bank, and Silvergate Capital Corporations. *Financial Internet Quarterly, 19*(2), 36–45.

Krause, D. (2024a). *Mainstreaming cryptocurrency: The state of Wisconsin Investment Board's Pioneering Investment in Bitcoin ETFs*. Available at SSRN https://ssrn.com/abstract=4852566.

Krause, D. (2024b). *Unlocking Ethereum's potential: The rise of spot ETFs in cryptocurrency investment* (June 06, 2024). Available at SSRN: https://ssrn.com/abstract=4856380.

Lai, Y., Yang, J., Liu, M., Li, Y., & Li, S. (2023). Web3: Exploring decentralized technologies and applications for the future of empowerment and ownership. *Blockchains, 1*(2), 111–131.

Liu, W., Cao, B., & Peng, M. (2023). *Web3 technologies: Challenges and opportunities*. IEEE Network.

Mazur, M., & Polyzos, E. (2024). Non-fungible tokens (NFTs). In *The Elgar companion to decentralized finance, digital assets, and Blockchain technologies* (pp. 280–297). Edward Elgar Publishing.

Riaza, B. P., & Gnabo, J. Y. (2023). Decentralized autonomous organizations (DAOs): Catalysts for enhanced market efficiency. *Finance Research Letters, 58*, 104445.

Schickler, J. (2023, September 7). MiCA, EU's comprehensive new crypto regulation. *CoinDesk*. https://www.coindesk.com/learn/mica-eus-comprehensive-new-crypto-regulation-explained/

Stanley, J. G. (2024). A disruptive ripple in the SEC's regulation of crypto assets. *North Carolina Banking Institute, 28*(1), 467.

Tapscott, A. (2023). *Web3: Charting the internet's next economic and cultural frontier*. Harper Business.

Wan, S., Lin, H., Gan, W., Chen, J., & Yu, P. S. (2023). Web3: The next internet revolution. *arXiv preprint arXiv:2304.06111*.

Weyl, E. G., Ohlhaver, P., & Buterin, V. (2022). Decentralized society: Finding web3's soul. *Available at SSRN 4105763*.

David Krause founded the AIM Program in 2004 and was its director until 2022, establishing it as a premier offering for the university. Prior to joining Marquette, Krause was active in several businesses he co-founded that were engaged in manufacturing, health care, medical devices, and financial services. Krause received his BBA, MBA, and Ph.D. degrees in the field of finance. He has concentrated his studies in the areas of investments, economics, and statistics. Over the years he has been published in numerous academic and trade journals. He is currently an Expert level candidate in the Certificate in Investment Performance Measurement (CIPM) program credentialed by the Chartered Financial Analyst (CFA) Institute. He also writes Level II and III investment ethics cases for the CFA Institute. In addition to his academic and business pursuits, David Krause has served on various corporate, charitable, civic boards and foundations.

From the Exclusion of the Concept of Blockchain to the Delimitation of the Concept of Distributed Ledger Technology Under MiCAR: Brief Notes

Diogo Pereira Coelho

1 Introduction

Over the last few years, since the creation and reception of blockchain technology, as well as financial operations related to crypto-assets, numerous atypical and differentiated legal situations have arisen, including camouflaged complex legal situations of a financial nature that are, in every way, identical to traditional securities. As one might expect, these situations have raised pertinent legal questions, especially regarding their definition and respective legal framework. In response, on September 24, 2020, the European Commission presented the MiCAR proposal[1] which, in essence, is a "light" version of the combination of the E-Money Directive,[2] the

[1] Proposal for a Regulation of the European Parliament and of the Council on Markets in Crypto-assets and amending Directive (EU) 2019/1937, https://eur-lex.europa.eu/legal-content/EN/TXT/?uri=CELEX%3A52020PC0593 (Accessed 10.09.24).

[2] Directive 2009/110/EC of the European Parliament and of the Council of 16 September 2009 on the taking up, pursuit and prudential supervision of the business of electronic money institutions amending Directives 2005/60/EC and 2006/48/EC and repealing Directive 2000/46/EC, https://eur-lex.europa.eu/legal-content/PT/TXT/?uri=CELEX%3A32009L0110 (Accessed 10.09.24).

Diogo Pereira Coelho is Founding Partner at Sypar, Lawyer, PhD Student in Law and Taxation (Crypto Taxation) and holds a Master's Degree in Law and Legal Practice in the specialty of Corporate Law.

D. P. Coelho (✉)
Sypar, Lisbon, Portugal

A. Zarifis, X. Cheng (eds.), *Fintech and the Emerging Ecosystems*, Financial Innovation and Technology, https://doi.org/10.1007/978-3-031-83402-8_10

Prospectus Regulation,[3] MiFID II,[4] MAR[5] and the Directive on Payment Services in the Internal Market.[6]

In March 2022, proposals for amendments were tabled by the European Parliament[7] and in October 2022 the final version was approved by the Council of the European Union.[8] The MiCAR proposal was finally voted on and approved by the European Parliament in April 2023,[9] having been formally approved by the Council

[3] Regulation (EU) 2017/1129 of the European Parliament and of the Council of 14 June 2017 on the prospectus to be published when securities are offered to the public or admitted to trading on a regulated market, and repealing Directive 2003/71/EC, https://eur-lex.europa.eu/legal-content/PT/TXT/?uri=CELEX%3A02017R1129-20211110 (Accessedm 10.09.24); & Commission Delegated Regulation (EU) 2019/980 of 14 March 2019 supplementing Regulation (EU) 2017/1129 of the European Parliament and of the Council as regards the format, content, scrutiny and approval of the prospectus to be published when securities are offered to the public or admitted to trading on a regulated market, and repealing Commission Regulation (EC) No 809/2004, https://eur-lex.europa.eu/legal-content/PT/TXT/?uri=CELEX%3A02019R0980-20200917 (Accessed 10.09.24).

[4] Directive 2014/65/EU of the European Parliament and of the Council of 15 May 2014 on markets in financial instruments and amending Directive 2002/92/EC and Directive 2011/61/EU, https://eur-lex.europa.eu/legal-content/PT/TXT/?uri=celex%3A32014L0065 (Accessed 10.09.24).

[5] Regulation (EU) No 596/2014 of the European Parliament and of the Council of 16 April 2014 on market abuse (market abuse regulation) and repealing Directive 2003/6/EC of the European Parliament and of the Council and Commission Directives 2003/124/EC, 2003/125/EC and 2004/72/EC, https://eur-lex.europa.eu/legal-content/pt/TXT/?uri=CELEX%3A32014R0596 (Accessed 10.09.24).

[6] Directive (EU) 2015/2366 of the European Parliament and of the Council of 25 November 2015 on payment services in the internal market, amending Directives 2002/65/EC, 2009/110/EC and 2013/36/EU and Regulation (EU) No 1093/2010, and repealing Directive 2007/64/EC, https://eur-lex.europa.eu/legal-content/PT/TXT/?uri=CELEX%3A02015L2366-20151223 (Accessed 10.09.24).

[7] Specifically, see Committee on Economic and Monetary Affairs (ECON), Amendments 001-001, Report, Stefan Berger A9-0052/2022, Markets in Crypto-assets (MiCAR), Proposal for a regulation, COM (2020)0593 - C9-0306/2020 - 2020/0265(COD), 12.04.22, https://www.europarl.europa.eu/doceo/document/A-9-2022-0052-AM-001-001_EN.pdf (Accessed 10.09.24); most of these amendments suggested by ECON in its first proposal were not taken into account in the final vote by the European Parliament in April 2023, only those included in the second amendment proposal. See Committee on Economic and Monetary Affairs (ECON), Amendments 2, Irene Tinagli, Report, Stefan Berger A9-0052/2022, Markets in Crypto-Assets (MiCAR), Proposal for a regulation, COM (2020)0593 - C9-0306/2020 - 2020/0265(COD), 12.04.22, https://www.europarl.europa.eu/doceo/document/A-9-2022-0052-AM-002-002_PT.pdf (Accessed 10.09.24).

[8] Council of the European Union, Information note, Proposal for a Regulation of the European Parliament and of the Council on Markets in Crypto-assets, and amending Directive (EU) 2019/1937 (MiCAR) - Letter to the Chair of the European Parliament Committee on Economic and Monetary Affairs, Interinstitutional File: 2020/0265 (COD), https://data.consilium.europa.eu/doc/document/ST-13198-2022-INIT/en/pdf (Accessed 10.09.24).

[9] See European Parliament, Markets in crypto-assets (MiCAR), Think Thank, European Parliamentary Research Service, 2023, https://www.europarl.europa.eu/thinktank/pt/document/EPRS_ATA(2023)745716 (Accessed 10.09.24); & European Parliament, Crypto-assets: green light to new rules for tracing transfers in the EU, Press Release, 2023, https://www.europarl.europa.eu/news/en/press-room/20230414IPR80133/crypto-assets-green-light-to-new-rules-for-tracing-transfers-in-the-eu (Accessed 10.09.24). See also Pereira Coelho D, A aprovação do

of the European Union in May 2023[10] and published in the Official Journal of the European Union in June of the same year.[11] The legal definition of "crypto-asset" introduced, along with the legal subcategories chosen and defined by the European legislator (i.e. asset-referenced crypto-assets, e-money tokens, utility tokens and "other crypto-assets"), have been touted as the "backbone" of MiCAR. This is understandable, as it is these legal definitions, along with the definition of DLT, that will allow the legal classification and legal framework of crypto-assets to be delimited, including the scope of application of MiCAR. However, these definitions have many inaccuracies and leave plenty of doubts as to their extraordinary scope. In this sense, only by truly understanding the logic and principles of the distributed ledger technology and the crypto-asset in question, will it be possible to properly ascertain the legal consequences that may arise from its operation and, consequently,

---

regulamento MiCA: algumas notas, Observador, May 2023, https://observador.pt/opiniao/a-aprovacao-do-regulamento-MiCAR-algumas-notas/ (Accessed 10.09.24). On the subject of the new legal framework, see Garcia Rolo A, A proposta de Regulamento europeu sobre mercados de criptoativos: breve sumário e análise, in Revista de Direito das Sociedades (RDS), February 2021, https://www.revistadedireitodassociedades.pt/artigos/a-proposta-de-regulamento-europeu-sobre-mercados-de-criptoativos-breve-sumario-e-analise (Accessed 10.09.24); Maia G, Vieira dos Santos J, MiCA and DeFi ("Proposal for a Regulation on Market in Crypto-assets" and "Decentralized Finance"), in Revista Electrónica de Direito, N.° 2 (Vol.28), June 2022, https://cij.up.pt/client/files/0000000001/4-guilherme-maia_1922.pdf (Accessed 10.09.24); Vieira dos Santos J, Challenges in Imposing Requirements on Offerors of Crypto-assets, in Fintech Regulation and the Licensing Principle, Moura Vicente D, Pereira Duarte D, Granadeiro C, European Banking Institute, CIDP, 2023, https://ebi-europa.eu/wp-content/uploads/2023/02/eBook-22Fintech-Regulation-Licensing-Principle-2-2023.pdf (Accessed 10.09.24); Vieira dos Santos J, Regulação dos criptoativos, in Caderno do Mercado de Valores Mobiliários, No. 64, 2019, https://www.cmvm.pt/pt/EstatisticasEstudosEPublicacoes/CadernosDoMercadoDeValoresMobiliarios/Documents/CMVM-CADERNOS-n64.pdf (Accessed 10.09.24); Vieira dos Santos J, Regulação de Formas de Financiamento Empresarial FinTech - Em especial o Crowdfunding e as Initial Coin Offering, Instituto do Conhecimento, No. 8, Almedina, Abreu Advogados, 2022; Tomczak T, Crypto-assets and crypto-assets' subcategories under MiCA Regulation, in Capital Markets Law Journal, Vol. 17, No. 3, 2022, https://academic.oup.com/cmlj/article/17/3/365/6609567 (Accessed 10.09.24); Zetzsche D A, Annunziata F, Arner D W, Buckley, R P, The Markets in Crypto-Assets Regulation (MICAR) and the EU Digital Finance Strategy, in EBI Working Paper Series 2020 - no. 77, 2020, https://papers.ssrn.com/sol3/papers.cfm?abstract_id=3725395 (Accessed 10.09.24); Garcia Rolo A, Criptoativo – conceito, modalidades, regime e distinção de figuras afins, in CIDP Research Paper Series, CIDP, No. 18, July 2022, https://papers.ssrn.com/sol3/papers.cfm?abstract_id=4123583 (Accessed 10.09.24).

[10] Council of the European Union, Infographic – Cryptoassets, 2023, https://www.consilium.europa.eu/pt/infographics/crypto-assets/ (Accessed 10.09.24).

[11] The new rules came into force 20 days after publication and will apply after a transition period of 12 months (for stablecoins) and 18 months (for other crypto-assets). See Regulation (EU) 2023/1114 of the European Parliament and of the Council of 31 May 2023 on markets in crypto-assets, and amending Regulations (EU) No 1093/2010 and (EU) No 1095/2010 and Directives 2013/36/EU and (EU) 2019/1937, https://eur-lex.europa.eu/eli/reg/2023/1114/oj (Accessed 10.09.24).

define its legal classification and an appropriate legal framework within the scope of the definitions adopted in MiCAR.[12]

This article aims to contribute to the understanding of the legal definition of DLT with a view to facilitating the case-by-case analysis of the legal framework of crypto-assets (whose scope and legal definition will not be discussed in depth), as well as to scrutinize the legislator's option to leave out the concept of blockchain and the possible problems that may result from it.

2 Brief Introduction to Concept of Blockchain

2.1 The Origin of Decentralization, Blockchain and Cryptocurrencies

The need "to coordinate activities between a large number of people led to the invention of institutions and the creation of models of trust and relationships based on intermediation", i.e. centralized models based on the centralization of information.[13] Modern forms of social, economic and political organization depend on these models.[14] It so happens that the financial crisis of 2007–2008 and the great recession that followed left the population very distrustful of the financial markets and the financial institutions themselves. As it turned out, this distrust was (and still is) justified by the danger associated with excessive centralization[15] and the concealment of data records.[16] In this scenario, blockchain technology, which, abstractly, comprises a technological platform where the coordination of activities between individuals takes place directly between individuals, without resorting to intermediary coordination mechanisms,[17] has presented itself as a vehicle for

[12] Vieira dos Santos J, Challenges in Imposing Requirements . . . , op. cit. note 9, 64.

[13] Martins P, Introdução à Blockchain – Bitcoin, Criptomoedas, Smart contracts, Conceitos, Tecnologia, Implicações, Data Protection, FCA – Editora de Informática, 1.ª Edição, 2018, 143.

[14] See Martins P, Introdução à Blockchain . . . , op. cit., note 13, 143; & Atzori M, Blockchain Technology and Decentralized Governance: Is the State Still Necessary?, University College of London - Center for Blockchain Technologies, 2015, 6, https://papers.ssrn.com/sol3/papers.cfm?abstract_id=2709713 (Accessed 10.09.24).

[15] The centralist model of the economy is characterized by the problem of information asymmetry. As a rule, economic entities or agents are the sole holders of the only databases where their activity is recorded. In general, these databases are not shared with other entities or economic agents. See Martins P, Introdução à Blockchain . . . , op. cit., note 13, 142.

[16] Akgiray V, Blockchain Technology and Corporate Governance - Technology, Markets, Regulation and Corporate Governance, Corporate Governance Committee, OECD, 2018, 4, https://one.oecd.org/document/DAF/CA/CG/RD(2018)1/REV1/En/pdf (Accessed 10.09.24).

[17] Martins P, Introdução à Blockchain . . . , op. cit., note 13, 144.

decentralization, i.e. a process of eliminating individuals or mechanisms that play a role in coordinating activities between individuals.[18]

What distinguishes decentralized networks from traditional centralized networks is that, through algorithms,[19] data records can be collaboratively created by all participants. It is the participants themselves who share the information, and this, in a network that can consist of an infrastructure made up of several networks, geographies, institutions or even social bodies.[20] Within these networks, participants can access and view registrations or changes to registrations while still keeping those same registrations safe from unauthorized access via cryptographic keys[21] and digital signatures (which, in turn, control each participant's respective access and power over form and content[22]). The initial notoriety achieved by blockchain technology was due precisely to the use of this "decentralized" data recording system, which put the phenomenon of the issuance and dissemination of Bitcoin (BTC) and the accelerated dissemination of other cryptocurrencies into the background until today.[23] In fact, due to the strong connection between the two phenomena, there was initially an incorrect idea that blockchain and Bitcoin were indistinguishable, which is not the case in reality.[24]

---

[18] Martins P, Introdução à Blockchain..., op. cit., note 13, 144; & Akgiray V, Blockchain Technology..., op. cit. note 16, 6–7.

[19] A computer algorithm is a set of sequential, logical and unambiguous operations which, when applied to a set of data, make it possible to find the solution to a problem in a finite number of steps. In other words, it is an ordered and finite set of well-defined instructions designed to perform a particular task, namely problem solving. In this respect, see Oliveira Ascensão J, A Protecção Jurídica dos Programas de Computador, Ordem dos Advogados Portugueses, 1988, 73, https://portal.oa.pt/upl/%7B639e8fc8-d372-43d0-8a42-c429d91445f8%7D.pdf (Accessed 10.09.24).

[20] Piazza F S, Bitcoin and the Blockchain as Possible Corporate Governance Tools: Strengths and Weaknesses, in Penn State Journal of Law & International Affairs, Issue 2, Volume 5, 2017, 274, https://elibrary.law.psu.edu/cgi/viewcontent.cgi?article=1163&context=jlia (Accessed 10.09.24).

[21] Cryptography is a branch of mathematics dedicated to the study of principles and techniques for creating sufficiently secure information processing systems, i.e. systems capable of transforming a message that is intelligible to everyone into a message that is only intelligible to one or more people, in whole or in part. The authenticity, reliability and integrity of messages are the fundamental problems that cryptography deals with. See Martins P, Introdução à Blockchain..., op. cit., note 13, 19-20.

[22] Piazza F S, Bitcoin and the Blockchain..., op. cit. note 20, 274.

[23] Mendes Correia F, A tecnologia descentralizada de registo de dados (blockchain) no setor financeiro, in FinTech – Desafios da Tecnologia Financeira, Menezes Cordeiro A, Perestrelo de Oliveira A, Pereira Duarte D, CIDP, Almedina, 1.ª Edição, 2018, 69. In this regard, it should be noted that although the BTC was created between 2008 and 2009, it was not known to the general public. Only after the concept was tested and put into circulation on black markets, such as Silk Road (one of the digital black markets on the famous deepweb or darkweb), which accepted the virtual currency as a payment method, did it begin to spread throughout the virtual community. The initial value of BTC was $0.30. See BTCSoul, The story of Silk Road: how Bitcoin took the darknet economy to the next level, 2018, https://www.btcsoul.com/noticias/a-historia-da-silk-road-como-o-bitcoin-levou-a-economia-da-darknet-a-outro-nivel/ (Accessed 10.09.24).

[24] Piazza F S, Bitcoin and the Blockchain..., op. cit. note 20, 274.

The blockchain as we know it today (and therefore BTC) was developed by an individual (or several individuals or entities?) using the pseudonym "Satoshi Nakamoto",[25] who published the technical whitepaper describing the protocol on the internet in 2008 (still during the financial crisis). This protocol was implemented in 2009 and, since then, several other versions[26] of cryptocurrencies have been created, which are nicknamed altcoin, in clear reference to the bitcoin alternative element.[27]

2.2 *Blockchain's Potential as a Disruptive Technology*[28]

Over the last few years, it has been argued that these technological innovations can affect the financial markets and the very structure of companies in such a profound way that only the revolution created by the US Securities Act of 1933[29] and

[25] The true identity of the designer (or designers) is still unknown. After publishing the protocol and exchanging a few messages with Gavin Andresen, a software developer to whom he handed over control of the source code repository and key alert functions of the software, he disappeared to, in his words, "move on to other things". Allegedly, both the CIA and the NSA, despite their attempts, have been unable to identify the creator. See L.S., Who is Satoshi Nakamoto?, The Economist newspaper, https://www.economist.com/the-economist-explains/2015/11/02/who-is-satoshi-nakamoto (Accessed 10.09.24).

[26] Among the best known are ETH (Ether) and LTC (Litecoin).

[27] It should be noted in this regard that the existing altcoins are listed on the CoinMarketCap platform, https://coinmarketcap.com/, which is a Dow Jones Industrial Average (DJIA)-style index of the main indicators of crypto-asset market movements. See Piazza F S, Bitcoin and the Blockchain . . . , op. cit. note 20, 265–266.

[28] The term "disruptive" is relatively new in this sector and, in other words, means causing a break with the standards, models or technologies already established in the market, describing a technological innovation, product or service with so-called "disruptive" characteristics, because they are diverse, revolutionary, innovative or never before thought of or applied in that specific context. See Dufloth R, Novas tecnologias e o futuro do profissional do Direito, Mgalhas, 2017, https://pt.linkedin.com/pulse/novas-tecnologias-e-o-futuro-do-profissional-direito-rodrigo-dufloth (Accessed 10.09.24). In this regard, it should be noted that the best-known way of measuring progress in computer processing power is Moore's law. Gordon E. Moore predicted that the number of transistors in chips would increase by 100% at the same cost every 18 months. However, information technology is exceeding what Moore's law itself predicted. Unlike hardware, for example, which has seen significant increases in computer memory capacity and the amount of digital information that can be transmitted over fiber optic cables, software is seeing the effectiveness of some algorithms grow at a rate that exceeds all predictions. See Ford M, Robôs – a ameaça de um futuro sem emprego (Rise of the Robots), tradução de José Vale Roberto & João Quina Edições, Bertrand Editora, 1.ª Edição, 2016, 93.

[29] In short, the Securities Act of 1933 regulates the initial offering of securities, providing for the prohibition of offering or selling securities that are not previously registered with the SEC and, in addition, the duty to disclose a prospectus. See Ferreira Gomes J, Os deveres de informação sobre negócios com pares relacionadas e os recentes Decretos-Leis n.°s 158/2009 e 185/2009, in Revista de Direito das Sociedades, Ano I – Número 3, Almedina, 2009, 590–591.

the Securities Exchange Act of 1934[30] can "rival".[31] The European Commission itself has already admitted that the potential scope of application of blockchain is quite vast and should be closely monitored, as it offers considerable potential to promote simplicity and efficiency through the creation of new infrastructures and processes. The Commission also stressed that these technologies could become a central element of future financial services infrastructures and that in-depth collaboration between incumbents, innovators and regulators will be necessary to ensure the success and take advantage of the implementation of the most promising applications.[32]

On the other hand, it is also not unreasonable to draw a parallel between the phenomenon of blockchain technology and the phenomenon of the Transmission Control Protocol and Internet Protocol (TCP/ IP), i.e. the communication technology that "created" the internet, an essential tool in the daily lives of human beings and companies.[33] It is fair to assume that, between the 1970s and 1980s, only a

[30] The Securities Exchange Act of 1934 has a broader remit, requiring listed companies to establish and maintain a system of continuous disclosure of information. It also requires the submission of annual and quarterly reports to the SEC, as well as other matters. See Ferreira Gomes J, Os deveres de informação sobre negócios..., op. cit. note 29, 590–591.

[31] Yermack D, Corporate Governance and Blockchains, NBER Working Paper No. 21802, National Bureau of Economic Research, 2015, 6–7, https://www.nber.org/papers/w21802 (Accessed 10.09.24).

[32] European Commission, Communication from the Commission to the European Parliament, the Council, the European Central Bank, the European Economic and Social Committee and the Committee of the Regions - FinTech Action plan: For a more competitive and innovative European financial sector, (COM/2018/0109 final), 2018, https://eur-lex.europa.eu/legal-content/PT/TXT/?uri=COM%3A2018%3A109%3AFIN) (Accessed 10.09.24). In particular, see point 2.3.

[33] This technology was introduced in 1970 as an electronic mail protocol (Advanced Research Projects Agency Network—ARPAnet). At the time, it was met with a high degree of skepticism by telecommunications companies, which continued to invest heavily in traditional methods. Then, in 1980, new technology companies began using the TCP/ IP protocol suite to build local peer-to-peer email networks. These networks would first be internal and later for localized use in other industries. The speed and capacity of communication increased almost infinitely and, as a result, there were huge productivity gains. Dedicated lines, circuit-switching equipment, fax machines, telex machines and the like became obsolete and relics of the past very quickly. In 1990 the World Wide Web (commonly abbreviated "www"), based on Hypertext Transfer Protocol (HTTP) and HyperText Markup (HTML) protocols, emerged, catapulting TCP/ IP-based technologies into the knowledge and use of the general public and marking the beginning of disruption and transformation. Publicized by the development and marketing of internet applications by companies such as Netscape, Sun and Microsoft, information and the number of internet users grew very quickly. Lower connectivity costs combined with the powerful development of application tools began the disruption and eventual replacement of existing business models. To name a few, Napster, eBay, Priceline, Google, Amazon, Facebook, Apple, Alibaba, Baidu, Weibo and Tancent were and, for the most part, still are the new base platforms for internet business models. The brand and physical scale are no longer commercially important, so those models that couldn't keep up or resist this new internet-driven world were forced to leave the stage. The most important factor in this fundamental transformation of the economy has been the ever-decreasing cost of connectivity, made possible by TCP/ IP technology. See Akgiray V, Blockchain Technology..., op. cit. note 16, 3–4.

minority of people imagined the enormous social and economic transformation that would take place after the implementation and application of the internet.[34] It is mainly in this sense that the parallel[35] between TCP/ IP technologies and blockchain can be drawn, not only in terms of technological potential, but, above all, in terms of the potential for transforming society and human and business relations. However, it should be noted that blockchain is not an alternative to TCP/ IP (at least, for now, as it presents the functionalities to do so), but a technology that develops in network protocols such as TCP/ IP. While TCP/ IP-based peer-to-peer (P2P) networks were designed to transfer information about assets, blockchain networks actually transfer the values of those assets,[36] and without backing them up. By allowing information and digital representations of value to be distributed and not copied, the backbone of a new type of internet has been created.[37]

2.3 *Functions and Main Features of Blockchain*

This type of decentralized network can be adapted to any degree or type of decentralization, depending on the form of access and usage rights, and it is possible to identify three formats of blockchain structures: (i) public blockchain, in which access does not require authorization and there is no owner or operator, with all participants having access to the same set of records and, in addition, freedom to enter and exit;[38] (ii) private blockchain, in which there is an owner or operator or there are multiple owners or operators, who provide access to authorized

---

[34] Akgiray V, Blockchain Technology . . . , op. cit. note 16, 4.

[35] It is relatively easy to find conceptual parallels between TCP/ IP and blockchain technologies. Specifically: (i) both technologies can be used on local or long-distance networks (just like TCP/ IP, the development and maintenance of blockchain is open and shared); (ii) there are volunteers all over the world who maintain the core software, i.e. just like when email emerged, Bitcoin was initially supported by an enthusiastic but relatively small community; (iii) TCP/ IP drastically reduced the cost of connectivity and therefore the cost of information, which allowed global access to information. The implementation of blockchain technology is therefore expected to drastically reduce the cost of transactions. By way of example, the entire process of trading a security can take days to clear, settle and finalize. The same transaction on a blockchain structure has the potential to be done in fractions of a second. See Akgiray V, Blockchain Technology . . . , op. cit. note 16, 4.

[36] Akgiray V, Blockchain Technology . . . , op. cit. note 16, 4.

[37] Terms such as "new internet", or "internet of trust", or "internet of value" are used, with some authors claiming that blockchain is the most disruptive technology since the creation of the aforementioned World Wide Web. See Bansal L, Blockchain: A New Type of Internet, Interconnections – The Equinix Blog, 2017 https://blog.equinix.com/blog/2017/10/05/blockchain-a-new-type-of-internet/ (Accessed 10.09.24); & Akgiray V, Blockchain Technology . . . , op. cit. note 16, 3.

[38] Bitcoin can be considered an example of a public blockchain. See Akgiray V, Blockchain Technology . . . , op. cit. note 16, 7.

participants, and only they can own a copy of the records;[39] (iii) hybrid blockchain, where we are dealing with a combination of a public and private blockchain, with participants being able to reap the benefits of both formats.[40] The blockchain therefore does not need a central registry or a single person responsible for the data entered and stored in the system, which is, among other things, a feature that sets this technology apart.[41]

According to this logic, "each participant is responsible for maintaining and updating part (or all) of the database", and the validity and reliability of the records derive from the harmony "between the individual entries of each member, rather than from a hierarchical criterion".[42] The irreversibility and immutability of the data registered on the network are explained by the fact that we are dealing with a database distributed and shared between countless computers, updated and registered by various processing units. At the same time, these processing units jointly check the veracity of all the entries in a given data record (i.e. whether they make sense with previous entries) through a kind of secure cross-checking of data called consensus. In the case of Bitcoin, the consensus mechanism used is called proof of work (PoW), and in the case of Ethereum, it is called proof of stake (PoS).[43] In other words, the blockchain uses data encryption and time validation methods through the juxtaposition of timestamps at key moments when data is entered, changed or deleted.[44] The entry of new data into the database, based on a principle of multilateral consensus, depends on the universal validation of this new

---

[39] An example is Nasdaq Linq. See Nasdaq, Nasdaq Linq enables first-ever private securities issuance documented with blockchain technology, Press release, 2015, https://ir.nasdaq.com/news-releases/news-release-details/nasdaq-linq-enables-first-ever-private-securities-issuance (Accessed 10.09.24).

[40] Zilavy T, What Is A Hybrid Blockchain And Why You Need To Know About It?, Altcoin Magazine, 2018, https://medium.com/altcoin-magazine/what-is-a-hybrid-blockchain-and-why-you-need-to-know-about-it-c7b887d2bae (Accessed 10.09.24); & Sagirlar G, Carminati B, Ferrari E, Sheehan J D, Ragnoli E, Hybrid-IoT: Hybrid Blockchain Architecture for Internet of Things – PoW Sub-blockchains, University of Insubria, IBM Research, 2018, 6-8, https://arxiv.org/abs/1804.03903 (Accessed 10.09.24).

[41] Mendes Correia F, A tecnologia descentralizada..., op. cit. note 23, 70; & Schrepel T, Collusion by blockchain and smart contracts, in Harvard Journal of Law and Technology (33 Harv. J.L. & Tech. 117), 2019, 120, https://papers.ssrn.com/sol3/papers.cfm?abstract_id=3315182 (Accessed 10.09.24).

[42] Mendes Correia F, A tecnologia descentralizada..., op. cit. note 23, 70.

[43] Vilaça Pacheco A, in Bitcoin, Editora Self, 1.ª Edição, 2018, 73-74. The issue of consensus is perhaps the technical specificity with the greatest degree of difficulty. The consensus mechanism is the general agreement on which a given blockchain infrastructure operates, i.e. the mechanism that determines how participants interact in a blockchain infrastructure. The most common consensus mechanisms are Proof of Work, Proof of Stake, Proof of Burn, Proof of Authority, Proof of Capacity or Proof of Storage. However, there are new mechanisms being introduced on a weekly basis. See also Thibault S, Collusion by blockchain and smart contracts, op. cit. note 41, 120.

[44] Mendes Correia F, A tecnologia descentralizada..., op. cit. note 23, 70.

information by the other participants.[45] Once this consensus has been reached, the new information entered is added to the database and can only be altered or deleted through a new consensus.[46] In this sense, the blockchain works like a ledger, but in a decentralized, shared and universal way, which allows the creation of consensus and trust in direct communication between two parties (peer-to-peer), instead of the traditional placing of trust in intermediaries or any third parties, even if they are imbued with conferred authority or increased credibility.[47]

The aim is to stop relying on people, i.e. intermediaries, but rather on mathematics, with a scope of application that goes far beyond the issuance of cryptocurrencies.[48] The decentralized database is therefore considered to be a reliable tool by nature, since distribution, shared records and databases have the function of creating a global and secure indicator for all movements that occur in a given entity.[49]

3 From the Exclusion of the Concept of Blockchain to the Delimitation of the Concept of Distributed Ledger Technology Under MiCAR: Brief Notes

3.1 Distinction Between Blockchain Technology and Distributed Ledger Technology

Regardless of any connection between the two phenomena, in general, distributed ledger technology (DLT) can be designed for multiple purposes, such as decentralized record keeping, management and automatic control of flows, group access and sharing, or even individual knowledge of information.[50] Although Bitcoin was

---

[45] With the application of blockchain and after validation through the consensus mechanism, there is no need for an authorized intermediary to confirm registrations. In essence, there is no need for a central database or bureaucratic repository of transactions and records. See Akgiray V, Blockchain Technology…, op. cit. note 16, 6–7.

[46] Mendes Correia F, A tecnologia descentralizada…, op. cit. note 23, 70.

[47] Williams S, It's Time We Got Real About Blockchain Technology, The Motley Fool, 2018, https://www.fool.com/investing/2018/05/17/its-time-we-got-real-about-blockchain-technology.aspx (Accessed 10.09.24).

[48] Atzori M, Blockchain Technology and Decentralized…, op. cit. note 14, 2.

[49] Thibault S, Collusion by blockchain and smart contracts, op. cit. note 41, 120–121.

[50] In this regard, although blockchain was initially proposed as a method of validating the ownership of crypto-assets such as BTC, after years of use in this regard, it has been recognized as an alternative with the potential to take on various forms of record-keeping, offering advantages in terms of cost, speed, data integrity (compared to classic methods) and a wide scale of use in the most diverse areas of business. As has been researched over the last few years, blockchain technology is suitable for registering ownership of a wide range of assets, including shares, debt securities, ownership of movable property and even real estate. Governments themselves are studying the possibility of creating blockchain infrastructures for public registry purposes,

the first real example of blockchain application, the initial idea of this technology had already been created in 1991 with the origin of DLT.[51] In fact, blockchain is just one type of DLT. As a rule, most create immutable public records, include time stamps and aim to guarantee security against attempts to corrupt data, including via cryptography. In fact, cryptography, which is the science of secure communication, was already a fundamental component of DLTs even before the emergence of blockchain, Bitcoin and other crypto-assets. Like blockchain, earlier DLTs also use various cryptographic methods to guarantee security and privacy. These methods include hashing (via mathematical algorithms),[52] digital signatures and public key cryptography. The main innovation introduced by blockchain and Bitcoin was the combination of these cryptographic methods with the concept of a decentralized, tamper-resistant ledger through the proof-of-work consensus mechanism. This combination provided a more robust and secure solution for decentralized digital transactions. As explained in the previous points, since the introduction of Bitcoin, subsequent blockchain projects have explored and expanded different cryptographic mechanisms and methods, including advanced algorithms, zero-knowledge proofs, ring signatures, among others. These innovations are aimed precisely at improving privacy, scalability and security within specific blockchain implementations. In this sense, the main differentiating element lies in the level of encryption, as certain types of DLT may not fully encrypt the data[53] or, at least, with the same degree of immutability or reliability that results from the cryptographic methods applied in most *blockchain* technologies. As such, it can be said that although blockchain has not necessarily introduced new cryptographic mechanisms compared to previous DLTs, it has introduced multiple advanced combinations of cryptographic mechanisms. Another differentiating element, less important but worth mentioning, lies in the way in which transaction record data is entered and structured. In general, in the case of the blockchain, it is in blocks, *i*.e. the blocks of data interconnected in a chain create the distributed ledger. There are other types of DLT that use another type of data structure to create the distributed ledger, so to be considered a DLT, the technology does not need to be structured in blocks.

including land registry, birth registry, driving licenses, academic qualifications, etc. See Yermack D, Corporate Governance and Blockchains, op. cit. note 31, 2; & Guadamuz A, Marsden C, Blockchains and Bitcoin: regulatory responses to cryptocurrencies, Sussex Research Online, ISSN 1396-0466, 2015, 31 http://sro.sussex.ac.uk/id/eprint/58872/1/bitcoin.pdf (Accessed 10.09.24).

[51] Stuart Haber & W. Scott Stornetta have proposed a structure for recording the date and time of the creation of intellectual property, as a digital document, with the aim of fixing property rights with the creator before it can be copied by others. See Yermack D, Corporate Governance and Blockchains, op. cit. note 31, 6–7.

[52] By way of example, BTC uses Bitcoin's SHA-256, Ethereum 1.0 used Ethash and, currently, Ethereum 2.0 uses Keccak-256. See van der Linden T, Shirazi T, Markets in crypto-assets regulation: Does it provide legal certainty and increase adoption of crypto-assets?, in Financial Innovation, volume 9, Article number: 22, 2023, 4, https://jfin-swufe.springeropen.com/articles/10.1186/s40854-022-00432-8 (Accessed 10.09.24).

[53] Tomasz T, Crypto-assets and crypto-assets . . . , op. cit. note 9, 368.

In short, the main differentiating elements are decentralization, data registration methods via a multilateral consensus mechanism,[54] encryption methods and temporal validity. These elements, as well as ensuring decentralization, make the technology (theoretically) impenetrable to internal or external attempts to corrupt data,[55] so they confer a fairly high degree of immutability and reliability to the information. It is in this logic that the literature has broadly defined blockchain as a type of technology (or network) for the distributed (or decentralized) and electronic recording, processing and storage of data, which allows the distribution and verification of digital information representing value or rights, structured in blocks of data encrypted via cryptographic methods with hash functions, without copying them (i.e. without backup) and in an automatic, permanent, transparent, instantaneous and tamper-proof way.[56] Strictly speaking, it has simply been defined as a type of DLT consisting of a network/chain made up of an interconnection of data blocks on transactions encrypted using cryptographic methods.

3.2 *Definition of Distributed Ledger Technology Under MiCAR*

The definition of this technology remains remarkably difficult, given its complex and cross-cutting nature, made up of various individual and connected elements, which, in itself, constitutes a huge obstacle in explaining and, consequently, regulating it. As such, the legislator decided to divide the legal definition of DLT into four related definitions, which are set out in Article 3(1)(1), (2), (3) and (4) of MiCAR. These definitions derive from Article 2 of the pilot regime for market infrastructures based on distributed ledger technology.[57] Specifically, the concept

---

[54] The database cannot be corrupted by a single participant, nor can one or more participants exercise a position of dominance, highlighting the necessary and intentionally multilateral character, if we wish, fully, indistinctly and almost totally... democratic. See Mendes Correia F, A tecnologia descentralizada..., op. cit. note 23, 70.

[55] Since the information contained in the blockchain as a shared and continuously reconciled database is not stored or even protected in terms of access to information, the records kept and democratically updated are truly public and easily verifiable and reliable. As it is a decentralized database, there is no centralized version that can be hacked, so it is also not vulnerable to possible cybercrime attempts. See Williams S, It's Time We Got Real About Blockchain..., op. cit. note 47; & Mendes Correia F, A tecnologia descentralizada..., op. cit. note 23, 70.

[56] See Mendes Correia F, A tecnologia descentralizada..., op. cit. note 23, 70; Thibault S, Collusion by blockchain and smart contracts, op. cit. note 41, 119; Vieira dos Santos J, Challenges in Imposing Requirements..., op. cit. cit. note 9, 31; & Engrácia Antunes J, As Criptomoedas, in Revista da Ordem dos Advogados (ROA), Lisboa, A. 81, Jan./Jun. 2021, 119, https://portal.oa.pt/media/133308/jose-engracia-antunes.pdf (Accessed 10.09.24).

[57] Regulation (EU) 2022/858 of the European Parliament and of the Council of 30 May 2022 on a pilot regime for market infrastructures based on distributed ledger technology, and amending Regulations (EU) No 600/2014 and (EU) No 909/2014 and Directive 2014/65/EU, https://eur-lex.europa.eu/eli/reg/2022/858/oj (Accessed 10.09.24).

of DLT is defined and divided as follows: (i) "Distributed ledger technology" or "DLT", consists of a "technology that enables the operation and use of distributed ledgers"; (ii) "Distributed ledger", constitutes an "information repository that keeps records of transactions and that is shared across, and synchronised between, a set of DLT network nodes using a consensus mechanism"; (iii) "Consensus mechanism", consists of the "rules and procedures by which an agreement is reached, among DLT network nodes, that a transaction is validated"; & (iv) "DLT network node", constitutes "device or process that is part of a network and that holds a complete or partial replica of records of all transactions on a distributed ledger".

As might be expected, in the spirit of the principle of technological neutrality, no reference is made to blockchain as a subcategory of the broad notion of DLT. The main feature that makes up its specific functional definition, including as a differentiating element from other types of DLTs, i.e. advanced cryptographic mechanisms, is also not included. In the initial MiCAR proposal, in its article 3(1)(1), as well as in the initial proposal for a pilot regime for DLT-based infrastructures,[58] in its article 2(1), DLT is defined as "type"/ "class" of technologies which "support the distributed recording of encrypted data" ended up not accompanying the final version of both regulations. As analyzed in the previous points, the failure to include this element raises multiple questions regarding the extraordinary scope of the legal definition of DLT and, above all, of crypto-asset. According to Article 3(1)(2) of MiCAR, in addition to DLT, crypto-assets may also be based on another "similar technology", which, combined with the lack of the differentiating element of cryptography, makes both legal definitions seem to be extraordinarily broad and, at the same time, unclear.[59] MiCAR seems to cover any type of digital asset, as long as it is issued through any type of DLT or any type of "similar technology" and is not excluded from its scope of application. In this logic that, despite these issues, does not seem to conflict with the principle of technological neutrality, any digital asset that is not considered a digital representation of value or rights based on blockchain, but rather on other types of DLT, or other similar technologies (regardless of what this may mean) without any function or characteristic associated with blockchain technology, will inevitably be connoted with the terms "crypto" or even "cryptocurrencies". In certain cases, this circumstance may not make sense in formal terms, may not be justified in material terms or may even be financially disadvantageous for the issuer. Distinguishing blockchain as one of the subcategories of DLT, associating designations beginning with "crypto" exclusively with blockchain-based digital representations of value or rights appears to be able to mitigate this problem, as all other non-blockchain-based digital representations

---

[58] Proposal for a Regulation of the European Parliament and of the Council on a pilot regime for market infrastructures based on distributed ledger technology, https://eur-lex.europa.eu/legal-content/EN/TXT/?uri=CELEX%3A52020PC0594 (last consulted 10.09.24).

[59] van der Linden T, Shirazi T, Markets in crypto-assets..., op. cit 54, 22.

of value or rights could be simply referred to as "digital assets",[60] which can be considered a broader concept. The indeterminacy of these concepts could limit innovation in the European space, since any type of DLT technology, or similar, that issues digital assets representing value or rights will eventually be subject to a robust legal regime (which implies high initial costs in terms of due diligence and compliance and, most likely, the "death of the business at birth").[61] While DLT has had multiple years to develop, other "similar technologies" will be immediately subject to a regime that may not even be adequate.[62]

4 Conclusion

The legal definitions adopted in MiCAR seem to be too imprecise and often do not even seem to be compatible with each other or with other regimes, and it is not sufficiently clear how they are related. Neither the legal definition of DLT included in the pilot regime, nor the one included in MiCAR, make any special reference to blockchain technology, or to the main characteristics that make up its specific functional definition, including what seems to be the main differentiating element, i.e. advanced cryptographic mechanisms. Intentionally or not, this choice made by the legislator, which seems to be supported by the spirit of the principle of technological neutrality, makes the legal definition of DLT and, therefore, of crypto-asset, extraordinarily broad and comprehensive. As cartoonish as it may seem, the current definition of crypto-asset may come to encompass digital assets based on technologies similar to DLTs but whose main component is not even advanced cryptographic mechanisms. They will still be referred to as "crypto" assets or "crypto" tokens. This lack of harmony in aligning the economic and technical perspectives results in serious problems in delimiting the definitions and, consequently, in determining the scope of application of MiCAR.

---

[60] A term commonly known in this ecosystem and used by the literature as a broad concept to encompass, for example, crypto-assets, NFTs, stablecoins, deposit tokens, CBDCs, and any other type of digital representation of value or rights.

[61] MiCAR's own recital (95), while admitting the importance of ensuring "confidence in markets in crypto-assets and the integrity of those markets", and that it is "necessary to lay down rules to deter market abuse for crypto-assets that are admitted to trading", also admits that crypto-asset issuers and CASPs are often SMEs, so that "it would be disproportionate to apply all the provisions" of MAR to these companies. See the Market Abuse Regulation and also the Commission Recommendation of 6 May 2003 concerning the definition of micro, small and medium-sized enterprises, https://eur-lex.europa.eu/legal-content/PT/TXT/?uri=celex%3A32003H0361 (Accessed 10.09.24).

[62] Tomczak T, Crypto-assets and crypto-assets . . . , op. cit. note 8, 368.

Diogo Pereira Coelho is a Founding Partner of Sypar and a lawyer specializing in IT, Digital, Tax, Criminal and Administrative Offences Law, with expertise in areas related to Web3 and Web4 like FinTech, the metaverse and AI. He worked at BNP Paribas as a Business Implementation Manager and as an Associate Lawyer at Carlos Pinto de Abreu e Associados. He also holds pedagogical certifications and lectured at IDS from 2018 to 2022. He holds a Law degree and a Master's in Corporate Law from the University of Lisbon and is currently pursuing a PhD in Law and Taxation at the University of Seville (crypto-taxation). He has postgraduate qualifications in Company Law, Tax Law, Criminal Law and Compliance from prestigious Portuguese universities, and he is an active member of several legal and tech associations. Diogo is fluent in Portuguese and German, with advanced knowledge of English and knowledge of Spanish.

Part II
Fintech Utilising AI and the Metaverse

An Introduction to Robo-Advisors, Notable Fintech Implementations, and Underlying Theory

Fabio S. Dias

1 What Are Robo-Advisors?

Robo-advisors represent a revolutionary shift in the financial advisory landscape, leveraging advanced computer algorithms to provide automated investment advice and manage portfolios. These digital platforms leverage algorithms and artificial intelligence to provide automated, low-cost, and efficient investment solutions, democratizing access to financial advisory services.

Complex mathematical models and historical data are used to analyse market trends, delivering investment recommendations that align with an individual client's risk tolerance and financial goals. Robo-advisors typically offer a range of investment options, including index funds and exchange-traded funds (ETFs).

Unlike traditional human financial advisors, robo-advisors operate around the clock and often come with lower fees. This automated approach appeals particularly to investors who prefer a passive investment strategy or those who cannot afford continuous personal monitoring of their portfolio development.

1.1 Market Growth and Projections

The robo-advisory market has seen substantial growth in recent years and is expected to continue this upward trajectory. According to a 2024 report by Statista (Robo-Advisors—Worldwide, 2024), the assets under management (AUM) in the Robo-Advisors market are projected to reach an impressive US$1802.00 billion

F. S. Dias (✉)
University of Surrey, Guildford, UK
e-mail: f.dias@surrey.ac.uk

A. Zarifis, X. Cheng (eds.), *Fintech and the Emerging Ecosystems*, Financial Innovation and Technology, https://doi.org/10.1007/978-3-031-83402-8_11

in 2024. This market is anticipated to experience a compound annual growth rate (CAGR) of 6.68% from 2024 to 2028, resulting in a projected total AUM of US$2334.00 billion by the end of 2028. Additionally, the number of users in the robo-advisory market is expected to climb to 34.130 million by 2028. On average, the assets under management per user are estimated to be around US$55.16k in 2024. From a global perspective, the United States leads the market, with AUM projected to reach US$1,459,000.00 million in 2024.

1.2 Notable Fintechs in Robo-Advisory Implementation

Several Fintech companies have gained market share in the robo-advisory industry. As these platforms evolve, they will likely play an even more significant role in shaping the future of personal finance and investment management.

Some of them are:

Betterment
Betterment is one of the pioneers in the robo-advisory space, known for its user-friendly platform and robust investment strategies. Founded in 2008, Betterment has consistently emphasized low-cost investment solutions and personalized financial planning. The platform uses sophisticated algorithms to manage clients' portfolios, focusing on diversification, tax efficiency, and risk management. Betterment offers various services, including goal-based investing, retirement planning, and socially responsible investment options. The platform's commitment to transparency and customer service has made it a popular choice among investors looking for reliable and affordable financial advisory services.

Wealthfront
Wealthfront is another significant player in the robo-advisory market, offering a comprehensive suite of financial planning tools and investment management services. Established in 2008, Wealthfront has built a reputation for innovation and technological excellence. The platform provides automated portfolio management, utilizing a passive investment strategy primarily composed of ETFs. Wealthfront's features include tax-loss harvesting, direct indexing, and personalized financial advice through its Path tool, which helps clients plan for various financial goals, such as buying a home or saving for retirement. Wealthfront's focus on automation and low fees has attracted a large user base, making it one of the leading robo-advisors in the industry.

1.3 *Advantages of Robo-Advisors*

Robo-advisors offer several advantages over traditional financial advisors, making them an attractive option for many investors:

1. **Cost efficiency**: Robo-advisors typically charge lower fees than human advisors, making investment management more accessible to a broader audience.
2. **24/7 availability**: These platforms operate continuously, providing round-the-clock monitoring and adjustments to clients' portfolios.
3. **Passive investment strategy**: Ideal for investors who prefer a hands-off approach, robo-advisors handle all aspects of portfolio management, from asset allocation to rebalancing.
4. **Personalized recommendations**: Using data-driven algorithms, robo-advisors tailor investment advice to individual clients' risk tolerance and financial goals.
5. **Diverse investment options**: Most robo-advisors offer a range of investment choices, including index funds and ETFs, which provide broad market exposure and reduce risk through diversification.
6. **Tax efficiency**: Many platforms incorporate tax optimization strategies, such as tax-loss harvesting, to enhance after-tax returns.

2 A Brief Literature Review

This brief literature review synthesizes the current academic research on robo-advisory Fintechs, examining their operational frameworks, technological underpinnings, regulatory challenges, and impacts on traditional financial advisory models. By analyzing a diverse array of scholarly sources, this review aims to elucidate the transformative potential and limitations of robo-advisors, offering a comprehensive understanding of their role in the contemporary financial landscape.

The implementation of robo-advisory services depends on intricate quantitative methods (Beketov et al., 2018). As robo-advisors are automated platforms that provide financial planning and investment management services with minimal human intervention, they need to leverage sophisticated algorithms and data analysis.

Key points from the literature on such models include:

1. **Quantitative techniques**: The core of robo-advisors lies in their quantitative methods. These methods include mean-variance optimization, Black-Litterman models, and Monte Carlo simulations. Each technique plays a crucial role in asset allocation, risk assessment, and portfolio optimization, ensuring that investment strategies are tailored to individual risk preferences and financial goals.
2. **Algorithmic efficiency**: The efficiency and accuracy of these algorithms are vital. They analyze large datasets to predict market trends, assess risk factors, and optimize investment portfolios. This data-driven approach helps in mini-

mizing human biases and errors, leading to more reliable financial advice and management.
3. **Customization and accessibility**: Robo-advisors offer a high degree of customization, making sophisticated financial strategies accessible to a broader audience. Users can receive personalized investment advice based on their financial situation, goals, and risk tolerance without the need for high fees typically associated with traditional financial advisors.
4. **Regulatory and ethical considerations**: The article also touches on the importance of regulatory frameworks to ensure the ethical deployment of robo-advisors. Compliance with financial regulations is essential to maintain transparency, protect consumer data, and ensure the accuracy of the financial advice provided.

Robo-advisors represent a significant advancement in the field of asset management, blending quantitative finance with cutting-edge technology to democratize financial planning and investment management.

2.1 Quantitative Techniques in Robo-Advisors

Robo-advisors have revolutionized the financial planning and investment management industry by offering sophisticated, automated services that were once exclusive to high-net-worth individuals. The core of these services lies in the use of advanced quantitative methods. These techniques include mean-variance optimization, Black–Litterman models, Monte Carlo simulations, and more advanced machine learning methods, all of which play a crucial role in asset allocation, risk assessment, and portfolio optimization.

Mean-Variance Optimization
Introduced by Harry Markowitz in 1952, mean-variance optimization is a fundamental technique in modern portfolio theory. This method helps in creating an efficient frontier, representing the set of optimal portfolios that offer the highest expected return for a given level of risk. Robo-advisors use this technique to balance the trade-off between risk and return, aligning investment strategies with an individual's risk tolerance and financial goals.

Black–Litterman Model
The Black–Litterman model is an enhancement of the mean-variance optimization framework, developed by Fischer Black and Robert Litterman. This model addresses some of the shortcomings of mean-variance optimization, such as the sensitivity to input assumptions. By incorporating both market equilibrium and investor views, the Black-Litterman model produces more stable and realistic estimates of expected returns. Robo-advisors utilize this model to refine their asset allocation strategies, ensuring they are more resilient to market fluctuations.

Monte Carlo Simulations

Monte Carlo simulations are used to assess the potential future performance of an investment portfolio under various scenarios. By generating thousands of random scenarios for asset returns and economic conditions, this technique helps in understanding the range of possible outcomes and the probabilities of different returns. Robo-advisors leverage Monte Carlo simulations to provide investors with insights into the potential risks and rewards of their investment strategies over time.

Advanced Machine Learning Methods

Robo-advisors are increasingly incorporating advanced machine learning techniques to enhance their portfolio optimization processes. Notably, two Random Forest models are used to implement optimal portfolio rules for time-varying expected returns and volatility.

1. **Random forest for excess return forecasting**: This model forecasts monthly excess returns using macroeconomic factors, such as payout yields. By analyzing a vast array of economic indicators, the model provides more accurate predictions of future returns compared to traditional methods.
2. **Random forest for volatility estimation**: This model estimates the prevailing volatility, which is crucial for risk management. Accurate volatility predictions enable robo-advisors to adjust portfolio allocations dynamically, ensuring that risk levels are maintained within the desired range.

Machine Learning Portfolio Allocation

Some machine learning models have demonstrated the potential to offer substantial improvements over traditional buy-and-hold strategies (Dias & Peters, 2020). By accurately forecasting returns and volatility, these models enable better reward-risk timing. This approach enhances utility, improves risk-adjusted returns, and reduces maximum drawdowns, providing significant benefits to investors (Pinelis & Ruppert, 2022).

One of the most recently documented approaches used for portfolio allocation based on machine learning is based on a combination of the factors below:

Machine learning techniques: The use of advanced machine learning methods, particularly Random Forest models, in portfolio management, is based on employing these models to forecast monthly excess returns using macroeconomic factors such as payout yields and to estimate prevailing volatility.

Time-varying expected returns and volatility: Optimal portfolio rules are implemented using two separate Random Forest models. One model predicts the expected returns while the other estimates the volatility. This dual-model approach allows for a more dynamic and responsive investment strategy that adjusts to changing market conditions.

Performance improvements: There are mensurable improvements in risk-adjusted returns, and maximum drawdowns achieved by employing machine learning models for reward-risk timing (Pinelis & Ruppert, 2022). These improvements are compared to traditional buy-and-hold strategies, showing the advantages of using machine learning for more accurate forecasts and risk assessments.

Random Forests for Portfolio Allocation

In the realm of portfolio allocation, machine learning has become an invaluable tool, offering sophisticated methods to optimize investment strategies. Among these methods, the Random Forest model stands out for its unique advantages, making it particularly suited for the complexities of financial data.

Understanding Random Forests

Random Forest is an ensemble learning method that builds multiple decision trees during training and merges their outputs to improve the model's performance and stability. Here's why Random Forest is preferred over other machine learning models for portfolio allocation:

1. **Non-metric characteristics**: Random Forests are non-metric, meaning they do not assume any specific distribution of the data. This characteristic is crucial for financial data, which often deviate from normal distributions and exhibit patterns that are hard to capture with parametric models.
2. **Scale invariance**: Decision trees, the building blocks of Random Forests, are scale-invariant. This means that rescaling the features (e.g., converting dollar amounts to thousands of dollars) does not affect their predictions. This invariance simplifies the preprocessing steps required for financial data, which can vary widely in scale.
3. **Fewer parameters to optimize**: Compared to models like deep neural networks, Random Forests require tuning fewer parameters. Deep neural networks can have hundreds of parameters and various configurations of hidden layers and neurons, making them complex and computationally intensive. In contrast, Random Forests are relatively straightforward, focusing on optimizing a smaller set of parameters, such as the number of trees and the maximum depth of each tree.

Dealing with Noisy Financial Data

Financial data are notoriously noisy, with risk premia difficult to forecast due to the diminishing signal-to-noise ratio in well-known variables. Additionally, potential shifts in data distributions complicate risk premia estimation. Here's how Random Forests handle these challenges:

1. **Mitigating noise**: Random Forests can find complex signals within noisy data by growing multiple trees with random subsets of variables (random subspace method). This approach helps to identify robust patterns that may not be apparent in the entire dataset. By averaging the predictions of multiple trees, Random Forests reduce the impact of noisy or irrelevant features, leading to more stable and accurate predictions.
2. **Adaptability to changing relationships**: Financial markets are dynamic, with relationships between predictors and target variables like excess returns shifting over time. A single decision tree might accurately predict returns based on certain variables during specific periods, but these relationships may not hold

consistently. Random Forests address this by growing many trees with different variables. Even if some trees fail to capture the changing relationships, the overall prediction from the forest remains robust. This adaptability ensures that the model can handle shifts in data distributions better than models relying on static relationships.

3. **Reducing overfitting**: While a single decision tree may overfit to idiosyncratic patterns in the training data, a Random Forest mitigates this risk by averaging the results of multiple trees. This ensemble approach helps in generalizing better to out-of-sample data, thereby improving the model's performance in real-world scenarios.

Practical Example: Predicting Excess Returns
Consider a scenario where a Random Forest model is used to predict excess returns based on macroeconomic factors such as inflation, term spread, and dividend yield. In certain market environments, the relationship between these predictors and excess returns may vary. For example, during high inflation periods, the term spread might be a significant predictor, whereas, in stable economic conditions, the dividend yield might be more relevant.

By growing many trees with different combinations of these predictors, a Random Forest can capture the varying importance of these factors over time. If some trees rely heavily on inflation and term spread, and others on dividend yield, the ensemble model can balance these relationships, providing more consistent and reliable predictions across different market conditions.

2.2 *Further Considerations*

Random Forests offer several advantages for portfolio allocation, including non-metric characteristics, scale invariance, fewer parameters to optimize, and robustness to noisy financial data. Their ability to adapt to changing relationships between predictors and target variables makes them particularly well-suited for financial markets. By leveraging the power of Random Forests, investors can achieve more stable and accurate portfolio allocations, ultimately leading to better investment outcomes.

The transformative impact of AI and big data on the finance industry is profound, driving significant advancements and changes across various facets of financial operations. AI enhances financial modeling by leveraging machine learning (ML) algorithms that surpass traditional statistical methods. These traditional methods often rely on fixed assumptions and predefined functional forms, limiting their ability to adapt to complex and evolving financial data. In contrast, ML techniques can process and analyze large datasets, identifying intricate patterns and making more accurate predictions. This allows financial institutions to create more robust and dynamic models, improving decision-making processes and forecasting.

Risk management also benefits from AI's capabilities. AI systems can analyze vast amounts of historical and real-time data to identify potential risks and predict future scenarios. This predictive power is crucial for assessing market conditions and anticipating financial downturns or crises. Furthermore, AI can automate the monitoring of transactions, detecting anomalies that may indicate fraudulent activities. This real-time surveillance enhances the ability to mitigate risks swiftly and efficiently, protecting both institutions and consumers from potential losses.

In the realm of trading strategies, AI has revolutionized how trades are executed and strategies are developed. Algorithmic trading, particularly high-frequency trading (HFT), relies on AI to execute trades at lightning speeds, capitalizing on small price discrepancies that occur within fractions of a second. AI-driven quantitative trading strategies analyze historical data and market trends to make informed trading decisions, often outperforming human traders. These AI systems continuously learn and adapt, refining their strategies to stay ahead of market changes and competitors.

However, integrating AI into finance is not without its challenges. Data privacy is a paramount concern, given the sensitive nature of financial information. Ensuring that this data is protected from breaches and misuse is critical, and firms must navigate complex regulatory landscapes that govern data privacy. Ethical considerations also play a significant role, as AI models can inadvertently perpetuate biases present in historical data, leading to unfair or discriminatory outcomes. Ensuring transparency and accountability in AI decision-making processes is essential to maintain trust and fairness in financial operations.

Moreover, the regulatory framework surrounding AI in finance is still evolving. Financial institutions must stay updated on regulatory developments and ensure compliance with a myriad of global standards. This includes adhering to data privacy regulations like GDPR in Europe and other local guidelines that may affect how AI can be deployed and used in financial services.

In summary, AI and big data are driving a transformative impact on the finance industry, enhancing financial modeling, risk management, and trading strategies. While traditional statistical methods are constrained, AI offers a more dynamic and accurate approach to analyzing complex financial data. Nonetheless, integrating AI into finance comes with significant challenges, including data privacy, ethical considerations, and the need for robust regulatory frameworks. As the technology continues to evolve, addressing these challenges will be crucial for maximizing the benefits of AI in finance.

2.3 The Promises and Pitfalls of Robo-Advising

Another study emphasized the complexity of robo-advising tools and their varying impacts on different types of investors (D'Acunto et al., 2019). It highlighted the need for understanding both the advantages and potential drawbacks as these tools become more ubiquitous globally. By tailoring portfolios to individual holdings and preferences, robo-advisors can significantly enhance diversification and reduce behavioral biases, offering substantial benefits to investors. However, the increased engagement required and the appeal to already active, wealthy investors suggest areas where robo-advisors may need to evolve to better serve a broader audience.

Robo-advisors represent a significant advancement in financial technology, offering personalized, algorithm-driven investment management that can enhance diversification, improve returns, and mitigate behavioral biases. However, they also present challenges, such as requiring increased investor attention and potentially appealing primarily to already active, wealthy individuals. As robo-advisors continue to grow in popularity, understanding these promises and pitfalls will be crucial for investors and the financial industry alike. The main promises and pitfalls observed are:

Promises

Diversification benefits: A study examining the introduction of a wealth-management robo-adviser revealed that investors who adopted robo-advising experienced significant diversification benefits.

Improved portfolio performance: Ex ante undiversified investors increased their stock holdings, leading to portfolios with lower volatility and better returns. Already well-diversified investors, while holding fewer stocks, also saw a reduction in volatility and increased their trading activity.

Behavioral biases reduction: Adopters of robo-advising tools exhibited a decline in common behavioral biases such as the disposition effect, trend chasing, and the rank effect. This behavioral shift underscores the potential of robo-advisors to foster more rational investment behavior.

Pitfalls

Active and wealthy bias: The study found that adopters tended to be more active investors with greater assets under management compared to non-adopters. This indicates that while robo-advisors are accessible, they may primarily appeal to a subset of the investor population that is already engaged and financially well-off.

Behavioral Triggers: Post-adoption, investors showed increased attention to their investments, as evidenced by more frequent online account logins. This increased engagement, while potentially beneficial, may also lead to overtrading or heightened anxiety about market fluctuations.

3 The Customization of Investment Portfolios by Robo-Advisors

The advent of robo-advisors has revolutionized the investment landscape, providing an accessible, efficient, and cost-effective way for individuals to manage their investments. Unlike traditional financial advisors who offer personalized advice through face-to-face interactions, robo-advisors use sophisticated algorithms to create customized investment portfolios based on the client's financial goals, risk tolerance, and preferences.

The traditional (human-led) process for building customised investment portfolios is based on model portfolios and investment factors (Lawler et al., 2020). Robo-advisors follow a similar process, using client questionnaires, portfolio optimization, and model portfolios (Phoon & Koh, 2018).

3.1 The Client Questionnaire: Gathering Essential Information

The journey of building a customized portfolio with a robo-advisor begins with the client completing a detailed questionnaire. This initial step is crucial as it provides the robo-advisor with the necessary information to understand the client's financial situation, investment goals, risk tolerance, and preferences. The questionnaire typically includes the following components:

1. **Demographic Information**: Questions about the client's age, income, employment status, and financial dependents help the robo-advisor gauge the client's investment horizon and potential future financial needs.
2. **Investment Goals**: Clients are asked about their primary objectives for investing, such as saving for retirement, purchasing a home, funding education, or simply growing wealth. Understanding these goals allows the robo-advisor to tailor the investment strategy to meet specific future needs.
3. **Risk Tolerance**: Behavioral questions assess how comfortable the client is with potential losses. For example, "How much of a loss would make you uncomfortable?" This helps in determining the client's ability and willingness to take on risk, which is essential for setting appropriate volatility targets.
4. **Tax Circumstances**: Information about the client's tax situation, such as their tax bracket and any specific tax considerations, helps in optimizing the portfolio for tax efficiency.
5. **ESG Preferences**: With increasing awareness about sustainable investing, clients may express preferences for Environmental, Social, and Governance (ESG) focused investments. The questionnaire might include questions to determine the client's interest in incorporating ESG factors into their portfolio.

3.2 Portfolio Optimization: Balancing Risk and Return

Once the questionnaire is completed, the robo-advisor uses the gathered data to build a customized investment portfolio. This involves setting a volatility target for the client, which reflects the level of risk they are willing to take. The process of portfolio optimization aims to maximize the expected return while ensuring that the portfolio's volatility does not exceed the client's risk tolerance. Here's how it works:

1. **Defining volatility targets**: Based on the client's risk tolerance, the robo-advisor sets a target for the portfolio's volatility. Volatility, often measured as the standard deviation of returns, represents the degree of variation in the investment's value over time. A lower volatility target corresponds to a more conservative portfolio, while a higher target indicates a willingness to accept more risk for potentially higher returns.
2. **Solving the optimization problem**: The core of portfolio optimization is to find the allocation of assets that maximizes the expected return subject to the volatility constraint and other preferences indicated by the client. This involves mathematical techniques and algorithms that solve for the optimal mix of investments. The optimization problem can be formulated as follows:

$$\max_{\mathrm{w}} \mathbf{w}^T \mu$$

Subject to:

$$\mathbf{w}^T \sum \mathbf{w} \leq \sigma_{\text{target}}^2$$

$$\mathbf{w}^T \mathbf{1} = 1$$

$$\mathbf{w} \geq 0$$

where

- w is the vector of asset weights.
- μ is the vector of expected returns for each asset.
- Σ }Σ is the covariance matrix of asset returns.
- σ_{target}^2 is the target volatility.

3. **Model portfolios**: The optimal solution found by the robo-advisor is usually a linear combination of model portfolios. A model portfolio is a pre-constructed mix of assets designed to meet specific investment objectives and risk profiles. By combining different model portfolios, the robo-advisor can create a customized solution that aligns with the client's unique circumstances.

3.3 Understanding Model Portfolios

In financial advisory services, a model portfolio represents a collection of investments that are chosen to reflect a particular investment strategy, risk tolerance, or time horizon. These portfolios are designed by financial experts and serve as building blocks for creating personalized investment strategies. Here's why model portfolios are important:

1. **Efficiency**: Using model portfolios allows robo-advisors to quickly generate customized solutions without needing to start from scratch for each client. This efficiency reduces costs and makes professional portfolio management accessible to a broader audience.
2. **Diversification**: Model portfolios are typically well-diversified, containing a mix of asset classes such as stocks, bonds, and other securities. Diversification helps in managing risk and enhancing returns over time.
3. **Expertise**: Model portfolios are crafted based on extensive research and analysis by financial professionals. They reflect best practices in asset allocation and are regularly updated to adapt to changing market conditions.

3.4 The Role of Markowitz Theory

Robo-advisors have democratized access to sophisticated investment management, offering customized portfolios tailored to individual needs and preferences. By starting with a comprehensive client questionnaire, robo-advisors gather essential information that feeds into the portfolio optimization process. Utilizing principles from Modern Portfolio Theory and leveraging the efficiency of model portfolios, robo-advisors create investment strategies that aim to maximize returns while managing risk.

The principles of portfolio optimization used by robo-advisors are rooted in Modern Portfolio Theory (MPT), developed by Harry Markowitz in the 1950s (Markowitz, 1952). Markowitz's theory emphasizes the importance of diversification and the trade-off between risk and return. The key concept introduced by Markowitz is the efficient frontier, which represents the set of optimal portfolios that offer the highest expected return for a given level of risk. By using MPT, robo-advisors can identify the most efficient portfolio allocation for their clients, balancing the desire for returns with the need to manage risk.

3.5 Volatility vs. Maximum Drawdown Targets

While volatility is a common risk measure used in portfolio optimization, some robo-advisors may use maximum drawdown targets instead. Maximum drawdown represents the largest peak-to-trough decline in the portfolio's value over a specified period. Although drawdown is a useful measure of risk, it poses certain challenges in optimization:

1. **Non-convexity**: The maximum drawdown is not a convex function, meaning it can have multiple local minima and maxima. This non-convexity makes

it difficult to find the global optimal solution using standard optimization techniques, which are designed to work with convex problems.
2. **Complexity**: Solving for the optimal portfolio with maximum drawdown constraints requires more complex algorithms and computational power, potentially increasing the costs and complexity of the robo-advisor's operations.

Convexity is a crucial property in optimization problems because it ensures that any local minimum is also a global minimum. This simplifies the search for the optimal solution and guarantees that the algorithms used will converge to the best possible outcome. In the context of portfolio optimization:

1. **Simplifies computation**: Convex optimization problems can be solved more efficiently using well-established mathematical techniques. This efficiency is vital for robo-advisors, which need to process and analyze large amounts of data quickly.
2. **Ensures optimality**: With convex problems, robo-advisors can be confident that the solutions they find are truly optimal, providing the best possible outcomes for their clients given the specified constraints.
3. **Reduces risk**: Convexity reduces the risk of the optimization algorithm getting stuck in a suboptimal solution, ensuring that clients receive portfolios that effectively balance risk and return.

While volatility targets are commonly used in this optimization process, some robo-advisors may also consider maximum drawdown targets, despite the added complexity. The importance of convexity in optimization cannot be overstated, as it ensures that the solutions found are both efficient and optimal.

3.6 Balancing Practicality and Criticism in Robo-Advisory Portfolios

Markowitz theory, introduced in the 1950s and the backbone of Modern Portfolio Theory (MPT), has garnered its share of critics over the years. Some argue that its assumptions are too simplistic or that it doesn't adequately capture the complexities of financial markets. However, it remains a solid foundation for constructing robo-advisory portfolios, primarily because it avoids the pitfalls of overfitting data, a crucial aspect given the limited and potentially unstable nature of financial return observations.

Markowitz theory suggests that an optimal portfolio can be constructed by balancing expected returns against risk, measured by the variance or standard deviation of returns. Despite its foundational role in finance, it has faced several criticisms:

1. **Assumption of normal distribution**: Critics point out that financial returns do not always follow a normal distribution. Real-world returns often exhibit skewness and kurtosis (fat tails), which are not accounted for in MPT.
2. **Static nature**: MPT assumes a static view of the world, where asset returns and covariances are constant over time. However, financial markets are dynamic and constantly evolving.
3. **Risk measurement**: Using standard deviation as a proxy for risk has been questioned, as it treats upside and downside volatility equally, while investors are typically more concerned with downside risk.

Despite these criticisms, MPT is still widely used in robo-advisory platforms because it provides a straightforward and robust framework for diversification, a key principle in risk management.

One significant advantage of using Markowitz theory in robo-advisory portfolios is its resistance to overfitting. Overfitting occurs when a model is too closely tailored to historical data, capturing noise rather than underlying patterns. This can lead to poor performance when the model is applied to new, unseen data.

In financial markets, overfitting is a particular concern because:

1. **Limited data**: Financial return data is inherently limited. While stock market history spans over a century, the usable data set for many assets is much shorter. This limited data makes it easy to overfit a model to past returns.
2. **Structural breaks**: Financial markets experience structural breaks—sudden shifts in the underlying processes generating the data. A structural break can render historical data irrelevant for future predictions, leading to significant model inaccuracies.

A structural break is a significant and lasting change in the statistical properties of a time series, such as the mean or variance. These breaks can be caused by major economic events, policy changes, or technological advancements.

For example, the end of the Bretton Woods system in 1971 is a classic instance of a structural break. Bretton Woods established fixed exchange rates and a gold-backed dollar. Its collapse led to floating exchange rates and a fundamentally different global financial system. Portfolios optimized using data from the Bretton Woods era would be ill-suited for the post-Bretton Woods environment, highlighting the challenges posed by structural breaks.

When constructing portfolios, especially in a robo-advisory context, it is crucial to account for the limited and potentially unstable nature of financial data. Markowitz theory helps in this regard by promoting diversification and avoiding complex models that risk overfitting.

1. **Data limitations**: Given the finite amount of historical data, models that rely heavily on past performance may not generalize well. Markowitz's approach, which focuses on mean-variance optimization, uses relatively simple statistical measures that are less likely to be distorted by limited data.
2. **Adaptability to structural breaks**: While no model can fully predict structural breaks, a diversified portfolio based on Markowitz theory is better positioned to

adapt to changing conditions. Diversification reduces dependence on any single asset or market condition, providing a buffer against unexpected shifts.

Convexity is a crucial property in optimization problems. A function is convex if a line segment between any two points on the function lies above or on the graph. Convex problems are easier to solve because any local minimum is also a global minimum, ensuring that optimization algorithms can find the best solution efficiently.

In the context of portfolio optimization:

1. **Simplifies computation**: Convex optimization problems can be solved using efficient algorithms, reducing computational costs and time. This is particularly important for robo-advisors, which need to process large volumes of data quickly.
2. **Ensures robust solutions**: Convexity guarantees that the solutions found are globally optimal, providing the best possible risk-return trade-off for the client.

Non-convex problems, like those involving maximum drawdown constraints, are more complex. They can have multiple local minima, making it challenging to find the global optimum. This complexity can lead to suboptimal portfolio choices and increased computational requirements.

3.7 *Integrating ESG Preferences*

Robo-advisors also incorporate Environmental, Social, and Governance (ESG) factors into portfolio construction based on client preferences. ESG investing focuses on companies with positive environmental practices, social responsibility, and good governance. Integrating ESG preferences requires additional constraints in the optimization problem, but the principles of Markowitz theory still apply.

1. **Enhanced risk management**: ESG factors can serve as additional measures of risk. Companies with strong ESG practices may be less prone to regulatory fines, reputational damage, and operational disruptions.
2. **Alignment with client values**: Incorporating ESG preferences ensures that the portfolio aligns with the client's values, enhancing their satisfaction and engagement with the investment process.

4 Conclusion

As technology continues to evolve, the capabilities of robo-advisors will only improve, providing even more personalized and effective investment solutions. For investors, this means greater accessibility to professional-grade portfolio management, tailored to their unique financial goals and risk tolerance.

While Markowitz theory has its limitations and critics, it remains a foundational tool in the construction of robo-advisory portfolios. Its ability to balance risk and return through diversification helps avoid overfitting and provides robust solutions in the face of limited and unstable financial data. By understanding and mitigating the effects of structural breaks, such as the end of the Bretton Woods system, robo-advisors can create adaptable and resilient portfolios.

Moreover, the convexity of the optimization problem ensures that the solutions found are efficient and globally optimal. Incorporating client preferences, including ESG factors, further customizes the portfolios, aligning them with individual values and enhancing the overall investment experience.

In the dynamic and complex world of finance, the principles of Markowitz theory, coupled with modern computational techniques, provide a solid foundation for robo-advisors to deliver personalized and effective investment strategies. As technology continues to evolve, the ability to integrate more data, adapt to structural breaks, and incorporate diverse preferences will only enhance the effectiveness of robo-advisory services, democratizing access to sophisticated portfolio management for all investors.

References

Beketov, M., Lehmann, K., & Wittke, M. (2018). Robo advisors: Quantitative methods inside the robots. *Journal of Asset Management, 19*, 363–370.

D'Acunto, F., Prabhala, N., & Rossi, A. G. (2019). The promises and Pitfalls of Robo-advising. *The Review of Financial Studies, 32*(5), 1983–2020.

Dias, F. S., & Peters, G. W. (2020). A non-parametric test and predictive model for signed path dependence. *Computational Economics, 56*, 461–498.

Lawler, B., Mossman, B., Nolan, P., & Ang, A. (2020). Factors and advisor portfolios. *The Journal of Wealth Management, 22*(4), 37–61.

Markowitz, H. M. (1952). Portfolio selection. *The Jornal of Finance, 7*(1), 77–91.

Phoon, K., & Koh, F. (2018). Robo-advisors and wealth management. *The Journal of Alternative Investments, 20*(3), 79–94.

Pinelis, M., & Ruppert, D. (2022). Machine learning portfolio allocation. *The Journal of Finance and Data Science, 8*, 35–54.

Robo-Advisors - Worldwide. (2024). Retrieved from Statista: https://www.statista.com/outlook/dmo/fintech/digital-investment/robo-advisors/worldwide

Fabio S. Dias is a Senior Lecturer of Finance and Econometrics at the University of Surrey, Guildford (UK). Prior to joining the university, he was a Senior Manager for Analytics & Modelling at Lloyds Banking Group. He started his banking career as a developer for the Front Office Technology at Credit Suisse, where he eventually was promoted to Vice President.

Artificial Intelligence in Financial Technology: Challenges, Opportunities, and Global Trends

Sonam Rani, Gaurav Gupta, Sailaja Bohara, and Amitabh Bhargava

1 Introduction

Artificial intelligence (AI) has emerged as a transformative force in the financial technology (Fintech) industry, driving significant advancements, and reshaping traditional financial services. AI encompasses a range of technologies that model complex abilities, offering solutions that enhance efficiency, reduce costs, and improve customer experiences in the financial sector (Ahmed et al., 2022; Shao et al., 2022). The integration of AI within Fintech has enabled the development of innovative services, such as algorithmic trading, robo-advisors, and automated customer service, all of which contribute to a more dynamic and responsive financial ecosystem (Cao et al., 2020).

The convergence of AI and Fintech represents a critical shift in the way financial services are delivered, with AI playing a pivotal role in enhancing the accessibility and effectiveness of these services. Financial institutions are increasingly leveraging AI to manage vast amounts of data, optimize operations, and provide personalized financial solutions to consumers (Flavián et al., 2022).

This integration not only improves operational efficiency but also poses new challenges, including ethical considerations and the need for robust regulatory frameworks to manage the socio-economic impacts of AI-driven financial technologies. Understanding the role of AI in Fintech is therefore crucial for academics, industry professionals, and policymakers aiming to navigate this rapidly evolving landscape.

S. Rani · G. Gupta (✉) · S. Bohara · A. Bhargava
Amity University, Noida, India
e-mail: abhargava@gn.amity.edu

A. Zarifis, X. Cheng (eds.), *Fintech and the Emerging Ecosystems*, Financial Innovation and Technology, https://doi.org/10.1007/978-3-031-83402-8_12

2 Objective

1. To explore the prospects and emerging trends in AI-driven Fintech solutions, identifying opportunities for further research and development that can contribute to a more user-centric and inclusive financial ecosystem.
2. To highlight the theoretical foundations underlying the integration of Artificial Intelligence (AI) in Fintech, utilizing the TCCM framework to identify and categorize the key theories driving innovation and change in the industry.
3. To explore the contextual factors influencing the adoption and impact of AI in the Fintech sector, with a particular focus on how varying characteristics such as market maturity, regulatory environment, and consumer behavior shape the development and implementation of AI-driven financial solutions.

3 Research Methodology

This study employs a systematic literature review to thoroughly explore the topic at hand. We focused on two major online databases: Scopus and Web of Science, with a primary emphasis on Scopus due to its broader subject matter coverage. Scopus, as highlighted by Singh et al. (2021), and Martín-Martín et al. (2018), offers 20% more research articles than Web of Science. In our search, Scopus yielded six times more articles than Web of Science using the specified keywords.

One of the advantages of Scopus is its extensive array of fields that allow for advanced bibliometric analysis. We conducted our search on Scopus using specific keywords in the article titles, such as "AI," "financial technology," "Fintech," "FINtech," and "Artificial Intelligence." Initially, this search produced 947 articles.

To refine the results, we applied stricter filters. We selected only articles and review articles published in journals, excluding conference papers. We further narrowed our selection to documents written in English and focused on the business and management domains. This filtering process reduced the number of articles to 317. After applying additional filters to focus on top journals, the count was further reduced to approximately 127 papers. Following a final review, we excluded articles related to financial services, resulting in a final selection of 88 research articles that specifically focused on AI, financial technology, and Fintech and finally we took 10 highly cited authors' papers for TCCM.

Notably, we did not use Cite Score as a criterion for selection due to the limited number of articles available on the topic. In addition to the Scopus search, we manually searched for relevant articles in each journal that appeared in our results, ensuring that no significant studies were overlooked, particularly those dealing with AI in the hospitality sector.

To aid in theory development, we employed the TCCM framework, which stands for Theory, Context, Characteristics, and Methodology. This framework was used to summarize and systematically organize the information from the research articles.

We categorized the articles in an Excel spreadsheet by author(s), title, publication year, source title, key findings, applied theories, the context in which financial inclusion and financial literacy are discussed, characteristics of financial inclusion, financial literacy, individual well-being, and research methodology, following the approach established by Martín-Martín et al. (2018).

3.1 Software Used

VOSviewer: VOSviewer is a software tool designed to assist users in visualizing and building bibliometric networks. It presents bibliometric data in the form of easily comprehensible and interpretable networks or maps. VOSviewer offers various output options, including bibliographic coupling by author and country, co-citation, citation, and graphical representations of keyword occurrence within the data.

3.2 Output

The output from the analysis of the bibliometric Excel is presented in different clusters, displaying various information. Figure 1 presents the data related to the most productive countries regarding the highest amount of publications, whether a single country or a multiple-country publication.

In Fig. 1, The network visualization illustrates global research collaboration patterns among various countries. The United States and the United Kingdom are shown as dominant players with strong bilateral connections, indicating a significant research partnership. Other notable clusters include India-centric collaborations involving countries like Finland, Bahrain, and Vietnam, as well as a separate cluster centered around Spain. The map highlights the diversity and widespread nature of international research efforts, showcasing both established and emerging hubs of

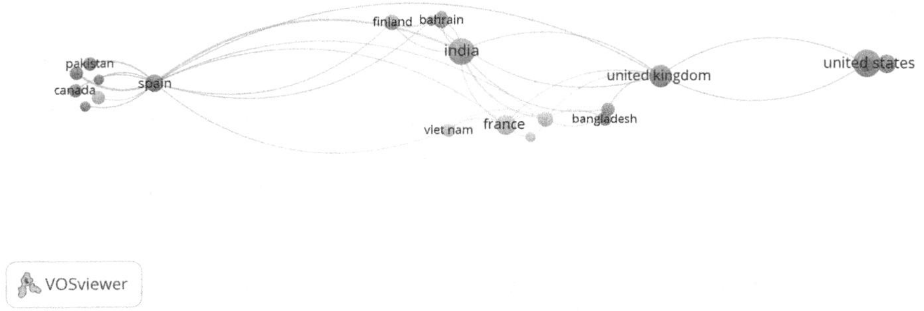

Fig. 1 Top most productive countries with the highest amount of publication (see online version for colors)

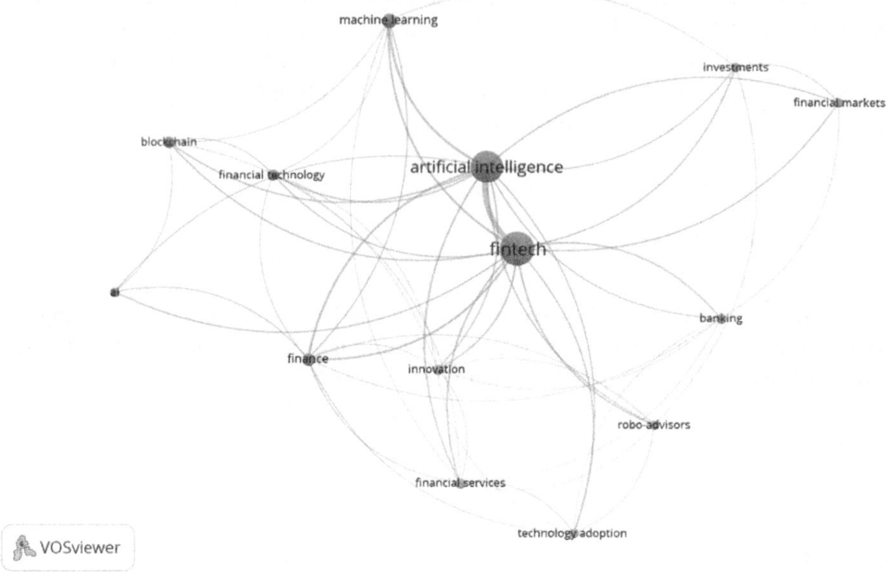

Fig. 2 Occurrence of all keywords in the bibliometric analysis (see online version for colors)

collaboration. The thickness of the connecting lines emphasizes the strength of these collaborations, with the United States and United Kingdom leading as central nodes in the global research network.

In Fig. 2, The central nodes of the network, "fintech" and "artificial intelligence," are the most prominent, indicating their pivotal role in the research landscape. These nodes are closely connected to other key topics such as "machine learning," "blockchain," and "financial technology," reflecting the integration of advanced technologies in the fintech domain. The map also shows connections between fintech and traditional financial sectors, with nodes like "banking," "financial services," and "investments." The keyword "innovation" links various concepts, underscoring its importance in the development and adoption of fintech solutions. The network reveals how contemporary research in fintech is deeply intertwined with technological advancements, particularly in artificial intelligence and blockchain, while also maintaining strong ties to traditional financial concepts.

In Fig. 3, The network reveals two distinct clusters of researchers who are interconnected through their collaborative work. The first cluster, shown in red, includes prominent authors such as Luis V. Casalino, Carlos Flavian, Daniel Belanche, and Cheng Xi Aw. These researchers are closely linked, indicating frequent collaborations within this group. The second cluster, shown in green, includes researchers like Heinz Herrmann, Georgios Sermpinis, and Arvind Ashta, who are also well-connected within their group. The connections between these two clusters suggest that while they primarily collaborate within their respective groups, there are also some cross-collaborations, particularly involving Luis V. Casalino,

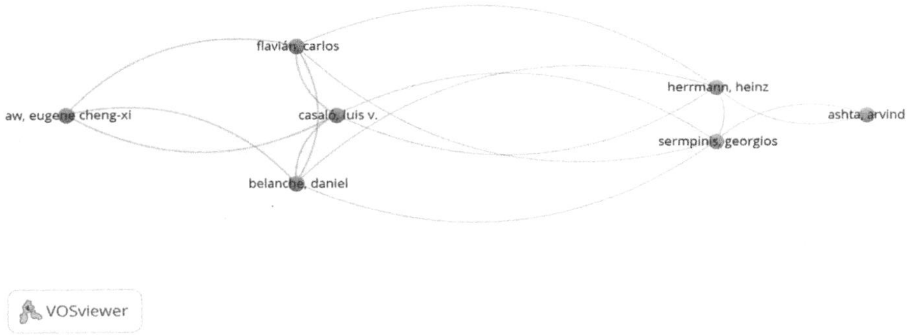

Fig. 3 Highest amount of citation authors (see online version for colors)

who appears to serve as a bridge between the two clusters. This network highlights the collaborative nature of research in this domain, with key individuals facilitating connections across different research groups.

4 TCCM Framework

The TCCM (Theory, Context, Characteristics, and Methodology) framework is utilised to systematically analyse the existing literature on the implementation of financial technology (FinTech) and artificial intelligence (AI) in the financial sector, particularly focusing on accounting, auditing, and financial inclusion. This framework provides a structured approach to understanding the theoretical foundations, research contexts, key findings, and methodological approaches employed in the studies (Table 1).

Theory (T)
The studies collectively highlight the critical role of AI and emerging technologies in reshaping financial services, regulatory practices, and consumer behavior. Carlos Flavián et al. (2022) employ the Technology Readiness Index (TRI) to explore how customers' readiness to adopt AI-driven services, such as robo-advisors, is influenced by their attitudes toward technology. Their findings on the roles of optimism and discomfort in technology adoption underscore the nuanced ways customers interact with AI in financial services. Herrmann and Masawi (2022), through bibliometric analysis, examine the convergence of AI and Fintech, demonstrating AI's disruptive impact on the financial sector and mapping the global research landscape in these fields. Building on this, Liu et al. (2023) introduce the concept of personalized regulation using AI, contrasting it with traditional regulatory approaches. They argue that AI can tailor financial risk management, providing a more nuanced regulatory framework that balances risk containment with economic development, especially for underprivileged sectors. In a related

Table 1 TCCM Table (Theory, Context, Characteristics & Methodology)

Authors/Year	Theory	Context	Characteristics/findings	Methodology
Ashrafi and Kabir (2023)	Technology Readiness Index (TRI) is used to understand customers' adoption of AI-driven services like robot-advisors.	Explores AI-managed investments in the banking and financial sectors, focusing on how customers' readiness affects their intent to use robot advisors.	Optimism increases, and insecurity decreases, customers' intent to use robo-advisors. Discomfort surprisingly increases adoption.	Quantitative analysis of 404 potential customers using TRI framework. Post-hoc analysis on service awareness and labeling.
Aw et al. (2023)	No single theoretical framework uses bibliometric techniques to analyze AI and Fintech convergence.	Focuses on AI's role in financial operations within the BFSI sectors, highlighting AI as a disruptive force.	AI and Fintech dominate academic discourse with strong international research collaboration.	Bibliometric analysis of 298 papers using VOSviewer, focusing on global research landscapes.
Belanche et al. (2019)	Personalized regulation using AI to tailor financial risk management, contrasting with traditional approaches.	Examines China's P2P lending sector, focusing on regulatory shifts and their impact on borrowers' economic development.	Advocates for AI-driven personalized regulation to balance credit risk containment and borrower protection.	Empirical analysis using credit application data, demonstrating AI's role in personalized regulation.
Flavián et al. (2021) Haider et al. (2020)	AI-enhanced financial decision-making to improve loan assessments, particularly in natural disasters.	Studies AI's role in reducing delinquency rates in the aftermath of natural disasters.	AI significantly benefits financially vulnerable borrowers by providing tailored risk assessments.	Empirical research with a credit-scoring company, comparing AI-empowered lenders with others.
	Privacy and justice perspective to investigate consumer resistance to robo-advisors.	Analyzes consumer resistance in the digital transformation of the banking and finance industry.	Perceived fairness reduces privacy concerns and intrusiveness, lowering resistance to robo-advisors.	Quantitative research with 200 consumers using PLS-SEM to test relationships between variables.

Herrmann and Masawi (2022)	Dual-factor theory to study robo-advisory service adoption.	Investigate factors influencing robo-advisory service adoption among consumers.	Trust, complexity, and perceived value/risk impact adoption intentions.	Data was collected via Google Forms and analyzed using PLS-SEM and SMART PLS 3.3.4.
Liu et al. (2023)	No single framework, discusses AI adoption in BFSI and academic research gaps.	Examines the disparity between AI adoption in BFSI and academic research, focusing on Responsible AI in practice.	Highlights the underrepresentation of insurance and the need for Responsible AI governance.	Review-based methodology analyzing literature on AI in BFSI.
Liu et al. (2024)	Agile and Fintech theory applied in Islamic banking research.	Focuses on the impact of Fintech in revolutionizing Islamic banking in Bahrain.	Islamic banks need to adopt Fintech to stay competitive.	Secondary data analysis emphasizing the necessity for agility in Islamic banks.
Nguyen et al. (2023)	Combines Islamic finance principles with AI and NLP for Fintech implementation.	Analyzes AI and NLP in Islamic Fintech for mitigating COVID-19's impact.	AI and NLP enhance economic support through Islamic finance solutions.	Uses interdisciplinary approaches combining AI with Islamic finance principles.
Rabbani and Khan (2020)	Technology Acceptance Model (TAM) extended with subjective norms to predict robo-advisor adoption.	Research diverse customer reactions to robo-advisors in the Fintech industry.	Attitudes, subjective norms, and familiarity with robots drive adoption.	Data was collected via web survey and analyzed using structural equation modeling.
Roszkowska (2020)	Audit-related causes of financial scandals and technological solutions.	Examines how technologies like blockchain, AI, and IoT can prevent financial scandals.	Emerging technologies can significantly enhance financial statement reliability.	Uses case studies and interdisciplinary literature review to propose advancements

Source: Author's Analysis

study, Liu et al. (2024) apply AI-enhanced financial decision-making to improve loan assessments during natural disasters, highlighting AI's potential to enhance the resilience of vulnerable borrowers through accurate risk assessments. Aw et al. (2023) contribute to this discussion by exploring privacy and justice perspectives in the context of consumer resistance to robo-advisors. They connect psychological barriers to AI adoption with perceived fairness, privacy concerns, and intrusiveness, showing how these factors drive resistance to new technologies. Similarly, Ashrafi and Kabir (2023) use dual-factor theory to study the determinants of robo-advisory service adoption, analyzing how perceived value, risk, and innovation resilience influence users' behavioral intentions. This complements Flavián et al.'s findings by focusing on the cognitive processes underlying technology adoption. Furthering the discussion on AI's impact, Nguyen et al. (2023) highlight the theoretical gap between AI adoption in the BFSI sector and academic research, emphasizing the need for Responsible AI (RAI) frameworks. Their work aligns with Herrmann and Masawi's focus on the global research landscape by addressing the ethical implications of rapid AI adoption in finance. Rabbani and Khan (2020) apply Agile and Fintech theory within Islamic banking, demonstrating how Fintech innovations can revolutionize the sector, echoing the broader theme of adapting traditional financial practices to new technological paradigms, as seen in the works of Flavián and Liu. Finally, Haider et al. (2020) integrate Islamic finance principles with AI and NLP, proposing an AI-based Fintech model to mitigate the impact of crises like COVID-19. This reflects the ongoing theme of combining technology with traditional financial practices to address modern challenges. Belanche et al. (2019), using the Technology Acceptance Model (TAM), explore how attitudes and subjective norms influence robo-advisor adoption, connecting with Flavián et al. and Ashrafi & Kabir by examining the psychological and social factors affecting technology acceptance in financial services. Paulina Roszkowska (2020) rounds out this exploration by analyzing how emerging technologies like blockchain, AI, and IoT can prevent financial scandals, reinforcing the idea that technological advancements can enhance the reliability of financial practices. Together, these studies underscore a shared focus on understanding how AI and other technologies can be responsibly and effectively integrated into financial systems to enhance service delivery, risk management, and regulatory frameworks.

Context (C)

The studies collectively examine the integration of AI and emerging technologies within various financial contexts, emphasizing their transformative potential across different sectors. Carlos Flavián et al. (2022) investigate the rapidly growing automation of services, particularly in the banking and financial investment sectors, focusing on AI-managed investments and how customers' technology readiness affects their intent to use robo-advisors. Herrmann and Masawi (2022) explore the intersection of AI and Fintech within the BFSI (Banking, Financial Services, and Insurance) sectors, highlighting AI's role as a disruptive force in global financial operations. Liu et al. (2023) situate their study within China's peer-to-peer (P2P) lending sector, particularly examining the impact of a sudden regulatory shift that led to the industry's shutdown. They focus on how this change affected the economic potential of borrowers, especially those who were underprivileged. Building on this, Liu et al. (2024) place their research in the context of natural disasters, analyzing AI's role in improving loan assessments and reducing delinquency rates, particularly for financially vulnerable borrowers. Aw et al. (2023) address the challenges of consumer resistance to Fintech services, such as robo-advisors, within the broader digital transformation of the banking and finance industry, emphasizing the importance of understanding psychological and perceptual barriers to technology adoption. Ashrafi and Kabir (2023) focus on the factors influencing consumer adoption of robo-advisory services, placing their study in the context of the growing importance of trust, innovation resilience, and perceived value in the financial services industry. Nguyen et al. (2023) examine the disparity between AI adoption in the BFSI sector and the corresponding academic research, particularly noting the underrepresentation of the insurance sector and the emerging need for Responsible AI frameworks. Rabbani and Khan (2020) explore the role of Fintech in revolutionizing Islamic banking in Bahrain, positioning their study within the context of a sector that must adapt to stay competitive. Haider et al. (2020) focus on the integration of AI and NLP with Islamic finance principles to develop Fintech solutions that address the economic impact of crises like COVID-19. Belanche et al. (2019) investigate the adoption of robo-advisors within the broader Fintech industry, examining how customer attitudes and subjective norms shape adoption. Lastly, Paulina Roszkowska (2020) contextualizes her study within the realm of financial scandals, exploring how technologies like blockchain, AI, and IoT can enhance the reliability of financial statements and prevent future scandals.

Characteristics/Findings (C)

The methodologies employed in these studies are diverse, reflecting the varied contexts and research questions. Carlos Flavián et al. (2022) use a quantitative research design, analyzing data from 404 North American potential customers of robo-advisors to test their hypotheses, including post-hoc analysis on service awareness and labeling. Herrmann and Masawi (2022) conduct a bibliometric analysis using VOSviewer software, examining 298 papers from the Scopus database to analyze global research trends in AI and Fintech. Liu et al. (2023) employ an empirical analysis of individual credit applications to assess the impact of China's P2P lending regulations, using AI to predict financial risks and demonstrate personalized regulation. Liu et al. (2024) adopt an empirical research design in collaboration with a credit-scoring company, tracking loan applications and analyzing delinquency rates among borrowers affected by natural disasters, comparing outcomes between AI-empowered and non-AI lenders. Aw et al. (2023) utilize a quantitative research approach, collecting data from 200 consumers via an online survey and analyzing the results using Partial Least Squares Structural Equation Modeling (PLS-SEM) to test the relationships between various perceptions and resistance to robo-advisors. Ashrafi and Kabir (2023) also use a PLS-SEM methodology, analyzing data collected through social media-distributed Google Forms and evaluating it with SMART PLS 3.3.4. Nguyen et al. (2023) conduct a comprehensive literature review, critically analyzing existing research and trends in AI adoption within the BFSI sector, focusing on the evolution of AI and the challenges of implementing Responsible AI. Rabbani and Khan (2020) use secondary data analysis to explore the need for agility and Fintech adoption in Islamic banking. Haider et al. (2020) combine interdisciplinary approaches, integrating AI and NLP with Islamic finance principles to develop a Fintech model for crisis mitigation. Belanche et al. (2019) collect data via a web survey from 765 customers and use structural equation modeling and multisample analyses to test their hypotheses on robo-advisor adoption. Finally, Paulina Roszkowska (2020) employs case studies and an interdisciplinary literature review to propose how emerging technologies can enhance the reliability of financial statements and prevent scandals.

Methods (M)
The findings across these studies reveal critical insights into how AI and emerging technologies influence financial services and consumer behavior. Carlos Flavián et al. (2022) find that technological optimism increases customers' intention to use robo-advisors, while insecurity decreases it. Interestingly, they also discover that technological discomfort positively influences adoption, suggesting that the passive role customers play in AI-driven services may reduce barriers to technology adoption. Herrmann and Masawi (2022) identify that AI and Fintech are dominant themes in academic discourse, with significant contributions from the United States, China, and India, highlighting strong international collaboration in these fields. Liu et al. (2023) advocate for AI-driven personalized regulation, suggesting it can mitigate adverse effects on borrowers' economic development while managing credit risks more effectively than traditional approaches. In their subsequent study, Liu et al. (2024) find that AI significantly benefits financially vulnerable borrowers by providing tailored risk assessments, particularly in the aftermath of natural disasters. Aw et al. (2023) show that perceived fairness (justice) negatively impacts privacy concerns and perceived intrusiveness, which in turn reduces consumer resistance to robo-advisors. Ashrafi and Kabir (2023) reveal that trust, complexity, and perceived value are crucial factors influencing the adoption of robo-advisory services, with innovation resilience moderating these effects. Nguyen et al. (2023) highlight the underrepresentation of the insurance sector in AI research and emphasize the urgent need for Responsible AI frameworks in financial services, especially in decentralized finance (DeFi). Rabbani and Khan (2020) emphasize the necessity for Islamic banks to embrace Fintech innovations to remain agile and competitive. Haider et al. (2020) demonstrate that combining AI and NLP with Islamic finance principles, such as Zakat and Qardh-Al-Hasan, can effectively mitigate the economic impact of crises like COVID-19. Belanche et al. (2019) find that attitudes, subjective norms, and familiarity with robots are key drivers of robo-advisor adoption, with perceived ease of use significantly influencing these factors. Lastly, Paulina Roszkowska (2020) suggests that emerging technologies like blockchain, AI, and IoT can significantly enhance the reliability of financial statements and prevent scandals similar to those involving Enron and Arthur Andersen. Together, these findings underscore the transformative potential

of AI and emerging technologies in enhancing financial services, managing risks, and addressing consumer concerns, while also highlighting the need for responsible and context-sensitive regulatory frameworks.

5 Discussion

The collective research highlights the profound impact of AI and emerging technologies on financial services, regulatory practices, and consumer behavior. Carlos Flavián et al. (2022) illustrate how technology readiness, particularly optimism and discomfort, influences the adoption of AI-driven services like robo-advisors, revealing the complexity of consumer interactions with technology. This is echoed by Aw et al. (2023), who explore the psychological and perceptual barriers to AI adoption, emphasizing the importance of perceived fairness and privacy concerns in shaping consumer resistance. Meanwhile, Herrmann and Masawi (2022) and Nguyen et al. (2023) expand the discussion to a macro level, analyzing the global research landscape and identifying gaps between AI's rapid adoption in the BFSI sector and the slower pace of corresponding academic research, particularly in the insurance sector. The studies by Liu et al. (2023, 2024) add another dimension by exploring AI's role in personalized regulation and financial decision-making. Their findings suggest that AI can offer more tailored and effective solutions in both regulatory frameworks and disaster recovery, particularly for financially vulnerable populations. This focus on personalized, context-sensitive applications of AI is further supported by Ashrafi and Kabir (2023), who analyze the factors influencing the adoption of robo-advisory services, emphasizing the role of trust and perceived value in driving consumer behavior. The work of Rabbani and Khan (2020) and Haider et al. (2020) highlights the unique challenges and opportunities presented by Fintech in Islamic banking. They demonstrate that AI and Fintech innovations can revolutionize traditional financial practices, offering agile and innovative solutions, especially during crises like COVID-19. Finally, Paulina Roszkowska (2020) broadens the discussion by examining how emerging technologies like blockchain, AI, and IoT can enhance the reliability of financial statements and prevent financial scandals, reinforcing the importance of technological advancements in maintaining financial integrity.

6 Research Implications

These studies collectively suggest several avenues for future research. First, the nuanced findings by Flavián et al. (2021) and Aw et al. (2023) on consumer behavior indicate a need for deeper exploration into the psychological factors that influence technology adoption in financial services. Understanding how optimism, discomfort, fairness, and privacy concerns interact to shape consumer behavior can provide valuable insights for developing more effective AI-driven services. The research gaps identified by Herrmann and Masawi (2022) and Nguyen et al. (2023) highlight the need for more focused academic inquiry into the adoption of AI in underrepresented sectors like insurance. Moreover, the call for Responsible AI frameworks underscores the importance of investigating the ethical and governance challenges associated with AI's rapid integration into financial services. The findings from Liu et al. (2023, 2024) on personalized regulation and disaster recovery suggest that future research should explore the broader applications of AI in regulatory frameworks and crisis management. Additionally, the intersection of Fintech and Islamic finance, as discussed by Rabbani and Khan (2020) and Haider et al. (2020), offers a fertile ground for research into how AI and Fintech can be adapted to meet the specific needs of different cultural and religious contexts. Finally, Roszkowska's (2020) examination of emerging technologies in auditing points to the potential for interdisciplinary research that combines technological advancements with financial integrity and governance. This could lead to the development of more robust systems for preventing financial scandals and improving the reliability of financial reporting.

7 Practical Implications

From a practical standpoint, the findings suggest that financial institutions should focus on developing more comprehensive strategies for the deployment of RPA and AI technologies. These strategies should include training programs that enhance both technological and human capabilities, ensuring a balanced approach to risk management. The successful integration of AI in financial inclusion initiatives, as demonstrated by studies in the dataset, indicates that financial institutions and policymakers should leverage these technologies to improve access to financial services, particularly in regions where traditional financial infrastructure is lacking. Furthermore, the insights gained from the combination of Islamic finance principles with AI could be applied to develop new financial products and services that are both culturally relevant and technologically advanced. Financial institutions should also consider adopting machine learning techniques to better understand and predict customer behaviors, leading to more personalized and effective financial services. The practical application of these findings can significantly enhance the resilience and inclusivity of financial systems, making them better equipped to handle future economic challenges.

8 Conclusion

The dataset provides a comprehensive overview of the current state of research in financial literacy, inclusion, and the implementation of AI and RPA in the financial sector. The findings highlight the critical challenges and opportunities presented by these technologies, particularly in enhancing financial decision-making and inclusion. The research and practical implications drawn from the dataset underscore the importance of continued exploration into the integration of AI in financial practices, with a particular focus on addressing disparities and enhancing financial resilience. As the financial landscape continues to evolve, the insights provided by this research will be invaluable in shaping future policies and strategies that promote a more inclusive and technologically advanced financial system.

References

Ahmed, S., Alshater, M. M., El Ammari, A., & Hammami, H. (2022). Artificial intelligence and machine learning in finance: A bibliometric review. *Research in International Business and Finance, 61*, 101646.

Ashrafi, D. M., & Kabir, M. R. (2023). Human or AI? Understanding the key drivers of customers' adoption of financial robo-advisory services: The role of innovation resilience. *Journal of Global Business and Technology, 19*(1), 18–40.

Aw, E. C.-X., Kam, T., Tan, G. W.-H., & Ooi, K.-B. (2023). Counteracting dark sides of robo-advisors: Justice, privacy and intrusion considerations. *International Journal of Bank Marketing, 41*(4), 789–809.

Belanche, D., Casaló, L. V., & Flavián, C. (2019). Artificial intelligence in FinTech: Understanding robo-advisors adoption among customers. *Industrial Management & Data Systems, 119*(7), 1411–1430.

Cao, L., Yuan, G., Leung, T., & Zhang, W. (2020). Special issue on AI and FinTech: the challenge ahead. *IEEE intelligent systems, 35*(2), 3–6.

Flavián, C., Pérez-Rueda, A., Belanche, D., & Casaló, L. V. (2022). Intention to use analytical artificial intelligence (AI) in services: The effect of technology readiness and awareness. *Journal of Service Management, 33*(2), 293–320.

Haider, M., Khan, S., Rabbani, M. R., & Thallasinos, Y. E. (2020). An artificial intelligence and NLP-based Islamic FinTech model combining Zakat and Qardh-Al-Hasan for countering the adverse impact of COVID-19 on SMEs and individuals. *International Journal of Economics and Business Administration, 8*(2), 348–361.

Herrmann, H., & Masawi, B. (2022). Three and a half decades of artificial intelligence in banking, financial services, and insurance: A systematic evolutionary review. *Strategic Change, 31*(6), 549–569.

Liu, Y., Li, X., & Zheng, Z. (2023). Consequences of China's 2018 online lending regulation and the promise of PolicyTech. *Information Systems Research.*

Liu, Y., Li, X., & Zheng, Z. (2024). Smart natural disaster relief: Assisting victims with artificial intelligence in lending. *Information Systems Research, 35*(2), 489–504.

Martín-Martín, A., Orduna-Malea, E., Thelwall, M., & Delgado López-Cózar, E. (2018). Google Scholar, Web of Science, and Scopus: A systematic comparison of citations in 252 subject categories. *Journal of Informetrics, 12*(4), 1160–1177.

Nguyen, D. K., Sermpinis, G., & Stasinakis, C. (2023). Big data, artificial intelligence and machine learning: A transformative symbiosis in favor of financial technology. *European Financial Management, 29*(2), 517–548.

Rabbani, M. R., & Khan, S. (2020). Agility and Fintech is the future of Islamic finance: A study from Islamic banks in Bahrain. *International Journal of Scientific and Technology Research, 9*(3), 6955–6957.

Roszkowska, P. (2020). Fintech in financial reporting and audit for fraud prevention and safeguarding equity investments, *Journal of Accounting & Organizational Change* (Vol. 17 No. 2, pp. 164–196).

Shao, S., Shi, Z., & Shi, Y. (2022). Impact of AI on employment in the manufacturing industry. *International Journal of Financial Engineering, 9*(3), 2141013.

Singh, V. K., Singh, P., Karmakar, M., Leta, J., & Mayr, P. (2021). The journal coverage of Web of Science, Scopus and Dimensions: A comparative analysis. *Scientometrics, 126*(6), 5113–5142. https://doi.org/10.1007/s11192-021-03948-5

Sonam Rani is an accomplished Assistant Professor at Amity University Uttar Pradesh, Greater Noida Campus. She brings over a decade of experience in the education industry, specializing in accounting, banking, and finance. With a robust academic background, including UGC-NET and ongoing Ph.D. studies, she is deeply committed to advancing knowledge and fostering student success. Her teaching philosophy integrates real-world applications with theoretical insights, ensuring a dynamic and impactful learning experience. She is proficient in advanced Excel, SPSS, and Tally, which she incorporates into the curriculum to enhance practical skills. Her dedication to research is evident through her publications in Scopus-indexed journals, contributions to book chapters, and securing copyrights and patents to her credit.

Gaurav Gupta holds a doctorate in Marketing from Punjabi University, Patiala, and has also studied at Wilkes University, Pennsylvania, USA, and IIM-Kozhikode. He has presented research at IIM-Ahmedabad, IIM-Indore, IIM-Bangalore, and internationally at the University of Ljubljana, Slovenia, and Wolkite University, Ethiopia. His papers are published in ABDC listed/Scopus Indexed journals, and he serves as an editor with Taylor and Francis Group. Dr. Gupta has received fellowships from the European Union, IIM-Bangalore, and ICSSR (Ministry of HRD, India). He is a member of the Advisory Board for Cleveland Professional University, USA. Currently, he is associated with Amity University, Noida, and previously worked with Christ University. His interests include Brand Management, Marketing Research, AI and Marketing, with several publications and presentations to his credit.

Sailaja Bohara with nine years of experience in marketing, excels in both quantitative and qualitative research. She has published extensively in top-tier journals and is an Assistant Professor at Amity Business School, Amity University, Greater Noida. Dr. Sailaja is proficient in marketing research, critical thinking, problem-solving, and data analysis. Her expertise includes report and content writing, and she is skilled in using IT tools like MS Office, SPSS, AMOS, and PL-SEM.

Amitabh Bhargava is a senior executive with over 26 years of leadership experience in academia and corporate sectors. He has expertise in core academics, corporate-academia relations, strategic planning, and industry interface, with a focus on establishing Centers of Excellence, digital marketing, and media. Dr. Bhargava has a proven track record of collaborating with C-level executives, solving critical challenges, and meeting stakeholder expectations. His specialization lies in management, particularly marketing management. He has published numerous research papers in reputed journals, including SCI, WOS, and Scopus, and holds three Indian patents. Dr. Bhargava earned his Ph.D. in Management from Banasthali Vidyapith, Rajasthan, and currently serves as an Associate Professor and Head of Institution for the Management Domain at Amity University, Greater Noida Campus.

Metaverse: Where Is It Going to Add Value for the Financial Services Industry and Banks?

Anna Omarini and Gulnaz Rakhmatullina

1 Introduction

The concept of the metaverse has gained a lot of traction and interest in the last few years because of the number of investments and level of interest displayed by multinational companies. While there are many definitions to refer to it, we can converge on the idea that the metaverse is an immersive shared virtual space where various activities (e.g., creating, learning, playing, shopping, socializing, and working) can be carried out with the help of augmented reality (AR) and virtual reality (VR) services (see Damar, 2021). Therefore, it represents the convergence of trends and a range of technologies that are in place and growing exponentially.

As a result, numerous businesses in various industries are exploring the concept and its possible applications to their businesses. Each one can take advantage of the metaverse, mainly because the concept is not owned or restricted to any person, country, or business, allowing new ideas to be implemented. As with any major innovation, the potential evolution of the metaverse is still to be seen but should not be ignored. There are already a wide range of use cases, with gaming, developing events, and commerce being the immediate ones. However, its evolution goes from a near-term to long-term opportunities to be implemented and accepted by the market. In dealing with its evolution, also the financial services industry can take advantage of it.

The goal of this chapter is to create a comprehensive framework of value creation in the metaverse and apply this framework to the financial services sector. By merging Stakeholder Theory and Service-Dominant (S-D) Logic, we first proposed that value is co-created in the metaverse through the cooperation and resource

A. Omarini (✉) · G. Rakhmatullina
Bocconi University, Milan, Italy
e-mail: anna.omarini@unibocconi.it

A. Zarifis, X. Cheng (eds.), *Fintech and the Emerging Ecosystems*, Financial Innovation and Technology, https://doi.org/10.1007/978-3-031-83402-8_13

integration of different stakeholders, such as the company and its employees, customers, and collaborators. Furthermore, we created a comprehensive framework that classifies the value created by distinguishing between customer vs. company value orientation, as well as value created for the physical vs. virtual worlds. Finally, we applied the proposed framework to the financial services sector and provided examples by plotting them in the framework. We believe that our article benefits academic literature and industry participants by explaining how the metaverse can create value and providing a comprehensive framework of value creation in the metaverse that can be applied to any industry.

The rest of the chapter is structured as follows. The second section presents an overview of the metaverse. The third and fourth sections describe the theoretical background and the proposed value-creation framework in the metaverse. The fourth section applies the proposed framework to the financial services industry, while the final section concludes with a discussion and future challenges.

2 The Metaverse Overview

2.1 Timeframe

Over the past few years, the term "metaverse" has gained significant attention, becoming a buzzword. However, it's important to note that virtual worlds where people can gather, socialize, play, and work have existed for several decades already, primarily within the gaming industry (Wang et al., 2022). The roots of virtual worlds can be traced back to the 1970s and 1980s when the first text-based multiplayer dungeon (MUD) games were created. These were followed by an appearance in the 1980s–1990s of a wide range of virtual games, including shooting games, fantasy role-playing games, massively multiplayer online role-playing games (MMORPGs), and social virtual worlds. At the same time, during the early 1990s, there was a surge of excitement around virtual reality (VR) technologies, with the emergence of companies like WorldsChat and Alphaworld. However, this initial hype about VR technologies subsided by the mid-1990s due to the high costs and limited advancements in available technologies, which decreased the interest of companies and investors.

Even if prototypes of the metaverse existed decades ago, the phenomenon of metaverse reached the peak of its popularity only in the 2020s. Several factors have contributed to this growth. First, the emergence, improvement, and adoption of technologies such as augmented reality (AR), virtual reality (VR), mixed reality (XR), and haptic technologies have elevated the virtual world experience to new levels. Second, the increased adoption of cryptocurrencies and virtual economies has facilitated transactions within virtual worlds. Third, changes in consumer behavior and the accelerated digital activities resulting from the COVID-19 pandemic (Mancuso et al., 2023) have further fueled interest in the metaverse. Additionally, the active engagement of younger digital-native generations, like Generation Z, has played a role in driving the popularity of the metaverse. Finally, the overall hype surrounding the metaverse, generated by companies, media, and users, reached new heights when Mark Zuckerberg announced in October 2021 that Facebook would be rebranded as Meta and made substantial investments in the metaverse (Damar, 2021).

Since 2021, numerous companies have ventured into virtual worlds to engage with customers, conduct marketing activities, and sell virtual items. Notable tech giants such as Meta (formerly Facebook), Microsoft, Apple, Tencent, Alibaba, Sony, and Nintendo are all actively involved in building metaverses. Fashion brands have started selling NFTs on platforms like Sandbox, Decentraland, etc. Additionally, gaming worlds like Fortnite, Decentraland, and Roblox have made significant contributions to the creation of immersive virtual experiences. For instance, Meta launched the Horizon Workroom Beta, introducing the concept of a virtual office, while platforms like Fortnite have hosted virtual concerts attracting thousands of attendees. As a result of the involvement of major technological giants as well as the appearance of new start-ups (Ferrigno et al., 2023), the market landscape has changed by creating new market opportunities for the companies in the new virtual worlds as well as providing options to create omnichannel experiences by integrating the virtual and physical worlds. As a result, if by mid-2022, investments in the metaverse reached $120 billion, forecasts indicate that by 2030, the metaverse's value could ascend to $5 trillion (Ferrigno et al., 2023).

2.2 *The Metaverse Definition*

Defining the metaverse is a complex task as there is no universally accepted definition, and perspectives on it vary depending on one's point of view and purpose.

One of the points of disagreement is the level of interconnectedness between the virtual and physical worlds within the metaverse. Initially derived from Neal Stephenson's 1992 novel "Snow Crash," the metaverse was described as a three-dimensional virtual world and a gigantic virtual universe parallel to the world in which "Meta" means virtual and abstract, and "verse" means universe where users can get together to play games, socialize, and work (Polyviou & Pappas, 2023). Thus, originally, the concept of metaverse was as a separate parallel virtual world that could drastically differ from the physical world. However, contemporary interpretations of the metaverse focus on the seamless integration of both realms using various technologies. Mark Zuckerberg, for example, envisions the metaverse as an immersive ecosystem where avatars and holograms enable work, interaction, and socialization through shared experiences.

Another point of disagreement is the role of immersion and immersive technologies. Originally, the metaverse was thought of as a parallel virtual world that could be accessed only with the help of immersive technologies, such as VR.

Nowadays, some companies, like Meta, rely heavily on virtual and augmented reality technologies to provide virtually interconnected experiences that characterize the metaverse (Gauttier et al., 2024), while other companies, such as Roblox and Sandbox, claim themselves to be the metaverses even though they provide access to their worlds also through mobile devices without relying on immersive technologies. Thus, some experts argue that the platform can be called a metaverse even if it does not necessarily use technologies such as AR and VR (Park & Kim, 2022), while others argue that such a perspective collides with the immersive nature of a metaverse and its ability to merge physical and virtual worlds and it ignores important aspects of integration, immersion, and perceived presence by the user (Dwivedi et al., 2022).

The third point of disagreement is the aspect of decentralization. It is expected by some experts that Web 3.0 and metaverse will be structured in a decentralized way with the use of blockchain technologies (Ritterbusch & Teichmann, 2023); however, at the same time Meta (former Facebook), for example, claimed the metaverse as its own, establishing its own governance (Gauttier et al., 2024).

The final significant disagreement pertains to whether the current metaverses can truly be considered "the" metaverse, as the original concept referred to a single virtual world parallel to the physical world. According to some experts, we are already experiencing the metaverse, while others claim that the metaverse is still under development. At the same time, some people characterize the metaverse as a single virtual world, while others as a hyperconnected shared digital space blending physical and virtual realities (Barrera & Shah, 2023). Today, numerous companies create their own metaverses that are not interconnected; therefore, there is still a doubt whether a collection of these not connected virtual worlds will become a single metaverse or whether we will have several separate metaverses just as they exist today.

In this article, we define the metaverse as a permanent and immersive mixed-reality world where people can interact synchronously with other people and objects beyond the limitations of time and space by using avatars and immersion-supporting devices, platforms, and infrastructures (Kaplan & Haenlein, 2009). We look at a metaverse from the holistic point of view as an integration of many virtual worlds, open or closed, and technologies that provide an environment interconnected with the physical world and that can be accessed with or without AR/VR/XR technologies.

2.3 The Metaverse Features

Compared to early virtual worlds, contemporary metaverses have distinct characteristics. They offer more natural and immersive experiences, accessible not only through personal computers but also through portable devices such as mobile phones. They have become more economically efficient, thanks to the development of blockchain and virtual currencies, ensuring more stable and improved provision of services. Additionally, metaverses have garnered increased interest due to the growing demand for virtual worlds following the COVID-19 pandemic (Dwivedi et al., 2022).

Within the metaverse, users are represented by ***digital avatars*** that can experience digital life in ***virtual environments***, engage in various activities, consume ***products and services***, and participate in ***digital economic interactions*** facilitated by ***technologies*** and ***metaverse engines*** (Wang et al., 2022).

To experience the metaverse, users need to create their digital representations, or avatars. These avatars can be human-like or have any imaginary forms, be similar to the user or not. In the metaverse worlds, users can represent themselves anonymously and play different personalities, however, in the majority of cases, the role of avatar in the metaverse is self-representation. Thus, by using the avatars, users represent themselves, explore the environment, and interact with companies, objects, or other participants in the metaverse.

Virtual environments in the metaverse can simulate real spaces, mirror the physical world, or be entirely imaginative, featuring unique spatial and temporal dimensions (Wang et al., 2022). Virtual worlds, such as several gaming platforms, could have characteristics of fantasy worlds, where users are represented by fantasy characters. However, current metaverse worlds, such as Meta or Decentraland, are closer to the real world, with more realistic features where users can create more realistic avatars, spaces, and experiences.

By using the metaverse platforms, the firms can provide virtual spaces and services that support both the physical and virtual worlds. For example, users can obtain knowledge and learn skills to be used in physical worlds (training programs, education), check and experience the virtual prototypes of physical products (clothes, cars, apartments), or communicate with avatars in virtual worlds to get physical world services. Simultaneously, the metaverse offers a parallel virtual world with its own activities and offerings. Virtual offerings could be products (skins, clothes, accessories, moves, or emojis for avatars, virtual art, etc.) or services (games, social dating, online museums, and online concerts) created by virtual service providers or the users themselves. The products and services on the metaverse can be obtained for free, exchanged, or purchased using cryptocurrencies or metaverse-specific currencies.

Technologies play a key role in providing a metaverse experience. For example, digital twins provide representation of the real world; VR/AR/XR create 3D experiences and immersion; high-speed internet and 5G improve the reliability, speed, and latency of connections; AI enables the large-scale metaverse creation; and blockchain and NFTs provide improved means for economic transactions, while Metaverse engine uses big data from the real world as an input to create experiences in the virtual world (Wang et al., 2022). The development of technologies made a remarkable change to the previous version of metaverses and brought interactive experiences that break the boundaries between physical and virtual worlds, where companies can create new products and experiences and link their offerings between these two worlds with the help of creating synergies (Koohang et al., 2023).

As a result of technological and social development, the concept of metaverse has changed from a narrow single-world perspective to a broader perspective of interconnected worlds, from pure VR experiences to experiences converging many other technologies, such as AR and MR with a focus on social and interactive nature of the environments (Barrera & Shah, 2023). All these developments expanded the boundaries of the metaverse concept, merging physical and virtual worlds, and creating opportunities for different stakeholders to interact, create partnerships, and create value.

3 Value Creation in the Metaverse

3.1 Theoretical Background

To analyze how value can be created for companies in the metaverse, we used Stakeholder Theory alongside Service-Dominant (S-D) Logic.

According to Stakeholder Theory, which was developed by R. Edward Freeman in his book "Strategic Management: A Stakeholder Approach" (1984), companies should focus on creating value not only for shareholders but for all companies' stakeholders, such as customers, suppliers, employees, and other groups affected by company operations. Stakeholder Theory defines stakeholders as individuals or groups with legitimate interests in various aspects of company activities, who participate in those activities to obtain benefits (Donaldson & Preston, 1995). Moreover, this theory emphasizes that there is no prioritizing of benefits of any stakeholder over another, and companies practicing stakeholder management are relatively successful in performance terms such as profitability, stability, growth, etc. (Donaldson & Preston, 1995).

Service-Dominant Logic (S-D Logic), which was developed by Vargo and Lusch (2004) and continues to expand nowadays, further develops Stakeholder Theory by positing that value is co-created through the interactions of actors, defined as entities performing similar resource-integration and service exchange practices. According to Service-Dominant (S-D) logic, the value is a change in benefit experienced by a particular actor and it is influenced by the combination of other resources and interactions with other actors (Nariswari & Vargo, 2023). Service, on the other side, is the application of resources by one actor for its own benefit or the benefit of others (Nariswari & Vargo, 2023). As a result, the value is collaboratively created by resource-integrating actors that perform the exchange of services.

These two theories are particularly applicable to the metaverse for several reasons:

- All interactions in the metaverse are digital and are based on the exchange of services, where companies provide services either to support physical or virtual operations. These services can range from supporting physical operations, such as virtual touch points with customers and training and education of customers

and employees to virtual-only services, such as providing environments, products, and other services to create virtual interactions with stakeholders
- Value in the metaverse is created for different stakeholders. The metaverse operations benefit not only the companies that provide services to customers but also a wide range of other stakeholders, such as customers, employees, suppliers, partners, etc.
- Value in the metaverse is co-created by the interaction and active participation of different stakeholders. For example, companies do not create metaverse offerings by themselves, but actively cooperate with platform providers, suppliers, and other service providers to co-create and deliver the services to end-users. At the same time, end-users actively participate in the development, customization, and use of those offerings
- Value is co-created by integrating various resources of the involved stakeholders. Apart from interaction and cooperation between each other, stakeholders also incorporate different types of resources available to create value. This includes not only financial resources, but also resources such as expertise, knowledge, and skills unique to each type of stakeholder.

3.2 The Main Stakeholders

The stakeholders within the metaverse can be classified from a firm's perspective into several categories: firms providing products and services, firms' customers, metaverse platforms, and firms' partners and collaborators.

Firms Providing Products and Services
Firms that offer products and services in the metaverse encompass a diverse range of industries and offerings starting from fashion brands providing digital skins and clothing for avatars and ending with pop stars creating virtual concerts and performances. By using the metaverse platforms and technologies, firms can provide product/services to support their physical operations or expand their offerings into the virtual world. For instance, Tesla utilized digital twins for their physical cars to enhance customer service by providing proper and on-time maintenance assistance (Gilboa, 2022), while Marriott Hotels to stimulate customer intention to buy has developed VRoom Service, VR Postcard, and teleportation cabins that enable customers to explore 3D travel destinations and experience their luxury resorts before making a purchase (Dwivedi et al., 2022).

At the same time, some companies are entering the virtual world to offer standalone virtual products and services. Disney's chief technology officer Tilak Mandadi, for example, has announced plans to build a "theme park metaverse" as the next phase for Disney's theme parks (Ning et al., 2023). In 2019, Fabricant, the only digital fashion brand at that moment, introduced the first digital blockchain dress titled "Iridescence," which was sold for $9500. After that moment, many fashion brands, such as Adidas, Nike, Gucci, Balenciaga, Luis Vuitton, and others, introduced fully digital products/NFTs. Some brands, like Adidas and Dolce & Gabbana, granted the holders of NFTs access to physical merchandising, other benefits, or "physical twins," while others offered virtual products and NFTs available only for virtual world use. Apart from fashion, NFTs have expanded into the art world. For example, the British auction house Sotheby's launched "Sotheby's Metaverse" section, where it held a special auction titled "Natively 9 Digital 1.2: The Collectors," with 53 pieces from NFT art collections on display at one time (Ning et al., 2023).

Firms' Customers
Customers are users of the metaverse who explore virtual spaces, interact with others, and consume environments, products, services, and content within the metaverse. It is important to mention that if currently the metaverse users are a very niche market, consisting mainly of gamers, in the future the metaverse users' population might expand drastically. It can be expected that when more companies enter the metaverse, creating the network effect, and when the digitally native population, such as Generation alpha, becomes financially active, the metaverse might become more attractive for the customers, dissolving the boundaries between the virtual and physical worlds in the same way as it happened between online and brick-and-mortar channels (Dwivedi et al., 2022). Consumers in the future may switch easily between physical vs virtual worlds channels, products, and selves (Belk, 2013; Dwivedi et al., 2022), which can result in the metaverse becoming just another part of a company's omnichannel strategy.

Firms' Employees
Firms' employees represent another important stakeholder group. Immersive technologies and metaverse platforms offer opportunities for firms to engage with their employees and facilitate interactions among them. For instance, Accenture, in partnership with Microsoft, has launched a virtual space called "the Nth floor" where employees can experience virtual meetings and digital office environments focused on social interaction (Buchholz et al., 2022). BCG Gamma, the artificial intelligence division of BCG, has established its first office in The Sandbox, a metaverse platform, which will be used as a meeting point for conferences and internal meetings. Samsung and Hyundai had job fairs in the metaverse platform, called "Gather Town," which was used for the recruiting purposes of new employees (Handley, 2021).

Metaverse and technologies that are used alongside can be utilized by employees not only for social interaction, but also for increased productivity, decreased waste, and improved cooperation. For example, in the fashion market, using 3D prototyping allows designers to visualize the final product and experiment with different fabrics and patterns before the product is manufactured (Papahristou & Bilalis, 2017). In industrial markets, Boeing, for example, has announced that it will use VR at scale to engineer its next aircraft, powering an immersive digital twin of the product (Bobier et al., 2022).

Metaverse Platforms

Metaverse platforms are the providers of virtual environments that enable interactions between firms, users, and other stakeholders. These platforms, such as Roblox, Decentraland, Meta, and Fortnite, etc., offer virtual spaces where users can meet, socialize, and engage with content created by the platforms themselves, end-users, or firms. From one side, the platforms provide technological resources, such as the provision and update of technological infrastructure for stakeholders to interact and allow external stakeholders to visualize and co-create offerings using more comfortable, interactive, and realistic experiences (Mancuso et al., 2023). On another side, the platforms create value by management of knowledge resources of external stakeholders (Mancuso et al., 2023). Until now, management of knowledge has been considered to be performed by organizations such as platforms and service providers. However, current metaverse platforms also provide technology and an environment for external stakeholders, such as users, to create value and co-create the offerings that help the platforms and service providers design and manage successful VR/AR content (Mancuso et al., 2023). As a result, value is created not only by the interaction of platforms and service providers but also by the interaction between service providers and users (Schöbel & Leimeister, 2023), where the platform and service providers split the control rights related to their joint value-creating activities (Schöbel & Leimeister, 2023).

Firms' Partners: Suppliers, Intermediaries, and Collaborators

Firms' suppliers, intermediaries, and collaborators play a vital role in the metaverse ecosystem. While metaverse platforms are often the primary partners for firms, there are additional collaborations involving designers of virtual products, technology suppliers, software and hardware providers, and companies offering complementary services. Collaborations can range from creating virtual collections to acquiring firms specializing in virtual products and NFTs. For example, to create its first digital dress Fabricant collaborated with Dapper Labs and artist Johanna Jaskowska, to launch its virtual collection, Adidas collaborated with a few top projects like Bored Ape Yacht Club, Mutant Ape Yacht Club, Pixel Vault NFT, while instead of collaborating, Nike has acquired RTFKT, the company creating virtual sneakers and NFTs.

In summary, the metaverse ecosystem encompasses various stakeholders, each contributing to the development and growth of the metaverse as a transformative digital space. In this digital space, by collaborating with platform providers and virtual content providers, companies have an opportunity to improve their internal operations, engage customers, and expand their product offerings. Platforms give permission and opportunity to companies, customers, and intermediaries to interact with each other by providing an immersive and engaging environment. Virtual artists and content providers become new suppliers for companies to create new products and experiences for their customers and employees. Cryptocurrency providers verify financial transactions between different parties in the platform. Customers and employees can interact with other parties in an engaging environment to consume the company offerings and co-create the company value. As a result, metaverses provide a hybrid engagement in a complex network, where a range of participants governs partnerships and develops innovations and value through joint-actor interactions (Dwivedi et al., 2023).

4 Value-Creation Framework in the Metaverse

Our research presents a conceptual framework illustrated in Fig. 1, which classifies the value generated through the utilization of the metaverse. The framework distinguishes between customer and company value orientation, as well as value created for the physical and virtual worlds. Additionally, we have organized examples of value creation for various stakeholders into four distinct quadrants.

The metaverse offers unique opportunities for companies to co-create value with various stakeholders, including customers, employees, internal departments, and collaborators. Here's how it can support both physical and virtual operations:

Quadrant 1: Improving Customer Experience
This quadrant explores how the metaverse can complement the physical world and be a channel to generate additional touchpoints with customers to support the company's physical operations. Examples of these touchpoints include product information, service support, and new marketing/advertising opportunities.

Fig. 1 Metaverse value creation

The metaverse can be used as a valuable tool for providing customers with additional product information. This can be achieved through digital representations of products, enabled by digital twins, or via virtual simulations. For instance, customers can virtually experience hotel rooms or explore properties such as new apartments without needing physical visits. Similarly, simulated VR environments allow customers to test-drive cars, providing an immersive experience and aiding in the decision-making process. VR technology can provide an immersive experience, transport users to artificially constructed environments, and create artificial scenarios and storytelling. This could be very beneficial for customers who want to try the experience before making a purchase.

In addition to product information, companies can provide service support and enhance customer service for physical products with the help of virtual touchpoints and new technologies. Using VR technologies during calls might help the parties to feel more present and engaged, while using other types of technologies, including QR codes, AR, XR, and digital twins, can help resolve issues faster.

The metaverse can also be used as an additional channel for the company's marketing initiatives. For example, technologies such as AR and VR create more immersive and engaging virtual environments compared to regular digital environments, which can result in higher customer engagement and more successful advertising outcomes. Advertising in the virtual environment can be highly customized based on customer backgrounds and previous behavior, giving an opportunity to show different advertisement placement and provide interaction with various avatars influencers in the virtual world to different customers. In addition to advertising, the virtual world can be used as a customer education tool. Users can access information about the company through social interaction in virtual worlds. This way, customers can learn about the company's history, specific events, or obtain any other company-related information.

To sum up, the value in this quadrant is co-created by companies and customers. On one side, through the use of the metaverse, customers receive benefits in the form of additional product and service support that enhance their experiences. On the other side, customers participate in creating overall value by providing additional information/feedback to the company and increased engagement, which could lead to higher loyalty and increased revenue flows. As a result, companies can create more company-customer interactions and touchpoints, which is an important element in building both customer and brand equity.

Quadrant 2: Extending Customer Experience

This quadrant focuses on the potential opportunities that arise only in the virtual world, providing companies with a completely new environment to engage with customers and create value.

By providing virtual-only products and services, companies can expand the boundaries limited by the physical world and extend their portfolios into the virtual world. Companies can provide customers with very imaginative, creative, and unique offerings, such as virtual services and virtual products that are impossible in the real world, due to laws of nature (Dwivedi et al., 2023). While virtual services can include a wide range of activities to support operations in virtual environments, virtual products can be with or without NFT technology. The difference between just virtual products and NFTs is that NFTs allow consumers to acquire, possess, and trade unique virtual artifacts that are identified through blockchain technology (Chohan & Paschen, 2021; Dwivedi et al., 2022). It is worth mentioning that while virtual products have less value than their physical equivalents, the NFTs can reach very high price points due to their unique identifiers (Dwivedi et al., 2022; Hofstetter et al., 2022).

Apart from providing virtual products and services, companies can effectively reach and engage their target audience in the metaverse by creating virtual content that utilizes additional touchpoints and strategic advertising placements. This is why many companies entering the metaverse choose to develop games on gaming metaverse platforms. Through interaction with brand-related gaming content, customers can enjoy extended periods of engagement, experience the brand interaction in more natural settings (where interactions with the brand are voluntary and not perceived as traditional advertisements), and ultimately have a more positive customer experience. By creating new gaming content, apart from having touchpoints with current customers, metaverse platforms give opportunities to companies to reach new target audiences. For example, platforms like Roblox and Fortnite provide access to younger digital-native demographics who will become financially active in the future. Companies can engage with these audiences through in-game advertising, virtual products/services/NFTs, or special events, ultimately boosting brand awareness. Even if these audiences do not represent the primary market for certain companies, establishing a presence on metaverse platforms enables reaching and engaging potential future customers.

Companies and customers co-create value in this quadrant because while companies provide the virtual tools, such as virtual products/services and environments, customers are the ones who actively participate not only in creation of their virtual environments and experiences but also in exposing those experiences to others through social interaction and user generated content. As a result, with the help of new virtual offerings, customers engage in new environments and experiences and at the same time provide new revenue streams for companies.

Quadrant 3: Improving Business Operations

This quadrant explores how the metaverse can complement the physical world and improve a company's internal processes to create efficiency and benefit internal stakeholders.

One aspect of improving business operations through the metaverse is the opportunity to increase transparency and information flow, resulting in reduced costs, improved efficiency, higher coordination, and increased sustainability. One example of this could be creating digital twins. Digital twins have wide-ranging applications across industries such as automotive, e-commerce, healthcare, manufacturing, and logistics (Dwivedi et al., 2022; Liu et al., 2021). Digital twins, which are replicas of actual physical objects, environments, and people in virtual form (Dwivedi et al., 2022), can have applications in many industries and can help companies improve operations and reduce costs. For instance, using a 3D digital twin instead of the physical prototype can help to reduce the waste of materials, time spent, and be more sustainable. In operations and supply chain management, digital twins facilitate collaboration through transparent data sharing and product traceability. By incorporating information from all parties involved in the production process, from suppliers of raw materials to retailers selling the product to the end-users, digital twins enhance supply chain operations, reduce lead time, and decrease costs. Additionally, digital twins can be widely used in product maintenance. By having full information about the condition of an item/product (either company equipment or final product), companies can predict its future condition by running simulations of possible scenarios in different environments and prevent possible risks. Additionally, by creating virtual prototypes of the products, especially in the new product development stage, companies can avoid waste and more accurately understand the products' future demand by concept testing and collecting immediate feedback customers (Dwivedi et al., 2023).

Another aspect of improving business operations is the creation of virtual office spaces and environments. By providing virtual spaces for their employees, companies give them the opportunity to collaborate despite distance and provide an immersive feeling of colleagues' presence that regular digital channels, such as online calls, cannot provide. New virtual spaces can be also used for holding recruiting events as well as trainings, helping create environments and simulations not possible or very costly to run in the physical world.

As a result, the value in this quadrant is created by providing additional benefits to company stakeholders such as employees, different departments within the company, and company partners such as suppliers and intermediaries. Additionally, the total value created can reach higher outcomes when all parties actively use these metaverse solutions and integrate their own resources into better implementation of those solutions.

Quadrant 4: Extending Business Operations

This quadrant emphasizes the value that companies can generate by collaboration with new companies in the metaverse and providing virtual-only offerings.

Entering a new market means having opportunities to establish new collaborations. In the metaverse world, new collaborators include new companies that support the company operations in the virtual world, such as hardware/software providers, new suppliers or designers, metaverse platform providers, and the full spectrum of other companies that provide complementary services on metaverse platforms (Dwivedi et al., 2022). The biggest collaborators for companies in virtual worlds are metaverse/gaming platforms. Many companies enter the metaverse via partnering with metaverse/gaming platforms that provide virtual space, help create special experiences such as games and events, and serve as retail platforms for the sale of company products. However, apart from metaverse/gaming platforms, there is a wide range of other collaborators helping companies create virtual offerings in the metaverse. Together, these collaborators co-create value in this quadrant by providing new virtual offerings to customers, and the value of these offerings highly depends on the level of cooperation, resource integration, and interaction between the company and new collaborators.

In summary, the metaverse provides companies the opportunity to co-create value with their stakeholders. By creating virtual touchpoints, interactive experiences, and collaborative environments, companies can enhance both physical and virtual operations. This not only increases stakeholders' engagement but also creates competitive advantages and drives innovation and efficiency across the business ecosystem.

5 An Application of the Framework to the Financial Service Industry

The financial service industry is not new to technology innovation, which has often introduced new ways of doing banking, and metaverse falls into this category. Metaverse is a significant technology and a strategical shift on the future of banking. Its potential lies in how it will enable banks to differentiate themselves from others also rebuilding community and reignite conversations with their customers at a time when banking has become perceived as commoditized and drained of emotional salience. The metaverse could put human beings back into the conversation in ways that would simply not be possible in app alerts or text messages.

In the last few years, the interlinking of finance and technology has fundamentally transformed the industry in the ways its services can be conceived, produced, delivered, and consumed, from the one hand. And from the other hand, it has also started transforming the ways customers do their banking until reach a point where all of this can make the model of financial intermediation evolving.

The digital vortex is the inevitable movement of many industries where business models, the set of offerings, and value chains are digitized to the maximum extent possible, where all these create new disruptions and blur the lines between industries.

Banks around the world are sitting up and paying attention to the latest developments in the metaverse. The metaverse promises to eliminate the friction that exists between today's many digital platforms and to reinvent how data moves and is used across digital experiences. It will radically change how banks interact with customers, what products and services they offer, how they make and distribute them, and how they operate their organizations. In this process, the metaverse will also create new industries and new ways of working and engaging with others.

There are several reasons that call for a proper definition of metaverse in banking and financial services. Based on the framework in Fig. 1, we can take a wider perspective to contextualize it into the industry. This is because the customers and market in the banking industry are constantly in need of new technological innovations related to banking. This would force banks continuously trying to upgrade their metaverse banking in many ways by searching for advancement ideas once it is implemented.

In particular, metaverse can be one of the many possible expressions coming out from the FinTech definition that the Financial Stability Board gave in 2017 when it stated that: "FinTech is a technologically enabled financial innovation that could result in new business models, applications, processes, or products with an associated material effect on financial market and institutions and the provision of financial services." The statement is useful and consistent with the way the industry is evolving. In this case, the magnitude of technology can become even deeper and more pervasive with more challenges and opportunities. It is contended that the development outlook of metaverse banking is highly dependent on the development potentials of its two core components, which are metaverse and online banking services. Moreover, and in parallel with the other industries, new financial concepts of service, business models, and new markets may arise, where the richness of it is driven by the evolutionary progression from Web2 to Web3 and further. According to Accenture (2022), some 47% of bankers believe that customers will use AR/VR as an alternative channel for transactions by 2030.

Technology has always been considered in its early stage a feature nice versus must have, then the more this feature becomes a habit into a customer everyday banking, the more the industry and its players need to look at it as a way eligible to make the industry evolving. This time the scenario is even.

As usual, the initial approach to innovation may be that of understanding the "tool" then its magnitude further tailoring it into each industry and specific company profile.

The Accenture Technology Vision survey for 2022 found that 67% of global banking executives agreed that the metaverse will have a positive impact on their organizations, while 38% said it will be a breakthrough or transformational. Around 92% agreed future digital platforms need offering unified experiences that enable interoperability of customers' data across different platforms and spaces.

According to Infosys (2022, p.5), banks in North America are focusing on how to use metaverse technologies to build an additional channel for customers to let them access existing banking functions (such as payments, balance check, and customized financial advice) rather than develop new business models. However, some others are considering investments in the decentralized financial instruments, such as blockchain, non-fungible tokens (NFTs), and cryptocurrencies.

In some countries, such as Indonesia, several state-owned banks have attempted entrance to the metaverse. The metaverse is expected to offer a notable change for financial inclusion in Indonesia, because it has removed the limitations of space and time (Anggara et al., 2022, p. 408)

At this stage of our analysis, it is useful to consider metaverse a feature to have versus a new banking channel like mobile banking, branch banking, and ATM channel of banking. In this case, metaverse works "*as for users to experience the banking services in the metaverse similar to real-life traditional banking services if they opted to do so. However, no matter how real the traditional banking services can be felt in the metaverse, any banking services executed through metaverse banking should be considered online banking services. This is because the information arising in the metaverse is measured in bits, digitally processed and stored online.*" This banking channel is "*actualized through the integration of metaverse and online banking services, enabled by a mix of numerous advanced technologies that provides customers with synchronous banking services accompanied with 3D experiences in a virtual world.*" (Zekree et al., 2021, pp. 178–181).

Here, banks will be able to thrive by delivering the level of personalized service and deep emotional engagement that characterized branch banking in the predigital era.

At present, there are some players investigating which metaverse use cases they can leverage without high levels of cost or risk before using immersive technologies to transform how they interact with both customers and employees.

5.1 How to Frame Metaverse into the Financial Services Industry

This topic can be addressed from two perspectives; from the one hand, metaverse is able to offer new options to banks, and on the other hand, this is causing banks some pitfalls into their risk management approaches and regulating concerns.

Our purpose is to focus only on the idea of metaverse as a framework for new business opportunities. Therefore, we can frame them by using the four quadrants highlighted in Fig. 1. They are:

1. New touch points/features for customers
2. New markets
3. New modes/features of operations and
4. New collaborators for developing business ecosystems

It is worth clarifying that even though we classify these opportunities in different quadrants, there is the need to consider that the different financial services are strictly linked to each other from the one hand. And from the other hand, behind any real versus virtual/remote interaction there is always some need of financial needs to fulfill and here it comes the opportunity for banks to re-intermediate themselves into their customers' everyday lives.

The clue is to read each quadrant as enabler for the others and look for a big picture of metaverse into a single company strategy.

When we think of metaverse as a touchpoint and/or a feature, this means exploring metaverse for future opportunities, from the one hand, by start interacting with customers differently, engaging them into a new delivery channel, and for the other hand, looking for the bank to makeover or strengthen its brand image. This is the case of JP Morgan, which in early 2022 entered the metaverse by developing an immersive lounge in Decentraland to explore the opportunities for both consumers and brands alike. There is also the case of HSBC, which has invested in The Sandbox to develop innovative customers' brand experiences. Another interesting example is that of Ally Bank, which developed a financial learning experience game to teach financial literacy in the metaverse.

Under this framework, there is also the case of enabling virtual interactions with customers and stakeholders, such as using their avatars to speak with bank relationship manager or investment advisor via video chat. Alternatively, it could involve developing a virtual house tour with a mortgage broker in real time. This example is going to look forward to developing partnerships with a focus on an ecosystemic approach.

The virtual banking branch has the potential to increase bank scalability by relying on a connectivity-based business model reaching a broader community by utilizing increasingly developed technology, as well as deepening relationships with customers through more accessible interactions. There are some banks already developing these initiatives such as JP Morgan, KB Kookmin Bank, and Shinhan Bank in the South Korea. The metaverse is also expected to become a game changer for financial inclusion in Indonesia, where it is considered useful to reach customers from all over Indonesia, so that banks are expected to be local in serving the community by providing banking education and other digital services that can be accessed anytime and anywhere (Anggara et al., 2022, pp. 419–420).

When thinking of new markets, there are different opportunities and implications in terms of developing banking services and products tailored to the context. This is the case of the evolution of payment systems, and here, it comes the need to understand which money is going to be adapted and adopted in the metaverse as more commercial initiatives (such as gaming, virtual concerts, etc.) are going to be conceived, produced, and delivered for metaverse markets.

At present, consumers can spend money in the metaverse in different digital worlds. Most of these are "closed" in the sense that money can go in but it cannot come out; and this is a weakness for the customer.

For example, in the summer of 2021 a digital Gucci handbag was sold in the online game Roblox for $4115—more than its real-world counterpart. Since Roblox is a closed digital world, the owner of that bag cannot take it anywhere else in the metaverse.

Other metaverses, such as Horizon World, let people converting digital assets into real-life currencies.

However, not all "open" parts of the metaverse are equal. "Permissioned" platforms like Horizon Worlds retain legal ownership of all goods on their platforms. Users can still sell "their" goods, but the sales fees are many times higher compare to those on "permissionless" platforms like Decentraland, where the users hold actual legal custody of their digital assets.

Regardless, a central authority in the open parts of the metaverse does not manage ownership of assets in these open worlds. Instead, it is recorded on a public blockchain. Most of the potential for payments in the metaverse centers on the blockchain, which underpins digital assets like cryptocurrency and non-fungible tokens (NFTs). Blockchain in the metaverse creates several possibilities for payments players. Customers could access digital ATMs in the metaverse that are linked to their real-world bank accounts. They would use their real banking PINs to pull real money out of their real accounts and put them in their digital wallets. However, they could put much more than just fiat currencies like euros or pounds in their metaverse wallets—including cryptocurrencies and other digital assets like NFTs.

As these digital assets become more widely understood and used, the demand and value for banks to ensure the safekeeping of these assets will increase materially. Banks could start thinking of developing an approach to digital asset custody.

Systems to send and receive payments that bridge this mix of currencies and assets, both within the metaverse and between the metaverse and the real world, are still theoretical at this point.

Therefore, we can summarize there are two ways of approaching the need of payments: from the one hand, there is the old money joining the metaverse. This is the case of aligning banks with new providers such as Square App, which has a blockchain-based payment system, and in this case, we have a Payment-as-a-Service platform provider, which acts as a bridge for using existing infrastructure. This example shows how partnership is mandatory in metaverse, so that a collaborative approach is needed even more compared to the real world. On the other hand, there is new money, which has the inner qualities to be immediately eligible of being used in metaverse (think of retail Central Bank Digital Currency—CBDC—, cryptocurrency, or any other). On this point, also, authorities such as the Central Banks can come to play a role in this new market environment, and this is especially useful the more traffic is developing on these platforms.

Based on the possible application of NFTs for banks in the area of credit cards, banks could create branded NFTs that are tied to a particular card or line of credit, making it easier for customers to manage their financial transactions. This could include things like setting spending limits on certain purchases, setting reminders for when payments are due, or tracking spending trends over time (Belk et al., 2022).

Immediately linked to payments, the ecosystems may require having also a lending system, and in this regard, the opportunity for metaverse to be a tool for financial inclusion can require developing another piece of the financial metaverse, which is an AI-based machine learning credit scoring. Because the need is to give answer in real time, then these tools can gather data from past transactions, social networks, and also integrating other platforms and/or database, where the consumer has had his/her transactions' experiences.

Moving from outside focus to an inside company's focus, then new modes of operations from metaverse may also change the way banks interact with their employees and this goes straight to the need for improving the employee experiences. This comes by developing virtual spaces with connections among employees belonging to different departments, business units, and/or located in different geographies. Moreover, thinking of new ways of training, developing, and onboarding as well as enhancing experiences in recruitment process. This is the case of Bank of America, which held immersive training, simulating customer service scenarios for branch employees so they can detect emotions and adjust behaviors accordingly.

However, metaverse can be also applied in many different ways (Dubei et al., 2022). Some first movers in the banking industry are already exploring the metaverse, with the wide range of applications they are experimenting with showing the versatility of the technology. KB Kookmin Bank—one of the biggest financial institutions in South Korea—offers a virtual bank where customers can access personalized financial information and interact one-on-one with its financial advisors in VR.

BNP Paribas, meanwhile, has launched a virtual reality app that enables retail banking users to access their account activity and transaction records in a VR environment.

Bank of America offers VR training in nearly 4300 financial centers nationwide. The training technology allows the bank's employees to practice a range of routine to complex tasks and simulate client interactions through a virtual environment.

JP Morgan has opened an Onyx lounge in the metaverse, a virtual lounge in the blockchain-based world of Decentraland. Similar to its real-world function, the bank can facilitate cross-border payments, foreign exchange, financial assets creation, trading, and safekeeping. Onyx is a blockchain-based platform for wholesale payments transactions.

HSBC is investing in a plot of land at The Sandbox metaverse, which it will develop to engage with sports, e-sports, and gaming fans. The bank says the partnership with The Sandbox will enable it to create innovative brand experiences for new and existing customers. Gucci, Warner Music Group (WMG), The Walking Dead, Snoop Dogg, and Adidas are among the other brands that are working with The Sandbox.

Furthermore, for banks, apart from becoming a useful medium to interact with their customers and retain them, it also opens up new avenues of revenue, such as cross-selling insurance policies, crypto investments, and investing in NFTs.

When banks look at metaverse for engaging and communicate with customers, this is a tool for collecting useful data from their feedback.

Metaverse also offers shared ledger solutions through its all-inclusive digital identity verification for customers by integrating a trusted identity mechanism. This saves time and money that is spent on a manual KYC process, while subsequently reducing the carbon footprint of each company. This also allows for more transparency in transactions between different parties and helps reduce fraud since all parties have a clear record of ownership and past transactions. Additionally, metaverse incorporates smart contract functionality so that once specific conditions are met on one side of an agreement (i.e., the bank or utility company), it automatically triggers processes on the other side of the transaction (i.e., the customer). The bank or utility company can then provide the customer with an instant notification of transfer, from the moment the customer agrees to a contract through to when the money is transferred, allowing for instant contract fulfillment (Subramanian & Subramanian, 2022).

Finally, also the mortgage business can be redefined by metaverse. A mortgage is a financial product that allows people to buy houses with borrowed money. Traditionally, the mortgage has been provided by banks and other financial institutions, who assess the risk of lending to individual borrowers to determine how much money they are willing to offer, at what rates of interest, and over what period. Metaverse may impact this traditional concept by using blockchain technology, which is going to redefine mortgages as we know them today (Melnyk et al., 2022). With metaverse, lenders can quickly assess a borrower's creditworthiness based on factors such as their income history, job stability, credit score, and total assets—without having to rely on traditional methods like paperwork or lengthy appointments with bank loan officers (Renduchintala et al., 2022). Furthermore, the use of smart contracts on metaverse will ensure that all terms and conditions of the loan are transparent and fair while helping to reduce fraud and minimize the risk of loan default. As a result, the mortgage on metaverse will be faster, easier, efficient—offering people greater access to homeownership at lower costs overall (Mystakidis, 2022).

All the above has highlighted the most positive side of the metaverse into the industry; however, it can also be outlined the other side of the coin. This comes overall from the need that both banks and customers are prioritizing security and privacy, and for banks, also governance and regulations, overall if we think of the use of personal data, either they are financial and healthcare data.

The metaverse integrates several systems and applications across different platforms, which increases the potential risk of cybercrime, especially in the financial and banking sectors. Just like social media or interactions in the real world, metaverses may well expose brands including banks to a range of reputational and legal risks, as well as money laundering, fraud, and the privacy risks attached to tracking and retaining the richer data banks may gather from customers in the metaverse.

Trust will be paramount to adoption of the new experiences banks and other brands are beginning to build. For these reasons, it is imperative that the metaverse is developed with responsibility at the core. From ownership of data to inclusion and diversity, to sustainability and risk management, and through to security and personal safety, this work must begin now.

5.2 *From Present to Future*

The banking sector stands at a pivotal juncture, facing a dynamic landscape that is both challenging and ripe with opportunity. Banks are navigating the complexities of economic pressures, regulatory reforms, and technological advancements, testing their resilience in the process. The industry's ability to integrate new technologies, such as blockchain and digital currencies, while maintaining financial stability, will be crucial.

As banks chart their course through these transformative times, their success will hinge on their capacity to balance risk with innovation, ensuring they remain robust and relevant in an ever-evolving financial world.

The evolution of metaverse in banking will depend on the different horizon we undertake so that we can highlight different bank's driven terms of opportunities schemes.

Some banks already recognize the potential of the metaverse to offer customers and clients a new way of experiencing and accessing their products and services; however, at this stage there is still the need to understand before acting. Consequently, there are many examples overall on the scene of the ways banks are developing business use cases and defining value-driven customer journeys within the metaverse, especially if we think of the many and different generations.

Based on the above, metaverse, like each major previous wave of innovation before it, is less a substitute for location and more a complement to it. In order to think strategically about the metaverse and location, it is important to understand the way the two act as complements to one another. It is useful to think of both as a channel—each good for transmitting different kinds of information while metaverse can be an improvement on what came before, the metaverse still will be insufficient to replace the fidelity of the physical world. Once point is crucial and fundamental to think about and this is that the metaverse offers rich new opportunities for gathering data to improve consumer engagement and experiences (Boutenko et al. 2022).

This can help banks understand their customers' needs and preferences in a better way, which can lead to improved services and more personalized offerings. In addition, the metaverse allows banks to integrate with other financial systems easily and applications, reducing costs while improving efficiency. Overall, these benefits make the metaverse a compelling choice for use in the banking industry, also from making account transactions to facilitating cross-border payments and digital identity verification.

As previously mentioned, one of metaverse's key value propositions is its ability to integrate with other VR platforms (such as Oculus Rift, HTC Vive, and PlayStation VR). This means that users can have a seamless experience where they can switch between different tools without having to take off their headsets or log into multiple channels.

Here it comes two critical dimensions for the development of metaverse in banking.

One dimension concerns the development of a continuum customer experience, which is going to be the next era of digital transformation, but enriching the human experience with new possibilities. The new customer experience can be defined both by the level of hybridization between physical reality and digital reality and by the level of immersiveness of the experience narrative. This requires answering some of the following critical questions:

- How can companies create new fair value (functional, social or hedonic) by combining atoms and bits?
- How can companies create new value by enriching in a transparent and fair manner the degree of sensorial involvement (cognitive or emotional) in new augmented spaces?

- What would be scalability of metaverse use, and types of metaverse infrastructure (open versus closed)?
- How security and privacy concerns will be managed and treated in metaverse?
- How much governance and standards can affect the role and the evolution of metaverse in the market (strict rules versus open mkt), and who is going to define them?
- How can interoperability concerns be treated, and how it can be scaled up in the future?
- What would be the future payments system in metaverse, and how it can benefit different stakeholders?

This is a critical point because these digital initiatives may improve customer transactional experience from one hand, but there is a conspicuous side effect of losing the human touch with customer on the other hand, which permeates the entire process. Due to the digitalization of services, many banks downsized their physical locations due to the online rendering of many services that reduced physical customer visits to the bank. Reduction in physical contact with bank employees and bank premises increased emotional detachment from the bank as a brand. This requires of having a balance approach, which comes from understanding more and more the customer base.

A further dimension refers to the continuum between centralization and decentralization of the solutions in question, or the degree of control (technical and strategic) in the hands of each player: with what methods and with how many degrees of freedom will a company be able to capture part of the value generated? The theme refers to revenue models, but also to the so-called Web3, that is, all those transformations of the network supported by blockchain technologies, with their distributed certification of ownership and rights.

Both of these dimensions highlight the other side of the metaverse in banking. Just like in the real world, user data will be an important currency in the metaverse, because data are the prices, and data ownership is a strategic advantage. Based on this, users need to be aware in the virtual world just as they are in the real one: companies have a great interest in obtaining even more information about consumers.

If the metaverse(s) is the new iteration of the internet, it will attract great scrutiny from global regulators and policymakers. All the challenges of the Web2 internet could be magnified in the metaverse, as well as all the different technologies available on it and related implications on data management.

Once more, consumers need to protect themselves, even from being tracked from the metaverse into reality, so that regulators and legislators have the duty to clarify also across country borders what happens to their digital identity when a customer click on something in a metaverse or buys something if this counts as implied consent to the assignment of all his/her data. A clear regulatory framework is mandatory.

6 Conclusions

Just like any innovation, the metaverse creates new opportunities for players in different industries. Understanding who the players are and how they can benefit from the metaverse is crucial to the metaverse development. The goal of this chapter was to develop a comprehensive framework of value creation in the metaverse and apply this framework to the financial services market. We looked at the value creation in the metaverse through the lens of Stakeholder theory and Service-Dominant (S-D) Logic. We suggested that the value in the metaverse can be co-created through the active participation, interaction, collaboration, and resource integration of different stakeholders, such as companies, customers, employees, and collaborators. Furthermore, we developed a 2 $\times$ 2 framework that can be used for understanding value-creation opportunities in the metaverse by categorizing them into physical vs. virtual world support and customer vs. company orientation opportunities. Finally, we emphasized how financial institutions could benefit the value creation in each quadrant of the proposed framework.

Financial institutions could easily and meaningfully be part of the metaverse in several ways. Since traditional financial institutions have access to sophisticated infrastructure, they can help enable metaverse use cases, including custody, benchmark, and administrative capabilities as well as offering financial-related services to corporations with a presence in the metaverse. According to Citi (2022), as the metaverse develops, a spectrum of financial services will be needed to support its activities. Metaverse finance (MetaFi) will likely be a combination of decentralized finance (DeFi), centralized finance (CeFi), and traditional finance (TradFi), with new products specifically designed to meet the unique needs of the new ecosystem. Additionally, since the metaverse will need a strong digital identity standard as it powers an open economic system where decentralized reputation is a sine-qua-non feature, banks, with their perfected know-your-customer (KYC) processes, could play a crucial role in setting those standards. As a result, from initial capital formation to supporting commerce within the metaverse, financial services can play an important role in the evolution.

In the meantime, the concerns regulators and consumers already hold today around privacy, bias, fairness, and the human impact of digital platforms will become more acute as the metaverse further blurs the line between people's physical and digital lives. Thus, banks should prepare for high levels of regulatory scrutiny of the metaverse and be ready to respond rapidly to new regulations.

We believe that our chapter adds value for industry participants and academic researchers. Due to the novelty of the topic, academic literature on the metaverse is very fragmented and underdeveloped. We believe that the framework proposed in this chapter, the example of its use in the financial services market, and the academic theories applied create a comprehensive explanation of value creation in the metaverse, which contributes to academic literature. Additionally, our chapter benefits industry players by providing a comprehensive framework that clarifies the value-creation opportunities that can be implemented in companies' metaverse strategies.

The success of developing and scaling the metaverse as a new business ecosystem is largely dependent on the understanding of how value is created and how different stakeholders could benefit from that. We hope our study serves as a valuable resource for industry participants and scholars, aiding in the successful development and expansion of the metaverse as a vibrant, collaborative, and sustainable business ecosystem.

References

Accenture. (2022, April). The ultimate guide to banking in the metaverse. Retrieved from https://bankingblog.accenture.com/ultimate-guide-to-banking-in-the-metaverse

Anggara, M. R. H., Davie, M. R., Margani, M., Arystiana, D. M. A., & Aulia, M. (2022). The presence of commercial banks in metaverse's financial ecosystem: Opportunities and risks. *Journal of Central Banking Law and Institutions, 1*(3), 405–430. https://doi.org/10.21098/jcli.v1i2.16. e-ISSN: 2809-9885, p-ISSN: 2827-7775.

Barrera, K. G., & Shah, D. (2023). Marketing in the metaverse: Conceptual understanding, framework, and research agenda. *Journal of Business Research, 155*, 113420.

Belk, R. (2013). Extended self in a digital world. *Journal of Consumer Research, 40*(3), 477–500.

Belk, R., Humayun, M., & Brouard, M. (2022). Money, possessions, and ownership in the metaverse: NFTs, cryptocurrencies, Web3 and Wild Markets. *Journal of Business Research, 153*, 198–205. https://doi.org/10.1016/j.jbusres.2022.08.031

Bobier, J. F., Merey, T., Robnett, S., Grebe, M., Feng, J., Rehberg, B., Woolsey, K., & Hazan, J. (2022). *The corporate Hitchhiker's guide to the metaverse. Boston Consulting Group.*

Boutenko, V., Florida, R., & Jacobson, J. (2022, August 6). The metaverse will enhance—not replace—companies' physical locations. *Harvard Business Review*. Retrieved from https://hbr.org/2022/08/the-metaverse-will-enhance-not-replace-companies-physical-locations

Buchholz, F., Oppermann, L., & Prinz, W. (2022). There's more than one metaverse. *i-com, 21*(3), 313–324.

Chohan, R., & Paschen, J. (2021). What marketers need to know about non-fungible tokens (NFTs). *Business Horizons*. https://doi.org/10.1016/j.bushor.2021.12.004

Citi. (2022, March). Metaverse and money. Decrypting the future, Report. www.citi.com

Damar, M. (2021). Metaverse shape of your life for future: A bibliometric snapshot. *Journal of Metaverse, 1*(1), 1–8.

Donaldson, T., & Preston, L. E. (1995). The stakeholder theory of the corporation: Concepts, evidence, and implications. *Academy of Management Review, 20*(1), 65–91.

Dubei, V., Mokashi, A., Pradhan, S. R., Gupta, P., & Walimbe, R. (2022). Metaverse and banking industry—2023 The year of metaverse adoption. *Applied Sciences and Technology, 4*(10), 62–73. ISSN: 2668-778X, Technium, www.techniumscience.com

Dwivedi, Y. K., Hughes, L., Baabdullah, A. M., Ribeiro-Navarrete, S., Giannakis, M., Al-Debei, M. M., & Wamba, S. F. (2022). Metaverse beyond the hype: Multidisciplinary perspectives on emerging challenges, opportunities, and agenda for research, practice and policy. *International Journal of Information Management, 66*, 102542.

Dwivedi, Y. K., Hughes, L., Wang, Y., Alalwan, A. A., Ahn, S. J., Balakrishnan, J., Barta, S., Belk, R., Buhalis, D., Dutot, V., Felix, R., Filieri, R., Flavián, C., Gustafsson, A., Hinsch, C., Hollensen, S., Jain, V., Kim, J., Krishen, A. S., ... Wirtz, J. (2023). Metaverse marketing: How the metaverse will shape the future of consumer research and practice. *Psychology & Marketing, 40*(4), 750–776.

Ferrigno, G., Di Paola, N., Oguntegbe, K. F., & Kraus, S. (2023). Value creation in the metaverse age: a thematic analysis of press releases. *International Journal of Entrepreneurial Behavior & Research, 29*(11), 337–363.
Freeman, R. E. (1984). *Strategic management: A stakeholder approach.* Pitman.
Gauttier, S., Simouri, W., & Milliat, A. (2024). When to enter the metaverse: Business leaders offer perspectives. *Journal of Business Strategy, 45*(1), 2–9.
Gilboa, E. (2022, September 12). From Tesla to NVIDIA, digital twins are a complexity solver. Lightlytics.com. Retrieved from https://www.lightlytics.com/post/from-tesla-to-nvidia-digital-twins-are-a-complexity-solver#:~:text=Tesla%20%2D%20a%20digital%20twin%20for%20every%20car%20made.&text=These%20allow%20the%20company's%20AI,stations%20for%20repairs%20and%20maintenance.
Handley, L. (2021, November 30). Looking for a job? You might get hired via the metaverse, experts say. CNBC.com. Retrieved from https://www.cnbc.com/2021/11/30/looking-for-a-job-you-might-get-hired-via-the-metaverse-experts-say.html.
Hofstetter, R., de Bellis, E., Brandes, L., Clegg, M., Lamberton, C., Reibstein, D., Rohlfsen, F., Schmitt, B., & Zhang, Z. J. (2022). Crypto-marketing: How non-fungible tokens (NFTs) challenge traditional marketing. *Marketing Letters.* https://doi.org/10.2139/ssrn.4055610
Infosys. (2022). Banking in the metaverse. From buzzword to business case: Why banks are optimistic but cautious about the metaverse, Report. www.infosys.com
Kaplan, A. M., & Haenlein, M. (2009). The fairyland of second life: Virtual social worlds and how to use them. *Business Horizons, 52*(6), 563–572.
Koohang, A., Nord, J., Ooi, K., Tan, G., Al-Emran, M., Aw, E., Baabdullah, A. M., Buhalis, D., Cham, T. -H., Dennis, C., Dutot, V., Dwivedi, Y. K., Hughes, L., Mogaji, E., Pandey, N., Phau, I., Raman, R., Sharma, A., Sigala, M., ... Wong, L. (2023). Shaping the metaverse into reality: A holistic multidisciplinary understanding of opportunities, challenges, and avenues for future investigation. *Journal of Computer Information Systems, 63*(3), 735–765.
Liu, M., Fang, S., Dong, H., & Xu, C. (2021). Review of digital twin about concepts, technologies, and industrial applications. *Journal of Manufacturing Systems, 58*, 346–361.
Mancuso, I., Petruzzelli, A. M., & Panniello, U. (2023). Digital business model innovation in metaverse: How to approach virtual economy opportunities. *Information Processing & Management, 60*(5), 103457.
Melnyk, M., Kuchkin, M., & Blyznyukov, A. (2022). Commercial banks: Traditional banking models vs. FinTechs solutions. *Financial Markets, Institutions and Risks, 6*(2), 122–129. https://doi.org/10.21272/fmir.6(2).122-129.2022
Morgan, J. P. (2022, January 18). https://www.jpmorgan.com/content/dam/jpm/trea sury-services/documents/opportunities-in-the-metaverse.pdf.
Mystakidis, S. (2022). Metaverse. *Encyclopedia, 2*, 486–497. https://doi.org/10.3390/encyclopedia2010031
Nariswari, A., & Vargo, S. L. (2023). Service-dominant logic. In *Elgar encyclopedia of services.* Edward Elgar.
Ning, H., Wang, H., Lin, Y., Wang, W., Dhelim, S., Farha, F., & Daneshmand, M. (2023). A survey on the metaverse: The state-of-the-art, technologies, applications, and challenges. *IEEE Internet of Things Journal, 10*(16), 14671–14688.
Papahristou, E., & Bilalis, N. (2017). Should the fashion industry confront the sustainability challenge with 3D prototyping technology. *International Journal of Sustainable Engineering, 10*(4-5), 207–214.
Park, S.-M., & Kim, Y.-G. (2022). A metaverse: taxonomy, components, applications, and open challenges. *IEEE Access, 10*, 4209–4251.
Polyviou, A., & Pappas, I. O. (2023). Chasing metaverses: Reflecting on existing literature to understand the business value of metaverses. *Information Systems Frontiers, 25*(6), 2417–2438.
Renduchintala, T., Alfauri, H., Yang, Z., Pietro, R. D., & Jain, R. (2022). A survey of Blockchain applications in the FinTech sector. *Journal of Open Innovation: Technology, Market, and Complexity, 8*(4), 185.

Ritterbusch, G. D., & Teichmann, M. R. (2023). Defining the metaverse: A systematic literature review. *IEEE Access, 11*, 12368–12377.

Schöbel, S. M., & Leimeister, J. M. (2023). Metaverse platform ecosystems. *Electronic Markets, 33*(1), 12.

Subramanian, H., & Subramanian, S. (2022). Improving diagnosis through digital pathology: Proof-of-concept implementation using smart contracts and decentralized file storage. *Journal of medical Internet Research, 24*(3), e34207.

Vargo, S. L., & Lusch, R. F. (2004). Evolving to a new dominant logic in marketing. *Journal of Marketing, 68*(Jan), 1–17.

Wang, Y., Su, Z., Zhang, N., Xing, R., Liu, D., Luan, T. H., & Shen, X. (2022). A survey on metaverse: Fundamentals, security, and privacy. *IEEE Communications Surveys & Tutorials, 25*(1), 319–352.

Zekree, M., Zainurin, L., Masri, M. H., Azrin Besar, M. A., & Anshari, M. (2021). Towards an understanding of metaverse banking: a conceptual paper. *Journal of Financial Reporting and Accounting*. https://doi.org/10.1108/JFRA-12-2021-0487. Emerald.

Anna Omarini's expertise is in bank strategy and management, FinTech, digital transformation, digital business models, Open Banking/Open Finance, and payments. She has been carrying out her expertise and experience in four major activities: research, teaching, advisory, and being an independent board member of banks and financial institutions.

She is a Researcher with Tenure at Bocconi University—where she is also the Director for the elective courses Bank and FinTech: Vision and Strategy, and FinTech for Banking and Financial Transformation—and an academic expert on her related research issues.

She is also the author of several books, articles, and chapters, and a speaker and a chairperson at several national and international conferences.

She is a reviewer for several national and international journals on her research topics, an editorial board member for several journals, and member of numerous associations, organizations, and scientific committees.

Since January 2024, she has been a member of the Central Bank Digital Currency (CBDC) Academic Advisory Group (AAG) of the Bank of England and the UK Treasury, and a member of the scientific committee of ItaliaFintech, a non-profit organization for the evolution of FinTech in the financial services industry. She has also experience as an independent board member in banks and FinTech companies.

Gulnaz Rakhmatullina holds a Bachelor's degree in Marketing/Consumer Science from the University of Wisconsin, Madison, and an MBA from Manchester Business School. She has 7 years of industry experience in market research and strategic marketing. Currently, she is pursuing a PhD at Bocconi University with a research focus on "Technologies & Innovations in Retail/the Metaverse."

Part III
Fintech Management, Consumer Behaviour, Regulation and Cybersecurity

The Digital Evolution of Italian Financial Services: Client Behavior and Market Shifts

Laura Grassi, Filippo Renga, Alessandro Faes, and Claudio Garitta

1 Introduction

In an era where digital transformation is reshaping industries across the globe, the financial sector is no exception. The shift from traditional to digital and hybrid models is not just a trend but a fundamental evolution driven by consumer demand and technological innovation. This chapter delves into how various types of clients, from individual "retail" consumers to small and medium-sized enterprises (SMEs), are responding to and contextually driving this digitalization. Understanding these dynamics is crucial for financial operators as they strategize for the future, balancing between digital and physical channels while considering the complexities of the services offered. We will explore these dynamics through the specific case of Italy.

The Italian Scenario

Italy's financial sector has a deep historical significance, often credited as the birthplace of modern banking. Notably, Banca Monte dei Paschi di Siena, established in 1472, remains the oldest bank still in operation today, a testament to Italy's long-standing influence in global finance (Treanor, 2016).

In recent years, Italy's financial sector has mirrored broader European trends, particularly in the rationalization of bank branches. The number of bank branches in Italy has seen a significant decline, from 30,740 in 2014 to 20,160 by the end of 2023 (Banca d'Italia, 2024). This contraction reflects a broader shift across the Eurozone, where the total number of bank offices has decreased dramatically since the 2008 financial crisis, dropping from approximately 186,000 to around 106,000 by 2023. Italy's figures, while above the Eurozone average in 2008 with 57.7 offices

L. Grassi (✉) · F. Renga · A. Faes · C. Garitta
Politecnico di Milano, Milan, Italy
e-mail: laura.grassi@polimi.it

A. Zarifis, X. Cheng (eds.), *Fintech and the Emerging Ecosystems*, Financial Innovation and Technology, https://doi.org/10.1007/978-3-031-83402-8_14

per 100,000 inhabitants, declined to 34.2 per 100,000 inhabitants by 2023, slightly above the European average (ECB, 2024).

This decline in physical branches is accompanied by a reduction in bank staff across the Eurozone, a pattern seen in Italy as well. Italian banks have seen their workforce shrink from 303,595 employees in 2014 to 262,250 in 2023 (Banca d'Italia, 2024). This reduction in both physical branches and personnel highlights the industry's ongoing adaptation to digitalization and changing consumer preferences.

2 Retail Consumers

2.1 Consumers' Use of Digital Financial Channels

Before COVID-19, digital financial channels in Italy were primarily embraced by individuals who were cost-conscious, logical, financially knowledgeable, and well-versed in digital technologies (Filotto et al., 2021). Today, however, the majority of customers expect that their product and service needs in any industry should be fulfilled on their own schedule, at their preferred locations, and at a fair price (Vincent Jaiwant, 2023). Financial services are no exception. As a result, digitalization has become a central aspect of the financial habits of Italian consumers. With banks encouraging customers—especially those requiring minimal direct support—to transition to digital services, a significant portion of the population has already adapted. For example, data collected from Italian banks show that online banking customers in 2023 have increased by 47% compared to 2019, with the amount of online transactions rising by 142% and online onboarding up by 203% over the same period. In 2023, as many as 66% of Italian banking customers (up 3 p.p. from 2022) have used at least one digital banking channel and 57% (up 2 p.p. from 2022) have used mobile banking specifically, underscoring the growing dominance of mobile access in the online banking experience.

Despite this, Italian consumers also show varying degrees of digital engagement with different financial services through digital channels. For instance, 75% of consumers have conducted a bank transfer digitally at least once, while 16% are aware of this service but do not use it, and only 9% are unaware of its existence. However, more complex services, such as remote loan applications, see lower engagement. Only 24% of Italians have applied for a loan remotely, despite 39% knowing of its availability, and just 23% have invested their savings through digital channels. These figures suggest a continued need for physical interaction, especially for more complex financial services. Even in the insurance sector, where digital penetration is increasing (Chang, 2023), only 44% of consumers have activated insurance policies via digital channels.

Going more in depth in the lending vertical, the adoption and preference of digital over traditional channels also vary depending on the type of lending service. For example, when it comes to activating a credit line, 56% of Italian consumers want the possibility to visit a branch, while 29% ask for digital channels. Furthermore, 20% can accept to manage their cases remotely, but using more traditional means such as telephone or email. This trend is even more pronounced with more complex services like mortgages, where 70% of consumers require an in-person visit to branches. Age also plays a significant role in these preferences. Younger consumers (18–24 years old), as predictable (Hosen et al., 2023), are more inclined toward digital channels, with 60% favoring digital credit line applications, compared to 28% who prefer a physical branch. However, as the complexity of the service increases, even younger consumers show a preference for in-person interactions. For example, 44% of younger consumers prefer in-branch service for mortgage applications, closely matching the 49% who favor digital channels.

Also in the insurance sector, while there is a growing tendency to use digital channels, the degree of complexity of the policy often dictates the preferred method of engagement. For simpler policies, such as travel insurance, 59% of consumers prefer autonomous activation via an app or website, while 29% still opt for agency or branch services. Conversely, for more sensitive and thus complex policies like life insurance, 60% of consumers prefer to interact physically at a branch, with only 25% choosing digital options.

2.2 *Embedded Finance and Embedded Insurance*

The evolution of distribution models and service delivery channels in the financial sector extends beyond the traditional physical-digital dualism to include innovative concepts such as embedded finance and insurance. Embedded finance or insurance refers to the integration of financial products directly into the customer journey of another, typically non-financial, operator. For example, the option to purchase insurance while booking a trip is something 58% of Italian consumers would consider. More broadly, 78% of consumers would evaluate an embedded insurance proposal, whether it is linked to purchasing a car from a dealership (34%), offered by a telecom operator (18%), or by a utility provider at the activation of a service (12%). Consumer openness to embedded finance is also notable, particularly in the context of credit services. Approximately 72% of consumers are willing to consider requesting financing through non-financial players. This willingness varies by the type of operator and the specific loan offered. For instance, 53% would be open to financing from a car dealer when purchasing a vehicle, while 20% might consider doing so through an e-commerce platform. However, only 7% would contemplate using social networks, and a mere 3% would consider an online game for such services. When it comes to investment services, the willingness to engage with embedded finance drops significantly. Only 22% of consumers would consider investments proposed by non-financial entities, indicating a strong trust in the traditional banking sector for these sensitive financial services. Applications for managing cards and payments see the highest engagement, with a 10% willingness to consider them, but interest in other non-financial players remains low.

2.3 Sharing of Consumer Data

Data sharing and management are fundamental to the new financial models, including embedded finance and the offering of various value-added services (Grassi, 2024). In the context of Open Banking and Open Finance (see Box 1), consumers are expected to be free to request that their banks share their data to obtain value-added services from other operators. However, in Italy, data sharing remains a significant hurdle. The majority of consumers are not willing to allow their bank to share their current account data, whether with other banks (74%), account aggregators (79%), or non-financial operators (87%). For those few consumers who are open to data sharing, economic incentives tend to be the primary motivator, rather than the desire for more personalized products.

To establish a true Open Finance system that offers value-added services (Grassi et al., 2022), banks might also find it beneficial to enrich their existing customer data with additional sensitive information, always with the consumer's consent and in compliance with privacy regulations. A closer relationship between the consumer and the bank can increase willingness to share data. Currently, 29% of consumers believe they already share sensitive information, such as health, travel, or family data, with their bank, and another 15% are open to doing so, typically in exchange for more advantageous services. Nevertheless, the majority of Italian consumers (56%) remain opposed to sharing such data. In the insurance sector, consumer data play an even more crucial role, directly influencing premium calculations by insurance companies. Sharing personal and sensitive data can enhance the personalization and efficiency of services. In this context, 91% of consumers are willing to share at least one piece of sensitive information with their insurance company, particularly in areas where customers are already accustomed to such exchanges, like driving style data for bonus-malus policies. Although offering a reward may encourage customers to share data, the type of data being shared still plays a significant role in their willingness to do so (Grassi, 2024). Indeed, other types of sensitive data, such as home security information, see less willingness to share, although 59% of consumers are generally open to sharing data if it results in more convenient services. Conversely, data considered particularly sensitive, such as family-related information (and it applies also to social network data), are met with strong resistance, with 87% of consumers refusing to share it.

Box 1. Open Banking and Open Finance

Open Banking involves enabling the sharing of financial data among players in the banking ecosystem. This phenomenon was originally made possible by the PSD2 (Payment Services Directive 2), the second European directive on payment services, which has recently evolved into the PSD3. Open Banking operates on the principle that banking and payment information should be

(continued)

accessible to customers freely, without the constraints that previously existed. Since the implementation of PSD2 in 2019, banks have been required to share certain information about their customers' accounts and payments through APIs (Application Programming Interfaces), provided that customer consent is obtained. The Fintech services enabled by Open Banking and the opening of APIs are fundamentally three types:

- Account Information: Access to current accounts through applications other than those provided by banks.
- Payment Initiation: The ability to initiate payment orders from one's current account through other applications.
- Fund Confirmation: The ability to verify the availability of funds to cover the amount required for a transaction.

Open Finance, similarly, is based on the principle that data provided by and created on behalf of financial services customers are owned and controlled by the customers themselves. However, unlike Open Banking, Open Finance extends beyond banking data to encompass all financial activities. This includes data related to credit services, investments, insurance, and even sensitive personal information such as family details, health data, or information from other sources (e.g., social networks, real-time location data).

In Europe, the European Commission has prioritized Data Strategy and Open Finance, laying the groundwork for new services that will lead to improved financial products, better-targeted advice, broader consumer access, and increased efficiency in business-to-business transactions. On June 28, 2023, the Commission presented a legislative proposal for a financial data access framework, known as FIDA (Financial Data Access). This framework aims to establish clear and simple rights and obligations for managing customer data sharing in the financial sector beyond payment accounts. Key elements to be established include:

- The option, but not the obligation, for customers to share their financial data with third parties.
- The requirement for data holders to make customer data available to third parties upon customer request.
- Full control for customers over who accesses their data and for what purpose.
- Standardization of customer data and technical interfaces.

2.4 The Knowledge and Use of Digital Services in Finance and Insurance

In Italy, the most well-known and widely used digital services among consumers in the finance and insurance sectors primarily relate to payments. Payments made in stores via smartphone or smartwatch and money transfers through non-banking apps are familiar to the majority of consumers (87% and 80% respectively), with high usage rates (63% and 55%). However, newer services that combine payment and credit, such as Buy Now Pay Later, though well-known (64%), show relatively lower usage at 37%. As we move toward more advanced services like account aggregators and instant insurance, both awareness and usage are lower, although these figures have grown significantly in recent years. Specifically, awareness of account aggregators stands at 49% with 25% usage, while instant insurance awareness is at 35% with 14% using the service. More complex services, such as those related to cryptocurrencies and decentralized finance, have very limited rates of use and awareness among the general population. This suggests that while basic digital services are becoming mainstream, there is still a significant gap in the adoption of more advanced or novel digital financial products. When observing the use of different digital services, Italian consumers can be categorized into three main groups. The first group consists of those who are not very open to digital services; they have not used any of the listed services and have very limited digital experience in the financial sector (28%). The second group includes consumers who use digital channels, but only for basic functions like payments and transfers (33%), showing some openness to digitalization but with limited engagement in innovative services. Finally, the third group comprises consumers who actively use Fintech and Insurtech services (39%), such as account aggregation and instant insurance, demonstrating a higher level of financial and digital sophistication.

Among the most significant digital innovations for analyzing consumer openness is the concept of behavioral policies in insurance. In these offerings, the insurance premium is calculated based on the customer's behavior, which is monitored through devices connected to the insurer. These services require considerable data sharing and management and aim to encourage lower-risk behaviors. Notably, there is a very high propensity among consumers toward car insurance policies that adopt this model (86%). However, for home insurance policies where devices measure behaviors like frequently leaving doors open, and for health policies that might monitor physical activity or parameters such as blood pressure, consumer interest remains relevant but drops to 48% and 42%, respectively.

3 SMEs and Micro-enterprises

3.1 The Use of Digital Financial Channels by SMEs and Micro-enterprises

The use of digital financial channels is also prevalent among small and medium-sized enterprises (SMEs) in Italy, although the extent varies depending on the complexity of the service. For simple tasks, such as communicating with the bank, a vast majority of SMEs (77%) prefer to use online channels. However, when it comes to more complex services like invoice advances and loan applications, the use of digital channels decreases significantly, with only 44% and 36% of SMEs, respectively, utilizing these methods. Despite having access to digital channels, more than a third of SMEs (38%) still prefer to visit a branch to request a loan, and 17% rely exclusively on physical branches, expressing satisfaction with this arrangement. There is a small but notable unmet demand for digital services, with approximately 5% of SMEs wishing to request a loan digitally but being unable to do so at present. The situation differs somewhat when it comes to micro-enterprises, which are typically less structured and often consist of individual entrepreneurs. For basic activities like bank communication, only 63% of micro-enterprises use online channels, with an additional 5% expressing a desire to do so but lacking the capability. The rest prefer in-person visits to branches. This lower propensity to use digital channels compared to SMEs is also evident in other services such as loan applications, where less than a third (27%) apply online. On the other hand, 56% prefer to handle these tasks in person, either because they only have access to physical branches (20%) or because they opt for direct interaction despite having digital options available (36%). The unmet demand for digital services remains low in this segment, with only 8% wishing to request loans online but unable to do so.

In the insurance sector, SMEs show a slightly greater preference for direct interaction with branches or agencies compared to the banking sector. For general communication with insurers, 66% of SMEs use online channels, with another 7% expressing a wish to do so. Digital channels are preferred for lower-value activities such as policy renewal (61%), verification (59%), and modification (50%). However, when it comes to more complex tasks requiring consultation, such as policy activation, the preference for in-person branch visits prevails. Additionally, claims management represents an area of significant unmet digital demand, with 16% of SMEs wanting to manage claims online but currently lacking the option. For micro-enterprises, the inclination toward digital channels in the insurance sector is even more limited. Only 53% of micro-enterprises use online channels for communication with their insurer, with another 6% wishing they could do so. The rest prefer physical visits to branches or agencies. This pattern is consistent across other services, such as policy activation, where only 23% use online methods, while 43% prefer in-person agency visits, despite having digital options available. An additional 20% are satisfied with only having a physical option.

3.2 Financial Consultancy for SMEs and Micro-enterprises

Financial consultancy plays a critical role in supporting small and medium-sized enterprises (SMEs) and micro-enterprises in Italy, with these businesses often relying on personalized advice to meet their complex needs. A majority of SMEs (89%) utilize services aimed at analyzing their insurance needs, with 55% doing so through the same intermediary from whom they purchased the policy, and 35% through a different consultant. In comparison, micro-enterprises, which typically have less complex organizational structures and simpler needs, show a lower but still significant reliance on personalized support, with 73% utilizing such services. In the banking sector, the personal relationship between SMEs and their banks is also fundamental. A significant 81% of SMEs identify a trusted individual within their bank who they can rely on to solve specific problems or address needs. Only 4% of SMEs do not have such a figure and do not feel the need for one, while another 3% have never found one. The remaining 12% use a different bank from their main one to find this reference figure. The situation is similar for micro-enterprises, further underscoring the crucial role that banks play as a point of reference for small businesses. The need for an expert within the bank who understands the sector or supply chain in which the business operates is slightly less critical but still important. Just over half of SMEs (53%) find such an expert in their primary bank, while a considerable 32% find this expertise in another bank they interact with. This highlights the priority that business activities often place on specialized knowledge over digitalization. For micro-enterprises, the importance of this expert figure is somewhat reduced, with 23% of micro-enterprises not expressing interest in such a role, compared to 7% of SMEs. This difference further illustrates the simpler and less specific financial needs of micro-enterprises.

3.3 Ecosystem Services in Marketplace Mode

Ecosystem services in marketplace mode are becoming increasingly significant for SMEs as financial institutions explore new ways to offer integrated solutions to businesses. In Italy, small and medium-sized enterprises (SMEs) have shown interest in such services, particularly those that provide comprehensive support across various aspects of business operations. Among the most desired ecosystem services by SMEs are consultancy on financial needs (30%) and business risk management (20%), both of which are crucial in the insurance sector. Other services that SMEs find valuable include payment cards for business expenses (17%) and accounting support services (14%). Despite this, 22% of SMEs report no interest in any ecosystem services in marketplace mode. In contrast, micro-enterprises demonstrate significantly less demand for these services, with 50% indicating no interest in any of the ecosystem offerings. The services that do attract some attention among micro-enterprises, though at lower levels than SMEs, include consultancy on financial needs (19%), accounting support (14%), and electronic invoicing (12%). This difference in demand highlights the varied needs and resources between SMEs and micro-enterprises, with the latter group often requiring more basic support services and showing less interest in comprehensive ecosystem solutions.

3.4 The Financial and Non-financial Operators that SMEs Turn to

Small and medium-sized enterprises (SMEs) in Italy typically rely on traditional financial operators when seeking loans and insurance policies, reflecting a cautious approach to financial innovation. Nearly all SMEs (95%) turn to conventional banks for loans, with a significant portion (52%) also relying on a known consultant. However, there is a growing segment of SMEs (32%) that have already experimented with innovative banks, and only 6% of these would avoid repeating the experience in the future. This trend suggests a gradual but notable shift toward considering less traditional operators. For instance, while 40% of SMEs are willing to approach an innovative bank, 18% would consider seeking a loan from non-specialized operators such as e-commerce platforms. The scenario is similar in the insurance sector, where the vast majority of SMEs (93%) still prefer traditional insurance companies. A very high percentage (82%) also considers independent consultants or agencies, highlighting the strength of these channels. Although only 27% have experimented with innovative insurance providers, there is significant openness to considering them in the future, with 40% indicating they might explore this option, and only 4% dismissing the idea entirely.

3.5 Sharing Data of SMEs and Micro-enterprises

Data sharing has become an increasingly important aspect of the relationship between SMEs and financial operators, particularly within the frameworks of Open Banking and Open Finance (see Box 1). A significant number of SMEs in Italy (56%) believe they already share their company data in real-time with their bank, while an additional 18% would be open to doing so without hesitation. However, data sharing with insurance companies is less common, with only 34% of SMEs currently engaging in this practice. Still, there is a notable willingness to expand this, with 32% of SMEs considering it. On the other hand, the willingness to share data with innovative operators is almost nonexistent, with 86% of SMEs expressing reluctance to do so. For micro-enterprises, the situation is somewhat different. A smaller percentage (40%) believes they already share their data with their bank, and 17% are open to the idea, but a significant 42% are resistant to sharing their data. In the insurance sector, data sharing is even less prevalent among micro-enterprises, with nearly half (48%) unwilling to share their data with insurance companies, and an overwhelming majority (89%) are not willing to share their data with other operators. This highlights a clear divide between the levels of data sharing among SMEs and micro-enterprises, with the latter group being much more cautious and selective in their willingness to engage with new financial technologies.

4 Startups and Innovative Players

4.1 A Broad Overview of the Italian Landscape

As customers are requesting more and more digital, secure and enjoyable financial services, startups and scaleups emerged as key players to offer these services themselves or to partner with incumbents (Lee & Shin, 2018). By 2023, the Italian Fintech & Insurtech landscape included 622 startups and scaleups, either founded by Italian entrepreneurs or based in Italy. Unlike previous years, which saw consistent growth in the number of startups, 2023 experienced a plateau. On one hand, this can be interpreted as a sign of market maturity: more startups are recognizing opportunities for growth and synergies within larger financial or industrial groups. On the other hand, it suggests a natural market consolidation, where ideas that failed to gain traction are exiting the stage, potentially indicating a need for greater cohesion within the Italian ecosystem.

The business models of Italian Fintech and Insurtech startups are distinguished by their diversity and adaptability. These companies are not merely digitizing traditional financial services; they are reimagining how these services can be delivered more efficiently, personally, and in line with the digital lifestyles of today's consumers. Notably, approximately 19% of these startups are already utilizing Generative AI—a technology with the potential to revolutionize financial services by enabling highly personalized and predictive offerings. This technology allows startups to create customized financial solutions that can adapt in real-time to the evolving needs and behaviors of consumers. For example, AI-driven financial planning tools can provide personalized advice that evolves as a consumer's financial situation changes, offering a level of customization that traditional models struggle to achieve.

However, the journey for these startups is not without challenges. Access to funding remains a critical issue, especially in light of the global decline in startup investments. In 2023, Italian Fintech and Insurtech startups collectively raised 174 million euros—a significant 81% decrease from the previous year. This funding shortfall underscores the difficulties these startups face in securing the capital needed to scale their operations and bring their innovations to market. Yet, this challenge also presents an opportunity for startups to focus on sustainable growth. By adopting more conservative financial strategies and forming strategic partnerships, startups can mitigate the risks associated with rapid expansion. Partnerships with traditional financial institutions, for example, can provide access to larger customer bases, established distribution networks, and crucial industry expertise, all of which are vital for navigating the complex regulatory landscape—a significant barrier for many startups.

Regulatory compliance, while essential, can be particularly burdensome for smaller companies with limited resources. Startups must develop a comprehensive understanding of the regulatory environment and possess the agility to adapt quickly to changes. Regulatory sandboxes, which allow startups to test their innovations in a controlled setting, offer a flexible framework that can help alleviate some of these challenges, enabling innovation within a safer, more manageable context.

As competition within the financial services market intensifies, startups face the additional pressure of distinguishing themselves in a crowded field. They must compete not only with established financial institutions but also with other innovative companies, both domestically and internationally. This competitive environment drives innovation but also raises the stakes, making it imperative for startups to differentiate themselves through unique value propositions and superior customer experiences. Achieving profitability in such a landscape remains a crucial milestone. While these startups are often seen as disruptors, bringing fresh ideas and innovative solutions to market, reaching sustainable profitability can be challenging (Garitta and Grassi, 2025). In 2023, approximately 35% of Italian Fintech and Insurtech startups reported reaching break-even, reflecting the sector's growing maturity. This is a significant achievement, particularly in a landscape where many struggle to transition from innovative concepts to profitable business models. However, due to the relatively small size of many Italian Fintech ventures, profitability is often dependent on securing partnerships with a few key customers.

International expansion presents both opportunities and challenges for these startups. As they seek to grow beyond their domestic market, they must navigate different regulatory environments and adapt their products to meet the diverse needs of international customers. Despite these hurdles, expanding internationally is increasingly seen as essential for long-term growth. Currently, only 41% of Italian Fintech startups operate outside of Italy, reflecting both the challenges of entering new markets and the cautious approach many take when considering international opportunities. Yet, for those that do expand, the rewards can be substantial—access to larger customer bases, diversified revenue streams, and the ability to tap into emerging markets. Moreover, as the regulation is harmonized within the European Union borders, it is even easier to enter other markets.

Strategic collaborations play a crucial role in the growth and success of these startups. The importance of partnerships is underscored by the fact that 82% of Italian startups have at least one strategic partner, with 27% of these partners also investing in the startups' capital. This deepening integration between startups and traditional financial institutions suggests that the future of financial services will likely involve a hybrid model where traditional and digital services are closely intertwined. Partnerships are not only a means to expand customer bases and enter new markets, but they also provide startups with the expertise and resources needed to navigate complex regulatory environments and scale their operations more effectively.

4.2 A Focus on Insurtech Ventures

The Insurtech segment is showing as well significant potential for growth. In 2023, the 109 Insurtech startups surveyed raised a total of 25 million euros, with a projected revenue growth of 128% over the previous year. This impressive growth underscores the dynamic nature of the insurance technology market and the increasing demand for digital insurance solutions.

Despite this growth, the path to profitability remains challenging for many Insurtech startups. Only 24% of these companies have reached break-even, highlighting the long road to economic sustainability in this sector. However, the potential for growth is considerable, particularly as consumers become more comfortable with digital insurance products. The ability to offer personalized, data-driven insurance solutions that can be tailored to individual needs is a key differentiator for Insurtech startups.

One of the distinguishing features of the Insurtech segment is its greater propensity for international expansion. Nearly 44% of Insurtech startups are already offering their services outside of Italy, and many others have plans to expand internationally in the near future. This focus on global markets is driven by the need to tap into larger customer bases and to leverage the benefits of regulatory harmonization within the European Union. Expanding into international markets presents both opportunities and challenges, requiring a deep understanding of local regulations, customer preferences, and competitive dynamics.

4.3 Our Outlook

As the digital financial ecosystem continues to evolve, the role of startups and scale-ups will become increasingly central. These entities are not just innovators; they are change-makers, pushing the boundaries of what is possible in financial services and setting new standards for customer experience, efficiency, and personalization.

Looking ahead, the success of these startups will depend on their ability to navigate the challenges of funding, regulation, and competition while capitalizing on the opportunities presented by technological advancements and changing consumer behaviors. The potential for growth in the Fintech and Insurtech sectors is immense, but realizing this potential will require a combination of innovation, strategic partnerships, and a deep understanding of the global financial landscape.

For traditional financial institutions, engaging with startups offers a pathway to innovation and competitiveness in an increasingly digital world. By collaborating with startups, these institutions can enhance their digital offerings, improve customer engagement, and position themselves as leaders in the evolving financial ecosystem.

About the Research Center

Established in 2015 at Politecnico di Milano, the Fintech & Insurtech Observatory is the baseline for studying and advancing digital innovation within the Italian and broader European financial and insurance ecosystems. The Observatory plays a crucial role in collecting and analyzing data on various aspects of innovation, offering valuable insights that inform academic research, guide market practitioners, and assist regulatory supervisors. Each year, the Observatory conducts a comprehensive analysis of all Italian Fintech and Insurtech startups, leveraging a proprietary database to shed light on trends in funding, the evolution of business models, and the adoption of new technologies. Through its extensive research and unique relationships with key industry players—including banks, insurance companies, and technology providers—the Observatory possesses a thorough understanding of the major trends affecting financial incumbents. Additionally, it closely examines client preferences and behaviors in response to the opportunities presented by financial innovation, as well as the shifts occurring within traditional financial institutions. Unless otherwise noted, the data presented in this chapter are drawn from surveys conducted on a representative sample of Italian consumers and small and medium-sized enterprises.

References

Banca d'Italia. (2024). *Banche e Istituzioni Finanziarie: Articolazione territoriale*. https://www.bancaditalia.it/pubblicazioni/banche-istfin/2024-banche-istfin/statistiche_STAATER_20240329.pdf

Chang, V. Y. L. (2023). Do InsurTech startups disrupt the insurance industry? *Finance Research Letters, 57*, 104220. https://doi.org/10.1016/j.frl.2023.104220

European Central Bank (ECB). (2024). *The changing landscape of bank offices in the euro area*. https://data.ecb.europa.eu/blog/blog-posts/changing-landscape-bank-offices-euro-area

Filotto, U., Caratelli, M., & Fornezza, F. (2021). Shaping the digital transformation of the retail banking industry. Empirical evidence from Italy. *European Management Journal, 39*(3), 366–375. https://doi.org/10.1016/j.emj.2020.08.004

Garitta, C., & Grassi, L. (2025). Predicting break-even in FinTech startups as a signal for success. *Finance Research Letters, 74*, 106735

Grassi, L. (2024). In a world of Open Finance, are customers willing to share data? An analysis of the data-driven insurance business. *Eurasian Business Review*. https://doi.org/10.1007/s40821-024-00263-w

Grassi, L., Figini, N., & Fedeli, L. (2022). How does a data strategy enable customer value? The case of FinTechs and traditional banks under the open finance framework. *Financial Innovation, 8*(1), 75. https://doi.org/10.1186/s40854-022-00378-x

Hosen, M., Lim, A.-F., Jannat, T., Khan, N. R., & Pek, C.-K. (2023). Millennials fintech services adoption: What matters most? In M. A. Al-Sharafi, M. Al-Emran, G. W.-H. Tan, & K.-B. Ooi (Eds.), *Current and future trends on intelligent technology adoption* (Vol. 1128, pp. 229–243). Springer. https://doi.org/10.1007/978-3-031-48397-4_12

Lee, I., & Shin, Y. J. (2018). Fintech: Ecosystem, business models, investment decisions, and challenges. *Business Horizons, 61*(1), 35–46. https://doi.org/10.1016/j.bushor.2017.09.003

Treanor, J. (2016). https://www.theguardian.com/business/2016/dec/22/monte-dei-paschi-the-history-of-the-worlds-oldest-bank

Vincent Jaiwant, S. (2023). Changing structure of consumer buying behaviour and expectation in the digital era. In G. Singh, R. Goel, & V. Garg (Eds.), *Industry 4.0 and the digital transformation of international business* (pp. 207–215). Springer. https://doi.org/10.1007/978-981-19-7880-7_12

Laura Grassi is the Director of the Fintech & Insurtech Observatory and a Associate Professor at the Politecnico di Milano, specializing in Banking and Fintech. She also serves as the Director of the Executive MBA Evening Program at the Graduate School of Management and acts as the Scientific Director of multiple digital finance master's programs, collaborating with several financial institutions. Recently, she joined the European Banking Authority's (EBA) Banking Stakeholder Group (BSG).

Laura's research and professional interests lie at the intersection of digital innovation and financial services, focusing on areas such as Fintech, Banking, and Corporate Governance. She plays an active role in fostering the growth of Fintech and Insurtech startups and leads several applied research initiatives, including Horizon Europe projects. Throughout her career, Laura has been dedicated to advancing digital transformation in finance, both through her academic leadership and impactful research.

Holding a PhD, MSc, and BSc in Management Engineering, all with honors from the Politecnico di Milano, Laura has published extensively on cutting-edge topics like open finance, decentralized finance (DeFi), and the role of technology in transforming the financial sector.

Filippo Renga is the Co-Founder of the Digital Innovation Observatories of the School of Management of Politecnico di Milano, where he started and coordinated the Observatories on Smart AgriFood, Fintech & Insurtech, Travel Innovation, and Mobile (Mobile & App Economy, Marketing & Service, Payment & Commerce, Banking, Enterprise).

He is also a coordinator of the Paths of Excellence at the Cremona Campus of the same University and co-author of various academic articles on Mobile services. He is the Co-Founder of 5 startups with a turnover of more than 35 million € to date.

Alessandro Faes is a Researcher within the Fintech & Insurtech Observatory of the School of Management of Politecnico di Milano, where he has focused for over five years on Open Finance, broadened competition in financial services, customer behavior in banking and insurance, RegTech and Financial Identity, and sustainability. A graduate in Economics and Social Sciences at Bocconi University, he is currently a PhD Candidate in Management Engineering at Politecnico di Milano.

Claudio Garitta is a PhD candidate in Management Engineering at the Politecnico di Milano. He holds a degree in Management Engineering from the same institution, with a specialization in Finance. Since 2021, he has been part of the Fintech & Insurtech Observatory at the Politecnico di Milano, where his research mainly focuses on the innovation driven by startups, particularly in evaluating their growth strategies and market impact.

Building Trust in AI: Leadership Insights from Malaysian Fintech Boards

Alex Zarifis and Larisa Yarovaya

1 Introduction

The adoption of new technology is a key priority for businesses that aspire to remain competitive in the long term. There are numerous examples from the past where companies failed to embrace new technologies, leading to their products becoming obsolete and their market share shrinking. Perhaps, the most well-known one, Kodak's reluctance to adopt digital photography technology caused the company to lose its dominance in the camera market. Similarly, Nokia's slow response to the rise of smartphones led to its decline in the mobile phone industry.

In the past decade, two major trends have taken many industries by storm: the adoption of blockchain technology and the rise of artificial intelligence (AI). Blockchain is revolutionizing sectors such as finance, supply chain management, and healthcare by providing greater transparency, security, and decentralization. Meanwhile, AI is transforming industries by enhancing efficiency, automating processes, and driving innovation. Recent research by Naeem et al. (2025) indicates that the growth of AI generates a strong contagion effect on other innovative sectors, such as cryptocurrency, blockchain, robotics, and the metaverse. This can be interpreted from both return and risk perspectives. The former suggests that investment in AI can positively affect the growth of other innovative sectors, while the latter indicates that during periods of increased uncertainty and crisis, these sectors may be vulnerable to risks transmitted from the AI sector. Therefore, the

---

A. Zarifis (✉)
University of Southampton, Southampton, UK

Cambridge Centre for Alternative Finance, Cambridge, UK
e-mail: a.zarifis@soton.ac.uk

L. Yarovaya
Centre for Digital Finance, University of Southampton, Southampton, UK

A. Zarifis, X. Cheng (eds.), *Fintech and the Emerging Ecosystems*, Financial Innovation and Technology, https://doi.org/10.1007/978-3-031-83402-8_15

interplay between AI adoption and the Fintech sector is particularly important for corporate managers of Fintech firms to consider, when weighing the potential for growth against the associated risks of exposure to the AI sector.

Several factors influence the pace at which firms adopt new technologies and the success of these endeavours. One factor that has received relatively less attention in research is trust—whether it is trust in the technology itself, trust in the firms implementing it, or trust among stakeholders involved in its use. Trust is a multidimensional characteristic, making it difficult to study and isolate its specific role from other, more quantifiable macro- and microeconomic factors. Additionally, trust has a strong cultural dimension, which further complicates its analysis. This research identifies practical ways leaders can build trust in AI with shareholders, staff, and customers.

Trust in technology evolves over time, and various scandals, fraud cases, and scams can significantly slow down the pace of its adoption. Negative events can create scepticism, causing individuals and businesses to hesitate in embracing new technologies.

In September 2024, an unusual case of alleged financial fraud with Artificial Intelligence (AI), including alleged wire fraud and money laundering, has emerged: A man was accused of using AI to create dozens of fake bands, fake songs, and fake listeners, attracting around 7.6 million pounds (GBP) (Kumar, 2024). This case illustrates the almost limitless scale AI can offer, the almost unlimited speed AI can offer, and how AI, at least for a period of time, can convince humans and safety checks made by information systems that it is human. Probably more importantly however, it illustrates how quickly using AI and automation can land you in court.

While the finance literature on trust is relatively extensive, research on the role of trust in the Fintech field remains limited. A study by Jalan et al. (2023) showed that societal trust and cultural values influence cryptocurrency adoption, and the negative impact of mistrust has also been documented. A similar parallel can be drawn with the adoption of AI; however, the existing literature is still limited and niche. For example, Klingbeil et al. (2024) examine the relationship between trust and overreliance on AI, while Choung et al. (2024) explore the role of trust in public acceptance of AI-powered surveillance technology. Given the breadth of AI applications and its transformative power across industries, understanding the mechanisms for establishing trust in AI is crucial.

There are many challenges a board of a financial services company in Asia faces such as the typical concerns of the economy, staff and allocating resources. Additionally, technology-related issues such as cybersecurity, privacy and AI are high on the agenda (EY, 2024). Globally, most boards struggle to fully understand how they should utilize AI and apply governance to it (van Giffen & Ludwig, 2023). Moving too fast without clarity may increase both traditional risks, and new ones Generative AI introduces, while moving too slowly may render the organization obsolete (Khanna et al., 2024). Leadership is needed during this transition particularly from those that can deeply influence strategic decisions. It is important to get the strategic decisions right, and also to lead the financial organization through a digital transformation.

1.1 Additional Risks from AI and the Need for Trust

There may be additional liabilities for boards, if decisions based on AI go wrong (Herrmann & Masawi, 2022). This adds more complexity to risk management. Shareholders can claim a board knew, or should have known, of the dangers involved in a decision. Board members may have to consider whether their insurance covers potential claims. These changes to the board's role, and the uncertainty it may bring, must not prevent them from instilling trust in the process of digital transformation in finance with AI (Zarifis & Cheng, 2024).

As the role of AI increases, the reliance on human involvement often decreases, leading to heightened dependence on AI systems. This shift can create a feeling of lost control and potentially increase risks, or at least perceived risk. In the past, the risks were typically associated with a process failing, such as a money transfer not being completed successfully. However, with AI, the scope of risks is broader. With AI the risks now extend beyond whether a process is completed to the reasons behind the actions. For example, an insurer may understand why they rejected a customer when using traditional automation, but this rationale is not always clear with AI systems. AI introduces various additional risks, including legal and regulatory challenges, as well as risks to reputation, finances, and ethical behaviour.

There are many tensions in AI adoption that leaders need to contend with. Moving quickly may give a competitive advantage but may reduce trust (Khanna et al., 2024). This is due to not having time to build trust and problems that a rushed implementation may cause. Using AI more broadly may increase the reward but also the risk.

Given the complex and delicate balance an organization must strike when using AI, this is a process where a wise and experienced board can, and must, have an active leadership role. What is gained by AI is important, but what is lost by automating and replacing people may not be reversible. Skills, knowledge, and wisdom may be lost irreversibly. Therefore, this research attempts to answer the following question:

What are the most effective ways for a board to build trust in AI use in Fintech for shareholders, staff, and customers?

1.2 How Leaders Can Build Trust in AI

This research interviewed 21 Malaysian Fintech board members to identify the most effective, practical, ways for a board to build trust for shareholders, staff, and customers. Due to the strong linkages between trust and cultural values in technology adoption (Jalan et al., 2023), this study sheds light on building trust in AI within the unique context of Malaysian Fintech firms. To gain a nuanced understanding of the trust-building mechanisms, we conducted interviews with 21 Malaysian Fintech board members and analysed this primary data. This qualitative research design enables us to uncover various angles and dimensions of the interplay between trust and leadership in the complex context of the Fintech industry in Malaysia, which operates within relatively unexplored and unique cultural settings.

The findings show significant overlap between the effective overall implementation and governance of AI. However, several issues are identified that relate specifically to how AI innovations should be communicated to build trust. The findings also indicate that certain applications of Generative AI are more conducive to building trust in AI, even if they are more restrained and limited in scope, and some of Generative AI's performance may be sacrificed as a result. Thus, there are trade-offs between unleashing Generative AI in all its capacity and a more constrained, transparent, and predictable application that builds trust in customers, staff, and shareholders. This balancing act, between a fast adoption of Generative AI and a more cautious, controlled approach is at the heart of the challenge the board faces.

Leaders and corporate boards must build trust by providing a suitable strategy and an effective implementation, while maintaining a healthy level of scepticism based on an understanding of AI's limitations. This balance will lead to more stable and sustainable trust.

The next section reviews the literature on the role of board members in building trust in AI and Fintech. This is followed by the methodology section, which explains the qualitative approach taken in detail. Then, we discuss the results where characteristic quotes illustrate the beliefs of the board members. Finally, the practical implications for board members are offered.

2 Theoretical Foundation

The literature on AI adoption and associated opportunities and challenges is rapidly expanding. While precious research indicates that there are these different perspectives on the challenges to trust in AI (Felzmann et al., 2019), it does not provide a clear understanding of what these challenges are. This gap is particularly evident in the context of Fintech in Malaysia. Therefore, an exploratory approach using interviews will help identify the relevant issues for boards of directors in Malaysia.

2.1 How AI and Fintech Are Disrupting Finance and the Role of Board Members in Fintech

Out of the five priorities identified by Asian board members, two are technology related: (1) Cybersecurity and data privacy and (2) technology innovation (EY, 2024). In Asia, as in other regions of the world, AI and other innovative technologies such as blockchain and the Internet of Things (IoT) are accelerating the pace of digital transformation making most board members believe that their business model will need to change (EY, 2024). Nevertheless, globally, most boards hesitate to act decisively to transform their business model to fully utilize the emerging technologies (Khanna et al., 2024). Akyildirim et al. (2020) identified and analysed numerous cases of superficial and misleading changes in corporate identity towards blockchain and cryptocurrency that did not go beyond crypto-related name changes. The actual changes to the business model were minimal or non-existent, and this attempt to partake in the hype around crypto and blockchain technology has been referred to as '*crypto exuberance*' (Akyildirim et al., 2020).While similar malicious intentions and motives may be present among firms attempting to associate themselves with AI to boost equity and attract investors, some barriers to implementing actual changes to the business model could be genuine. For example, boards in Asia acknowledge that the challenges ahead require them to receive additional training (Russell Reynolds Associates, 2021), while the correct training maybe lacking either in terms of expertise or resources. Research has identified four dimensions to how a board should implement AI governance: (1) strategy and competitiveness, (2) capital allocation, (3) AI risks and (4) technology competence (van Giffen & Ludwig, 2023). Evaluating the risks from AI can be particularly challenging. There are risks of mistakes caused by AI due to the choice of algorithms, using data that is not representative, and interpretation of the results by humans (Herrmann & Masawi, 2022).

2.2 Challenges to Trust in AI for Shareholders

Each of the stakeholders-shareholders, staff, and customers can be unique and differ from one another. Hence, the associated challenges of building trust in AI could differ across each stakeholder group.

Apart from the benefits AI brings to organizations, it also brings several risks that may concern *shareholders*. Evidence shows that the technical knowledge of boards in Asia is important and influences how effectively AI is implemented (Li et al., 2021). As AI is causing transformational changes, reshaping business models in finance (Zarifis & Cheng, 2024), shareholders expect the board to have the knowledge and navigate these changes effectively. Therefore, from the shareholders perspective, there are additional risks due to the transformation AI causes.

As AI can appear to be a black box, it is essential that regulators in highly regulated sectors of the economy, such as finance, are provided with transparency (Weber et al., 2024). The board must assure the shareholders that this is happening and that no unnecessary additional risks are emerging.

Shareholders may feel that the organization has taken on unnecessary additional risks with the way AI is utilized without their knowledge, which may even lead them to take legal action (Irvin et al., 2023). It is therefore important to have regular and clear updates and inform shareholders about the cases of AI adoption. This can be easy if the way AI is implemented is transparent to the board themselves, but much harder if the implementation is indeed a black box.

Finally, boards of directors are increasingly using AI to fulfil their own role of leadership and governance of a Fintech (Hilb, 2020). The board will have to show to shareholders that the quality of the leadership and governance has not been reduced with the use of AI.

2.3 Challenges to Trust in AI for Staff

Unlike most other information systems, AI can cause a sense of losing control among *staff* (Grove et al., 2020). This loss of control can make staff worry about the possible negative outcomes the use of AI can have on themselves and other stakeholders. With AI increasingly taking on roles performed by humans, there is a risk that staff may be blamed for mistakes made by the AI (Ashta & Herrmann, 2021). While there is evidence that in general, people trust information systems too much, assuming they are always right even when there are indications to the contrary (Howard, 2024), particular caution should be exercised in the case of AI. Staff should not accept the information provided by AI without critical assessment by the team and relevant decision-makers. Klingbeil et al. (2024) show that overreliance on AI advice might negatively affect human cooperation and create a conflict with available contextual information against the company's own interest.

An organization's information systems, particularly those at the enterprise level such as enterprise resource planning software (ERP), are a way to impose the organizations plans. If staff increasingly hesitate to utilize the information from AI, or use it incorrectly, there will be problems. As interactions between humans are reduced in the workplace due to increased digitalization and automation, building relationships sufficiently to have trust in each other may be harder (World Economic Forum, 2023).

2.4 Challenges to Trust in AI for Customers

The interaction between an organization and its *customers* is becoming more faceless but also more data intensive. When customers trust AI, they are more likely to use the service (Chi et al., 2023), but when AI is used in financial services it can cause distrust (Zarifis et al., 2021).

Most implementations of AI create the risk of causing financial harm to customers but in some cases, such as when developing medicines, physical harm can also be caused (Irvin et al., 2023).

A related question, to what are the challenges to trusting AI from the customer's perspective, is how much should the customer trust AI when making significant decisions such as whether to get a mortgage (Norkute et al., 2023). Therefore, this is not a narrow question of building trust in a technology the board know is reliable and predictable. It may be better to not focus on building blind trust with customers, but be transparent and explain how AI makes decisions. While transparency is not only usually effective in building trust, it is also an ethical approach to take. However, transparency is not guaranteed to be helpful in all contexts and can be counterproductive (Felzmann et al., 2019). Someone playing the role of devil's advocate may claim that in some cases if customers know how AI works, they will trust and respect the decisions less. Explainable AI (XAI) is not always easy to achieve and may not always be wanted. This lack of clarity in how to build trust with consumers for AI illustrates how the board of directors need to play a hands-on role and utilize their knowledge and judgement. It could be argued that if it is hard to build trust in the AI used, then maybe the focus should be on building trust in the organization. So, instead of telling customers trust the Fintech because of its AI, trust the Fintech despite of its AI because it is hard to explain how the AI works.

3 Method

3.1 Data Analysis

This research applies a qualitative method involving interviews to explore the leadership role of the board of directors in building trust in AI in Fintech in Malaysia. Qualitative case study analysis is used to analyse the interviews, using the Malaysian Fintech sector as a case of the leadership role of the board of directors (Eisenhardt, 1989; Monteiro, 2022). While AI is impacting most if not all sectors of the economy, the way it is utilized—and the opportunities and threats it brings—varies depending on the contexts. Therefore, it is important to focus on one specific case to draw accurate and representative conclusions. The qualitative data analysis software NVivo 14 (https://lumivero.com/products/nvivo/) was used to identify common themes in the interview transcripts.

3.2 Data Collection

The literature suggest that different stakeholders may have different concerns when it comes to the increasing role of AI in finance. The most effective ways for a board to build trust in AI use in Fintech may be different for shareholders, staff, and customers. Therefore, the research question needs to be answered three times, first for shareholders, then for staff and finally for customers. The issues that emerge from the literature review form the basis for the semi-structured interview questions. The semi-structured questions used in the interview are presented in Table 1.

This research interviewed 21 Malaysian Fintech board members, from 9 different boards, to identify the most effective ways for a leader to build trust for shareholders, staff and customers based on their experience. The number of interviews was limited to 21 as the topics became saturated and the same themes were repeatedly emerging (Miles & Huberman, 1994). To be selected for the interview, one of the requirements was that the prospective participants had to work in Fintech companies that were business-to-consumer (B2C) and not business-to-business (B2B), as these are two very different scenarios with different dynamics in the relationship between the Fintech organization and the stakeholders. The interviews were carried out in English and lasted from 36 to 51 min. The demographic information of the participants is presented in Table 2. The transcripts were anonymized, and

Table 1 Semi-structured interview questions

Part A: General questions
QA1: Are you on the board of directors of a Fintech organization?
QA2: What does your organization do?
QA3: What is your role?
QA4: Is your organization in Malaysia?
QA5: What is your age?
QA6: What is your education level?
QA7: What is your income?
Part B: Questions on AI and trust
QB1A: How do you use AI in your organization?
QB1B: How do you use Generative AI in your organization?
QB2A: Have you encountered challenges to trust in AI from the shareholders perspective? If you have, what are they?
QB2B: Have you found effective ways to build trust in AI for stakeholders? If you have, what are they?
QB3A: Have you encountered challenges to trust in AI from the staff's perspective? If you have, what are they?
QB3B: Have you found effective ways to build trust in AI for staff? If you have, what are they?
QB4A: Have you encountered challenges to trust in AI from the customer's perspective? If you have, what are they?
QB4B: Have you found effective ways to build trust in AI for customers? If you have, what are they?
Part C: Final question for unstructured comments
QC1: Do you want to say anything else related to these issues that I have not asked you about?

Table 2 Demographic information of participants

Measure	Variable	Participants	Percentage
Gender	Female	5	24%
	Male	16	76%
Age	25–39	3	14%
	40–59	12	57%
	60 or older	6	29%
Educational level (highest qualification)	University bachelor's degree	12	57%
	University postgraduate degree	9	43%
Yearly income(Malaysian Ringgit)	RM 90,001–120,000	4	14%
	RM 120,001–150,000	6	32%
	RM 150,001–180,000	10	33%
	Over RM 18,0001	1	5%
Malaysian nationality and Malaysian resident		19	89%
Without Malaysian nationality but a Malaysian resident		2	11%

the participants' privacy was protected in line with GDPR guidelines (European Parliament, 2016).

4 Analysis and Results

The literature on AI adoption and trust suggest that different stakeholders may have different concerns when it comes to the increasing role of AI in finance. The participants interviewed were asked about how they build trust in each of the three main stakeholders separately. The empirical data collected suggests that the main ways to build trust in AI can be separated into two steps: First, by building trust with an effective and trustworthy implementation of AI, and second, building trust by communicating how AI is used in a way that addresses the stakeholders' concerns. Their responses, and the lessons extracted from them, are presented in the following sections.

4.1 How Leaders Can Build Trust in AI with Shareholders

4.1.1 Implementation: Building Trust in the AI Implementation Process with Stakeholders

Most of the board members interviewed (15/21) spoke about the trade-off between the benefits of AI and the risks. Those who made this point see this as an area where they must have input in the process and show leadership. One board member interviewed commented:

> We talk about this (AI adoption) a-lot we react to competitors we react to what suppliers tell us we react to what our people tell us. It should be controlled it should be managed it should be managed how we managed risk before. We are accountable for it (AI adoption) we are regulated we will not take on more risk.

There were many comments from most interviewees (20/21) on how they are adapting their operations to implement AI in a trustworthy way. Most comments were about how the people involved are adapting, but some also discussed the technology more specifically. Some comments focused the people involved are:

> We learn how AI can help us . . . .we brought one new board member from IT...
>
> We were advised to have a dedicated committee on AI that will help us stay on-top of things we will have good chats to make good decisions at the right time.
>
> HR are aware of us wanting to attract AI experts in various roles seniorities divisions...if we have the right talent that gives us and shareholders confidence and trust in what we are trying to do.
>
> It needs to be a smooth process to make trust with everyone we need to have a smooth fast onboarding so the APIs and partners deliver that for us. They do it better and it is not our core process.

> Most shareholders will not get involved in day to day running of the business. If we make the right adjustments to keep up or even take a step a leap ahead of our competitors with AI they will continue to trust us or trust us more.

A comment more focused on how the technology will be implemented is:

> We want it to work for us but we don't want to go down the route of having many customizations because those will be our responsibility forever whenever there is a problem we will have to fix it ourselves.

Therefore, based on the comments of the interviewees, the ways to build trust in the AI implementation process for stakeholders are:

1. Use AI in a way that does not increase financial or other risks.
2. Build in-house expertise, don't rely on one consultant or technology provider.
3. Make a new committee focused on the governance of AI and data. Accurately evaluate new risks (compliance, etc.).
4. Develop a framework of AI risk that the board will use to evaluate and communicate risks from AI implementations. Management should regularly update the framework.
5. Renew board and bring in more technical knowledge, and have sufficient competence in AI. Keep up with developments in technology. Ensure all board members understand how Generative AI and traditional AI work.
6. Make the right strategic decisions and collaboration for the necessary technology and data (e.g. through APIs, etc.).

4.1.2 Communication: Building Trust in AI by Communicating Its Role More Clearly to Shareholders

Most of the interviewees (13/21) spoke about the importance of having a clear and consistent message to build trust with shareholders:

> Our reports and the website need to mention AI so people including the shareholders know we are using it drawing the benefits.
>
> We use many partners (to implement AI ourselves and for services using AI) but when it comes to our core business we have not handed it over to AI we use AI but we have not handed over our core business shareholders should know this . . .
>
> The regulation with data needs to be considered...following the regulation creates trust with the government shareholders everyone.
>
> Some people want to use AI for almost everything they don't understand the problems things can unravel. We don't want people (to believe that) the shareholders to think that...

Therefore, based on the comments of the interviewees, the ways to build trust in AI with shareholders by communicating the role of AI can be done in the following ways:

1. Clear vision on AI use. Illustrate sound business judgement. Showcase the organization's AI talent.

2. Clear boundaries on what AI does and does not do. Show willingness to enforce these.
3. Illustrate an ability to follow developments: Show similar cases of AI use from competitors, or companies in other areas.
4. If trust is concentrated on specific leaders that will have a smaller influence with the increased use of AI, the trust lost must be re-built.
5. Be transparent about AI risks, so shareholders can also evaluate them as accurately as possible.

4.2 *How Leaders Can Build Trust in AI with Staff*

4.2.1 Implementation: Building Trust in the AI Implementation Process for Staff

All the board members interviewed are aware of several concerns staff have about the use of AI, and how it affects them:

> There's an element of experimentation with all this but we are committed to moving forward, our staff know that they can't stop it change is a part of life.
>
> Most of our staff are finance professionals they're experts on the tools they use but not all tech . . .
>
> They (staff) get promotions and bonuses from their performance. Through all the change from AI but also crypto the economy the evaluation needs to be attractive . . .
>
> They (staff) have similar concerns to us so we need to talk about how it affects them and us.
>
> I have been asked if we are training AI on their behaviour and if AI will replace them once it is trained and if this is ethical. We don't want to do something not ethical.

Therefore, based on the comments of the interviewees, the ways to build trust in the AI implementation process for staff are:

1. Show long-term financial commitment to AI initiatives.
2. Encourage mindset of experimentation but with an awareness of the risks such as privacy, data protection laws and ethical behaviour.
3. Involve staff in process of digital transformation. Share new progress and new insights gained to illuminate the way forward.
4. Make AI ethics committee with staff from a variety of seniorities.
5. Give existing staff the necessary skills to effectively utilize Generative AI, rather than hiring new people with technological knowledge that do not know the business. Educate staff on when to not follow, and when to challenge the findings of AI.
6. Key performance indicators (KPIs) need to be adjusted. Some tasks become easier with AI, but the process of digital transformation is time consuming.

4.2.2 Communication: Building Trust in AI with Staff by Communicating the Role of AI

While there are real challenges for staff with the increasing use of AI, and staff want effective solutions, most of the board members interviewed (16/21) believe that how the change is articulated to staff is also critical:

> We are looking at alternative solutions with AI and we will continue to be open to looking at alternative solutions but we need to be clear on the strategy so we optimize the resources we have and staff understand that.
>
> With changes like this there are always many problems and we try to have a friendly culture where people are not scared of talking about the problems so we fix them.
>
> I want us (the board and other staff) to not be scared of how we use AI in the future but vigilance is also necessary we don't want to be asleep while the plane is on autopilot (we must not trust AI blindly).

Therefore, based on the comments of the interviewees, building trust in AI with staff by communicating the role of AI, can be done in the following ways:

1. Communicate a clear coherent, long-term vision, with a clear role for staff. The steps towards that vision should reflect the technological changes, business model changes, and the changes in their roles.
2. Be open and supportive to staff reporting problems, so whistleblowing is avoided.

4.3 How Leaders Can Build Trust in AI with Customers

4.3.1 Implementation: Building Trust in the AI Implementation Process for Customers

Most of the board members interviewed (18/21) spoke about transparency extensively as a way to build trust for customers in AI. A related point was also made about setting boundaries for what AI can and cannot do. Having these boundaries also helps in making AI decisions more explainable:

> We are comfortable with AI in financial advice and most of our customers are we need to be at the same point with Generative AI.
>
> They (customers) can't trust us if they don't know what we do (to make financial decisions) they ask us especially when there is a dip.

Therefore, based on the comments of the interviewees, the ways to build trust in the AI implementation process for consumers are:

1. Avoid using unsupervised Generative AI to complete tasks on its own.
2. Only use AI with clear transparent processes, and predictable outcomes, to complete tasks on its own.
3. Have clear guidelines on how staff can utilize Generative AI, covering what manual checks they should make.
4. Monitor competition and don't fall behind in how trust in AI is built.

4.3.2 Communication: Building Trust in AI by Communicating Its Role More Clearly to Customers

Several of the interviewees (12/21) stated that the use of AI and Generative AI needs to be explained, and customers must be reassured that this is done ethically and respectfully:

> People hate that moment when they realize they are not talking to a real person they feel misled you need to tell them from the start what is what.
>
> They need to know we use AI but all the things that made them trust us before and put their money with us still apply.

Therefore, based on the comments of the interviewees, building trust in AI with customers by communicating the role of AI can be done in the following ways:

1. Explain where Generative AI and other AI are used and how.
2. Emphasize the values and ethics of the organization and how they still apply when Generative AI or other AI is used.

5 Discussion and Conclusion

The magnitude of the digital transformation and the risks involved requires leadership from the board of directors. Globally, most boards struggle to fully understand how they should show leadership in how they utilize AI and apply governance to it.

Tables 3, 4, and 5 illustrate how a board should build trust in AI for shareholders, staff, and consumers. Leaders should build trust in two ways: First, by building trust with an effective and trustworthy implementation of AI, and second, building trust by communicating how AI is used in a way that addresses the stakeholder's concerns. The findings show that there is a significant overlap with good overall implementation and governance of AI. There are, however, several issues identified that are specific ways to communicate how AI is used and to build trust. The findings also show that some ways of applying Generative AI are more conducive to trust in AI, even if they may be a more restrained and limited application, and some of Generative AI's performance is sacrificed. There are, therefore, some trade-offs between unleashing Generative AI in all its capacity and a more constrained, transparent, and predictable application that builds trust with customers, staff, and shareholders. This balancing act, between a fast adoption of Generative AI and a more cautious adoption of a more controlled AI, is at the heart of the challenge the board faces.

Based on the directors interviewed, more technical knowledge of the technology is needed on boards. This finding supports previous research on boards in China (Li et al., 2021) and suggests this also applies to Malaysia. The message that comes out strongly is that board members with their experience in making strategic decisions with long-term implications are critical, but new knowledge needs to be gained.

Table 3 How leaders can build trust in AI with shareholders

Implementation
1. Use AI in a way that does not increase financial or other risks
2. Build in-house expertise, don't rely on one consultant or technology provider
3. Make a new committee focused on the governance of AI and data. Accurately evaluate new risks (compliance, etc.)
4. Develop a framework of AI risk that the board will use to evaluate and communicate risks from AI implementations. Management should regularly update the framework
5. Renew board and bring in more technical knowledge, and have sufficient competence in AI. Keep up with developments in technology. Ensure all board members understand how Generative AI and traditional AI work
6. Make the right strategic decisions, and collaboration, for the necessary technology and data (e.g. through APIs, etc.)
Communication
1. Clear vision on AI use. Illustrate sound business judgement. Showcase the organization's AI talent
2. Clear boundaries on what AI does and does not do. Show willingness to enforce these
3. Illustrate an ability to follow developments: Show similar cases of AI use from competitors, or companies in other areas
4. If trust is concentrated on specific leaders that will have a smaller influence with the increased use of AI, the trust lost must be re-built
5. Be transparent about AI risks so shareholders can also evaluate them as accurately as possible

Table 4 How leaders can build trust in AI with staff

Implementation
1. Show long-term financial commitment to AI initiatives
2. Encourage mindset of experimentation but with an awareness of the risks such as privacy, data protection laws and ethical behaviour
3. Involve staff in process of digital transformation. Share new progress and new insights gained to illuminate the way forward
4. Make AI ethics committee with staff from a variety of seniorities
5. Give existing staff the necessary skills to effectively utilize Generative AI, rather than hiring new people with technological knowledge that do not know the business. Educate staff on when to not follow, and when to challenge the findings of AI
6. Key performance indicators (KPIs) need to be adjusted. Some tasks become easier with AI, but the process of digital transformation is time consuming
Communication
1. Communicate a clear coherent, long-term vision, with a clear role for staff. The steps towards that vision should reflect the technological changes, business model changes, and the changes in their roles
2. Be open and supportive to staff reporting problems, so whistleblowing is avoided

Building evidence-based trust, and supporting healthy distrust in AI, is important. Blind trust in AI and the assumption that it works like another technology that operates in a predictable way, such as statistical analysis of investments provided by a financial investment app, are also unhealthy. Therefore, leaders and boards, in particular, must build trust by providing a suitable strategy and an effective implementation, while at the same time, avoid crushing a healthy level of distrust based on an understanding of AI's limitations. A blind distrust must not be replaced

Table 5 How leaders can build trust in AI with customers

Implementation
1. Avoid using unsupervised Generative AI to complete tasks on its own
2. Only use AI with clear transparent processes, and predictable outcomes, to complete tasks on its own
3. Have clear guidelines on how staff can utilize Generative AI, covering what manual checks they should make
4. Monitor competition and don't fall behind in how trust in AI is built
Communication
1. Explain where Generative AI and other AI are used and how
2. Emphasize the values and ethics of the organization and how they still apply when Generative AI, or other AI, is used

by a blind trust. Therefore, a level of trust as close to the abilities and limitations of the AI used is ideal. This will be a more stable and sustainable trust. This delicate balance is based on good judgement, which is where a board with their experience often excel. This is one more time when they must raise to the challenge and show leadership.

Limitations and future research: The findings support how leaders, particularly board members, build trust in AI for finance and Fintech in Malaysia. The findings may apply to other regions, but future research should confirm this. While many of the findings may apply to other sectors of the economy and other countries, they will be more relevant to sectors with similar characteristics such as the high level of risk and the high level of trust necessary.

The authors thank the Institute of Corporate Directors Malaysia for their support, and for featuring this research: https://pulse.icdm.com.my/article/how-leadership-in-financial-organisations-build-trust-in-ai-lessons-from-boards-of-directors-in-fintech-in-malaysia/

References

Akyildirim, E., Corbet, S., Sensoy, A., & Yarovaya, L. (2020). The impact of blockchain related name changes on corporate performance. *Journal of Corporate Finance, 65*. https://doi.org/10.1016/j.jcorpfin.2020.101759

Ashta, A., & Herrmann, H. (2021). Artificial intelligence and fintech: An overview of opportunities and risks for banking, investments, and microfinance. *Strategic Change, 30*(3), 211–222. https://doi.org/10.1002/jsc.2404

Chi, O. H., Chi, C. G., Gursoy, D., & Nunkoo, R. (2023). Customers' acceptance of artificially intelligent service robots: The influence of trust and culture. *International Journal of Information Management, 70*, 102623. https://doi.org/10.1016/j.ijinfomgt.2023.102623. Elsevier.

Choung, H., David, P., & Ling, T. W. (2024). Acceptance of AI-powered facial recognition technology in surveillance scenarios: Role of trust, security, and privacy perceptions. *Technology in Society, 79*.

Eisenhardt, K. M. (1989). Building theories from case study research. *Academy of Management Review, 14*(4), 532–550. https://doi.org/10.5465/amr.1989.4308385

European Parliament. (2016). *EU General Data Protection Regulation GDPR, Official Journal of the European Union.*

EY. (2024). *Asia-Pacific Board priorities: Balancing growth with economic volatility.*

Felzmann, H., Villaronga, E. F., Lutz, C., & Tamò-Larrieux, A. (2019). Transparency you can trust: Transparency requirements for artificial intelligence between legal norms and contextual concerns. *Big Data and Society, 6*(1), 1–14. https://doi.org/10.1177/2053951719860542

Grove, H., Clouse, M., Schaffner, L., & Xu, T. (2020). Monitoring AI progress for corporate governance. *Journal of Governance and Regulation, 9*(1), 8–17. https://doi.org/10.22495/jgrv9i1art1

Herrmann, H., & Masawi, B. (2022). Three and a half decades of artificial intelligence in banking, financial services, and insurance: A systematic evolutionary review. *Strategic Change, 31*(6), 549–569. https://doi.org/10.1002/jsc.2525. Wiley.

Hilb, M. (2020). Toward artificial governance? The role of artificial intelligence in shaping the future of corporate governance. *Journal of Management and Governance, 24*(4), 851–870. https://doi.org/10.1007/s10997-020-09519-9. Springer.

Howard, A. (2024). In AI we trust—Too much? *MIT Sloan Management Review*, 1–9.

Irvin, S., Tucker, S., Engvall, D., & Dapaah-Afriyie, D.; Farley, E. (Ed.). (2023). AI comes to the board room in a black box: Are the personal assets of directors at risk in AI-related claims? *JOLT Digest*, 2–16.

Jalan, A., Matkovskyy, R., Urquhart, A., & Yarovaya, L. (2023). The role of interpersonal trust in cryptocurrency adoption. *Journal of International Financial Markets, Institutions & Money, 83*. https://doi.org/10.1016/j.intfin.2022.101715

Khanna, T., Beckerle, M. C., Sakkab, N. Y. (2024, September–October). Boards need a new approach to technology. *Harvard Business Review*, 1–16.

Klingbeil, A., Grutzner, C., & Schreck, P. (2024). Trust and reliance on AI—An experimental study on the extent and costs of overreliance on AI. *Computers in Human Behavior, 160*.

Kumar, A. (2024) AI tools, fake songs, and $ 10M fraud: US musician indicted for royalty scam. *Business Standard*, 1.

Li, J., Li, M., Wang, X., & Thatcher, J. B. (2021). Strategic directions for AI: The role of CIOs and boards of directors. *MIS Quarterly: Management Information Systems, 45*(3), 1603–1643. https://doi.org/10.25300/MISQ/2021/16523

Miles, M. B., & Huberman, A. M. (1994). *Qualitative data analysis*. Sage.

Monteiro, E. (2022). Qualitative research methods in information systems: A call for phenomenon-focused problematization. *MIS Quarterly, 46*(4).

Naeem, M., Arfaoui, N., & Yarovaya, L. (2025). The contagion effect of artificial intelligence across innovative industries: From blockchain and metaverse to cleantech and beyond. *Technological Forecasting and Social Change, 210*, 123822.

Norkute, M., Designer, L., & Labs, T. R. (2023). The road to building trust with AI systems. *Thomson Reuters Labs*, 1–7.

Russell Reynolds Associates. (2021). *Boards in Malaysia.*

van Giffen, B., & Ludwig, H. (2023). How boards of directors govern artificial intelligence. *MIS Quarterly Executive, 22*(4), 251–272. https://doi.org/10.17705/2msqe.00085

Weber, P., Carl, K. V., & Hinz, O. (2024). Applications of explainable artificial intelligence in finance—A systematic review of finance, information systems, and computer science literature. *Management Review Quarterly, 74*, 867–907. https://doi.org/10.1007/s11301-023-00320-0. Springer.

World Economic Forum. (2023). *Measuring digital trust: Supporting decision-making for trustworthy technologies.*

Zarifis, A., & Cheng, X. (2024). The five emerging business models of Fintech for AI adoption, growth and building trust. In A. Zarifis, D. Ktoridou, L. Efthymiou, & X. Cheng (Eds.), *Business digital transformation* (pp. 73–97). Springer. https://doi.org/10.1007/978-3-031-33665-2_4

Zarifis, A., Kawalek, P., & Azadegan, A. (2021). Evaluating if trust and personal information privacy concerns are barriers to using health insurance that explicitly utilizes AI. *Journal of Internet Commerce, 20*(1), 66–83. https://doi.org/10.1080/15332861.2020.1832817

Dr. Alex Zarifis' research and teaching are on the practical applications of technology in business. Before the University of Southampton, he worked at several academic institutions including the University of Cambridge, the University of Manchester and the University of Mannheim. He is currently a research affiliate of the Cambridge Center for Alternative Finance (CCAF).

He has explored cryptoassets such as cryptocurrencies since 2012. As part of this research, he published the first peer-reviewed research on trust in digital currencies in the world in 2014. He also participated in creating the first government recognized, university degree on blockchain technologies in the world.

Dr. Alex has published extensively on trust in different technologies and business models. His research has explored the role of trust in AI, blockchain, financial technology (Fintech) and insurance technology (Insurtech).

Dr. Larisa Yarovaya is an Associate Professor of Finance and the Director of the Centre for Digital Finance at Southampton Business School, University of Southampton, UK. Larisa is also an Advisory Board member of the British Blockchain Association, which also serves as the secretariat of the All-Party Parliamentary Group on Blockchain Technologies.

With a profound expertise in international finance and Fintech, Larisa has contributed significantly to the academic landscape, authoring over 80 papers and co-editing the book 'Cryptocurrency and Blockchain Technology'.

Recognized for her outstanding contributions, Larisa has earned a spot in Stanford's top 2% Global Scientists list, and her research has garnered more than 10,000 citations. Larisa is also ranked among the top 5 in the Top 200 Young Economists by RePEc, selected from a pool of 14,784 economists who have published their first work within the last 10 years.

Her impactful work has been widely disseminated through esteemed media outlets such as BBC, MarketWatch, FT Live, CBC, Euronews, and Bloomberg, showcasing her influence in both academic and public spheres. She has also appeared as an expert in the CNBC series on 'Ethereum' and 'Stablecoins'. Larisa is actively engaged in policy debates and consultancy to influence the regulatory landscape in the United Kingdom and abroad.

Opportunities and Challenges of Fintech in Southeast Asia

Jianzheng Shi and Yue Wang

1 Introduction

As China's "Belt and Road Initiative" advances and its strategic partnership with ASEAN continues to deepen, an increasing number of Chinese enterprises are designating Southeast Asia as their primary expansion target. The historical ties between China and Southeast Asian nations, rooted in maritime trade established in the fifteenth century, are both enduring and robust. In recent years, Southeast Asia's rapid economic growth has positioned it as a global focal point for economic development and a crucial initial node on China's Maritime Silk Road. Chinese enterprises and investment institutions have been actively establishing their presence across the region, from Jakarta to Manila, and from Hanoi to Phnom Penh, vying for market share and talent acquisition.

Three pivotal factors—geographical proximity, demographic composition, and economic development potential—render Southeast Asia an ideal arena for Chinese Fintech expansion. Historically, China and Southeast Asian nations have maintained close exchanges in political, economic, and cultural spheres. The region, home to over 20 million individuals of Chinese descent, represents one of the world's most concentrated overseas Chinese communities, providing an unparalleled foundation for bilateral business interactions. Moreover, the Southeast Asian region is characterized by a substantial population base and a youthful age structure, offering significant economic development potential. From an economic perspective, nations such as Indonesia, Vietnam, and the Philippines have registered GDP growth rates exceeding 6%, demonstrating robust growth trajectories. Furthermore, these coun-

J. Shi (✉) · Y. Wang
Singapore University of Social Sciences, Singapore, Republic of Singapore
e-mail: jzshi001@suss.edu.sg

A. Zarifis, X. Cheng (eds.), *Fintech and the Emerging Ecosystems*, Financial Innovation and Technology, https://doi.org/10.1007/978-3-031-83402-8_16

tries' substantial investments in digital infrastructure and increasing mobile internet penetration rates have created a conducive environment for Fintech enterprises.

In recent years, as domestic online financial regulations in China have become increasingly stringent, some Fintech firms have strategically initiated or been compelled to pursue overseas development strategies. The intense competition within the domestic market, coupled with escalating regulatory and compliance costs, has precipitated a strategic shift toward overseas markets. In this context, Southeast Asian countries, particularly Indonesia, the Philippines, and Vietnam, have naturally emerged as preferred destinations due to their large populations, significant internet user bases, relatively lenient regulatory environments, and underdeveloped financial services sectors.

Consequently, this report will focus on five representative Southeast Asian nations—Singapore, Vietnam, Indonesia, the Philippines, and Cambodia. It will provide a detailed analysis of their regulatory policies, examine case studies of Fintech development, assess Chinese enterprises that have established a presence in Southeast Asia, and offer a comprehensive evaluation of the business environments in these nations. This multifaceted approach aims to provide a nuanced understanding of the opportunities and challenges present in the Southeast Asian Fintech landscape for Chinese enterprises seeking expansion in the region.

2 Brief Overview of the Overall Situation in Southeast Asia

Southeast Asia, a term that emerged in the late stages of World War II, encompasses 11 countries. These 11 Southeast Asian countries can be divided into mainland countries (such as Thailand, Myanmar, Vietnam, etc.) and island countries (such as Indonesia, the Philippines, Brunei, etc.). The World Bank's statistics for per capita GDP in 2017 rank as follows: Singapore, Brunei, Malaysia, Thailand, Indonesia, Philippines, Laos, Vietnam, East Timor, Cambodia, and Myanmar. Each country has a long history and is an emerging economy. Apart from Singapore, all other countries are developing nations. Table 1 shows the overview of key Southeast Asian countries.

Southeast Asia's geographic location is significant and, in recent history, has gradually developed into one of the world's important sea and air transportation hubs. The region's strategic position has amplified its influence, serving as a global trade and transport route nexus.

There is significant variation among Southeast Asian countries in terms of scale, population, and economy. At the same time, Southeast Asia has the largest number of overseas Chinese in the world, with more than 20 million ethnic Chinese in the region. Additionally, there are over 2 million Indians and over 1 million immigrants from other countries, making the cultural environment relatively complex with significant differences in religious beliefs.

According to a joint study by Google US and Temasek Holdings of Singapore, the total transaction volume of Southeast Asia's internet economy reached $72

Table 1 Overview of key Southeast Asian countries

Category	Singapore	Malaysia	Thailand	Indonesia	Philippines	Vietnam	Cambodia
Land area (square km)	7800	329,613	513,120	1,904,560	300,000	331,212	181,035
Population size (2021)	5,896,686	32,776,194	69,635,763	276,361,783	113,046,913	97,338,579	16,718,965
Total GDP (billion USD)	337.5	354.3	505.9	1111	367.8	340.6	27.3
GDP per capita (USD)	57,714	10,880	7196	4028	3249	3499	1631
GDP growth rate (%)	−5.4	−5.6	−6.1	−2.1	−9.5	2.9	−3.1
Exchange rate (2021)	1.34 SGD	4.18 MYR	32.87 THB	14,220 IDR	50.10 PHP	23,070 VND	4,120 KHR

billion in 2018. This internet economy mainly includes online tourism, e-commerce, online media, and ride-hailing services. With an increasing number of consumers using smartphones to access the internet, the size of Southeast Asia's internet economy is expected to exceed $240 billion by 2025.

In particular, Indonesia's growth stands out. By 2025, Indonesia's internet economy is projected to grow to $100 billion, accounting for two-fifths of the entire Southeast Asian region. With the development of the internet economy, Fintech has gradually risen in the Southeast Asian market.

From 2014 onwards, Fintech has shown a high-speed growth trend. By 2018, Fintech in Southeast Asia had a record year in terms of transaction financing, with an overall increase of 143%. The ASEAN Fintech Census 2018 report published by Ernst & Young shows that the top five sub-areas of cumulative Fintech investment in Southeast Asian countries are payments, investment tech, insurtech, consumer finance, and alternative lending.

Overall, whether it's the advantages brought by the natural environment and geographical location or the dividend effects of the economy and population, all indicate that Southeast Asia has a favorable investment environment for Fintech. With the continuous improvement of technology and financial levels in Southeast Asian countries, the development of the internet economy is thriving, driving the steady development of Fintech. The Fintech market in Southeast Asia is in excellent shape, and Fintech companies from various countries are gradually laying out their operations in Southeast Asia.

3 Overview of Financial Technology Development in Southeast Asian Countries

The current landscape of financial technology development across Southeast Asian nations exhibits notable disparities. Singapore emerges as the preeminent performer, demonstrating comprehensive leadership across various domains. Its consistent recognition by major international organizations and institutions as one of the foremost regions for Fintech development underscores its dominant position.

Indonesia and the Philippines, characterized as nascent Fintech markets, possess significant advantages stemming from their substantial population bases and high internet penetration rates. These factors contribute to their considerable developmental potential. The demographic dividend and technological readiness in these nations create a fertile environment for Fintech innovation and adoption.

Conversely, countries such as Vietnam and Cambodia are in the incipient stages of Fintech development, with limited scope in their financial technology operations. The Fintech ecosystems in these nations are still evolving, presenting both challenges and opportunities for growth.

Looking ahead, the influx of capital is anticipated to play a pivotal role in fostering the development of Fintech start-ups across the region. This financial impetus is expected to catalyze innovation, enhance technological infrastructure, and accelerate the maturation of Fintech services in less developed markets. The heterogeneous nature of Fintech development in Southeast Asia necessitates tailored approaches for each market. While Singapore serves as a benchmark for regional excellence, the emerging markets offer unique opportunities for rapid growth and innovation. The nascent markets, despite their current limitations, hold potential for significant future expansion, particularly with the anticipated influx of investment capital.

3.1 Singapore

Singapore, as the most economically advanced nation in Southeast Asia and a globally significant financial hub, has established itself as a leader in financial technology (Fintech) innovation and regulation. The Monetary Authority of Singapore (MAS), serving as the nation's central banking institution, plays a pivotal role in shaping the financial landscape through its multifaceted responsibilities. These encompass formulating and implementing monetary policy, overseeing the payment system, issuing currency, regulating financial institutions, and managing the country's foreign exchange reserves.

The Fintech sector in Singapore has experienced exponential growth, largely attributed to the proactive and innovative regulatory approach adopted by MAS. A key initiative in this regard is the implementation of a "regulatory sandbox." This framework allows Fintech companies to test and develop innovative financial services within a controlled environment, subject to business reporting requirements. This approach significantly mitigates regulatory barriers and fosters an ecosystem conducive to Fintech innovation and entrepreneurship.

Singapore's preeminence in the Southeast Asian Fintech landscape is further evidenced by its concentration of Fintech enterprises. The city-state hosts the largest number of Fintech companies in the region, encompassing a diverse array of sectors including payments, technological support services, and peer-to-peer lending platforms. This diversity reflects the comprehensive nature of Singapore's Fintech ecosystem and its capacity to support various facets of financial innovation.

The mobile payment market in Singapore exhibits particular dynamism, with a proliferation of widely adopted payment applications. Notable among these are Grab, PayLah!, and Apple Pay, each contributing to the increasing digitalization of financial transactions in the country. This robust mobile payment ecosystem underscores Singapore's advanced digital infrastructure and the population's high technological literacy.

Furthermore, Singapore's position as a Fintech leader is reinforced by its role as a hub for high-level Fintech summits and conferences. These events serve as crucial platforms for knowledge exchange, networking, and showcasing cutting-edge financial technologies. The frequency and caliber of these summits significantly enhance Singapore's influence in shaping global Fintech trends and policies. Singapore's comprehensive approach to Fintech development, combining supportive regulatory frameworks, a diverse ecosystem of Fintech companies, a thriving mobile payment market, and its role as a global Fintech thought leader, solidifies its position at the forefront of financial innovation in Southeast Asia and beyond.

3.2 Vietnam

Fintech development in Vietnam is in a stage of rapid growth. This is mainly due to the Vietnamese government's strong support for financial technology innovation, as well as the opportunities brought about by technological developments such as digitization and mobile payment. Here are a few major trends as in Table 2.

Mobile and digital payments: With Vietnam's growing middle class and increased mobile phone penetration, digital payments are growing rapidly. Payment companies such as MoMo, ZaloPay, and VNPay have made some significant inroads in this space.

Investment in Fintech companies: Fintech companies in Vietnam have received a large amount of domestic and foreign investment in recent years. Investors see huge potential in Vietnam's huge population, untapped market, and Fintech sector.

Development of Fintech regulations: The Vietnamese government is actively developing and revising Fintech-related regulations to encourage more innovation and promote the development of the Fintech industry while protecting consumer rights and preventing risks.

Financial Inclusion: Fintech has the potential to help Vietnam tackle the problem of "unbanking," where a large population does not have bank accounts. Viet Nam's large unbanked population can be provided with financial services through Fintech solutions such as mobile payments and internet banking.

Table 2 Policy content table based on the timeline provided in the image

Year	Policy content
2011	The government issued an overall plan for electronic payment to promote the development of e-commerce
2012	The government introduced laws on non-cash payments and electronic wallets, and issued documents to guide non-cash payment regulations
2014	The government issued guidelines on third-party payment platforms
2016	The Prime Minister signed Vietnam's 5-year plan to build a cashless society
2017	The State Bank of Vietnam and Vietnam National Payment Corporation set up a Fintech steering committee

3.2.1 Enterprises Layout in Vietnam

Ant Financial: In November 2017, Ant Financial reached a cooperation with the National Payment. Corporation of Vietnam (NAPAS) allows Chinese tourists to use Alipay when traveling in Vietnam.

JD Finance: In 2017, it invested in Tiki.vn, a well-known e-commerce platform in Vietnam. Tencent: In November 2017, WeChat officially announced a cooperation agreement with VIMO. VIMO is the first and currently the only authorized payment intermediary in Vietnam that cooperates with both WeChat Pay and Alipay.

Crowd: In February 2018, Zhangzhong Financial Services launched the cash loan idong in Vietnam. The loan amount of idong is 500,000 VND (equivalent to about 147 yuan), and the loan period is 7/14 days.

3.3 Indonesia

Indonesia, comprised of approximately 17,508 islands, is the world's largest archipelago nation. As of 2017, it had a population exceeding 261 million people, making it the biggest economy in Southeast Asia and a member of the G20. As a founding member of the Association of Southeast Asian Nations (ASEAN), Indonesia plays a significant role in the region. Roughly 87% of Indonesians practice Islam, making Indonesia the world's most populous Muslim-majority nation. Diplomatic relations between Indonesia and China were established in 1950.

Indonesia's financial system comprises commercial banks, rural banks, finance companies, insurance companies, pension funds, and financial markets. Here are some key banking institutions:

Bank Indonesia: This is the central bank of the country, responsible for setting and implementing monetary policy, supervising, and managing the nation's financial system.

Bank Mandiri: As the largest commercial bank in Indonesia, it provides a variety of retail and commercial banking services.

Bank CIMB Niaga: One of the largest foreign banks in Indonesia, it's also one of the earliest foreign banks to enter the Indonesian market.

The Financial Services Authority of Indonesia (OJK) oversees financial services regulation in the country. The agency is tasked with creating and enforcing policies to ensure stability and fairness in the Indonesian financial services industry.

Indonesia has demonstrated a proactive stance toward the development of financial technology (Fintech), with the sector experiencing substantial growth by 2021, particularly in mobile payments and online lending. The Financial Services Authority (OJK) has implemented a dedicated regulatory sandbox, facilitating the testing and promotion of novel Fintech products and services within a controlled environment. Concurrently, the government has instituted various policies and regulations to stimulate digitalization and innovation in the financial sector. The rapid increase in mobile and internet penetration has been a key catalyst for

Indonesia's burgeoning Fintech landscape, with digital payments at the forefront of this transformation. The sector has witnessed a significant influx of investments and start-ups, facilitating the development of advanced solutions in peer-to-peer lending, insurtech, and robo-advisory services, among others.

To foster a conducive environment for Fintech growth, the Indonesian government has been actively revising regulatory frameworks and establishing innovation hubs. The creation of the Fintech Office by OJK represents a crucial initiative, providing a centralized platform for regulatory processes and nurturing an ecosystem conducive to Fintech innovation and expansion. Furthermore, traditional banking institutions in Indonesia have begun to forge strategic collaborations with Fintech firms to digitize their operations and enhance the efficiency of their financial services. This trend suggests a future banking landscape that will be predominantly digital and potentially dominated by non-traditional players. This transition aligns with the government's vision of cultivating a digital economy, capitalizing on the vast potential presented by Indonesia's large, youthful population, and expanding middle class.

The convergence of these factors—supportive regulatory frameworks, increasing digital penetration, strategic partnerships, and favorable demographics—positions Indonesia as a pivotal market in the Southeast Asian Fintech ecosystem. The country's trajectory in Fintech development not only reflects its commitment to financial innovation but also underscores its potential to emerge as a significant player in the global digital economy.

3.3.1 Enterprises Layout in Indonesia

Alibaba: In 2015, Alibaba signed an agreement with DOKU to track and simplify payments for Indonesian customers. In 2016, Alibaba acquired a controlling stake in Lazada, the largest e-commerce company in Southeast Asia, and increased its capital by US $1 billion. The company's main market is Indonesia. In May 2017, HelloPay merged with Alipay to form Alipay, trying to expand Alipay to Southeast Asia. In July 2017, Alibaba invested another US $1 billion in Lazada, a Southeast Asian e-commerce platform, increasing its stake in Lazada from 51 to 83%. On March 21, 2018, the electronic wallet DANA jointly launched by Ant Financial and Indonesian Emtek Group was officially launched.

Tencent: In 2013, Tencent formed a joint venture company with PTGlobal Mediacom, the largest media group in Indonesia, with the purpose of promoting WeChat in the Indonesian market and further expanding the local social media market. It is expected to expand WeChat payment in Indonesia in the future. In July 2017, Tencent invested US $100 million to US $150 million in Go-Jek, an Indonesian online car-hailing giant, with the aim of entering the mobile phone terminal service market in Southeast Asia.

Advance AI: Indonesia is the first stop for ADVANCE.AI to go overseas. In order to ensure the operation, promotion, and service of the product, the team established a joint venture company in Indonesia and formed a team of about 200 people.

ADVANCE.AI mainly provides services to internet companies and internet financial institutions with standardized products in Indonesia.

Tong shield: In 2018, Tongdun Technology received a lot of goods in overseas markets, and successively established subsidiaries in Indonesia, Singapore, and Malaysia.

Hengchang: Entered Indonesia in 2018, and obtained the OJK registration number in April 2019, with a registered capital of 10 billion Indonesian rupiah. With the help of domestic funds, it has developed businesses including super loans, collections, and cash loans. It is a new member of the Indonesian Technology Finance Association (AFPI) and technology accumulation, opened in Indonesia.

3.4 Philippines

The Philippines is a multi-ethnic archipelagic country in Southeast Asia, with an area of 299,700 square kilometers. Statistics from the International Monetary Fund (IMF) show that the GDP growth rate of the Philippines in 2018–2019 is expected to be 6.7%. The total population is 105.7 million, the Malay branch accounts for 85% of the national population, and the foreign descendants mainly include Chinese, Arabs, Indians, Americans, and Spaniards. The Philippines, which faces the mainland across the sea, has a deep historical relationship with China. The founding father "Fuxi Rizal", the patriot "Roman Wang Bin", and the former president "Aquino III" are all descendants of the Chinese. Although the Chinese population is only about one million, through generations of travel to Southeast Asia and hard work, 70% of the Philippine economy is related to the Chinese, including aviation, supermarkets, banks, catering, mining, food, etc. Around eight to nine out of 10 Filipino Chinese are from Fujian, and the same percentage are from Quanzhou Sanyi as history reported. English and Tagalog are the official languages, and the Philippines is the fifth largest English-speaking country in the world. The Philippines is a diverse country, successively colonized by Spain, Japan, and the United States. At the same time, in 1450, the Arabs brought Islamic culture and political power to the southern Mindanao region of the Philippines. About 85% of Philippine citizens believe in Catholicism, 4.9% believe in Islam, and a small number of people believe in independent religion and Protestantism. In modern times, the Philippines was deeply influenced by American colonization. Coupled with its diverse historical culture and popular English environment, the Philippines was once known as the "Four Asian Tigers," and Manila was even more known as the "Little New York of Asia." The Philippines is a major member of ASEAN and one of the 24 member countries of the Asia-Pacific Economic Cooperation (APEC). It is a developing country, an emerging industrial country, and one of the emerging markets in the world. It established diplomatic relations with China on June 9, 1975. In recent years, the two countries have had both friction and cooperation in diplomacy. However, with the advancement of international cooperation under the

"Belt and Road Initiative", bilateral relations between China and the Philippines are expected to achieve greater development.

The banking system in the Philippines consists of commercial banks, rural banks, and trust companies. Here are some of the main banks:

Bangko Sentral ng Pilipinas (BSP): This is the central bank of the Philippines. It is responsible for setting and implementing monetary policies, as well as supervising and managing the country's financial system. Established in 1949, the BSP also provides liquidity and emergency loan assistance to banking institutions.

BDO Unibank: As the largest commercial bank in the Philippines, it offers a wide range of retail and commercial banking services. BDO Unibank, incorporated in 1968, also provides investment banking services, private banking services, leasing and finance, investment advisory, and more.

Bank of the Philippine Islands (BPI): One of the oldest commercial banks in the country, BPI provides a variety of retail and commercial banking services. Founded during the Spanish Colonial period, BPI has a long history dating back to 1851. It offers a comprehensive range of financial products and solutions, including corporate banking, investment banking, and asset management.

The Philippines has a well-established financial system, and as a result, it has been a significant player in Southeast Asia's banking industry. It has a mix of local and foreign banks, and the Bangko Sentral ng Pilipinas has worked diligently to maintain stability and confidence in the country's financial system. Over the years, they have implemented various reforms and regulations to modernize and improve the banking sector, which has led to a robust and resilient system.

However, the rural banking sector is another critical component of the Philippine banking system, focusing on the rural and less developed regions of the country. These banks play a crucial role in promoting rural development by providing necessary banking services to rural communities. This structure helps ensure financial inclusion, allowing more Filipinos access to banking services and credit, which can be particularly beneficial for farmers and small businesses.

Regarding financial technology (Fintech), both the Philippines and Indonesia have made significant strides. In the Philippines, the central bank has actively promoted the use of digital payments and has established regulations to foster a safe and inclusive digital financial ecosystem. They've launched initiatives like the National Retail Payment System (NRPS), aiming to increase the share of digital transactions in the country. On the other hand, Indonesia's Fintech sector has achieved substantial growth, particularly in areas like mobile payments and online lending. The Financial Services Authority of Indonesia (OJK) established a regulatory sandbox to test and promote new Fintech products and services in a controlled environment. The government has also pushed for policies and regulations encouraging digitalization and innovation.

3.4.1 Platform Development Status

Loansolutions, founded by JP Bisson in January 2014, is an online lending platform with loan products including personal loans, vehicle, business, home, cash, salary, student, sailor, car loan, and car insurance. In addition, the company provides financial advisory services to help borrowers from inquiry to final loan acquisition. In 2016, Loansolutions entered into a partnership with local financial services firm JK Capital Finance, Inc., a partnership aimed at making its capital more inclusive.

Acudeen: In March 2016, co-founded by Magellan Fetalino III and Mario Salazar, it is positioned as an online platform for receivables discounts, allowing fast transactions with receivables financing within 5–7 days, giving SMEs better control of cash flow. So far, Acudeen has displayed a total of 1669 invoices and a transaction value of nearly 120 million Philippine pesos on its website.

Fund Ko was established in 2016 as a subsidiary of Guevent Investments Development Corporation (GIDC). Its loan products are personal, cash-back, business, and working student loans. Through FundKo, borrowers can apply for loans of PHP 1000–2000 for 3–10 months at interest rates as low as 1% per month. In addition, borrowers can apply without submitting collateral. FundKo lenders can also provide additional funding to SMEs for their expansion, refurbishment, and other business funding needs.

Good Credit: An e-Gift Voucher program based on multiple repayment models, all transactions are done through a mobile application. It provides various financial services around P2P participation in B2B and B2C scenarios. Borrowers can directly receive fast cash assistance in the form of GK's model focuses on small amounts (like 500–1000 Philippine pesos face value) and pays out in overpayment plans (commonly known as 4GIVES). Through this model, GK users (borrowers) will have enough time to arrange their liabilities, unlike credit cards that need to pay fees at the end of the month.

Uploan launched in 2017 targets the withholding salary loan market, providing investment for both institutional and retail investors. Through Uploan's platform, investors can fund loans against personal salary for different risk criteria and loan tenors.

Money Match launched in 2017, the initial investment amount is 5000 pesos. The return rate of the project is between 12 and 36%, with an average return rate of 24%. It belongs to Fintech Global Resources, Inc.

3.4.2 Domestic Enterprises Layout in the Philippines

Ant Financial: In February 2017, Ant Financial and the digital financial company Mynt reached a strategic cooperation. The latter owns GCash, the largest e-wallet in the Philippines. Ant Financial Inc. and Ant Global Inc. 45% of the shares, and Ayala, the second largest enterprise group in the Philippines, holds 10% of the shares.

Tencent: In October 2018, Tencent and KKR acquired part of the equity of Voyager Innovations Inc., a payment innovation company under PLDT (Philippine

Long Distance Telephone Company), for US $175 million. Founded in 2013, Voyager owns e-wallet PayMaya, remittance service Smart Padala, lending platform Lendr, and enterprise solution PayMaya Business.

Crowd: In May 2018, the Philippine cash loan product "PondoPeso" was launched, with a daily interest rate of 3–5%. At present, there are hundreds of local employees.

MinTech: In 2017, it entered the local market research, and the APP "Peso2Go" was launched in mid-2018 to start the cash loan business. Over 100,000 Google Play downloads, 3.7 rating. Mainly provide 140–500 yuan, 7–14 days of loan interest rate above 3%, the product is currently hundreds of orders per month. The identity is mainly verified through manual credit review, and bad debts are reduced by strengthening collection. The first excess is about 30%, and the team has more than 50 people.

Hengchang: Hengchang's 100%-owned Philippine company successfully obtained two licenses for Lending and Financing in 2019, with a registered capital of more than 20 million pesos. Hengchang's local firm is the only Chinese-owned member of Fintech PH, the Philippine Fintech Association.

3.5 Cambodia

The Kingdom of Cambodia, situated in Southeast Asia, shares borders with Laos to the north, Vietnam to the northeast and east, and Thailand to the west and northwest. Phnom Penh serves as both its capital and largest urban center. With a population of approximately 16 million, Cambodia's economy predominantly relies on the textile industry, agriculture, and tourism sectors. The Cambodian financial system, while still in a developmental phase, is primarily composed of the National Bank of Cambodia (NBC) and various commercial banks. The NBC, as the central bank, is tasked with formulating and implementing monetary policy, regulating domestic financial institutions, and promoting financial stability and sustainable economic growth.

Among the prominent commercial banks, Phnom Penh Commercial Bank stands out as one of the largest, offering a diverse range of retail and corporate banking services. Its significant role in promoting financial inclusivity contributes substantially to Cambodia's economic development. ACLEDA Bank, evolving from a microfinance service provider to a comprehensive banking institution, has emerged as the largest retail bank in Cambodia. It has been instrumental in advancing financial inclusion, particularly by extending financial services to the unbanked and underbanked segments of the population.

The Cambodian financial landscape has been experiencing notable growth and evolution. Efforts to enhance financial inclusion and banking penetration have intensified, particularly with the advent of digital banking and Fintech solutions. ACLEDA Bank, for instance, has pioneered mobile banking services, thereby improving the accessibility and convenience of banking for its customers.

From a regulatory perspective, the NBC has been proactive in establishing a conducive environment that fosters the stability and integrity of the Cambodian banking system. This includes the implementation of appropriate prudential standards, effective supervision mechanisms, and robust risk management practices. Moreover, the NBC has demonstrated a progressive stance toward digital innovation. The launch of the Bakong project, a blockchain-based peer-to-peer payment and money transfer platform, represents a pioneering initiative in the country. This development signifies the positive strides being made toward digital transformation and financial inclusion in Cambodia.

The evolving financial sector in Cambodia, characterized by the expansion of traditional banking services and the integration of innovative digital solutions, reflects the country's commitment to financial development and inclusion. As this sector continues to mature, it is likely to play an increasingly crucial role in Cambodia's overall economic growth and development trajectory.

4 Summary and Observations

Southeast Asian nations exhibit significant heterogeneity in terms of population demographics, economic structures, and cultural landscapes. However, a common thread among these diverse countries is the relatively underdeveloped state of modern financial services. The rapid evolution of the new economy, particularly in e-commerce and digital retail, has catalyzed the growth of a modern consumer base, thereby establishing a favorable foundation and external environment for the proliferation of financial technology.

Despite the limited penetration of traditional financial services, Southeast Asia's internet industry and new economy sectors are experiencing unprecedented growth. The confluence of improving infrastructure, a substantial internet user base, and the emergence of multiple novel technology application scenarios present immense potential for the development and application of financial technologies, notably in mobile payments and online lending.

Singapore, as a highly developed and open regional hub, has consistently been recognized by international organizations and institutions as one of the most promising regions for Fintech development. Regulatory bodies have implemented "sandbox" frameworks to further stimulate Fintech innovation. In the mobile payment sector, GrabPay and PayLah! have emerged as market leaders, while Funding Societies and Seedin have established themselves at the forefront of Singapore's online lending industry.

Indonesia and the Philippines, with their large populations, represent emerging Fintech markets with substantial growth potential. The Indonesian Financial Services Authority (OJK) has implemented stringent entry requirements for new registrants, drawing lessons from China's P2P lending experience. The Philippines maintains a relatively lenient approach to online lending regulation, although the absence of a unified personal identity system and limited credit information pose significant challenges.

Vietnam and Cambodia are still in the nascent stages of Fintech development, with limited operational scope in the sector. These markets anticipate capital infusion to foster the growth of start-ups.

Chinese enterprises, ranging from internet giants to Fintech companies, and from PE/VC investments to telecommunications technology exports, are poised to increase their investment in Southeast Asia. Publicly available information indicates that companies such as Ant Financial, Baidu, Tencent, JD Finance, Lufax, Yixin, and Hengchang have all initiated overseas expansion, with a particular focus on the Southeast Asian market.

The internationalization of Southeast Asian Fintech companies presents both opportunities and challenges. These entities must prioritize regulatory compliance, cultural integration, and the pursuit of mutual benefit. Given the considerable variation in historical circumstances, business environments, and market dynamics across Southeast Asian countries, coupled with the rapidly evolving nature of the Fintech industry, successful international expansion necessitates a profound understanding of local policies and markets. Proactive participation in industry self-regulatory associations, establishment of Chinese commercial associations and exchange platforms, and fostering peer exchanges are crucial strategies. Moreover, in the process of team building and daily operations management, it is imperative to recruit and cultivate local talent aggressively, leveraging their inherent advantages as natives to facilitate genuine integration into local society and markets, thereby ensuring the company's sustainable development.

Recommended Reading

Chia, R., & Goh, G. G. (2020). Fintech development and regulatory challenges in ASEAN: A case study of Singapore, Malaysia, and Indonesia. *Journal of Asian Finance, Economics, and Business, 7*(4), 267–276.

Chia, R., & Lim, D. (2020). Financial technology (FinTech) and the ASEAN Economic Community: Regulatory challenges and opportunities. *Asia-Pacific Journal of Business Administration, 12*(2), 127–140.

De Rezende Rocha, R., Calado, L., & Cerdeira, J. O. (2020). Fintech in emerging markets: A systematic review and future research agenda. *International Journal of Information Management, 54*, 102165.

Fatimah, R. (2019). The impact of financial technology (fintech) on financial inclusion: A literature review. *Journal of Asian Finance, Economics, and Business, 6*(4), 139–147.

Lai, V. S., Ooi, K. B., & Chong, A. Y. (2017). An empirical analysis of the factors influencing the intention to use fintech services. *Journal of Innovation & Knowledge, 2*(3), 132–141.

Maghzi, A., Emrouznejad, A., & Cabanda, E. (2020). The role of fintech in sustainable development: A systematic review and bibliometric analysis. *Technological Forecasting and Social Change, 160*, 120262.

Pham, M., & Rosenboom, N. (2019). Fintech development in Southeast Asia: A comparative analysis of Indonesia, Malaysia, and Vietnam. *Journal of Asian Finance, Economics, and Business, 6*(3), 101–112.

PwC. (2019). Fintech in ASEAN: From start-up to scale-up. Retrieved from https://www.pwc.com/sg/en/publications/assets/asean-fintech-report-2019.pdf

Shi, J., & Wang, Y. (2023). Chance or challenge for fintech in SEA. *Eximia, 11*, 181–192.

Tan, A. Y., & Argudo, M. V. (2019). Exploring factors influencing fintech adoption in Southeast Asia. *Journal of Asian Finance, Economics, and Business, 6*(3), 61–70.

World Bank Group. (2020). East Asia and Pacific economic update: Fighting poverty through digital transfer. Retrieved from https://openknowledge.worldbank.org/handle/10986/34421

Dr. Jianzheng Shi is a distinguished scholar in the fields of fintech, blockchain, and digital asset management. Now pursuing a DBA at the Singapore University of Social Sciences, where he also serves as an Adjunct Professor. Dr. Shi holds a PhD by Portfolio in Fintech from the Swiss School of Business Research and a Professional Doctorate in Fintech from the European International University. Dr. Shi's research focuses on the intersection of financial technology, blockchain systems, and digital economics. His work explores the implications of emerging technologies on financial systems, regulatory frameworks, and economic structures. He has published seminal papers on fintech and web3 related. In addition to his academic pursuits, Dr. Shi brings valuable industry experience from his tenure at global technology leaders such as Huawei and Apple. Dr. Shi is actively engaged in the academic community, serving as an editor for Technium Science and a peer reviewer for the *International Journal of Science and Research.*

Dr. Yue Wang is Head of Doctor of Business Administration Programme at the School of Business, Singapore University of Social Sciences (SUSS). She holds a PhD in Marketing, Master's degree in Economics from the National University of Singapore, and a Bachelor's degree in Economics from Huazhong University of Science and Technology. Her interdisciplinary research focuses on the intersection of fintech, blockchain, AI, and their impacts on consumer behavior, business models, and society at large. Dr. Wang's recent work explores the impact of AI on various aspects of business and society, including AI-assisted therapy, blockchain-enabled AI ecosystems, and the use of AI in team dynamics and critical thinking. In her teaching, Dr. Wang is passionate about preparing students for the AI-driven future of business. She has developed and teaches courses on AI and Marketing 5.0, Marketing for the Future Economy, and Contemporary Topics in Business and Management, integrating cutting-edge AI applications into the curriculum. As an AI enthusiast, she has conducted AI workshops at SUSS, been invited to speak on AI-related topics at various institutions, and proactively works with AI start-ups to integrate AI into real-world business applications.

New Cooperation Models Between Banks and Fintech: A Path Toward Digital Transformation in the Emerging Financial Ecosystem

Agata Wolska

> *Digital transformation is no longer a choice for banks; it's a strategic imperative to survive and thrive in the digital age.*
>
> *— Kristalina Georgieva, Managing Director of the International Monetary Fund (IMF)*

1 Introduction

The financial services sector has undergone significant transformation, driven by the rise of financial technology (FinTech) companies and the introduction of new banking regulations such as PSD2. By requiring banks to open their payment services to third parties, PSD2 has fueled competition and paved the way for Open Banking. However, Open Banking is more than just a regulatory outcome–it reflects a fundamental shift in mindset that prioritizes transparency, innovation, and customer empowerment. Recent studies highlight that Open Banking, alongside broader digital transformation efforts, has profoundly reshaped the competitive landscape. These shifts compel banks to rethink their strategies, embrace new technologies, and enhance customer experiences to maintain their competitive edge.

The emergence of innovative players in the financial technology (Fintech) sector has challenged traditional banking models. These players offer digital-first solutions that are faster, more accessible, and more personalized than conventional banking services. As a result, banks and Fintech companies are now viewed not as competitors in a zero-sum game but as potential partners capable of reshaping the financial ecosystem.

The innovations brought by Fintech have disrupted traditional banking models and have opened up new opportunities for financial inclusion, efficiency, and enhanced customer experience (Mărăcine et al., 2020; Sajid et al., 2023; Yin, 2022).

A. Wolska (✉)
Kozminski University, Warsaw, Poland
e-mail: awolska@kozminski.edu.pl

A. Zarifis, X. Cheng (eds.), *Fintech and the Emerging Ecosystems*, Financial Innovation and Technology, https://doi.org/10.1007/978-3-031-83402-8_17

The dilemma, however, lies in the complex nature of this partnership. Banks, with their established infrastructures and regulatory experience, are typically slow to adapt to the rapid pace of technological change. At the same time, Fintech companies, known for their agility and innovation, often lack the deep-rooted customer trust and regulatory know-how that banks possess. This creates a **strategic tension**: how can banks and Fintechs cooperate in ways that leverage their respective strengths while mitigating their weaknesses.

This question is crucial because the integration of banks and Fintechs could be the key to driving the **digital transformation of the financial ecosystem**. By working together, these entities have the potential to create seamless, customer-centric financial services that are both secure and innovative. Cooperation models such as partnerships, acquisitions, or API-driven ecosystems are already emerging, but the challenge remains to find the most effective ways to harness this synergy without compromising on regulatory compliance, cybersecurity, or customer trust.

2 The Beginning of Digital Transformation in the Banking Sector

Digital transformation in banking is not just about modernizing technology but reimagining the entire customer experience.
— David Vélez, CEO of Nubank

A significant observation about the role of technology in modern banking and business sectors is that technology serves as the primary driving force in various business sectors, especially in banks. Implementing new digital technologies not only enhances the efficiency and effectiveness of services but also significantly influences banks' products and delivery methods (European Central Bank, 1999). The utilization of digital technologies for innovation has initiated a series of enhancements, which subsequently affect banks' profitability.

Digital banking emerged with the introduction of web-based services in the 1990s. The 1990s also saw the launch of the first mobile banking services, which used SMS and WAP for basic account services (Łasak & Williams, 2023).

Smartphones, especially after the release of the iPhone in 2007, gained popularity following the financial crisis, providing consumers with internet access and computing power wherever and whenever they wanted. Some key data points to consider include: 97% of adult Americans own a mobile phone, 85% of adult Americans own a smartphone, and 62% of them have purchased the device.[1] Throughout most of that decade, individuals utilized a combination of web and mobile channels without a distinct preference for one over the other. According to the American Bankers Association (ABA), in 2023, 48% of bank customers indicated that their primary

[1] https://www.statista.com/statistics/201183/forecast-of-smartphone-penetration-in-the-us/

channel for accessing their bank account was mobile, 23% indicated the online channel and only 9% would go to a bank branch.[2]

According to Statista Mobile banking usage increased overall between 2019 and 2024 among bank account holders in the United States, though at a slow pace. The share of bank account holders who processed banking matters on their smartphone or tablet was 63% in the first quarter of 2024, 5 percentage points more than in the first half of 2019. While mobile banking usage increased, the popularity of branch banking decreased during the same period.[3]

Digitalization is impacting banks, banking sectors, and the financial system at large. Newly unleashed competitive forces require incumbents to reassess opportunities and threats, strengths and weaknesses, ultimately leading to a transformation of business models (Łasak & Williams, 2023).

The developments in finance after the 2008 Global Financial Crisis (GFC) demonstrate the significant impact of digitalization. The use of new technologies in financial services has transformed the industry, leading to the decentralization of market structures by breaking down traditional banking services. Globally, banks have undergone digital transformation in response to competition from digital-first companies and disruptive Fintechs. This shift has focused on improving personalization, enhancing customer experience, and implementing advanced technologies such as wearables and artificial intelligence (Van De Venn, 2023).

It has also involved adopting innovations like decentralized finance (DeFi) and blockchain, which present new challenges such as data security and regulatory compliance. Digitalization started as a response to inefficiencies but has evolved into a competitive necessity, fundamentally reshaping the global banking landscape.

3 How Fintech Companies Are Transforming Financial Services

> Fintech companies are transforming financial services by leveraging data to deliver personalized and real-time solutions, unlike anything traditional banks can offer.
> — Christine Lagarde, President of the European Central Bank

The rapid evolution of technology has reshaped the financial industry landscape, bringing innovative solutions to meet consumers' changing demands. The Fintech revolution has questioned the role of traditional players in promoting financial inclusion and fostering the growth of alternative financial services and products.

While the regulated traditional banking channel has been engaged in meeting the challenges of inclusive growth, the emergence of technology-driven solutions has the potential to redefine service quality and product delivery through innovative use of technology in the design and delivery of financial products and services (Mehro-

[2] https://www.aba.com/about-us/press-room/press-releases/consumer-survey-banking-methods-2023

[3] https://www.statista.com/statistics/1394885/mobile-banking-penetration-in-us/

tra, 2019). The recent surge in digitization within the banking industry, particularly in payments, alongside the adoption of access and network technologies, has given rise to numerous opportunities for emerging entities such as Fintech.

The notion of Fintech, derived from financial technology, signifies the convergence of finance and information technology, representing a symbiotic relationship between the two domains.

Another definition of Fintech refers to the application of technology to provide financial services. Fintech is a term used to describe technology startups entering the market to compete with traditional banks and financial institutions. These startups offer various services, including mobile payment solutions, crowdfunding platforms, online portfolio management, and international money transfers (Anyfantaki, 2016).

Fintech has emerged as a transformative force, disrupting the traditional banking sector and presenting new opportunities for financial institutions to enhance their offerings and maintain competitiveness (Allen et al., 2021; Saini, 2023). Fintech firms operate very differently than banks. They are skilled at customizing solutions and offering bespoke options based on the sophisticated use of data about their customers.

The growth of Fintech has been driven by several factors, including the widespread adoption of smartphones, the rise of cloud computing, and the increasing use of artificial intelligence and machine learning (Allen et al., 2021). Fintech companies have leveraged these technologies to develop user-friendly, efficient, and cost-effective financial services that challenge the dominance of traditional banks (Allen et al., 2021; Srinivasan & Rajarajeswari, 2021).

During the COVID-19 pandemic, there has been a rapid increase in the use of Fintech as people seek out contactless and digital financial solutions. This acceleration of digitalization has brought about significant changes in consumer behavior. Consumers had to quickly adapt to digital channels for financial transactions and interactions with financial service providers, a shift that would have otherwise taken years. The rapid growth of e-commerce has led to the need for financial solutions to meet the demands of online consumers, particularly during and after the pandemic. In response to these changes, banks and technology firms have been developing new financial services to cater to the needs of digital customers.

Before the pandemic, banks had already been increasing their IT expenditure and investing heavily in new technologies to adapt to digitalization. Banks view new technology as a way to enhance service quality and operational efficiency while also creating new revenue streams. However, the rise of new competitors, particularly technology companies such as Fintech and BigTech, implies that market competition and structures will keep evolving. Therefore, to compete effectively, traditional banks must continue embracing digitalization's transformational impact. Fintech firms have been able to design specialized digital platforms (Mărăcine et al., 2020), reach previously underserved customer segments, improve customer selection and profiling, reduce operating costs, and optimize business processes. Fintech encompasses new mobile payments, virtual currencies (e.g., Bitcoin), advanced transactions, B2C and B2B banking, and innovations in investment funds and database management (CB Insights, 2019). Banks need to continuously adapt and use digital products to remain competitive and relevant in the technology-driven financial landscape (Sajid et al., 2023).

Banks have a choice to make—they can either embrace technological advancements to connect with a wider market and service providers, or they can stick to their current approach by focusing on developing competitive solutions for all customer and product segments while restricting access to their systems.

The emergence of Fintech is reshaping the financial industry, bringing forth both opportunities and challenges for traditional banks. To succeed in this changing landscape, banks can enhance their value, elevate customer experience, and maintain their competitive advantage by embracing technological advancements and establishing strategic partnerships with Fintech companies (Brandl & Hornuf, 2020; Nambiar & Bolar, 2022).

Cooperation models between banks and Fintech firms have become a pivotal strategy. A significant model is the partnership strategy, which allows banks to utilize Fintech capabilities in various sectors such as payments, lending, and wealth management. Traditional banks have acknowledged the significance of adopting Fintech and have commenced partnering with Fintech startups to elevate their services. These alliances enable banks to access innovative technologies, enhance customer experience, and improve operational efficiency.

4 The Rise of Blockchain-Enabled Payment Solutions in Traditional Finance

Traditional banks and financial institutions are increasingly exploring the potential of blockchain technology to create innovative payment solutions. For example, Visa's B2B Connect, launched in 2019, is a blockchain-enabled platform that facilitates cross-border transactions between banks without the need for a card. Similarly, Mastercard's Send utilizes a private blockchain to enable near real-time cross-border payment transfers between various payment accounts worldwide. These initiatives demonstrate that traditional financial players are embracing blockchain technology to streamline payment processes, reduce costs, and enhance the efficiency of international transactions.[4]

The financial sector has recognized the significant potential of blockchain technology to revolutionize various business functions, including finance (Weerawarna et al., 2023). Blockchain's ability to provide secure, immutable, decentralized, and transparent data services has made it an attractive technology for financial institutions seeking to address dynamic changes and meet the demands of modern distributed industries. By implementing blockchain-based solutions, traditional banking systems can gain a competitive advantage in securing transactions at a lower cost compared to traditional methods (Weerawarna et al., 2023). Many banks have started to cooperate with FinTech companies, invest in blockchain-

[4] https://www.bvnk.com/blog/blockchain-cross-border-payments

based startups, or even develop their own blockchain-based platforms to experiment with this emerging technology (Weerawarna et al., 2023; Wu & Duan, 2019). For example, Santander partners with Ripple to bring certainty and speed to international payments.

"We want to be at the forefront of the merging of finance and technology," explained One Pay FX Chief Technology Officer Ed Metzger. "But our innovation is always customer-led. Customers told us that the international payments process could be better. So, we partnered with Ripple to explore how blockchain could make transactions faster, cheaper, and more transparent."[5]

Blockchain technology can revolutionize various aspects of the financial industry, from cross-border payments to securities trading and asset management. The unique features of blockchain, such as its decentralized, secure, and transparent nature, make it an attractive solution for financial institutions seeking to optimize their operations and offer more efficient services to their customers. As blockchain continues gaining traction in the financial sector, we expect to see more traditional banks and financial institutions embracing this innovative technology to streamline their operations, enhance customer experiences, and maintain their competitive edge in the rapidly evolving financial landscape (Polyviou et al., 2019; Varma et al., 2022; Weerawarna et al., 2023).

5 The Role of Open Banking and Regulatory Frameworks in Shaping the Future of Finance

> Open banking is a game-changer for financial inclusion, offering individuals and businesses access to a broader range of services and creating new opportunities for underserved populations.
>
> —Charlotte Crosswell, CEO of Innovate Finance

The rapid growth of e-commerce has underscored the need for financial solutions that meet online shoppers' expectations, particularly during and after the pandemic. Furthermore, the implementation of the PSD2 regulation in 2015 paved the way for Open Banking, enabling third-party providers to offer financial services on sales platforms. Integrating purchase and payment transactions on a single platform without requiring access to a bank has become increasingly important. In response to these demands, Embedded Finance and BaaS (Banking as a Service) have emerged as innovative ways to provide financial services.

The second Payment Services Directive (PSD2) is a regulatory framework for payment services, which was approved by the European Parliament and European Council in late 2015 and came into force on 13 January 2016. Market participants

[5] https://ripple.com/insights/santander-partners-with-ripple-to-bring-certainty-and-speed-to-international-payments/

needed to comply with the majority of the requirements set out in the legislation on January 13, 2018.[6]

PSD2 aims to further integrate and support an efficient EU payments market while promoting competition in an environment witnessing the emergence of new players such as FinTech startups and a new generation of payment products and services. Regulators anticipate that PSD2 will drive innovation in the sector, leading to increased transparency, enhanced security, improved service quality, and more favorable user pricing.

The introduction of PSD2 in Europe was motivated by the need to address challenges in the payment market brought by its predecessor, the Payment Services Directive. The PSD2 framework facilitated a financial data-sharing economy, with the philosophy of leveling the playing field by allowing new players (Fintech) in the financial market. This resulted in heightened competition, potentially leading to lower consumer prices and fostering innovation.

PSD2 has provided open banking with a stable regulatory framework. It has mandated that banks must provide access to payment data for AISPs and PISPs through a secure interface. The additional services offered include giving consumers a comprehensive overview of their financial situation and analyzing their spending patterns, expenses, and financial needs.[7]

PSD2 has set up a regulatory framework to support the Open Banking initiative in Europe, with a specific emphasis on payment services and data access.

Open Banking does not have a legal definition, but its core principle involves banks sharing customer data with other parties with the customer's permission. It is a business model characterized by banks sharing and using permission data with third-party developers and firms to develop applications and services. Its core philosophy is based on the sharing of customer data by banks with other parties with the customer's permission. Open Banking is understood as a business model featuring the following characteristics:

> Open banking is defined as the sharing and leveraging of customer-permissioned data by banks with third-party developers and firms to build applications and services[8]

Other doctrinal texts have similarly referred to Open Banking as "*A collaborative model in which banking data is shared through APIs between two or more unaffiliated parties to deliver.*"[9]

> Open banking is the ability to securely share your financial accounts' data to access innovative financial experiences. Traditionally, only you and your bank could access your

---

[6] https://www.fca.org.uk/firms/payment-services-regulations-e-money-regulations

[7] https://ec.europa.eu/commission/presscorner/detail/de/qanda_23_3544

[8] Basel Committee on Banking Supervision, Report on open banking and application programming interfaces, 2019, available at: https://www.bis.org/bcbs/publ/d486.htm, last visited 16 March, 2023, p. 19.

[9] Laura Brodsky and Liz Oakes, Data sharing and open banking, Mckinsey & Company, 2017, available at: https://www.mckinsey.com/industries/financial-services/our-insights/data-sharing-and-open-banking, last visited 16 March, 2023.

> financial data. Open banking allows the customer to share that data with another financial service provider—either a different financial institution or third party, and empowers you to use your own data for your own benefit. Third-party providers can include various Fintechs, currency exchanges, merchants, and other digital platforms.[10](Mastercard)

> Open banking presents an entirely different model. In this approach, customer data is controlled by the customer, who can then share this data with various financial institutions or even nonfinancial organizations. This sharing typically takes place through APIs (Application Programming Interfaces). Open banking is designed to remove traditional limitations by giving customers more options and flexibility in financial services. (Zeynalova, 2024)

Open Banking is a collaborative model in which banking data is shared through APIs between unaffiliated parties to enhance capabilities and market experiences. The term Open Banking was officially coined by the Competition and Markets Authority (CMA) in the United Kingdom in 2017. This came after the CMA ordered the nine largest banks in the United Kingdom to adopt standardized APIs to offer improved products and pricing (Quiñones, 2024). Open Banking is largely about creating ecosystems and using data intelligently to deliver new products to customers and encourage competition. The primary goals of regulatory frameworks that delineate open banking typically involve the promotion of innovation and the cultivation of competition, thereby leading to the emergence of novel products and services offered at competitive price points, all to the advantage of consumers. Open Banking presents a completely different model. In this approach, customer data are controlled by the customer, who can then share this data with various financial institutions. Open Banking has the potential to drive innovation, pushing major banks to improve their services and compete with smaller and newer banks. This benefits consumers by potentially lowering costs and providing access to better technology and customer service.

Prior to the introduction of Open Banking, financial institutions traditionally held exclusive control over customer data within a closed infrastructure. This control allowed them to use the data to create and develop financial products and services. The shift to Open Banking means that banks need to create Application Programming Interfaces (APIs) that allow third parties to access customer data, so they can offer financial and related services. This change challenges banks to move beyond their usual ways of working and face increased competition. The introduction of Open banking has given consumers the power to manage and access their financial information across different platforms, improving their experience with a more seamless and personalized approach.

Banks should leverage the potential of open banking APIs to partner with Fintech companies. In such a situation, customers can access a unified solution, leading to greater satisfaction. Moreover, by collaborating with Fintech firms, banks can better cater to specific customer interests.

[10] https://www.mastercard.com/news/perspectives/2024/open-banking-101/

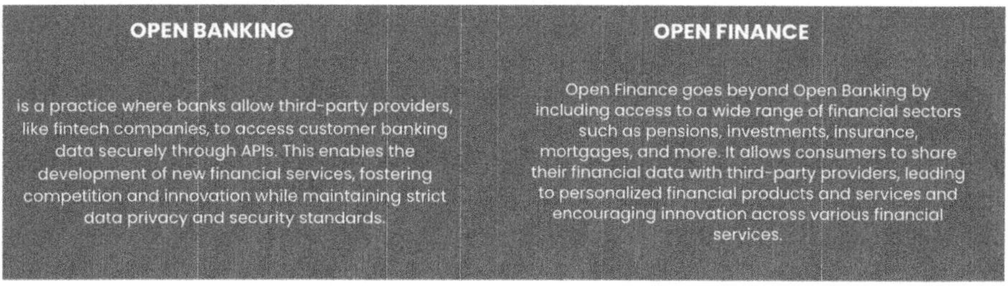

Fig. 1 Open banking and open finance (own source)

6 Unlocking Financial Innovation with Fintech and Open Finance

Open Finance is the next step after Open Banking. It builds on the principles of Open Banking and the PSD2 regulation to enable the sharing of financial information for services beyond banking. Unlike Open Banking, Open Finance includes access to sectors such as pensions, investments, insurance, mortgages, and more. This allows consumers to securely share their financial data with third-party providers, leading to the development of personalized financial products and services and fostering innovation in various financial areas (Fig. 1).

The promise of open finance lies in its potential to enhance customer data access, sharing, portability, and interoperability, thereby leveling the informational playing field and fostering greater competition between incumbent financial institutions and a new breed of Fintech disruptors (Awrey & Macey, 2022). By harnessing the power of new platform technology, open finance seeks to revolutionize the financial services industry, offering consumers more choices and better solutions for their financial needs, from fast payments to borrowing, investing, and budget management (Awrey & Macey, 2022).

7 The Platform Revolution: The Emergence of Sharing Economy

> The platform revolution is reshaping industries by creating new business models that leverage the power of network effects and data sharing.
> — Geoffrey G. Parker, Author of "Platform Revolution"

The sharing economy, a fundamental part of the platform revolution, has had a significant impact on various sectors such as mobility, hospitality, and financial services. Companies like Uber and Airbnb have disrupted their industries by using digital technologies, introducing new market coordination methods, and taking advantage of peer-to-peer services. These sharing economy platforms have shown the potential to transform traditional industries by decentralizing products and services. The sharing economy is an economic model that promotes cooperation rather than competition (Parker et al., 2016).

Alongside the growth of the sharing economy, the financial services industry has undergone a transformative shift driven by the emergence of financial technology companies. This digital disruption, often called the Fintech revolution, has fundamentally changed the retail banking model (Ferrari, 2016). Fintech firms have introduced innovative services, such as peer-to-peer lending, robo-advisory platforms, and cross-border trade finance solutions, challenging the traditional banking paradigm. As Bill Gates famously stated, "Banking is necessary, banks are not,"[11] this phrase encapsulates the profound changes occurring in the financial sector. The technological advancements underpinning the Fintech revolution have enabled the digitization of financial services, allowing for the development of new market structures, business models, and customer experiences. The rise of Banking as a Service has further blurred the boundaries between traditional financial institutions and Fintech players, as banks now offer their infrastructure and capabilities to third-party service providers. Consequently, the financial landscape is being reshaped, with incumbent banks facing increased competition from agile, technology-driven Fintech firms that cater to the evolving needs of consumers.

Banking as a Service (BaaS) expands the range of financial services available to customers, enhancing transparency and fostering competition in the financial services industry. This model benefits traditional banks and third-party companies, enabling them to deliver top-tier services to their clientele.

Open banking APIs are crucial for BaaS (banking as a service), which falls under the broader concept of open banking. With BaaS, banks open their APIs to Fintech firms, facilitating the offering of banking services embedded within the Fintech companies' financial products. This goes beyond simply sharing data—BaaS encompasses the core functionality of financial services. Third-party firms can utilize existing banking products or create new financial instruments tailored to their business needs. They leverage APIs to tailor banking information and infrastructure for specific purposes (Fig. 2).

8 From Traditional Banks to Embedded Finance

> Payments and lending will continue to be the largest embedded financial services, but the growth of adjacent value-added services, including insurance, tax, and accounting, will bolster them.
>
> —Bain & Company (2022)

The promise of embedded finance extends beyond the immediate benefits to stakeholders. Indeed, Fintech has given rise to new forms of currencies and new

[11] Bill Gates stated, "**Banking is necessary, banks are not**," in an interview published in 1994 in the book "*The Road Ahead*."

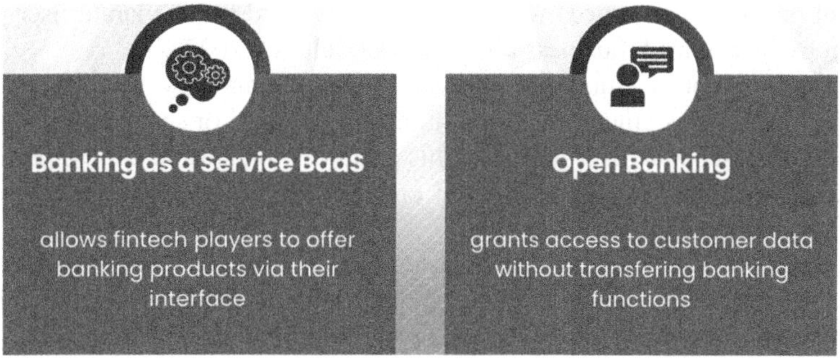

Fig. 2 Banking as a service and open banking (own source)

ways of allocating capital, managing risks, and carrying out financial transactions, leading to a digital transformation of the financial sector (Alexander & Karametaxas, 2021). This transformation provides consumers with better-targeted services and lower prices, facilitates access to credit for small and medium-sized enterprises, enhances the productivity of traditional financial institutions, and, more fundamentally, offers new possibilities of including more individuals and enterprises in the financial system (Alexander & Karametaxas, 2021).

The embedded finance revolution is primarily about the smooth movement of money that keeps our society functioning. The barriers that slow it down are disappearing (Sieber & Guibaud, 2022). The rise of embedded finance represents a new era, not only for banking transactions but also for how consumers and businesses build and manage relationships with financial services more broadly. Embedded finance improves upon Fintech because companies successfully employing embedded finance start with a significant customer base (Sieber & Guibaud, 2022).

According to Bain & Company, financial services embedded into e-commerce and other software platforms accounted for $2.6 trillion, or nearly 5%, of total US financial transactions in 2021, and by 2026, it is projected to exceed $7 trillion, according to our research.[12]

Bain & Company defines embedded finance as a nonfinancial software platform providing an adjacent financial service, for which it takes some degree of economic ownership. This allows the platform's customers to take advantage of a value-added offering within the native customer journey (Bain & Company, 2022).

Embedded finance, an emerging trend in the financial services industry, offers a compelling value proposition for various stakeholders. As per Deloitte, embedded finance utilizes technology to create a digital ecosystem where customers can access

[12] Embedded Finance: What It Takes to Prosper in the New Value Chain, *2022 Bain & Company, Inc.*

financial products or services without being redirected to a separate user journey relevant to their non-FS business transactions (Deloitte, 2022).[13]

As Deloitte notes, embedded finance utilizes technology to create a digital ecosystem where customers can access financial products or services without being redirected to a separate user journey. This seamless integration can be particularly beneficial for small and medium-sized enterprises, which often face barriers to accessing traditional financial services.

According to VISA, embedded finance offers a win-win-win scenario for three parties. Providers benefit from a low-cost distribution channel, enablers tap into the growing trend for convenience and simplicity, distributors create better engagement on their platforms, and end-users gain instant access to contextualized financial services automatically and in one place.[14]

Embedded finance has emerged as a transformative trend in the financial services industry, offering a win-win-win scenario for providers, enablers, distributors, and end-users (Capponi et al., 2023). Providers benefit from a low-cost distribution channel, tapping into the growing consumer demand for convenience and simplicity. Enablers, such as Fintech companies, are able to leverage this trend to create innovative financial products and services that are seamlessly integrated into the customer's primary user journey (Mehrotra, 2019).

A perfect example is embedded payments within a retailer's mobile app that allow consumers to make instant, contactless purchases with digital wallets or embedded lending products, such as Klarna or digital private label credit cards, quickly becoming a common practice.

For distributors, embedded finance enhances customer engagement by offering contextual financial services directly within their platforms or applications. This improves the user experience and generates additional revenue streams for the distributor. Finally, end-users gain instant access to personalized financial services, eliminating the need to navigate separate user journeys or platforms. The rise of embedded finance is driven by the exponential facilitation of the value chain proposition for customers, as argued by Kaal (Anagnostopoulos, 2018). The conventional methods of performing financial services are being challenged by more modern, technology-empowered channels that better meet consumer expectations. The economic business model has shifted to a platform-based model. The power of customer connection is shifting from banks to the brands offering embedded services. This presents a challenge for traditional banks (Łasak & Williams, 2023, 58).

Providers like financial institutions can leverage embedded finance as a low-cost distribution channel to reach a wider customer base (Awrey & Macey, 2022). Enablers, the technology companies that facilitate the integration of financial services, can tap into the growing demand for convenience and simplicity. Distributors,

[13] Embedded Finance Strategic regulatory considerations for financial services firm, Deloitte, 2022.

[14] Embedded Finance, what are the emerging opportunities in this new value chain, VISA, 2023

the platforms that embed financial services, can create better customer engagement by offering contextualized financial products and services automatically and in one place. Ultimately, end-users, the customers, gain instant access to a seamless and integrated financial experience, enjoying the benefits of increased accessibility and convenience (Feyen et al., 2021). Some examples:

- Stripe enables platforms to integrate financial services, allowing their business customers to easily send, receive, and store funds.
- Shopify is expanding its partnership with Stripe to power Shopify Balance, a business account designed for independent businesses and entrepreneurs.
- Stripe is providing standardized access to banking capabilities via APIs by expanding its bank partner network to include Goldman Sachs Bank USA and Evolve Bank & Trust as US partners.
- Stripe is expanding its bank partner network with Citibank N.A. and Barclays as global expansion partners.[15]

9 Securing the Fintech Ecosystem: Open Banking, Authentication, and Safe Transactions

The Fintech industry has experienced rapid growth and innovation, revolutionizing the way financial services are delivered. However, this expansion has also brought increased concerns about cybersecurity and the need to ensure the safety and security of financial transactions (Arner et al., 2017). One of the key challenges facing the Fintech ecosystem is the need to balance technological innovation with robust security measures to protect consumer data and financial assets.

Fintech companies must adopt advanced authentication methods, such as biometric authentication, multi-factor authentication, and blockchain-based identity management systems to mitigate these risks. These approaches can help to ensure that only authorized individuals can access sensitive financial information and conduct transactions, reducing the risk of fraud and unauthorized access.

Ensuring regulatory compliance is a critical aspect of safeguarding the Fintech ecosystem. Regulatory bodies around the world have implemented various guidelines and standards to address the unique security and privacy challenges posed by Fintech (Berkmen et al., 2019; Gai et al., 2018; Prastyanti et al., 2023).

Open Banking allows banks and financial sectors to easily access customers' financial data easily, revolutionizing the industry. It also provides customers with convenient cloud access to a wide range of financial services from various providers. Storing sensitive services and data on cloud servers has its pros and cons. It can facilitate fine-grained access to services and data anywhere and anytime, supporting the open banking system. However, data privacy and secrecy are a challenge.

[15] https://stripe.com/en-pl/newsroom/news/treasury

Therefore, efficient access control is necessary to protect cloud-hosted sensitive financial data from unauthorized customers (Riad & Elhoseny, 2022).

Fintech companies must comply with regulations such as the General Data Protection Regulation in Europe, the Payment Card Industry Data Security Standard for payment card transactions, anti-money laundering, and Know Your Customer requirements. This is essential for maintaining trust and operating within the legal framework.

The regulatory trends are all aimed at ensuring security while providing a seamless banking experience for customers. In addition, with the move toward open banking, customers and third-party service providers will have more access to and control over their information than ever before. As a result, it will be increasingly critical for banks, Fintech firms, and non-banking institutions to adapt to this change. Expectations to improve data usability and transparency for customers will override the traditional approach of retaining as much proprietary information as possible in-house. AI-powered biometric systems enhance transaction security by using unique biological traits, such as fingerprints and facial recognition. Securing the Fintech ecosystem is crucial for the continued growth and adoption of innovative financial services. By addressing the challenges of open banking, authentication, and secure transactions, the industry can build a more trustworthy and resilient financial ecosystem that benefits both consumers and financial service providers (Mittal & Gupta, 2023; Saini, 2023).

10 Conclusions

The convergence of Fintech and Open Finance is unleashing a wave of financial innovation that is reshaping the industry. By harnessing technology, embracing open platforms, and fostering financial inclusion, the future of finance holds the promise of a more accessible, personalized, and equitable financial landscape. Banks need to learn to adapt to remain relevant in the new hierarchy. Fintech companies need to shape the financial products that the consumer-facing businesses will ultimately deliver. Once financial services can be delivered through a company or product consumers use every day, there is a tremendous opportunity to reach a greater number of people than ever before. There is already evidence from early success stories that more progress is possible. The emergence of embedded finance represents a significant shift in the financial services industry, offering a range of benefits for providers, enablers, distributors, and end-users. Beyond the immediate advantages, embedded finance also holds the potential to drive financial inclusion, empowering previously underserved populations and contributing to broader economic development. However, the rapid pace of innovation in this space necessitates a careful and balanced approach to regulation, ensuring that the benefits of embedded finance are realized responsibly and sustainably. The rise of embedded finance is also closely linked to the broader trend of financial inclusion enabled by Fintech innovations. Digital transformation has democratized financial services, providing underserved and unbanked populations with affordable and accessible financial products (Salampasis & Mention, 2018). This has the potential to drive inclusive economic growth and move toward a more equitable society (Salampasis & Mention, 2018).

The emergence of Fintech and open finance is the key to unlocking a more inclusive, equitable, and democratized financial system that empowers individuals and enterprises to thrive in the global digital economy (Alexander & Karametaxas, 2021; Awrey & Macey, 2022; Mehrotra, 2019; Salampasis & Mention, 2018).

References

Alexander, K., & Karametaxas, X E. (2021, April 2). Digital transformation and financial inclusion. *Informa*, 273–290. https://doi.org/10.4324/9780429325670-15

Allen, F., Gu, X., & Jagtiani, J. (2021). A survey of fintech research and policy discussion. *Review of Corporate Finance, 1*(3–4), 259–339. Available at: https://doi.org/10.1561/114.00000007. Now Publishers

Anagnostopoulos, I. (2018, November 1). Fintech and regtech: Impact on regulators and banks. *Journal of Economics and Business, 100*, 7–25. https://doi.org/10.1016/j.jeconbus.2018.07.003. Elsevier BV

Anyfantaki, S. (2016). The evolution of financial technology (FinTech). *Economic Bulletin, 44*, 47–62. https://EconPapers.repec.org/RePEc:bog:econbl:y:2016:i:44:p:47

Arner, D W., Barberis, J., & Buckley, R P. (2017, January 1). FinTech and RegTech in a nutshell, and the future in a sandbox. *Research Foundation Briefs*. https://doi.org/10.2139/ssrn.3088303. RELX Group.

Awrey, D., & Macey, J. (2022, January 1). The promise and perils of open finance. https://doi.org/10.2139/ssrn.4045640. RELX Group.

Bain & Company. (2022). *Embedded finance: What it takes to prosper in the new value chain*. https://www.bain.com/contentassets/a5ad904e61324de88b62707de879f174/bain_brief_embedded-finance.pdf

Berkmen, P., Beaton, K., Gershenson, D., Granado, J. A. D., Ishi, K., Kim, M., Kopp, E., & Rousset, M. (2019, January 1). Fintech in Latin America and the Caribbean: Stocktaking. *International Monetary Fund, 19*(71), 1–1. https://doi.org/10.5089/9781498303248.001

Brandl, B., & Hornuf, L. (2020). Where did FinTechs come from, and where do they go? The transformation of the financial industry in Germany after digitalization. *Frontiers in Artificial Intelligence, 3*. Available at: https://doi.org/10.3389/frai.2020.00008. Frontiers Media.

Capponi, A., Iyengar, G., & Sethuraman, J. (2023, January 1). Decentralized finance: Protocols, risks, and governance. *Foundations and Trends® in Privacy and Security, 5*(3), 144–188. https://doi.org/10.1561/3300000036. Now Publishers.

CB Insights. (2019). *FinTech trends to watch in 2019*. Research report. https://www.cbinsights.com/research/report/fintech-trends-2019/

Deloitte. (2022). *The ecosystem imperative: Embedded finance—customer relationships and value web dynamics*. https://www2.deloitte.com/content/dam/Deloitte/us/Documents/finance-transformation/us-the-ecosystem-imperative-embedded-finance.pdf

European Central Bank. (1999). *The effects of technology on the EU banking systems*. European Central Bank. https://www.ecb.europa.eu/pub/pdf/other/techbnken.pdf

Ferrari, R. (2016, March 18). FinTech impact on retail banking—From a universal banking model to banking verticalization. In S. Chishti & J. Barberis (Eds.), *The FinTech book: The financial technology handbook for investors, entrepreneurs and visionaries* (pp. 248–252). Wiley. https://doi.org/10.1002/9781119218906.ch65

Feyen, E., Frost, J., Gambacorta, L., Natarajan, H., & Saal, M. (2021, July 13). Fintech and the digital transformation of financial services: implications for market structure and public policy. Federal Reserve Bank of St. Louis. https://www.bis.org/publ/bppdf/bispap117.htm

Gai, K., Qiu, M., & Sun, X. (2018, February 1). A survey on FinTech. *Journal of Network and Computer Applications, 103*, 262–273. https://doi.org/10.1016/j.jnca.2017.10.011. Elsevier.

Łasak, P., & Williams, J. (2023). *Digital Transformation and the Economics of Banking* (1st ed.). Routledge/W. W. Norton.

Mărăcine, V., Voican, O., & Scarlat, E. (2020). The digital transformation and disruption in business models of the banks under the impact of FinTech and BigTech. *Proceedings of the International Conference on Business Excellence, 14*(1), 294–305. Available at: https://doi.org/10.2478/picbe-2020-0028. De Gruyter Open.

Mehrotra, A. (2019, April 1). Financial inclusion through FinTech—A case of lost focus. In *2019 international conference on automation, computational and technology management (ICACTM)*. https://doi.org/10.1109/icactm.2019.8776857

Mittal, P., & Gupta, S. (2023, June 25). FinTech and digital finance: Foes or friends after COVID-19 pandemic? *Business, Management and Economics Research, 9*, 13–21. https://doi.org/10.32861/bmer.91.13.21

Nambiar, K. B., & Bolar, K. (2022). Factors influencing customer preference of cardless technology over the card for cash withdrawals: an extended technology acceptance model. *Journal of Financial Services Marketing, 28*(1), 58–73. Available at: https://doi.org/10.1057/s41264-022-00139-y. Palgrave Macmillan.

Parker, G., Van Alstyne, M., & Choudary, S. (2016). *Platform revolution: How markets are transforming the economy and how to make them work for you*. W. W. Norton.

Polyviou, A., Velanas, P., & Soldatos, J. (2019, October 25). Blockchain technology: Financial sector applications beyond cryptocurrencies. In *Proceedings of the 3rd annual decentralized conference on blockchain and cryptocurrency*. https://doi.org/10.3390/proceedings2019028007

Prastyanti, R. A., Rezi, R., & Rahayu, I. (2023, June 27). Ethical Fintech is a new way of banking. *Kontigensi Jurnal Ilmiah Manajemen, 11*(1), 255–260. https://doi.org/10.56457/jimk.v11i1.353

Quiñones, J. D. S. (2024). *Rethinking the right to data portability in the transition from open banking to open finance in the EU*. Editora Dialéctica.

Riad, K., & Elhoseny, M. (2022). A blockchain-based key-revocation access control for open banking. *Wireless Communications and Mobile Computing, 2022*, 1–14. https://doi.org/10.1155/2022/3200891

Saini, A. (2023). The Fintech revolution and the future of banking and financial institutions: A quantitative investigation. *Psychology and Education, 55*(1). Available at: https://doi.org/10.48047/pne.2018.55.1.53.

Sajid, R., Ayub, H., Malik, B. F., & Ellahi, A. (2023). The role of Fintech on bank risk-taking: Mediating role of bank's operating efficiency. *Human Behavior and Emerging Technologies, 2023*, 1–11. Available at: https://doi.org/10.1155/2023/7059307. Wiley.

Salampasis, D., & Mention, A. (2018, January 1). FinTech: Harnessing innovation for financial inclusion. In D. L. K. Chuen & R. Deng (Eds.), Handbook *of blockchain, digital finance, and inclusion* (pp. 451–461). Elsevier. https://doi.org/10.1016/b978-0-12-812282-2.00018-8

Sieber, S., & Guibaud, S. (2022). *Embedded finance* (1st ed.). Wiley.

Srinivasan, K., & Rajarajeswari, S. (2021). Financial technology in Indian finance market. *International Journal of Engineering and Management Research, 11*(2), 206–211. Available at: https://doi.org/10.31033/ijemr.11.2.29.

Van De Venn, P. (2023). The evolution of digital banking. *Journal of Digital Banking, 7*(4), 365. https://doi.org/10.69554/uloc7565

Varma, P., Nijjer, S., Sood, K., Grima, S., & Rupeika-Apoga, R. (2022, September 20). Thematic analysis of financial technology (Fintech) influence on the banking industry. *Risks, 10*(10), 186. https://doi.org/10.3390/risks10100186. Multidisciplinary Digital Publishing Institute.

Weerawarna, R., Miah, S. J., & Shao, X. (2023, February 9). Emerging advances of blockchain technology in finance: a content analysis. *Personal and Ubiquitous Computing, 27*(4), 1495–1508. https://doi.org/10.1007/s00779-023-01712-5. Springer.

Wu, B., & Duan, T. (2019, March 1). The application of blockchain technology in financial markets. *Journal of Physics: Conference Series, 1176*, 042094. https://doi.org/10.1088/1742-6596/1176/4/042094. IOP.

Yin, M. (2022). Fintech opportunities for commercial banks under the COVID-19. Available at: https://doi.org/10.23977/msied2022.010.

Zeynalova, A. (2024). From closed banking to open banking: Risks and opportunities. *Journal of Applied Business Taxation and Economics Research, 3*(3), 303–316. https://doi.org/10.54408/jabter.v3i3.278

Agata Wolska has extensive banking experience, having worked in banks and Fintech companies since 2004, including US Bank, Bank of Valletta, Vodeno, Ebury UK Ltd, Raiffeisen Bank, and HSBC. Throughout her career, she has successfully led numerous digital transformation initiatives, implementing innovative strategies and advanced technologies that have significantly contributed to the growth of the companies she has worked with. Agata is currently pursuing her doctoral studies at Kozminski University in Poland, focusing on the impact of Open Banking on various economies.

Fintech, Banks and Mobile Operators: Interplays for Increasing Financial Inclusion

Charles Bélanger, Arvind Ashta, and Geri Mason

1 Introduction: The Raison D'être of Fintech

The business model of many high-technology industries, including telecoms, profits from network effects, such as positive consumption (Birke, 2009) and production externalities, commonly called network externalities (Economides, 1996; McIntyre & Srinivasan, 2017). These network externalities are common on platforms with two-sided markets (Eisenmann et al., 2006). The concept is fairly easy to understand. If only one person has a phone, they cannot telephone anybody. With an increase in the number of people with phones, the phone's utility has increased for the first person. However, with competition coming in, telecom operators can either fragment the market or encourage interoperability.

In an inter-operability market, mobile telephone operators are highly susceptible to churn (Wieland, 2007) and are, therefore, interested in promoting customer loyalty. To increase loyalty, telecoms introduce additional value-added services to influence customer satisfaction, trust, commitment, corporate image, and switching costs (Kaur & Soch, 2012). An example of increased value addition that would lead to high switching costs is to provide more services that are exclusive to the platform and which would fragment the market for the extra products while retaining interoperability for the basic product (Ashta & Bélanger, 2024; Babus & Parlatore, 2022; Chen & Duffie, 2021). For telecoms, one example is to provide

C. Bélanger
Burgundy School of Business, Dijon, France

A. Ashta (✉)
BHAI: Building Humane Advances and Institutions, Toulouse, France

G. Mason
Seattle Pacific University, Seattle, WA, USA
e-mail: geri@spu.edu

A. Zarifis, X. Cheng (eds.), *Fintech and the Emerging Ecosystems*, Financial Innovation and Technology, https://doi.org/10.1007/978-3-031-83402-8_18

financial services like mobile payments (Yeboah-Asiamah et al., 2018). Beyond this, it nowadays also includes services such as games, news, educational services, job adverts, shopping, tele-doctor, and farming information (Safaricom, 2024). Such extra services are in several cases provided by Fintech partners that have a Business-to-Customers (B2C) model.

The provision of mobile payment services had an unintended effect: it reached the financially excluded in rural areas, the old and the poor, who have mobile phones but may not have a bank account and promoted financial inclusion by reaching new markets (Dong et al., 2019). Aspects of financial inclusion included increased savings, borrowing, and receiving remittances among people experiencing poverty (Munyegera & Matsumoto, 2018; Ouma et al., 2017). It has become a classic example of a disruptive innovation (Christensen, 2006; Lee et al., 2023). Mobile money addressed affordability and access, reducing institutional voids in resource-constrained environments (David-West et al., 2019).

With time, many of the mobile financial service providers became significant players in their own right, such as Alipay (Ant Financial), JD Finance, Baidu, and WeChatPay (Tencent) in China (Bu et al., 2023; Wang & Chang, 2018). They benefitted from their own network externalities: the availability of many complementary services led to the impression that mobile banking is easy to use (Ewe et al., 2015). Along with mobile-money-backed players, we have seen independent Fintech players that have grown fast, such as the Swedish Fintech company Klarna (taken over by Paypal), N26 in Germany, Revolut in the UK, among many others. The market capitalization of Revolut is estimated at $40 billion, more than that of Société Générale's market capitalization (Quinio & Levingston, 2024).

While financial inclusion is vital for reducing poverty and inequality (Mishra, 2014), there is a limit to increasing financial inclusion in developing countries through B2C Fintech because of a lack of infrastructure. Figures 1 and 2 compare

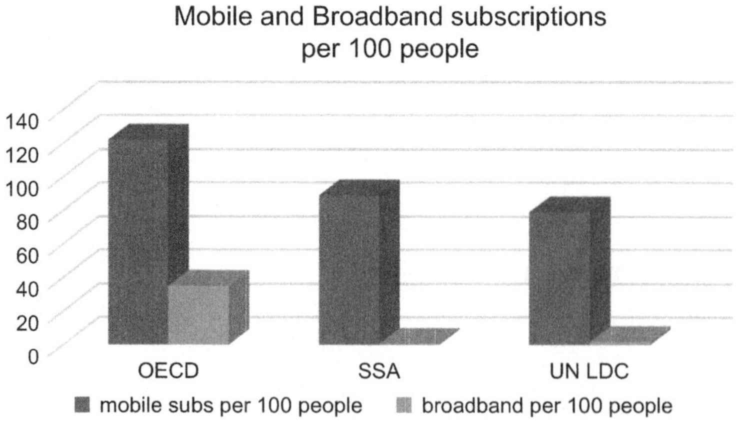

Fig. 1 Mobile and broad Band subscriptions (based on data from World Bank (2022))

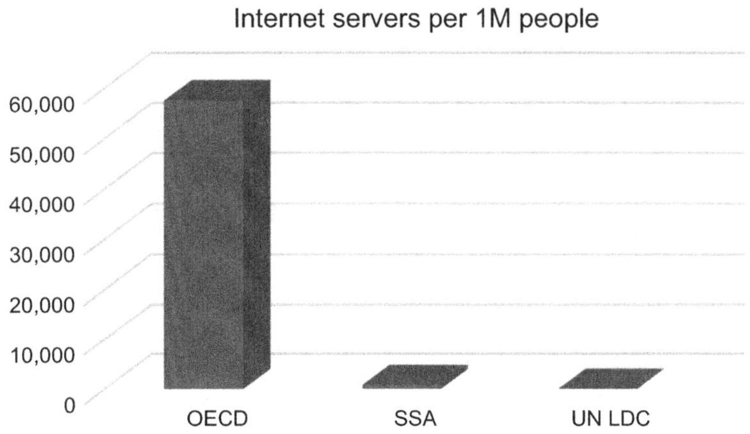

Fig. 2 Internet servers availability (based on data from World Bank (2022))

digital access in OECD countries to that of Sub-Saharan Africa and all countries classified as Less Developed Countries by the UN (World Bank, 2022). While broadband access and mobile subscriptions are increasing in SSA and other microfinance markets, it is by no means comparable to OECD country digital access. In particular, the lack of secure internet servers poses additional risk to digital financial transactions. In a time when digitization is accelerating, security concerns should be added to our care for the marginalized and financially excluded.

The objective of this study is to understand what is happening in the Fintech and adjacent markets (telecoms, financial services) and how this may impact financial access. In the next section, we review the literature on the growth of Fintechs and these adjacent markets and fine-tune our research question. We then provide a brief note on our qualitative research methodology, before providing our findings and discussing these. The conclusion opens up the subject to further inquiry.

2 Literature Review

Researchers have been looking at the risks created by the growth in Fintech, in particular on the financial services industry. They have also been speculating on the possible interplay between Fintech, the financial service providers and telcos.

Fintech creates growth risks. The growth in size and number of these Fintech players leads to new types of risks: the disruption of banks and the closing of many of the Fintech payers who do not innovate rapidly (Bu et al., 2023). We have seen Klarna's valuation fall from $35 billion to $6.7 billion (Quinio & Levingston, 2024) and that of Affirm (another big BNPL provider in the US) from $45 billion to $9.5 billion in the last three years (Franklin & Acton, 2024). Some banks bought out

Fintech operators, such as BNP buying out Nickel (Ashta & Courtois, 2020). The market dynamics are complex.

In the developing world, such disruptions and risks may impact the long tail of poor customers who have recently been included in the financial system. Indeed, in West Africa, microfinance outreach is reducing, banking outreach is growing marginally, but e-money services are growing exponentially (Ndione et al., 2024). As a result, in this region, financial access is growing only due to e-money suppliers. Several microfinance institutions that were providing essential services to the financially excluded are closing in the most advanced East African markets (Central Bank of Kenya, 2023), which reduces options for the customers that are the less digitally included—like the old and the poor, often in rural areas. These unprofitable customers were included because MFIs used to cross-subsidize their less profitable mostly rural and group lending operations with their individual-lending urban operations (Armendáriz & Szafarz, 2009). It becomes in this context especially important for the financial institutions (banks and microfinances) to reduce their operational costs through sustaining innovations, which are often provided by partner Fintechs focused on Business-to-Business (B2B) services, for example, for scoring or workflow management.

Overreliance on Fintech solutions within the financial inclusion realm is not only cannibalizing more traditional, face-to-face MFI operations, but by doing so is ensuring that the digitally excluded remain financially excluded as well. According to the World Bank, only 55% of the population of West and Central Africa have access to electricity (World Bank, 2022), an essential ingredient of Fintech. When looking at exclusively the rural population (often the target of more traditional microfinance activities), this coverage drops to only 25% of the rural population with access to electricity (World Bank, 2022). A lack of access to electricity is a commonly used indicator of poverty. The poorest therefore will be excluded from financial inclusion initiatives that are overly reliant on Fintech and electricity access. This raises serious concerns over calls to digitalize for the sake of efficient operations and even more so when it is for the purpose of expanding financial inclusion. In order to expand inclusion, the needs of those excluded, beginning with those most marginalized, should be prioritized.

Will Fintech growth disrupt the financial services market? More recent research looks at churn rates and customer loyalty within the mobile payment industry (Amoroso et al., 2023). Improving customer loyalty requires continuous technological innovation to improve the customer experience (Wang & Chang, 2018) and to introduce gamification (Dzandu et al., 2022). Technological innovations that will enhance customer experience often focus on interface design, system quality, security assurance, and service quality (Zhou et al., 2021). Interface design is where we see various new Fintech ventures now being successful in Africa (Participant A, personal communication, 2024). Performance and effort expectancy are antecedents to using mobile money (Senyo & Osabutey, 2020). These initiatives reinforce the importance of implementing innovations to improve current technologies, which is often a precondition to disruptive innovation (Christensen, 2006). Markets are therefore pushing MFIs further into Fintech development and adoption despite concerns over inclusion in order to retain current customers, an essential component of any business model but even more so in one designed to subsidize marginalized clients.

This increase in mobile payments with innovative features is affecting banks (Mbiti & Weil, 2015). They are threatened that Fintech mobile operators will enter the banking market (Ashta & Biot-Paquerot, 2018). Indeed, in several markets, mobile money operators sponsor incubators to come up with new Fintech payment solutions (Molla & Biru, 2023). However, recent research in Sub-Saharan Africa shows that banking services, microfinance services, and e-money service providers are independent of each other and do not disrupt each other (Mashamba & Gani, 2023; Ndione et al., 2024). Perhaps this is because banks are collaborating with Fintechs (coopetition) to come up with innovations that would help them defend their markets (Geurts et al., 2022). However, some banks are also collaborating with Telcos, especially if the bank is not present in the retail market. For example, the investment bank Goldman Sachs collaborated with ApplePay to introduce Buy-Now-Pay-Later loans to ApplePay's clients. This seems to have not worked ultimately, as ApplePay is withdrawing from the market and closing down the collaboration (Franklin & Acton, 2024).

In less-developed countries in other regions, banks are now reaching previously unserved customers by digitalization (Gupta & Kanungo, 2022). Research in Indonesia indicates that banks need to educate their customers on this issue and influence their attitudes toward using financial technology (Juwita et al., 2023). Indeed, financial education has been a key type of technical assistance for several donors (Swiss Capacity Building Facility, 2024), and it often shows the best results in impacting outreach (Kaiser & Menkhoff, 2017). In Asia, access to electricity is much less limited (World Bank, 2022). However, oversaturation in microfinance markets makes the primary concern financial literacy and over-indebtedness rather than inclusion. Many MFIs have converted into for-profit institutions and there are reports across countries of predatory lending behaviors (Phillips et al., forthcoming).

It is useful to conceptualize the competitive interplay between Fintechs, Banks, and Telcos. Table 1 summarizes key internal factors of influence within telcos and financial institutions, with regards to different types of issues and solutions. The table further categorizes the B2C Fintechs jointly with the telcos, and the B2B Fintechs jointly with the financial institutions—in line with the examples provided above and showing that more disruptive B2C innovations (DI) are most often implemented jointly with the telcos, while sustaining innovations (SI) are implemented rather with B2B Fintechs and financial institutions. Solutions are further organized by type of innovation, being either sustaining or disruptive (Christensen, 2006). It shows that most solutions concern sustaining innovations (as opposed to disruptive innovations), especially for key issues such as churn for the telcos, and cross-subsidization for the banks. This shows that survival has become the focus of most institutions; a focus on survival precludes any efforts to increase financial inclusion, the original purpose of microfinance.

Recurrent internal factors of influence include multi-disciplinary working groups and partnerships. Those are important because the new available technologies

Table 1 Summary internal factors of influence per players, issues, solutions

Player	Issues	Solutions (and type of innovation -either SI or DI[a]) & internal factors of influence
Telcos & B2C Fintechs	Churn (Wieland, 2007)	Loyalty, customer experience & gamification (SI) : Studies, satisfaction monitoring, incentives, products, partnerships (Jaspers et al., 2012)
		Quality network & service (SI): Selection of technologies, maintenance, etc.
		Interface (SI): Ease of access, multi-disciplinary working groups (Noviaristanti et al., 2024)
	Value addition (Kaur & Soch, 2012)	New products and services (SI & DI): Partnerships, build competencies, independent governance, incubation (Noviaristanti et al., 2024)
	Market fragmentation (Ashta & Bélanger, 2024; Babus & Parlatore, 2022; Chen & Duffie, 2021)	Locking customers & stickiness (SI & DI): Strategy, negotiation (Jaspers et al., 2007)
Financial Institutions & B2B Fintechs	New markets (Munyegera & Matsumoto, 2018; Ouma et al., 2017)	Products or systems (SI & DI): Partnerships (B2B Fintechs), flexibility competences customer-interacting staff
		Financial incentives and subsidies (DI): Technical assistance, Loan guarantee, Subsidized funding, KPIs, grants for incubation, Financial incentives for teams or specific staff (Armendáriz & Szafarz, 2009)
		Coopetition to find innovation to defend their market (SI & DI): Joint venture (Babu et al., 2020)
	Cross-subsidy (Bu et al., 2023)	Segmentation (SI): Flexibility competences customer-interacting staff (Vanderstraeten et al., 2016)
		Business models improvements (SI): Partnerships and incubation (Vanderstraeten et al., 2016)
		Financial and technological education (SI & DI): Cross-functional teams (Vanderstraeten et al., 2016)

Source: Authors' own work

[a] *SI* Sustaining innovation, *DI* Disruptive innovation

require a unique coordination between operational/business skillset and technological skillset—e.g., to design a Fintech business model, or to implement innovations to improve customer interface. Some of those solutions have already been studied in the context of telcos and banking.

More specifically, regarding telcos, (Noviaristanti et al., 2024) studied the set-up of corporate accelerators in telco businesses, to build new competencies, to facilitate partnerships with sub-businesses implementing innovations, and to complement and leverage existing resources. Jaspers et al. (2007) assessed the collaboration between telcos and new entrants to complement their offer, showing how it was increasing the value of their services / make them more competitive.

Regarding financial institutions, (Armendáriz & Szafarz, 2009) studied donor intervention in mission-driven organizations, and showed how those may come to deviate from their initial social objective. They identified different explanations such as the nature of their mission and the cost to serve different types of clients depending on their regions and income level. We see this in the Fintech context, as institutions deviate from low-tech inclusion strategies in order to embrace Fintech solutions that increase efficiency and current client retention. Babu et al. (2020) studied strategic alliances between telcos and financial institutions with a focus on the value added to the final customers. Vanderstraeten et al. (2016) investigated incubators with a focus on the flexibility of their business model and the multidisciplinary nature of their staff.

This leads to the research question: in such a fast-growing, complex market, what are the factors that lead to changes in the microfinance marketplace?

3 Methodology

To explore the factors enabling or inhibiting successful disruptive and sustaining innovations for financial inclusion—with a specific focus on the interplay between telcos, mobile money, and financial services—a qualitative research approach was employed in the form of semi-structured interviews. Interviews were conducted in person at conferences held in Kigali, Rwanda, and Tel Aviv, Israel in May and June 2024, leveraging the physical presence of key stakeholders in the financial technology and banking sectors. The analysis of the interviews uses a three-dimensional framework (Corley & Gioia, 2011; Gioia et al., 2013).

Seven respondents, including CEOs, IT managers, and innovation leaders from Fintechs and microfinance institutions and associations, were selected to provide a comprehensive understanding of the challenges and opportunities in implementing mobile money solutions and enhancing customer experiences through technology. Each respondent signed a consent form prior to the interviews, acknowledging their participation and the recording of their responses. We started to see saturation (recurrent themes coming—less new information coming up) after 7 interviews. Elite respondents are difficult to find and are selected based on convenience and snowballing (Harvey, 2011). Therefore, seven interviews were considered sufficient.

The semi-structured format of the interviews allowed for flexibility in probing deeper insights while maintaining consistency across sessions. A standardized background and set of questions were shared with the participants before the interviews. The primary questions aimed to identify the internal factors that enable or inhibit successful disruptive innovation for financial inclusion within microfinance institutions (MFIs), Fintechs, banks, and telecommunications companies. Sub-questions included identifying three types of disruptive innovations utilized by microfinance institutions, outlining the key challenges and opportunities associated with these innovations; identifying three types of sustaining innovations used by microfinance institutions and discussing their respective challenges and opportunities; and determining which innovations are most likely to support financial institutions in responding to competitive threats posed by Fintechs, mobile money, and telcos, including the reasons for their effectiveness.

Each interview was recorded with informed consent, transcribed verbatim, and analyzed qualitatively to extract contextual insights using the tool of ChatGPT4.0. This methodology facilitated a thorough understanding of the landscape of financial inclusion innovations from the perspective of industry experts, specifically highlighting how mobile money and telecommunications infrastructure can be leveraged to enhance access to financial services and address customer needs effectively.

4 Results

The interviews conducted with various Fintech leaders provided significant insights into how disruptive and sustaining innovations can influence the competitive dynamics between Fintechs, banks, and microfinance institutions, particularly in relation to telcos, data connection, and mobile money.

One CEO (Interviewee 1) emphasized the transformative potential of mobile banking platforms as a solution to enhance customer access to banking services, thus reducing churn in underserved markets. This individual noted that mobile services, facilitated by robust data connections provided by telecom operators, allow financial institutions to maintain a presence in rural areas without the need for physical branches. The convenience of mobile banking is especially critical in regions where traditional banking infrastructure is lacking, highlighting the synergy between telecommunications and financial services. However, they also pointed out challenges such as digital literacy and the need for regulatory support, which could impact mobile money adoption.

An IT manager (Interviewee 2) echoed similar sentiments by identifying infrastructure, particularly data connectivity, as a crucial factor in maintaining customer loyalty. This individual highlighted that reliable internet and mobile data services are essential for enabling effective digital banking solutions. The interaction between telcos and banks is significant; improved data services can lead to better user experiences and increase the adoption of mobile money services, like SMS banking and wallet solutions. They underscored the necessity for financial institutions to invest in educational initiatives that help users understand and utilize these mobile services effectively.

One country director (Interviewee 3) pointed to the role of user-friendly interfaces and mobile applications as critical tools for enhancing customer experiences in mobile money services. They highlighted that the widespread availability of chat applications like WhatsApp allows customers to engage with financial services without installing separate banking apps, thus lowering the barriers to entry. This not only helps in customer retention but also ensures that users in low connectivity areas can still access essential services.

The importance of leveraging mobile technology to reach new markets was highlighted by a founder (Interviewee 4). They discussed strategies aimed at tapping into smaller farmers and underserved communities, facilitated by mobile money platforms. These platforms allow financial institutions to offer tailored products directly to users, transforming how services are delivered. The agility offered by mobile money solutions helps microfinance institutions efficiently bridge service gaps and address specific market needs, reducing reliance on traditional banking methods.

Another co-founder (Interviewee 5) emphasized the significance of integrating low-tech solutions, such as USD mechanisms and stable coin wallets, into mobile money applications to serve low-income users without smartphones. They indicated that such innovations enable financial institutions to penetrate new markets by utilizing existing telecommunications infrastructure and mobile wallet networks. The co-founder also pointed to the role of partnerships between Fintechs and telcos, which can enhance market access and provide consumers with seamless access to financial services.

Furthermore, a co-founder (Interviewee 6) highlighted the growing relevance of climate risk assessment tools as part of innovative mobile money offerings. They stressed that integrating these tools can help microfinance institutions better evaluate the specific risks faced by agricultural customers, leading to more informed lending decisions and ultimately contributing to financial stability for users reliant on farming. This can enhance the operational capacity of financial institutions in rural areas where data on climate conditions may be sparse and in need of fusion with financial services.

Finally, another co-founder (Interviewee 7) commented on the potential for financial institutions to leverage economies of scale in their partnership with telecom providers. They emphasized that using a robust telecommunications network enhances customer outreach, enabling institutions to efficiently manage costs while delivering services that meet the specific needs of underserved communities. This relationship is crucial in ensuring that financial services continue to be innovative and adaptable to the evolving landscape of digital finance.

Throughout the interviews, several recurring themes emerged regarding the challenges and solutions faced by financial institutions in relation to telcos, data connections, and mobile money. A common issue was the need for improved digital literacy among customers, which was highlighted by multiple participants (Interviewees 1, 2, and 5) as a barrier to adopting new technologies. Moreover, the discussion frequently highlighted user experience challenges, particularly in navigating financial platforms via mobile services. General concerns for the constraints for financial inclusion were expressed by most (Interviewees 1, 2, 3, 5, and 7).

Additional themes on enhancing products and services were present. Interviewees 3, 4, and 6 all offered examples of specialized Fintech to serve particular customer niches better, enhancing retention and reducing churn. Solutions such as robust mobile banking platforms, intuitive chatbots for customer support, and personalized financial products emerged as effective strategies to bridge the technological gap and enhance access to financial services in markets increasingly reliant on mobile money and telecommunications. These insights demonstrate the complex yet vital interplay between financial services and the telecommunications sector in fostering financial inclusion.

5 Discussion of Themes, Concepts and Dimensions

Table 2 presents the results based on the interviews, structured around themes, concepts, and dimensions.

The findings from the interviews reveal multiple first-order themes that reflect the practical challenges and opportunities faced by Fintech and microfinance institutions in the context of financial inclusion.

The themes of Mobile Banking Platforms and User Experience Tools exemplify how disruptive innovations can enhance customer access, reinforcing the importance of developing tailored services that meet unique market needs. As noted above, such innovations target the reduction of churn by increasing customer loyalty through enhanced incentives and experience (Wieland, 2007). This showcases the prevalence of SI in the Fintech marketplace. While survival is a key operational outcome, microfinance mandates increased financial inclusion. Retention and satisfaction of existing customers fall short of the mark.

The use of Climate Risk Assessment Tools (Interviewee 6) and represented an innovative approach to product development that aligns with ongoing environmental challenges, showcasing how financial institutions can develop new frameworks for delivering services while simultaneously addressing climate vulnerabilities. Interviewee 4 also emphasized tailoring products to meet the needs of small farmers. These niche approaches can be both SI and DI (Noviaristanti et al., 2024), depending on the reach of financial inclusion among the particular farm communities served by these organizations. The productivity gains such innovations provide are certainly a desirable supplement to the baseline goal of financial inclusion. Value addition (Kaur & Soch, 2012) is an important contribution of Fintech.

The concept of data connectivity was a concern raised by most interviewees; this highlights the necessity for robust telecommunications infrastructure to support these innovations effectively, ensuring that financial services are accessible and usable in various contexts, especially in rural areas. Financial inclusion remains the primary purpose of MFI, and Fintech should be assessed for its ability to contribute

Table 2 Themes, concepts, and dimensions

1st Order Themes (Informant Quotes)	2nd Order Concepts	3rd order Dimensions
"Mobile banking platforms help expand access for underserved markets." (Interviewee 1)	Disruptive Innovation	Innovation
"Replacing branches with mobile platforms minimizes costs and enhances convenience." (Interviewee 1)		
"Integrating climate risk tools allows better evaluation of agricultural customers." (Interviewee 6)	Innovative Product Development	
"These tools enable informed lending decisions amidst climate uncertainties." (Interviewee 6)		
"WhatsApp chatbots provide a low-barrier way for customers to access services." (Interviewee 3)	Customer Engagement	Customer Orientation
"Simplifying user access ensures retention and addresses churn." (Interviewee 3)		
"The need for digital literacy programs cannot be overstated." (Interviewee 2)	Awareness & Training	
"Investing in financial education improves service adoption and usage." (Interviewee 5)		
"Reliable data connections are crucial for effective digital banking services." (Interviewee 2)	Infrastructure Dependence	Strategic Considerations
"The strength of the telecom network directly influences financial service usability." (Interviewee 2)		
"Collaborating with telcos enables better reach in underserved areas." (Interviewee 6)	Strategic Collaborations	
"Mobile money platforms are essential in reaching remote populations effectively." (Interviewee 4)		

Source: Authors' own work

to this goal additively. Infrastructure barriers to such sources of inclusion should be taken seriously as the digitization of the microfinance industry progresses. Interviewees also expressed concern regarding the digital literacy of clients (Interviewees 1, 2, and 5), mirroring donor concerns (Swiss Capacity Building Facility, 2024). Customer Education emerged as a crucial element in facilitating the adoption of new services, indicating a significant gap in digital literacy that must be addressed. This is another vital concern if true financial inclusion is to be achieved, rather than innovation solely for the survival of the organization.

Additionally, the findings emphasized the significance of Partnerships with Telecoms, illustrating that collaboration is vital for expanding outreach and effectively addressing customer needs. Vanderstraeten et al. (2016) emphasize the importance of partnerships between financial institutions and B2B Fintechs. This is a third configuration with an emphasis on partnership between the Telecoms and financial institutions. This re-emphasizes the importance of digital access and the co-reliance between these two industries, which will only increase as more physical branches close their doors (Central Bank of Kenya, 2023).

In summary, these themes, concepts, and dimensions collectively illustrate a nuanced understanding of the interplay between Fintechs and traditional financial services, emphasizing the importance of innovation, strategic collaboration, and customer orientation in fostering financial inclusion. The primary goal of financial inclusion must remain at the forefront of such innovation and become the rigorous standard by which such partnerships and innovations are measured.

6 Concluding Remarks: Where Are We Going?

In the Bottom of the Pyramid markets, governments aim for development and poverty reduction while businesses aim to maximize earnings (Ahmad, 2014). Therefore, policy recommendations need to keep in mind that governments stimulate financial access provision by allowing private operators to make a profit. Our findings show that the respondents in our case study are very sensitive to increasing access and using this technology. It is essential that we understand the motivations for these collaborations so that we may return to the touchstone of purpose. MFI CEOs/directors, IT managers, and founders interviewed agree that digital literacy and financial inclusion remain top priorities for their organizations. However, they need support from the government and multilateral donors to increase basic infrastructure.

More research is warranted to understand the impacts of mobile money initiatives on financial inclusion, particularly in rural areas where access to technology and financial literacy can significantly influence outcomes. It is imperative to document impacts on financial inclusion as physical branches close and organizations convert to a more digitized model of services. If financial markets have been digitally saturated, financial inclusion may only be achieved by increasing digital literacy or by non-digital tools. Exploring strategies for increasing digital literacy and its potential to mitigate these losses is also imperative. Furthermore, increasing digital literacy has the potential to expand the network effects of Fintech advancements, as it decreases network effect barriers. Understanding these dynamics will be essential for developing strategies that prioritize the most marginalized customers while fostering innovation in the financial landscape.

Comparing the findings from these interviews with existing theories on network effects and market dynamics reveals critical areas for further research. Moving forward, one should assess how and why internal and external factors drive the collaboration between (i) telcos and B2C Fintechs, (ii) financial institutions and B2B Fintechs, and (iii) telcos and financial institutions. Specifically, there is a need for a deeper exploration of how telcos can effectively collaborate with Fintechs to create interoperable systems that enhance customer retention and reduce churn in two-sided markets. Innovative solutions to reach a client niche such as small farmers, or that truly disrupt the industry and increase financial inclusion, need to be better understood and celebrated. Such disruptive innovations will always be necessary for a thriving microfinance industry. However, to the extent that more and more innovations are for the sake of organizational survival, we must proceed with caution and be ready to reevaluate MFI motives and metrics.

Microfinance gained popularity through the Grameen Bank's work four decades ago; the emphasis of this early microfinance was financial inclusion and entrepreneurship. It is essential to interrogate the Fintech trends so that those promoting financial inclusion may be propagated and those detracting from it may be re-evaluated. Financial sustainability has been a key element of the microfinance promise (Morduch, 1999) for many years, but it is a necessary and not sufficient condition. If the fullness of the promise, financial inclusion, and entrepreneurship, are not delivered on, financial sustainability alone is not enough.

Fintech is proffered as a solution to the focus on customer retention, yet it is manifesting as inter-MFI competition, particularly in West African countries. Such an industry trajectory is becoming increasingly similar to sub-prime lending in the United States or United Kingdom, which has had dire results. This easy-access, tech-supported lending will become increasingly consumption-based, devolving into quick transactions with no care for financial health, financial literacy, or other dimensions of human development. The original Grameen model included health, sanitation, family planning, and solidarity measures in its agreements with borrower groups, a set of conditions known as the 16 Decisions (Mason et al., 2024). This original model of microfinance, the root of the Year of Microcredit in 2005 and the Nobel Peace Prize in 2006, is a much more holistic approach in which financial access and entrepreneurship are part of a matrix of human development. Innovations that can incorporate and/or enhance other aspects of human development would be disruptive and impactful. For example, embedding health care training or educational tools into Fintech could return financial inclusion to the holistic roots planted by the Grameen Bank 16 Decisions. The time is ripe for an examination of Fintech and the course that the combination of microfinance and technology has charted for the future of the industry.

References

Ahmad, M. U. (2014). Business below the Pyramid. *FIIB Business Review, 3*(1), 27–34. https://doi.org/10.1177/2455265820140104

Amoroso, D., Lim, R., Lei, J., & Saxena, A. (2023). A Study of satisfaction and loyalty for continuance intention of mobile wallet in India. *International Journal of E-Adoption, 15*(1), 1–18.

Armendáriz, B., & Szafarz, A. (2009). *Microfinance mission drift.* Research Institute in Management Sciences. https://www.researchgate.net/profile/Ariane-Szafarz/publication/46465801_On_Mission_Drift_In_Microfinance_Institutions/links/0a85e52dfbdb370487000000/On-Mission-Drift-In-Microfinance-Institutions.pdf

Ashta, A., & Bélanger, C. (2024). *The ICE age: A case study on profiting in fragmented markets.* A₹tha (March 2024) Indian Institute of Management Calcutta, p 4.

Ashta, A., & Biot-Paquerot, G. (2018). FinTech evolution: Strategic value management issues in a fast changing industry. *Strategic Change, 27*(4), 301–311. https://doi.org/10.1002/jsc.2203

Ashta, A., & Courtois, T. (2020). Lessons from an Incumbent taking over a challenger. *Entreprendre & Innover, 3*, 56–65.

Babu, M. M., Dey, B. L., Rahman, M., Roy, S. K., Alwi, S. F. S., & Kamal, M. M. (2020). Value co-creation through social innovation: A study of sustainable strategic alliance in telecommunication and financial services sectors in Bangladesh. *Industrial Marketing Management, 89*, 13–27.

Babus, A., & Parlatore, C. (2022). Strategic fragmented markets. *Journal of Financial Economics, 145*(3), 876–908.

Birke, D. (2009). The economics of networks: A survey of the empirical literature. *Journal of Economic Surveys, 23*(4), 762–793. https://doi.org/10.1111/j.1467-6419.2009.00578.x

Bu, Y., Du, X., Li, H., Yu, X., & Wang, Y. (2023). Research on the FinTech risk early warning based on the MS-VAR model: An empirical analysis in China. *Global Finance Journal, 58*. https://doi.org/10.1016/j.gfj.2023.100898

Central Bank of Kenya. (2023). *Financial sector stability report.* https://www.centralbank.go.ke/uploads/financial_sector_stability

Chen, D., & Duffie, D. (2021). Market fragmentation. *American Economic Review, 111*(7), 2247–2274.

Christensen, C. M. (2006). The ongoing process of building a theory of disruption. *Journal of Product Innovation Management, 23*(1), 39–55. https://doi.org/10.1111/j.1540-5885.2005.00180.x

Corley, K. G., & Gioia, D. A. (2011). Building theory about theory building: What constitutes a theoretical contribution? *Academy of Management Review, 36*(1), 12–32. https://doi.org/10.5465/amr.2009.0486

David-West, O., Iheanachor, N., Umukoro, I. O. (2019). Mobile money as a frugal innovation for the bottom of the pyramid – Cases of selected African countries. *Africa Journal of Management, 5*(3) 274–302. https://doi.org/10.1080/23322373.2019.1652023

Dong, Y., Chung, M., Zhou, C., & Venkataraman, S. (2019). Banking on "Mobile Money": The implications of mobile money services on the value chain. *Manufacturing & Service Operations Management, 21*(2), msom.2018.0717. https://doi.org/10.1287/msom.2018.0717

Dzandu, M. D., Hanu, C., & Amegbe, H. (2022). Gamification of mobile money payment for generating customer value in emerging economies: The social impact theory perspective. *Technological Forecasting and Social Change, 185*, 122049. https://doi.org/10.1016/j.techfore.2022.122049

Economides, N. (1996). The economics of networks. *International Journal of Industrial Organization, 14*(6), 673–699.

Eisenmann, T., Parker, G., & Van Alstyne, M. W. (2006). Strategies for two-sided markets. *Harvard Business Review*. https://www.binhphuongnguyen.com/wp-content/uploads/2021/07/HBR-Strategy-for-2-side-market-Egg-and-Chicken-Dilemma-Startup.pdf

Ewe, S. Y., Yap, S. F., & Lee, C. K. C. (2015). Network externalities and the perception of innovation characteristics: Mobile banking. *Marketing Intelligence & Planning, 33*(4), 592–611.

Franklin, J., & Acton, M. (2024, June 17). *Apple scraps 'buy now, pay later' service in US just months after rollout*. https://www.ft.com/content/aa6dc2cf-bb8e-4ed7-be25-d725eba37aa8

Geurts, A., Broekhuizen, T., Dolfsma, W., & Cepa, K. (2022). Tensions in multilateral coopetition: Findings from the disrupted music industry. *Industrial Marketing Management, 105*, 532–547. https://doi.org/10.1016/j.indmarman.2022.06.020

Gioia, D. A., Corley, K. G., & Hamilton, A. L. (2013). Seeking qualitative rigor in inductive research: Notes on the Gioia methodology. *Organizational Research Methods, 16*(1), 15–31.

Gupta, S., & Kanungo, R. P. (2022). Financial inclusion through digitalisation: Economic viability for the bottom of the pyramid (BOP) segment. *Journal of Business Research, 148*, 262–276. https://doi.org/10.1016/j.jbusres.2022.04.070

Harvey, W. S. (2011). Strategies for conducting elite interviews. *Qualitative Research, 11*(4), 431–441.

Jaspers, F., Hulsink, W., & Theeuwes, J. (2007). Entry and innovation in maturing markets: Virtual operators in mobile telecommunications. *Technology Analysis & Strategic Management, 19*(2), 205–225. https://doi.org/10.1080/09537320601168144

Jaspers, F., Prencipe, A., & Ende, J. (2012). Organizing interindustry architectural innovations: Evidence from mobile communication applications. *Journal of Product Innovation Management, 29*(3), 419–431. https://doi.org/10.1111/j.1540-5885.2012.00915.x

Juwita, R., Kusumah, A. D., Aqila, T. S., Tsabitah, H., & Syauqi, M. F. (2023). The intention to use mobile banking as a financial technology service among Islamic bank users. *The Indonesian Capital Market Review, 15*(1), 3.

Kaiser, T., & Menkhoff, L. (2017). Does financial education impact financial literacy and financial behavior, and if so, when? *The World Bank Economic Review, 31*(3), 611–630.

Kaur, H., & Soch, H. (2012). Validating antecedents of customer loyalty for Indian cell phone users. *Vikalpa: The Journal for Decision Makers, 37*(4), 47–62. https://doi.org/10.1177/0256090920120404

Lee, C.-C., Ni, W., & Zhang, X. (2023). FinTech development and commercial bank efficiency in China. *Global Finance Journal, 57*, 100850.

Mashamba, T., & Gani, S. (2023). Fintech, bank funding, and economic growth in Sub-Saharan Africa. *Cogent Economics & Finance, 11*(1), 2225916. https://doi.org/10.1080/23322039.2023.2225916

Mason, G., Phillips, R., & Davy, D. (2024). *The shift from grassroots third sector microfinance to corporatized microfinance- The forgotten 16 Decisions and the loss of social solidarity*. Working Paper.

Mbiti, I., & Weil, D. N. (2015). Mobile banking: The impact of M-Pesa in Kenya. In *African successes, Volume III: Modernization and development* (pp. 247–293). University of Chicago Press. https://www.degruyter.com/document/doi/10.7208/9780226315867-009/pdf?licenseType=restricted

McIntyre, D. P., & Srinivasan, A. (2017). Networks, platforms, and strategy: Emerging views and next steps. *Strategic Management Journal, 38*(1), 141–160. https://doi.org/10.1002/smj.2596

Mishra, P. K. (2014). Exclusion to inclusion: An economic paradigm for India. *FIIB Business Review, 3*(4), 3–15. https://doi.org/10.1177/2455265820140401

Molla, A., & Biru, A. (2023). The evolution of the Fintech entrepreneurial ecosystem in Africa: An exploratory study and model for future development. *Technological Forecasting and Social Change, 186*, 122123. https://doi.org/10.1016/j.techfore.2022.122123

Morduch, J. (1999). The microfinance promise. *Journal of Economic Literature, 37*(4), 1569–1614.

Munyegera, G. K., & Matsumoto, T. (2018). ICT for financial access: Mobile money and the financial behavior of rural households in Uganda. *Review of Development Economics, 22*(1): 45–66. https://doi.org/10.1111/rode.12327

Ndione, M., Ashta, A., & Bako Liba, B. B. (2024). Banks, microfinance institutions and fintech: How the ratio of male and female entrepreneurs moderates their capacity for financial inclusion. *Cogent Economics & Finance, 12*(1), 2402031. https://doi.org/10.1080/23322039.2024.2402031

Noviaristanti, S., Acur, N., Mendibil, K., & Miranda, E. (2024). The network orchestration role of accelerators for value creation. *IEEE Transactions on Engineering Management*. https://ieeexplore.ieee.org/abstract/document/10416427/

Ouma, S. A., Odongo, T. M., & Were, M. (2017). Mobile financial services and financial inclusion: Is it a boon for savings mobilization? *Review of Development Finance*.https://doi.org/10.1016/J.RDF.2017.01.001

Phillips, R., Mason, G., & Davy, D. (forthcoming). *Civil society and poverty: Contextual challenges in Cambodia. (Varieties of Civil Societies Across Asia)*. Routledge.

Quinio, A., & Levingston, I. (2024, June 20). *Revolut seeks valuation of more than $40bn in employee share sale*. https://www.ft.com/content/9e613f65-cdf5-4b3d-9ac7-cfb39cde3159
Safaricom. (2024). *All products*. https://www.safaricom.co.ke/personal/all-products
Senyo, P., & Osabutey, E. L. C. (2020). Unearthing antecedents to financial inclusion through FinTech innovations. *Technovation, 98*. https://doi.org/10.1016/j.technovation.2020.102155
Swiss Capacity Building Facility. (2024). *How we work – How we fund*. https://www.scbf.ch/overview
Vanderstraeten, J., van Witteloostuijn, A., Matthyssens, P., & Andreassi, T. (2016). Being flexible through customization- The impact of incubator focus and customization strategies on incubate survival and growth. *Journal of Engineering and Technology Management, 41*, 45–64.
Wang, M., & Chang, Y. (2018). *Technology leadership, brand equity, and customer loyalty towards fintech service providers in China*. https://scholar.archive.org/work/lzit73z5ongrparspmcbu4gvru/access/wayback/https://aisel.aisnet.org/cgi/viewcontent.cgi?article=1362&context=amcis2018
Wieland, K. (2007). Telecom sector among "worst" for churning. *Telecommunications - International Edition, 41*(3), 11–11.
World Bank. (2022). *World Development Indicators, access to electricity West and Central Africa* [Dataset].
Yeboah-Asiamah, E., Narteh, B., & Mahmoud, M. A. (2018). Preventing customer churn in the mobile telecommunication industry: Is mobile money usage the missing link? *Journal of African Business, 19*(2), 174–194. https://doi.org/10.1080/15228916.2018.1440462
Zhou, Q., Lim, F. J., Yu, H., Xu, G., Ren, X., Liu, D., Wang, X., Mai, X., & Xu, H. (2021). A study on factors affecting service quality and loyalty intention in mobile banking. *Journal of Retailing and Consumer Services, 60*, 102424.

Charles Belanger has over 18 years of senior management and consulting experience in 40 countries in Latin America, the Middle East, and Sub-Saharan Africa. Charles implemented more than 30 projects on research, impact, policymaking, digital services, and innovation for development partners and financial institutions, such as UNCDF, IFC World Bank, IFAD, LuxDev, IDB Invest, AFD, FINCA, Baobab, Vision Fund, Vodacom-MPESA, and Equity Bank. Charles is currently pursuing a Doctorate in Business Administration (DBA) at the Burgundy School of Business, Université Bourgogne Franche-Comté in Dijon, France. His thesis project explores the context and role of fintechs in sustaining and/or disrupting innovations to advance financial inclusion in East Africa. Charles published several articles about financial inclusion, on the topics of banks' downscaling through equity investment, democratization of women through microfinance, conflict management, and technologies for financial institutions to reach the last mile. He is based in Nairobi, Kenya.

Arvind Ashta is a researcher and consultant in development studies. He was a professor of Finance at the Burgundy School of Business in Dijon, France and a member of its research center CEREN, EA 7477 for over two decades. He has over a hundred publications in international academic journals and has authored and edited a few books. The essence of his research interests hovers around microfinance, social entrepreneurship, and fintech. He is a member of research associations such as CERMi, RRI, and the anti-poverty working group at PRME. He is on the editorial board of many academic journals. He chairs the advisory board of MF Strategy and has founded BHAI (Building Humane Advances and Institutions). He is based in Toulouse, France.

Geri Mason is a professor and researcher in development economics. Her fields of research interest include sustainable development, microfinance/financial inclusion, poverty, and responsible management education. Dr. Mason's teaching specialties are development economics, social and cultural systems, and undergraduate capstone research. Her published research focuses on the economics of microfinance and development, encompassing current debates in microfinance. Articulating her passion for poverty and economic development, parallel research examines methodologies for integrating poverty into management education, particularly through economics. She is an active member of the Collaborative for Econometrics and Integrated Development Studies (CEIDS), the Anti-poverty working group in PRME, as well as the PRME Champion lead for Seattle Pacific University. She consults with development organizations such as Vision Fund International and Agros International on program design and evaluation.

Understanding the RegTech Drivers in the Financial Ecosystem

Iván Sosa and Sergio Sosa

1 Introduction

The rapid advancement of digital technologies has profoundly reshaped industries, especially the financial sector, where regulatory requirements are constantly evolving. As the complexity of compliance requirements increases, organizations increasingly turn to regulatory technology (RegTech) to manage these challenges.

Existing literature established the foundations of RegTech by detailing its evolution through distinct phases. From its initial approach in the standardization of financial reporting to its current role as a sophisticated ecosystem integrating advanced technologies, the definition of RegTech is achieved by emphasizing the dynamic interplay between regulation and technology. This definition also emphasizes RegTech's unique position within the financial industry by highlighting its critical role in the current regulatory landscape.

However, despite the increasing relevance of RegTech, there is a notable gap in understanding its adoption drivers and the extent of its impact on compliance processes. This chapter addresses this gap by exploring the critical drivers of RegTech adoption in the financial ecosystem and assessing how these drivers have revolutionized the efficiency and effectiveness of the phases of regulatory compliance processes in the financial landscape. To approach this gap, this chapter proposes this research question:

I. Sosa (✉)
Camilo Jose Cela University, Madrid, Spain
e-mail: ivan.sosa@ucjc.edu

S. Sosa
InsurTech Research Institute, Madrid, Spain

A. Zarifis, X. Cheng (eds.), *Fintech and the Emerging Ecosystems*, Financial Innovation and Technology, https://doi.org/10.1007/978-3-031-83402-8_19

RQ.1.- What are the most significant drivers of RegTech adoption in the financial ecosystem?

The core research question drives the chapter by contributing significantly to the understanding of RegTech's impact on regulatory compliance processes in the financial ecosystem. For this reason, by examining the evolution of RegTech and sectoral dimensions in the theoretical framework, this research aims to identify the most significant drivers of RegTech adoption and explore how these drivers influence the efficiency and effectiveness of compliance processes in the findings and contributions sections.

Therefore, this chapter contributes to the field by providing actionable insights for industry stakeholders, offering practical direction on leveraging RegTech to improve compliance management, as this field is often considered the most stringent in terms of regulatory requirements. Furthermore, these contributions are essential for practitioners and policymakers as they navigate the challenges and opportunities presented by RegTech dynamics in a rapidly evolving regulatory landscape.

2 Theoretical Framework

Regulatory Technology (RegTech) is an emerging field that utilizes information technology and digital innovations to enhance regulatory compliance processes (Solms, 2020), involving the use of computing and network-based information systems to streamline regulatory compliance, monitoring, reporting, and supervision (Miglionico, 2020). The emergence of Regulatory Technology (RegTech) can be traced through a phased evolution (Grassi & Lanfranchi, 2022), each marked by significant shifts in focus and technological adoption within the regulatory and financial landscape.

From 2009 to 2014, the first phase was dominated by implementing the eXtensible Business Reporting Language (XBRL), a pivotal technology that laid the groundwork for RegTech by standardizing financial reporting. In the aftermath of the 2007–2008 financial crisis, there was a strong push towards creating a unified financial reporting framework that regulators could easily access and analyze across various jurisdictions, including China, Spain, and the United States (Liu et al., 2014). XBRL's ability to link financial data with unique identifiers facilitated seamless data exchange across systems, significantly reducing information production costs and enhancing transparency (Hao et al., 2014). Despite its benefits, this period also saw concerns about the reliability and consistency of data in XBRL format, highlighting the early challenges of using technology for regulatory purposes (Bartley et al., 2011). The second phase, beginning in 2015, marked the formal emergence of RegTech as a distinct field. This was catalyzed by the UK Financial Conduct Authority's (FCA) call for input on RegTech development, which spurred academic and industry interest in technologies like Artificial Intelligence (AI), Big Data, and Distributed Ledger Technology (DLT) as foundational elements of RegTech solutions (Arner et al., 2017). These technologies were key to addressing complex regulatory challenges such as anti-money laundering (AML) and risk assessment, particularly emphasizing the critical role of data in ensuring regulatory compliance (Barberis & Arner, 2016). The third phase, from 2018 to 2020, saw a dramatic increase in RegTech literature, with nearly 60% of relevant publications emerging (Grassi & Lanfranchi, 2022). This phase revisited core RegTech concepts while delving into risks like data privacy and cybersecurity and introduced the concept of SupTech—RegTech used by regulators for supervision (Anagnostopoulos, 2018). The current phase, starting in 2021, is characterized by a deeper focus on specific RegTech applications, such as supporting Environmental, Social, and Governance (ESG) reporting through DLT and crisis resolution (ResTech), reflecting a maturing field that increasingly relies on quantitative methodologies to refine its approaches (Cerchiaro et al., 2021; Loiacono & Rulli 2022).

This phased analysis of the emergence of RegTech (Grassi & Lanfranchi, 2022) highlights its evolution from a technology focused on financial reporting standardization to a sophisticated ecosystem that integrates advanced technologies to address complex regulatory challenges across sectors. However, while academic contributions during these phases reflect the growing importance of RegTech in shaping the future of regulatory compliance and oversight, they need to reflect the increasing complexity of regulatory requirements and the growing reliance on advanced technologies to manage compliance efficiently.

For this reason, the comprehensive RegTech framework developed by Grassi and Lanfranchi (2022) provides a fundamental structure for understanding the multi-faceted nature of regulatory technology in today's complex financial ecosystem. This significant framework is based on four key dimensions that are central to the evolving academic debate. These dimensions combined form a robust framework that is essential for analyzing comprehensively the current and future impact of RegTech on the financial industry. As it systematically explores the convergence of regulation and technology, the critical role of data, the involvement of diverse stakeholders, and the balance between benefits and risks, this framework provides a holistic view that is indispensable for both academics and practitioners seeking to navigate the evolving regulatory technology landscape.

The first dimension of RegTech centers on integrating regulation and technology, fundamentally transforming how regulatory processes are managed across industries. RegTech is defined by its role in driving digital innovation, enhancing digital reporting, and reshaping regulatory systems through the deployment of automated, non-invasive, and scalable digital solutions (Kavassalis et al., 2018; Arner et al., 2020). These technologies enable real-time, dynamic, and seamless operations, crucial for adapting to evolving regulatory demands (Chiu & Deipenbrock, 2021). A significant debate within the literature is whether RegTech should be considered a subset of Fintech. While some scholars view RegTech as inherently connected to Fintech due to their shared technological foundations, others argue that RegTech has distinct origins and functions, having emerged primarily in response to top-down regulatory demands rather than bottom-up technological innovation (Arner et al., 2017). This distinction highlights the unique role of RegTech in creating a new regulatory paradigm applicable beyond the financial sector. RegTech solutions address various regulations, including privacy issues such as GDPR. They can be tailored to specific regulations like Know Your Customer (KYC) or encompass multiple regulatory frameworks simultaneously (Buckley et al., 2020). These solutions leverage a wide array of advanced technologies, including big data, artificial intelligence, machine learning, distributed ledger technology (DLT), blockchain, smart contracts, and APIs, which facilitate integration and interoperability across systems (Battanta et al., 2020). Real-world applications of these technologies include the use of Big Data and AI to enhance fraud detection and policy assessment, and employing blockchain to automate authentication processes traditionally managed by regulators (Michaels & Homer, 2018).

The second dimension of RegTech focuses on the pivotal role of data, which is essential for effectively deploying these technological solutions in regulatory compliance. As data becomes increasingly central, RegTech shifts traditional paradigms, such as the Know Your Customer (KYC) model, towards more data-centric approaches, exemplified by the Know Your Data (KYD) framework (Arner et al., 2017). This shift highlights the emergence of a data ecosystem where information is seamlessly shared among regulators, industry associations, and investors, forming the backbone of integrated, technology-driven regulation (Yang & Li, 2018). In RegTech, data comes in various forms—structured, unstructured, qualitative, quantitative, granular, or aggregated (EIOPA, 2020). The diversity of data sources, which include regulatory databases, internal communications, and even satellite positioning, underscores the complexity and breadth of data management required in this domain (Currie et al., 2018). RegTech's capability to automate data collection is transformative, enabling regulators to pull data directly from financial institutions' systems and integrate it with customer data (FINRA, 2018). Given the reliance on data, ensuring its quality and integrity is critical. RegTech solutions often focus on data improvement processes, including aggregation, big data processing, and advanced modeling techniques (Yang & Li, 2018). Additionally, the proper management, storage, and protection of this data are essential, with RegTech tools supporting these technical aspects to maintain data security and compliance (Omarova, 2020). Ultimately, the automation and enhancement of data analysis through RegTech lead to more informed regulatory decisions, underscoring the fundamental role of data in transforming regulatory processes within the financial ecosystem.

The third dimension of RegTech focuses on the diverse stakeholders involved and the wide range of applications it encompasses. At its core, RegTech is particularly pertinent to the financial sector, given the industry's heavily regulated nature. Within this domain, RegTech has found applications across various subsectors, including banking, payments, securities, lending, trading, and insurance, effectively supporting intermediaries, regulated entities, and firms required to manage extensive regulatory data (Buckley et al., 2020). However, the influence of RegTech extends beyond these traditional sectors, offering significant opportunities for unregulated entities such as technology companies, consulting firms, startups, and service providers. These organizations can leverage RegTech to monitor data, ensure internal and external communications compliance, and enhance overall data integrity (Micheler & Whaley, 2020). RegTech's applications span five critical functions: compliance, monitoring, risk management, reporting, and operations. In compliance, RegTech enhances organizational readiness for new regulations and facilitates regulatory intelligence by offering a structured and accessible catalog of requirements (Currie & Seddon, 2021). Emerging areas such as Know Your Customer (KYC), Anti-Money Laundering (AML), and customer due diligence have benefited from innovations like biometric verification and advanced data analytics to detect insider trading (Arner et al., 2017). Additionally, RegTech aids in monitoring risks by providing alerts and monitoring internal communications for potential threats (FINRA, 2018). It also plays a vital role in risk management, helping organizations identify and mitigate various risks, from cybersecurity to operational challenges (Butler & Brooks, 2018). Moreover, RegTech has significant implications for regulators and supervisory bodies, often referred to as authorities. These bodies utilize RegTech (or SupTech, when applied by regulators) to enhance policy-making, streamline enforcement operations, and ensure real-time market monitoring and fraud prevention (Zeranski & Sancak, 2021).

The fourth dimension of the RegTech framework encompasses the benefits and risks associated with Regulatory Technology (RegTech), which is critical in understanding its role within the financial and regulatory landscape. The benefits of RegTech are widely recognized and include enhanced efficiency and effectiveness in regulatory compliance, greater accuracy, transparency, and manageability of data, and significant reductions in costs and time associated with compliance processes. These advantages are achieved through automation, the use of AI and machine learning (ML), and the ability to concentrate resources on high-risk areas, leading to improved internal governance and decision-making processes (Chao et al., 2022). RegTech also offers competitive advantages by enhancing consumer protection, improving customer experience, and contributing to a broader economic growth and stability (Arner et al., 2019). However, these benefits are accompanied by several risks. Integrating advanced technologies in regulatory processes introduces operational risks, cyber risks, data privacy concerns, and the potential for algorithmic biases. The reliance on technology also poses challenges, such as the high initial investment costs, the risk of over-reliance on technological solutions leading to a loss of human expertise, and the potential for systemic risks if these technologies are applied uncritically (Deshpande, 2020). Additionally, the uneven adoption of RegTech across different organizations could lead to disparities in regulatory compliance, with smaller firms or regulators potentially being excluded due to resource constraints (Micheler & Whaley, 2020). The risks are further compounded by the possibility of creating monopolistic tendencies in the market if only a few firms dominate the RegTech space. Then, while RegTech presents significant opportunities for enhancing regulatory compliance and efficiency, it also introduces a complex array of risks that must be carefully managed to avoid.

Therefore, RegTech represents a significant advancement in the regulatory practice landscape, offering technological solutions to meet the evolving regulatory requirements in various industries. Its impact on regulatory, monitoring, reporting, and supervision is profound, making it a critical component in the digital transformation of compliance processes in the financial industry. Nevertheless, to date, the drivers of RegTech within the financial ecosystem have not been investigated, representing a critical gap in the field of research. While RegTech is widely recognized for its transformative impact on regulatory compliance, monitoring, reporting, and supervision, there is limited understanding of the driving capabilities that boost its adoption in the financial ecosystem. For this reason, identifying and analyzing these drivers is essential to understanding how RegTech can be leveraged most effectively to improve the efficiency and effectiveness of the regulatory compliance processes.

3 Research Strategy

The research strategy aims to develop an inductive conceptual framework to understand how RegTech dynamics have impacted the financial ecosystem. To this purpose, applying grounded theory methodology (GTM), the global RegTech firms have been analyzed, revealing significant findings to understand the most significant drivers of RegTech adoption and how these firms impact the efficiency and effectiveness of the regulatory compliance processes.

The selected sample comprises 100 of the world's most innovative RegTech companies in 2024. For this purpose, the annual TOP 100 Global RegTech Report published by Fintech Global, considered a leading global provider of RegTech information services, has been used to build the database to approach this research.

Since the existing limitation in the RegTech research, a qualitative investigation has been carried out implementing a Grounded Theory Methodology (GTM) to develop the theory inductively from data (Corbin & Strauss, 2008; Glaser & Strauss, 2009). For this reason, an exploratory research design has been defined in line with the flexibility of GTM (Birks et al., 2013) since data collection and analysis are closely related to GTM. The phases of this methodology are described below:

3.1 Open Coding

Firstly, based on the terms of the "OPEN CODING" procedure, this process has been carried out by analyzing, comparing, and conceptualizing data to classify the "Dimensions" into seven theory blocks that represent similar themes. For this purpose, the data have been segmented, examined, and broken down into discrete parts, closely examined to reach and elaborate the main "Blocks of Theory" (7). Subsequently, a meticulous analysis of the data has been carried out to identify and conceptualize the meanings of the content of each block (7) in terms of similarities and differences until it has been possible to group the concepts of the "Dimensions" into a total of 45 "Categories" that represent similar ideas.

3.2 *Axial Coding*

At a second level, based on the terms of the "AXIAL CODING" procedure, the process of reassembling the data that has been fractured during the "Open Coding" process and identifying the relationships with the "Categories" (45) obtained at the first level has been carried out. For this purpose, relationships have been established across the categories to adequately interpret that the categories are connected and interlinked, resulting in 15 "Innovations." This has allowed the integration of the 45 "Categories" into subcategories (15 "Innovations") to understand and refine the complexity that is occurring related to the RegTech dynamics.

3.3 *Selective Coding*

Finally, at a third level, based on the terms of the "SELECTIVE CODING" procedure, the process has been carried out by integrating the 15 "Innovations" (subcategories) into seven core categories defined as "Drivers" to understand what drives RegTech in the financial ecosystem. This process represents the final step of the data analysis, which explains and validates the existing relationship statements between its "Categories" (45) and "Subcategories" (15 "Innovations"). This methodology has made it possible to establish seven (7) central explanatory categories ("Drivers"), in which all the "Categories" (45) and "Innovations" (15) converge, detailing their connections in the findings and contributions section.

4 Findings

The adoption of Regulatory Technology (RegTech) in the financial ecosystem is supported by seven key drivers (see Fig. 1). These drivers are instrumental in shaping the implementation and utilization of RegTech solutions, ensuring that financial organizations can efficiently manage regulatory compliance. These drivers underscore the transformative impact of RegTech on regulatory compliance strategies, highlighting the importance of technology in enhancing efficiency, accuracy, and effectiveness in managing compliance. The most significant drivers are:

4.1 *Compliance Automation*

This driver involves the use of technology to streamline and automate compliance processes. This includes automated data collection, reporting and compliance with regulatory requirements, reducing manual workload and minimizing human error.

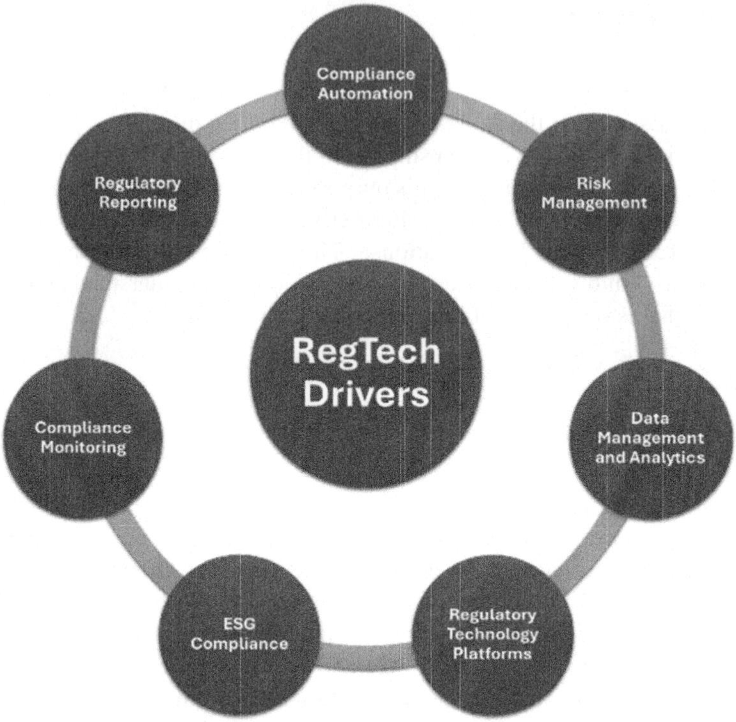

Fig. 1 RegTech Adoption Drivers. Source: Own Elaboration

Automation tools can quickly adapt to changing regulations, ensuring that financial organizations are compliant with the regulatory standards. RegTech innovations boosted by this driver are:

4.1.1 KYC Solutions

Specializing in automated solutions for Know Your Customer (KYC) processes, customer due diligence, and identity verification.

4.1.2 AML Solutions

Offering automated Anti-Money Laundering (AML) solutions for transaction monitoring, suspicious activity detection, and compliance with AML regulations.

4.1.3 Regulatory Reporting Automation

Providing automation tools for regulatory reporting, ensuring accurate and timely submission of regulatory requirements.

Among the RegTech companies analyzed, *ACTICO's* platform aligns with innovation in KYC solutions by leveraging intelligent automation and digital decision-making to improve customer due diligence and identity verification processes. Through machine learning and automated decision-making, this firm effectively streamlines KYC operations, ensuring compliance and reducing operational risk. *Alessa* exemplifies innovation in AML Solutions by offering automated tools for transaction monitoring, suspicious activity detection, and regulatory compliance. By streamlining compliance and fraud prevention processes, it enables financial institutions to effectively tackle money laundering and reduce associated risks, supporting global financial crime prevention efforts. *Fintellix's* expertise in multinational data management and regulatory reporting aligns closely with the innovation of regulatory reporting automation. By providing scalable, end-to-end solutions, it ensures accurate and timely submission of regulatory requirements, helping financial institutions efficiently meet complex compliance obligations across multiple jurisdictions.

4.2 Risk Management

This driver refers to the use of advanced technologies to identify, assess, and mitigate compliance risks. This includes tools to monitor and analyze risk factors, predict potential compliance issues, and implement strategies to proactively address these risks. Effective risk management helps financial organizations avoid sanctions, reduce operational losses, and maintain their reputation. RegTech innovations boosted by this driver are:

4.2.1 Fraud Detection

Focusing on fraud detection solutions using advanced analytics, machine learning, and AI to identify and prevent fraudulent activities.

4.2.2 Cybersecurity

Offering cybersecurity solutions to protect financial institutions from cyber threats data breaches and ensure compliance with data security regulations.

4.2.3 Risk Assessment and Monitoring

Providing tools for risk assessment, monitoring, and mitigation, including credit risk, operational risk, and compliance risk.

More specifically, *Third Line Analytics 's* "AlertSpeed" solution exemplifies innovation in fraud detection by utilizing advanced entity resolution and machine learning (ML) technologies. The platform's real-time transaction screening and behavior-based ML align with cutting-edge RegTech advances, aimed at identifying and preventing fraudulent activity with high accuracy and reducing false positives. *CalQRisk's* comprehensive GRC software aligns with innovation in cybersecurity by offering robust solutions that protect financial institutions from cyber threats and data breaches. By integrating cybersecurity within its modular platform, it ensures compliance with data security regulations, mitigating associated risks. *CleverChain* exemplifies innovation in risk assessment and monitoring by offering advanced tools to assess, monitor, and mitigate credit, operational, and compliance risks. Its modular anti-money laundering platform integrates financial crime expertise with automated decision-making, enhancing due diligence and risk assessment across multiple industries globally.

4.3 Data Management and Analytics

This driver involves the systematic collection, storage and analysis of large volumes of data to ensure regulatory compliance. RegTech solutions provide sophisticated data analytics capabilities that help organizations interpret complex data sets, identify compliance trends and make informed decisions. This enables adequate data management to ensure the accuracy, integrity and security of regulatory data. RegTech innovations boosted by this driver are:

4.3.1 Big Data Analytics

Leveraging predictive analytics to forecast regulatory trends, identify risks, and optimize compliance strategies.

4.3.2 Artificial Intelligence (AI)

Utilizing AI technologies for automating compliance processes, enhancing decision-making, and improving operational efficiency.

For instance, *ION* exemplifies the application of big data analytics by processing large volumes of real-time market data to monitor orders and trades across multiple trading venues. Its solutions enable investment firms to leverage predictive analytics, anticipate regulatory trends, identify risks, and optimize compliance strategies, especially in intraday exposure management and risk prioritization. *Cognitive View* typifies RegTech's use of AI technologies to automate compliance and risk monitoring. Its AI-powered generative platform significantly reduces compliance professionals' workload by automating review processes and improving decision-making through multiple communication channels, thereby improving operational efficiency and ensuring compliance with global regulatory standards.

4.4 Regulatory Technology Platforms

This driver refers to global solutions that integrate various RegTech tools and services to provide a centralized approach to compliance management. These platforms offer a range of functionalities, such as compliance tracking, reporting, risk assessment, and audit management. They provide a unified interface for organizations to effectively manage their compliance processes. RegTech innovations boosted by this driver are:

4.4.1 Integrated Compliance Platforms

Offering comprehensive RegTech platforms integrating multiple compliance solutions, risk management tools, and regulatory reporting capabilities.

4.4.2 Regulatory Change Management

Providing solutions for tracking regulatory changes, managing compliance updates, and ensuring regulatory alignment.

Notably, *ComplyCube* modeled the integrated compliance platforms concept by providing a comprehensive RegTech solution that integrates multiple compliance processes, risk management tools, and regulatory reporting capabilities. The platform's automation, AI, and machine learning functionalities align seamlessly with various industries, delivering agile and efficient compliance management that empowers operational excellence. *Compliance.ai* exemplifies regulatory change management innovation by offering advanced solutions designed specifically for the banking, financial services, and insurance industries. Its unique Expert-In-The-Loop methodology integrates expert monitoring with machine learning, enabling clients to proactively manage and adapt to regulatory changes in real-time, thereby mitigating compliance risk and ensuring regulatory alignment.

4.5 ESG Compliance

This driver refers to adherence to regulations and standards related to environmental protection, social responsibility, and corporate governance. RegTech solutions in this area help organizations monitor and report on their ESG performance, ensuring they meet regulatory requirements and align with stakeholder expectations. RegTech innovations boosted by this driver are:

4.5.1 ESG Reporting Solutions

Specializing in Environmental, Social, and Governance (ESG) reporting tools to help organizations comply with ESG frameworks, sustainability standards, and disclosure requirements.

For instance, *Novatus Global* leverages its specialized expertise and technology tools to develop ESG reporting solutions that comply with environmental, social, and governance (ESG) frameworks. By integrating its advisory expertise, the firm ensures that clients effectively comply with sustainability standards and disclosure requirements, driving actionable and compliant ESG reporting outcomes. *Greenomy* exemplifies innovation in ESG reporting solutions by providing advanced tools that streamline compliance with CSRD and EU taxonomy frameworks. Its SaaS portal integrates complex regulatory requirements into a unified data model, enhanced by generative AI, enabling efficient and comprehensive ESG reporting for global corporations and financial institutions.

4.6 Regulatory Reporting

This driver involves the accurate and timely submission of compliance-related information to regulatory authorities. RegTech tools facilitate the automation of reporting processes, ensuring that organizations can generate and submit reports in the required formats and within specified deadlines. These tools help reduce the complexity and cost associated with regulatory reporting. RegTech innovations boosted by this driver are:

4.6.1 Transaction Reporting

Focusing on transaction reporting solutions for regulatory compliance, trade reporting, and transaction data management.

4.6.2 Regulatory Data Management

Offering data management solutions for regulatory reporting, data governance, and data quality assurance.

Regarding the RegTech companies analyzed, *Qomply's* technology exemplifies innovation in transaction reporting by automating the validation of transaction reports through an extensive set of rules. Its solution ensures accurate, complete, and compliant reporting, streamlining the reporting process while reducing errors and costs for financial institutions. *CUBE* illustrates innovation in regulatory data management by providing comprehensive solutions supporting regulatory reporting, data governance, and quality assurance. Leveraging advanced technologies such as AI and machine learning, this firm is a critical resource for regulatory intelligence, ensuring clients maintain robust and compliant regulatory inventories globally.

4.7 Compliance Monitoring

This driver consists of continuously observing and assessing an organization's compliance with regulatory requirements. RegTech solutions provide real-time monitoring capabilities, enabling organizations to quickly detect and address compliance issues. These tools typically include alerts and notifications to ensure that non-compliances are quickly identified and resolved, maintaining the integrity of the compliance program. RegTech innovations boosted by this driver are:

4.7.1 Real-Time Monitoring

Providing real-time monitoring solutions for compliance activities, regulatory changes, and risk alerts.

4.7.2 Compliance Dashboards

Offering interactive dashboards for monitoring compliance metrics, regulatory obligations, and audit trails.

Most specifically, *EverC's* AI-powered solutions, particularly *MerchantView*, align closely with real-time monitoring innovation by automatically analyzing merchant activities and URLs to detect money laundering and other risks. This continuous, real-time assessment improves compliance by quickly identifying and mitigating potential regulatory threats. *Arctic Intelligence* platform exemplifies compliance dashboard innovation by providing real-time, interactive dashboards that monitor compliance metrics, regulatory obligations, and audit trails across multiple industries and countries, thereby improving financial crime risk management.

Therefore, the findings of this research emphasize that the adoption of RegTech in the financial ecosystem is not merely a response to increasing regulatory requirements, but a strategic transformation driven by technological drivers. The identified drivers—compliance automation, risk management, data management and analytics, regulatory technology platforms, ESG compliance, regulatory reporting, and compliance monitoring—play a critical role in reshaping how companies approach regulatory compliance. As a result, the adoption of RegTech across the financial ecosystem is driven by the combination of these drivers, each of which contributes to a more robust and efficient compliance framework. These drivers address the immediate challenges posed by regulatory requirements and enable organizations with the tools necessary to navigate the future of regulatory compliance. For this reason, as the regulatory landscape continues to evolve, RegTech's importance as a strategic enabler of compliance will consolidate its role as an indispensable component of the financial ecosystem.

5 Contributions

The primary drivers of Regulatory Technology (RegTech) adoption across the financial ecosystem are multifaceted and rely on leveraging the regulatory phases identified through the compliance process. Therefore, it is understood that RegTech firms involve the use of computing and network-based information systems to streamline regulatory compliance, monitoring, reporting, and supervision (Miglionico, 2020). These are the phases of the regulatory compliance processes. Considering that RegTech is an emerging field that utilizes information technology and digital innovations to enhance regulatory compliance processes (Solms, 2020), the RegTech drivers are defined to address the challenges within each of these phases. For this reason, exploring these phases is essential for developing a comprehensive regulatory compliance strategy and leveraging RegTech drivers to their full potential within the financial ecosystem. The essence of how RegTech drivers are integrated to the different phases of the regulatory compliance processes has been conceptualized in Fig. 2.

5.1 Regulatory Phase

The regulatory phase is a foundational stage in the compliance process. It encompasses the development and implementation of policies, risk assessments, and establishing the necessary controls to ensure that an organization adheres to all relevant regulations and standards. This phase is critical as it defines the foundation for all subsequent compliance activities, ensuring the organization is prepared to tackle regulatory obligations (Table 1).

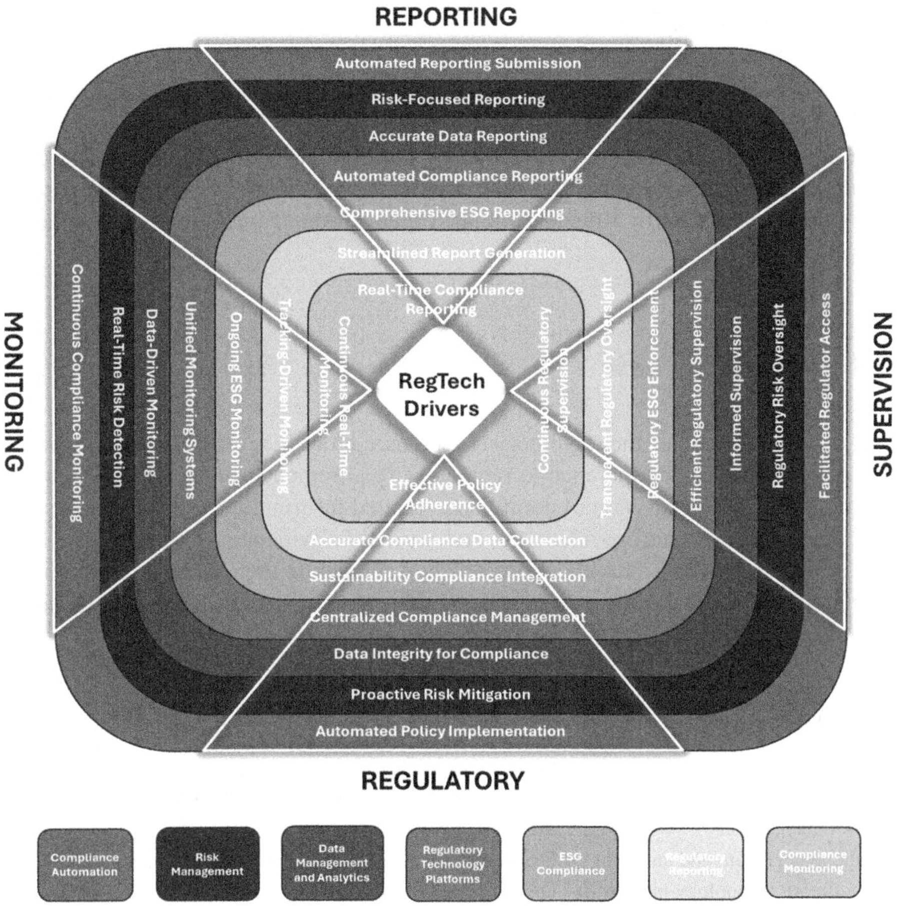

Fig. 2 RegTech Drivers Across Compliance Phases: An Integrated Approach. Source: own elaboration

Table 1 Overview of RegTech drivers in the compliance regulatory phase

RegTech driver	Process definition
Compliance automation	Streamlining policy execution and control implementation.
Risk management	Identifying and addressing risks during compliance.
Data management and analytics	Ensuring accuracy and accessibility of compliance data.
Regulatory technology platforms	Integrating tools for streamlined policy execution.
ESG compliance	Aligning policies with ESG standards.
Regulatory reporting	Ensuring reliable data for regulatory obligations.
Compliance monitoring	Ensuring that implemented policies and controls are effective.

Source: Author's elaboration

5.2 Monitoring Phase

The monitoring phase is a critical component of the regulatory compliance process. It involves continuous monitoring and auditing of the organization's activities to ensure ongoing compliance with regulatory requirements. This proactive approach ensures that regulatory obligations are consistently met and minimizes the risk of non-compliance, thereby safeguarding the organization against potential regulatory breaches (Table 2).

5.3 Reporting Phase

The reporting phase of the regulatory compliance process is crucial for demonstrating an organization's adherence to regulatory requirements through the systematic compilation and submission of compliance-related information. This phase ensures that organizations can provide clear and verifiable evidence of their compliance activities to regulators and other stakeholders, enhancing the reliability of reporting and reducing errors to ensure that organizations consistently tackle their regulatory obligations (Table 3).

Table 2 Overview of RegTech drivers in the compliance monitoring phase

RegTech driver	Process definition
Compliance automation	Real-time monitoring through automation.
Risk management	Monitoring compliance risks continuously.
Data management and analytics	Using analytics to identify compliance trends and risks.
Regulatory technology platforms	Offering centralized real-time monitoring.
ESG compliance	Continuously tracking ESG-related activities.
Regulatory reporting	Tracking reporting requirements and deadlines.
Compliance monitoring	Providing continuous real-time monitoring of compliance activities.

Source: Author's elaboration

Table 3 Overview of RegTech drivers in the compliance reporting phase

RegTech driver	Process definition
Compliance automation	Ensuring timely and accurate regulatory reports.
Risk management	Highlighting potential risks in compliance reports.
Data management and analytics	Providing reliable data for regulatory submissions.
Regulatory technology platforms	Simplifying reporting through integrated platforms.
ESG compliance	Facilitating detailed ESG disclosures.
Regulatory reporting	Automating the creation and submission of reports.
Compliance monitoring	Documenting compliance activities and deviations in real-time.

Source: Author's elaboration

Table 4 Overview of RegTech drivers in the compliance supervision phase

RegTech driver	Process definition
Compliance automation	Enabling real-time supervision through automated systems.
Risk management	Supporting regulators in assessing organizational risks.
Data management and analytics	Empowering regulators with comprehensive data analysis.
Regulatory technology platforms	Providing regulators with a unified compliance interface.
ESG compliance	Supporting regulators in ensuring ESG adherence.
Regulatory reporting	Offering clear insights for adequate supervision.
Compliance monitoring	Allowing regulators to monitor compliance activities in real-time.

Source: Author's elaboration

5.4 *Supervision Phase*

The supervision phase, characterized by the supervisory role of external regulatory bodies, is crucial for enforcing compliance, as regulators observe compliance activities and take corrective actions when necessary. The application of SupTech is becoming prevalent at this stage, enabling more effective enforcement and ensuring that organizations maintain ongoing compliance (Table 4).

From the preceding, each phase represents a critical and interdependent aspect of the regulatory compliance process that can be substantially enhanced by adopting RegTech drivers. These drivers are pivotal in increasing the efficiency, accuracy, and overall effectiveness of managing complex regulatory requirements. For this reason, understanding these four phases is crucial for developing a comprehensive approach to the regulatory compliance processes and effectively leveraging RegTech within the financial ecosystem.

Consequently, RegTech has been instrumental in supporting financial institutions in managing new risks, compliance efforts, and regulations, leading to automation and increased efficiency (Grassi & Lanfranchi, 2022). In the financial sector, the increasing use of RegTech solutions by institutions aims to comply more efficiently with regulations, particularly in areas like anti-money laundering compliance, influencing the evolution of financial crime over the next decade (Kurum, 2020). By automating data collection, analysis, and reporting, RegTech empowers financial institutions to stay updated with regulations, identify compliance gaps, and demonstrate adherence to regulators effectively (Josyula, 2023). Furthermore, RegTech firms have significantly impacted the financial sector by streamlining Know Your Customer (KYC) and Customer Due Diligence (CDD) processes, thereby reducing compliance costs and enhancing operational efficiency (Sushkova, 2021).

The existing financial RegTech solutions have been well-developed with the ability to conduct automated data distribution and regulatory reporting through big data analytics, real-time reporting, risk exposure assessment, potential threat prediction, real-time monitoring, tracking of compliance states and future regulations, and auditing with the adoption of multiple technologies (Li et al., 2023).

These technologies have also facilitated the development of innovative solutions for compliance with regulatory requirements, leading to increased competition in financial markets and improved consumer benefits (Lee, 2020). Mainly because RegTech automates various regulatory compliance activities that were previously manual, such as regulatory interpretation and regulatory reporting, amidst the challenges of the increasing volume of regulations and operational data (Firmansyah & Arman, 2023). Moreover, the integration of Artificial Intelligence (AI) and Machine Learning (ML) in RegTech solutions has enabled financial institutions to ease the regulatory burden and achieve high levels of compliance success (Singh, 2023).

As a result, RegTech innovations are reshaping compliance within the financial sector, presenting opportunities for institutions to enhance efficiency and reduce operational costs (Olawale et al., 2024). For this reason, as the number of regulations and associated compliance costs continue to rise, Regulatory Technology (RegTech) has gained significant traction among banks (Douaihy & Rowe, 2023).

Therefore, it is understood that scholars advocate for integrating compliance considerations into strategic decision-making processes to ensure alignment with regulatory mandates and minimize exposure to regulatory enforcement actions (Muslim, 2024). Consequently, if RegTech refers to the use of technology to assist organizations in meeting regulatory compliance requirements (Li et al., 2023), mapping organizational processes with applicable regulatory guidelines is an important step in regulatory compliance management (Sapkota et al., 2013).

6 Conclusion

This chapter has comprehensively explored the critical drivers behind regulatory technology (RegTech) adoption within the financial ecosystem, focusing on understanding how these drivers reshape regulatory compliance processes.

To this purpose, a grounded theory methodology has been employed to develop an inductive conceptual framework that has captured the complexity of RegTech dynamics. The research has identified seven core drivers of RegTech adoption through open coding, axial coding, and selective coding processes. These drivers have been categorized into specific RegTech innovations within the financial ecosystem, providing a solid academic structure to support the research findings and contributions.

Research findings have revealed that RegTech adoption is not simply a response to regulatory pressures but a strategic transformation that enables financial organizations to effectively navigate a complex compliance landscape. This transformation is driven by a combination of drivers, including compliance automation, risk management, data management and analytics, regulatory technology platforms, ESG compliance, regulatory reporting, and compliance monitoring. Each of these drivers plays a crucial role in improving regulatory compliance by enhancing companies' efficiency, accuracy, and responsiveness.

The contributions of this research lie in its detailed analysis of the drivers of RegTech adoption and the development of a comprehensive framework that integrates these drivers across the different phases of compliance: regulation, monitoring, reporting, and supervision. These contributions are significant for academia and practical application, as they provide industry stakeholders with actionable insights to leverage RegTech drivers in regulatory compliance processes through the integrated framework developed in this research.

Therefore, as the financial ecosystem continues to evolve, the insights obtained from this research will be instrumental in informing future regulatory strategies and driving innovation in compliance management. Mainly because RegTech firms, as emphasized in this chapter, are not only enablers of compliance with regulatory requirements, but also drivers of companies that are set to redefine the regulatory compliance landscape.

References

Anagnostopoulos, I. (2018). Fintech and regtech: Impact on regulators and banks. *Journal of Economics and Business, 100*, 7–25. https://doi.org/10.1016/j.jeconbus.2018.07.003

Arner, D. W., Barberis, J., & Buckley, R. P. (2017). FinTech, RegTech, and the reconceptualization of financial regulation. Northwestern Journal of International Law & Business, *371*. Retrieved from: https://bit.ly/4cvLoAN

Arner, D. W., Buckley, R. P., Zetzsche, D. A., & Veidt, R. (2020). Sustainability, FinTech and financial inclusion. *European Business Organization Law Review, 21*(1), 7–35. https://doi.org/10.1007/s40804-020-00183-y

Arner, D. W., Zetzsche, D. A., Buckley, R. P., & Barberis, J. N. (2019). The identity challenge in finance: From analogue identity to digitized identification to digital KYC utilities. *European Business Organization Law Review, 20*(1), 55–80. https://doi.org/10.2139/ssrn.3224115

Barberis, J., & Arner, D. W. (2016). FinTech in China: From shadow banking to P2P lending. In *Banking beyond banks and money* (pp. 69–96). Springer. https://doi.org/10.1007/978-3-319-42448-4_5

Bartley, J., Chen, A., & Taylor, E. (2011). A comparison of XBRL filings to corporate 10-Ks: Evidence from the voluntary filing program. *Accounting Horizon, 25*(2), 227–245. https://doi.org/10.2308/acch-10028

Battanta, L., Giorgino, M., Grassi, L., & Lanfranchi, D. (2020). RegTech: Case studies of cooperation with Banks in Italy. In *European conference on innovation and entrepreneurship* (pp. 112–119). Academic Conferences International Limited. Retrieved from: https://bit.ly/4crkoCh

Birks, D., Fernandez, W., Levina, N., & Nasirin, S. (2013). Grounded theory method in information systems research: Its nature, diversity and opportunities. *European Journal of Information Systems, 22*(1), 1–8. https://doi.org/10.1057/ejis.2012.48

Buckley, R. P., Arner, D. W., Zetzsche, D. A., & Weber, R. H. (2020). The road to RegTech: The (astonishing) example of the European Union. *Journal of Banking Regulation, 21*(1), 26–36. https://doi.org/10.1057/s41261-019-00104-1

Butler, T., & Brooks, R. (2018). On the role of ontology-based RegTech for managing risk and compliance reporting in the age of regulation. *Journal of Risk Management in Financial Institutions, 11*(1), 19–33. https://doi.org/10.69554/LXST2119

Cerchiaro, D., Leo, S., Landriault, E., & De Vega, P. (2021). DLT to boost efficiency for financial intermediaries. An application in ESG reporting activities. *Technology Analysis & Strategic Management, 7*, 1–14. https://doi.org/10.1080/09537325.2021.1999921

Chao, X., Ran, Q., Chen, J., Li, T., Qian, Q., & Ergu, D. (2022). Regulatory technology (RegTech) in financial stability supervision: Taxonomy, key methods, applications and future directions. *International Review of Financial Analysis, 80, 102023*. https://doi.org/10.1016/j.irfa.2022.102023

Chiu, I. H., & Deipenbrock, G. (2021). *Routledge handbook of financial technology and law* (1st ed.). Routledge. Retrieved from: https://bit.ly/3SSWtoA

Corbin, J., & Strauss, A. L. (2008). *Basics of qualitative research: Techniques and procedures for developing grounded theory* (3rd ed.). Sage Publications. https://doi.org/10.4135/9781452230153

Currie, W. L., Gozman, D. P., & Seddon, J. J. (2018). Dialectic tensions in the financial markets: A longitudinal study of pre-and post-crisis regulatory technology. *Journal of Information Technology, 33*(4), 304–325. https://doi.org/10.1057/s41265-017-0047-5

Currie, W. L., & Seddon, J. J. (2021). Exploring technological instantiation of regulatory practices in entangled financial markets. *Journal of Information Technology, 37*(1). https://doi.org/10.1177/02683962211027308

Deshpande, A. (2020). AI/ML applications and the potential transformation of Fintech and Finserv sectors. In *13th CMI Conference on Cybersecurity and Privacy (CMI) - Digital Transformation - Potentials and Challenges. Copenhagen, Denmark. pp.* 1–6.https://doi.org/10.1109/CMI51275.2020.9322734.

Douaihy, H., & Rowe, F. (2023). Institutional pressures and regtech challenges for banking: The case of money laundering and terrorist financing in Lebanon. *Journal of Information Technology, 38*(3), 304–318. https://doi.org/10.1177/02683962231152968

EIOPA. (2020). Supervisory technology strategy. *European Insurance and Occupational Pensions Authority*. Retrieved from: https://bit.ly/4dsv2dx

FINRA. (2018). Technology based innovations for regulatory compliance ("RegTech") in the securities industry. *Financial Industry Regulatory Authority. Retrieved from:*https://bit.ly/3Z7SubN

Fintech Global. (2024). The world's most innovative RegTech companies that every financial institution needs to know about in 2024. *RegTech 100 Companies Report. Retrieved from:*https://bit.ly/3YKHO2v

Firmansyah, B., & Arman, A. (2023). Generic solution architecture design of regulatory technology (regtech). *Indonesian Journal of Electrical Engineering and Informatics, 11*(2). https://doi.org/10.52549/ijeei.v11i2.4533

Glaser, B. G., & Strauss, A. (2009). The discovery of grounded theory: Strategies for qualitative research. *Aldine Transaction Publishers*. Retrieved from https://bit.ly/3M4vti4

Grassi, L., & Lanfranchi, D. (2022). Regtech in public and private sectors: The nexus between data, technology and regulation. *Journal of Industrial and Business Economics, 49*(3), 441–479. https://doi.org/10.1007/s40812-022-00226-0

Hao, L., Zhang, J. H., & Fang, J. B. (2014). Does voluntary adoption of XBRL reduce cost of equity capital? *International Journal of Accounting and Information Management.*https://doi.org/10.1108/IJAIM-11-2012-0071

Josyula, H. P. (2023). Fraud detection in fintech leveraging machine learning and behavioral analytics. *Research Square*. https://doi.org/10.21203/rs.3.rs-3548343/v1

Kavassalis, P., Stieber, H., Breymann, W., Saxton, K., & Gross, F. J. (2018). An innovative RegTech approach to financial risk monitoring and supervisory reporting. *The Journal of Risk Finance.*https://doi.org/10.1108/JRF-07-2017-0111

Kurum, E. (2020). Regtech solutions and aml compliance: What future for financial crime? *Journal of Financial Crime, 30*(3), 776–794. https://doi.org/10.1108/jfc-04-2020-0051

Lee, J. (2020). Access to finance for artificial intelligence regulation in the financial services industry. *European Business Organization Law Review, 21*(4), 731–757. https://doi.org/10.1007/s40804-020-00200-0

Li, J., Maiti, A., & Fei., J. (2023). Features and scope of regulatory technologies: Challenges and opportunities with industrial internet of things. *Future Internet, 15*(8), 256. https://doi.org/10.3390/fi15080256

Liu, C., Luo, X. R., Sia, C. L., O'Farrell, G., & Teo, H. H. (2014). The impact of XBRL adoption in PR China. *Decision Support Systems, 59*, 242–249. https://doi.org/10.1016/j.dss.2013.12.003

Loiacono, G., & Rulli, E. (2022). ResTech: Innovative technologies for crisis resolution. *Journal of Banking Regulation, 23*, 227–243. https://doi.org/10.1057/s41261-021-00154-4

Michaels, L., & Homer, M. (2018). Regulation and supervision in a digital and inclusive world. In *Handbook of Blockchain, digital finance, and inclusion* (Vol. 1, pp. 329–346). Academic Press. *Retrieved from:*https://bit.ly/3YQ2RRo

Micheler, E., & Whaley, A. (2020). Regulatory technology: Replacing law with computer code. *European Business Organization Law Review, 21*(2), 349–377. https://doi.org/10.1007/s40804-019-00151-1

Miglionico, A. (2020). Automated regulation and supervision: The impact of regtech on banking compliance. *European Business Law Review, 31*(4), 641–662. https://doi.org/10.54648/eulr2020025

Muslim, M. (2024). Managerial finance tactics in the era of enhanced regulation following financial scandals. *Advances in Management & Financial Reporting, 2*(1). https://doi.org/10.60079/amfr.v2i1.202

Olawale, O., Ajayi, F. A., Udeh, C. A., & Odejide, O. A. (2024). Regtech innovations streamlining compliance, reducing costs in the financial sector. *GSC Advanced Research and Reviews, 19*(1), 114–131. https://doi.org/10.30574/gscarr.2024.19.1.0146

Omarova, S. T. (2020). Technology v technocracy: Fintech as a regulatory challenge. *Journal of Financial Regulation, 6*(1), 75–124. https://doi.org/10.1093/jfr/fjaa004

Sapkota, K., Aldea, A., Younas, M., Duce, D., & Bañares-Alcántara, R. (2013). RP-Match: A framework for automatic mapping of regulations with organizational processes. In *IEEE 10th International Conference on e-Business Engineering* (pp. 257–264). ICEBE. https://doi.org/10.1109/icebe.2013.39

Singh, C. (2023). Artificial intelligence and deep learning: Considerations for financial institutions for compliance with the regulatory burden in the United Kingdom. *Journal of Financial Crime, 31*(2), 259–266. https://doi.org/10.1108/jfc-01-2023-0011

Solms, J. V. (2020). Integrating regulatory technology (regtech) into the digital transformation of a bank treasury. *Journal of Banking Regulation, 22*(3), 191–207. https://doi.org/10.1057/s41261-020-00138-w

Sushkova, O. B. (2021). Legal risks of using regulatory technologies in business and professional activities. *SHS Web of Conferences, 106*, 02013. https://doi.org/10.1051/shsconf/202110602013

Yang, D., & Li, M. (2018). Evolutionary approaches and the construction of technology-driven regulations. *Emerging Markets Finance and Trade, 54*(14), 3256–3271. https://doi.org/10.1080/1540496X.2018.1496422

Zeranski, S., & Sancak, I. E. (2021). Prudential supervisory disclosure (PSD) with supervisory technology (SupTech): Lessons from a FinTech crisis. *International Journal of Disclosure and Governance, 18*(4), 315–335. https://doi.org/10.1057/s41310-021-00111-7

Iván Sosa is an outstanding professional with 14 years of experience dedicated to the insurance sector. Known for his strategic leadership, he has successfully led projects addressing the challenges of digital transformation, significantly advancing the sector. Beyond his corporate roles, Ivan is actively involved in academic research focused on the InsurTech ecosystem and its impact on the insurance industry. His dual business consulting and academic engagement background positions him as an influential player in the evolving XTech landscape. Iván holds a master's degree in marketing and sales management from IMF Business School and a bachelor's degree in business administration from Rey Juan Carlos University.

Sergio Sosa is an accomplished expert in actuarial analysis and risk management, known for his leadership at MetLife in product development and actuarial process automation. His career involves diverse fields, including managing foreign exchange and cryptocurrency trading functions, highlighting his adaptability in evolving environments. Sergio's technical skills in Python, R, and SQL complement his innovative problem-solving approach. With a master's degree in actuarial science and finance and an MBA in equities and trading, he brings a deep understanding of financial markets, positioning him as an up-and-coming professional with an in-depth knowledge of financial markets and risk assessment.

Cybersecurity in Fintech from a Corporate Finance Perspective

Narmin Nahidi

1 Introduction

The financial implications of cybersecurity risks are a critical concern for Fintech firms, which are uniquely vulnerable to cyber threats due to their reliance on digital technologies and the sensitive nature of the data they handle. In the Fintech sector, the potential costs associated with cyber breaches can be substantial, encompassing both direct and indirect financial impacts. These costs are not only immediate but can also have long-term repercussions on a firm's financial health and market position. Therefore, understanding and mitigating these risks is essential for the sustainability and growth of Fintech firms. This introduction will explore the various facets of the financial implications of cybersecurity risks, including the direct costs of breaches, the importance of effective risk management, the role of regulatory compliance, and the need for continuous investment in cybersecurity technologies.

The cost of cyber breaches and effective risk management are paramount concerns in the Fintech industry. Cyber breaches can lead to severe financial repercussions, including fines, legal fees, and remediation expenses. These direct costs often arise immediately after a breach is detected and can be substantial. Furthermore, these breaches can disrupt business operations and lead to significant financial losses. Firms may also face regulatory fines if they fail to comply with data protection laws, further exacerbating the financial strain. Additionally, legal fees can accumulate rapidly as companies seek to navigate the complex legal landscape following a breach. The remediation process often requires substantial investment in cybersecurity measures to prevent future incidents. Companies may

N. Nahidi (✉)
University of Exeter, Exeter, UK

ESC Clermont Business School, Clermont-Ferrand, France
e-mail: n.nahidi@exeter.ac.uk

A. Zarifis, X. Cheng (eds.), *Fintech and the Emerging Ecosystems*, Financial Innovation and Technology, https://doi.org/10.1007/978-3-031-83402-8_20

need to hire external experts to conduct forensic investigations, adding to the overall cost burden. High-profile incidents underscore the extensive financial impacts of inadequate cybersecurity measures. These incidents highlight how cyber breaches can escalate into significant financial liabilities, with long-term repercussions on a company's financial health. The immediate costs can be debilitating, but the long-term effects, such as increased insurance premiums and ongoing legal battles, further strain financial resources. Beyond the immediate financial outlay, breaches result in a loss of consumer confidence, which has a tangible impact on market share and revenue streams. Companies often face increased scrutiny from regulatory bodies post-breach, leading to more stringent compliance requirements and higher operational costs. The reputational damage can be enduring, necessitating extensive public relations efforts to restore brand image. The fallout from such incidents may also lead to a decline in stock prices, adversely affecting shareholders and the firm's market valuation. Moreover, the resources diverted to address these crises can hinder a company's ability to invest in growth opportunities, thus impacting its competitive positioning in the market.

Indirect costs, including reputational damage and the erosion of customer trust, are often more insidious and challenging to quantify. Reputational damage can lead to a loss of business as customers migrate to competitors who are perceived as more secure. This erosion of confidence can be particularly devastating for Fintech firms, whose business models heavily rely on digital trust. Customer acquisition costs can skyrocket as firms strive to rebuild their reputation and regain market share, often requiring substantial investments in marketing and public relations campaigns. Consequently, effective risk management strategies become imperative to prevent such adverse outcomes. Effective risk management necessitates the identification, assessment, and mitigation of cyber risks through strategies like penetration testing, threat modeling, and incident response planning. These proactive measures help firms understand their security posture, prioritize areas needing improvement, and prepare for potential cyber incidents.

Integrating cybersecurity into enterprise risk management frameworks is essential for a proactive stance in mitigating potential threats. Enterprise risk management (ERM) frameworks provide a holistic approach to identifying and managing risks across an organization. By embedding cybersecurity within ERM, firms can ensure that cyber risks are evaluated alongside other business risks, such as financial and operational risks. This integration facilitates a comprehensive understanding of the risk landscape and promotes a coordinated response to threats, thus enhancing the firm's overall resilience. The evolving threat landscape requires Fintech firms to adapt their risk management strategies continually. Cyber threats are becoming increasingly sophisticated, with attackers employing advanced techniques to breach defenses. As a result, firms must invest in cutting-edge technologies and continuously update their security protocols to stay ahead of potential threats. This ongoing investment is critical to maintaining a robust security posture and protecting financial assets and customer data.

2 Financial Implications of Cybersecurity Risks in Fintech

2.1 *Cost of Cyber Breaches and Risk Management*

Cyber breaches can inflict severe financial repercussions on Fintech firms, encompassing both direct costs, such as fines, legal fees, and remediation expenses, and indirect costs, including reputational damage and erosion of customer trust (Sampat et al., 2024; Teigland et al., 2018). These direct costs often arise immediately after a breach is detected and can be substantial. These breaches can disrupt business operations and lead to significant financial losses. Firms may also face regulatory fines if they fail to comply with data protection laws, further exacerbating the financial strain (Quach et al., 2022). Additionally, legal fees can accumulate rapidly as companies seek to navigate the complex legal landscape following a breach. The remediation process often requires substantial investment in cybersecurity measures to prevent future incidents. Companies may need to hire external experts to conduct forensic investigations, adding to the overall cost burden. For instance, legal fees accrue rapidly as firms navigate complex regulatory landscapes to address compliance issues. Remediation expenses involve the technical effort to close security gaps and the operational disruptions caused by such incidents.

High-profile incidents, such as the Equifax data breach, underscore the extensive financial impacts of inadequate cybersecurity measures. In Equifax's case, the breach led to over $700 million in settlements and remediation costs. This example highlights how cyber breaches can escalate into significant financial liabilities, with long-term repercussions on a company's financial health. The immediate costs can be debilitating, but the long-term effects, such as increased insurance premiums and ongoing legal battles, further strain financial resources. Beyond the immediate financial outlay, the breach resulted in a loss of consumer confidence, which had a tangible impact on Equifax's market share and revenue streams. Companies often face increased scrutiny from regulatory bodies post-breach, which can lead to more stringent compliance requirements and higher operational costs. Additionally, the reputational damage can be enduring, necessitating extensive public relations efforts to restore brand image. The fallout from such incidents may also lead to a decline in stock prices, adversely affecting shareholders and the firm's market valuation. Moreover, the resources diverted to address these crises can hinder a company's ability to invest in growth opportunities, thus impacting its competitive positioning in the market.

Indirect costs, including reputational damage and the erosion of customer trust, are often more insidious and challenging to quantify. Reputational damage can lead to a loss of business as customers migrate to competitors who are perceived as more secure. For Fintech firms, whose business models heavily rely on digital trust, this erosion of confidence can be particularly devastating. Customer acquisition costs can skyrocket as firms strive to rebuild their reputation and regain market share, often requiring substantial investments in marketing and public relations campaigns. Consequently, effective risk management strategies become imperative to prevent such adverse outcomes. Effective risk management necessitates the identification, assessment, and mitigation of cyber risks through strategies like penetration testing, threat modeling, and incident response planning (Ralston et al., 2007). Penetration testing involves simulated cyberattacks to identify vulnerabilities before malicious actors can exploit them. This proactive measure helps firms understand their security posture and prioritize areas needing improvement. Threat modeling, on the other hand, provides a structured approach to identifying potential threats and vulnerabilities, allowing firms to develop targeted defenses. These strategies are fundamental to preparing for and responding to potential cyber incidents.

Incident response planning is another critical component of cybersecurity risk management. It involves preparing for potential cyber incidents by developing protocols for detection, containment, and recovery. An effective incident response plan ensures that firms can respond swiftly and efficiently to minimize the impact of a breach. This preparedness not only reduces the immediate financial damage but also helps maintain customer trust by demonstrating a firm's commitment to protecting its data. Integrating these plans within a broader risk management framework is essential for a coordinated approach to cyber threats. Integrating cybersecurity into enterprise risk management frameworks is essential for a proactive stance in mitigating potential threats. Enterprise risk management (ERM) frameworks provide a holistic approach to identifying and managing risks across an organization (Almeida et al., 2019). By embedding cybersecurity within ERM, firms can ensure that cyber risks are evaluated alongside other business risks, such as financial and operational risks. This integration facilitates a comprehensive understanding of the risk landscape and promotes a coordinated response to threats, thus enhancing the overall resilience of the firm.

Moreover, the financial implications of cyber breaches extend beyond the immediate aftermath of an incident. Firms often face long-term challenges, such as increased scrutiny from regulators and heightened expectations from stakeholders regarding cybersecurity measures (Kianpour & Raza, 2024). Regulatory bodies may impose more stringent requirements on firms that have experienced breaches, leading to higher compliance costs. Additionally, stakeholders, including investors and customers, may demand greater transparency and assurance about the firm's cybersecurity posture, necessitating ongoing investments in security infrastructure and practices. These evolving demands underscore the necessity of continuous improvement in cybersecurity measures.

The evolving threat landscape requires Fintech firms to continually adapt their risk management strategies. Cyber threats are becoming increasingly sophisticated, with attackers employing advanced techniques to breach defenses (Tounsi & Rais, 2018). As a result, firms must invest in cutting-edge technologies and continuously update their security protocols to stay ahead of potential threats. This ongoing investment is critical to maintaining a robust security posture and protecting financial assets and customer data. Firms must be vigilant and proactive to ensure they can counteract emerging threats effectively.

The financial repercussions of cyber breaches also underscore the importance of a well-defined governance structure for cybersecurity (Appiah et al., 2022;

Ngozi Samuel Uzougbo et al., 2024). Senior leadership involvement is crucial in driving a culture of security and ensuring that cybersecurity is prioritized at the highest levels of the organization. By establishing clear governance frameworks and accountability, firms can enhance their resilience against cyber threats and better manage the financial impacts of breaches. Leadership commitment is vital to fostering a security-conscious organizational culture.

The cost of cyber breaches and the necessity of effective risk management are paramount concerns for Fintech firms. Direct costs, such as fines and remediation expenses, coupled with indirect costs like reputational damage, highlight the severe financial impact of cyber incidents. Implementing comprehensive risk management strategies, including penetration testing, threat modeling, and incident response planning, is essential. Moreover, integrating cybersecurity into enterprise risk management frameworks and maintaining a proactive stance on evolving threats can help mitigate these risks. A well-defined governance structure and continuous investment in cybersecurity are critical to safeguarding financial assets and maintaining customer trust in the Fintech industry. By addressing these areas comprehensively, Fintech firms can better navigate the complexities of the cybersecurity landscape.

2.2 *Regulatory Compliance and Financial Impact*

Compliance with cybersecurity regulations is both a legal obligation and a fundamental component of risk management in the Fintech industry (AlBenJasim et al., 2023; Didenko, 2020). Adherence to these regulations ensures that Fintech firms maintain the integrity, confidentiality, and availability of sensitive financial data. Regulatory compliance involves significant investments in technology, personnel, and processes to meet stringent security standards. These efforts are crucial for legal adherence and fostering trust among stakeholders, including customers, investors, and regulatory bodies. The financial implications of compliance are substantial; however, the costs associated with non-compliance can be far more detrimental, encompassing fines, legal fees, and reputational damage (Brewster, 2013).

The General Data Protection Regulation (GDPR) is one of the most comprehensive data protection laws, impacting Fintech firms operating within the European Union or handling the data of EU citizens. Compliance with GDPR requires firms to implement robust data protection measures, conduct regular audits, and ensure transparent data processing practices. For instance, in 2019, Google faced a €50 million fine for GDPR violations related to inadequate transparency and consent practices (Daigle & Khan, 2020). This example underscores the financial risks of non-compliance and highlights the importance of adhering to regulatory standards to avoid such penalties. Similarly, China's Cybersecurity Law mandates stringent requirements for data localization, security assessments, and critical information infrastructure protection. Fintech companies operating in China must store data within the country and undergo periodic security evaluations to comply with these regulations. In 2021, Didi, a leading Chinese ride-hailing company, faced severe regulatory scrutiny and was fined $1.2 billion for violations, including data security lapses. This incident demonstrates the significant financial impact regulatory non-compliance can have, reinforcing the necessity for Fintech firms to align with local cybersecurity laws.

The United States also has several cybersecurity regulations that Fintech firms must navigate, such as the Gramm-Leach-Bliley Act (GLBA) and the California Consumer Privacy Act (CCPA). The GLBA requires financial institutions to protect consumer financial information, while the CCPA enhances privacy rights and consumer protection for residents of California. In 2020, Morgan Stanley was fined $60 million by the Office of the Comptroller of the Currency (OCC) for failing to properly decommission data centers, resulting in potential exposure of sensitive client information. This case illustrates the critical financial and operational risks associated with regulatory non-compliance in the US context. Beyond avoiding fines and legal consequences, regulatory compliance offers significant benefits that can outweigh the costs. For example, firms that comply with regulations often enjoy enhanced risk management, which can lead to lower insurance premiums and increased investor confidence. Demonstrating a commitment to regulatory compliance can also provide a competitive advantage, as customers and partners prefer to engage with companies that prioritize data security. This proactive approach to compliance not only mitigates financial risks but also positions firms favorably in the market, fostering long-term growth and stability.

3 Investment Strategies in Cybersecurity Technologies

3.1 Evaluating ROI and Budget Allocation

Investment in cybersecurity technologies is indispensable for Fintech firms, yet determining the return on investment (ROI) poses a significant challenge. ROI analysis entails evaluating potential cost savings from prevented breaches, improved operational efficiency, and heightened customer trust (Lee, 2021). Effective budget allocation for cybersecurity necessitates prioritizing high-risk areas, leveraging cost-efficient solutions, and aligning expenditures with overall business objectives. A nuanced understanding of the financial trade-offs inherent in cybersecurity investments is crucial for optimizing budgetary allocations. Understanding the importance of cybersecurity investments begins with recognizing the multifaceted nature of cyber threats and the diverse array of technologies required to combat them (Dunn Cavelty & Wenger, 2020; Thakur, 2024). Fintech firms must invest in a range of security measures, encompassing firewalls, encryption, advanced threat detection systems, and incident response capabilities. Each of these components plays a critical role in forming a comprehensive cybersecurity strategy, yet they represent substantial costs that must be meticulously justified through rigorous return on investment (ROI) analysis. Firstly, firewalls serve as a fundamental barrier, preventing unauthorized access to a firm's network. They scrutinize incoming and outgoing traffic based on predetermined security rules, thus blocking malicious traffic while allowing legitimate communication. The investment in sophisticated firewall technologies is crucial, as they provide the first line of defense against external threats. However, the costs associated with acquiring, implementing, and maintaining these systems are significant. These costs include the initial purchase price and ongoing expenses related to updates, monitoring, and management. Justifying these expenditures requires a clear understanding of the potential cost savings from thwarted cyberattacks and the value of maintaining network integrity.

Encryption technologies are equally vital, ensuring that sensitive data is rendered unreadable to unauthorized users. This includes data at rest, in transit, and during processing (Dunn Cavelty & Wenger, 2020). Implementing robust encryption mechanisms protects financial information, customer data, and proprietary business intelligence from interception and theft. However, encryption solutions can be costly, involving substantial investments in hardware, software, and expertise to deploy and manage effectively. ROI analysis for encryption must consider the potential financial impact of data breaches that could occur in the absence of such measures, as well as the enhanced trust and compliance with regulatory requirements that strong encryption can provide. Advanced threat detection systems represent another crucial element of a Fintech firm's cybersecurity arsenal. These systems employ machine learning and artificial intelligence to identify and respond to sophisticated threats in real time (OPenAI, 2024). They can detect anomalies and potential security incidents that traditional systems might miss. The implementation of these advanced technologies involves significant costs, including the procurement of sophisticated software, the integration of these systems into existing infrastructures, and the ongoing expenses for tuning and updating these solutions. The ROI for advanced threat detection systems is often realized through the prevention of high-impact security incidents, which can save the firm substantial sums in potential breach costs and associated damages (Ainslie et al., 2023). Incident response capabilities are also indispensable for Fintech firms, enabling them to swiftly and effectively address security breaches. This involves establishing protocols and teams dedicated to detecting, containing, and mitigating cyber incidents. Investments in incident response include the development of incident response plans, training for staff, and the acquisition of tools that facilitate rapid and effective responses. The costs of maintaining an incident response team and the associated infrastructure are considerable. However, the value derived from minimizing the impact and duration of security incidents, preserving customer trust, and avoiding regulatory penalties can significantly justify these expenditures.

One of the primary challenges in evaluating the ROI of cybersecurity investments is quantifying the benefits derived from risk reduction (Garvey et al., 2012; Lee, 2021). Unlike other business investments that produce clear and measurable outcomes, the benefits of cybersecurity are often intangible and difficult to quantify. For instance, how does one measure the value of a prevented data breach? While it is possible to estimate the costs associated with data breaches, including regulatory fines, remediation expenses, and lost business, the actual value of a breach that does not occur remains speculative. To address this challenge, firms can use several methods to approximate the potential savings and benefits derived from avoided breaches. One approach involves calculating the average cost of a data breach within the industry, using insights from reports like IBM's Cost of a Data Breach Report (Algarni et al., 2021; Phillips & Tanner, 2019; Wang et al., 2019). By understanding the average cost per breached record and the total number of records a firm holds, companies can estimate their potential financial exposure. Scenario analysis is another method where firms create hypothetical breach scenarios to evaluate potential impacts, considering factors such as the type of data compromised and the scale of the breach. Additionally, historical data from past breaches can provide benchmarks for estimating the financial impact of future incidents. Risk assessment frameworks like the FAIR (Factor Analysis of Information Risk) model also aid in quantifying the value of prevented breaches, translating qualitative risk assessments into quantitative financial metrics (Kandasamy et al., 2020; Wang et al., 2020).

Moreover, firms can consider the indirect benefits of preventing data breaches, such as maintaining customer trust and protecting brand reputation. The loss of customer trust can have long-term financial repercussions, including decreased customer retention, lower acquisition rates, and reduced revenue. By investing in cybersecurity measures that prevent breaches, firms can preserve their reputation and avoid costs associated with rebuilding trust and regaining market share. Regulatory compliance is another critical aspect of measuring the value of preventing data breaches (La Torre et al., 2018). Compliance with data protection regulations, such as GDPR and CCPA, requires firms to implement stringent security measures. Non-compliance can result in substantial fines and legal penalties, which can be avoided through effective cybersecurity investments (Barrett et al., 2018). Thus, by preventing data breaches, firms can ensure regulatory compliance and avoid the financial consequences of non-compliance, thereby providing a clearer justification for the costs associated with robust security measures. In addition to risk reduction, improved operational efficiency is another key benefit of cybersecurity investments. Advanced cybersecurity technologies can streamline operations by automating threat detection and response, reducing the need for manual intervention. This not only enhances the firm's security posture but also frees up resources that can be redirected toward other critical business functions. For example, implementing automated security monitoring tools can significantly reduce the time and effort required to manage and respond to security incidents, thereby improving overall operational efficiency.

Heightened customer trust is a crucial yet often overlooked, benefit of robust cybersecurity measures. In the Fintech industry, where trust and security are paramount, demonstrating a strong commitment to cybersecurity can enhance customer confidence and loyalty. Customers are more likely to engage with firms that prioritize the protection of their personal and financial information. This trust translates into increased customer retention and acquisition, ultimately driving revenue growth. Effective budget allocation for cybersecurity involves a strategic approach that prioritizes high-risk areas and leverages cost-efficient solutions. Fintech firms must conduct thorough risk assessments to identify the most critical vulnerabilities and allocate resources accordingly. For instance, if a firm determines that its customer data storage systems are particularly vulnerable to cyberattacks, it should prioritize investments in data encryption and access controls to mitigate this risk. Leveraging cost-efficient solutions is also essential for optimizing cybersecurity budgets (Rashid et al., 2021). This involves evaluating the cost-effectiveness of different technologies and solutions to ensure that the firm is getting the best value for its investment. For example, open-source security tools may offer comparable protection to proprietary solutions at a fraction of the cost. Additionally, cloud-based security services can provide scalable and cost-effective protection without the need for significant upfront investments in hardware and software.

By aligning cybersecurity investments with the firm's broader business objectives, these expenditures are positioned not just as necessary expenses but as strategic contributions that drive the firm's growth and long-term success. Instead of being perceived solely as cost centers—areas that drain resources without generating direct profit—cybersecurity initiatives become integral to protecting valuable assets, maintaining customer trust, and ensuring regulatory compliance. This alignment fosters resilience against cyber threats, ultimately supporting business continuity and enabling the firm to seize new opportunities confidently, thus enhancing both competitive advantage and profitability.

A nuanced understanding of the financial trade-offs inherent in cybersecurity investments is crucial for optimizing budgetary allocations. Firms must balance the need for robust security with the financial constraints they face. This requires a careful analysis of the costs and benefits of different security measures and an understanding of how these investments impact the firm's overall financial health. For instance, while investing in the latest cybersecurity technologies may provide the highest level of protection, it may not be financially feasible for all firms. In such cases, firms must find a balance between cost and effectiveness to ensure that they are adequately protected without compromising their financial stability. Evaluating the ROI of cybersecurity investments is a complex and challenging task, but it is essential for Fintech firms to make informed decisions about their cybersecurity strategies (Mirza et al., 2023; Murinde et al., 2022). Firms can optimize their cybersecurity budgets and enhance their overall security posture by understanding the multifaceted benefits of cybersecurity, prioritizing high-risk areas, leveraging cost-efficient solutions, and aligning expenditures with business objectives. Effective cybersecurity investments protect the firm's assets and data and support its growth and success in a highly competitive industry.

3.2 Cost-Benefit Analysis and Case Studies

Conducting a rigorous cost-benefit analysis aids Fintech firms in making informed decisions regarding cybersecurity investments by juxtaposing implementation costs against the potential financial impacts of cyber incidents. Techniques such as net present value (NPV) and internal rate of return (IRR) are instrumental in assessing the financial viability of cybersecurity projects (Belay et al., 2022). Empirical case studies, such as the successful implementation of multi-factor authentication (MFA) by leading Fintech firms, demonstrate the tangible benefits of strategic cybersecurity investments, including enhanced security and increased customer confidence. A cost-benefit analysis of cybersecurity investments begins with identifying and quantifying the costs associated with implementing various security measures. These costs can include initial setup expenses, ongoing maintenance and support fees, and the costs of personnel required to manage and operate the security systems. For example, the implementation of an advanced threat detection system may involve substantial upfront costs for purchasing the necessary hardware and software, as well as ongoing expenses for system updates and technical support. In addition to direct costs, firms must also consider the potential financial impacts of cyber incidents that could be prevented by security investments. This includes estimating the costs associated with data breaches, such as regulatory fines, legal fees, remediation expenses, and the loss of business due to reputational damage. For instance, a data breach that exposes sensitive customer information could result in significant fines under regulations like the GDPR, as well as substantial legal and remediation costs. By comparing these potential costs to the costs of implementing security measures, firms can determine the financial benefits of their investments.

Net present value (NPV) is a useful technique for assessing the financial viability of cybersecurity projects. NPV calculates the present value of future cash flows generated by the investment minus the initial costs. A positive NPV indicates that the investment is expected to generate a net financial benefit over its lifetime. For example, if the NPV of implementing a multi-factor authentication (MFA) system is positive, it suggests that the cost savings from prevented breaches and improved customer trust outweigh the initial and ongoing costs of the system. Internal rate of return (IRR) is another important technique for evaluating cybersecurity investments. IRR measures the expected rate of return on an investment, considering the timing and magnitude of cash flows. An IRR that exceeds the firm's required rate of return indicates that the investment is financially viable. For instance, if the IRR of a new encryption system is higher than the firm's cost of capital, it suggests that the investment will generate sufficient financial returns to justify the expenditure.

Empirical case studies provide valuable insights into the tangible benefits of strategic cybersecurity investments. One notable example is the successful implementation of multi-factor authentication (MFA) by a leading Fintech firm. MFA significantly enhances security by requiring users to provide multiple forms of verification before accessing sensitive information. This reduces the risk of unauthorized access and data breaches. In this case, the Fintech firm experienced a substantial decrease in security incidents following the implementation of MFA, leading to significant cost savings and increased customer confidence. Another case study involves a Fintech firm that invested in a comprehensive security information and event management (SIEM) system. The SIEM system provided real-time monitoring and analysis of security events, enabling the firm to detect and respond to threats more quickly and effectively. As a result, the firm was able to prevent several potential breaches and avoid the associated costs. The implementation of the SIEM system also improved the firm's compliance with regulatory requirements, reducing the risk of fines and legal repercussions. A further example is the adoption of advanced encryption technologies by a Fintech company to protect customer data. The investment in encryption not only safeguarded the firm's data from cyber threats but also enhanced its reputation for security. Customers felt more confident in the firm's ability to protect their personal and financial information, leading to increased customer loyalty and retention. The firm also reported a notable reduction in customer churn and an increase in new customer acquisitions, demonstrating the positive impact of strong cybersecurity measures on business performance.

Cost-benefit analysis and case studies highlight the importance of strategic cybersecurity investments for Fintech firms. By evaluating the financial impacts of cyber incidents and the costs of implementing security measures, firms can make informed decisions about their cybersecurity strategies. Techniques like NPV and IRR provide a framework for assessing the financial viability of these investments, while empirical case studies demonstrate the tangible benefits of robust cybersecurity measures. Ultimately, strategic investments in cybersecurity not only protect the firm's assets and data but also enhance its overall business performance and competitiveness in the market.

4 Impact on Corporate Valuation and Investor Confidence

4.1 Influence on Corporate Valuation

A firm's cybersecurity posture exerts a significant influence on its corporate valuation. In today's digital economy, where data breaches and cyber threats are increasingly common, investors and stakeholders closely scrutinize a company's cybersecurity measures. Companies that exhibit robust cybersecurity protocols are perceived as lower-risk investments, which can positively impact their market value (Kostyuk & Wayne, 2020). Conversely, data breaches often precipitate declines in stock prices and market capitalization, as they reveal vulnerabilities and expose the company to financial and reputational damage (Ashraf, 2022). This section explores the correlation between cybersecurity practices and corporate valuation, emphasizing the necessity of strong cybersecurity frameworks in maintaining and enhancing corporate value. The correlation between cybersecurity and corporate valuation is evident in the market's reaction to data breaches. When a company suffers a breach, it is not uncommon to see immediate declines in its stock price as investors react to the anticipated costs and potential loss of customer trust. One example is the 2013 Target data breach, which led to a significant drop in the company's stock value, losing over $4 billion in market capitalization in the weeks following the incident. This immediate market reaction underscores how critical cybersecurity is to investor confidence and perceived corporate stability. Moreover, the long-term impacts of data breaches on corporate valuation can be profound. Companies may face ongoing costs related to legal actions, regulatory fines, and the need for extensive remediation efforts. These costs can erode profit margins and reduce the resources available for growth initiatives. For example, Equifax's 2017 data breach resulted in over $1.4 billion in costs related to security upgrades, legal fees, and fines, significantly impacting its financial health and market position. Such extended financial burdens highlight the long-term risks associated with poor cybersecurity practices.

Beyond the direct financial costs, data breaches can lead to a loss of customer trust, which is critical for sustaining business operations and revenue. When customers lose faith in a company's ability to protect their personal information, they may take their business elsewhere, leading to reduced revenues and market share. This erosion of trust can be challenging to rebuild, further compounding the negative impact on corporate valuation. Companies like Yahoo, which experienced massive data breaches, faced not only immediate financial repercussions but also long-term challenges in regaining user trust and rebuilding their brand reputation. Additionally, robust cybersecurity measures can enhance a company's valuation by positioning it as a market leader in security and data protection (Corallo et al., 2020; Tao et al., 2019). Investors and customers are increasingly prioritizing security, and companies that demonstrate strong cybersecurity practices can differentiate themselves from competitors. This differentiation can lead to increased market share and higher valuations as investors perceive these companies as safer and more reliable investments. For instance, companies like IBM and Microsoft have leveraged their strong cybersecurity frameworks to build trust and attract investments, thereby enhancing their corporate valuation.

The regulatory environment also plays a significant role in influencing corporate valuation through cybersecurity practices. Regulatory bodies worldwide have implemented stringent data protection laws, such as the GDPR in Europe and CCPA in California. Compliance with these regulations is not only a legal requirement but also a factor that investors consider when evaluating a company's risk profile. Non-compliance can result in substantial fines and penalties, further impacting corporate valuation. Companies that proactively invest in meeting and exceeding regulatory requirements can mitigate these risks and enhance their attractiveness to investors. Cybersecurity's impact on mergers and acquisitions (M&A) is profound. Companies with strong cybersecurity practices are often more attractive targets for acquisition, as they pose lower risks to the acquiring entity. Conversely, companies with poor cybersecurity records may see reduced valuations or face significant scrutiny during the due diligence process, potentially derailing deals. The Verizon acquisition of Yahoo is a prime example, where the discovery of massive data breaches led to a $350 million reduction in the acquisition price, highlighting how cybersecurity issues can directly influence corporate valuation during M&A activities.

Investor sentiment towards cybersecurity has evolved significantly, with many now viewing robust cybersecurity as a critical component of good corporate governance. Investors are increasingly integrating cybersecurity metrics into their investment decision-making processes, evaluating how well companies manage and mitigate cyber risks. This shift reflects a broader recognition that cybersecurity is integral to a company's overall risk management strategy and financial health. As a result, companies that excel in cybersecurity governance can attract a more extensive and diversified investor base, positively impacting their valuation. A firm's cybersecurity posture significantly influences its corporate valuation (Berkman et al., 2018; Hasan et al., 2021). Robust cybersecurity measures can enhance market value by reducing risk, building customer and investor trust, and ensuring compliance with regulatory standards. Conversely, data breaches can lead to substantial declines in stock prices, long-term financial burdens, and erosion of customer trust, all of which negatively impact corporate valuation. As such, strong cybersecurity frameworks are essential for maintaining and enhancing corporate value in the digital age.

4.2 Role in Mergers and Acquisitions

Cybersecurity due diligence constitutes a critical component of mergers and acquisitions (M&A) within the Fintech sector. In an era where data breaches and cyber threats are rampant, prospective acquirers meticulously assess the target company's cybersecurity practices to identify risks that could potentially affect the transaction's value. The financial implications of cybersecurity in M&A underscore the importance of thorough due diligence and the adoption of best practices to ensure successful transactions (Vu et al., 2024). The integration of cybersecurity into the M&A due diligence process begins with a comprehensive assessment of the target company's security posture. This involves evaluating the effectiveness of existing security measures, the history of any past breaches, and the potential vulnerabilities that could be exploited post-acquisition. During the acquisition of a Fintech firm, acquirers might scrutinize the firm's encryption practices, incident response protocols, and compliance with relevant cybersecurity regulations. This thorough examination helps identify any latent risks that could jeopardize the value of the acquisition.

One of the primary concerns in M&A transactions is the potential for undisclosed cyber risks. A company with a history of unreported breaches or weak cybersecurity practices may pose significant risks to the acquiring firm. The discovery of such issues during due diligence can lead to renegotiations of the deal terms, adjustments in the purchase price, or even the abandonment of the transaction. For example, Verizon's acquisition of Yahoo was notably affected by the disclosure of significant data breaches, leading to a $350 million reduction in the acquisition price. This case illustrates the critical financial implications of cybersecurity risks in M&A transactions. The integration phase post-acquisition presents additional cybersecurity challenges (Goldman, 2012). The merging of IT systems, networks, and data from two distinct entities can create new vulnerabilities and increase the attack surface. Ensuring that the target company's cybersecurity practices align with those of the acquiring firm is essential to mitigate these risks. This may involve implementing comprehensive security assessments, integrating security technologies, and harmonizing security policies and procedures. Failure to effectively manage these integration challenges can result in security gaps that adversaries could exploit.

The importance of cybersecurity in M&A extends beyond the initial due diligence and integration phases. Ongoing monitoring and assessment of the acquired entity's cybersecurity posture are crucial to maintaining a strong security framework. This includes regular audits, vulnerability assessments, and updates to security policies to address emerging threats. Acquirers must also ensure that the acquired company's employees are adequately trained in cybersecurity best practices to foster a culture of security awareness. Continuous improvement of cybersecurity measures is vital to protect the value of the acquisition and prevent potential financial and reputational damage. Regulatory considerations play a significant role in the cybersecurity due diligence process (Bechara & Schuch, 2020). Different jurisdictions have varying requirements for data protection and cybersecurity compliance, which must be accounted for during the M&A process. For instance, acquiring a company that operates in the European Union entails compliance with the GDPR, which mandates stringent data protection measures. Similarly, acquisitions involving companies in the United States may require adherence to regulations such as the CCPA. Failure to comply with these regulations can result in significant fines and legal consequences, further emphasizing the need for thorough cybersecurity due diligence.

The financial implications of cybersecurity in M&A transactions are multifaceted. Poor cybersecurity practices can lead to substantial financial losses, including regulatory fines, legal fees, and remediation costs. Additionally, the reputational damage resulting from a data breach can erode customer trust and impact the long-term success of the acquisition. Conversely, companies with strong cybersecurity frameworks can enhance the value of the transaction by demonstrating their commitment to data protection and risk management. This can result in higher valuations and more favorable deal terms. Cybersecurity due diligence also includes evaluating the target company's third-party relationships (Vitunskaite et al., 2019). Vendors, suppliers, and partners can introduce additional cyber risks, and it is essential to assess the security practices of these third parties. For example, if the target company relies heavily on third-party service providers, acquirers must ensure that these providers adhere to robust cybersecurity standards. This assessment helps mitigate the risks associated with supply chain vulnerabilities and ensures that the acquired entity's security posture is not compromised by third-party weaknesses. In addition to traditional cybersecurity assessments, advanced threat intelligence and cyber risk quantification tools can enhance the due diligence process. These tools provide deeper insights into the target company's cyber risk profile by analyzing threat data, identifying potential attack vectors, and quantifying the financial impact of cyber risks. By leveraging these advanced technologies, acquirers can make more informed decisions and better assess the potential risks and rewards of the transaction. The role of cybersecurity in M&A transactions is to protect the value of the acquisition and ensure the long-term success of the combined entity (DePamphilis, 2011). Thorough cybersecurity due diligence helps identify and mitigate risks, align security practices, and foster a culture of security awareness. By prioritizing cybersecurity throughout the M&A process, firms can enhance their resilience against cyber threats and safeguard their investments.

4.3 Investor Perspectives and Managing Relations

Investors are increasingly cognizant of cybersecurity risks and their potential impacts on financial performance. As the digital landscape evolves, investors have become more aware of how cybersecurity incidents can affect a company's valuation, operational stability, and market reputation. Effective communication of a firm's cybersecurity strategies can enhance transparency and foster investor trust, which is crucial for attracting and retaining investment (Huda, 2023; Radu & Smaili, 2022). In today's financial environment, where information asymmetry can lead to heightened risks, investors seek assurances that companies are not only aware of cyber threats but are also proactively addressing them through comprehensive and robust cybersecurity measures. Fintech firms must demonstrate their commitment to cybersecurity through regular reporting and comprehensive disclosures (Ng & Kwok, 2017). This involves providing detailed reports on the firm's cybersecurity posture, including information on security policies, incident response plans, and recent security assessments. An example of this is firms could include cybersecurity metrics in their annual reports or provide dedicated cybersecurity reports. Transparency in these disclosures helps to build investor confidence by showing that the firm is actively managing cyber risks. Regular updates on cybersecurity initiatives and improvements can also reassure investors that the firm is continually enhancing its security measures in response to evolving threats.

Proactive engagement with stakeholders is another crucial aspect of managing investor relations in the context of cybersecurity. This can involve regular meetings with investors to discuss cybersecurity strategies and respond to their concerns. As an illustration, firms can organize webinars or conference calls with cybersecurity experts to explain the steps being taken to protect the company's assets and data. Additionally, creating channels for ongoing communication, such as dedicated investor relations websites or newsletters focused on cybersecurity, can keep investors informed and engaged. By maintaining an open dialogue, firms can address investor queries promptly and provide reassurances about their cybersecurity efforts.

Managing investor relations entails a strategic approach to transparency and communication about cybersecurity measures. This includes aligning the firm's cybersecurity disclosures with broader business objectives and ensuring that they reflect a genuine commitment to security. For instance, firms should avoid overly technical jargon in their communications and instead focus on how cybersecurity efforts contribute to business resilience and long-term value creation. By framing cybersecurity within the context of business strategy, firms can help investors understand the importance of these measures and their role in safeguarding financial performance. The role of regulatory bodies in shaping investor perspectives on cybersecurity cannot be overlooked. Regulations such as the Sarbanes-Oxley Act in the United States require public companies to disclose material risks, including those related to cybersecurity. Compliance with these regulations not only ensures legal adherence but also signals to investors that the firm is serious about its cybersecurity responsibilities. Case in point, the U.S. Securities and Exchange Commission (SEC) has emphasized the importance of clear and timely disclosures regarding cybersecurity risks and incidents. Adhering to these guidelines helps firms to build credibility and trust with investors. Additionally, cybersecurity ratings provided by third-party organizations can influence investor perceptions. These ratings assess the security posture of companies based on various criteria, including vulnerability management, incident response, and compliance with industry standards. High ratings can enhance a firm's reputation and attract more investment, while poor ratings can deter potential investors. For instance, Moody's Investors Service has begun incorporating cybersecurity risk assessments into its credit rating process, reflecting the growing importance of cybersecurity in investment decisions. Fintech firms can leverage strong cybersecurity ratings to showcase their commitment to security and differentiate themselves from competitors.

The financial implications of cybersecurity breaches further underscore the importance of effective investor communication. High-profile data breaches can lead to significant financial losses, regulatory fines, and reputational damage, all of which can negatively impact investor confidence and stock prices. By proactively communicating their cybersecurity strategies and demonstrating resilience, firms can mitigate the adverse effects of incidents on investor relations. This proactive approach can include sharing lessons learned from past incidents and outlining steps taken to prevent future breaches. Investors also appreciate firms that integrate cybersecurity into their overall risk management frameworks. This integration demonstrates that cybersecurity is not treated as an isolated issue but as a critical component of the firm's risk management strategy. Firms can highlight how their cybersecurity efforts align with other risk management initiatives, such as business continuity planning and disaster recovery. This holistic approach reassures investors that the firm is well-prepared to handle various risks, thereby enhancing investor confidence. Specifically, a Fintech firm that showcases its comprehensive risk management framework, including cybersecurity, can attract risk-averse investors looking for stable and secure investment opportunities. Furthermore, the growing trend of Environmental, Social, and Governance (ESG) investing has increased the focus on cybersecurity. ESG investors consider cybersecurity to be part of the governance criteria when evaluating potential investments. Firms that demonstrate strong cybersecurity governance practices, such as board-level oversight and regular security audits, are more likely to attract ESG-focused investors. By aligning cybersecurity efforts with broader ESG goals, Fintech firms can tap into the growing pool of ESG investment capital. For example, firms that publicly commit to cybersecurity best practices and report on their progress can enhance their appeal to socially responsible investors. Investors are increasingly aware of the significant impact cybersecurity can have on financial performance and corporate valuation. Effective communication and transparency about cybersecurity strategies, coupled with proactive engagement with stakeholders, are essential for fostering investor trust and confidence. Regulatory compliance, third-party cybersecurity ratings, and integration of cybersecurity into broader risk management and ESG frameworks further enhance investor relations. By adopting these practices, Fintech firms can navigate the complex landscape of cybersecurity risks and maintain strong, trust-based relationships with their investors.

5 Conclusion

The financial implications of cyber breaches extend beyond the immediate aftermath of an incident. Firms often face long-term challenges, such as increased scrutiny from regulators and heightened expectations from stakeholders regarding cybersecurity measures. Regulatory bodies may impose more stringent requirements on firms that have experienced breaches, leading to higher compliance costs. Additionally, stakeholders, including investors and customers, may demand greater transparency and assurance about the firm's cybersecurity posture, necessitating ongoing investments in security infrastructure and practices. These evolving demands underscore the necessity of continuous improvement in cybersecurity measures. The evolving threat landscape necessitates that Fintech firms continually adapt their risk management strategies. Cyber threats are becoming increasingly sophisticated, with attackers employing advanced techniques to breach defenses. Consequently, firms must invest in cutting-edge technologies and continuously update their security protocols to stay ahead of potential threats. This ongoing investment is critical to maintaining a robust security posture and protecting financial assets and customer data. Firms must be vigilant and proactive to ensure they can counteract emerging threats effectively. The importance of a well-defined governance structure for cybersecurity cannot be overstated. Senior leadership involvement is crucial in driving a culture of security and ensuring that cybersecurity is prioritized at the highest levels of the organization. By establishing clear governance frameworks and accountability, firms can enhance their resilience against cyber threats and better manage the financial impacts of breaches. Leadership commitment is vital to fostering a security-conscious organizational culture.

The necessity of effective risk management in the Fintech industry is underscored by the severe financial impact of cyber incidents. Direct costs, such as fines and remediation expenses, coupled with indirect costs like reputational damage, highlight the critical need for comprehensive risk management strategies. Implementing strategies such as penetration testing, threat modeling, and incident response planning is essential for mitigating these risks. Moreover, integrating cybersecurity into enterprise risk management frameworks and maintaining a proactive stance on evolving threats can help mitigate these risks. A well-defined governance structure and continuous investment in cybersecurity are critical to safeguarding financial assets and maintaining customer trust in the Fintech industry. By addressing these areas comprehensively, Fintech firms can better navigate the complexities of the cybersecurity landscape. This holistic approach to cybersecurity not only protects the firm's assets and data but also supports its growth and success in a highly competitive industry. The ability to manage and mitigate cyber risks effectively is a crucial factor in ensuring the long-term stability and profitability of Fintech firms. This strategic approach to cybersecurity can provide a significant competitive advantage, positioning firms as leaders in the industry and fostering investor confidence.

References

Ainslie, S., Thompson, D., Maynard, S., & Ahmad, A. (2023). Cyber-threat intelligence for security decision-making: A review and research agenda for practice. *Computers and Security, 132*, 103352. https://doi.org/10.1016/j.cose.2023.103352

AlBenJasim, S., Dargahi, T., Takruri, H., & Al-Zaidi, R. (2023). FinTech cybersecurity challenges and regulations: Bahrain case study. *Journal of Computer Information Systems, 00*(00), 1–17. https://doi.org/10.1080/08874417.2023.2251455

Algarni, A. M., Thayananthan, V., & Malaiya, Y. K. (2021). Quantitative assessment of cybersecurity risks for mitigating data breaches in business systems. *Applied Sciences (Switzerland), 11*(8). https://doi.org/10.3390/app11083678

Almeida, R., Teixeira, J. M., Mira da Silva, M., & Faroleiro, P. (2019). A conceptual model for enterprise risk management. *Journal of Enterprise Information Management, 32*(5), 843–868. https://doi.org/10.1108/JEIM-05-2018-0097

Appiah, G., Amankwah-Amoah, J., & Liu, Y. L. (2022). Organizational architecture, resilience, and cyberattacks. *IEEE Transactions on Engineering Management, 69*(5), 2218–2233. https://doi.org/10.1109/TEM.2020.3004610

Ashraf, M. (2022). The role of peer events in corporate governance: Evidence from data breaches. *The Accounting Review, 97*(2), 1–24. https://doi.org/10.2308/TAR-2019-1033

Barrett, K. L., Lynch, M. J., Long, M. A., & Stretesky, P. B. (2018). Monetary penalties and noncompliance with environmental Laws: A mediation analysis. *American Journal of Criminal Justice, 43*(3), 530–550. https://doi.org/10.1007/s12103-017-9428-0

Bechara, F. R., & Schuch, S. B. (2020). Cybersecurity and global regulatory challenges. *Journal of Financial Crime, 28*(2), 359–374. https://doi.org/10.1108/JFC-07-2020-0149

Belay, A. M., Puranik, S., Gallart-Fernández, R., Tuiskula, H., Melendez, J., Lamprinos, I., Díaz-González, F., & Smolnikar, M. (2022). Developing novel technologies and services for intelligent low voltage electricity grids: Cost–benefit analysis and policy implications. *Energies, 15*(1). https://doi.org/10.3390/en15010094

Berkman, H., Jona, J., Lee, G., & Soderstrom, N. (2018). Cybersecurity awareness and market valuations. *Journal of Accounting and Public Policy, 37*(6), 508–526. https://doi.org/10.1016/j.jaccpubpol.2018.10.003

Brewster, R. (2013). Pricing compliance: When formal remedies displace reputational sanctions. *Harvard International Law Journal, 54*(2), 259–314.

Corallo, A., Lazoi, M., & Lezzi, M. (2020). Cybersecurity in the context of industry 4.0: A structured classification of critical assets and business impacts. *Computers in Industry, 114*, 103165. https://doi.org/10.1016/j.compind.2019.103165

Daigle, B., & Khan, M. (2020). The EU general data protection regulation: An analysis of enforcement trends by EU data protection authorities. *United States International Trade Commission Journal of International Commerce and Economics*, 1–38. https://www.usitc.gov/journals.

DePamphilis, D. M. (2011). *Mergers, acquisitions, and other restructuring activities: An integrated approach to process, tools, cases, and solutions* (6th ed., pp. 1–753). Academic Press. https://doi.org/10.1016/C2010-0-67115-X

Didenko, A. N. (2020). Cybersecurity regulation in the financial sector: Prospects of legal harmonization in the European Union and beyond. *Uniform Law Review, 25*(1), 125–167. https://doi.org/10.1093/ulr/unaa006

Dunn Cavelty, M., & Wenger, A. (2020). Cyber security meets security politics: Complex technology, fragmented politics, and networked science. *Contemporary Security Policy, 41*(1), 5–32. https://doi.org/10.1080/13523260.2019.1678855

Garvey, P. R., Moynihan, R. A., & Servi, L. (2012). Model based systems engineering with Department of Defense Architectural Framework. *Systems Engineering, 14*(3), 305–326. https://doi.org/10.1002/sys

Goldman, E. H. (2012). The effect of acquisition decision making on security posture. *Information Management and Computer Security, 20*(5), 350–363. https://doi.org/10.1108/09685221211286520

Hasan, S., Ali, M., Kurnia, S., & Thurasamy, R. (2021). Evaluating the cyber security readiness of organizations and its influence on performance. *Journal of Information Security and Applications, 58*, 102726. https://doi.org/10.1016/j.jisa.2020.102726

Huda, M. (2023). Trust as a key element for quality communication and information management: Insights into developing safe cyber-organisational sustainability. *International Journal of Organizational Analysis*.https://doi.org/10.1108/IJOA-12-2022-3532

Kandasamy, K., Srinivas, S., Achuthan, K., & Rangan, V. P. (2020). IoT cyber risk: A holistic analysis of cyber risk assessment frameworks, risk vectors, and risk ranking process. *Eurasip Journal on Information Security, 2020*(1). https://doi.org/10.1186/s13635-020-00111-0

Kianpour, M., & Raza, S. (2024). More than malware: Unmasking the hidden risk of cybersecurity regulations. *International Cybersecurity Law Review, 5*(1), 169–212. https://doi.org/10.1365/s43439-024-00111-7

Kostyuk, N., & Wayne, C. (2020). The microfoundations of state cybersecurity: Cyber risk perceptions and the mass public. *Journal of Global Security Studies, 6*(2), ogz077. https://doi.org/10.1093/jogss/ogz077

La Torre, M., Dumay, J., & Rea, M. A. (2018). Breaching intellectual capital: Critical reflections on big data security. *Meditari Accountancy Research, 26*(3), 463–482. https://doi.org/10.1108/MEDAR-06-2017-0154

Lee, I. (2021). Cybersecurity: Risk management framework and investment cost analysis. *Business Horizons, 64*(5), 659–671. https://doi.org/10.1016/j.bushor.2021.02.022

Mirza, N., Elhoseny, M., Umar, M., & Metawa, N. (2023). Safeguarding FinTech innovations with machine learning: Comparative assessment of various approaches. *Research in International Business and Finance, 66*(October 2022), 102009. https://doi.org/10.1016/j.ribaf.2023.102009

Murinde, V., Rizopoulos, E., & Zachariadis, M. (2022). The impact of the FinTech revolution on the future of banking: Opportunities and risks. *International Review of Financial Analysis, 81*(June 2021), 102103. https://doi.org/10.1016/j.irfa.2022.102103

Ng, A. W., & Kwok, B. K. B. (2017). Emergence of Fintech and cybersecurity in a global financial Centre: Strategic approach by a regulator. In Journal of financial regulation and compliance (25, 4, pp. 422–434). Emerald Group Publishing Ltd. doi:https://doi.org/10.1108/JFRC-01-2017-0013.

OPenAI. (2024). ChatGPT: Generative Pre-trained Transformer 4. *Website*.

Phillips, R., & Tanner, B. (2019). Breaking down silos between business continuity and cyber security. *Journal of Business Continuity and Emergency Planning, 12*(3), 224–232.

Quach, S., Thaichon, P., Martin, K. D., Weaven, S., & Palmatier, R. W. (2022). Digital technologies: Tensions in privacy and data. *Journal of the Academy of Marketing Science, 50*(6), 1299–1323. https://doi.org/10.1007/s11747-022-00845-y

Radu, C., & Smaili, N. (2022). Board gender diversity and corporate response to cyber risk: Evidence from cybersecurity related disclosure. *Journal of Business Ethics, 177*(2), 351–374. https://doi.org/10.1007/s10551-020-04717-9

Ralston, P. A. S., Graham, J. H., & Hieb, J. L. (2007). Cyber security risk assessment for SCADA and DCS networks. *ISA Transactions, 46*(4), 583–594. https://doi.org/10.1016/j.isatra.2007.04.003

Rashid, Z., Noor, U., & Altmann, J. (2021). Economic model for evaluating the value creation through information sharing within the cybersecurity information sharing ecosystem. *Future Generation Computer Systems, 124*, 436–466. https://doi.org/10.1016/j.future.2021.05.033

Sampat, B., Mogaji, E., & Nguyen, N. P. (2024). The dark side of FinTech in financial services: A qualitative enquiry into FinTech developers' perspective. *International Journal of Bank Marketing, 42*(1), 38–65. https://doi.org/10.1108/IJBM-07-2022-0328

Tao, H., Bhuiyan, M. Z. A., Rahman, M. A., Wang, G., Wang, T., Ahmed, M. M., & Li, J. (2019). Economic perspective analysis of protecting big data security and privacy. *Future Generation Computer Systems, 98*, 660–671. https://doi.org/10.1016/j.future.2019.03.042

Teigland, R., Siri, S., Larsson, A., Puertas, A. M., & Bogusz, C. I. (2018). *The rise and development of FinTech: Accounts of disruption from Sweden and beyond*. https://doi.org/10.4324/9781351183628.

Thakur, M. (2024). Cyber security threats and counter measures in digital age. *Journal of Applied Science and Education (JASE), 04*(042), 1–20. https://doi.org/10.54060/a2zjournals.jase.42http://creativecommons.org/licenses/by/4.0/

Tounsi, W., & Rais, H. (2018). A survey on technical threat intelligence in the age of sophisticated cyber attacks. *Computers & Security, 72*, 212–233. https://doi.org/10.1016/j.cose.2017.09.001

Uzougbo, N. S., Ikegwu, C. G., & Adewusi, A. O. (2024). Cybersecurity compliance in financial institutions: A comparative analysis of global standards and regulations. *International Journal of Science and Research Archive, 12*(1), 533–548. https://doi.org/10.30574/ijsra.2024.12.1.0802

Vitunskaite, M., He, Y., Brandstetter, T., & Janicke, H. (2019). Smart cities and cyber security: Are we there yet? A comparative study on the role of standards, third party risk management and security ownership. *Computers and Security, 83*, 313–331. https://doi.org/10.1016/j.cose.2019.02.009

Vu, G. T. M., Hoang, K., & Hoang, H. V. (2024). Merger and acquisition, firm-level cybersecurity risk, and research and development intensity. *Managerial and Decision Economics, March*, 3094–3106. https://doi.org/10.1002/mde.4190.

Wang, J., Neil, M., & Fenton, N. (2020). A Bayesian network approach for cybersecurity risk assessment implementing and extending the FAIR model. *Computers and Security, 89*, 101659. https://doi.org/10.1016/j.cose.2019.101659

Wang, P., D'Cruze, H., & Wood, D. (2019). Economic costs and impacts of business data breaches. *Issues in Information Systems, 20*(2), 162–171. https://doi.org/10.48009/2_iis_2019_162-171

Narmin Nahidi is a dedicated academic and professional with a Ph.D. in Finance from Ca' Foscari University of Venice. Currently a faculty member at the University of Exeter, she also serves as an Adjunct Professor of Corporate Finance and Fintech at ESC Clermont Business School. Her teaching career spans various institutions. With expertise in Corporate Finance, Financial Technology, Behavioral Finance, and Sustainability, her research also covers Gender

Economics and Neurofinance. Dr. Nahidi holds a Senior Fellowship from the Higher Education Academy and is a Chartered Management & Business Educator (CMBE) and supervises PhD students. She is actively involved in academic service, journal editorial work, and professional associations like FMA and AFA.

The manufacturer's authorised representative in the EU is Springer Nature Customer Service Centre GmbH, Europaplatz 3, 69115 Heidelberg, Germany. If you have any concerns regarding our products, please contact ProductSafety@springernature.com

Printed and bound by CPI Group (UK) Ltd, Croydon, CR0 4YY
30/09/2026
02225595-0018